The Integration of Immigrants into AMERICAN SOCIETY

Panel on the Integration of Immigrants into American Society

Mary C. Waters and Marisa Gerstein Pineau, *Editors*

Committee on Population

Division of Behavioral and Social Sciences and Education

The National Academies of
SCIENCES · ENGINEERING · MEDICINE

THE NATIONAL ACADEMIES PRESS
Washington, DC
www.nap.edu

THE NATIONAL ACADEMIES PRESS 500 Fifth Street, NW Washington, DC 20001

This activity was supported by the Carnegie Corporation of New York, the National Science Foundation, the Russell Sage Foundation, and the U.S. Citizenship and Immigration Services of the U.S. Department of Homeland Security, with additional support from the National Academy of Sciences Kellogg Fund. The contribution of the Eunice Kennedy Shriver National Institute of Child Health and Human Development in sponsoring the planning meeting for this activity is also acknowledged. Any opinions, findings, conclusion, or recommendations expressed in this publication do not necessarily reflect the views of the organization or agencies that provided support for the project.

International Standard Book Number-13: 978-0-309-37398-2
International Standard Book Number-10: 0-309-37398-0
Library of Congress Control Number: 2015958960
Digital Object Identifier: 10.17226/21746

Additional copies of this report are available from the National Academies Press, 500 Fifth Street, NW, Keck 360, Washington, DC 20001; (800) 624-6242 or (202) 334-3313; http://www.nap.edu.

Printed in the United States of America

Suggested citation: National Academies of Sciences, Engineering, and Medicine. (2015). *The Integration of Immigrants into American Society.* Panel on the Integration of Immigrants into American Society, M.C. Waters and M.G. Pineau, Eds. Committee on Population, Division of Behavioral and Social Sciences and Education. Washington, DC: The National Academies Press. doi: 10.17226/21746.

The National Academies of
SCIENCES · ENGINEERING · MEDICINE

The **National Academy of Sciences** was established in 1863 by an Act of Congress, signed by President Lincoln, as a private, nongovernmental institution to advise the nation on issues related to science and technology. Members are elected by their peers for outstanding contributions to research. Dr. Ralph J. Cicerone is president.

The **National Academy of Engineering** was established in 1964 under the charter of the National Academy of Sciences to bring the practices of engineering to advising the nation. Members are elected by their peers for extraordinary contributions to engineering. Dr. C. D. Mote, Jr., is president.

The **National Academy of Medicine** (formerly the Institute of Medicine) was established in 1970 under the charter of the National Academy of Sciences to advise the nation on medical and health issues. Members are elected by their peers for distinguished contributions to medicine and health. Dr. Victor J. Dzau is president.

The three Academies work together as the **National Academies of Sciences, Engineering, and Medicine** to provide independent, objective analysis and advice to the nation and conduct other activities to solve complex problems and inform public policy decisions. The Academies also encourage education and research, recognize outstanding contributions to knowledge, and increase public understanding in matters of science, engineering, and medicine.

Learn more about the National Academies of Sciences, Engineering, and Medicine at **www.national-academies.org**.

PANEL ON INTEGRATION OF IMMIGRANTS INTO AMERICAN SOCIETY

MARY C. WATERS (*Chair*), Department of Sociology, Harvard University

RICHARD ALBA, Department of Sociology, Graduate Center of the City University of New York

FRANK D. BEAN, Center for Research on Immigration, Population and Public Policy, University of California, Irvine

IRENE BLOEMRAAD, Department of Sociology, University of California, Berkeley

MICHAEL FIX, Migration Policy Institute

NANCY FONER, Department of Sociology, Hunter College, and Graduate Center of the City University of New York

CHARLES HIRSCHMAN, Department of Sociology at the Daniel J. Evans School of Governance and Public Policy, University of Washington

DANIEL T. LICHTER, Department of Policy Analysis and Management, Department of Sociology, and the Cornell Population Center, Cornell University

DOUGLAS S. MASSEY, Department of Sociology and Public Affairs and the Woodrow Wilson School, Princeton University

CECILIA MENJIVAR, Department of Sociology, University of Kansas

S. KARTHICK RAMAKRISHNAN, Department of Public Policy and Political Science, University of California, Riverside

AUDREY SINGER, Metropolitan Policy Program, Brookings Institution

DAVID T. TAKEUCHI, Boston College School of Social Work

KEVIN J.A. THOMAS, Department of Sociology, Demography, and African Studies, and the Population Research Institute, Pennsylvania State University

STEPHEN TREJO, Department of Economics, University of Texas at Austin

RICHARD WRIGHT, Department of Geography and Public Affairs, Dartmouth College

HIROKAZU YOSHIKAWA, Department of Globalization and Education at the Steinhardt School and Global TIES for Children Center, New York University

MARISA GERSTEIN PINEAU, *Study Director*
THOMAS J. PLEWES, *Senior Staff Officer*
MARY GHITELMAN, *Program Assistant*
TINA M. LATIMER, *Program Coordinator*

v

Preface

In the years since the publication of the institution's last major report on immigration, *The New Americans* (National Research Council, 1997), there have been massive shifts in the demographics, legal status, geographic location, and overall impact of immigration. These shifts have raised new concerns about the integration of immigrants in the United States. The aim of this project was therefore to facilitate a more informed and fact-based discussion of this topic.

The panel formally met six times over the period from January 2014 to March 2015 in order to collect information to assist in its deliberations and to prepare this report. During this time, an active national debate over the course of U.S. immigration policy was ongoing, highlighted by the November 2014 announcement by President Obama of the Immigration Accountability Executive Action, intended to provide relief from deportation for parents of citizen children and people who arrived as children and to prioritize the deportation of felons, along with further strengthening border enforcement. These actions could significantly affect the path to integration into U.S. society of millions of immigrants, particularly those in the country without proper documentation. The Executive action also expanded the population eligible for the Deferred Action for Childhood Arrivals (DACA) Program and extended the period of DACA and work authorization, from 2 to 3 years and allowed parents of U.S. citizens and lawful permanent residents who have been present in the country since January 1, 2010, to request deferred action and employment authorization for 3 years under the new Deferred Action for Parental Accountability (DAPA) Program. However, the expansion of DACA and establishment of

DAPA were quickly blocked by federal courts. At the time this report was completed, the implementation of the Executive action was unsettled, and its possible effects are unknown.

At the same time he announced the Executive action, President Obama established the White House Task Force on New Americans, an interagency group tasked with reviewing the federal government's immigrant integration efforts in order to make recommendations to improve these services. The task force released an initial report in April 2015, and its findings and recommendations are cited throughout this report. The Task Force will report its final findings and recommendations to the President in November 2015.

The panel's charge was to address the questions of immigrant integration in multiple domains. We did this by our own research, by inviting leading researchers to meetings to offer their perspectives on these questions, and by commissioning papers to address specific issues. The presentations and subsequent panel deliberations gave the panel the opportunity to develop the perspectives and articulate the challenges shared here. This volume is the product of that study process, and drafting the report was a collaborative enterprise.

We thank everyone who made presentations to the panel, including Erwin de Leon, The Urban Institute; Roberto Gonzalez, Harvard Graduate School of Education; Robert P. Jones, Public Religion Research Institute; Ali Noorani, National Immigration Forum; Jeffrey Passel, Pew Research Center; Anne Piehl, Rutgers University; Alex Piquero, University of Texas at Dallas; and Veronica Terriquez, University of Southern California. A special note of appreciation is owed to those who contributed commissioned papers: Catherine Barry, U.S. Department of Veterans Affairs; Leighton Ku, George Washington University; and Charis Kubrin, University of California, Irvine. We particularly thank Cristina Rodriguez of Yale University who prepared a paper for us on the legal aspects of immigrant integration that was the foundation of Chapter 2; this report is very much strengthened by her contributions. We also thank Youngmin Yi, Department of Sociology, Cornell University, who prepared three tables for Chapter 6.

This report was authored by the committee. Despite having many other responsibilities, members of the committee generously donated their time and expertise to the project. Members contributed to the study by drafting and revising chapters, providing background readings, leading discussions, making presentations, and critically commenting on the various report drafts. The perspectives that members brought to the table were instrumental in synthesizing ideas throughout the committee process. The committee worked together remarkably well and with a great commitment to balance and to reviewing the available evidence to draw conclusions on a very complex and contentious topic. It was a pleasure to serve with them.

Several members of the staff of the National Academies of Sciences, Engineering, and Medicine made significant contributions to the report. The panel was established under the auspices of the Committee on Population, directed by Thomas Plewes, who was instrumental in developing the study and providing guidance and support to the staff throughout the project. We are all greatly indebted to our study director, Marisa Gerstein Pineau, who worked tirelessly, wrote brilliantly, edited ruthlessly, and with great humor and equanimity managed a task that never should have been possible in such a short period of time. Special thanks are due to Danielle Johnson, Tina Latimer, and Mary Ghitelman, who provided logistics and report preparation support throughout the project. Kirsten Sampson Snyder ably guided the volume through report review, Robert Katt served as editor, and Yvonne Wise managed the report production process.

The project was undertaken with the support of the Carnegie Corporation of New York, the National Science Foundation (NSF), the Russell Sage Foundation, and the U.S. Citizenship and Immigration Services (USCIS). Particular thanks go to Geri Mannion of the Carnegie Corporation of New York; Patricia White of NSF; Aixa Cintron-Velez of the Russell Sage Foundation; and Jason Ackleson, Delancey Gustin, Michael Hoefer, Tiffany Lightbourn, Laura Patching, and Nathan Stiefel of USCIS, all of whom represented these sponsoring organizations throughout the study development and information gathering processes and made innumerable contributions to the final product. Patricia White also provided the panel with original analysis of polling data for our report while on sabbatical at the National Academies of Sciences, Engineering, and Medicine. We are grateful to them and their organizations for their support.

This report has been reviewed in draft form by individuals chosen for their diverse perspectives and technical expertise, in accordance with procedures approved by the institution's Report Review Committee. The purpose of this independent review is to provide candid and critical comments that will assist the institution in making its published report as sound as possible and to ensure that the report meets institutional standards for objectivity, evidence, and responsiveness to the study charge. The review comments and draft manuscript remain confidential to protect the integrity of the deliberative process.

We thank the following individuals for their review of this report: Claire D. Brindis, Bixby Center for Global Reproductive Health and Adolescent and Young Adult Health-National Resource Center, University of California, San Francisco; Katharine M. Donato, Department of Sociology, Vanderbilt University; Elena Fuentes-Afflick, Pediatrics and Academic Affairs, University of California, San Francisco; Tomás Jiménez, Department of Sociology, Stanford University; Michael Jones-Correa, Department of Government, Cornell University; John R. Logan, Spatial Structures in the

Social Sciences, Department of Sociology, Brown University; Emilio A. Parrado, Department of Sociology and Population Studies Center, University of Pennsylvania; Manuel Pastor, Sociology and American Studies and Ethnicity and Program for Environmental and Regional Equity and Center for the Study of Immigrant Integration, University of Southern California; Giovanni Peri, Department of Economics and Temporary Migration Cluster, University of California, Davis; Zhenchao Qian, Department of Sociology and Institute for Population Research, Ohio State University; and David D. Yao, Industrial Engineering and Operations Research, Columbia University.

Although the reviewers listed above provided many constructive comments and suggestions, they were not asked to endorse the contents of this volume before its release. The review of this report was overseen by Michael Hout of the Department of Sociology, New York University, and Ellen W. Clayton of the Center for Biomedical Ethics and Society, Vanderbilt University. Appointed by the National Academies of Science, Engineering, and Medicine, they were responsible for making certain that an independent examination of this report was carried out in accordance with institutional procedures and that all review comments were carefully considered. Responsibility for the final content rests entirely with the authors.

Mary C. Waters, *Chair*
Panel on the Integration of Immigrants
into American Society

Contents

xi

Summary

The United States prides itself on being a nation of immigrants, and the nation has a long history of successfully absorbing people from across the globe. The successful integration of immigrants and their children contributes to economic vitality and to a vibrant and ever-changing culture. Americans have offered opportunities to immigrants and their children to better themselves and to be fully incorporated into U.S. society, and in exchange *immigrants* have become *Americans*—embracing an American identity and citizenship, protecting the United States through service in its military, fostering technological innovation, harvesting its crops, and enriching everything from the nation's cuisine to its universities, music, and art.

2015 marked the 50th anniversary of the passage of the Immigration Act of 1965, which began the most recent period of mass immigration to the United States. This act abolished the restrictive quota system of the 1920s and opened up legal immigration to all the countries in the world, helping to set the stage for a dramatic increase in immigration from Asia, Africa, Latin America, and the Caribbean. At the same time, it limited the numbers of legal immigrants coming from countries in the Western Hemisphere, thus establishing restrictions on immigrants across the U.S. southern border and setting the stage for the rise in undocumented border crossers. Although the Immigration Act of 1965 exemplified the progressive ideals of the 1960s, the system it engendered may also hinder some immigrants' and their descendants' prospects for integration.

Today, the 41 million immigrants in the United States represent 13.1 percent of the U.S. population. The U.S.-born children of immigrants, the second generation, represent another 37.1 million people, or 12 percent of the population. Thus, together the first and second generations account for one out of four members of the U.S. population. Whether they are successfully integrating is therefore a pressing and important question.

To address this question, the Panel on the Integration of Immigrants into American Society was charged with (1) summarizing what is known about how immigrants and their descendants are integrating into American society; (2) discussing the implications of this knowledge for informing various policy options; and (3) identifying any important gaps in existing knowledge and data availability. Another panel appointed under the National Academies of Sciences, Engineering, and Medicine will be publishing its final report later this year; that report will examine the economic and fiscal impacts of immigration and present projections of immigration and of related economic and fiscal trends in the future. That report will complement but does not overlap with this panel's work on immigrant integration.

The panel defines integration as the process by which members of immigrant groups and host societies come to resemble one another. That process, which has both economic and sociocultural dimensions, begins with the immigrant generation and continues through the second generation and beyond. The process of integration depends upon the participation of immigrants and their descendants in major social institutions such as schools and the labor market, as well as their social acceptance by other Americans. Greater integration implies movement toward parity of critical life opportunities with the native-born American majority. Integration may make immigrants and their children better off and in a better position to fully contribute to their communities, which is no doubt a major objective for the immigrants themselves. If immigrants come to the United States with very little education and become more like native-born Americans by getting more education, they are considered more integrated. They are also considered better off, because more education improves their well-being. However, integration does not always improve well-being. For example, immigrants on average come to the United States with better health than native-born Americans, but as they integrate in other ways, they also become less healthy. Therefore, their well-being (as measured by health) declines. So, to the extent that available data allow, the panel measured two separate dimensions of change—integration and well-being. The first dimension, integration, speaks to whether immigrants and the native-born become more like one another; the second dimension, well-being, examines whether immigrants are better or worse off over time.

Integration is a two-way process: it happens both because immigrants experience change once they arrive and because native-born Americans change in response to immigration. The process of integration takes time, and the panel measured the process in two ways: for the first generation, by examining what happens in the time since arrival; for the second and third generations—the children and grandchildren of immigrants—by comparisons across generations.

PATTERNS OF INTEGRATION

Overall, the panel found that current immigrants and their descendants are integrating into U.S. society. This report documents the course and extent of integration, and the report's chapters draw 18 formal conclusions with regard to integration. Across all measurable outcomes, integration increases over time, with immigrants becoming more like the native-born with more time in the country, and with the second and third generations becoming more like other native-born Americans than their parents were.

For the outcomes of educational attainment, income, occupational distribution, living above the poverty line, residential integration, and language ability, immigrants also increase their well-being as they become more similar to the native-born and improve their situation over time. Still, the well-being of immigrants and their descendants is highly dependent on immigrant starting points and on the segment of American society—the racial and ethnic groups, the legal status, the social class, and the geographic area—into which they integrate. There are three notable outcomes where well-being declines as immigrants and their descendants converge with native-born Americans: health, crime, and the percentage of children growing up with two parents. We discuss these outcomes below.

Education

Despite large differences in starting points among the first generation, there has been strong intergenerational progress in educational attainment. Second generation members of most contemporary immigrant groups meet or exceed the schooling level of typical third+ generation native-born Americans. This is true for both men and women.

However, this general picture masks important variations between and within groups. One difference from earlier waves of immigration is the large percentage of highly skilled immigrants now coming to the United States. More than a quarter of the foreign-born now has a college education or more, and they contribute a great deal to the U.S. scientific and technical workforce. These immigrants' children also do exceptionally well educationally and typically attain the top tiers of the occupational distribution.

Other immigrants start with exceptionally low levels of education. This is particularly true for foreign-born Mexicans and Central Americans, who on average have less than 10 years of education. These immigrants' children progress a great deal relative to their parents, with an average education of more than 12 years, but they do not reach parity with the general population of native-born. This outcome mostly reflects the low levels of schooling, English proficiency, and other forms of human capital their parents bring to the United States.

Employment and Earnings

Immigrant men have higher employment rates than the second and higher generations. This employment advantage is especially dramatic among the least educated immigrants, who are much more likely to be employed than comparably educated native born men, indicating that they are filling an important niche in our economy. For second+ generation men, the trajectories vary by ethnicity and race. By this measure, Asian men are successfully integrating with the non-Hispanic white population, and Hispanic men are making gains once their lower education is taken into account. However, second generation blacks appear to be integrating with the general black native-born population, where higher education does not translate into higher employment rates. Among women the pattern is reversed, with a substantially lower employment rate for immigrants than for the native-born, but employment rates for second and higher generation women moving toward parity with the general native-born population, regardless of race.

Foreign-born workers' earnings improve relative to the native-born the longer they reside in the United States. These overall patterns, however, are still shaped by racial and ethnic stratification. Earnings assimilation is considerably slower for Hispanic (predominantly Mexican) immigrants than for other immigrants. And although Asian immigrants and their descendants appear to do just as well as native-born whites, these comparisons become less favorable after controlling for education. Asian Americans' schooling advantage can obscure the fact that, at least among men, they tend to earn somewhat less than third+ generation non-Hispanic whites with the same level of education.

Occupations

The occupational distributions of the first and second generations reveal a picture of intergenerational improvement similar to that for education and earnings. The groups concentrated in low-status occupations in the first generation improve their occupational position substantially in the second generation, although they do not reach parity with third+ generation Americans. Second generation children of immigrants from Mexico and Central America have made large leaps in occupational terms: 22 percent of second generation Mexican men and 31 percent of second generation men from Central America in 2003-2013 were in professional or managerial positions. Like their foreign-born fathers, second generation men were overrepresented in service jobs, although they have largely left agricultural work. Second generation Mexican men were also less likely than their immigrant parents to take jobs in the informal sector and were more likely to receive health and retirement benefits through their employment. The occupational leap for second generation women for this period was even greater, and the gap separating them from later generation women narrowed greatly.

The robust representation of the first and second generations across the occupational spectrum in these analyses implies that the U.S. workforce has been welcoming immigrants and their children into higher-level jobs in recent decades. This pattern of workforce integration appears likely to continue as the baby boom cohorts complete their retirement over the next two decades.

Poverty

Immigrants are more likely to be poor than the native-born, even though their labor force participation rates are higher and they work longer hours on average. The poverty rate for foreign-born persons was 18.4 percent in 2013, compared to 13.4 percent for the native-born. However, the poverty rate declined over generations, from over 18 percent for first generation adults (immigrants) to 13.6 percent in the second generation and 11.5 percent by the third+ generation. These overall patterns vary by race and ethnic group, with a troubling rise in poverty for the black second+ generations relative to the black first generation. The panel's analysis also shows progress stalling among Asian Americans between the second and third generations. Overall, first generation Hispanics have the highest poverty rates, but there is much progress from the first to the second generation.

Residential Integration

Over time most immigrants and their descendants gradually become less segregated from the general population of native-born whites and more dispersed across regions, cities, communities, and neighborhoods. Earnings and occupation explain some but not all of the high levels of foreign-born segregation from other native-born residents. Length of residence also matters: recently arrived immigrants often choose to live in areas with other immigrants and thus have higher levels of residential segregation from native-born whites than immigrants who have been in the country for 10-20 years. Race plays an independent role—Asians are the least segregated in metropolitan areas from native-born whites, followed by Hispanics and then black immigrants, who are the most segregated from native-born whites. New research also points to an independent effect of legal status, with the undocumented being more segregated than other immigrants.

Language

Language diversity in the United States has grown as the immigrant population has increased and become more varied. Today, about 85 percent of the foreign-born population speaks a language other than English at home. The most prevalent language (other than English) is by far Spanish: 62 percent of all immigrants speak Spanish at home.

However, a more accurate measure of language integration is English-language proficiency, or how well people say they speak English. There is evidence that integration is happening as rapidly or faster now than it did for the earlier waves of mainly European immigrants in the 20th century. Today, many immigrants arrive already speaking English as a first or second language. Currently, about 50 percent of the foreign-born in surveys report they speak English "very well" or "well," while less than 10 percent say they speak English "not at all." There are significant differences in English proficiency by region and country of birth: immigrants from Latin America and the Caribbean generally report lower rates of English-language proficiency than immigrants from other regions, and they are most likely to say they speak English "not at all."

The second+ generations are generally acquiring English and losing their ancestors' language at roughly the same rates as their historical predecessors, with English monolingualism usually occurring within three generations. Spanish speakers and their descendants, however, appear to be acquiring English and losing Spanish more slowly than other immigrant groups. Yet even in the large Spanish-speaking concentration in Southern California, Mexican Americans' transition to English dominance is all but complete by the third generation; only 4 percent still speak primarily Spanish at home, although 17 percent reported they can speak Spanish very well.

Despite the positive outlook for linguistic integration, the barriers to English proficiency, particularly for low-skilled, poorly educated, residentially segregated, and undocumented immigrant populations, are cause for concern. Funding for English-as a second-language classes has declined even as the population of English-language learners (ELL) has grown. The number of children who are ELL has grown substantially in recent decades, presenting challenges for many school systems. Since 1990, the school-age ELL population has grown at a much faster rate than the school-age population overall. Today, 9 percent of all students in the K-12 system are ELL. Their relative concentration varies widely by state and district. Overall resources for education in English as a second language are limited for both adults and children.

Health

Foreign-born immigrants have better infant, child, and adult health outcomes than the U.S.-born population in general and better outcomes than U.S.-born members of their ethnic group. In comparison with native-born Americans, the foreign-born are less likely to die from cardiovascular disease and all cancers combined; they experience fewer chronic health conditions, lower infant mortality rates, lower rates of obesity, and fewer functional limitations. Immigrants also have a lower prevalence of depression and of alcohol abuse.

Foreign-born immigrants live longer, too. They have a life expectancy of 80.0 years, 3.4 years more than the native-born population, and this immigrant advantage holds across all the major ethnoracial categories. Over time and generations, these advantages decline as their health status converges with the native-born.

Even though immigrants generally have better health than native-born Americans, they are disadvantaged when it comes to receiving health care to meet their preventive and medical health needs. The Affordable Care Act (ACA) seems likely to improve this situation for many poor immigrants, but undocumented immigrants are specifically excluded from all coverage under the ACA and are not entitled to any nonemergency care in U.S. hospitals.

Crime

Increased prevalence of immigrants is associated with lower crime rates—the opposite of what many Americans fear. Among men ages 18-39, the foreign-born are incarcerated at a rate that is one-fourth the rate for the native-born. Cities and neighborhoods with greater concentrations of immigrants have much lower rates of crime and violence than comparable nonimmigrant neighborhoods. This phenomenon is reflected not only across space but also over time. There is, however, evidence that crime rates for the second and third generation rise to more closely match the general population of native-born Americans. If this trend is confirmed, it may be an unwelcome aspect of integration.

Family Patterns

The panel's analysis indicates that immigrant family-formation patterns change over time. Immigrant divorce rates and out-of-wedlock birth rates start out much lower than the rates for native-born Americans generally, but over time and over generations these rates increase, while the likelihood of living in extended families with multiple generations under one roof declines. Thus immigrant children are much more likely to live in families with two parents than are third generation children. This is true overall and within all of the major ethnic and racial groups. Two-parent families provide children with a number of important advantages: they are associated with lower risks of poverty, more effective parenting practices, and lower levels of stress than are households with only one or no parents. The prevalence of two-parent families continues to be high for second generation children, but the percentage of children in two-parent families declines substantially between the second and third generations, converging toward the percentage for other native-born families. Since single-parent families are more likely to be impoverished, this is a disadvantage going forward.

CAUSES FOR CONCERN

The panel identified three causes for concern in the integration of immigrants: the role of legal status in slowing or blocking the integration of not just the undocumented but also their U.S.-citizen children; racial patterns in immigrant integration and the resulting racial stratification in the U.S. population; and the low percentage of immigrants who naturalize, compared with other major immigrant-receiving countries.

Legal Status

As the evidence examined by the panel made clear, an immigrant's legal status is a key factor in that individual's integration trajectory. Immigration statuses fall into four rough categories: permanent, temporary, discretionary, and undocumented. These statuses lie on a continuum of precariousness and security, with differences in the right to remain in the United States, rights to benefits and services from the government, ability to work, susceptibility to deportation, and ability to participate fully in the economic, political, social, and civic life of the nation. In recent decades, these statuses have multiplied due to changes in immigration policy, creating different paths and multiplying the roadblocks to integration into American society.

People often transition between different immigration statuses. Over half of those receiving lawful permanent resident (LPR) status in 2013 were already residing in the United States and adjusted their status to permanent from a visa that allowed them to work or study only temporarily in the United States. Many immigrants thus begin the process of integration into American society—working, sending their children to school, interacting with neighbors, and making friends—while living with a temporary status that does not automatically put them on the path to LPR or citizenship. Likewise, some undocumented immigrants live here for decades with no legal status while putting down deep roots in American society. Currently, there are insufficient data on changes in the legal status of immigrants over time to measure the presumably large effects of those trajectories on the process of integration.

Since the mid-1990s, U.S. immigration policy has become more punitive toward the undocumented, and interior enforcement policies have attempted to prevent their employment and long-term residence in this country. An estimated 11.3 million (26%) of the foreign-born in the United States are undocumented. Their number rose rapidly from the 1990s through 2007, reaching a peak of 12.2 million, but then fell with the Great Recession in 2008 and a sharp decline in immigration from Mexico, plateauing at 11.3 million since then. Although undocumented immigrants come from all over the globe and one in ten undocumented immigrants come from Asia, more than three-quarters are from North and Central America. The majority of the undocumented residents in the United States today—about 52 percent—are from Mexico.

It is a political, not a scientific, question whether we should try to prevent the integration of the undocumented or provide a path to legalization, and thus not within this panel's purview. However, the panel did find evidence that the current immigration policy has several effects on integration. First, it has only partially affected the integration of the undocumented, many of whom have lived in the United States for decades. The shift in recent years to a more intense regime of enforcement has not prevented the undocumented from working, but it has coincided with a reduction in their wages. Undocumented students are less likely than other immigrants to graduate from high school and enroll in college, undermining their long-term earnings capacity.

Second, the immigration impasse has led to a plethora of laws targeting the undocumented at local, state, and federal levels. These laws often contradict each other, creating variation in integration policies across the country. Some states and localities provide in-state college tuition for undocumented immigrants, some provide driver's licenses, and some are declaring themselves to be sanctuary cities. In other localities, there are restrictive laws, such as prohibitions on renting housing to undocumented immigrants or aggressive local enforcement of federal immigration laws.

Finally, the current system includes restrictions on the receipt of public benefits, and those restrictions have created barriers to the successful integration of the U.S.-citizen children of the undocumented, even though, as citizens, it is in the country's best interest that these children integrate successfully. Today, 5.2 million children in the United States reside with at least one undocumented immigrant parent. The vast majority of these children—4.5 million—are U.S.-born citizens. Included in this total are almost 7 percent of students in kindergarten through high school (K-12), presenting important challenges for schools, including behavioral issues among these children. Policies designed to block the integration of undocumented immigrants or individuals with a temporary status can have the unintended effect of halting or hindering the integration of U.S. citizens and LPRs in mixed-status families. Laws are often designed to apply to individuals, but their effects ripple through households, families, and communities, with measurable long-term negative impacts on children who are lawful U.S. citizens.

Race

The panel found that patterns of immigrant integration are shaped by race. Although there is evidence of integration and improvement in socioeconomic outcomes for blacks, Latinos, and Asians, their perceived race still matters, even after controlling for all their other characteristics. Black immigrants and their descendants are integrating with native-born non-Hispanic whites at the slowest rate. Asian immigrants and their descendants are integrating with native-born non-Hispanic whites most quickly, and Latinos are in between. The panel found some evidence of racial discrimination against Latinos and some evidence that their overall trajectories of integration are shaped more by the large numbers of undocumented in their group than by a process of racialization. At this time, it is not possible with the data available to the panel to definitively state whether Latinos are experiencing a pattern of racial exclusion or a pattern of steady progress that could lead to a declining significance of group boundaries. What can be reasonably concluded is that progress in reducing racial discrimination and disparities in socioeconomic outcomes in the United States will improve the outcomes for the native-born and immigrants alike.

Naturalization Rates

Birthright citizenship is one of the most powerful mechanisms of formal political and civic inclusion in the United States. Yet naturalization rates in the United States lag behind other countries that receive substantial numbers of immigrants. The overall level of citizenship among working-age immigrants (15-64 years old) who have been living in the United States for at least 10 years is 50 percent. After adjustments to account for the undocumented population in the United States, a group that is barred by law from citizenship, the naturalization rate among U.S. immigrants rises slightly but is still well below many European countries and far lower than other traditional receiving countries such as Australia and Canada. This is surprising since the vast majority of immigrants, when surveyed, report wanting to become a U.S. citizen. Moderate levels of naturalization in the United States appear to stem not from immigrants' lack of interest or even primarily from the bureaucratic process of applying for citizenship but from somewhere in the process by which individuals translate their motivation to naturalize into action. Further research is needed to clearly identify the barriers to naturalization. Low naturalization rates have important implications for political integration because the greatest barriers to immigrants' political participation, especially participation in elections, are gaining citizenship and registering to vote after becoming a citizen.

EFFECT OF IMMIGRATION ON SOCIETY

Previous immigration from around the globe changed the United States. It is much more difficult to see and to measure the ways in which immigration is changing the country now because it is notoriously hard to measure cultural changes while they are occurring. It is also difficult because the United States is a very heterogeneous society already, and new immigration adds to that diversity. It is difficult to measure the society that immigrants are integrating into when the society itself does not remain static. The major way in which the panel outlines how immigration has affected American society is by documenting the growth in racial, ethnic, and religious diversity in the U.S. population, which has resulted in increased intergroup contact and the transformation of American communities and institutions.[1]

In 1970, 83 percent of the U.S. population was non-Hispanic white; today, that proportion is about 62 percent, and immigration is responsible for much of that change, both directly through arrival of foreign-born immigrants and indirectly through the higher birth rates of immigrants and their children. Hispanics have grown from just over 4.5 percent of the total U.S. population in 1970 to about 17 percent today. Asians are currently the fastest-growing immigrant group in the country, as immigration from Mexico has declined; Asians represented less than 1 percent of the population in 1970 but are 6 percent today. Black immigration has also grown. In 1970, blacks were just 2.5 percent of the foreign-born; today, they are 9 percent of immigrants residing in the United States.

Ethnic and racial diversity resulting from immigration is no longer limited to a few states and cities that have histories of absorbing immigrants. Today, new immigrants are moving throughout the country, including into areas that have not witnessed a large influx of immigrants for centuries.

---

[1] As discussed above, this report does not examine the effects of immigration on the U.S. economy. That is the charge of the other National Academies of Sciences, Engineering, and Medicine panel.

This new pattern has changed the landscape of immigration. The states with the fastest growth rates of immigrant population today are primarily in the South. The presence of racial- and religious-minority immigrants in new localities and in nonmetropolitan areas raises new challenges of integration and incorporation for many communities and small towns that are unaccustomed to substantial minority and immigrant populations. At the same time, there are many localities in new destination areas that have adopted welcoming strategies to encourage immigrant workers and foster their integration into the community.

In urban areas across the country, immigrants and descendants have been "pioneer integrators" of previously all-white or all-black spaces. The result is that many neighborhoods are more diverse now than they have ever been, and the number of all-white census tracts has fallen. Yet racial segregation is still prevalent throughout the country, with blacks experiencing the most segregation from whites, followed by segregation of Hispanics and then Asians from the non-Hispanic white population.

While three-quarters of all immigrants are Christian, immigration is also bringing new religious diversity to the United States. Four percent of the foreign-born are Muslim, and although Muslim immigrants are doing better than the national average in education and income, they do report encountering high levels of prejudice and discrimination. Religious diversity is especially notable among Asian immigrants, with sizable numbers of Hindus, Buddhists, and those who do not identify with any religion. Participation in religious organizations helps immigrants and may shore up support for the religious organizations they support, even as native-born Americans' religious affiliation declines.

Immigrants have also contributed enormously to America's shifting patterns of racial and ethnic mixing in intimate and marital relationships. Marriages between the native-born and immigrants appear to have increased significantly over time. Today, about one of every seven new marriages is an interracial or interethnic marriage, more than twice the rate a generation ago. Perhaps as a result, the social and cultural boundaries between native-born and foreign-born populations in the United States are much less clearly defined than in the past. Moreover, second and third generation individuals from immigrant minority populations are far more likely to marry higher generation native-born partners than are their first generation counterparts. These intermarriages also contribute to the increase in mixed-race Americans.

An additional important effect of intermarriage is on family networks. A recent survey reported that more that 35 percent of Americans said that one of their "close" kin is of a different race. Integration of immigrants and their descendants is a major contributor to this large degree of intermixing. In the future, the lines between what Americans today think of as separate ethnoracial groups may become much more blurred. Indeed, immigrants become Americans not just by integrating into our neighborhoods, schools, and workplaces, but also into our families. Very quickly, "they" become "us."

THE NEED FOR BETTER DATA

The panel was handicapped in its work by the dearth of available longitudinal data to measure immigrant integration. This is a long-standing problem that has become increasingly critical as immigration to the United States has increased and as immigrants have become dispersed throughout the country. The panel made several specific recommendations for data collection that are outlined in detail in Chapter 10. These include the following:

- That the federal government collect data on generational status by adding a question on birthplace of parents to the American Community Survey, in order to measure the integration of the second generation.
- That the Current Population Survey test and if possible add a question on legal statuses at entry or at present, leaving those in undocumented status to be identified by process of elimination, and that other major national surveys with large numbers of immigrants also add a question of this type to identify legal status.
- That any legislation to regularize immigrant status in the future for the undocumented include a component to survey those who apply and to follow them to understand the effects of legalization.
- That administrative data held by U.S. Citizenship and Immigration Services on visa type be linked to census and other government data, as other countries have done, and that such data be made available to researchers in secure data enclaves. Such data would significantly help federal, state, and local officials understand and develop policies to improve the integration of immigrants into U.S. society.

1

Introduction

The United States is a country that has been populated, built, and transformed by successive waves of migration from almost every part of the world. This reality is widely recognized in the familiar image of the United States as a "nation of immigrants" and by the great majority of Americans, who fondly trace their family histories to Asia, Africa, or Europe or to a mix of origins that often includes an ancestry from one or more of the many indigenous peoples of the Americas. The American national mosaic is one of long standing. In the 18th century, Jean de Crèvecoeur (1981 [1782]) observed that in America, "individuals of all nations are melted into a new race of men." More than two centuries later, the American experiment of *E Pluribus Unum* continues with one of the most generous immigration policies in the world, one that includes provisions for diversity, refugees, family reunification, and workers who bring scarce employment skills. The United States is home to almost one-fifth of the world's international migrants, including 23 million who arrived from 1990 to 2013 (United Nations Population Division, 2013). This figure (23 million net immigrants) is three times larger than the number of immigrants received by any other country during that period.

The successful integration of immigrants and their children contributes to the nation's economic vitality and its vibrant and ever-changing culture. The United States has offered opportunities to immigrants and their children to better themselves and to be fully incorporated into this society; in exchange *"immigrants"* have become *"Americans"*—embracing an American identity and citizenship, protecting the United States through service in its military, building its cities, harvesting its crops, and enriching everything from the nation's cuisine to its universities, music, and art.

This has not always been a smooth process, and Americans have sometimes failed to live up to ideals of full inclusion and equality of opportunity for immigrants. Many descendants of immigrants who are fully integrated into U.S. society remember the success of their immigrant parents and grandparents but forget the resistance they encountered—the riots where Italians were killed, the branding of the Irish as criminals who were taken away in "paddy wagons," the anti-Semitism that targeted Jewish immigrants, the racist denial of citizenship to Chinese immigrants, and the shameful internment of Japanese American citizens. This historical amnesia contributes to the tendency to celebrate the nation's success in integrating past immigrants and to worry that somehow the most recent immigrants will not integrate and instead pose a threat to American society and civic life.

2015 was the 50th anniversary of the passage in 1965 of the Hart Celler Act, which amended the Immigration and Nationality Act of 1952 (INA) and began the most recent period of mass immigration to the United States. These amendments abolished the restrictive quota system of the 1920s and opened up legal immigration to all countries in the world, setting the stage for a dramatic increase in immigration from Asia and Africa. At the same time, they limited the numbers of legal immigrants permitted from countries in the Western Hemisphere, establishing restrictions on immigrants across the U.S. southern border and setting the stage for the rise in undocumented border crossers.

Today, the approximately 41 million immigrants in the United States represent 13.1 percent of the U.S. population, which is slightly lower than it was 100 years ago. An estimated 11.3 million of these immigrants—over 25 percent—are undocumented. The U.S.-born children of immigrants, the second generation (see Box 1-1), represent another 37.1 million people, 12 percent of the population. Together, the first and second generations account for one of every four members of the U.S. population.

The numbers of immigrants coming to the United States, the racial and ethnic diversity of new immigrants, and the complex and politically fraught issue of undocumented immigrants have raised questions about whether the nation is being as successful in absorbing current immigrants and their descendants as it has been in the past. Are new immigrants and their children being well integrated into American society? Do current policies and practices facilitate their integration? How is American society being transformed by the millions of immigrants who have arrived in recent decades?

To address these issues, the Panel on the Integration of Immigrants into American Society was tasked with responding to the following questions:

BOX 1-1
Definition of "Generations"

This report follows the standard scholarly definition of "generation." The first generation are the foreign-born (the immigrants), the second generation are the U.S.-born (native-born) children of immigrants, and the third generation are the grandchildren of the immigrants. Scholars also make a distinction for immigrants who come as children as the 1.5 generation (Waters, 2014).[1] Using these generational designations, one can see that the major ethnic and racial groups in the United States vary a great deal by generation. In 2014, 90 percent of whites were third generation or higher, 4 percent were first generation, and 6 percent were second generation. Blacks were 10 percent first generation, 6 percent second, and 85 percent third generation or higher. Hispanics are very heterogeneous with regard to generation. In 2014, one-third were long-time U.S. residents with at least three generations of residence in the United States; another third were the children of immigrants (although many of them were adult children, since immigration from Latin America has been ongoing throughout the 20th and 21st centuries), and another third were foreign-born. Asians are the ethnoracial category most heavily influenced by recent immigration, with only 1 in 10 being third generation or higher in 2014, while almost two-thirds were foreign-born and almost one-third were second generation.

---

[1]Portes and Rumbaut (2006) formally defines the 1.5 generation as those who immigrated between the ages of 6 and 12; using the term 1.75 to apply to those who came from infancy to age 5, and the 1.25 generation to be from ages 13-18. In practice, researchers use different age cut-offs for the 1.5 generation, often lumping together children who arrived up to age 12 as the 1.5 generation (Portes and Rumbaut, 2001).

1. What has been the demographic impact of immigration, in terms of the size and age, sex, and racial/ethnic composition of the U.S. population from 1970 to 2010? What are the likely changes in the future?
2. What have been the effects of recent immigration on the educational outcomes, employment, and earnings of the native-born population?[1]
3. How has the social and spatial mobility of immigrants and the second generation changed over the last 45 years?

---

[1]The native-born population includes the second and third generation descendants of foreign-born immigrants. For more information about how the panel uses "generations" in this report, see Box 1-1.

4. How has the residential integration (or segregation) of immigrants and their descendants changed over the last 45 years? How has immigration affected residential segregation patterns within native-born racial and ethnic communities?
5. How rapidly are recent immigrants and their descendants integrating into American society, as measured by competency in English language, educational attainment, rate of naturalization, degree of intermarriage, maintenance of ethnic identity, health outcomes, and other dimensions?
6. How has immigration affected American institutions, including civil society, and economic and political organizations? What role do mediating institutions play in the integration process? How responsive are these institutions to the needs of immigrants and their descendants?
7. How has immigration affected the stock and growth of scientific and technological skills in universities, research organizations, and private businesses? Is it possible to measure the impact of immigration on the pace of technological change and innovation?
8. What are the general attitudes and public perceptions of native-born Americans toward (a) legal and illegal immigration and (b) how immigrants shape American society? How do these perceptions compare with the statistical record?
9. How does legal status affect immigrants' and their descendants' ability to integrate across various dimensions?
10. For each of these questions, how do outcomes vary by gender, race and ethnicity, social class, geography, and other social categories?
11. What additional data are needed for research on the role and impact of immigration on American society?

In the sections below, the panel sets up the context for answering these questions. First, we lay out the definition of integration we will use throughout the report. Second, we address the question of demographic changes in the United States since 1970. Third, we discuss demographic projections for the U.S. population based on current and predicted immigration trends. Fourth, we examine native-born attitudes toward immigration and immigrants themselves. Finally, we discuss the implications of these conditions for immigrant integration. The final section outlines the rest of the report.

INTEGRATION

"Integration"[2] is the term the panel uses to describe the changes that both immigrants and their descendants—and the society they have joined—undergo in response to migration. The panel defines integration as the process by which members of immigrant groups and host societies come to resemble one another (Brown and Bean, 2006). That process, which has both economic and sociocultural dimensions, begins with the immigrant generation and continues through the second generation and beyond (Brown and Bean, 2006). The process of integration depends upon the participation of immigrants and their descendants in major social institutions such as schools and the labor market, as well as their social acceptance by other Americans (Alba et al., 2012). Greater integration implies parity of critical life chances with the native-born American majority. This would include reductions in differences between immigrants or their descendants vis-a-vis the general population of native-born over time in indicators such as socioeconomic inequality, residential segregation, and political participation and representation. Used in this way, the term "integration" has gained near-universal acceptance in the international literature on the position of immigrants and their descendants within the society receiving them, during the contemporary era of mass international migration.

Integration is a two-fold process: it happens both because immigrants experience change once they arrive and because native-born Americans change in response to immigration. The process of integration takes time, and the panel considers the process in two ways: for the first generation, by examining what happens in the time since arrival; for the second and third generations—the children and grandchildren of immigrants—by comparisons across generations.

Integration may make immigrants and their children better off and in a better position to fully contribute to their communities, which is no doubt a major objective for the immigrants themselves. If immigrants come to the United States with very little education and become more like native-born Americans by getting more education, one would say they are more integrated. And they would also probably be viewed as being better off, because more education improves their well-being. But immigrants also, on average, come to the United States with better health than native-born Americans. As they become more like native-born Americans they become less healthy. They become more integrated and their well-being declines. So, to the extent that available data allow, the panel measured two separate

---

[2] "Assimilation" is another term widely used for the processes of incorporation of immigrants and their children and the decline of ethnic distinctions in equality of opportunity and life chances. For this report, "integration" is used as a synonym for "assimilation" as defined by Alba and Nee (2003).

dimensions of change: integration and well-being. The first asks whether immigrants and the native-born become more like one another; the second asks whether immigrants are better or worse off over time.

This report investigates whether immigrants and their children are becoming more like the general population of native-born Americans across a wide range of indicators: attitudes toward social issues, citizenship, crime, education, family structure, health, income, language, occupations, political participation, religion, and residence. Of course this is a complicated process to measure, in part because immigrants are very diverse themselves and have very different starting points in all of these domains when they arrive and because immigrants change at different paces across domains and individuals, but also because Americans are also changing. The convergence between immigrants and later generation Americans may happen because immigrants change once they get here, because native-born Americans change in response to immigration, or both. There is no presumption that change is happening in one direction only.

Indeed, bidirectional change is often easier to see in hindsight than in real time. Looking back, one can now see how the absorption of immigrants in the 19th and 20th centuries changed American culture. Many foods, celebrations, and artistic forms considered quintessentially American today originated in immigrant homelands. Current immigrants continue to contribute to the vibrancy and innovation of American culture as artists, engineers, and entrepeneurs. One-fourth of the American Nobel Prize winners since 2004, and a similar proportion of MacArthur "Genius" Awardees (which are given to people in a range of fields including the arts) have been immigrants to the United States. The foreign-born (see Box 1-2) are also overrepresented among authors of highly cited scientific papers and holders of patents (Smith and Edmonston, 1997, p. 385; Chellaraj et al., 2008; Stephan and Levin, 2001, 2007; Hunt and Gauthier-Loiselle, 2010; Kerr, 2008). To the extent that one can document changes among the native-born in the 21st century due to immigration, the panel attempts to do so, but we also suspect that many of the changes happening right now will only be visible to future historians as they look back.

Examining integration involves assessing the extent to which different groups, across generations or over time within the same generation, come to approximate the status of the general native-born population. Equality between immigrants and the native-born should not be expected in the first generation because immigrants have different background characteristics: they are younger, their education may not have been in American schools, and they may initially lack proficiency in English. But one can measure progress toward that equality among immigrants and their descendants. To measure equality of opportunity between the native-born and immigrant generations, the report employs conditional probabilities and other means to measure the likelihood of outcomes net of prior characteristics. (For in-

BOX 1-2
Immigrants versus Foreign-Born

Although this study addresses *immigrant* integration, most of the data presented in this report refers to counts of the *foreign-born*. Not all foreign-born people are immigrants, although all immigrants are, by definition, foreign-born. Some people counted by the census as foreign-born are in the United States only temporarily (see Chapter 3 for a list of all the temporary statuses that can characterize the foreign-born) and do not intend to make the United States their permanent home. The data refer to the foreign-born because of the nature of national data collection efforts, which ask respondents about their place of birth rather than their legal status or intention to remain in the United States. More specifically, the data in this report are largely based on census and survey data on the stock of foreign-born persons in the United States. Changes in the numbers of foreign-born persons over time (between censuses and surveys) are used to measure flows of immigration. There are, however, a number of limitations of census and survey data for the study of immigration (discussed in detail in Chapter 10). Even the official census definition of foreign-born—all persons who are not U.S. citizens at birth—is different from the common understanding that the foreign-born persons are those born outside the 50 states. The native-born population includes persons born in the 50 states and U.S. territories (e.g., American Samoa, Puerto Rico, etc.) and those born abroad with at least one parent who is a U.S. citizen.

The major limitation of Decennial Census, American Community Survey, and Current Population Survey data for the study of immigration is that the current visa status (and visa status at time of arrival) of respondents is not ascertained. Current citizenship and year of arrival are measured in most data sources, although with some significant variations in the wording of the question. In general, it is impossible to distinguish between legal permanent residents (green card holders), persons on nonimmigrant visas for work or study that is supposed to be temporary, and persons who do not have a current visa or are visa over-stayers, referred to in this report as undocumented immigrants. Therefore, undocumented immigrants are included in census data, but there is no way to distinguish them from other immigrant categories. In addition, some undocumented people do not answer the census. The best estimates are that about 10-15 percent of the undocumented do not answer the census and are thus undercounted (Passell and Cohn, 2011). Nonetheless, it is common statistical practice to refer to the foreign-born population as determined by a census or survey as "immigrants," despite the heterogeneity of the "foreign-born" category. As noted throughout this report, there is considerable mobility across these statuses, and current visa status does not always predict who stays permanently.

stance, does an immigrant from China with a college degree earn as much as a native-born white with a college degree?) These conditional probabilities are typically estimated for different generations of an immigrant-origin group, with statistical controls for differences from the general native-born population in demographic characteristics and skill levels.

DEMOGRAPHIC CHANGES IN THE
FOREIGN-BORN POPULATION SINCE 1970

The demographic make-up of the United States in the early 21st century is incredibly diverse compared to mid-20th century America. In many ways, the composition of the contemporary United States is more similar to the polyglot nation of the early 20th century, when major waves of immigrants were drawn by greater economic and political opportunities in the United States than were available in their countries of origin. The desire for religious freedom, flight from persecution, and family ties are also important factors spurring migration (Massey, 1999; Portes and Rumbaut, 2014; Grasmuck and Pessar, 1991). Today as in the past, nearly one in seven Americans is foreign-born. But today's immigrants are more likely to come from Latin America or Asia than from Europe, are more likely to be female, are much less likely to be white, and are more geographically dispersed than the immigrants who arrived at the turn of the 20th century. Meanwhile, the development of federal immigration law since that era (discussed in Chapter 2) has led to the rapid growth of an undocumented-immigrant population whose experiences differ from immigrants with legal status in fundamental ways (see Chapter 3).

In this section, the panel reviews the demographic changes among the foreign-born since 1970. We discuss both flows and stocks of immigrants. Flows are the numbers of arrivals and departures each year or in a designated period (e.g., decades). Stock refers to the number of foreign-born in the population at a point in time, usually based on counts in the census or other surveys such as the Current Population Survey. Both flows and stocks have measurement problems. For example, flows of immigrants as measured by administrative data of the U.S. Citizenship and Immigration Services of the Department of Homeland Security include only those immigrants who lawfully enter the United States with a visa of some kind, either permanent or temporary. The panel had less information on how many people leave the United States. Another substantial problem is that these flow data do not count those who enter without inspection, as undocumented immigrants. The stock data are based on the foreign-born as measured in censuses and surveys, but they include anyone residing in the United States, including those who do not plan to stay and do not consider themselves immigrants. Nevertheless, stock and flow data do provide different but complementary perspectives on the composition of the foreign-born population. Flow data represent the recent history of immigration. Stock data provide a snapshot of the current and future composition of the foreign-born.

The next section begins by discussing the rapid growth of immigration in recent decades and then examines the ways in which these immigrants are different from previous waves of immigrants, how they differ from the native-born, and how they are changing the overall demographics of the United States.

In the 50 years since the 1965 amendments to the INA passed, the demographics of immigration—and in consequence, the demographics of the United States—have changed dramatically. Before that law passed, the number of Americans who were foreign-born had declined steadily, shrinking from over 14 million in 1930 to less than 10 million in 1970 (see Figure 1-1). As a share of the total population, the foreign-born peaked at almost 15 percent at the turn of the 20th century and declined to less than 5 percent in 1970. After 1970, the number of foreign-born increased rapidly, doubling by 1990 to 19.9 million and doubling again by 2007 to 40.5 million.

Since the beginning of the Great Recession in 2007, net immigration to the United States appears to have plateaued and undocumented immigra-

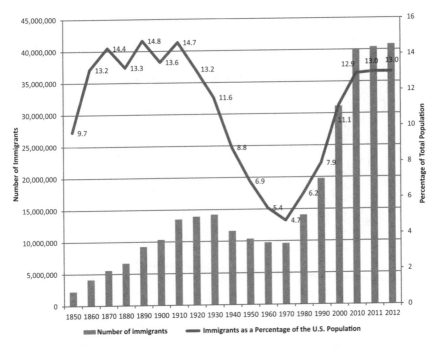

FIGURE 1-1 Number of immigrants and immigrants as percentage of the U.S. population, 1850 to 2013.
SOURCE: Original figure based on U.S. Census Bureau data.

tion appears to have declined, at least temporarily. In 2012, there were 41.7 million foreign-born in the United States, a relatively small 5-year increase compared to the rapid growth over the previous two decades. Today, 13 percent of the U.S. population is foreign-born, a proportion that is actually slightly lower than it was 100 years ago (Figure 1-1).

Regions and Countries of Origin

The vast majority of immigrants in 1900 arrived from Europe; today, the majority come from Latin America and Asia. In 1960, over 60 percent of immigrants were from Europe (see Figure 1-2), and the top five countries of birth among the foreign-born were Canada, Germany, Italy, Poland, and the United Kingdom.[3] By 1970, Europeans comprised less than 50 percent of the foreign-born, and that percentage declined rapidly in the following decades. Meanwhile the share of foreign-born from Latin America and Asia has grown rapidly. Forty-four percent of the foreign-born in the United States in 2011 were from Latin America, and 28.6 percent were from Asian countries. The top five countries of birth among the foreign-born in 2010 were China, India, Mexico, the Philippines, and Vietnam. And while immigration from Africa is proportionately much smaller, the number of immigrants from that continent has also increased steadily since 1970.

Mexican immigration has been the driver for the dramatic growth in migration from Latin America since 1970. Today, almost one-third of the foreign-born are from Mexico (see Figure 1-3). Immigration from other parts of Latin America also increased: since 1990, the number of Central American immigrants in the United States has nearly tripled (Stoney and Batalova, 2013). However, a major demographic shift in migration flows is occurring as Mexican immigration, in particular, has slowed and Asian immigration has increased. Between 2008 and 2009, Asian arrivals began to outpace immigration from Latin America; and in 2010, 36 percent of immigrants arrived from Asian countries, versus 31 percent from Latin America (see Figure 1-4). In 2013, China replaced Mexico as the top sending country for immigrants to the United States (Jensen, 2015).

Race and Ethnicity

The United States has a long history of counting and classifying its population by race and ethnicity, beginning with the first Decennial Census in 1790 (Prewitt, 2013). However, the categories of race and their interpretation have changed over time—in no small part due to immigration and the absorption of people from different parts of the world. The meaning of

---

[3] See https://www.census.gov/how/pdf//Foreign-Born--50-Years-Growth.pdf [September 2015].

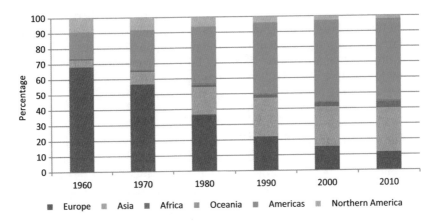

FIGURE 1-2 Immigrant population by region of birth, 1960 to 2010.
SOURCE: Original figure based on U.S. Census Bureau data.

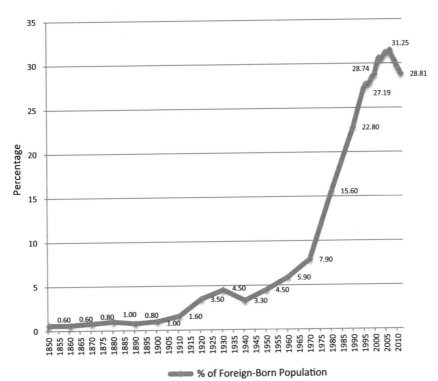

FIGURE 1-3 Mexican-born as percentage of the foreign-born population.
SOURCE: Data are from Jeffrey Passel (Pew Research Center) presentation to the
Panel on the Integration of Immigrants into American Society on January 16, 2014.

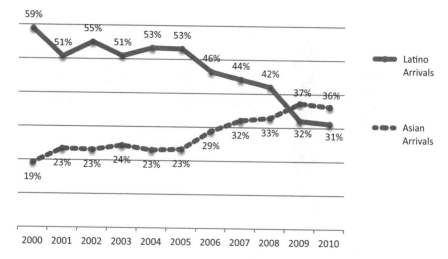

FIGURE 1-4 Latino and Asian arrivals as share of all immigrant arrivals, 2000-2010. SOURCE: Data are from Jeffrey Passel (Pew Research Center) presentation to the Panel on the Integration of Immigrants into American Society on January 16, 2014.

the term "race" itself has also changed. At the height of immigration from Europe, different national-origin groups such as the Irish, Poles, and Italians were considered "races" in popular understanding and by many social scientists, although these beliefs were not formalized in the official census classifications (Snipp, 2003; Perez and Hirschman, 2009).

This report uses the federal (as defined by the Office of Management and Budget) race and ethnic categories, with Hispanics as an independent category alongside the major race groups (see Box 1-3). The panel uses the terms "race and ethnicity" and "ethnoracial categories" to refer to this classification scheme. For example, we report on the ethnoracial categories—white non-Hispanic, black non-Hispanic, Asian non-Hispanic, American Indian non-Hispanic, and Hispanic—when we are reporting on race and ethnic characteristics of the population. We use the terms "Hispanic" and "Latino" interchangeably to refer to the same group, as these terms are used to varying degrees in different parts of the country or are preferred by different individuals.

The racial and ethnic categorizations of the population are a good example of how immigration changes American society and American society changes immigrants. Census and survey data on race and ethnicity are based on the subjective identities (self-reports) of respondents who complete written forms or respond to interviewer questions, and respondents are free to check any listed category or to write in any group identity that

---

BOX 1-3
Racial and Ethnic Categories

In 1978, the Office of Management and Budget (OMB) issued OMB Statistical Directive No. 15, which stipulated the racial and ethnic categories to be used to classify the population for federal statistical purposes. That directive defined five racial categories (American Indian/Alaskan Native, Asian and Pacific Islander, Black, White, and Other) and one ethnic classification (Hispanic or Latino, and Not Hispanic or Latino). This classification was revised in 1997 to separate Pacific Islanders from Asians in the new category, Native Hawaiian and Pacific Islander. The 1997 revision of Statistical Directive No 15 allows respondents to the census and federal surveys to report one or more races (Office of Management and Budget, 1997a, 1997b). The statistical convention to classify Hispanics as an ethnic group and not as a race is rooted in history, including a challenge from the Mexican government to the U.S. government around the use of "Mexican" as a racial category in the 1930 census. "Hispanic" has been measured separately ever since (Choldin, 1986). The issue of how to classify Hispanics reflects a larger political debate about whether Latino or Hispanic immigrants are being "racialized" into a more durable racial boundary and identity or whether they are evolving as an ethnic group, similar to Italians and Poles before them (Perlmann, 2005; Telles and Ortiz, 2008; Massey and Sánchez, 2010).

---

is not listed. Many immigrants remark that they learn their "official" ethnoracial identity soon after they arrive and are asked about it constantly: on government forms, when they register their children for school, on employment applications, etc. Many come to understand and identify with a racial or ethnic category that was often unfamiliar or meaningless before they immigrated. Black immigrants from Africa or the Caribbean had not thought of themselves as African Americans before immigrating to the United States, and the category "Asian" is often new to many people who had thought of themselves as Chinese or Pakistani before their arrival. In this sense, one can speak of people being "racialized" as they come to the United States. They may also face racial discrimination, based on neither their identity as immigrants nor their national origin identity but rather on their new "racial identity."

The shift from European to Latin American and Asian migration has also significantly changed the racial and ethnic make-up of the United States (see Figures 1-5 and 1-6). In 1970, 83 percent of Americans were non-Hispanic white; today, that proportion is 62.4 percent. In 1970, Lati-

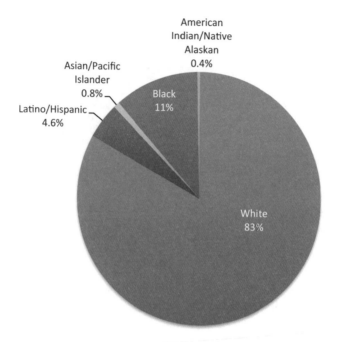

FIGURE 1-5 Racial and ethnic composition of the United States, 1970.
SOURCE: Data from U.S. Census Bureau Decennial Census, 1970. Also see Gibson and Jung (2002).

nos were approximately 4.6 percent of the total U.S. population.[4] In 2013, Latinos made up 17 percent of the U.S. population, with foreign-born Latinos accounting for 6 percent of the population, or about one-third of all Latinos.[5] Since 2000, the native-born Latino population grew at a faster rate than the foreign-born because of both a decline in migration from Mexico and an increasing number of native-born children of Latino immigrants. Overall, Latino population growth between 2000 and 2010 accounted for more than half of the nation's population growth (Passel et al., 2011).

Asians, meanwhile, have become the fastest-growing racial group in

---

[4]The 1970 Decennial Census marked the Bureau's first attempt to collect data for the entire Hispanic/Latino population. However, there were problems with data collection. For further discussion, see http://www.pewsocialtrends.org/2010/03/03/census-history-counting-hispanics-2/ [September 2015].

[5]See http://www.pewhispanic.org/2014/04/29/statistical-portrait-of-hispanics-in-the-united-states-2012/, Table 1 [September 2015].

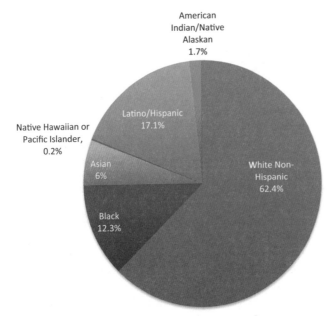

FIGURE 1-6 Racial and ethnic composition of the United States, 2013.
SOURCE: Data from American Community Survey, 2013. Available: http://www.
census.gov/acs/www/ [October 2015].

the United States (Passel, 2013). In 1970 Asians accounted for less than 1 percent of the U.S. population, a reflection of long-term discriminatory regulations that banned most Asian immigration (see Chapter 2). In 2010, they made up almost 6 percent of the U.S. population, and 74 percent of them were foreign-born (Passel, 2013).

The proportion of foreign-born among blacks in the United States is much smaller: only 9 percent in 2013. However, the number of black immigrants has increased steadily since 1970,[6] and immigrants accounted for at least 20 percent of the growth of the black population between 2000 and 2006 (Kent, 2007).

Overall, racial and ethnic minorities accounted for 91.7 percent of the nation's population growth between 2000 and 2010 (Passel et al., 2011). Non-Hispanic whites are now a minority of all births, while fertility rates for Latinos, in particular, remain relatively high (Monte and Ellis, 2014).[7] Today, there are four states where the majority of the population

---

[6]See http://www.census.gov/newsroom/press-releases/2014/cb14-184.html [September 2015].
[7]See https://www.census.gov/newsroom/press-releases/2015/cb15-113.html [September 2015].

is "minority"—California, Hawaii, New Mexico, and Texas—plus the District of Columbia (Desilver, 2015). It is not a coincidence that most of these states also have large immigrant populations. As discussed further below, the United States will be even more racially and ethnically diverse in the future, due to immigration, intermarriage, and fertility trends.

Age

The foreign-born population is now much younger than it was 50 years ago (Grieco et al., 2012).[8] The median age for the foreign-born declined dramatically after the 1965 amendments to the INA, dropping from 51.8 years in 1970 to 39.9 in 1980.[9] Before 1970, over half of all foreign-born in the United States were over the age of 50 (see Figure 1-7) and the foreign-born were mostly European immigrants who arrived during the earlier wave at the turn of the 20th century. By 2000, only 20 percent were in this age category, while 70 percent were between the ages of 18 and 54. However, after bottoming out at 37.2 years in 1990, the median age of the foreign-born began to creep upward as the proportion under the age of 18 declined. In 2012, the median age of the foreign-born was 41.4 years, compared to 35.9 years among the native-born.[10, 11]

Part of the explanation for the higher median age of the foreign-born is the large number of second generation Americans under the age of 18, which pulls down the median age of the native-born (see Figure 1-8). The vast majority of immigrants are of child-bearing age, and immigrants generally have higher fertility rates than the native-born (see Figure 1-9). In 2013, 37.1 million Americans, or about 12 percent of the population, were members of the second generation, and one-fourth of all children in the United States (17.4 million) had at least one foreign-born parent.[12] This has particular significance for the future racial and ethnic composition of the country because so many of the second generation are racial and ethnic minorities. The panel discusses the implications of this increasing diversity

---

[8]The median age for foreign-born from Mexico and Central America is the lowest at 38, while the median age for foreign-born from the Caribbean is the highest at 47. See http://www.pewhispanic.org/2013/01/29/statistical-portrait-of-the-foreign-born-population-in-the-united-states-2011/ [September 2015].

[9]See http://www.census.gov/content/dam/Census/library/working-papers/2012/demo/POP-twps0096.pdf [September 2015].

[10]See http://www.migrationpolicy.org/article/frequently-requested-statistics-immigrants-and-immigration-united-states [September 2015].

[11]Since the children of immigrants born in the United States count as native-born, and the majority of those immigrating are adults, the median age for immigrants is generally higher than it is for the native-born.

[12]See https://www.census.gov/population/foreign/files/cps2010/T4.2010.pdf [September 2015].

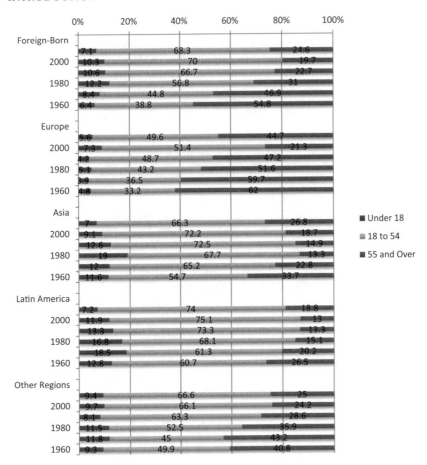

FIGURE 1-7 Age distribution of the foreign-born by region of origin, 1960-2010. SOURCE: Data from U.S. Census Bureau Decennial Census 1960-2000 and American Community Survey, 2010. Also see Grieco et al. (2012).

among the native-born in the population projections below and in the chapters that follow.

Gender

The gender ratio for the foreign-born is generally balanced, with 101 males for every 100 females (see Table 1-1).[13] The native-born population, on the other hand, skews toward more females, with a gender ratio of 95

---

[13] See http://www.migrationpolicy.org/article/sex-ratios-foreign-born-united-states [September 2015].

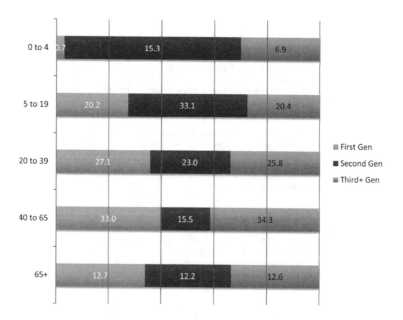

FIGURE 1-8 Age distribution by generation: Percentage in each age group.
SOURCE: Data from Current Population Survey, 2010. Available: https://www.
census.gov/population/foreign/files/cps2010/T4.2010.pdf [October 2015].

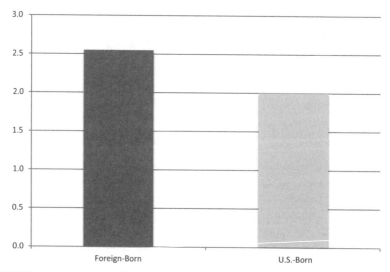

FIGURE 1-9 General fertility rates per thousand women.
SOURCE: Data from 2008-2012 American Community Survey.

males per 100 females. As the ratios by age in Table-1-1 show, these ratios vary by age because women live longer than men and because the age structure of migrants is concentrated in the young-adult working ages. Thus, a better measure is to examine gender ratios that have been age standardized. Donato and Gabaccia (2015, p. 154) created age-standardized gender ratios for the years 1850-2010, and these are plotted in Figure 1-10.

Gender ratios for all of the foreign-born have varied over time, with the percentage of women among immigrants growing. The gender composition among immigrants shifted from male dominated toward gender balanced in the 1930s and was gender balanced by the 1970s. Unstandardized rates show women at above 50 percent of the stock of immigrants beginning in 1970; standardized rates indicate a gender balanced stock where women comprise about 50 percent of the foreign-born after 1970 (Donato et.al., 2011).

As Donato and colleagues (2011, 2015) point out, because Mexicans are such a large percentage of recent immigrant flows after 1970 and because they are a much more male-dominated migration stream, it is useful to separate the gender ratio for all immigrants from the gender ratio for Mexican migrants (Figure 1-10). The lines diverge beginning in 1970 when men were predominant among the Mexican foreign-born, whereas among the rest of the foreign-born women's share continued to grow. By 2010 the percentage of females was 50 percent for all the foreign-born in the United States and was slightly higher at 51 percent when Mexicans are excluded.

Nonetheless, the gender ratios for specific source countries vary widely. India (138 males per 100 females) and Mexico (124 per 100) have male-to-female gender ratios well above the median, as do El Salvador (110 males per 100 females) and Haiti (109 per 100). Germany (64 males per 100 females), South Korea (65 per 100), the Dominican Republic (68 per 100), the Philippines (71 per 100), and Japan (74 per 100) all have much lower ratios of males to females, indicating that more females than males may be immigrating from those countries but also reflecting the age structures of the different immigrant populations (older populations in source countries such as Germany and Japan will reflect the demographic that women live longer than men in those countries).

The gender-balanced immigrant population of today reflects a complex mix of factors including shifts in labor demand, civil strife around the world leading to more refugees, and increased state regulation of migration (Donato and Gabaccia, 2015, p. 178; Oishi, 2005). Many women immigrate and work. No matter how they enter—on a family preference visa, as a close relative exempt from numerical limitations, without legal documents, or with an H-1B or other employment worker visa—most are employed in the United States after entering and are therefore meeting market demands for labor. The increasing percentage of women among immigrants

TABLE 1-1 Male to Female Ratio among Immigrants to the United States, 1870-2000

| | Males per 100 Females among U.S. Immigrants | | | | | | | | | | | | | |
	1870	1880	1890	1900	1910	1920	1930	1940	1950	1960	1970	1980	1990	2000
Total	117.4	119.1	121.2	119.5	131.1	122.9	116.6	111.8	103.3	95.6	84.4	87.8	95.8	99.0
Under 15 years	103.5	102.0	103.1	101.9	102.2	102.0	102.0	102.1	104.1	102.5	102.7	104.7	106.0	104.6
15 to 64 years	119.1	117.5	120.8	121.7	133.9	124.7	117.3	112.7	103.7	92.9	83.8	91.9	101.6	103.9
15 to 44 years	114.3	115.7	122.5	121.8	137.2	123.3	114.6	99.5	89.4	83.5	80.8	97.6	109.6	110.2
15 to 24 years	101.5	102.2	104.1	98.3	126.6	97.0	96.4	93.9	82.5	86.2	88.1	110.2	121.9	121.3
25 to 44 years	119.3	120.2	130.5	131.0	141.3	130.5	118.5	100.1	90.5	82.7	78.4	92.5	105.6	106.9
45 to 64 years	134.7	121.2	117.2	121.4	126.5	127.4	121.4	123.0	111.3	99.7	87.8	80.4	83.3	89.9
65 years and older	111.4	109.8	112.2	108.5	105.3	104.7	107.7	104.9	102.3	100.0	82.4	69.7	64.1	65.6

SOURCE: Data from U.S. Census Bureau Decennial Census. Also see Gibson and Jung (2006), Hobbs and Stoops (2002), and Ruggles et al. (2010).

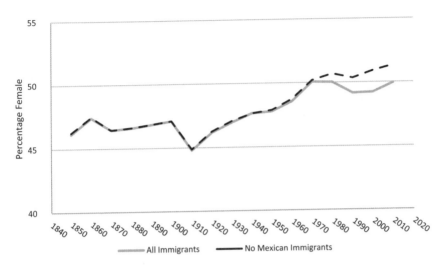

FIGURE 1-10 Standardized age ratios of the foreign-born by gender with and without Mexican foreign-born, 1850-2010.
SOURCE: Donato and Gabaccia (2015). Reprinted with permission.

thus reflects a much stronger demand for labor in a variety of occupations such as domestic service, child care, health care, factory assembly work, and food processing/production. The gender imbalance in deportations may also contribute to the feminization of Latino immigration, in particular (Mexican Migration Monitor, 2012). The increase in human trafficking in the United States and globally also contributes to the feminization of immigration (Pettman, 1996).

Geographic Dispersal

A key component of the story of recent immigration is the significant geographic dispersal of immigrants across the United States. Historically, immigrants tended to cluster in a handful of traditional gateway cities or states, such as California, Illinois, New York, and Texas. Although these states are still the most popular destinations and have the largest numbers of foreign-born, recent years have seen immigration to states that had not previously witnessed a large influx of foreign-born. The panel discusses this geographic dispersal in further detail in Chapter 5, but we highlight some of the most important trends here.

Six states—California, Florida, Illinois, New Jersey, New York, and Texas—attract the largest proportion of the foreign-born, but that share has declined in recent years, from 73 percent in 1990 to 64 percent in 2012.[14] The states with the fastest growth in immigrants today are in the South and West: Alabama, Arkansas, Georgia, Kentucky, Nebraska, Nevada, North Carolina, South Carolina, Tennessee, Utah, and Virginia. Although the numbers in many of these states are still relatively small, some saw more than 400 percent growth in their foreign-born population since 1990. The rapid growth of immigration in the South and Midwest and in the Mountain States has been dramatic in the last few decades. Many of these receiving communities were either all white or contained a mix of black and white residents but had virtually no Latino or Asian residents. The sudden influx of Latino and Asian immigrants, many of whom are undocumented, has challenged long-established racial and social hierarchies, has posed new problems for school systems who had not previously dealt with children in need of instruction in English as a second language, and sometimes has led to negative attitudes and anti-immigrant backlash. Other communities, particularly declining rural areas, have welcomed the new influx as a way to revitalize small communities that were experiencing long-term population decline.

Immigration has also broadened from traditional gateway cities, such as Chicago, Los Angeles, and New York City, to other metropolitan areas—including Atlanta, Dallas, Las Vegas, and Washington, D.C. Many immigrants to these metro areas are finding homes in the suburbs.[15] And while overall immigration to rural areas is relatively small, some rural counties have witnessed a surge in Latino immigration, particularly in places where meat processing plants are major employers.[16] This influx of immigrants has created new challenges for communities and local institutions that have not previously had to create or maintain integrative services (see Chapter 5).

Education

The European immigrants who arrived at the turn of the 20th century had less formal schooling than the native-born; on average, immigrants from southern, eastern, and central Europe had a little more than 4 years of education versus 8 years for the native-born (Perlmann, 2005). Rates of illiteracy in 1910 were less than 10 percent among immigrants from northwestern Europe and about 20 to 50 percent among immigrants from eastern and southern Europe (Lieberson, 1963, pp. 72-73). By 1920, with rising educational levels

---

[14] Data are from Jeffrey Passel, Pew Research Center, presentation to the Panel on the Integration of Immigrants into American Society on January 16, 2014.

[15] See http://www.migrationpolicy.org/article/twenty-first-century-gateways-immigrants-suburban-america [August 2015].

[16] See http://www.ers.usda.gov/topics/in-the-news/immigration-and-the-rural-workforce.aspx#Foreign [August 2015].

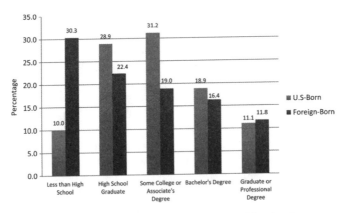

FIGURE 1-11 Educational attainment of U.S.-born and foreign-born over age 25, 2013.
SOURCE: Data from American Community Survey, 2013, 1-year estimates. Available: http://www.census.gov/acs/www/ [October 2015].

in Europe and the imposition of a literacy test in 1917, illiteracy was generally less than 2 to 3 percent for most immigrant streams from all European countries. The educational attainment of the second generation from European immigration generally matched the larger native-born population, demonstrating large strides in just one generation (Perlmann, 2005).

Since 1970, although immigrants' education level has increased, either before arrival or after they have reached the United States, immigrants are still overrepresented among the least educated: 31.7 percent have less than a high school degree, compared to 11 percent of the native-born.[17] However, the educational attainment of immigrants has risen since 1980 (Hall et al., 2011). In 2013, 28 percent had a bachelor's degree or higher, and a slightly higher proportion of immigrants than native-born had advanced degrees (see Figure 1-11). Meanwhile the largest proportion of the foreign-born are actually in the middle range of educational achievement: more than 40 percent have a high school diploma and/or some college.

Educational attainment varies a great deal in relation to immigrants' regions of origin. Despite some national variations, Asians and Europeans are generally as highly educated or more highly educated than native-born Americans. Almost 50 percent of the foreign-born from Asia and 39.1 percent from Europe have a bachelor's degree or higher, versus 27.9 percent of the U.S.-born population. But only 12.3 percent of Latin American immigrants have a bachelor's degree, and immigrants from Mexico and

---

[17]See http://www.census.gov/prod/2012pubs/acs-19.pdf [May 2015].

Central America, in particular, are much more likely to have very low levels of education. However, there is evidence that second generation Latinos make great strides in education, despite their parents' relatively low socioeconomic status. The panel discusses this further in Chapter 6.

Income

In addition to lower levels of education, European immigrants at the turn of the last century also earned less than their native-born counterparts (Perlmann, 2005). Immigrants from southern, eastern, and central Europe in particular tended to work in low-skilled jobs where wages were particularly low. However, wage inequalities between immigrants and the native-born declined over time, and the second generation nearly closed the wage gap, earning within 10 percent of the children of native-born Americans (Perlmann, 2005).

A similar pattern of intergenerational change over time occurs in earnings and household income when one examines changes between the first and second generation (see Chapter 6). Among the present-day first generation, the earnings of foreign-born workers are still generally lower than earnings of the native-born, and the gap is particularly large for men. The median income for full-time, year-round, native-born male workers is $50,534, compared to just $36,960 for foreign-born men (for comparisons for both men and women, see Figure 1-12). The income gap for foreign-born versus native-born is wider for men than for women. Nearly one-third of the foreign-born make less than $25,000 per year, compared to 19 percent of the native-born, and although almost 20 percent of immigrants make over $75,000, the native-born outpace them in every income category above $35,000 (see Figure 1-13).

Not surprisingly, native-born head of households also have higher incomes than those headed by the foreign-born. Overall, the average household income of the foreign-born was $48,137 in 2013, compared to $53,997 in native-born households. However, as with education, there is variation based on immigrants' region of origin. As Figure 1-14 shows, the median household incomes for immigrants from Asia, Canada, Europe, and Oceania (the region including Australia, Fiji, and New Zealand) are higher than native-born median household income, while the median immigrant household from Latin America had a much lower income than the median native-born household. Part of the explanation for this variation is the bimodal nature of the labor market and different immigrant groups' representation in particular types of occupations, as described below.

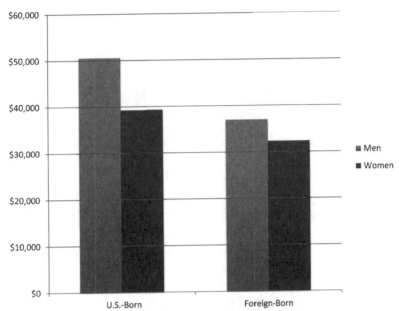

FIGURE 1-12 Median earnings by nativity and sex, 2013.
SOURCE: Data from American Community Survey, 2013, 1-year estimates. Available: http://www.census.gov/acs/www/ [October 2015].

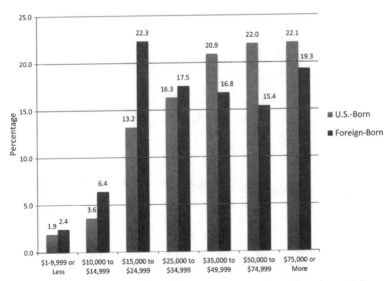

FIGURE 1-13 Yearly earnings for full-time, year-round workers by nativity.
SOURCE: Data from American Community Survey, 2013, 1-year estimates. Available: http://www.census.gov/acs/www/ [October 2015].

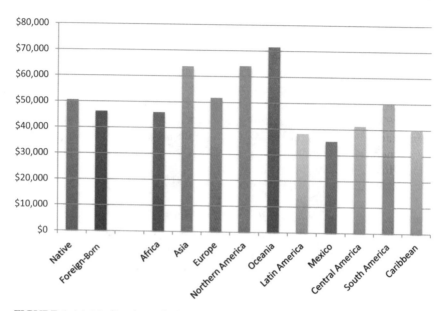

FIGURE 1-14 Median household income by nativity and region of origin, 2010. SOURCE: Data from American Community Survey, 2010. Available: http://www. census.gov/prod/2012pubs/acs-19.pdf [October 2015].

Occupation

A common perception of immigrant labor force participation is the concentration of immigrants in occupational niches. In fact, immigrants do not dominate in any single occupation, although there is geographical variation in the extent to which they are represented among agricultural workers, for instance, or health care workers. There are important variations by region of origin, however. Asian immigrants, particularly those from China and India, are overrepresented in professional occupations, including those in health care, engineering, and information technology. Immigrants from Latin America, meanwhile, are more concentrated in lower-skilled, lower-paying occupations in construction and in the service and retail industries (see Chapter 6 for further discussion).

Poverty

In recent decades, as immigration has been high, the U.S. poverty rate has also been stubbornly high. Rising income inequality and the declining wages of those with low education since the 1970s likely hit immigrants and their families particularly hard, as they are overrepresented among lower-educated workers. Unlike earlier European immigrants and their descendants, who benefited from the decline in income inequality and the growth in wages among those at the bottom of the labor market in the period beginning in the 1930s, current immigrants are entering a U.S. economy that sees declining fortunes at the bottom of the income distribution. Real wages for those without a college degree have fallen 26 percent since 1970, and for males without a high school degree they have fallen a remarkable 38 percent (Greenstone and Looney, 2011). Chapter 6 discusses intergenerational trends in poverty, which do show some progress over time. However, this progress begins at a low level, as the foreign-born are more likely than the native-born to be poor.

The poverty rate for immigrants is a cause for particular concern because many immigrants are barred from participation in social welfare programs that aid the impoverished. As Figure 1-15 illustrates, 18.7 percent of the foreign-born are impoverished, compared to 15.4 percent of the native-born, a difference of just over 3 percentage points, while the proportion of immigrants living within 200 percent of the poverty level is 6 percentage points higher than it is for the native-born. Considering that the poverty threshold for a family of four is $23,850 and 30 percent of immigrants make less than $25,000 a year, the higher proportion of immigrant households at or near poverty is unsurprising.

The differences in houshold income distribution relative to the poverty

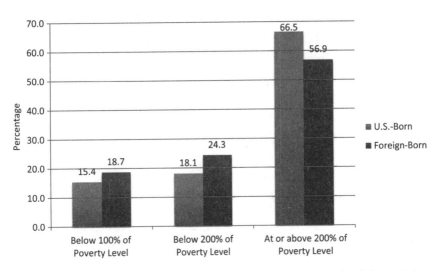

FIGURE 1-15 Percentage of households below or near poverty level, by nativity, 2013.
SOURCE: Data from American Community Survey, 2013, 1-year estimates. Available: http://www.census.gov/acs/www/ [October 2015].

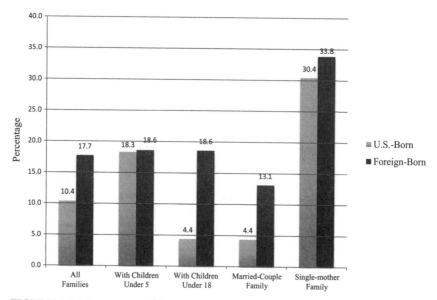

FIGURE 1-16 Percentage of families living in poverty, by nativity and family type, 2013.
SOURCE: Data from American Community Survey, 2013, 1-year estimates. Available: http://www.census.gov/acs/www/ [October 2015].

level becomes even more alarming for families with children. While 1 in 10 native-born families are impoverished, almost 18 percent of foreign-born families live below the poverty level (see Figure 1-16). The differences are particularly stark for families in which a married couple has children. Only 4.4 percent of native-born families with two parents are impoverished, but over 13 percent of foreign-born two-parent families live in poverty. This means a much larger proportion of children of foreign-born parents are living in poverty, even in cases where there is an intact household and both parents may be working. Although many of these children are U.S. citizens themselves, and some social welfare programs for children are available regardless of nativity (e.g., the Women, Infants, and Children Supplemental Nutrition Program of the Food and Nutrition Service; free and reduced school meals), the fact that their parents are often prevented from accessing social welfare programs makes these families' financial situations even more precarious (Yoshikawa, 2011).

Legal Status

A key finding in this report is the importance of legal status and its impact on immigrants' integration prospects. Although some distinctions in status existed in the past, the complicated system of statuses that exists today is unprecedented in U.S. history.

As discussed in detail in Chapter 2, an unintended consequence of the 1965 amendments to the INA and the immigration legislation that followed was to dramatically increase both legal *and* undocumented immigration to the United States. In response, rather than initiating overarching reform, the federal government has been reactive, creating piecemeal changes that grant certain groups or persons in specific situations various legal statuses. Some of these statuses provide clear pathways to lawful permanent residence and citizenship, but many are explicitly designed to be temporary and discourage permanent settlement in the United States. Meanwhile, federal, state, and local legislation has increasingly used legal status as a dividing line between those who can access various social services and those who are excluded from portions of the social safety net.

Chapter 3 outlines the current major legal statuses and examines how these statuses may aid or hinder immigrant integration. Legal status provides a continuum of integrative potential, with naturalized citizenship at one end and undocumented status at the other. However, many immigrants move back and forth along that continuum, gaining or losing statuses during the course of their residence in the United States. And despite the inherent uncertainty of temporary or undocumented statuses, it is important to understand that as long as immigrants reside in the United States, regardless of their legal status, immigrants are starting families, sending their children to schools, working in the labor market, paying taxes, attending churches, and participating in civic organizations. They interact on a daily basis across a variety of social environments with the native-born population. In effect, they are integrating into American society and culture.

Particularly important to the discussion of legal status and immigrant integration is the undocumented population. Between 1990 and 2007, the number of undocumented immigrants in the United States tripled (see Figure 1-17). Although unauthorized immigration declined somewhat after 2007 in response to the Great Recession, there are currently an estimated 11.3 million undocumented immigrants living in the United States (Passel et al., 2014). As noted above, this situation is unprecedented because, during the last great wave of immigration, there were relatively few obstacles to entry. The social and legal challenges facing undocumented immigrants create significant barriers to integration, a consequence discussed in detail in Chapter 3 and referred to throughout this report.

DEMOGRAPHIC PROJECTIONS

The increase in immigration since 1970 has its primary impact on the growth of the foreign-born population. But immigration also has secondary

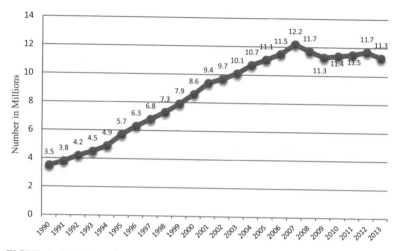

FIGURE 1-17 Number of undocumented immigrants in the United States, 1990-2013.
SOURCE: Data are from Jeffrey Passel (Pew Research Center) presentation to the Panel on the Integration of Immigrants into American Society on January 16, 2014. Also see Passel et al. (2014).

effects through the children and subsequent descendant of the foreign-born. The children of immigrants (or the second generation) are native-born and are American citizens at birth but can be considered as part of the broadly defined immigrant community. The second generation is generally reared within the culture and community of their immigrant parents, and their first language is often their parents' mother tongue, even as they usually make great strides in integrating into the American mainstream.

In 1970, the second generation population was about twice the size of the foreign-born population—almost 24 million. The large second generation population in the 1960s and 1970s was the product of the early 20th century immigrant wave from eastern and southern Europe. Almost all were adults and many were elderly. By the first decade of the 21st century, there was a new second generation population: the children of the post-1965 wave of immigrants from Latin America and Asia. Currently about one-quarter of all U.S. children are first generation or second generation immigrants.

Recent immigrants and their descendants will continue to affect the demography of the United States for many years to come. In late 2014 and early 2015, the U.S. Census Bureau released a new update of population projections from 2015 to 2060, with a primary emphasis on the impact of immigration on population growth, composition, and diversity (U.S. Census Bureau 2014a; Colby and Ortman, 2015). Historically, projections of net immigration to the United States were little more than conjectures based on recent trends and ad hoc assumptions. In recent years, the Census Bureau has adopted a new methodology based on a predictive model of future emigration rates from major sending countries and regions, informed by recent trends in immigration (U.S. Census Bureau, 2014b).

The Census Bureau projects that the number of foreign-born persons residing in the United States will increase from just over 41 million to more than 78 million between 2013 and 2060, with their population share rising from 13.1 percent to 18.8 percent (see Figure 1-18). Although the Census Bureau projects a slowing trend in the relative growth rate of the foreign-born population (from more than 2% to less than 1%) and a decline in absolute numbers of immigrants per year (from over 900,000 to less than 600,000), most of the growth of the U.S. population in the coming decades will be due to immigration, including both the increase from the immigrants themselves and the increase from their higher fertility rates. Fertility-related increase is projected to decline even faster as the population ages, and much of the projected natural increase of the native-born population is also due

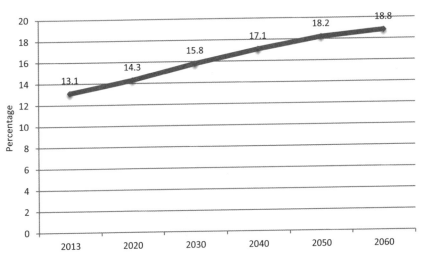

FIGURE 1-18 Projected growth in foreign-born as share of the total population, 2013-2060.
SOURCE: Data from U.S. Census Bureau, 2014 Population Projections. Available: http://www.census.gov/population/projections/data/national/2014/summarytables. html [October 2015].

to immigration. The Census Bureau projects that over 20 percent of the births in the United States between now and 2060 will be to foreign-born mothers (Colby and Ortman, 2015). Without new immigrants and their children, the United States is projected to experience population decline in the coming years.

The most controversial aspects of the new population projections are the impact of immigration on population diversity and the prediction that the U.S. population will become a majority minority population; that is, non-Hispanic whites will be less than half of the total population by the middle of the 21st century (Colby and Ortman, 2015, Table 2). However, a significant share of this change is due to the changes in the measurement of race and ethnicity in recent years.

There is little doubt that the massive wave of immigration of recent decades has changed the composition of the American population. In 2010, almost 15 million Americans claimed an Asian American identity and over 50 million reported themselves to be Hispanic (Humes et al., 2011). These numbers and future projections must be understood in light of a complex system of measurement of race and ethnicity in federal statistics, discussed above. As noted earlier, Hispanic ethnicity is measured on a separate census/survey question from race, so Hispanics may be of any race. In 2010, more than half (53%) of Hispanics reported that they were "white" on the race question, a little more than a third (36.7%) chose "Some Other Race" (many wrote in a Latin American national origin), and 6 percent chose multiracial (mostly "Some Other Race" and "white"). Multiple race reporting was only 2 to 3 percent in the 2000 and 2010 censuses, but it is projected to increase in the coming decades, perhaps to 6 percent, or 26 million Americans, in 2060 (Colby and Ortman, 2015, Table 2).

The Census Bureau projects that 28.6 percent of Americans will be Hispanic in 2060, 14.3 to 17.9 percent will be black, 9.3 to 11.7 percent will be Asian, 1.3 to 2.4 percent will be American Indian or Alaskan Native, and 0.3 to 0.7 percent will be Native Hawaiian or Pacific Islander. The range of uncertainty in these projections depends on how persons who claim multiple racial identities ("race alone or in combination" in census terminology) are counted. "One race" non-Hispanic whites are projected to be 43.6 percent of all Americans in 2060 (Colby and Ortman 2015, Table 2). However, all whites (including Hispanic whites and all multiracial persons who checked "white") are projected to be 74.3 percent of the American population in 2060 (Colby and Ortman 2015, Table 2).

It is impossible to predict the future ethnoracial population of the United States with numerical precision, but general trends are foreseeable. There will be more persons with diverse heritage, including a very large number of persons with ancestry from Latin America: likely more than a quarter of all Americans in 2060. Among the less predictable consequences are whether these ancestral origins will be important in terms of language, culture, residential location, or choice of marital partners.

AMERICAN ATTITUDES ABOUT IMMIGRATION

An important but misunderstood component of immigrant integration is native-born attitudes toward immigration and immigrants. Immigration has been hotly debated in American elections and in the media, and based on these debates, one might think that Americans are deeply concerned with the issue and that many, perhaps even the majority, are opposed to immigration. Polling data suggest that this is not the case: most Americans assess immigration positively. Figure 1-19 shows the results of a poll question, asked from 2001 to 2014, on Americans' overall assessment about whether "Immigration is a good thing or a bad thing for this country today." In every year of the polling period, a majority of Americans say that immigration is a good thing, reaching a high of 72 percent in 2013 before falling to 63 percent in 2014.

Polling results also show that an increasing number of Americans (57% in 2005, up from 37% in 1993) think that immigrants contribute to the United States, and one-half feel that immigrants pay their fair share of taxes. Yet this is counterbalanced by the significant proportion, 42 percent, who think immigrants cost taxpayers too much (Segovia and Defever, 2010, pp. 380-381). The majority of Americans do not believe that recent immigrants take jobs away from U.S. citizens, and they believe that the jobs immigrants take are ones that Americans do not want (Segovia and Defever, 2010, p. 383). When asked specifically about immigration and whether

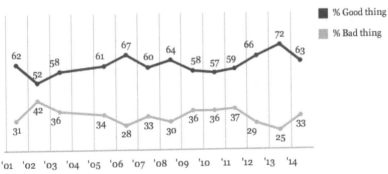

On the whole, do you think immigration is a good thing or a bad thing for this country today?

FIGURE 1-19 Impact of immigration on the United States, 2001-2014.
SOURCE: Saad (2014). Reprinted with permission.

illegal or legal immigration is a bigger problem, respondents in a 2006 Pew survey were much more likely to say that it was illegal immigration (60%) than legal immigration (4%), with 22 percent saying both were of equal importance and 11 percent saying neither (Pew Research Center, 2006; Segovia and Defever, 2010, p. 379).

Opinion polls since 1964 have asked questions to solicit respondents' assessment of their ideal level of immigration (Segovia and Defever, 2010; Saad, 2014). For example, "Should immigration be kept at the present level, increased, or decreased?" These opinions do not necessarily match the actions that Congress takes. In 1964, for example, just before the passage of the 1965 Immigration Act that vastly increased immigration to the United States, almost one-half of respondents (48%) *liked the present level* of immigration and 38 percent wanted a reduction (Lapinski et al., 1997, pp. 360-361).

More recent polling data from 1999-2014 show that the dominant view of the public about the desired level of immigration is for a decrease, followed closely by maintaining it at current levels (Saad, 2014). However, support for increasing immigration levels has been rising over the last 15 years. There has been a doubling of the percentage who said that the level should be increased, from 10 percent in 1999 to 22 percent in 2014. Not surprisingly, immigrants are more favorable toward maintaining current levels of immigration than are the native-born. Only 17 percent of the foreign-born, compared to 60 percent of the native-born, told pollsters in 2014 that immigrant levels should be decreased. Urban residents and the highly educated are more supportive of expanding immigration than are those in rural areas and those with less than a college education. (Saad, 2014, p. 5).

While Americans have generally preferred to decrease the number of immigrants coming to the United States, they have also tended to resist mass deportation as the solution to the problem of unauthorized immigration. For example, in the CBS/*New York Times Poll* in 2006 and 2007, the proportion favoring legalization was consistent at around 62 percent,[18] while the proportion favoring deportation was considerably lower, at around 33 percent.[19] In later years, the *New York Times Poll* split the legalization option into two possibilities: for immigrants to either (1) stay in the United States and eventually apply for citizenship or (2) stay but not qualify for

---

[18]Support for legalization was 62 percent in May 2006, 60 percent in March 2007, 61 percent in May 2007, and 65 percent in June 2007. See http://www.cbsnews.com/htdocs/pdf/poll_bush_050906.pdf, http://www.cbsnews.com/htdocs/pdf/052407_immigration.pdf, and http://www.cbsnews.com/htdocs/pdf/062807_immigration.pdf [September 2015].

[19]Support for deportation was 33 percent in May 2006, 36 percent in March 2007, 35 percent and 28 percent in May 2007. Sources: CBS News Poll webpages cited in the preceding footnote.

citizenship.[20] Less than a third of respondents preferred deportation over legalization, while nearly one-half supported legalization with a pathway to citizenship. Only about 19 percent favored legalization without the possibility of citizenship.

In general, most Americans do not think immigration is as important as many other issues facing the country. From 1994 to 2014, immigration is mentioned as the most important issue facing the country today by only about 1 percent to 3 percent of Americans. By contrast, the economy, unemployment, and health care consistently receive higher mentions.[21] Even at times when immigration reform is very much in the news and high on legislators' agenda; it is not the top issue for the vast majority of Americans.

Attitudes on immigration have recently become decoupled from strictly economic concerns. While restrictive attitudes on immigration tended to go up significantly during recessions and periods of high unemployment in the 1980s and 1990s (Lapinski et al., 1997), there is no clear relationship among aggregate economic output, unemployment, and immigration attitudes after 2001. Furthermore, observational and experimental studies of immigration opinion have found that personal economic circumstances bear little or no relationship to restrictive attitudes on immigration (Citrin et al., 1997; Hainmuller and Hiscox, 2010). There also is not a fixed relationship between local demographic composition and concentration of immigrants and attitudes toward immigrants. Rather, the broader political context (whether immigration is nationally salient and being widely debated and reported on) interacts with local demographics. Hopkins (2010) found that when immigration is nationally salient, a growing population of immigrants is associated with more restrictionist views, but demography does not predict attitudes when immigration is not nationally salient.

So even though immigration is rarely mentioned as an important policy issue by the American public, and despite consistent majority support for legalization of the undocumented, immigration remains a contentious topic. As past research has shown, this level of heightened attention and polarization on immigration is evident more among party activists than among the general electorate (Skocpol and Williamson, 2012; Parker and Barreto, 2014) and is often the result of agenda-setting and mobilization by key media personalities and political actors, rather than emerging from widespread popular sentiment (Hopkins, 2010; Gulasekaram and Ramakrishnan, 2015).

Concern about immigration is also fueled by misconceptions about

---

[20] See http://s3.documentcloud.org/documents/1302290/sept14b-politics-trn.pdf [September 2015].

[21] Panel's analysis of Gallup toplines obtained from Roper Center Public Opinion Archives, University of Connecticut, see http://www.ropercenter.uconn.edu/ [September 2015].

immigrants and the process of integration. Americans have been found to overestimate the size of the nonwhite population (Wong, 2007), to erroneously believe that immigrants commit more crime than natives (Simes and Waters, 2013), and to worry that immigrants and their children are not learning English (Hopkins et al., 2014). A sense of cultural threat to national identity and culture, rooted in a worry about integration, therefore seems to underly many Americans' worries about immigration (Hainmueller and Hopkins, 2014).

IMPLICATIONS

The United States has witnessed major changes in the demographic make-up of immigrants since 1970. Prior to the passage of the 1965 amendments to the INA, the majority of immigration to the United States originated from Europe. After 1965, the United States witnessed a surge of immigration from Latin America and Asia, creating a much more racially and ethnically diverse society. This new wave of immigration is more balanced in terms of gender ratios but varies in terms of skills and education, both from earlier immigration patterns and by region of origin. Immigrants are more geographically dispersed throughout the country than ever before. And since 1990 in particular, the United States has witnessed an enormous influx of undocumented immigrants, a legal category that was barely recognized 100 years ago.[22]

The demographic trends described above have broad implications for immigrant integration that cut across the various social dimensions discussed in this report. Just as in the past, American society is adjusting to the fact that a high proportion of the population is composed of immigrants and their descendants. But the differences between earlier waves of immigrants and more recent arrivals present new challenges to integration.

One key issue is the role of racial discrimination in the integration of immigrants and their descendants. Scholars debate how much racial and ethnic discrimination is directed toward immigrants and their children, whether immigration and the complexity it brings to our racial and ethnic classification system will ultimately lead to a blurring or hardening of the boundaries separating groups, what kinds of racial and ethnic distinctions that we see now will persist into the future, and what kinds will become less socially meaningful (for recent reviews, see Lee and Bean, 2012; Alba and Nee, 2009). Sometimes these questions are framed as a debate about

---

[22]Many scholars have described Chinese immigrants who arrived after the Chinese Exclusion Act of 1882 as the first "illegal aliens." Ngai (2004) describes the evolution of the term as having roots in the experiences of these Chinese immigrants and then being more broadly applied after the 1920s.

where the "color line" will be drawn in the 21st century. Will immigrants and their children who are Asian and Latino remain distinct, or will their relatively high intermarriage rates with whites lead to a blurring of the line separating the groups, similar in many ways to what happened to groups of European origin, who developed optional or voluntary ethnicities that no longer affect their life chances (Alba and Nee, 2003; Waters, 1990)? This debate also focuses on African Americans and the historically durable line separating them from whites, one enforced until recently by the legal prohibition on intermarriage between blacks and whites and the norm of the one-drop rule, which defined any racially mixed person as black (Lee and Bean, 2012).

There is evidence on both sides of this debate. High intermarriage rates of both Asians and Latinos with whites, as well as patterns of racial integration in some neighborhoods, point to possible future blurring of the boundaries separating these groups (see Chapter 8). The association between Latinos and undocumented immigration, however, may be leading to a pattern of heightened discrimination against Latinos. The negative framing of undocumented immigrants as illegal criminals, alien invaders, and terrorists, along with the conflation of undocumented and documented migrants in public discourse, contributes to the racialization of Latinos as a despised out-group. Discrimination against Hispanics may have been exacerbated by the criminalization of undocumented hiring and the imposition of employer sanctions under the Immigration Reform and Control Act of 1986, which encouraged employers either to avoid Latino immigrants who "looked Hispanic" (Lowell et al., 1995) or to pay lower wages to compensate themselves for the risk of hiring undocumented foreigners (Lowell and Jing 1994; Sorensen and Bean 1994; Fry et al., 1995; Cobb-Clark et al., 1995).

To the extent that immigrants today are racialized, they can be expected to be subject to systematic discrimination and exclusion, thus compromising their integration into U.S. society. Immigrants with darker skin earn significantly less than those with lighter skin in U.S. labor markets (Frank et al., 2010; Hersch, 2008; 2011). And stereotypical markers of Hispanic origin such as indigenous features and brown skin, have come to trigger discrimination and exclusion within American society (Chavez, 2008; Lee and Fiske, 2006; Massey, 2007, 2014; Massey and Denton, 1992; Massey and Sanchez, 2010; Turner et al., 2002).

Discrimination, skin color, and socioeconomic status may interact to particularly affect ethnoracial self-identification among Latin American immigrants, who come from a region where race is more often seen as a continuum than a dichotomy. For instance, upon arrival, many Latin American immigrants select "other" when asked about their race, corresponding to a racially mixed identity. However, with rising socioeconomic status, they are more likely to become familiar with U.S. racial taxonomies and select "white" as their racial identity (Duncan and Trejo, 2011; Pulido and Pastor, 2013). Investigators studying immigrant integration must therefore remember that self-identifications are both causes and consequences of integration and socioeconomic mobility, sometimes making it difficult to measure such mobility over time (discussed further in Chapter 6). Chapter 10 describes the kinds of longitudinal data on immigrants and their children that would enable much more accurate measurement of this change.

The ubiquity and the vagaries of racial and ethnic categorization in American society, along with the scarcity of data on immigration and especially on the second generation, means that there is often conceptual confusion in interpreting trends and statistics not only on racial and ethnic inequality but also on immigrant integration. For example, the gap between Hispanic and white graduation rates in the United States is sometimes interpreted to mean a deep crisis exists in our education system. But Latino graduation rates include about one-third of people who are foreign-born, many of whom completed their schooling in countries such as Mexico, with a much lower overall educational distribution. Throughout the report, the panel tries to specify the intersection between national origin and generation to analyze change over time among immigrants and their descendants. This careful attention to specifying the groups we are analyzing is made difficult by the scarcity of data sources containing the relevant variables. The most glaring problem is that the Decennial Census and American Community Survey do not contain a question on parental birthplace. We return to this issue in Chapter 10 when we discuss data recommendations.

The implications of this debate about the role of racial discrimination in limiting opportunities for immigrants and their children are profound. One out of four children today are the children of immigrants, and the question of whether their ethnoracial identity will hold them back from full and equal participation in our society is an open one. Throughout the report, the panel presents reasons for optimism about the ability of U.S. society to move beyond discrimination and prejudice, as well as particular reasons for concern that discrimination and prejudice will affect immigrants and their descendants negatively. While the panel cannot provide a definitive answer at this time, we do include the best evidence on both sides of this question.

REPORT ORGANIZATION

In the following chapters, the panel surveys the empirical evidence on how immigrant and generational status has been and continues to be predictive of integration into American society. In Chapter 2, we review the legal and institutional context for immigrant integration, including the historical construction of the U.S. immigration system, the emergence of the current system of legal statuses, and the tensions inherent in the uniquely American brand of "immigration federalism." Chapter 3 discusses the central role legal status plays in the integration of both immigrants and their descendants and examines the largest and most important legal statuses in detail. Chapter 4 details the political and civic dimensions of integration with a focus on naturalization. Chapter 5 focuses on the spatial dimensions of integration at each level of geography, emphasizing the importance of place and contexts of reception. Chapter 6 examines the socioeconomic dimensions of immigrant integration, including education, income, and occupation. Chapter 7 discusses sociocultural aspects of integration, including language, religion, attitudes of both immigrants and the native-born, and crime. Family dimensions, including intermarriage, fertility, and family form, are the focus of Chapter 8. Chapter 9 outlines the health dimensions of integration, including the apparent immigrant health paradox. Finally, in Chapter 10 the panel assesses the available data for studying immigrant integration and makes recommendations for improving available data sources.

REFERENCES

Alba, R., and Nee, V. (2003). *Remaking the American Mainstream: Assimilation and Contemporary Immigration*. Cambridge, MA: Harvard University Press.

Alba, R., Reitz, J.G., and Simon, P. (2012). National conceptions of assimilation, integration, and cohesion. In M. Crul and J. Mollenkopf (Eds.), *The Changing Face of World Cities: Young Adult Children of Immigrants in Europe and the United States* (pp. 41-61). New York: Russell Sage Foundation.

Brown, S.K., and Bean, F.D. (2006). Assimilation models, old and new: Explaining a long-term process. *Migration Information Source*, 3-41.

Chavez, C. (2008). Conceptualizing from the inside: Advantages, complications, and demands on insider positionality. *The Qualitative Report*, *13*(3), 474-494.

Chellaraj, G., Maskus, K.E., and Mattoo, A. (2008). The contribution of international graduate students to U.S. innovation. *Review of International Economics, 16*, 444-462.

Choldin, H.M. (1986). Statistics and politics: The "Hispanic issue" in the 1980 census. *Demography*, *23*(3), 403-418.

Citrin, J., Green, D.P., Muste, C., and Wong, C. (1997). Public opinion toward immigration reform: The role of economic motivations. *The Journal of Politics*, *59*(03), 858-881.

Cobb-Clark, D.A., Shiells, C.R., and Lowell, B.L. (1995). Immigration reform: The effects of employer sanctions and legalization on wages. *Journal of Labor Economics*, 472-498.

Colby, S.L., and Ortman, J.M. (2015). *Projections of the Size and Composition of the U.S. Population: 2014 to 2060*. Current Population Reports, P25-1143. Washington, DC: U.S. Census Bureau. Available: https://www.census.gov/content/dam/Census/library/publications/2015/demo/p25-1143.pdf [May 2015].

de Crèvecoeur, J. Hector St. John (1782). *Letters from an American Farmer and Sketches of Eighteenth-Century America*. London, UK: Davies & Davis.

Desilver, D. (2015). *Share of Counties Where Whites Are a Minority Has Doubled since 1980.* Washington, DC: Pew Research Center. Available: http://www.pewresearch.org/fact-tank/2015/07/01/share-of-counties-where-whites-are-a-minority-has-doubled-since-1980/ [July 2015].

Donato, K.M., and Gabaccia, D. (2015). *Gender and International Migration.* New York: Russell Sage Foundation.

Donato, K.M., Alexander, J.T., Gabaccia, D.R., and Leinonen, J. (2011). Variations in the gender composition of immigrant populations: How they matter. *International Migration Review, 45*(3), 495-526.

Duncan, B., and Trejo, S.J. (2011). Tracking intergenerational progress for immigrant groups: The problem of ethnic attrition. *American Economic Review: Papers and Proceedings, 101*(3), 603-608.

Frank, R., Akresh, I.R., and Lu, B. (2010). Latino immigrants and the U.S. racial order how and where do they fit in? *American Sociological Review, 75*(3), 378-401.

Fry, R., Lowell, B.L., and Haghighat, E. (1995). The impact of employer sanctions on metropolitan wage rates. *Industrial Relations: A Journal of Economy and Society, 34*(3), 464-484.

Gibson, C., and Jung, K. (2006). *Historical Census Statistics on the Foreign-Born Population of the United States: 1850-2000.* Population Division Working Paper No. 81. Washington, DC: U.S. Census Bureau.

Grasmuck, S., and Pessar, P.R. (1991). *Between Two Islands: Dominican International Migration.* Oakland: University of California Press.

Greenstone, M., and Looney, A. (2011). Trends: Reduced earnings for men in America. The *Milken Institute Review, Third Quarter,* 8-16. Available: http://www.hamiltonproject. org/files/downloads_and_links/07_milken_greenstone_looney.pdf [May 2015].

Grieco, E.M., Acosta, Y.D., de la Cruz, G.P., Gambino, C., Gryb, T., Larsen, L.J., Trevelyan, E.N., and Walters, N.P. (2012). *The Foreign-Born Population in the United States: 2010.* Washington, DC: U.S. Census Bureau. Available: https://www.census.gov/prod/2012pubs/acs-19.pdf [August 2015].

Gulasekaram, P., and Ramakrishnan, S.K. (2015). *The New Immigration Federalism.* Cambridge, UK: Cambridge University Press.

Hainmueller, J., and Hiscox, M.J. (2010). Attitudes toward highly skilled and low-skilled immigration: Evidence from a survey experiment. *American Political Science Review, 104*(01), 61-84.

Hall, M., Singer, A., De Jong, G.F., and Graefe, D.R. (2011). *The Geography of Immigrant Skills: Educational Profiles of Metropolitan Areas.* Washington, DC: Brookings Institution Press. Available: http://www.brookings.edu/~/media/research/files/papers/2011/6/immigrants-singer/06_immigrants_singer.pdf [May 2015].

Hainmueller, J., and Hopkins, D. (2014). Public attitudes toward immigration. *Annual Review of Political Science, 17,* 225-249.

Hersch, J. (2008). Profiling the new immigrant worker: The effects of skin color and height. *Journal of Labor Economics, 26,* 345-386.

Hersch, J. (2011). The persistence of skin color discrimination for immigrants. *Social Science Research, 40,* 1337-1349.

Hobbs, F., and Stoops, N. (2002). *Demographic Trends in the 20th Century.* Census 2000 Special Reports, CENSR-4. Washington, DC: US Census Bureau.

Hopkins, D.J. (2010) Politicized places: Explaining where and when immigrants provoke local opposition. *American Political Science Review, 104*(01), 40-60.

Hopkins, D.J., Tran, V.C., and Williamson, A.F. (2014). See no Spanish: Language, local context, and attitudes toward immigration. *Politics, Groups, and Identities, 2*(1), 35-51.

Humes, K.R., Jones, N.A., and Ramirez, R.R. (2011). *Overview of Race and Hispanic Origin: 2010*. 2010 Census Briefs, C2010BR-02. Washington, DC: U.S. Census Bureau. Available: http://www.census.gov/prod/cen2010/briefs/c2010br-02.pdf [August 2015].

Hunt, J., and Gauthier-Loisellem, M. (2010). How much does immigration boost innovation? *American Economic Journal: Macroeconomics, 2*(April), 31-56.

Jensen, E. (2015). *China Replaces Mexico as the Top Sending Country for Immigrants to the United States*. Washington, DC: U.S. Census Bureau. Available: http://researchmatters. blogs.census.gov/2015/05/01/china-replaces-mexico-as-the-top-sending-country-for-immigrants-to-the-united-states/ [July 2015].

Kent, M.M. (2007). Immigration and America's black population. *Population Bulletin, 62*(4). Available: http://www.prb.org/pdf07/62.4immigration.pdf [September 2015].

Kerr, W.R. (2008). Ethnic scientific communities and international technology diffusion. *The Review of Economics and Statistics, 90*(3), 518-537.

Lapinski, J.S., Peltola, P., Shaw, G., and Yang, A. (1997). Trends: Immigrants and immigration. *Public Opinion Quarterly*, 356-383.

Lee, J., and Bean, F.D. (2012). A postracial society or a diversity paradox? *Du Bois Review: Social Science Research on Race, 9*(02), 419-437.

Lee, T.L., and Fiske, S.T. (2006). Not an outgroup, not yet an ingroup: Immigrants in the stereotype content model. *International Journal of Intercultural Relations, 30*(6), 751-768.

Lieberson, S. (1963). *Ethnic Patterns in American Cities*. New York: Free Press of Glencoe.

Lowell, B.L., and Jing, Z. (1994). Unauthorized workers and immigration reform: What can we ascertain from employers? *International Migration Review*, 427-448.

Lowell, B.L., Teachman, J., and Jing, Z. (1995). Unintended consequences of immigration reform: Discrimination and Hispanic employment. *Demography, 32*(4), 617-628.

Massey, D.S. (1999). Why does immigration occur?: A theoretical synthesis. In C. Hirschman, P. Kasinitz, and J. DeWind (Eds.), *The Handbook of International Migration* (pp. 34-52). New York: Russell Sage Foundation.

Massey, D.S. (2007). *Categorically Unequal: The American Stratification System*. New York: Russell Sage Foundation.

Massey, D.S. (2014). The racialization of Latinos in the United States. In S.M. Bucerius and M. Tonry (Eds.), *The Oxford Handbook on Ethnicity, Crime, and Immigration* (pp. 21-40). New York: Oxford University Press.

Massey, D.S., and Denton, N.A. (1992). Racial identity and the spatial assimilation of Mexicans in the United States. *Social Science Research, 21*(3), 235-260.

Massey, D.S., and Sánchez, M. (2010). *Brokered Boundaries: Immigrant Identity in Anti-Immigrant Times*. New York: Russell Sage Foundation.

Mexican Migration Monitor. (2012). *Hitting Homes: The Impact of Immigration Enforcement*. Los Angeles: Universit of Southern California Tomas Rivera Policy Institute and Colegio de la Frontera Norte.

Monte, L.M., and Ellis, R.R. (2014). *Fertility of Women in the United States: 2012*. Washington, DC: U.S. Census Bureau. Available: https://www.census.gov/content/dam/Census/library/publications/2014/demo/p20-575.pdf [August 2015].

Ngai, M.M. (2004). *Impossible Subjects: Illegal Aliens and the Making of Modern America*. Princeton, NJ: Princeton University Press.

Office of Management and Budget. (1997a). Recommendations from the Interagency Committee for the Review of the Race and Ethnic Standards to the Office of Management and Budget concerning changes to the standards for the classification of federal data on race and ethnicity. *Federal Register, 62*(131), 36874-36946.

Office of Management and Budget. (1997b). Revisions to the standards for the classification of federal data on race and ethnicity. *Federal Register, 62*(210), 58782-58790.

Oishi, N. (2005) *Women in Motion: Globalization, State Policies and Labor Migration in Asia.* Stanford, CA: Stanford University Press.

Parker, C.S., and Barreto, M.A. (2014). *Change They Can't Believe in: The Tea Party and Reactionary Politics in America.* Princeton, NJ: Princeton University Press.

Passel, J. (2013). *The Rise of Asian Americans.* Washington, DC: Pew Research Center. Available: http://www.pewsocialtrends.org/files/2013/04/Asian-Americans-new-full-report-04-2013.pdf [August 2015].

Passel, J., and Cohn, D. (2011). *Unauthorized Immigrant Population: National and State Trends, 2010.* Washington, DC: Pew Research Center. Available: http://www.pewhispanic.org/2011/02/01/unauthorized-immigrant-population-brnational-and-state-trends-2010/ [August 2015].

Passel, J., Cohn, D., and Lopez, M.H. (2011). *Hispanics Account for More than Half of Nation's Growth in Past Decade.* Washington, DC: Pew Research Center. Available: http://www.pewhispanic.org/2011/03/24/hispanics-account-for-more-than-half-of-nations-growth-in-past-decade/ [August 2015].

Passel, J., Cohn, D., Krogstad, J.M., and Gonzalez-Barrera, A. (2014). *As Growth Stalls, Unauthorized Immigrant Population Becomes More Settled.* Available: http://www.pewhispanic.org/2014/09/03/as-growth-stalls-unauthorized-immigrant-population-becomes-more-settled/ [September 2015].

Perez, A.D., and Hirschman, C. (2009). The changing racial and ethnic composition of the U.S. population: Emerging American identities. *Population and Development Review,* 35, 1-51.

Perlmann, J. (2005). *Italians Then, Mexicans Now: Immigrant Origins and the Second-Generation Progress, 1890-2000.* New York: Russell Sage Foundation.

Pettman, J.J. (1996). *Worlding Women: A Feminist International Politics.* London, UK: Routledge.

Pew Research Center. (2006). *America's Immigration Quandary.* Washington, DC: Pew Research Center for the People and the Press and Pew Hispanic Center. Available: http://www.people-press.org/files/legacy-pdf/274.pdf [July 2015].

Portes, A., and Rumbaut, R.G. (2001). *Legacies: The Story of the Immigrant Second Generation.* Berkeley: University of California Press.

Portes, A., and Rumbaut, R.G. (2006). *Immigrant America: A Portrait.* Berkeley: University of California Press.

Portes, A., and Rumbaut, R.G. (2014). *Immigrant America.* 4th Edition. Berkeley: University of California Press.

Prewitt, K. (2013). *What is Your Race?: The Census and Our Flawed Efforts to Classify Americans.* Princeton, NJ: Princeton University Press.

Pulido, L., and Pastor, M. (2013). Where in the world is Juan and what color is he? The geography of Latina/o racial subjectivity in Southern California. *American Quarterly,* 65(2), 309-341. Available: http://muse.jhu.edu/login?auth=0&type=summary&url=/journals/american_quarterly/v065/65.2.pulido.pdf [September 2015].

Ruggles, S., Alexander, J.T., Genadek, K., Goeken, R., Schroeder, M.B., and Sobek, M. (2010). *Integrated Public Use Microdata Series: Version 5.0* [Machine-readable database]. Minneapolis: University of Minnesota.

Saad, L. (2014). *More in U.S. Would Decrease Immigration than Increase.* Available: http://www.gallup.com/poll/171962/decrease-immigration-increase.aspx [August 2015].

Segovia, F., and Defever, R. (2010). The polls—trends: American public opinions on immigrants and immigration policy. *Public Opinion Quarterly,* 24(3) 375-394.

Simes, J.T., and Waters, M.C. (2013). The politics of immigration and crime. In S.M. Bucerius and M. Tonry (Eds.), *The Oxford Handbook on Ethnicity, Crime, and Immigration* (pp. 457-483). New York: Oxford University Press.

Skocpol, T., and Williamson, V. (2012). *The Tea Party and the Remaking of Republican Conservatism*. New York: Oxford University Press.

Smith, J.P., and Edmonston, B. (1997). *The New Americans: Economic, Demographic, and Fiscal Effects of Immigration*. Washington, DC: National Academy Press.

Snipp, C.M. (2003). Racial measurement in the American census: Past practices and implications for the future. *Annual Review of Sociology, 29*, 563-588.

Sorensen, E., and Bean, F.D. (1994). The Immigration Reform and Control Act and the wages of Mexican origin workers: Evidence from Current Population Surveys. *Social Science Quarterly, 75*(1), 1-17.

Stephan, P.E., and Levin, S.G. (2001).Exceptional contributions to U.S. science by the foreign-born and foreign-educated. *Population Research and Policy Review, 20*(1-2), 59-79.

Stephan, P.E., and Levin, S.G. (2007). Foreign scholars in the U.S.: Contributions and costs. In P.E. Stephan and R.G. Ehrenberg (Eds.), *Science and the University* (pp. 150-173). Madison: University of Wisconsin.

Stoney, S., and Batalova, J. (2013). Central American immigrants in the United States. *Migration Information Source*, March. Available: http://www.migrationpolicy.org/article/central-american-immigrants-united-states/ [August 2015].

Telles, E.E., and Ortiz, V. (2008) *Generations of Exclusion: Mexican Americans, Assimilation, and Race*. New York: Russell Sage Foundation.

Turner, M.A., Ross, S., Galster, G.C., and Yinger, J. (2002). *Discrimination in Metropolitan Housing Markets: National Results from Phase 1 of the Housing Discrimination Study*. Available: http://www.huduser.gov/portal/Publications/pdf/Phase1_Report.pdf [September 2015].

United Nations Population Division. (2013). The number of international migrants worldwide reaches 232 million. *Population Facts*, 2103/2. Available: http://esa.un.org/unmigration/documents/The_number_of_international_migrants.pdf [September 2015].

U.S. Census Bureau. (2014a). *Data on Population Projections: 2014 to 2060*. Population projections based on Census 2010. Available: https://www.census.gov/population/projections/data/national/ [September 2015].

U.S. Census Bureau. (2014b). *Methodology, Assumptions, and Inputs for the 2014 National Projections*. Available: https://www.census.gov/population/projections/files/methodology/methodstatement14.pdf [September 2015].

Waters, M.C. (1990). *Ethnic Options: Choosing Identities in America*. Berkeley: University of California Press.

Waters, M.C. (2014). Defining difference: The role of immigrant generation and race in American and British immigration studies. *Ethnic and Racial Studies, 37*(1), 10-26.

Wong, C.J. (2007). Little and big pictures in our heads about local context and innumeracy about racial groups in the United States. *Public Opinion Quarterly, 71*(3), 392-412.

Yoshikawa, H. (2011). *Immigrants Raising Citizens: Undocumented Parents of Young Children*. New York: Russell Sage Foundation.

2

Legal and Institutional Context for Immigrant Integration

The opportunities and barriers to immigrant integration in the United States today are shaped by historical, legal, economic, and institutional contexts. At present, immigration law is one of the most important of these contexts in that it creates varying degrees of stability and opportunities, with potentially profound implications for immigrant integration.

Legal status has varied over time in its consequences for immigrant integration. Early in the country's history there was little attention to legal status and noncitizens could even vote in federal elections. The U.S. Constitution does not forbid noncitizens from voting in federal elections and, until the 1920s, at least 22 states and federal territories, and possibly more, allowed noncitizens to vote at some point (Bloemraad, 2006; Hayduk, 2006). Various states and territories viewed alien suffrage as an incentive to encourage settlement. In the early 1800s, several states in the Midwest allowed male residents to vote, regardless of their citizenship status, and in the second half of the 19th century, 13 states implemented policies aimed at attracting immigrant residents by giving voting rights to "declarant aliens"—immigrants who had declared their intention to become U.S. citizens by filing "first papers" (Raskin, 1993).

The 1790 and 1870 Naturalization Acts restricted naturalization to only white and then subsequently black immigrants. The Chinese Exclusion Act of 1882 explicitly barred Chinese immigrants from citizenship through naturalization, and curtailed almost all Chinese migration, while the Immigration Act of 1917 delineated an "Asiatic Barred Zone" from which migration was prohibited. Asian immigrants challenged their ineligibility for naturalization, but court rulings such as *United States v. Bhagat Singh Thind*, 261 U.S. 204 (1923), upheld Asian immigrants' ineligibility for naturalization. Beyond setting up barriers to political integration, lack of U.S. citizenship could matter for jobs and owning property. In many Western states, noncitizens were barred from the right to own land. Thus, legal status also blocked Asian immigrants' economic and social integration into American society.[1] For white European immigrants who entered the United States without inspection to avoid the Quota Acts of the 1920s, there were relatively few repercussions, and they were often able to naturalize at a later date (Ngai, 2004; Kanstroom, 2010). In recent decades, however, the importance of legal status has grown, as have the variety of different legal statuses that immigrants can hold.

Since its inception, the United States has grappled with two sets of competing demands relevant to immigration: first, the conflict between federal and state rights, and second, the needs of immigration enforcement versus immigrant integration. Policy makers, bureaucrats, and immigrants also face laws and policies that are not targeted toward immigration per se but nevertheless have profound implications for immigrant integration. Beyond law, many institutions structure the life chances of immigrants and their children, including government agencies, nonprofits, informal associations, the overall economy, and the business sector. For example, immigrants in certain cities and counties can rely on significant support from local government agencies, while voluntary organizations, such as Catholic Charities, the International Rescue Committee, and the Hebrew Immigrant Aid Society have long worked in public-private partnerships to help settle refugees and displaced people moving to the United States. Integration therefore occurs within a patchwork of laws, policies, and agencies at multiple scales of governance, with variation across place and by designated legal status.

The legal framework for immigration in the United States is built on three levels: federal, state, and local. For much of the 19th century, immigration and naturalization laws were primarily instituted at the state and local level, with little federal oversight or intrusion, with the notable exception of exclusions from citizenship based on race.

By the turn of the 20th century, the federal government began to take a larger role in immigration, naturalization, and integration, primarily focused on restricting certain groups from entering the United States. Federal supremacy in defining conditions of entry continued through the 20th century, even as the shape of federal law changed from increasing restriction

---

[1] The U.S. Supreme Court affirmed, in *United States v. Wong Kim Ark*, 169 U.S. 649 (1898), that the children of immigrants born on U.S. soil are automatically U.S. citizens under the 14th Amendment, regardless of whether or not the immigrant parents were eligible for citizenship, as was the case for Asian immigrants (see Chapter 4).

through 1924, followed by small openings during World War II, to significant revisions starting in 1965. At the same time, states continued to play a significant role in regulating immigrants' access to licenses, public employment, benefits, and other aspects important to immigrant integration.

Today, immigrants' prospects for integration are shaped by continued dynamics of coordination and tension between federal, state, and local government and between dual interests in enforcement and integration. These tensions also reflect different economic costs and benefits. States and localities do not control who can enter the United States, but in some cases they may bear part of the fiscal burden of immigration (Smith and Edmonston, 1997).[2,3] States and localities have enacted their own complementary or conflicting policies and laws to address the needs of their communities in the perceived absence or inadequacy of federal action. Three important legal and institutional developments of the past 30 years stand out: (1) the proliferation of immigration statuses that provide different degrees of permanence and security; (2) the complex and at times contradictory policies and laws linked to those statuses; and (3) the broadening of grounds for removal and constraints on relief, with the related centrality of Executive action to immigrants' prospects. Each of these factors shapes or undermines opportunities for immigrant integration. Thus, while federal law continues to define the formal legal status of immigrants in the United States, policies at the state and local level are also central to their integration trajectory (Rodriguez, 2014).

This chapter analyzes the legal and institutional framework for immigration, beginning with a brief history of immigration policy in the United States and the development of what legal analysts call "immigration law" and "alienage law" as the federal government expanded its role in this arena. Next, it examines the proliferation of legal statuses since 1965. Last, it details the current framework for immigration federalism and the tension between two competing trends: increasing enforcement and federal supremacy over exit and entry, and the devolution of decisions about public benefits to states, coupled with the delegation of integration efforts to state and local government and nongovernmental organizations.

---

[2] For further information on the fiscal impacts of immigration on states, see http://www.ncsl.org/Portals/1/Documents/statefed/LiteratureReview_June%202013Final.pdf [August 2015].

[3] Estimating the fiscal impacts of immigration is the stated charge of the National Research Council's Panel on the Economic and Fiscal Effects of Immigration. That panel's final report is scheduled for release in 2016.

HISTORY OF IMMIGRATION POLICY IN THE UNITED STATES

The federal government did little to regulate immigration, citizenship, and integration in the first century after the nation's founding. With the exception of the 1790 Naturalization Act, the Alien and Sedition Act (1798), and various treaties and informal agreements, the federal government played a limited role (see Table 2-1). A federal immigration bureau was established only in 1890, followed by the federal naturalization service in 1906. Instead, states and localities were the "primary immigration regulators" (Neuman, 1993). Some tried to channel migration through regulation of shipping lines, while others focused on local rights or benefits tied to residency. Some populous states, like New York, had "robust" immigration and integration agencies (Law, 2013). Meanwhile the first federal naturalization legislation, enacted in 1790, gave authority over naturalization to any common law court of record in any state (this was amended in 1795 to include courts in the territories or a federal court), leading to wide variation in procedures and citizenship acquisition across the country (Raskin, 1993; Law, 2013). From the perspective of the contemporary period, this early period was remarkable for its lack of federal oversight and the relative unimportance of immigration status or citizenship. Residents' race, gender, and ownership of property were much more consequential for rights, access to benefits, and shaping life chances (Smith, 1999).

Development of Immigration Federalism, 1875-1970

After the Civil War, states began to pass laws attempting to regulate immigration both by requiring newcomers to post bonds upon entry and by attempting to control the privileges or rights given to noncitizens. This set the stage for conflict between federal and state control that still characterizes the regulation of immigration, alienage, and immigrant integration today. In 1875, the *Chy Lung v. Freeman* Supreme Court case (92 U.S. 275) proved a turning point in the balance of power over immigration because the court "emphatically stated that control over the admission of foreigners into the country was exclusively a federal responsibility" (Gulasekaram and Ramakrishnan, 2015). But it left open the possibility for limited state and local regulation, opening the door to a distinction between immigration law—regulation over exit and entry—and alienage law, which regulates noncitizens' access to social benefits and licenses and restricts their options relative to citizens (Rodriguez, 2014).

In addition, in 1875 Congress passed the first restrictive federal immigration law, the Page Act, which prohibited the entry of "undesirable" immigrants and targeted Asian migrants both at their ports of departure and at entry into the United States (Peffer, 1986). Subsequently, the execu-

TABLE 2-1 Significant Federal Immigration and Naturalization Statutes

Year	Law	Major Provisions
1790	Naturalization Act	Established criteria for U.S. citizenship through naturalization; restricted naturalization to any "free white person"
1868	Fourteenth Amendment of the U.S. Constitution	Enshrined the right of birthplace citizenship for any person born in the United States
1870	Naturalization Act	Broadened naturalization "to aliens of African nativity and to persons of African descent"
1875	Page Act	Banned "involuntary" immigration from Asian countries and transportation of women for prostitution; banned immigrants who had committed crime
1882	Chinese Exclusion Act	Restricted immigration from China; barred Chinese immigrants from naturalized citizenship
1891	Immigration Act of 1891	Established federal immigration bureaucracy
1906	Naturalization Act	Established a federal Naturalization Service to promote uniform naturalization practices
1917	Immigration Act of 1917	Further restricted Asian immigration; excluded various categories of persons based on disability or moral criteria; introduced literacy test
1924	Immigration Act of 1924	Established strict national origin quotas restricting large-scale immigration from eastern and southern Europe and effectively barred Asian immigration
1924	Labor Appropriation Act	Created Border Control
1952	Immigration and Nationality Act	Abolished race-based bars of immigration and naturalization; allowed limited Asian migration
1965	Hart Celler Act amending the Immigration and Nationality Act	Abolished national origin quotas; established a preference system based primarily on family reunification; some provisions for skilled labor and refugees; established first numerical limitation on Western Hemisphere migration, including migration from Mexico

continued

TABLE 2-1 Continued

Year	Law	Major Provisions
1980	Refugee Act	Established the criteria for admission of refugees and immigration based on humanitarian relief; created the federal Refugee Resettlement Program
1986	Immigration Reform and Control Act	Provided path to legalization for many undocumented persons and created sanctions for employers hiring unauthorized workers
1990	Immigration Act	Raised the quota ceiling on family-sponsored visas, created the diversity lottery; enacted new high-skilled visa categories; enacted new Temporary Protected Status designation
1996	Personal Responsibility and Work Opportunity Reconciliation Act	Restricted legal immigrants' access to social welfare benefits, and barred undocumented immigrants from most federal and state benefits; devolved authority on qualification for benefits to states
1996	Illegal Immigration Reform and Immigrant Responsibility Act	Expanded border protections and interior enforcement; permitted cooperative agreements among federal, state, and local authorities to aid immigration enforcement; expanded grounds for removal; created pilot program for E-Verify
1996	Antiterrorism and Effective Death Penalty Act	Made deportation of Lawful Permanent Residents convicted of an aggravated felony mandatory; expanded definition of aggravated felony
2001	USA Patriot Act	Reorganized federal immigration bureaucracy and created the Department of Homeland Security; expanded border enforcement and grounds for immigrant inadmissibility
2005	REAL ID Act	Created national standards for state-issued identification cards
2008	Secure Communities	Allowed for data sharing between states and localities and federal government to identify and deport immigrants with criminal convictions

tive and legislative branches built up the federal U.S. immigration system, while the judicial branch continued to develop the nuances of immigration and alienage jurisprudence. In 1882, the Chinese Exclusion Act barred most Chinese immigration and also specified that Chinese immigrants were ineligible for naturalization. Congressional restrictions on immigration from Asia expanded in subsequent decades, culminating in the Immigration Act of 1924, which enshrined national origin quotas that effectively barred any vestige of migration from Asia. It also sharply curtailed immigration from eastern and southern Europe (Ngai, 2014; Tichenor, 2009).

Supreme Court cases spurred the creation of two interrelated legal frameworks that continue to set the parameters for authority over immigration: preemption and alienage (see Table 2-2). In cases upholding the Chinese Exclusion Act, the Supreme Court made it clear that the power to enact immigration laws rests solely with the federal government because Congress possesses plenary authority to regulate entry, exit, and the terms of immigrants' presence under the Supremacy Clause of the Constitution; state and local laws cannot contradict or undermine federal immigration regulation (Rodriguez, 2014). A distinct alienage framework developed from another court case, *Yick Wo v. Hopkins*, 118 U.S. 356 (1886), in which the Supreme Court struck down a local San Francisco ordinance targeting Chinese-owned laundries. Thereafter, courts acknowledged federal dominance with respect to alienage (how citizens and immigrants can be treated differently) but allowed for some state and local control over the everyday lives of immigrants. While state laws and local ordinances that seek to regulate the entry or legal presence of immigrants are banned via preemption, the alienage framework allows some room for state and local laws that treat immigrants and citizens differently. State and local laws that seek to differentiate between citizens and noncitizens are subject to heightened review under the Equal Protection Clause of the 14th Amendment, to determine whether distinctions between citizens and aliens are justified (Rodriguez, 2014). Although the line separating immigration and alienage law remains blurry, the distinction carries consequences to the present day, as courts continue to struggle to delineate when and where states and localities have authority over the immigrants living in their jurisdictions.

Federal Laws and the Proliferation of Statuses, 1965 to Present

The 1965 Hart Celler Act eliminated national origin quotas, which many Americans had come to see as rooted in racist ideas about nonwhites and at odds with the spirit of the U.S. Constitution (Zolberg, 2006). The act was passed along with the Civil Rights Act of 1964 and the Voting Rights Act of 1965. Having opened the door to new migration, the United States entered the 1970s on an expansionary trajectory, as is evident in the immigration profile sketched in Chapter 1. However, statistical descriptions of the number, origins, and other demographic features of contemporary immigrants obscure another central immigration story unfolding since 1971: the development of an increasingly complex system with a proliferation of legal statuses, along with consequential distinctions between these statuses. These distinctions are based on immigration law, alienage provisions, and the consequences of legislation and regulations enacted in policy arenas beyond immigration.

On the legislative side, federal laws have led to increases in both legal and unauthorized immigration, while sometimes explicitly limiting, and at other times encouraging, state and local enforcement schemes (Rodriguez, 2014). The 1980 Refugee Act established formal criteria and legal statuses for the admission of refugees and migrants of humanitarian concern, including the establishment of an asylum system and the federal Office of Refugee Resettlement, an agency in the Department of Health and Human Services explicitly focused on assisting refugees with integration (see Table 2-1). The 1986 Immigration Reform and Control Act legalized the status of undocumented residents who could prove long-term residence and of certain migrant agricultural workers; it also created the first federal sanctions for employers knowingly hiring unauthorized workers. At the same time, this 1986 law left open the possibility for states to penalize businesses by restricting their operating licenses (see *Chamber of Commerce v. Whiting*, 2011; Table 2-2).

The 1990 Immigration Act created new high-skilled visa categories and a new diversity lottery to allow people from countries underrepresented in the United States to migrate legally; it also raised the quota on family-sponsored migrants. Demand for family sponsorship has nevertheless far outstripped supply, and there are large backlogs for countries with large numbers of immigrants. Wait times for particular family categories from countries with large immigration flows, such as Mexico and the Philippines, have often exceeded 20 years.[4] The 1990 Act also created Temporary Protected Status (TPS), a temporary status discussed further below.

Immigration Statuses

The federal government exerts profound influence over immigrant integration through the definition of status. A wide variety of statuses exist under federal immigration law, each of which establishes foundations for integration of varying stability and scope. These statuses fall into

---

[4]Priority dates for each category are listed in the State Department visa bulletins, updated monthly, see http://travel.state.gov/content/visas/english/law-and-policy/bulletin.html [October 2015].

TABLE 2-2 Key Supreme Court Federalism Cases for Immigration and Alienage

Year	Case/Opinion Citation	Law Contested	Outcome
1875	*Chy Lung v. Freeman*, 92 U.S. 275	California law requiring bond for certain arriving immigrants	Law struck down
1875	*Henderson v. Mayor of New York City*, 92 U.S. 259	New York law requiring bond for arriving immigrants	Law struck down
1886	*Yick Wo v. Hopkins*, 118 U.S. 356	San Francisco law regulating laundries	Law struck down
1889	*Chae Chan Ping v. United States*, 130 U.S. 581	Federal Chinese Exclusion Act	Law upheld
1893	*Fong Yue Ting v. United States*, 149 U.S. 698	Federal Chinese Exclusion Act	Law upheld
1896	*Wong Wing v. United States*, 163 U.S. 228	Federal Chinese Exclusion Act	Law upheld
1914	*Patsone v. Pennsylvania*, 232 U.S. 138	Pennsylvania law banning noncitizen hunting	Law upheld
1915	*Truax v. Raich*, 239 U.S. 33	Arizona law requiring businesses to hire mostly citizens	Law struck down
1927	*Ohio ex rel. Clarke v. Deckenbach*, 274 U.S. 392	Cincinnati law barring noncitizens from operating billiard halls	Law upheld
1941	*Hines v. Davidowitz*, 312 U.S. 52	Pennsylvania alien registration law	Law struck down
1948	*Takahashi v. Fish & Game Commission*, 334 U.S. 410	California law denying commercial fishing licenses to noncitizens	Law struck down
1948	*Oyama v. California*, 332 U.S. 633	California Alien Land Law barring noncitizens from owning land	Law struck down but only applied to U.S. citizens of Japanese descent
1971	*Graham v. Richardson*, 403 U.S. 365	Arizona and Pennsylvania laws denying public benefits to certain noncitizens	Laws struck down

continued

TABLE 2-2 Continued

Year	Case/Opinion Citation	Law Contested	Outcome
1973	*Sugarman v. Dougall*, 413 U.S. 93	New York law barring noncitizens from civil service positions	Law struck down
1976	*De Canas v. Bica*, 424 U.S. 351	California law penalizing employers for hiring unauthorized workers	Law upheld
1976	*Mathews v. Diaz*, 426 U.S. 67	Federal law denying Medicare benefits to certain noncitizens	Law upheld
1978	*Foley v. Connelie*, 435 U.S. 291	New York law barring noncitizens from becoming state troopers	Law upheld
1982	*Plyler v. Doe*, 457 U.S. 202	Texas law allowing state to not fund public education for undocumented children	Law struck down
1982	*Toll v. Moreno*, 458 U.S. 1	University of Maryland policy denying in-state status to nonimmigrants	Policy struck down
1995	*LULAC v. Wilson*, 908 F. Supp. 755, 786-787 (C.D. Cal)	California Proposition 187 denying benefits to, and increasing enforcement against, undocumented immigrants	Law struck down by lower courts
2011	*Chamber of Congress v. Whiting*, 563 U.S. ___	Arizona law sanctioning employers who hire undocumented workers	Law upheld
2012	*Arizona v. United States*, 567 U.S. ___	Arizona law enforcement bill targeted at undocumented immigrants	Parts of law struck down; provision requiring police to verify the citizenship status of anyone lawfully detained was upheld
2014	*Arizona DREAM ACT Coalition v. Brewer*, 13-16248 (9th Circuit Court of Appeals)	Arizona law denying drivers licenses to immigrants with Deferred Action for Childhood Arrivals	Blocked by lower courts

four approximate categories: permanent, temporary, discretionary, and undocumented.

Permanent Status

The paradigmatic immigration status is lawful permanent residency—often referred to as "having a green card." Lawful permanent resident (LPR) status historically has served as a way station to citizenship (Motomura, 2007) and has constituted the strongest anchor the law provides for noncitizens. The alienage law governing LPR status has been relatively stable for three decades because courts subject the distinctions drawn between citizens and LPRs by state and local governments to heightened review under the Fourteenth Amendment's Equal Protection Clause (*Graham v. Richardson,* 1971; Rodríguez and Rubio-Marin, 2011). Today this principle effectively means that any distinction drawn by states and localities without federal authorization, other than those that go to the heart of the state's definition of its political community (*Sugarman v. Dougall,* 1973; Table 2-2), are constitutionally invalid (Rodriguez, 2014).

Although Congress can place virtually any contingency on permanent status it deems appropriate, a limited but potentially consequential set of distinctions exists today. The primary "disabilities" that attend LPR status and likely affect integration prospects are the lack of voting and other political rights, constraints on access to certain public benefits, and most profoundly, the absence of the right to remain (Rodriguez, 2014).

Temporary Statuses

Alongside the regime of permanent immigration under lawful permanent residency, a complex system of temporary immigration statuses has taken shape. *Temporary visa* holders are entitled to only limited periods of presence in the United States. Some of these visas are granted for particular employment purposes, ranging from agricultural and service jobs to high-skilled technical and academic positions (Myers, 2006). The number of these temporary "nonimmigrants" dwarfs the number of LPRs admitted under the employment categories each year. In 2012, for example, more than 600,000 nonimmigrants were admitted for employment purposes, compared to 144,000 employment-based LPRs (although over 1 million LPRs were admitted in total, due to the system's heavy bias toward family immigration) (Wilson, 2013). Significant numbers of temporary visa workers eventually adjust to LPR status or develop ties to employers and U.S. citizens that lead to a desire to remain, making the integration question relevant (Myers, 2006, p. 11). And although some temporary visas only enable seasonal presence, many others, such as the H1-B visa, permit repeated renewals that can result in presence for a decade or more.

The largest nonemployment-based temporary status is *Temporary Protected Status*, created by Congress as part of the Immigration Act of 1990 (Public Law 101-649). TPS was designed as a mechanism to provide temporary protection to individuals who are unable to return to their home countries because of an armed conflict, environmental disaster, or other condition that is deemed temporary. Since 1990, various countries have been designated (and in some cases delisted from) the TPS category, and the continuing designation of some countries has led to large populations of temporary nonimmigrants with TPS residing in the United States for extended periods of time.

Constitutionally speaking, the equal protection constraints on state authority apply for the most part to all those lawfully present, including those in temporary statuses. Negative integration consequences can result from the perception that low-skilled immigrants will not be long-term residents and from the labor exploitation that could result from temporary visa workers' inability to change employers. To the extent that the legal structure fails to provide adequate avenues to long-term presence for those with temporary status who develop ties to the United States but lose their temporary status, these statuses also exacerbate the problem of undocumented immigration. However, policies designed to extend the rights granted LPR status throughout the legal-status system might result in less tolerance for immigration generally (Rodriguez, 2014; Ruhs, 2013).

Discretionary Statuses

The third category of immigration status under federal law is discretionary status: lawful status conferred through Executive discretion. The most important discretionary status is *deferred action status*. Unlike TPS, deferred action has no statutory foundation but is instead part of Executive authority to determine whether to initiate or pursue removal in a particular case. The executive branch has long relied on deferred action to manage its docket and provide a form of humanitarian relief, but until the Obama administration initiated Deferred Action for Childhood Arrivals (DACA) in 2012, it had not been used as a form of categorical relief. Under DACA, unauthorized immigrants between the ages of 15 and 30 who were brought to the United States as minors and meet certain criteria are granted both work authorization and temporary protection from deportation.[5] In November 2014, President Obama expanded DACA and created Deferred Action for

---

[5] See http://www.dhs.gov/news/2012/06/15/secretary-napolitano-announces-deferred-action-process-young-people-who-are-low [October 2015].

Parental Accountability for parents of U.S. citizens and LPRs, although as of April 2015, these changes have been halted by the courts. Notably, deferred action is not intended to result in permanent presence, and the fact that the Executive retains authority to terminate the statuses makes them inherently unstable, a distinction the panel discusses further in Chapter 3.

Undocumented Status

Undocumented status, also called "unauthorized" or "illegal," is the direct if unintended result of the development of legal statuses over the last century. Although the image of those in undocumented status is of migrants who *entered without inspection* by illicitly crossing the border, an estimated 45 percent of immigrants with this status entered the United States legally via other statuses and then fell "out of status" when those statuses expired or were revoked (visa overstayers).[6] Undocumented status may also be a starting point for transitions to other legal statuses, such as TPS, although it is much easier for visa overstayers to transition to other statuses than it is for those who entered without inspection. As discussed throughout the report, undocumented status offers few legal protections and is inherently unstable because the undocumented are at constant risk of deportation, which poses significant barriers to immigrant integration.

MODERN IMMIGRATION FEDERALISM: ENFORCEMENT VERSUS INTEGRATION

Since 1971, immigration federalism has been shaped by two trends. First, the federal government has continued to strengthen its control over immigration enforcement while continuing to expand the grounds for removal. Despite the steady increase in unauthorized immigration until the Great Recession in 2007 and the perception by many that the federal government has done little to secure the U.S. borders or enforce immigration law, there has been unprecedented growth in funding, technology, and personnel dedicated to enforcement over the past 20 years. In fiscal 2012, spending on immigration enforcement was almost $18 billion, exceeding by approximately 24 percent the combined total funding of the Federal Bureau of Investigation, Drug Enforcement Agency, U.S. Secret Service, U.S. Marshals Service, and Bureau of Alcohol, Tobacco, Firearms, and Explo-

---

[6] The Department of Homeland Security has not issued an estimate of the number of visa overstayers. Pew Research Center estimated 45 percent in 2006 (see Pew Research Center, *Modes of Entry for the Unauthorized Migrant Population.* Hispanic Trends Fact Sheet, see http://www.pewhispanic.org/2006/05/22/modes-of-entry-for-the-unauthorized-migrant-population/ [August 2015]).

sives, and 15 times the amount it spent in 1986, the year the Immigration Reform and Control Act was enacted (Meissner et al., 2013). Since 1990, millions of immigrants have been detained and deported from the United States. And when states have attempted to take a stronger role in enforcement, as Arizona did in 2010 with the passage of The Support our Law Enforcement and Safe Neighborhoods Act (SB 1070),[7] they have generally been blocked by the courts.[8]

Second, the federal government has devolved decisions about whether and which immigrants can access public benefits to states and localities, while simultaneously delegating the majority of integration services to state and municipal governments and nongovernmental organizations. So while the federal government maintains tight control over immigrant entry and exit, it has given states significant leeway in determining access to various social benefits and is often only indirectly involved in immigrant integration efforts. These two trends—federal enforcement and decentralized integrative strategies—are discussed in the next two sections.

Enforcement Federalism

As noted in Chapter 1, an important part of the context for immigrant integration today has been the increase in federal immigration enforcement, including the militarization of the U.S.-Mexico border, the increase in interior enforcement, and the unprecedented rise in deportations of noncitizens after 1990 (see Figure 2-1). And while the executive branch has increased funding and resources for immigration enforcement, Congress has steadily expanded the grounds for removal while limiting the avenues for relief. The Anti-Drug Abuse Act of 1988 played a pivotal role in creating the current legal framework because it created the concept of "aggravated felony" and rendered deportable any noncitizen convicted of a crime that falls within the definition. Congress expanded the scope of the definition dramatically in the ensuing years via the Antiterrorism and Effective Death Penalty Act (1996), the USA Patriot Act [Uniting and Strengthening America by Providing Appropriate Tools Required to Intercept and Obstruct Terrorism Act of 2001] and other legislation (see Table 2-1), while closing off most avenues of relief, including cancellation of removal and asylum and eliminating judicial review of discretionary denials generally (Legomsky, 2000).

The steady expansion of grounds for removal and corresponding limi-

---

[7] This Arizona statute was introduced in 2010 as Senate Bill 1070 and is therefore commonly called "SB 1070."

[8] The Obama administration's lawsuit against Arizona's Senate Bill 1070 was novel, as the government has historically relied on private litigants to bring preemption claims against state laws.

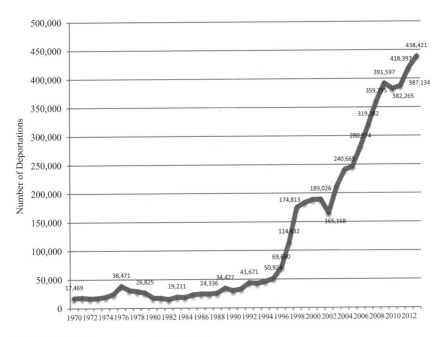

FIGURE 2-1 Deportations, 1970-2012.
SOURCE: Data from Office of Immigration Statistics (2014).

tation of relief have had serious consequences for immigrant's integration prospects because anyone who has not been naturalized is now theoretically deportable (Kanstroom, 2007). Both developments destabilize LPR status by rendering even long-time residents more easily removable. This increased uncertainty in turn has significant implications for immigrant families (see Chapter 3).

Congress has shown little if any interest in revisiting the grounds for removal, and the absence of legislative movement on this issue has resulted in what could be described as "compensation" by the executive branch (Cox and Rodriguez, 2009, pp. 519-528). The last three administrations have issued memoranda instructing prosecutors for the Immigration and Naturalization Service and its successor, Immigration and Customs Enforcement, to take factors such as family ties and links to the community into account when determining whether to initiate removal (Wadhia, 2010). Most recently, the Obama administration has issued a series of memoranda emphasizing that interior enforcement should be directed first and foremost at noncitizens who present national security or public safety risks. Despite the record number of removals under the Obama administration (Figure 2-1), the executive branch has also used its discretion to shift enforcement resources from the interior to the border (Rosenblum and Meissner, 2014), away from worksite raids and toward employer audits, and away from home raids toward reliance on the criminal justice machinery (Rodriguez, 2014; Chacón, 2006).

These discretionary moves may reduce the risk of removal and leave greater numbers of families and communities intact. Shifting resources away from targeting workplaces and homes can make enforcement operations less disruptive to immigrant communities, even if the number of removals continues to increase. And in theory, shifting resources away from interior enforcement to recent entrants at the border can provide significant relief for established immigrant families because the targets of interior enforcement are more likely to have community and family ties than recent entrants, although some (and perhaps many) of the latter may also be attempting entry (or re-entry) to the United States to reunite with families. However, executive discretion is a limited tool for immigrant integration because Congress has expanded the grounds for removal, and discretionary statuses provide no pathway to lawful permanent residence.

Federal and State Enforcement Strategies

Although the federal government has continually reasserted its supremacy in immigration enforcement, there have been efforts to leverage state and local encounters with immigrants to assist enforcement strategies. For instance, in 1996 the Illegal Immigration Reform and Immigration Responsibility Act authorized formal cooperation between federal and state and local authorities, including the 287(g)[9] agreements in which state and local police receive federal training for, and are authorized to perform, immigration functions. Even at the program's peak, the 287(g) Program was very limited in scope, and under the Obama administration attention initially shifted from the 287(g) Program to the Secure Communities Program.

Secure Communities took advantage of state and local enforcement resources by allowing state and local police to routinely share their arrest data with the Federal Bureau of Investigation, which in turn shared those data with the Department of Homeland Security (DHS) so it could be compared with DHS databases to determine if a person in state or local custody is removable. President Obama discontinued the program in a November 2014 Executive action, replacing it with the Priority Enforcement Program, which is intended to target only those who have been convicted of certain serious crimes or who pose a danger to national security. This Execu-

---

[9]This descriptor is a shorthand reference to the Immigration and Nationality Act, Section 287(g), codified at 8 U.S.C. § 1357(g).

tive action, which took effect on January 5, 2015, targets enforcement to "noncitizens who have been convicted of serious crimes, are threats to public safety, are recent illegal entrants, or have violated recent deportation orders" (Rosenblum, 2015). Although the data-sharing aspects of Secure Communities continue, DHS states that it will only seek notification about potentially removable persons rather than all undocumented people, except in special circumstances. For people who were already in detention before the Priority Enforcement Program (which replaced Secure Communities) went into effect on July 1, 2015, if Immigration and Customs Enforcement deems the case to be nonpriority, they might be released. If they are already in deportation proceedings, other factors come into play, such as the availability of legal counsel, in determining whether the case proceeds or is terminated (and the deportation stopped). As an Executive action, these changes also can change with a new president. Many aspects of this new policy are still unclear as of the time of this report.

The Supreme Court's decision in *Arizona v. United States* (Table 2-2) leaves open the realm of informal federal-state cooperation. In many areas of law enforcement, the federal government depends on state and local police to advance its objectives because the federal government does not have the resources or capacity to fully enforce its own laws. DHS depends on informal information-sharing from states and localities to identify removable noncitizens—a dependence that has become all the more significant as the grounds for removal have expanded (Motomura, 2012). In addition, federal law does require the federal government to accept inquiries from state and local police into the immigration status of those in police custody (8 U.S.C. § 1373(b)). The law therefore effectively requires the federal government to receive information from police that could prompt the initiation of removal.

Arizona v. United States also left in place SB 1070's Section 2(B), which requires police to inquire into the immigration status of anyone with whom they come into contact if there is reason to believe they are in the country unlawfully. Currently six states (Alabama, Arizona, Georgia, Indiana, South Carolina, and Utah) have passed laws that allow police to question individuals about their legal status. Several studies (Ayón and Becerra, 2013; Santos and Menjívar, 2013; Santos et al., 2013; Toomey et al., 2014) indicate that these SB 1070–inspired policies have had deleterious effects on Latino immigrant families' well-being. However, enthusiasm for enforcement may be on the wane, and many local police departments have taken a pragmatic approach to the law in order to limit its impact on immigrant communities (Trevizo and Brousseau, 2014). Meanwhile, the Supreme Court explicitly left open the possibility for lawsuits alleging civil rights and other constitutional violations. Alabama and South Carolina appear to have abandoned their own analogues to SB 1070, Section 2(B), in the wake of federal lawsuits.

Enforcement Resistance

Today, eagerness for enforcement in places like Arizona contrasts with resistance to enforcement elsewhere. By 2013, at least 70 jurisdictions nationwide had adopted ordinances that restrained public officials from inquiring into the immigration status of persons they encounter (Elias, 2013, p. 726), in the tradition of the sanctuary movement of the 1980s, when churches and some localities sought to shelter Central American refugees from removal (Rodríguez, 2008, pp. 600-605). The most recent and arguably most powerful manifestation of enforcement resistance has taken the form of so-called anti-detainer ordinances (Graber, 2012). Three states—California, Connecticut, and Colorado—and numerous cities, such as Chicago and Los Angeles, have adopted ordinances or statutes (sometimes known as TRUST Acts) that constrain the circumstances under which local police may hold persons pursuant to a detainer, usually permitting acquiescence to the federal request only in the case of serious offenses or where an outstanding order of removal exists (National Immigration Law Center, 2012).

Although some localities have treated detainers as mandatory, existing Supreme Court federalism precedents (e.g., *Printz v. United States*, 521 U.S. 898, 1997) likely would prevent DHS from attempting to make them so. And two federal district courts recently have issued opinions placing constitutional limits on detainers, which helped spur the changes to Secure Communities.[10] It is currently unclear whether these anti-detainer ordinances have become obsolete or will be revised to prohibit even notification in response to the changes to Secure Communities. As of the time this report was completed, several efforts were under way in the U.S. Senate to limit the power of municipalities to pass anti-detainer ordinances, which further clouds the future for enforcement resistance.

Other Forms of Autonomous State Action

In addition to the ongoing involvement of local law enforcement bureaucracies in immigration enforcement, recent legal developments have left some space for states and localities to adopt other enforcement measures.[11]

---

[10] See Jeh Johnson's memo in response to President Obama's Executive action. Available: http://www.dhs.gov/sites/default/files/publications/14_1120_memo_secure_communities.pdf [October 2015].

[11] States may also use their own criminal laws in ways that destabilize immigrant communities. Prosecutors in Maricopa County, Arizona, for example, have used the state's anti-smuggling law to crack down not only on those who transport unauthorized immigrants but on unauthorized immigrants themselves, for self-smuggling (Eagly, 2011, p. 1760). In 2006, voters in Arizona adopted a referendum categorically denying bail to unauthorized immigrants charged with certain crimes, including identity theft, sexual assault, and murder. Although

First, in 2011 the Supreme Court upheld Arizona's Legal Arizona Worker's Act (Table 2-2), which threatens to take away the business licenses of employers who hire unauthorized workers and requires employers to use the federal E-Verify database to determine whether a prospective employee is authorized to work. The statute is essentially unenforced (Gans, 2008, p. 14; Santa Cruz, 2010), but there is evidence suggesting that its existence prompted some immigrant workers to relocate to another state (Bohn et al., 2014; Lofstrom and Bohn, 2011) and may have motivated employers to fire or refuse to hire immigrants and even certain ethnic minorities (Menjívar, 2013) to avoid penalties. However, it did little to help the labor market outcomes of native low-skilled workers (Bohn et al., 2015) and might have increased immigrant workers' perception of vulnerability, pushing them further underground (Menjívar and Enchautegui, 2015).

Second, the federal courts have divided over whether laws that require landlords to verify immigration status and prohibit them from renting to unauthorized immigrants are preempted by *Arizona v. United States*, and the Supreme Court has declined to review these cases, leaving the issue undecided. These ordinances are arguably the most significant assaults on immigrants' presence enacted to date because they threaten the most serious human rights consequences. But few localities have adopted them, and their greatest impact may be not the imposition of homelessness but the potential displacement of immigrants to other locales—with corresponding economic consequences for the communities left behind (Capps et al., 2011; Singer et al., 2009). More research is needed on the actual effects of these laws on immigrant integration and mobility.

Finally, the latest aspect of federal-state contestation has arisen in response to DACA. As of early 2015, one state—Nebraska—still refuses to issue drivers' licenses to DACA recipients despite their lawful presence (although they still lack formal lawful status). Although the vast majority of states have moved quickly to make licenses available, this development reflects the persistence of the debate over the social position of undocumented immigrations. The Ninth Circuit Court of Appeals used the preemption framework to block Arizona's law, on the theory that denying them licenses would significantly undermine their ability to work and therefore conflict with federal policy that authorized their employment (*Arizona DREAM Act Coalition v. Brewer*, 757 F.3d 1053, 9th Cir. 2014).

---

an 11-member panel of the Ninth Circuit recently struck down that provision as "excessive" and therefore a violation of substantive due process, (*Lopez-Valenzuela v. Arpaio*, 2014 WL 5151625 [9th Cir. Oct. 15, 2014]), similar provisions exist in at least three other states.

Integration Federalism

Even as the federal government has moved to affirm its supremacy over immigration enforcement and limited the role of states in enforcement actions, it has devolved to states and localities the responsibility for decisions about access to various public benefits, while relying on state and local agencies and nongovernmental organizations to carry out its affirmative integrative programs. Integration federalism therefore reverses the burden of responsibility, decentralizing decisions about access to social goods that aid integration and leaving most of the affirmative integration work to institutions removed from direct federal control.

Affirmative Integration Programs

Unlike other countries with large immigrant populations, the United States has not constructed a centralized immigrant integration system, and "no single federal entity has been designated to lead the creation, implementation, and coordination of a national immigrant integration capability," (U.S. Government Accountability Office, 2011, p. 25). Instead, efforts to provide support for immigrants' adjustment to life in the United States are largely the province of state and local bureaucracies and the private sector, with limited federal support in the form of grants and information dissemination. (See Chapter 4 for more details on federal integration efforts for naturalization and civic inclusion.)

The federal government does maintain a variety of grant programs administered by its various agencies and designed to provide technical and cash assistance to service providers that work with immigrants, as well as to provide support for civics education and preparation for naturalization. And U.S. Citizenship and Immigration Services provide basic information to assist in the naturalization process. The panel discusses other federal integration programs below.

Federal Integration Strategies

The most robust federal integration program is specifically targeted toward refugees. The Bureau of Population, Refugees, and Migration within the State Department matches refugees with nongovernmental organizations under contract to provide housing, furnishings, food, and other essential services for 1 to 3 months. The Office of Refugee Resettlement within the Department of Health and Human Services also handles transitional assistance for "temporarily dependent refugees," and the Immigration and Nationality Act gives the Director of the Office of Refugee Resettlement the authority to provide cash, medical assistance, and social service assistance to refugees (Immigration and Nationality Act, Sections 412(c) and 412(e), codified at [8 USC 1522]). These benefits usually are run through state agencies and are designed to assist refugees who are ineligible for federal assistance programs (Bruno, 2011, p. 9). The State Department also strives to resettle refugees where they have families or where relevant ethnic communities exist, hence some of the unexpected settlement patterns of specific groups of immigrants (Patrick, 2004). The implications of these programs for refugees and asylees are discussed further in Chapter 3.

For most immigrants, however, state and local institutions and the private sector perform the bulk of what would be considered traditional affirmative integration functions, such as language and civics education, job training, and assistance accessing public benefits and institutions. This is in sharp contrast to most other immigrant-receiving countries such as Canada, Australia, and western European countries, which have more comprehensive government-run programs for immigrant integration.[12] Even the federal government's own integration policies rely heavily on state and local governments to implement and run these programs. Scholars and advocates for reform have noted and criticized the lack of federal coordination and leadership concerning immigrant integration (Bloemraad and De Graauw, 2011, pp. 10-11; Catholic Legal Immigration Network, Inc., 2007; Kerwin et al., 2011, pp. 6-9).

As noted in Chapter 1, President Obama's White House Task Force on New Americans recently undertook a review of immigration integration efforts across federal agencies in order to identify goals to strengthen integration and build "strong and welcoming communities" (White House Task Force on New Americans, 2015, p. 2). The report makes a series of recommendations to agencies to promote integration but does not call for a more centralized immigrant integration system. Federalizing the integration process ultimately requires a clear definition of what integration means and how it should be measured, or at least identification of those characteristics of integration that can be encouraged through government action. Whether greater centralization would promote better integration outcomes than the status quo also depends on which jurisdiction's programs are being evaluated; as discussed below, offices in states such as Illinois and New York may offer far more tailored and extensive integration assistance than the federal government could provide.

---

[12]While systematic studies comparing naturalization programs across countries have been done (Bloemraad, 2006), the panel did not find systematic cross-country studies comparing centralized as opposed to localized programs of immigrant integration. This area needs further research.

Adult Education and Workforce Training

In addition to civics and naturalization education efforts that are explicitly aimed at preparing immigrants for their potential roles as American citizens, the federal government plays a strong role in integration education via adult education and workforce training. The principal vehicle of support for adult education and training has been the Workforce Innovation and Opportunity Act of 2014[13] (WIOA) and its predecessor, the Workforce Investment Act of 1998. The two principal titles of interest here are Title I, which focuses on the provision of employment and training services for adults, and Title II,[14] which sets out the law's adult education and literacy programs: specifically adult basic education, adult secondary education, and English as a second language (ESL).

As discussed in Chapter 1, the large number of immigrants with low levels of education and/or limited English proficiency is not a new phenomenon or even a new cause for concern. What is relatively new is legislation explicitly designed to address these issues. Today, several pertinent trends underscore the needs of immigrant and limited English proficient (LEP) [15] adults for adult education and workforce training.

One such trend is the sustained concentration of immigrant workers in low-skill jobs: 57 percent in 2013. The shares of immigrant workers in middle- and high-skilled jobs in 2013 were 19 and 24 percent respectively. [16] Second, while the literacy, numeracy, and technological skills of *all* U.S. adults trail those of adults in many OECD countries surveyed by the Programme for the International Assessment of Adult Skills (PIAAC), immigrants' skills lagged those of the native-born. Immigrants made up 15 percent of the U.S. adult population in 2012 but were one-third of low-skilled adults according to the PIAAC, faring worse on this measure than immigrants in most other countries surveyed (Office of Career, Technical, and Adult Education 2015).[17] (The likely reason for this situation is that many immigrants to the United States are not as highly selected as immigrants to other receiving countries and thus contain more low-skilled people.) Third, 2013 American Community Survey data show that close

---

[13]Public Law 113-128 (2014), codified under USC 113.

[14]Since 1998, Title II of the Workforce Investment Act has been known as the Adult Education and Family Literacy Act.

[15]The term "limited English proficient" refers to persons ages 5 and older who reported speaking English "not at all," "not well," or "well" on the American Community Survey questionnaire. Individuals who reported speaking only English or speaking English "very well" are considered proficient in English.

[16]Analysis by Michael Fix and Jeanne Batalova, Migration Policy Institute, of the 2000 Census and 2007, 2010, and 2013 American Community Survey (ACS) data.

[17]PIAAC data also indicate that the second generation's literacy, numeracy, and technology skills catch up to that of the third generation native-born (Batalova and Fix, 2015).

to half (46%) of all full-time immigrant workers in the United States were LEP, while about a quarter of immigrant workers (23%) were low LEP—that is, they spoke little if any English.[18]

Fourth, higher levels of education attainment are no guarantee of literacy in English. According to the PIAAC, 22 percent of natives and 54 percent of immigrants with college degrees scored "below proficient" in English literacy (Batalova and Fix, 2015).

Adult Education Since the 18th century, educating adults and integrating newcomers have often been mutually reinforcing national and state policy objectives (Eyre, 2013). States created evening schools in the late 19th and early 20th centuries to provide language classes to new migrants, and the 1918 Immigration Act provided federal assistance to schools to offer English language, history, government, and citizenship classes to promote naturalization (Eyre, 2013). Since the 1960s "War on Poverty" and the 1964 enactment of the Economic Opportunity Act (Public Law 88-52), the federal government has provided substantial support to states to provide ESL training under the nation's adult basic education and workforce development law (McHugh et al., 2007). As more than 40 percent of the 1.6 million enrollees in adult education supported in part by federal funds were in ESL classes in 2013, it could be argued that federal and state support for these programs represents an often-overlooked cornerstone of national immigrant integration policy. State financial contributions to adult education, and presumably to ESL, vary widely. In California, for example, roughly 20 percent of overall spending on adult education comes from federal funds; in Texas the share is 75 percent. States also vary in terms of the number and shares of adult English learners enrolled in ESL classes and in the access states provide to adult education programs for undocumented immigrants (e.g., Arizona and Georgia ban their enrollment).

The economic returns to immigrants from learning their receiving country's language have been widely studied both in the United States and internationally (Chiswick and Miller, 2008, 2009, 2010). For instance, data from the 2001 Australian Census indicated that the earnings of immigrants who were proficient in the destination country language were 15 percent higher than those who were not proficient (Chiswick and Miller, 2008). And other studies have found that LEP high-skilled immigrants were twice as likely to work in unskilled jobs as those with equivalent skills who were English proficient (e.g., Wilson, 2013). (Chapter 7 discusses this topic further.)

Several trends in ESL education are critical to immigrant integration.

---

[18] Michael Fix and Jeanne Batalova, Migration Policy Institute, of 2013 American Community Survey.

First is the wide but declining reach of ESL programs funded under Title II of the WIOA. In program year 1999-2000, states enrolled 1.1 million adults in ESL classes, representing 38 percent of all students enrolled in adult education classes supported in part with federal funds. By program year 2013-2014, the number had fallen to 667,000 enrollees. ESL enrollees, however, represented a rising share of *all* adult education students: 42 percent in program year 2013-2014.[19]

Second, adult education for all adults—but especially for those with limited English skills—typically proceeds sequentially from English-language learning to obtaining a secondary-education credential (e.g., passing the General Education Development test), and then to postsecondary professional credentials or postsecondary education. This long, attenuated process often does not match the time and economic pressures many low-income adult immigrants experience today, making persistence and progress in ESL classes and low transfer rates from adult secondary education to postsecondary education a source of abiding policy concern. According to the most recent data, only 46 percent of adults in federally supported ESL programs completed the level in which they enrolled; 54 percent "separated before they completed" or "remained within level."[20] Commonly cited barriers to persistence and progress for low-wage immigrants include work conflicts and transportation and child care issues.

Workforce Training As noted above, the federal government's current principal vehicle for funding workforce training programs is the WIOA. Title I of that new law sets out the federal government's core programs in skills development, including employment and training for adults. While LEP individuals—many of whom are immigrants—have been a central focus of language and literacy programs, these populations historically were underrepresented in workforce training programs receiving support under the predecessor to the WIOA, the Workforce Investment Act. Despite the fact that LEP workers make up 35 percent of all workers lacking a high school degree, they represented just 3 percent of those receiving Title I services in 2012.

Implementation of the new workforce act (the WIOA) may expand ser-

---

[19] Migration Policy Institute tabulation of data for the 50 U.S. states and the District of Columbia from the U.S. Department of Education, Office of Vocational and Adult Education/ Division of Adult Education and Literacy, National Reporting System: "State Enrollment by Program Type (ABE, ESL, ASE): All States," program year 1999-2000 and 2013-2014. See https://wdcrobcolp01.ed.gov/CFAPPS/OVAE/NRS/reports/ [October 2015].

[20] Migration Policy Institute tabulation of data from U.S. Department of Education, Office of Career Technical, and Adult Education, National Reporting System: "Educational Gains and Attendance by Educational Functioning Level: All Regions," program year 2013-2014. See https://wdcrobcolp01.ed.gov/CFAPPS/OVAE/NRS/reports/ [October 2015].

vices to LEP adults and to immigrants, since this law's priorities for service prominently include "individuals who are English learners, individuals who have low levels of literacy, and individuals facing substantial cultural barriers" (Bird et al., 2015). The WIOA also adjusts state incentives in ways that may provide more of an incentive to serve populations that have low language and literacy skills. And the WIOA authorizes states to tie basic skills and workforce training together in ways that may make the credential attainment process less attenuated for LEP participants starting in ESL programs. However, the WIOA was not supported by additional funding, so these shifts will have to be initiated by states without new resources from the federal level.

Evaluation of Workforce Preparation Programs There have been few systematic studies in the United States of the impact of job training programs for LEP individuals and immigrants, in contrast to many other developed countries where both integration initiatives and their systematic evaluation are more common (Thomsen et al., 2013). One demonstration program was administered by the San Jose Center for Employment Training in the 1980s and 1990s. That program, which enrolled a large share of Hispanics, many of whom were LEP, integrated job training and English-language skills training. It produced "large and lasting impacts" according to two evaluations that employed random assignment evaluation methodologies (Wrigley et al., 2003).

Another more recent demonstration and evaluation was funded by the Department of Labor and examined workforce preparation programs' implementation and short-term outcomes at five demonstration sites. In general, English language proficiency increased but employment outcomes were mixed. For example, in Dallas, Texas, participants with follow-up data available (only 19% of the sample) saw a slight increase in wages, while at the remaining four sites, the impact on earnings was either not measured properly or the sample size was too small to generate statistically significant inferences (Grady and Coffey, 2009).

Perhaps the most carefully evaluated education and training program targeted in part to LEP populations has been Washington State's Integrated Basic Education and Skills Training (I-BEST) model. The model, which was created and introduced by the state's technical and community college system, combines adult education and college-level workforce training coursework. I-BEST involves co-teaching by basic skills faculty working with professional-technical faculty. It promotes integrated, contextualized language and work skills and takes into account learners' schedules and child care constraints. I-BEST has shown success in helping ESL and adult basic education students reach the goals of earning college credits and obtaining short-term credentials, as well as earning higher wages (Jenkins et al., 2009; Washington State Board for Community and Technical Colleges, 2012a, 2012b). Given the importance of these training programs for integration, best practices for such programs could be identified by conducting and compiling more evaluations like those conducted for the I-BEST Program in Washington State.

State and Local Integration Efforts

States and localities historically have been the public sector leaders in devising and implementing affirmative integration measures. In some cases, these measures are in tension with federal law and enforcement priorities, as discussed above. Here the panel examines how states and localities have responded to the presence and interests of undocumented immigrants. We then highlight some contemporary examples of more generally applicable state and local integration strategies.

Integrating Undocumented Immigrants Both Republican- and Democratic-leaning states have adopted laws that permit students who are undocumented immigrants to qualify for in-state tuition rates at public colleges and universities (20 states as of early 2015). Meanwhile, five states explicitly deny undocumented immigrants in-state tuition. And although Congress, through the Personal Responsibility and Work Opportunity Reconciliation Act (PRWORA), made undocumented immigrants ineligible for nonemergency state and local public benefits in 1996, it also authorized states to extend such benefits as long as they adopted laws that "affirmatively" provided for eligibility (Public Law 104-193, 110 State 2105, s. 411). Some states have enacted laws providing medical benefits, funded by the state and through the State Children's Health Insurance Program, to various categories of immigrants, including those granted deferred action (Mitnik and Halpern-Finnerty, 2010, p. 67).

Among the recent integrative strategies for undocumented immigrants are efforts to provide them with some form of identification. By 2015, 10 states and the District of Columbia had enacted laws making undocumented immigrants eligible for driver's licenses. Some local jurisdictions have complemented these efforts by issuing municipal identification cards, an identity document that can facilitate a range of activities that enhance integration, such as opening a bank account, signing a lease, and accessing municipal services such as hospitals and libraries (Center for Popular Democracy, 2013, pp. 49-51; de Graauw, 2014).

A significant potential limitation to the integrative value of driver's licenses and municipal identifications is that they "mark" undocumented immigrants. In the case of driver's licenses, Section 202 of the REAL ID Act of 2005 sets out uniform standards state licenses must meet in order to serve federal identification purposes (49 U.S.C. § 30301). A person must have a lawful immigration status in order to qualify for a fully compliant license, and states must somehow distinguish between licenses they issue that are not valid for federal purposes and those that are. As a result, in some jurisdictions the driver's licenses issued to undocumented immigrants vary in appearance from the standard license (National Immigration Law Center, 2013, p. 5). To counter this, officials in cities such as Los Angeles and New York have attempted to make municipal ID cards appealing to all city residents, including by attaching benefits such as museum entries to them (Center for Popular Democracy, 2013, p 19).

Finally, California has perhaps gone the furthest of any state with respect to immigrant integration. Overall, California has removed many barriers to education and employment for unauthorized immigrants. In addition to allowing in-state tuition and state financial aid to undocumented immigrants, it has also passed laws forbidding local landlord ordinances and mandates on the use of E-Verify by localities (Gulasekaram and Ramakrishnan, 2015). The state also allows undocumented immigrants to practice law and has mandated that all professional licensing boards in California consider applicants regardless of their immigration status (Ramakrishnan and Colbern, 2015). However, other state and local efforts at immigrant integration in California, such as allowing lawful permanent residents to serve on juries and allowing noncitizen parents to vote in school board elections, have failed to be enacted (Ramakrishnan and Colbern, 2015).

In New York, legislation proposed in 2014 that aims to create a form of state citizenship allowing all immigrants to vote in state elections, hold state office, and seek the protection of all state laws is unlikely to pass the legislature. While particular states are pushing further than ever before on immigrant integration, they still fall shy of the high-water mark set in the mid-1800s, when many states offered voting rights to certain noncitizens in state and federal elections (Raskin, 1993).

The efforts by state and local governments to facilitate the integration of both legal status and undocumented immigrants have yet to be systematically studied, so the panel cannot conclude whether they make a difference in the long-term integration of immigrants. The variation by state and locality provides an opportunity to undertake studies of the efficacy of different approaches to integration in the future.

Integration Agencies and Task Forces Numerous cities and states have created agencies, task forces, commissions, and other programs to promote immigrant integration. These programs vary widely in scope, but they generally involve "traditional" affirmative integration assistance, such as language and civics education, dissemination of financial services information, and assistance with the naturalization process (Rodriguez, 2014).

The states with the most developed task force and agency frameworks include Hawaii, Illinois, Maryland, Massachusetts, Michigan, New York, and Washington. The New York City Mayor's Office of Immigrants Affairs, founded in 1984, works with community-based organization and city agencies to "promote the well-being of immigrant communities."[21] During his tenure, Mayor Michael Bloomberg signed numerous executive orders in conjunction with this office, including orders that made city services accessible to all immigrants regardless of status, established protections from various forms of fraud, strengthened language access services for local residents seeking health and human services, and established centralized language access services for the city (Waters and Kasinitz, 2013). These orders provide a blueprint for what other localities might accomplish, given the scope of municipal government.

The Devolution of Public Benefits Determination to States and Localities

The law determining immigrants' access to public benefits is complex and governed by both legislation and jurisprudence. While federal laws have given states and localities permission to determine who accesses various benefits, the Supreme Court has handed down decisions sometimes prohibiting states from blocking access and at other times granting states leeway in determining who is eligible for these public goods (Table 2-2).

For instance, in the 1971 ruling on *Graham v. Richardson*, the Supreme Court invalidated state welfare schemes that barred certain LPR holders from receiving public benefits, while making it clear that any distinctions drawn between citizens and those with LPR status by state and local governments would be subjected to heightened review under the Fourteenth Amendment's Equal Protection Clause (Gulasekaram and Ramakrishnan, 2015; Rodriguez, 2014). However, in *De Cana v. Bica* (1976) the court ruled that the protections afforded LPR status in *Graham v. Richardson* neither extended to undocumented immigrants nor affected states' regulation of employment (Gulasekaram and Ramakrishnan, 2015). Then in *Plyler v. Doe* (1982), the court ruled that state and local governments could not deny undocumented children access to public education. Most recently, the court's ruling on the challenge to Arizona's SB 1070 substantially curtailed but did not eliminate state and local authority to enact laws or policies that amount to immigration regulation (Martin, 2012; Rodriguez, 2014).

Meanwhile, the PRWORA, passed by Congress in 1996, substantially

---

[21] See http://www.nyc.gov/html/imm/html/home/home.shtml [August 2015].

restricted even LPRs' access to means-tested benefits.[22] The PRWORA also devolved authority to state governments to determine whether LPRs and other "qualified aliens" should have access to federally funded state-run programs such as Temporary Assistance to Needy Families and Medicaid, as well as to state-funded benefits (Rodriguez, 2014). Many states reacted to these federal restrictions by providing state-funded programs (Borjas, 2002; Brown, 2013). Thus the devolution of public benefits and the decision over which immigrants can access these benefits has led to a patchwork system across the states in which immigrants' integration prospects are highly dependent on immigrants' status and geographic location.

SUMMARY AND CONCLUSIONS

Although courts and commentators have traditionally characterized immigration as an exclusively federal function, states and localities have been active participants throughout U.S. history in managing the consequences of immigration. The frameworks of legal status and the power the federal government wields to shape the terms and conditions of immigrant presence profoundly inform immigrants' prospect for integration by providing anchors of varying degrees of stability in the United States.

Conclusion 2-1 Three important legal and institutional developments of the past 30 years have implications for integration: (1) the proliferation of immigration statuses that provide different degrees of permanence and security and fall into four categories: permanent, temporary, discretionary, and undocumented; (2) the complex and at times contradictory policies and laws linked to those statuses; and (3) the broadening of grounds for removal and constraints on relief, with the related centrality of Executive action to immigrants' prospects.

Conclusion 2-2 The 11.3 million undocumented immigrants in the United States currently have few legal protections. Undocumented status is inherently unstable because undocumented immigrants are at constant risk of deportation, which poses significant barriers to immigrant integration.

In addition, federally supported adult education has proven to be a cornerstone of what can be seen as a rather skeletal federal immigrant integration policy. Yet LEP adults are generally underserved in federally

---

[22] Some of these restrictions have since been relaxed (Wasem, 2014, pp. 1-3), although most legal challenges to provisions of the law have failed, on the ground that they are rational exercises of Congress's power to regulate immigration (e.g., *City of Chicago v. Shalala*, 1996).

supported workforce development programs, and it remains to be seen whether the WIOA will expand the reach of workforce programs more widely to immigrant and LEP populations. Meanwhile, state and local efforts simultaneously challenge the complex balancing acts the federal government has struck and complement federal regulation by employing state and local institutions in the day-to-day work of integration. This form of integrative federalism leads to geographic variation in immigrants' integration prospects, with some states and localities providing more opportunities than others.

Conclusion 2-3 The patchwork of integration policies has not been systematically studied to determine which programs at the federal, state, or local level work best and with which populations. Rigorous evaluations of these programs could provide guidance for any attempt to institute new programs or to scale up existing programs to a higher level.

REFERENCES

Ayón, C., and Becerra, D. (2013). Mexican immigrant families under siege: The impact of anti-immigrant policies, discrimination, and the economic crisis. *Advances in Social Work, 14*(1), 206-228.

Batalova, J., and Fix, M. (2015). *Through an Immigrant Lens: PIAAC Assessment of the Competencies of Adults in the United States.* Washington, DC: Migration Policy Institute. Available: http://migrationpolicy.org/research/through-immigrant-lens-piaac-assessment-competencies-adults-united-states [September 2015].

Bird, K., Foster, M., and Ganzglass, E. (2015). *New Opportunities to Improve Economic and Career Success for Low-Income Youth and Adults: Key Provisions of the Workforce Innovation and Opportunity Act.* Washington, DC: Center for Law and Social Policy. Available: http://www.clasp.org/resources-and-publications/publication-1/KeyProvisions ofWIOA-Final.pdf [September 2015].

Bloemraad, I. (2006). *Becoming a Citizen: Incorporating Immigrants and Refugees in the United States and Canada.* Berkeley: University of California Press.

Bloemraad, I., and de Graauw, E. (2011). *Immigrant Integration and Policy in the United States: A Loosely Stitched Patchwork.* Berkeley: University of California Institute for Research on Labor and Employment.

Bohn, S., Lofstrom, M., and Raphael, S. (2014). Did the 2007 Legal Arizona Workers Act reduce the state's unauthorized immigrant population? *Review of Economics and Statistics, 96*(2), 258-269.

Bohn, S., Lofstrom, M., and Raphael, S. (2015). *Do E-Verify Mandates Improve Labor Market Outcomes of Low-Skilled Native and Legal Immigrant Workers?* Available: https://gspp.berkeley.edu/assets/uploads/research/pdf/p82.pdf [September 2015].

Borjas, G.J. (2002). Welfare reform and immigrant participation in welfare programs. *International Migration Review, 36*(4), 1093-1123.

Brown, H. (2013). The new racial politics of welfare: Ethno-racial diversity. *Immigration and Welfare Discourse Variation, 87*(3), 586-612.

Bruno, A. (2011). *U.S. Refugee Resettlement Assistance.* CRS No. R41570. Washington, DC: Congressional Research Service.

Capps, R., Rosenblum, M.R., Rodriguez, C., and Chishti, M. (2011) *Delegation and Divergence: A Study of 287(g) State and Local Immigration Enforcement.* Washington, DC: Migration Policy Institute.

Catholic Legal Immigration Network, Inc. (2007). *A More Perfect Union: A National Citizenship Plan.* Washington, DC: Author.

Catholic Legal Immigration Network, Inc. (2014). *States and Localities that Limit Compliance with ICE Detainer Requests.* Available: https://cliniclegal.org/sites/default/files/state_localities_that_limit_compliance_w_ice_detainers_6-2-14_0.pdf [September 2015].

The Center for Popular Democracy. (2013). *Who We Are: Municipal ID Cards as a Local Strategy to Promote Belonging and Shared Community Identity.* Available: http://popular democracy.org/news/who-we-are-municipal-id-cards-local-strategy-promote-belonging-and-shared-community-identity [September 2015].

Chacón, J.M. (2006). Unsecured borders: Immigration restrictions, crime control and national security. *Connecticut Law Review, 39*(5). Available: http://papers.ssrn.com/sol3/papers.cfm?abstract_id=1028569 [September 2015].

Chiswick, B.R., and Miller, P.W. (2008). *IZA Discussion Paper No. 3568: The Economics of Language: An Introduction and Overview.* Bonn, Germany: Institute for the Study of Labor. Available: http://repec.iza.org/dp3568.pdf [September 2015].

Chiswick, B.R., and Miller, P.W. (2009). The international transferability of immigrants' human capital. *Economics of Education Review, 28*(2), 162-169.

Chiswick, B.R., and Miller, P.W. (2010). Occupational language requirements and the value of English in the U.S. labor market. *Journal of Population Economics, 23*(1), 353-372.

de Graauw, E. (2014). Municipal ID cards for undocumented immigrants: Local bureaucratic membership in a federal system. *Politics & Society, 42*(3), 309-330.

Eagly, I.V. (2011). Local immigration prosecution: A study of Arizona before SB 1070. *UCLA Law Review, 58*(1), 1749-1817.

Elias, S.B. (2013). The new immigration federalism. *Ohio State Law Journal, 74,* 13-40.

Eyre, G.A. (2013). *An American Heritage Federal Adult Education: A Legislative History 1964-2013.* Washington, DC: U.S Department of Education, Office of Vocational and Adult Education. Available: http://lincs.ed.gov/publications/pdf/Adult_Ed_History_Report.pdf [September 2015].

Gans, J. (2008). *Arizona's Economy and the Legal Arizona Workers Act 14.* Tucson: University of Arizona's Udall Center for Studies in Public Policy. Available: http://udallcenter.arizona.edu/immigration/publications/2008_GANS_lawa.pdf [September 2015].

Graber, L. (2012). *All-in-One-Guide to Defeating ICE Hold Requests.* New York: National Immigration Project of the National Lawyers Guild. Available: http://www.nilc.org/document.html?id=673 [September 2015].

Grady, M., and Coffey, A.C. (2009). *Evaluation of the Limited English Proficiency and Hispanic Worker Initiative.* Prepared for the U.S. Department of Labor by Coffey Consulting, Bethesda, MD. Available: http://wdr.doleta.gov/research/FullText_Documents/Evaluation%20of%20the%20Limited%20English%20Proficiency%20and%20Hispanic%20Worker%20Initiative%20Final%20Report.pdf [September 2015].

Gulasekaram, P., and Ramakrishnan, S.K. (2015). *The New Immigration Federalism.* New York: Cambridge University Press.

Hayduk, R. (2006). *Democracy for All: Restoring Immigrant Voting Rights in the United States.* New York: Routledge.

Jenkins, D., Zeidenberg, M., and Kienzl, G. (2009). *Educational Outcomes of I-BEST, Washington State Community and Technical College System's Integrated Basic Education and Skills Training Program: Findings from a Multivariate Analysis*. Working paper no. 16, Community College Research Center, Teacher's College, Columbia University, New York. Available: http://ccrc.tc.columbia.edu/Publication.asp?uid=692 [September 2015].

Kanstroom, D. (2007). *Deportation Nation: Outsiders in American History*. Cambridge, MA: Harvard University Press.

Kerwin, D., Meissner, D., and McHugh, M. (2011). *Executive Action on Immigration: Six Ways to Make the System Work Better*. Washington, DC: Migration Policy Institute.

Law, A.O. (2013, August). *An Assessment of Antebellum Immigration Federalism and The Myth of the Weak State American Political Science Association Annual Meeting Paper*. Available: http://papers.ssrn.com/sol3/papers.cfm?abstract_id=2300567 [September 2015].

Legomsky, S.H. (2000). Fear and loathing in congress and the courts: Immigration and judicial review. *Texas Law Review, 78*, 1615.

Lofstrom, M., and Bohn, S. (2011). *Lessons from the 2007 Legal Arizona Workers Act*. San Francisco: Public Policy Institute of California.

Martin, D. (2012). Reading Arizona. *Virginia Law Review in Brief, 41*, 112.

McHugh, M., Gellatt, J., and Fix, M. (2007). *Adult English Language Instruction in the United States: Determining Need and Investing Wisely*. Washington, DC: Migration Policy Institute. Available: http://www.migrationpolicy.org/research/adult-english-language-instruction-united-states-determining-need-and-investing-wisely [September 2015].

Meissner, D., Kerwin, D.M., Chishti, M., and Bergeron, C. (2013). *Immigration Enforcement in the United States: The Rise of a Formidable Machinery*. Washington, DC: Migration Policy Institute.

Menjívar, C. (2013). When immigration policies affect immigrants' lives: Commentary. *Demography, 50*(3), 1097-1099.

Menjívar, C., and Enchautegui, M.E. (2015). Confluence of the economic recession and immigration laws in the lives of Latino immigrant workers in the United States. In M. Aysa-Lastra and L. Cachóno (Eds.), *Immigrant Vulnerability and Resilience* (series vol. 11, pp. 105-126). Cham, Switzerland: Springer.

Mitnik, P.A., and Halpern-Finnerty, J. (2010). Immigration and local governments: Inclusionary local policies in the era of state rescaling. In M. Varsanyi (Ed.), *Taking Local Control: Immigration Policy Activism in U.S. Cities and States* (pp. 51-72). La Jolla, CA: Center for Comparative Integration Studies.

Motomura, H. (2007). *Americans in Waiting: The Lost Story of Immigration and Citizenship in the United States*. New York: Oxford University Press.

Myers, D.W. (2006). *Temporary Worker Programs: A Patchwork Policy Response*. Washington, DC: Migration Policy Institute. Available: http://www.migrationpolicy.org/research/temporary-worker-programs-patchwork-policy-response [August 2015].

National Immigration Law Center. (2012). *The All-in-One Guide to Defeating ICE Hold Requests*. Available: http://www.ilrc.org/files/documents/all_in_one_guide_appendix_7.pdf [August 2015].

National Immigration Law Center. (2013). *Inclusive Policies Advance Dramatically in the States*. Available: http://www.nilc.org/document.html?id=963 [September 2015].

Neuman, G.L. (1993). The lost century of American immigration law (1776-1875). *Columbia Law Review*, 1833-1901.

Ngai, M.M. (2004). *Impossible Subjects: Illegal Aliens and the Making of Modern America*. Princeton, NJ: Princeton University Press.

Ngai, M.M. (2014). *Impossible Subjects: Illegal Aliens and the Making of Modern America*. (Updated edition with new Foreword.) Princeton, NJ: Princeton University Press.

Office of Immigration Statistics, U.S. Department of Homeland Security. (2014). *Yearbook of Immigration Statistics: 2013.* Available: http://www.dhs.gov/yearbook-immigration-statistics [May 2015].

Office of Career, Technical and Adult Education. (2015). *Making Skills Everyone's Business: A Call to Transform Adult Learning in the United States.* Washington, DC: U.S. Department of Education. Available: http://www2.ed.gov/about/offices/list/ovae/pi/AdultEd/making-skills.pdf [September 2015].

Patrick, E. (2004, June 1). *The U.S. Refugee Resettlement Program,* Washington, DC: Migration Policy Institute. Available: http://www.migrationpolicy.org/article/us-refugee-resettlement-program#8 [August 2015].

Peffer, G.A. (1986). Forbidden families: Emigration experiences of Chinese women under the Page Law, 1875-1882. *Journal of American Ethnic History,* 28-46.

Ramakrishnan, S.K., and Colbern, A. (2015). The California package: Immigrant integration and the evolving nature of state citizenship. *Policy Matters,* 6(3). Available: http://policymatters.ucr.edu/wp-content/uploads/2015/06/pmatters-vol6-3-state-citizenship.pdf [September 2015].

Raskin, J.B. (1993). Legal aliens, local citizens: The historical, constitutional, and theoretical meanings of alien suffrage. *University of Pennsylvania Law Review, 141*(4), 1391-1470.

Rodriguez, C.M. (2008). The significance of the local in immigration regulation. *Michigan Law Review,* 567-642.

Rodriguez, C.M. (2014). *Legal Frameworks Affecting Immigrant Integration: Federal Baselines and Local Variation.* Paper commissioned by the Panel on Integration of Immigrants into American Society, October, National Academies of Sciences, Engineering, and Medicine, Washington, DC.

Rodriguez, C., and Rubio-Marin, R. (2011). The Constitutional Status of Irregular Migrants: Testing the Boundaries of Human Rights Protection in Spain and the United States. In M. Dembour and T. Kelly (Eds.), *Are Human Rights for Migrants? Critical Reflections on the Status of Irregular Migrants in Europe and the United States* (pp. 73-98). New York: Routledge.

Rosenblum, M.R. (2015). *Understanding the Potential Impact of Executive Action on Immigration Enforcement.* Washington DC: Migration Policy Institute. Available: http://migrationpolicy.org/research/understanding-potential-impact-executive-action-immigration-enforcement [August 2015].

Rosenblum, M.R., and Meissner, D. (2014). *Deportation Dilemma: Reconciling Tough and Humane Enforcement.* Washington, DC: Migration Policy Institute. Available: http://www.migrationpolicy.org/research/deportationdilemma-reconciling-tough-humane-enforcement [August 2015].

Ruhs, M. (2013). *The Price of Rights: Regulating International Labor Migration.* Princeton, NJ: Princeton University Press.

Santa Cruz, N. (2010). Arizona has rarely invoked its last tough immigration law. *Los Angeles Times,* April 19. Available: http://articles.latimes.com/2010/apr/19/nation/la-na-employer-sanctions19-2010apr19 [September 2015].

Santos, C., and Menjívar, C. (2013). Youths' perspective on Senate Bill 1070 in Arizona: The socio-emotional effects of immigration policy. *Association of Mexican American Educators Journal, 7*(2), 7-17.

Santos, C., Menjívar, C., and Godfrey, E. (2013). Effects of SB 1070 on children. In L. Magãna and E. Lee (Eds.), *Latino Politics and Arizona's Immigration Law SB 1070* (pp. 79-92). New York: Springer.

Singer, A., Wilson, J.H., and DeRenzis, B. (2009). *Immigrants, Politics, and Local Responses in Suburban Washington.* Washington, DC: Brookings Institution Press. Available: http://www.brookings.edu/~/media/Research/Files/Reports/2009/2/25%20immigration%20singer/0225_immigration_singer.pdf [September 2015].

Smith, R.M. (1999). *Civic Ideals: Conflicting Visions of Citizenship in U.S. History.* New Haven, CT: Yale University Press.

Smith, J.P., and Edmonston, B.E. (1997). *The New Americans: Economic, Demographic, and Fiscal Effects of Immigration.* Washington, DC: National Academy Press.

Thomsen, S.L., Walter, T., and Aldashev, A. (2013). Short-term training programs for immigrants in the German welfare system: Do effects differ from natives and why? *IZA Journal of Migration, 2,* 24.

Tichenor, D.J. (2009). *Dividing Lines: The Politics of Immigration Control in America: The Politics of Immigration Control in America.* Princeton, NJ: Princeton University Press.

Toomey, R.B., Umaña-Taylor, A.J., Williams, D.R., Harvey-Mendoza, E., Jahromi, L.B., and Updegraff, K.A. (2014). Impact of Arizona's SB 1070 immigration law on utilization of health care and public assistance among Mexican-origin adolescent mothers and their mother figures. *American Journal of Public Health, 104*(S1), S28-S34.

Trevizo, P., and Brosseau, C (2014). SB 1070 frustrations at a boil for protestors, police. *Arizona Daily Star,* March 3. Available: http://azstarnet.com/news/local/border/SB-frustrations-at-a-boil-for-protesters-police/article_de89bccf-3544-5a74-849c-92a0369ebf6d.html [August 2015].

U.S. Government Accountability Office. (2011). *Immigrant Integration: U.S. Citizenship and Immigration Services Could Better Assess Its Grant Program.* GAO-12-274. Available: http://www.gao.gov/assets/590/587725.txt [September 2015].

Wadhia, S.S. (2010). The role of prosecutorial discretion in immigration law. *Connecticut Public Interest Law Journal, 9*(2), 243.

Washington State Board for Community and Technical Colleges. (2012a). *2012 I-BEST Review: Lessons Being Learned from Traditional Programs and New Innovations: Next Steps and Issues for Scaling Up.* Olympia: Author. Available: http://www.sbctc.ctc.edu/College/abe/2012I-BESTReview.pdf [September 2015].

Washington State Board for Community and Technical Colleges. (2012b). *Washington's Community and Technical Colleges Integrated Basic Education and Skills Training (I-BEST).* Fact sheet. Olympia: Author. Available: www.sbctc.edu/college/abepds/WEB_IBESTonepager_11.5.12.pdf [September 2015].

Wasem, R.E. (2014). *Noncitizen Eligibility for Federal Public Assistance: Policy Overview and Trends.* Washington, DC: Congressional Research Service.

Waters, M.C., and Kasinitz, P. (2013). Immigrants in New York City: Reaping the benefits of continuous immigration. *Daedalus, 142*(3), 92-106.

White House Task Force on New Americans. (2015). *Strengthening Communities by Welcoming All Residents: A Federal Strategic Action Plan on Immigrant and Refugee Integration.* Available: https://www.whitehouse.gov/sites/default/files/docs/final_tf_newamericans_report_4-14-15_clean.pdf [August 2015].

Wilson, J. (2013). *Immigration Facts: Temporary Foreign Workers.* Washington, DC: Brookings Institution Press. Available: http://www.brookings.edu/research/reports/2013/06/18-temporary-workers-wilson [August 2015].

Wrigley, H.S., Richer, E., Martinson, K., Kubo, H., and Strawn, J. (2003). *The Language of Opportunity: Expanding Employment Prospects for Adults with Limited English Skills.* Washington, DC: The Center for Law and Social Policy. Available: http://www.clasp.org/resources-and-publications/files/0148.pdf [September 2015].

Zolberg, A. (2006). *A Nation by Design: Immigration Policy in the Fashioning of America 1750-2000.* Cambridge, MA: Harvard University Press.

3

Legal Status and Immigrant Integration

L egal status affects immigrants' paths to integration in a variety of ways, across a wide range of activities, and with varying degrees of intensity. In areas that are fundamental for integration, such as employment, access to higher education, social services, and health care, legal status plays a significant role. In addition, the influence of legal status cuts across generations, with parents' undocumented status in particular affecting the development of children, even when the children are U.S. citizens.

While the previous chapter describes the history and current state of immigration policy, a wide body of research has also examined the impact of policy changes on immigrants and their descendants. These policy changes have contributed to the proliferation of legal statuses, with important consequences for immigrant integration. This chapter reviews the effects of legal status on opportunities for integration and examines the potential long-term consequences for immigrants and their descendants. It begins with a general introduction to the effects of legal status on various aspects of life that are crucial for integration. It then describes the categories of legal status and the opportunities and obstacles that legal statuses place on pathways to integration. The proliferation of different legal statuses interacts with integration trajectories in many ways, complicating any effort to pinpoint when integration into American society begins for individuals. More than half (52%) of people receiving lawful permanent resident (LPR) status do so after living in the United States for some period of time under a different legal status and adjusting to LPR status. And many undocumented people live in the United States for decades without officially "immigrating." Many people in temporary statuses have therefore begun integrating into American society before officially immigrating, and many people who are very integrated into our workplaces, neighborhoods, schools, and churches have never officially immigrated.

LEGAL STATUS AND ITS EFFECTS ON IMMIGRANT INTEGRATION

Increased immigration enforcement and restrictions on access to social benefits by legal status (see Chapter 2) channel immigrants either toward integration or, in its absence, to insecurity and dim prospects for the future. Immigrants living out-of-status or in temporary and discretionary statuses often face policies of deterrence that constrain their lives today as well as their opportunities for the future.

As discussed in Chapter 2, legal status has become increasingly important to immigrant integration. Most immigrants of the past did not face the complexities that the contemporary immigration system poses; when employment opportunities decreased, social programs were implemented to assist immigrants and aid integration (Fox, 2012). Presence in the country was generally enough to guarantee access to public benefits. But legislation enacted in 1996 under the Illegal Immigration Reform and Immigrant Responsibility Act (IIRIRA), the Personal Responsibility and Work Opportunity Reconciliation Act, and the Anti-Terrorism and Effective Death Penalty Act expanded the conditions under which unauthorized immigrants in local communities and jurisdictions face exclusion, while restricting even legal residents' access to social welfare benefits (see Table 3-1). Today, categories of admission and classification into different legal statuses have serious consequences for immigrants' everyday lives and the rights they are granted (Bosniak, 2007).

As described in Chapter 2, the federal government's definition of legal status establishes four general categories: permanent statuses, temporary, discretionary, and undocumented (see Table 3-2; also see Figure 3-1 for proportions in these categories). Permanent status is the strongest anchor the law provides because it allows labor mobility, confers significant constitutional rights and access to some public benefits, and can lead to naturalization provided that the LPR meets a set of additional requirements. Temporary statuses include a variety of employment-based and humanitarian-based admissions that confer lawful presence for limited periods of time, which are subject to review by Congress. Discretionary statuses grant temporary lawful status via executive discretion and as such can be terminated at any time. Although discretionary statuses provide temporary protection from removal, provided that holders meet certain requirements related to behavior and practices, these statuses grant the least degree of formal security.

Undocumented status offers no formal security at all, provides only some civil and labor rights, and poses a significant barrier for immigrant integration (Jones-Correa and de Graauw, 2013). While undocumented status is technically not a step toward legalization, in reality this status is where some immigrants start or, more significantly, where many find themselves at some point in the legalization process. Increasingly, laws have made it easier to shift from documented to undocumented status but not vice versa, placing many immigrants in undetermined legal statuses that can revert to undocumented status for long, indefinite periods of time (Menjívar, 2006). In consequence, this category is particularly dynamic and fluid.

There are two aspects of the current immigration system that magnify the importance of legal status today and its effects for the prospects of immigrant integration. First, on the legislative side there has been an expansion of temporary legal statuses with indefinite periods of extension as well as long waiting lines and backlogs for applications, particularly those submitted through family reunification, to be reviewed and adjudicated. This means that many immigrants who are legally present (but lack LPR status, see Chapter 2) may spend years, sometimes even decades, in uncertain situations, often lacking access to a range of social benefits. All legal statuses short of citizenship, including LPR, are intentionally designed to be temporary. Many people move through two or more statuses over the course of their lifetimes or even within a few years, although there is currently little data on the scale and length of these transitions (see Chapter 10 for further discussion of data needs and recommendations). Second, on the enforcement side, since the 1980s new strategies have expanded enforcement into the interior of the country, beyond the border with Mexico (Kanstroom, 2007; Massey, 2003).[1] This change heightens the importance of legal status for the daily activities of immigrants who are undocumented or hold temporary permits. More intensive and extensive enforcement strategies mean that individuals with less than permanent status face risk of deportation, and depending on local and state-level laws, they may also find their social rights severely curtailed. In several geographic areas throughout the country, enforcement has expanded to include a variety of public spaces, such as in traffic or on public transportation (Armenta, 2012; Ellis et al., 2014; Longazel, 2013; Menjívar and Abrego, 2012; Schmalzbauer, 2014; Steil and Ridgley, 2012), with negative consequences for the daily lives of immigrants, including constraints on the jobs they can secure and

---

[1] Although it is still too early to fully measure the impact of the November 2014 Executive action replacing Secure Communities with the Priority Enforcement Program, it may substantially reduce the threat of deportation to the majority of undocumented immigrants. The Migration Policy Institute estimates that approximately 13 percent of undocumented immigrants will be considered enforcement priorities under the new program, compared to 27 percent under the previous guidelines (for more details, see Rosenblum, 2015).

Temporary Resident				
Dual intent worker[a] (H-1B, etc.)	✓	K-12	✓	✓
Foreign student	✓	K-12	✓	Indirect
Other temporary worker	✓	K-12	✓	
Discretionary Status				
TPS	✓	K-12	✓	
DACA	✓	K-12		
DAPA	✓	K-12		
Undocumented	✓	K-12		

NOTES: TANF = Temporary Assistance to Needy Families, SNAP = Supplemental Nutrition Assistance Program, VAWA = Violence Against Women Act, TPS = Temporary Protected Status, DACA = Deferred Action for Childhood Arrivals, DAPA = Deferred Action for Parental Accountability, K-12 = primary and secondary education (kindergarten through 12th grade).

[a] "Dual intent worker" refers to temporary nonimmigrant visas for which an applicant is permitted to apply for a temporary work visa with the intent to eventually apply for lawful permanent residence.

TABLE 3-2 Visa Categories/Statuses

Name	Type of Immigrant/Eligibility	Pathway to LPR Status?
	LAWFUL PERMANENT RESIDENT (LPR) CATEGORIES	

Immigrant Categories Based on Family Relationships

Name	Type of Immigrant/Eligibility	Pathway to LPR Status?
Immediate relative immigrant visas, (IR-1–IR-5, CR-1)[a]	Visas are based on a close family relationship with a U.S. citizen described as an immediate relative (IR). The number of immigrants in these categories is not limited each fiscal year.	Yes. These categories require that an IR who is a U.S. citizen or an LPR file a Form I-130, Petition for Alien Relative for applicant.
Family preference immigrant visas (F1–F-4)[b]	• Visas for specific, more distant, family relationships with a U.S. citizen and for some specified relationships with an LPR. There are fiscal-year numerical limitations on these visas.	Yes. Same as for IR immigrant visas.
K visa[c]	• Visa for nonimmigrant fiancé(e)s or spouses of U.S. citizens and their accompanying minor children.	Yes. Applicants must apply for adjustment as soon as they marry their fiancé(e).
Widow/er of U.S. citizen[d]	Visas for widows or widowers who were married to a U.S. citizen at the time of the citizen's death. To immigrate, applicants must prove that they were legally married to the citizen and have not remarried and that they entered the marriage in good faith and not solely to obtain an immigration benefit.	Yes. Applicants file Form I-360, Petition for Amerasian, Widow(er), or Special Immigrant.

Employment-Based Immigrant Categories[e]

Name	Type of Immigrant/Eligibility	Pathway to LPR Status?
EB-1	• Persons with extraordinary ability in the sciences, arts, education, business, or athletics. • Outstanding professors and researchers with at least 3 years' experience in teaching or research and who are recognized internationally. • Multinational managers or executives who were employed for at least 1 year within the 3 years preceding their admission by an overseas affiliate, parent, subsidiary, or branch of the U.S. employer.	Yes, either through self-petition or employer petition.
EB-2	Professionals holding advanced degrees and persons of exceptional ability.	Yes. Same as for EB-1 visas.

TABLE 3-2 Continued

Name	Type of Immigrant/Eligibility	Pathway to LPR Status?
EB-3	Skilled workers, professionals, and unskilled workers (not temporary or seasonal).	Yes, through employer petition.
EB-4	Various specific worker categories, including but not limited to broadcasters in the U.S. employed by the International Broadcasting Bureau of the Broadcasting Board of Governors or a grantee of such organization; ministers of religion; certain employees or former employees of the U.S. government abroad; certain former employees of the Panama Canal Company or Canal Zone government; Iraqi and Afghan interpreters/translators who have worked directly with the U.S. Armed Forces or under Chief of Mission authority as a translator/interpreter for a period of at least 12 months and meet requirements (annual numeric limitation of 50 visas); certain Iraqi and Afghan nationals who have provided faithful and valuable service while employed by or on behalf of the U.S. government in Iraq or in Afghanistan and have experienced an ongoing serious threat as a consequence of that employment.	Yes, through employer petition.
EB-5	Immigrant investors must invest in a new commercial enterprise. "Commercial enterprise" means any for-profit activity formed for the ongoing conduct of lawful business. This definition includes a commercial enterprise consisting of a holding company and its wholly owned subsidiaries, provided that each such subsidiary is engaged in a for-profit activity formed for the ongoing conduct of a lawful business. Entrepreneurs must invest at least $1 million, or at least $500,000 in a targeted employment area (high unemployment or rural area).	Yes, through self-petition.

Other Immigrant Categories

Asylee*f*	Persons can apply for asylum if they suffered persecution or fear that they will suffer persecution due to race, religion, nationality, membership in a particular social group, or political opinion.	Yes. Asylees may apply 1 year after being granted asylum.

TABLE 3-2 Continued

Name	Type of Immigrant/Eligibility	Pathway to LPR Status?
Refugee[g]	A refugee is someone who meets all of the following conditions: • Is located outside the U.S. • Is of special humanitarian concern to the U.S. • Demonstrates that they were persecuted or fear persecution due to race, religion, nationality, political opinion, or membership in a particular social group. • Is not firmly resettled in another country. • Is admissible to the U.S.	Yes. Refugees must apply 1 year after coming to the U.S.
American Indian born in Canada[h]	Applicants may be eligible to receive LPR status as an American Indian born in Canada if they • have 50% or more of blood of the American Indian race, and • were born in Canada. Applicants must have proof of this ancestry based on familial blood relationship to parents, grandparents, and/or great-grand parents who are or were registered members of a recognized Canadian Indian Band or U.S. Indian tribe.	Yes. Applicants must tell the Customs and Border Protection officer that they are an American Indian born in Canada, provide documentation to support their claim, and state that they are seeking to enter to reside permanently in the U.S. Once in the U.S., applicants must schedule an Infopass appointment and appear in person at their local U.S. Citizenship and Immigration Services (USCIS) office.
Amerasian child of U.S. citizen[i]	Persons born in Korea, Vietnam, Laos, Kampuchea (Cambodia), or Thailand between January 1, 1951, and October 21, 1982, and fathered by a U.S. citizen can apply if they also meet all of the following conditions: • Have a financial sponsor in the U.S. who is 21 years of age or older, of good moral character, and is either a U.S. citizen or permanent resident. • Are admissible to the U.S. • Have an immigrant visa immediately available.	Yes. Applicants file Form I-360, Petition for Amerasian, Widow(er) or Special Immigrant.

TABLE 3-2 Continued

Name	Type of Immigrant/Eligibility	Pathway to LPR Status?
Armed Forces member[i]	Applicants must have originally enlisted in the U.S. Armed Forces outside the U.S. under a treaty or an agreement that was in effect on October 1, 1991, and served for a combined period of time of either • 12 years and, if already separated from service after these 12 years, must have separated only under honorable conditions; or • 6 years, if they are now on active duty, and have already re-enlisted for a total active duty service obligation of at least 12 years. Applicant must also meet all the following conditions: • Is a national of an independent state that maintains a treaty or agreement allowing nationals of that state to enlist in the U.S. Armed Forces each year (currently, only applies to nationals of the Philippines, the Federated States of Micronesia, and the Republic of the Marshall Islands). • Recommended by the executive branch of the Armed Services under which applicant serves or has served for this special immigrant status. • Is admissible to the U.S.	Yes. Applicants file Form I-360, Petition for Amerasian, Widow(er) or Special Immigrant.
Child of diplomat[k]	A person born to a foreign diplomatic officer in the U.S. The parent's accredited title must be listed in the State Department Diplomatic List, also known as the Blue List.	Yes. Applicants file, or have had filed on their behalf, Form I-360, Petition for Amerasian, Widow(er), or Special Immigrant.
Cuban native or citizen[l]	The Attorney General has the discretion to grant permanent residence to Cuban natives or citizens applying for a green card if they • have been present in the U.S. for at least 1 year; • have been admitted or paroled; or • are admissible as immigrants.	Yes. Cuban natives or citizens can apply for a green card while in the U.S. if they have been present in the U.S. for at least 1 year.

TABLE 3-2 Continued

Name	Type of Immigrant/Eligibility	Pathway to LPR Status?
Diversity Immigrant Visa Program ("green card lottery")[m]	The Diversity Immigrant Visa Program makes up to 50,000 immigrant visas available annually, drawn by random selection among all entries, to individuals who are from countries with low rates of immigration to the U.S. The program is administered by the U.S. Department of State. Most lottery winners reside outside the U.S. and immigrate through consular processing and issuance of an immigrant visa.	Yes. Applicants must establish that they • have been selected for a Diversity Visa by the State Department's lottery; • have an immigrant visa immediately available at the time of filing an adjustment application; • are admissible to the U.S.
Haitian refugee[n]	Under the 1998 Haitian Refugee Immigration Fairness Act, certain nationals of Haiti who had been residing in the U.S. since December 31, 1995, could become permanent residents.	Yes. Applicants must file Form I-485, Application to Register Permanent Residence or Adjust Status.
Help HAITI Act of 2010[o]	The Help Haitian Adoptees Immediately to Integrate Act of 2010 (Help HAITI Act of 2010) made it possible for certain Haitian orphans paroled into the U.S. to become LPRs and obtain green cards.	Yes. Applicants must have filed Form I-485, Application to Register Permanent Residence or Adjust Status, and supporting documentation on or before December 9, 2013.
Indochinese Parole Adjustment Act[p]	On November 1, 2000, Congress passed a law allowing certain individuals from Vietnam, Kampuchea (Cambodia), and Laos who did not receive asylum or refugee status to adjust their status to LPR.	Yes. Applicants must file Form I-485, Application to Register Permanent Residence or Adjust Status.

TABLE 3-2 Continued

Name	Type of Immigrant/Eligibility	Pathway to LPR Status?
Nicaraguan Adjustment and Central American Relief Act (NACARA), Section 203[q]	Section 203 of NACARA provides that certain nationals from Guatemala, El Salvador, and former Soviet bloc countries are eligible to apply for suspension of deportation or special rule cancellation of removal under the standards similar to those in effect prior to the enactment of the Illegal Immigration Reform and Immigrant Responsibility Act. An applicant who is granted suspension of deportation or cancellation of removal under NACARA may adjust his or her status to LPR. A qualified family member of an individual in this category is also eligible.	Yes. If USCIS grants an applicant relief under Section 203 of NACARA, applicant will be an LPR and can obtain an I-551, Permanent Residence Card.
S: Informant[r]	Applicants must have assisted a law enforcement agency as a witness or informant.	Yes. A federal or state law enforcement agency may submit an application for permanent residence on behalf of a witness or informant when the individual has completed the terms and conditions of the S classification.
Special Immigrant Juveniles (SIJ)[s]	The SIJ Program helps foreign children in the U.S. who have been abused, abandoned, or neglected. To petition for SIJ status, applicants must have a state court order that contains these findings: • Declares the applicant a dependent of the court or legally places them with a state agency, a private agency, or a private person. • Finds it is not in the applicant's best interests to return to applicant's home country (or the country in which applicant last lived). • Finds the applicant cannot be reunited with a parent for any one or more of the following reasons: abuse, abandonment, neglect, or similar reason under state law.	Yes. Once applicants meet all the eligibility requirements for SIJ status, applicants can establish eligibility for LPR status.

TABLE 3-2 Continued

Name	Type of Immigrant/Eligibility	Pathway to LPR Status?
V: Nonimmigrant spouse or child of LPR*t*	Allows the spouse or child of an LPR to live and work in the U.S. while waiting to obtain immigrant status.	Yes. The spouse or child of the LPR needs a Form I-130, Petition for Alien Relative, filed on their behalf on or before December 21, 2000, by the LPR relative and must have been waiting for their immigrant status for at least 3 years after the form was filed.
Victims of Crimes		
T: Victims of trafficking*u*	Applicants may be eligible if they meet all of the following conditions: • Are or were a victim of trafficking, as defined by law. • Are in the U.S., American Samoa, Commonwealth of the Northern Mariana Islands, or at a port of entry due to trafficking. • Complies with any reasonable request from a law enforcement agency for assistance in the investigation or prosecution of human trafficking (or they are under the age of 18, or they are unable to cooperate due to physical or psychological trauma). • Demonstrates that they would suffer extreme hardship involving unusual and severe harm if they were removed from the U.S. • Are admissible to the U.S. If not admissible, may apply for a waiver.	Yes. Applicants (1) must have been physically present in the U.S. for either (a) a continuous period of at least 3 years since the first date of admission as a T-1 nonimmigrant or (b) a continuous period during the investigation or prosecution of acts of trafficking, and the Attorney General has determined the investigation or prosecution is complete; (2) must have been a person of good moral character since first being admitted as a T-1 nonimmigrant; (3) must have complied with any reasonable request for assistance in the investigation or prosecution of acts of trafficking since first being admitted; (4) would suffer extreme hardship involving unusual and severe harm upon removal from the U.S.; and (5) must be admissible to the U.S. as a permanent resident.

TABLE 3-2 Continued

Name	Type of Immigrant/Eligibility	Pathway to LPR Status?
U: Victims of criminal activity[v]	Applicants may be eligible if they • are the victim of qualifying criminal activity; • have suffered substantial physical or mental abuse as a result of having been a victim of criminal activity that occurred in the U.S. or that violated U.S. laws; • have information about the criminal activity; • were helpful, are helpful, or are likely to be helpful to law enforcement in the investigation or prosecution of the crime; and • are admissible to the U.S. If not admissible, may apply for a waiver.	Yes. Applicants (1) must have been physically present in the U.S. for a continuous period of at least 3 years since the first date of admission; (2) must have not unreasonably refused to provide assistance in the criminal investigation or prosecution; (3) are not inadmissible under Section 212(a)(3)(E) of the Immigration Nationality Act; and (4) must have established that presence in the U.S. is justified on humanitarian grounds, to ensure family unity, or is in the public interest.
Violence Against Women Act (VAWA): Battered spouse, parent, or child[w]	Spouses, parents, and children may file for themselves if they are, or were, abused by a U.S. citizen or permanent resident. They may also file as an abused spouse if their child was abused by their U.S. citizen or permanent resident spouse. They may also include on their petition unmarried children who are under 21.	Yes. Once the VAWA self-petition is approved, the victim may file to become an LPR directly. Eligibility holds regardless of whether the victim entered the U.S. without inspection and admission or parole. VAWA self-petitioners do not need to show that illegal entry into the U.S. had a substantial connection to the domestic violence, battery, or extreme cruelty.

TABLE 3-2 Continued

Name	Type of Immigrant/Eligibility	Pathway to LPR Status?

TEMPORARY NONIMMIGRANT STATUSES

Nonimmigrant or Employment-Based Visa Categories with Regulatory Pathway to Lawful Permanent Residence

Name	Type of Immigrant/Eligibility	Pathway to LPR Status?
H-1B, Specialty workers[x,y,z]	Applicants must either • have completed a U.S. bachelor's or higher degree required by the specific specialty occupation from an accredited college or university; or • hold a foreign degree that is the equivalent to a U.S. bachelor's or higher degree in the specialty occupation; or • hold an unrestricted state license, registration, or certification that authorizes applicant to fully practice the specialty occupation and be engaged in that specialty in the state of intended employment; or • have education, training, or progressively responsible experience in the specialty that is equivalent to the completion of such a degree and have recognition of expertise in the specialty through progressively responsible positions directly related to the specialty.	Yes, if they are eligible under one of the employment immigration categories listed above.
H-1B2, DOD researcher and development project worker[aa]	Same as the conditions above for H-1B specialty workers.	Yes. See conditions above for H-1B.
H-1B3, fashion model[bb]	Applicants must be a fashion model of distinguished merit and ability.	Yes. See conditions above for H-1B.
L-1A, Intracompany transferee executive or manager[cc]	Applicants must • generally have been working for a qualifying organization abroad for one continuous year within the 3 years immediately preceding his or her admission to the U.S. in a specialized knowledge, executive, or managerial capacity • be seeking to enter the U.S. to provide services in an executive or managerial capacity to a branch of the same employer or one of its qualifying organizations.	Yes. See conditions above for H-1B.

TABLE 3-2 Continued

Name	Type of Immigrant/Eligibility	Pathway to LPR Status?
L-1B, Intracompany transferee with specialized knowledge[dd]	Applicants must • generally have been working for a qualifying organization abroad for one continuous year within the 3 years immediately preceding his or her admission to the U.S. in a specialized knowledge, executive, or managerial capacity; and • be seeking to enter the U.S. to provide services in a specialized knowledge capacity to a branch of the same employer or one of its qualifying organizations.	Yes. See conditions above for H-1B.
O, Individuals with extraordinary ability or achievement[ee]	To qualify, the beneficiary must demonstrate extraordinary ability by sustained national or international acclaim and must be coming temporarily to the U.S. to continue work in the area of extraordinary ability.	Yes. See conditions above for H-1B.
Special categories[ff]	Adjustment programs are limited to individuals who meet particular qualifications and/or apply during certain time frames. These categories include • Afghan/Iraqi translator • Armed Forces member • Broadcaster • International organization employee • Iraqi who assisted the U.S. government • Afghan who assisted the U.S. government • NATO-6 nonimmigrant • Panama Canal employee • Physician national interest waiver • Religious worker	Yes. Special immigrant classification requirements vary widely, and some may require the employer to file a Form I-360, Petition for Amerasian, Widow(er), or Special Immigrant. Most of these categories are EB-4 classifications of different designations and are either foreign national religious workers or employees and former employees of the U.S. government or benefiting the U.S. government abroad.
E-1, Treaty traders[gg]	A national of a treaty country (a country with which the U.S. maintains a treaty of commerce and navigation) can be admitted to the U.S. solely to engage in international trade on his or her own behalf.	Yes, if they are eligible under one of the employment-based immigration categories.

TABLE 3-2 Continued

Name	Type of Immigrant/Eligibility	Pathway to LPR Status?
E-2, Treaty investors[hh]	Allows a national of a treaty country (a country with which the U.S. maintains a treaty of commerce and navigation) to be admitted to the U.S. when investing a substantial amount of capital in a U.S. business.	Yes, if they are eligible under one of the employment-based immigration categories.
E-3, Certain specialty occupation professionals from Australia[ii]	Applies only to nationals of Australia who are coming to the U.S. solely to perform services in a specialty occupation. The specialty occupation requires theoretical and practical application of a body of knowledge in professional fields and at least the attainment of a bachelor's degree, or its equivalent, as a minimum for entry into the occupation in the U.S.	Yes, if they are eligible under one of the employment-based immigration categories.
TN, NAFTA professionals[jj]	Permits qualified Canadian and Mexican citizens to seek temporary entry into the U.S. to engage in business activities at a professional level. Among the types of professionals who are eligible to seek admission as TN nonimmigrants are accountants, engineers, lawyers, pharmacists, scientists, and teachers.	Yes, if they are eligible under one of the employment-based immigration categories.

TABLE 3-2 Continued

Name	Type of Immigrant/Eligibility	Pathway to LPR Status?
Student and Exchange Visas[kk]		
F-1, Academic students	Permits an applicant to enter the U.S. as a full-time student at an accredited college, university, seminary, conservatory, academic high school, elementary school, or other academic institution or in a language training program. Applicants must be enrolled in a program or course of study that culminates in a degree, diploma, or certificate, and their school must be authorized by the U.S. government to accept international students. Students may not work off campus during the first academic year, but they may accept on-campus employment subject to certain conditions and restrictions. F-1 students may engage in three types of off-campus employment after they have been studying for 1 academic year: • Curricular Practical Training; • Optional Practical Training (pre-completion or post-completion); or • Science, Technology, Engineering, and Mathematics (STEM) Optional Practical Training Extension.	Yes, if they are eligible under one of the employment or family-based categories discussed above.
M-1, Vocational students	Includes students in vocational or other nonacademic programs other than language training. M-1 students may engage in practical training only after they have completed their studies.	Yes, if they are eligible under one of the employment or family-based categories discussed above.

TABLE 3-2 Continued

Name	Type of Immigrant/Eligibility	Pathway to LPR Status?
J-1, Exchange visitors	Authorized for those who intend to participate in an approved program for the purpose of teaching, instructing or lecturing, studying, observing, conducting research, consulting, demonstrating special skills, receiving training, or to receive graduate medical education or training. J-1 nonimmigrants are sponsored by an exchange program that is designated as such by the U.S. Department of State. These programs are designed to promote the interchange of persons, knowledge, and skills in the fields of education, arts, and science. Examples of exchange visitors include, but, not limited to, professors or scholars, research assistants, students, trainees, teachers, specialists, nannies/au pairs, and camp counselors.	Exchange visitors may in some circumstances apply for adjustment of status to LPR, assuming they are not subject to the 2-year home residence requirement.

Nonimmigrant or Employment-Based Visa Categories with No Regulatory Pathway to LPR Status[ll]

CW-1, CNMI-only transitional worker[mm]	Employers in the Commonwealth of the Northern Mariana Islands (CNMI) can apply for temporary permission to employ foreign (nonimmigrant) workers who are otherwise ineligible to work under other nonimmigrant worker categories.	None.
E-2, CNMI-only investor[nn]	Allows foreign, long-term investors to remain lawfully present in the CNMI through December 2014 while they resolve their immigration status.	None.

TABLE 3-2 Continued

Name	Type of Immigrant/Eligibility	Pathway to LPR Status?
H-2A, Agricultural workers[oo]	To qualify workers under this category, employers must • offer a job that is of a temporary or seasonal nature; • demonstrate that there are not sufficient U.S. workers who are able, willing, qualified, and available to do the temporary work; • show that the employment of H-2A workers will not adversely affect the wages and working conditions of similarly employed U.S. workers; and • generally, submit with the H-2A petition a single valid temporary labor certification from the U.S. Department of Labor. (A limited exception to this requirement exists in certain "emergent circumstances.")	None.
H-2B, Nonagricultural workers[pp]	To qualify a worker under this category, an employer must establish that • there are not enough U.S. workers who are able, willing, qualified, and available to do the temporary work; • the employment of H-2B workers will not adversely affect the wages and working conditions of similarly employed U.S. workers; and • its need for the prospective worker's services or labor is temporary, regardless of whether the underlying job can be described as temporary. The employer's need is considered temporary if it is a one-time occurrence, a seasonal need, a peak load need, or an intermittent need.	None.
H-3[qq]	Allows foreign nationals to come temporarily to the U.S. as either a trainee to receive training in any field of endeavor, (other than graduate medical education or training, that is not available in the foreign national's home country) or a Special Education Exchange Visitor to participate in a special education exchange visitor training program that provides for practical training and experience in the education of children with physical, mental, or emotional disabilities.	None.

TABLE 3-2 Continued

Name	Type of Immigrant/Eligibility	Pathway to LPR Status?
I, Representatives of foreign media[rr]	Applicants must demonstrate that they are a bona fide representative of foreign media whose activities are essential to the functions of their organization. The consular officer at the U.S. embassy will determine whether an activity is qualifying in order to obtain a nonimmigrant visa.	None.
P-Visa[ss]	Applicants coming to the U.S. temporarily to perform • at a specific athletic competition as an athlete, individually or as part of a group or team, at an internationally recognized level of performance; • as a member of an internationally recognized entertainment group; • as a performer or group performing under a reciprocal exchange programs; or • as an artist or entertainer in a culturally unique program.	None.
Q, Cultural exchange[tt]	Only employers who administer cultural exchange programs are allowed to petition for Q nonimmigrants. The purpose is to facilitate the sharing of international cultures. Although employment-oriented, an integral part of the applicant's duties must have a cultural element. Applicants must be at least 18 years old and be able to communicate effectively about the cultural attributes of their country.	None.

TABLE 3-2 Continued

Name	Type of Immigrant/Eligibility	Pathway to LPR Status?
Temporary Protected Status (TPS)[uu]	The Secretary of Homeland Security may designate nationals of a foreign country for TPS due to conditions in the country that temporarily prevent the country's nationals from returning safely, or in certain circumstances, where the country is unable to handle the return of its nationals adequately. USCIS may grant TPS to eligible nationals of certain countries (or parts of countries), who are already in the U.S. Eligible individuals without nationality who last resided in the designated country may also be granted TPS. Countries currently designated for TPS are El Salvador, Guinea, Haiti, Honduras, Liberia, Nicaragua, Sierra Leone, South Sudan, Somalia, Sudan, and Syria. The Secretary may designate a country for TPS due to any one of the following temporary conditions in the country: • ongoing armed conflict (such as civil war); • an environmental disaster (such as earthquake or hurricane), or an epidemic; or • other extraorinary and temporary conditions. During a designated period, individuals who are TPS beneficiaries or who are found preliminarily eligible for TPS upon initial review of their cases (prima facie eligible) • are not removable from the U.S.; • can obtain an Employment Authorization Document; and • may be granted travel authorization. Once granted TPS, an individual also cannot be detained by the U.S. Department of Homeland Security (DHS) on the basis of his or her immigration status in the U.S. Once granted TPS, applicants must re-register during each re-registration period to maintain TPS benefits. This period varies by country and is determined by DHS. Re-registration periods vary from 16 months to 3.5 years before the current TPS expiration date.	TPS[vv]

TABLE 3-2 Continued

Name	Type of Immigrant/Eligibility	Pathway to LPR Status?
	DISCRETIONARY CATEGORIES	
Deferred Action for Childhood Arrivals (DACA)[ww]	Applicants who came to the U.S. as children and meet several guidelines may request consideration of deferred action for a period of 3 years, subject to renewal. They are also eligible for work authorization. An applicant may request DACA if the individual <ul><li>were under the age of 31 as of June 15, 2012;</li><li>came to the U.S. before reaching his or her 16th birthday;</li><li>has continuously resided in the U.S. from June 15, 2007, to the present time;</li><li>was physically present in the U.S on June 15, 2012, and at the time of making the request for consideration of deferred action with USCIS;</li><li>had no lawful status on June 15, 2012;</li><li>is currently in school, has graduated or obtained a certificate of completion from high school, has obtained a general education development certificate, or is an honorably discharged veteran of the U.S. Coast Guard or Armed Forces; and</li><li>has not been convicted of a felony, significant misdemeanor, or three or more other misdemeanors, and does not otherwise pose a threat to national security or public safety.</li></ul> Notes: In November 2014, President Obama announced an expansion of the DACA Program that eliminated the age limit and changed the date of continual residence. This expansion is currently blocked by federal court order.	None.

TABLE 3-2 Continued

Name	Type of Immigrant/Eligibility	Pathway to LPR Status?
Deferred Action for Parental Accountability (DAPA)[xx]	Applicants who are undocumented individuals living in the U.S. who, on November 20, 2014, are the parent of a U.S. citizen or LPR may request deferred action. An applicant can request deferred action and employment authorization if the applicant: • has continuous residence in the U.S. since January 1, 2010; • is the parent of a U.S. citizen or LPR born on or before November 20, 2014; and • is not an enforcement priority for removal from the U.S., pursuant to the November 20, 2014, Policies for the Apprehension, Detention and Removal of Undocumented Immigrants Memorandum. Notes: USCIS will consider each request for DAPA on a case-by-case basis. Enforcement priorities include (but are not limited to) national security and public safety threats. This status is currently blocked by the federal court order.	None.
Deferred Enforced Departure (DED)[yy]	DED allows qualified individuals to remain in the U.S. for limited periods of time according to a presidential directive. During the period ordered by the president, qualified individuals under DED generally may also apply for work authorization. Currently the only country covered by DED is Liberia.	None.

[a] See http://www.uscis.gov/green-card/green-card-through-family/green-card-immediate-relative-us-citizen [October 2015].

[b] See http://www.uscis.gov/green-card/green-card-through-family/green-card-family-member-us-citizen [October 2015].

[c] See http://www.uscis.gov/green-card/green-card-through-family/green-card-through-special-categories-family/k-nonimmigrant [October 2015].

[d] See http://www.uscis.gov/green-card/green-card-through-family/green-card-through-special-categories-family/widower [October 2015].

[e] Permanent residence categories based on employment in the United States. In most cases, an employer must sponsor the individual. An applicant may only self-petition in the EB-1 under the Extraordinary Ability category; EB-2 if seeking a National Interest Waiver; and EB-5 categories. For further details for each category, see http://www.uscis.gov/working-united-states/permanent-workers [October 2015].

[f] See http://www.uscis.gov/humanitarian/refugees-asylum/asylum [October 2015].

TABLE 3-2 Continued

[g] See http://www.uscis.gov/humanitarian/refugees-asylum/refugees [October 2015].

[h] See http://www.uscis.gov/green-card/other-ways-get-green-card/green-card-american-indian-born-canada [October 2015].

[i] See http://www.uscis.gov/green-card/other-ways-get-green-card/green-card-amerasian-child-us-citizen [October 2015].

[j] See http://www.uscis.gov/green-card/other-ways-get-green-card/green-card-armed-forces-member/green-card-armed-forces-member-meeting-certain-criteria.

[k]See http://www.uscis.gov/green-card/other-ways-get-green-card/green-card-person-born-foreign-diplomat-united-states/green-card-person-born-united-states-foreign-diplomat [October 2015].

[l] See http://www.uscis.gov/green-card/other-ways-get-green-card/green-card-cuban-native-or-citizen [October 2015].

[m] See http://www.uscis.gov/green-card/other-ways-get-green-card/green-card-through-diversity-immigration-visa-program/green-card-through-diversity-immigrant-visa-program [October 2015].

[n] See http://www.uscis.gov/green-card/other-ways-get-green-card/green-card-haitian-refugee [October 2015].

[o] See http://www.uscis.gov/archive/green-card-through-help-haiti-act-2010 [October 2015].

[p] See http://www.uscis.gov/green-card/other-ways-get-green-card/green-card-through-indochinese-parole-adjustment-act [October 2015].

[q] See http://www.uscis.gov/humanitarian/refugees-asylum/asylum/nacara-203-nicaraguan-adjustment-and-central-american-relief-act [October 2015].

[r] See http://www.uscis.gov/green-card/other-ways-get-green-card/green-card-informant-s-nonimmigrant [October 2015].

[s]See http://www.uscis.gov/green-card/special-immigrant-juveniles/special-immigrant-juveniles-sij-status [October 2015].

[t] See http://www.uscis.gov/green-card/green-card-through-family/green-card-through-special-categories-family/v-nonimmigrant [October 2015].

[u] See http://www.uscis.gov/green-card/other-ways-get-green-card/green-card-victim-trafficking-t-nonimmigrant [October 2015].

[v] The limit on the number of U visas that may be granted to principal petitioners each year is 10,000. However, there is no cap for family members deriving status from the principal applicant, such as spouses, children, or other eligible family members. For further details, see http://www.uscis.gov/green-card/other-ways-get-green-card/green-card-victim-crime-u-nonimmigrant [October 2015]._

[w] See http://www.uscis.gov/humanitarian/battered-spouse-children-parents [October 2015].

[x] See http://www.uscis.gov/working-united-states/temporary-workers/h-1b-specialty-occupations-dod-cooperative-research-and-development-project-workers-and-fashion-models [October 2015].

[y] The H-1B visa has an annual numerical limit "cap" of 65,000 visas each fiscal year. The first 20,000 petitions filed on behalf of beneficiaries with a U.S. master's degree or higher are exempt from the cap. Additionally, H-1B workers who are petitioned for or employed at an institution of higher education or its affiliated or related nonprofit entities, a nonprofit research organization, or a government research organization are not subject to this numerical cap.

[z] H-4 visas are available for spouses and children of H-1B specialty workers. H-4 visa holders' pathway to citizenship on dependent on their employed spouse or parent, and until recently H-4 visa holders were not granted work authorization. Beginning in May 2015, H-4 dependent spouses whose spouses had begun the process of seeking LPR status were permitted to apply for work authorization.

[aa] See http://www.uscis.gov/working-united-states/temporary-workers/h-1b-specialty-occupations-dod-cooperative-research-and-development-project-workers-and-fashion-models [October 2015].

TABLE 3-2 Continued

bb Ibid.

cc See http://www.uscis.gov/working-united-states/temporary-workers/l-1a-intracompany-transferee-executive-or-manager [October 2015].

dd See http://www.uscis.gov/working-united-states/temporary-workers/l-1b-intracompany-transferee-specialized-knowledge [October 2015].

ee See http://www.uscis.gov/working-united-states/temporary-workers/o-1-individuals-extraordinary-ability-or-achievement/o-1-visa-individuals-extraordinary-ability-or-achievement [October 2015].

ff See http://www.uscis.gov/green-card/green-card-through-job/green-card-through-special-categories-jobs [October 2015].

gg See http://www.uscis.gov/working-united-states/temporary-workers/e-1-treaty-traders [October 2015].

hh See http://www.uscis.gov/working-united-states/temporary-workers/e-2-treaty-investors [October 2015].

ii See http://www.uscis.gov/working-united-states/temporary-workers/e-3-certain-specialty-occupation-professionals-australia [October 2015].

jj See http://www.uscis.gov/working-united-states/temporary-workers/tn-nafta-professionals [October 2015].

kk Each of these categories has an equivalent visa category for immediate family members who are traveling to and residing in the United States with the visa holder. These visa categories are F-2, M-2, and J-2.

ll Although the following visa categories have no established regulatory pathway to lawful permanent residence, individuals in most categories may become eligible to apply for Adjustment of Status if they marry a U.S. citizen and are otherwise admissible to the United States, including those who have entered without inspection (undocumented) or overstayed their visa. In addition, individuals in some of these categories may apply for nonimmigrant visas with regulatory pathways to lawful permanent residence.

mm See http://www.uscis.gov/working-united-states/temporary-workers/cw-1-cnmi-only-transitional-worker [October 2015].

nn See http://www.uscis.gov/e-2c [October 2015].

oo See http://www.uscis.gov/working-united-states/temporary-workers/h-2a-agricultural-workers/h-2a-temporary-agricultural-workers [October 2015].

pp See http://www.uscis.gov/working-united-states/temporary-workers//h-2b-temporary-non-agricultural-workers [October 2015].

qq See http://www.uscis.gov/working-united-states/temporary-workers/h-3-nonimmigrant-trainee/h-3-nonimmigrant-trainee-or-special-education-exchange-visitor [October 2015].

rr See http://www.uscis.gov/working-united-states/temporary-workers/i-representatives-foreign-media [October 2015].

ss See http://www.uscis.gov/working-united-states/temporary-workers/p-1a-internationally-recognized-athlete; http://www.uscis.gov/working-united-states/temporary-workers/p-1b-member-internationally-recognized-entertainment-group/p-1b-member-internationally-recognized-entertainment-group; http://www.uscis.gov/working-united-states/temporary-workers/p-2-performer-or-group-performing-under-reciprocal-exchange-program/p-2-individual-performer-or-part-group-entering-perform-under-reciprocal-exchange-program; http://www.uscis.gov/working-united-states/temporary-workers/p-3-artist-or-entertainer-part-culturally-unique-program/p-3-artist-or-entertainer-coming-be-part-culturally-unique-program [October 2015].

tt See http://www.uscis.gov/working-united-states/temporary-workers/q-cultural-exchange [October 2015].

TABLE 3-2 Continued

uu See http://www.uscis.gov/humanitarian/temporary-protected-status-deferred-enforced-departure/temporary-protected-status [October 2015].

vv See http://www.uscis.gov/humanitarian/temporary-protected-status-deferred-enforced-departure/temporary-protected-status [October 2015].

ww See http://www.uscis.gov/humanitarian/consideration-deferred-action-childhood-arrivals-daca [October 2015].

xx See http://www.uscis.gov/immigrationaction [October 2015].

yy See http://www.uscis.gov/humanitarian/temporary-protected-status-deferred-enforced-departure/deferred-enforced-departure [October 2015].

their physical mobility (Hagan et al., 2011; Stewart, 2012). Whereas in the past immigrants in less permanent statuses were essentially "Americans in waiting" (Motomura, 2007), today functionally analogous immigrant groups are actively discouraged from putting down roots in the United States (Kanstroom, 2007).

Consequences for Integration

Legal status affects immigrants' opportunities to integrate across a wide variety of social dimensions. As discussed in detail in Chapter 4, only naturalized citizens are allowed to vote and fully participate in the U.S. political system. Legal status also defines access to social services (Capps et al., 2007; Hagan et al., 2003) and to health care (Cummings and Kreiss, 2008; Kandula et al., 2004; Viladich, 2012). Undocumented immigrants and those who are less than permanent residents are ineligible for medical care coverage, except emergency care and childbirth services. Immigrants in undocumented status or some temporary statuses, such as those who fall under Deferred Action for Childhood Arrivals (DACA), are not eligible for health care benefits through the Affordable Care Act[2] (see Chapter 9). The barriers immigrants face in accessing health care affect their children (Balcazar et al., 2015). Legal status also impacts housing, including ownership (McConnell, 2013, 2015), which has consequences for the neighborhoods in which immigrants live and the schools their children attend, as well as for housing conditions and overcrowding (Drever and Blue, 2011; McConnell, 2013; McConnell and Marcelli, 2007).

Legal status also can restrict access to higher education, with direct implications for immigrants' futures. Although all children in the United

---

[2]Throughout this report "Affordable Care Act" is used to refer to the combination of two separate pieces of legislation: the Patient Protection and Affordable Care Act (P.L. 111-148) and the Health Care and Education Reconciliation Act of 2010 (P.L. 111-152).

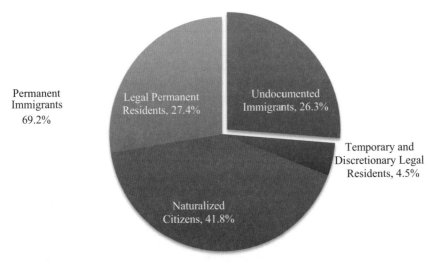

FIGURE 3-1 Proportions of immigrants in each general legal category, 2012.
NOTE: Although the data on stocks and flows of immigrants in the most statuses discussed in the text are from Office of Immigration Statistics Yearbook for 2013, the most recent data available for all categories are only available from Pew Research Center, and the most recent data are from 2012. However, the panel believes general proportions of immigrants in each category remained relatively stable between 2012 and 2013.
SOURCE: Data from Passel and Cohn (2014).

States, regardless of legal status, have the constitutional right to primary and secondary education (kindergarten through 12th grade, abbreviated as "K-12 education"), those in less permanent legal statuses have limited access to higher education, especially since several states do not extend to them the benefit of in-state tuition (see Chapter 2). As discussed further in Chapter 6, undocumented or uncertain legal status can thwart immigrants' initial optimism about educational opportunities in the United States, create higher barriers to social mobility (Hill and Torres, 2010; Menjívar, 2008; Gonzales, 2011), and impinge on educational attainment (Bean et al., 2011; Bean et al., 2015).

Legal status also dictates the kind of jobs immigrants can obtain and the wages they can earn (Donato et al., 1992, 2008; Donato and Massey, 1993; Donato and Sisk, 2012; Massey and Gelatt, 2010; Calavita, 2005; Flippen, 2014; Phillips and Massey, 1999; Massey et al., 2002; Takei et al., 2009; also see Chapter 6). Immigrants with postsecondary education or even professional degrees who are undocumented are often concentrated in low-paid and unstable jobs not commensurate with their education or experience. This occurs among immigrants who come to the United States with relatively higher levels of human capital (Menjívar, 2000), as well as those who acquire skills here (Abrego, 2014). Undocumented status in particular prevents them from acquiring jobs that are consistent with their expertise and degrees, potentially thwarting paths to socioeconomic mobility. The lack of labor rights associated with temporary visas and insecure legal status also negatively affects the occupational status and wages of immigrants (Gentsch and Massey, 2011).

Finally, all legal statuses short of citizenship are now subject to deportation due to changes in the law that make even LPRs deportable (see Chapter 2). And although most immigrants, even the undocumented, have the potential to "regularize" or legitimize their status and achieve LPR status via marriage, through an employer, or through family petitions, many face significant barriers to adjustment of status, including high fees, language barriers, technicalities about mode of entry and time of arrival, and lack of legal expertise. The complexities of the immigration system may themselves be barriers to integration (Table 3-2). In this way, legal status channels immigrants' access to society's benefits in the immediate future, with direct effects on the life prospects of immigrants and their descendants (Bean et al., 2013, 2015; Massey, 2007, 2013; Marquardt et al., 2011; Menjívar, 2012; Yoshikawa et al., 2013).

Intersections

The effects of legal status on integration also vary as status intersects with other social markers, such as gender, age, and national origin. They also differ by geography because states and localities vary in both enforcement practices and restrictions on various social welfare and civic benefits imposed on immigrants (see Chapter 2).

Legal status and gender interact in multiple ways (Salcido and Menjívar, 2012). For instance, 91 percent of deportees are men (Rosenblum and McCabe, 2014). Among Mexican nationals, 92 percent of those deported between 2009-2011 who had lived in the United States for more than a year were male, and among these, 72 percent were heads of households (Mexican Migration Monitor, 2012). The gender imbalance in deportation creates female-headed households, disrupting parent-child relationships and increasing the household's risk of poverty (Dreby, 2012; Enchautegui, 2013). Meanwhile, spouses of many temporary workers are prevented from accessing employment, a policy that disproportionately affects women. In the workplace, immigrant women who are undocumented face a range of constraints related to the combination of their legal status, entry into low-skill occupations, and work-family conflicts (Flippen, 2014), while men's wages are disproportionately affected by undocumented status compared with women (Donato et al., 2008). And immigrant women in domestic violence situations have been found to be less likely to report abuse when they are undocumented or in uncertain legal statuses (Bhuyan and Senturia, 2005; Erez and Globokar, 2009; Salcido and Adelman, 2004; Salcido and Menjívar, 2012).

National origin, as it intersects with enforcement practices, matters too. Ninety-one percent of the deported come from only four countries— El Salvador, Guatemala, Honduras, and Mexico—even though nationals from these countries make up just 73 percent of the undocumented population (Rosenblum and McCabe, 2014). In public discourse about immigration, undocumented immigrants are often conflated with Latinos, leading to racial profiling and discrimination that creates even higher barriers to integration (Chavez, 2001; 2007; Stumpf, 2006; Heyman, 2013).

Generation also matters, as young immigrants (the 1.5 generation, see Chapter 1) who are undocumented face different challenges than their counterparts who arrived as adults (Gleeson and Gonzales, 2012). Legal status constrains the social lives of young immigrants who, because of their status combined with the particular state in which they live, may be unable to obtain driver's licenses or formal identification documents, which denies them access to adult establishments. Thus, undocumented status affects young immigrants' socialization into adulthood (Abrego, 2006; Gonzalez and Chavez, 2012; Gleeson and Gonzalez, 2012). These effects vary by state and local residence, as states and localities have some leeway when it comes to administering social welfare programs and limiting employment and educational opportunities for immigrants.

Mixed-Status Families and Consequences for the Second Generation

The effects of legal status on immigrant integration reverberate beyond the individuals who hold these statuses, with consequences beyond the immigrant generation. These effects are particularly felt in mixed-status families where some members are undocumented and some are not (Dreby, 2012; Enriquez, 2015; Rodriguez and Hagan, 2004; Suárez-Orozco et al., 2011; Yoshikawa, 2011).

Mixed-status families take several forms. Many include undocumented parents and U.S.-born citizen children (or children with varied legal statuses). Mixed-status families also include unauthorized spouses of either citizens or LPRs who are barred from legal status because of the 3- and 10-year bars set out in the 1996 IIRIRA for immigrants who entered the country without inspection (Migration Policy Institute, 2014). Mixed-status families arrive at these formations through multiple paths and have varying opportunities to achieve legal status (Suárez-Orozco et al., 2011). Some of these family members are undocumented and have no opportunity to regularize their status; others hold temporary statuses or other dispensations; and others are trapped in the long waiting lines and backlogs of the immigration bureaucracy today.

In 2013, 5.2 million U.S. children resided with at least one undocumented immigrant parent. The vast majority of these children—4.5 million—were U.S.-born citizens, but 775,000 were estimated to have undocumented status themselves (Passel et al., 2014). Children with undocumented parents constitute nearly one-third of all children of immigrant parents and about 8 percent of all U.S.-born children. Thus, their parents' legal status can and will affect the prospects of a significant proportion of the U.S.-born second generation.

Mixed-status families present a unique opportunity to gauge the effects of legal status on short- and long-term patterns of immigrant incorporation as well as to capture the ripple effects of legal status beyond individuals and into the second generation. Children or spouses who are U.S. citizens or LPRs in these families often mediate between social institutions and their unauthorized relatives: translating documents, accompanying relatives to government offices, interpreting communications, and in general helping with daily life (Orellana et al., 2003; Menjívar, 2000). In this way, the U.S.-citizen and LPR children and spouses in immigrant families play the role of "brokers" by bridging undocumented family members to various key institutions in society and providing a link for eventual integration. Immigrant parents of U.S.-born children may entrust these children with responsibilities and decision making because of the children's ability—linguistically and culturally—to deal with institutions, organizations, and communities (Valenzuela, 1999).

Civic engagement and socialization in mixed-status families also "trickles up" from children to parents (Wong and Tseng, 2008); the children connect their parents to political institutions and community organizations, contributing to the parents' political socialization (Bloemraad and Trost, 2008). In these cases, the children's involvement beyond the home contributes to a sense of belonging and membership (Solis et al., 2013). By these means, the younger generation develops a sense of citizenship and provides paths for the rest of the family to advance their integration.

However, when parents are undocumented, their U.S.-born children often experience multiple negative effects, which in turn affect incorporation patterns for the second generation (Yoshikawa, 2011). Such negative effects include increased vulnerability of the parents and destabilization of the family (Thronson, 2008), increased risk of living in a one-parent household, and losses in income (Dreby, 2015; Landale et al., 2011). Thus, mixed-status families are also more likely to be impoverished than other families (Fix and Zimmerman, 2001). In addition, parents' undocumented status exerts substantial and lasting negative effects on their children's educational attainment (Bean et al., 2015). Even after controlling for measured and unmeasured factors that select into legalization, the adult second generation, Mexican American children whose parents remained undocumented attained 1.25 fewer years of completed schooling than their counterparts whose parents transitioned to a documented status (Bean et.al., 2011; Bean et al., 2015). This substantially diminishes the life chances of higher generation Mexican Americans, because such deficits are intergenerationally transmitted to children.[3]

Research in the area of child development shows that the legal status of parents also affects the developmental context of U.S.-born children. Parents' undocumented status is associated with lower levels of cognitive development and educational progress across early and middle childhood (Brabeck and Xu, 2010; Ortega et al., 2009; Yoshikawa, 2011). By adolescence, having an undocumented parent is associated with higher levels of anxiety and depressive symptoms (Potochnick and Perreira, 2010). These detrimental effects may occur through a variety of mechanisms. Parents may not access means-tested programs for their citizen children due to concerns about showing proof of earnings, which might identify their employers. In addition, fear of deportation can produce higher levels of chronic stress. Undocumented parents, relative to their documented low-income counterparts, experience worse job conditions and live in more-crowded housing conditions, both of which can translate into higher parental psychological distress and diminished learning opportunities for the children, such as subsidies for quality child care (Yoshikawa, 2011, Yoshikawa and Kalil, 2011).

Research suggests that the psychological trauma that some children in these families have experienced will be long lasting (Raymond-Flesch et al., 2014; Zayas, 2015), with the potential to alter these U.S. citizens' perceptions of who they are and their place in U.S. society (Menjívar and Lakhani, n.d.; Santos and Menjívar, 2013). Long-term effects can include decreased American identity on the part of children who live in contexts of heightened fear of deportations (Enchautegui and Menjívar, 2015; Santos and Menjívar, 2013). Despite the rights that come with birthright citizenship, U.S.-born children's opportunities are mediated and may be restricted by their parent's legal status (Yoshikawa, 2011).

In addition, the 774,000 minors who are undocumented face particular risks in both the short and long terms (Passel et al., 2014). As they pass through middle childhood and adolescence, they usually become aware of

---

[3] These deficits also dampen third-generation educational attainment, although research has not yet estimated the magnitude of this penalty because data on the migration status of the grandparents of the Mexican American third generation have heretofore not been collected.

their undocumented status and its implications for their current or future educational and employment prospects (Gonzales, 2011). This process of "learning to be illegal" has implications for psychological well-being, as some youth hide their status from peers, reduce their educational effort, and isolate themselves. And in families where children have different legal statuses, inequalities in rights and benefits may exacerbate discrepancies between siblings over the life course (Menjívar and Abrego, 2009).

These effects are not confined to just children in mixed-status families. Research has found that the implications of marriage to an undocumented immigrant for U.S.-citizen spouses and partners are direct and profound, as it can undermine certain social rights (e.g., the right to a family) that come with U.S. citizenship (Lopez, 2015; Schueths, 2012). The fear of deportation itself can reverberate to other family members who risk losing a close family member, with effects on perceptions of and relations with law enforcement agencies generally (Hacker et al., 2011). Although the research on mixed-status families is still relatively limited, indications from research in key areas that shape immigrant integration point to cumulative disadvantages that can negatively impact the integration of future generations descending from mixed-status families (O'Leary and Sanchez, 2011).

PERMANENT STATUSES

There are currently only two "permanent" legal statuses for immigrants: naturalized citizenship and LPR. Naturalization is often viewed as the end point of integration: the moment when an immigrant takes on the (nearly) full rights and responsibilities of being an American. LPR permanent residence grants immigrants many social benefits and a pathway to naturalization, but has much more limited rights. And while LPR status is intended as a way station to citizenship, in actuality many people remain in that status for extended periods of time, impeding their political integration (see Chapter 4). Below the panel discusses ways in which naturalized and LPR statuses potentially aid or impede immigrant integration; we also describe refugee and asylee statuses, both of which have a clear pathway to lawful permanent residence and are the focus of unique integration efforts by the federal government.

Naturalized Citizenship

In 2013, 779,929 people became naturalized citizens, a decline from the historical high point of 1,046,539 naturalizations in 2008. But in general the number of naturalizations has increased steadily since the 1990s (see Figure 3-2). An LPR wishing to apply for naturalization can do so after 5 years in LPR status (3 years if married to a U.S. citizen) or after serving in the U.S. Armed Forces (for further details, see Table 3-2). The demographics of naturalized citizens have changed considerably since 1970. Prior to that decade, the majority of naturalized citizens were born in European countries, reflecting the earlier waves of immigration. After 1970, the origin of new citizens shifted to Asia and Latin America (Table 3-2). There are currently 18.7 million naturalized citizens living in the United States. About a third of newly naturalized citizens are from Asia, and another third are from North America (which includes Mexico) (see Figure 3-3). The average naturalizing citizen is a married woman between the ages of 25 and 44 (see Lee and Forman, 2014).

With a few exceptions, naturalization extends rights similar to those obtained through citizenship by birth (for more details see Chapter 4). Citizens enjoy protection from deportation and have full access to social welfare benefits, creating stability and enhancing integration opportunities for both naturalized immigrants and their families (Table 3-1). Overall, 61 percent of eligible immigrants naturalize, although there is significant variation by region of origin (Gonzalez-Barrera et al., 2014). The panel discusses patterns of naturalization and potential explanations for disparate naturalization rates in detail in Chapter 4, but it is worth noting here that if

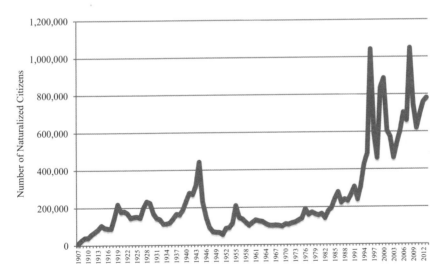

FIGURE 3-2 Persons naturalized, fiscal 1907 through 2013.
SOURCE: Data from Office of Immigration Statistics (2014). Available: http://www.dhs.gov/publication/yearbook-immigration-statistics-2013-naturalizations [October 2015].

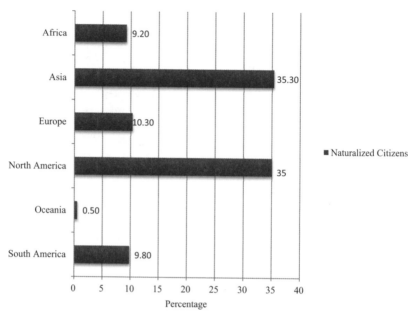

FIGURE 3-3 Newly naturalized citizens by region of origin, 2013.
SOURCE: Data from Office of Immigration Statistics (2014). Available: http://www.dhs.gov/publication/yearbook-immigration-statistics-2013-naturalizations [October 2015].

naturalization is a major marker of successful integration, these variations suggest that some groups are integrating more quickly than others.

Lawful Permanent Residence

LPR status grants indefinite legal residence to foreign-born individuals who have met a set of requirements. An applicant can become an LPR, or receive a "green card" in common parlance, via an assortment of family-based categories, employment-based categories, through diversity visas, or after adjusting from refugee or asylee status (see Figure 3-4, Table 3-2). LPR status can be issued to those residing outside the United States or to individuals already in the United States who are seeking to adjust their status; the latter are sometimes referred to as "adjustees" (Jasso, 2011).

The number of LPRs in the United States has generally grown since World War II, with some yearly variation and an enormous spike in the 1990s, the direct result of the one-time legalization opportunity offered under the 1986 Immigration Reform and Control Act (see Chapter 2). There

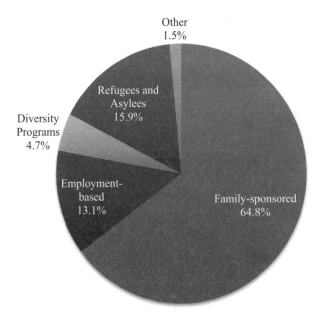

Other
1.5%

Refugees and
Asylees
15.9%

Diversity
Programs
4.7%

Employment-
based
13.1%

Family-sponsored
64.8%

FIGURE 3-4 Lawful permanent resident admissions by category of admissions, 2013.
SOURCE: Data from Office of Immigration Statistics (2014). Available: http://www.dhs.gov/yearbook-immigration-statistics-2013-lawful-permanent-residents [October 2015].

are 13.1 million LPRs living in the United States, and around 1 million people currently become LPRs every year (see Figure 3-5). More than 40 percent of new LPRs in 2013 were from Asia, and nearly 32 percent were from North America (see Figure 3-6).

LPR is the most stable legal status short of U.S. citizenship. LPRs have work authorization, are eligible for some public benefits, and can sponsor their spouses or unmarried children for permanent residence. LPR status therefore allows immigrants to put down more-permanent roots in the United States, potentially aiding their integration. And since adjustees make up the majority of new LPRs, a large portion of those receiving their "green card" have already begun the integration process (Martin and Yankay, 2014).

LPR status also provides a path to citizenship and political integration. Although LPRs cannot vote in elections that require voters to be U.S. citizens (e.g., they cannot vote in federal or state elections), there are a few jurisdictions in the country that allow LPRs to vote in local elections. They cannot run for political office but can and do participate in political

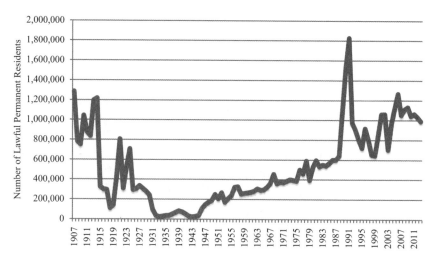

FIGURE 3-5 Persons granted lawful permanent residence, 1907-2013.
SOURCE: Data from Office of Immigration Statistics (2014). Available: http://www.
dhs.gov/yearbook-immigration-statistics-2013-lawful-permanent-residents [October
2015].

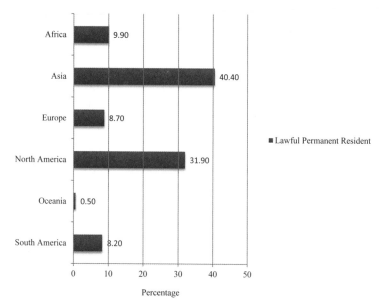

FIGURE 3-6 New lawful permanent residents by region of origin, 2013.
SOURCE: Data from Office of Immigration Statistics (2014). Available: http://www.
dhs.gov/yearbook-immigration-statistics-2013-lawful-permanent-residents [October
2015].

life (see Chapter 4). They can own property and travel any time but cannot be absent from the country for extended periods of time or relocate to another country to live there permanently without risking the loss of their LPR status. These requirements are conducive to permanent residence and integration (Aptekar, 2015).

However, since the IIRIRA passed in 1996, individuals with LPR status can be placed in removal proceedings if they are convicted of an "aggravated felony" (see Chapter 2), controlled substance violations (with the exception of possessing less than 30 grams of marijuana), certain firearm offenses, domestic violence, or two crimes involving moral turpitude. They may also face removal proceedings if they engage in document or marriage fraud, human trafficking, falsely claim U.S. citizenship, or violate laws relating to espionage, among other crimes. Thus, although lawful permanent residence is a "permanent" status, there are several exceptions today that make this status less permanent than it used to be.

In 1996, legislation also significantly limited LPRs' access to benefits (see Chapter 2). Since 1996, LPRs must wait 5 years to become eligible for Medicaid, food stamps, Supplemental Security Income, and the State Children's Health Insurance Program. The Personal Responsibility and Work Opportunity Reconciliation Act of 1996 also reduced food stamp allotments for mixed-status households, thus increasing food insecurity for U.S.-citizen children living in mixed-status families (Van Hook and Balistreri, 2006). Some of these benefits have since been restored, but several portions of these laws remain in place, and many adult immigrants continue to be ineligible for federal assistance programs.[4]

Moreover, the IIRIRA further instituted mechanisms that have limited the access of immigrant-sponsored relatives to public assistance. A U.S. citizen or LPR petitioning for a close family member (through family-based visas) must agree to support that person until he or she becomes a U.S. citizen or can be credited with 40 quarters of work (usually 10 years), and the petitioner must sign a legally enforceable affidavit of support that shows the petitioner has an income of at least 125 percent of the federal poverty level.[5] This requirement is intended to ensure that the sponsor will have enough resources to provide for the sponsored individual so that the

---

[4]In 2013, 16.7 percent of noncitizens (meaning immigrants who are eligible but have not naturalized) received Medicaid and 16.2 percent received food stamps. Overall, the proportion of noncitizens versus native-born receiving this type of assistance has barely changed since 1995: only 6.8 percent of all persons receiving Medicaid in 2013 were noncitizens (compared to 6.5% in 1995), and only 8.7 percent of those receiving food stamps in 2013 were noncitizens (Wasem, 2014). This suggests that concerns about immigrants disproportionately using social welfare services may be misplaced.

[5]See http://www.uscis.gov/green-card/green-card-processes-and-procedures/affidavit-support [January 2016].

individual will not become a public charge (Espenshade et al., 1997). It also makes it more difficult for low-income immigrants to sponsor relatives, delaying family reunification and/or contributing to more mixed-status families (Fix and Zimmerman, 2001).

These changes in access to social welfare benefits and in sponsorship requirements make it more difficult for immigrants with lower socioeconomic status to bring their family members to the United States and to access assistance if they subsequently experience unemployment or low wages. Delayed family reunification and the lack of a social safety net make even LPRs' prospects for full integration more difficult (Enchautegi and Menjívar, 2015).

Refugee and Asylum

Since 1948, the United States has provided relief for persons seeking refuge from persecution abroad. Today, two programs grant this relief: the refugee program grants entry to persons currently outside the United States, while those already within U.S. borders can apply for asylum (Table 3-2). Each year the President, in consultation with Congress, sets a limit for refugee admissions, generally between 70,000 and 80,000. However, the actual number admitted has fluctuated depending on the international and national political climate (Bruno, 2015). Refugee slots are also allotted regionally to ensure diversity; however, there are marked geographic concentrations. There is no cap on asylum approvals. Except for Cubans, groups of Latin American origin rarely receive either refugee or asylee status, regardless of conditions in the country of origin. By contrast, the 1966 Cuban Adjustment Act allows any Cuban national who arrives on U.S. soil to adjust to LPR status after 1 year.

Large numbers of refugees entered the United States in the 1970s and 1980s as a consequence of the Vietnam War and humanitarian emergencies worldwide. However, since 1990 the number of refugees entering the United States each year has shrunk considerably as the program added diversity quotas and reached a low point after 2001, in part due to changes in security procedures and admissions requirements and to changes in the national mood after the September 11, 2001, terrorist attacks ("9/11") (Bruno, 2015; Martin and Yankay, 2014). The number of people granted asylum has also fluctuated over the years, falling from a historical high of more than 39,000 in 2001 to around 25,000 to 29,000 in recent years (see Figure 3-7). The regions from which most refugees originate have changed considerably since 1990, when the largest number came from Europe. Today, most refugees and asylees are from Asia and Africa. Notably, immigrants originating in Latin America do not rank prominently in these visa allocations (see Figure 3-8).

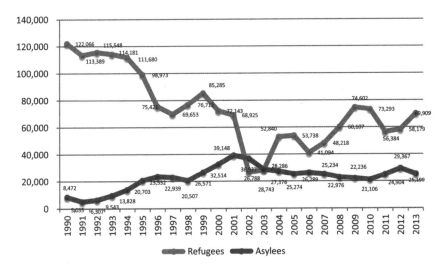

FIGURE 3-7 Refugee arrivals and persons granted asylum by region of origin, 1990-2013.
SOURCE: Data from Office of Immigration Statistics (2014). Available: http://www.dhs.gov/yearbook-immigration-statistics-2013-refugees-and-asylees [October 2015].

Refugees and asylees can receive assistance via the Office of Refugee Resettlement (ORR) in the U.S. Department of Health and Human Services, as the federal government assumes responsibility for their well-being (see Chapter 2). This is the *only* affirmative integration program at the federal level. ORR services include cash assistance, medical evaluations and health care assistance, assistance with accessing social welfare benefits, and assistance finding employment and setting up small businesses. Many of these programs are funded by ORR but run in partnership with states and localities.

Refugees approved for admission also receive assistance through the Department of State's Reception and Placement Program; this assistance includes rent, food, and clothing, as well as contacts with organizations that help them locate employment and obtain language skills. These organizations, usually composed of co-ethnics, mediate between the federal government and the refugees to provide refugees with a resettlement infrastructure familiar to them. Assistance beyond the first few months is coordinated between the federal government and the states where the refugees settle; it provides long-term cash and medical assistance, employment (they receive employment authorization upon arrival), and social services.

There is a clear path to U.S. citizenship for refugees and asylees and

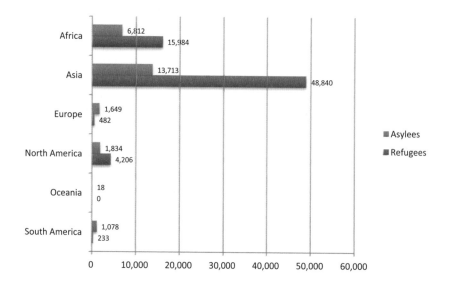

FIGURE 3-8 Refugee arrivals and persons granted asylum by region of origin, 2013.
SOURCE: Data from Office of Immigration Statistics (2014). Available: http://www.dhs.gov/yearbook-immigration-statistics-2013-refugees-and-asylees [October 2015].

a somewhat shortened time frame for naturalization. However, as with all categories short of naturalized U.S. citizen, refugees and asylees have no "right to remain." Refugees and asylees are subject to many of the same grounds of inadmissibility and removability as other noncitizen immigrants and can be subject to removal proceedings for criminal convictions and other violations, including immigration fraud.

Although refugees and asylees receive the most direct integrative assistance, they face the same potential barriers to integration as immigrants in other legal statuses (Portes and Zhou, 1993). For instance, many are black or Muslim (or both) and therefore may face discriminatory attitudes and may be stigmatized for outward demonstrations of their faith (McBrien, 2005). In addition, many refugees and asylees are fleeing violence and may have been forcibly separated from their homes. "Acute" refugees who flee suddenly with little preparation likely have very little in terms of material wealth and may have been separated from family members (Kunz, 1973). Acute refugees also generally have lower levels of education and skills than voluntary migrants (Zhou, 2001). And settlement of refugee populations in new gateway cities can strain local resources and create tensions with native-born populations (Singer and Wilson, 2007).

TEMPORARY STATUSES

The United States has a variety of temporary "nonimmigrant" statuses,[6] some of which have clearly established pathways to lawful permanent residence but the majority of which lack a clear regulatory pathway to permanent residence and citizenship. In addition, even statuses with a clear regulatory pathway often face long visa backlogs that make it difficult to predict when (or if, since they generally face restrictions on length of stay) they will be able to adjust their status to LPR (Menjívar, 2006). This section begins by discussing temporary statuses based on employment and education, including H1B specialty workers, H-2A agricultural workers, and international students. It then discusses Temporary Protected Status (TPS), a category that is intended to provide short-term relief to people escaping civil strife or natural disasters in their countries or origin but instead has become a long-term legal limbo for thousands of immigrants from Central America.

H-1B Temporary Worker

The most well-known employment-based nonimmigrant visa is the H-1B. The program was created in 1990 and has a ceiling quota of 65,000 new visas annually, with no cap on renewals or changes of employer (for details, see Table 3-2). An advanced-degree exemption allows for an additional 20,000 new visas to be issued each fiscal year. Over the past 15 years, demand for H-1B visas has far outstripped supply (with the exception of 2001 to 2003, when the cap on new visas was temporarily raised to 195,000); in 2015, U.S. Citizenship and Immigration Services (USCIS) received nearly 233,000 applications for new visas in fiscal 2016 and reached the cap a few days after filing season began. USCIS has created a lottery system to deal with the excess of annual applications for new H-1B visas.

In 2013, 474,355 nonimmigrants were "admitted" to the country via an H-1B visa (most were H-1B visa holders already present in the United States) (Figure 3-7). These numbers include both new H-1Bs subject to the annual caps, and renewals. The typical H1B visa holder is a college

---

[6] The panel does not offer detailed descriptions of every possible legal status in the immigration system because many categories apply to only a small number of individuals, and there is little to no data about how these legal statuses impact integration. Instead the analysis focuses on the largest and most politically prominent categories, for which data about integration are available. For a full list of legal statuses and a short statement about their pathways to citizenship, see Table 3-2.

educated male from India who works in STEM fields (O'Brien, 2013; for further details see U.S. Citizenship and Immigration Services, 2015).[7]

The H-1B visa is a "dual intent" visa, meaning it provides the opportunity for the highly skilled workers who hold them to regularize their status to LPR, provided that their employer has the ability and willingness to sponsor them. These are well-educated workers who are already trained in areas that complement the U.S. workforce and are deemed of special import for the economic future of the country (many H-IB workers were international students who attended U.S. universities). And even when H-1B visa holders have the same level of training as native-born professionals in the same field, the knowledge of a particular technological process or research area that an H-1B visa holder brings can be very different; they thus can contribute knowledge as collaborators rather than solely as competitors (Regets, 2007). Although further research is needed on these workers, the human capital they bring with them, combined with their strong connections to the U.S. labor market, likely aids their integration into U.S. society.

But while H-1B visa holders may benefit from potential LPR regularization through an employer, this is not a sure outcome. The long backlogs in the processing of applications and the per-country caps create bottlenecks in applications for lawful permanent residence, even as visa holders face a 6-year restriction on the length of time they can remain in this status. In addition, dependence on employer sponsorship can pose obstacles for those who want to apply for LPR status. Unfortunately USCIS does not track the number of H-1Bs who adjust to LPR, either via their employer or by other routes such as marriage to a U.S. citizen. The number who remain in the United States and the extent to which they and their families do successfully integrate is still an open question and additional research needs to be done on how these highly valued workers and their families are integrating.

Agricultural Worker (H-2A)

The United States has a wide variety of temporary employment-based visas with no clear regulatory pathway to lawful permanent residence. Although users of these visas may eventually adjust their status to other categories, and the existence of these categories indicates economic need for these workers, applicants for these visas are not permitted to express

---

[7]Exacerbating the gender imbalance in H-1B visas, until recently spouses of H-1B visa holders were not issued work permits. New USCIS rules indicate that effective May 26, 2015, holders of H-4 visas (dependent spouses of H-1B visa holders) are allowed to apply for work permits if their H-1B spouses have reached certain milestones in the LPR process. See http://www.uscis.gov/news/dhs-extends-eligibility-employment-authorization-certain-h-4-dependent-spouses-h-1b-nonimmigrants-seeking-employment-based-lawful-permanent-residence [August 2015].

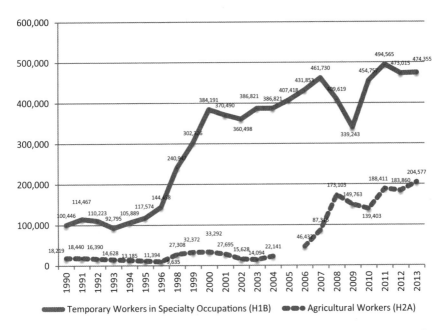

FIGURE 3-9 Annual number of admissions with visa type H-1B, temporary workers in specialty occupations, and H2A agricultural workers, 1990-2013. (Note: Data not available for H2A visas in 2005).
SOURCE: Data from Office of Immigration Statistics (2014). Available: http://www.dhs.gov/yearbook-immigration-statistics-2013-refugees-and-asylees [October 2015].

intent to permanently immigrate. These categories include H-2A agricultural workers; H-2B nonagricultural workers; O-visa performers, athletes, and academics; and TN NAFTA professionals from Mexico and Canada (see Table 3-2).

The largest and most prominent category in this set is the H-2A agricultural workers. The number of H-2A workers has skyrocketed since the mid-2000s (see Figure 3-9). The vast majority are low-skilled migrant workers from Mexico who work in the fruit and vegetable industry. Most H-2A workers are male, are over the age of 25, and have low levels of education.[8] And although *net* immigration rates from Mexico (in-migrants minus out-migrants) dropped to zero during the Great Recession, entries of Mexican temporary workers on H-1 and particularly H-2 visas have continued to increase (Massey, 2012).

_____

[8] See http://www.ncfh.org/docs/fs-Facts percent20about percent20Farmworkers.pdf [August 2015].

H-2A visas holders have no clear path to LPR or citizenship through their employment, are not eligible for most federal programs or state benefits, and have no legal right to remain in the country once their contracts expire. Overall, H-2A workers are encouraged to make their stays temporary and discouraged from putting down roots and integrating. However, many may settle in the United States anyway. Although some may shift their statuses via family ties or other forms of employment with clearer pathways to permanent residence, others may become "undocumented" visa overstayers if they do not leave the country when their visas (and contracts) expire. These visas may therefore be transitional statuses on pathways that provide more opportunities or higher barriers to integration, and further research on this status is warranted.

International Student

International students are an increasingly important part of the "nonimmigrant" population in the United States, both because their numbers are growing rapidly (see Figure 3-10) and because they are a key source of highly skilled labor in the United States. Student visas holders are not allowed to declare "dual intent" when they apply for visas, but despite this limitation, they have a well-traveled indirect path to other statuses, including H-1B and LPR (Ruiz, 2013).

In 2013, the United States admitted over 1.5 million foreign students, including undergraduate, graduate and vocational students. International students make up over 4 percent of all undergraduate and graduate students in the United States.[9] Almost 60 percent of all international students come from just five countries, and one-fourth come from China alone, although students arrive from every region of the world (see Figure 3-11; for further details on international students, see Ruiz, 2013).

Although foreign student visas do not have a direct path to LPR or citizenship, foreign students can seek temporary work authorization, can do a practicum in their field for up to 29 months after graduation, or can apply for H-1B visas, which can lead to employment-based LPR regularization opportunities. They can also seek LPR status through family-sponsored visas. Foreign students are self-selected for higher education and skills, which are positively correlated with integration. And foreign students' method of entry into the United States funnels them through a key integrating institution: schools of higher education. When, and if, foreign students graduate they are usually proficient in English (if they weren't before); are trained to fill skilled positions in the U.S. labor force, often in STEM fields; are bet-

---

[9] See http://www.iie.org/Who-We-Are/News-and-Events/Press-Center/Press-Releases/2014/2014-11-17-Open-Doors-Data [October 2015].

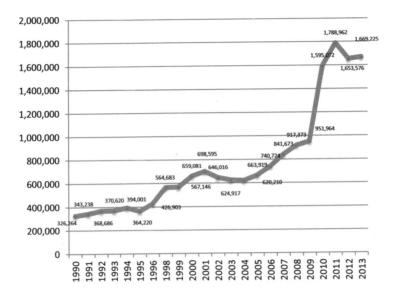

FIGURE 3-10 International students (F-1 visa), 1990-2013.
SOURCE: Data from Office of Immigration Statistics (2014). Available: http://www.
dhs.gov/yearbook-immigration-statistics-2013-refugees-and-asylees [October 2015].

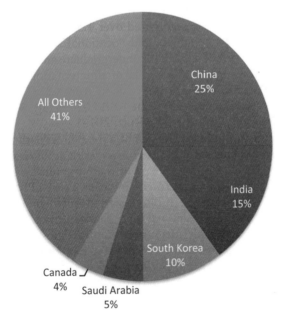

FIGURE 3-11 Countries of origin for international students, 2008-2012.
SOURCE: Adapted from Ruiz (2013).

ter acculturated to American social norms than their peers who were not educated in the United States; and may have formed intimate relationships with native-born students (see Chapter 8).

However, as with other temporary visas, foreign students are not eligible for federal benefits or state assistance, and if they apply for an H-1B visa, they face the same cap and lottery as other applicants. Foreign students also must remain enrolled in accredited educational institutions for the duration of their status, and when their visas expire they must either leave the country when their visa expires or risk falling out of status as visa overstayers. While international students enjoy several potential pathways to permanent status, they face the same barriers to social benefits and lack of stability as other temporary visa holders. And like all immigrants who are not naturalized citizens, they enjoy no "right to remain." There is currently little data on international students' integration, but as their numbers continue to grow, further research on these individuals would provide scholars, policy makers, and colleges and universities with valuable information about how this status interacts with immigrant integration.

Temporary Protected Status

Temporary Protected Status (TPS) is designed to address the shortcomings of refugee law, as TPS extends protection to some groups not covered under the conventional definition of refugees (see Chapter 2). TPS confers a work permit and allows recipients to work and live in the United States for a renewable period of 18 months. This dispensation was initially offered to immigrants from El Salvador in 1990. At the time, an estimated half-million Salvadorans were already residing in the United States with undocumented status after fleeing a violent civil war. The designation was extended through Deferred Enforced Departure and then terminated in 1994, but El Salvador was designated for TPS again in 2001 after devastating earthquakes in that country. Some countries have had continuous designation for many years; for instance, Somalia has been designated for TPS continuously since 1991. These immigrants must renew their permits every 18 months for a fee, and renewal deadlines vary by country.

In 2015, 11 countries were covered by TPS: 6 in Africa, 3 in Central America, 1 in the Caribbean, and 1 in the Middle East. An estimated 340,310 beneficiaries of TPS resided in the United States in 2014, and the vast majority were from El Salvador (see Figure 3-12) (Messick and Bergeron, 2014). USCIS does not publish numbers and characteristics of TPS beneficiaries as it does for other statuses, so additional demographics for this population are unavailable.

TPS aids immigrant integration by giving immigrants who would otherwise be undocumented a legal presence in the country, which affords them

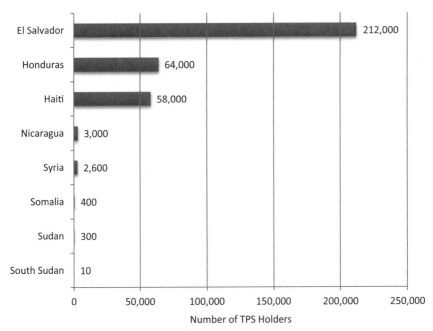

FIGURE 3-12 Estimated number of temporary protected status holders by country of origin, 2014.
SOURCE: Data from Messick and Bergeron (2014).

certain rights. TPS removes at least the immediate threat of deportation and grants recipients work authorization, making it easier to access legal employment and potentially better wages (Orrenius and Zavodny, 2014). However, aside from access to legal employment and a stay of deportation, most TPS holders have very limited rights—no more than those of immigrants in undocumented status.[10]

Although TPS seems to provide better economic opportunities for those who would otherwise be undocumented (Orrenius and Zavodny, 2014), the liminal legality of many Central Americans under TPS also constitutes a serious barrier to socioeconomic mobility and long-term integration (Menjívar, 2006). Furthermore, persons with TPS cannot petition for legal status for their family members, which serves as an additional reminder

---

[10]In 2013, the Sixth Circuit Court of Appeals, which covers parts of Kentucky, Michigan, Ohio, and Tennessee, found that immigrants with TPS who are immediate relatives of U.S. citizens *can* adjust their status to lawful permanent residence *(Flores et al. v. USCIS)*. A district court in Washington State made a similar determination in 2014. If policy changes are enacted in response to these court rulings allowing TPS holders in these districts to adjust their status, it would create an important geographic variation in the integrative prospects of TPS holders.

that the U.S. government considers them temporary visitors rather than permanent migrants and has the potential to restructure family composition in the long term (Enchautegui and Menjívar, 2015). Thus TPS confers partial inclusion while simultaneously affirming (with periodic reminders) that this status is temporary and partial.

DISCRETIONARY STATUSES

As described in Chapter 2, various presidential administrations since 1990 have created lawful statuses via executive discretion. Because these statuses are not created by legislation, they are subject to the discretion of the Executive, making them inherently unstable because the programs can be canceled at any time. They also do not provide any established regulatory pathway to lawful permanent residence. However, they do provide the right to work legally in the United States and some protection from deportation. The newest and largest status (in terms of eligible population) in this category is DACA.[11] Below, the panel describes the demographics of persons in the United States with this status and the aids and barriers to their integration.

Deferred Action for Childhood Arrivals

Since 2001 Congress has repeatedly considered and then failed to pass various versions of the DREAM Act (Development, Relief, and Education for Alien Minors), a legislative effort to provide legal status for undocumented persons who were brought to the United States as children and who meet certain educational and other criteria. In June 2012, President Obama announced an Executive action that provided relief from deportation and granted temporary work authorization for undocumented immigrants in this category (see Table 3-2 for details). The President updated and slightly expanded the program in a November 2014 Executive action, although as of February 2015 these changes were blocked by a federal judge.

When President Obama announced the June 2012 Executive action, an estimated 1.165 million people were immediately eligible to apply for

---

[11] In a November 2014 Executive action, President Obama also created Deferred Action for Parental Accountability for parents of U.S. citizens and LPRs. The Migration Policy Institute (2014) estimates that as many as 3.7 million parents may be eligible for the program. In February 2015, a federal district court in Texas issued an injunction against implementation of the program; and at the time of this report, the program remains in legal limbo.

DACA (Batalova et al., 2014).[12] By March 2015, almost 750,000 had applied, 64 percent of the estimated eligible population. The approval rate for DACA is almost 90 percent.[13,14] Notably, Latin American youth have been far more likely to apply for DACA than any other group, and three-fourths of all DACA applicants were born in Mexico (Singer et al., 2015). Although an estimated 10 percent of DACA-eligible persons are from Asia, they account for only 4 percent of applicants (see Figure 3-13). Women are more likely to apply for DACA than men, and the vast majority of applicants are low-income (for further details on the DACA eligible population and applicants, see Batalova, et al., 2014; Singer et al., 2015).

In some ways, DACA status parallels TPS (it even uses a similar application form and confers status for a similar length of time), as it provides temporary relief to a subset of the undocumented population but without a path to lawful permanent residence. The aids and barriers to integration that DACA recipients face are therefore similar to those who hold TPS, although DACA is an even more fragile status because it has no regulatory authorization from Congress, an issue made clear in the recent challenges to President Obama's November 2014 extensions of DACA.

Like TPS, DACA status may aid integration by granting immigrants legal presence in the Unites States, which affords them certain rights and protections. Indeed, comparisons of application rates by state suggest that the extra protections that DACA affords are a motivating factor for applying. For instance, Arizona, North Carolina, and Texas—all states with restrictive measures against undocumented immigrants—have a higher share of applicants in their estimated eligible populations than do California, Illinois, and New York, which are states with more welcoming political climates (Batalova et al., 2014; Singer et al., 2015). DACA removes the immediate threat of deportation and grants recipients work authorization,

---

[12]Estimates of the population immediately eligible for DACA are drawn from the most recent U.S. Census American Community Survey for 2013, with immigration status assigned based on responses to another national survey, the 2008 Survey of Income and Program Participation. The estimates have the same sampling and coverage errors as any other survey-based estimates that rely on ACS and other Census Bureau data. The Migration Policy Institute's estimates also use commonly accepted benchmarks from other research studies to determine the size of the unauthorized population and response rates to surveys. For more detail on the methodology, see *DACA at the Two-Year Mark: A National and State Profile of Youth Eligible and Applying for Deferred Action* from the Migration Policy Institute in 2014.

[13]Total numbers applying and approval rates calculated from USCIS data available at http://www.uscis.gov/sites/default/files/USCIS/Resources/Reports%20and%20Studies/Immigration%20Forms%20Data/Naturalization%20Data/I821d_performancedata_fy2015_qtr2.pdf [July 2015].

[14]The high approval rates for DACA applicants may reflect the fact that applicants are self-selected. See Singer et al. (2015) for information on what factors motivate and hinder DACA eligible individuals to apply.

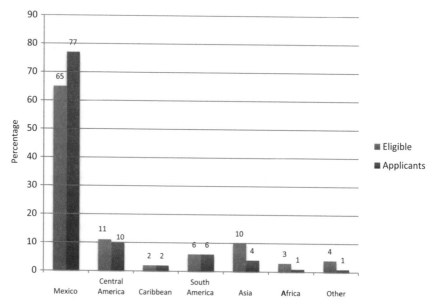

FIGURE 3-13 Percentage estimated eligible for DACA and percentage who have actually applied, by country and region of origin.
SOURCE: Data from Singer et al. (2015).

making it easier to access legal employment and better wages (Gonzalez and Bautista-Chavez, 2014). DACA status is also indirectly but strongly associated with a higher sense of national belonging (Wong and Valdivia, 2014; Teranishi et al., 2015) and civic participation (Wong and Valdivia, 2014).

Because attaining DACA status is directly linked to allowing its recipients to work, receipt of DACA leads most directly to a number of work-related benefits such as obtaining a first job or a better one (Wong and Valdivia, 2014), as well as higher earnings (Gonzales et al., 2014; Teranishi et al., 2015). Other benefits include obtaining health care through employment, more stability in transportation and housing, and greater participation in college activities (Gonzales et al., 2014; Raymond-Flesch et al., 2014; Teranishi et al., 2015). Early research therefore suggests that DACA can have a positive impact on immigrant integration.

However, there are important limits to DACA's integrative potential. First, this status is limited to undocumented people who are below a certain age and arrived within a particular time period. The educational requirement also limits its scope, especially since being undocumented poses significant challenges to educational attainment. Early research suggests that undocumented youth who do not meet the education requirements have more limited English skills, lower incomes, and are more likely to be in the labor force (Batalova et al., 2013). In addition, applicants must reapply every 2 years, highlighting the temporary nature of this status, which has no pathway to LPR status and citizenship. Also important, it is unclear whether future administrations will continue the program or if any future immigration reform by congress will make provisions for this population. And some eligible youth are not applying for DACA because they are worried about providing their information to the government and are holding out for comprehensive immigration reform that might offer better protections against deportation (Gonzalez and Bautista-Chavez, 2014).

DACA-eligible youth almost inevitably come from mixed-status families because most were brought to the United States by undocumented parents. Although DACA offers them some form of legal status, their family members continue to face deportation and limited opportunities. This ongoing instability and the constant fear of deportation for ineligible family members may further limit the integrative possibilities of this status.

UNDOCUMENTED IMMIGRANTS

The undocumented category is technically not a "legal" category but is indirectly established by immigration law as it creates categories of admission. As discussed in Chapter 1, the number of undocumented immigrants began to increase after the 1965 amendments to the Immigration and Nationality Act of 1952, which restricted immigration from Latin America. Between 1990 and 2007, the number of undocumented immigrants living in the United States tripled but then stalled and declined slightly, perhaps as a result of the Great Recession (see Figure 1-17 in Chapter 1). Although the majority of the undocumented are from Mexico and the popular stereotype is of migrants sneaking across the Southern Border, this category is composed of all individuals who entered the country without inspection, as well as visa overstayers; it thus includes people from every region of the world (see Figure 3-14).

The integrative prospects of undocumented immigrants tend to vary by geographic location, as discussed further in Chapter 5. As noted in Chapter 2, some states and municipalities grant the undocumented limited access to public assistance. As of early 2015, California, Colorado, Connecticut, the District of Columbia, Illinois, Maryland, Nevada, New Mexico, Utah, Vermont, Washington, offer access to driver's licenses regardless of legal status. Furthermore, California, Colorado, Connecticut, Illinois, Kansas, Maryland, Minnesota, Nebraska, New Mexico, New Jersey, New York, Oregon, Texas, Utah, Washington, and Wisconsin have statutes that condition eligibility for in-state tuition to attend college or university on attending and graduating from high school in the state, thus allowing stu-

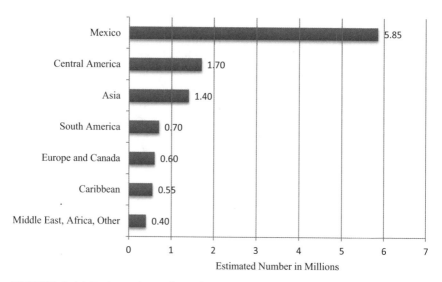

FIGURE 3-14 Estimated number of undocumented immigrants residing in the United States in millions by country and region of origin, 2012.
SOURCE: Data from Passel and Cohn (2014).

dents who cannot provide proof of citizenship or legal residence to claim this education benefit. Importantly, regardless of state of residence, undocumented children have a constitutional right to K-12 education as stipulated by *Plyler v. Doe* 457 U.S. 202 (1982).

The undocumented face unique barriers to integration, as by definition they are excluded from direct pathways to legalization. Perhaps the most important is the constant fear of deportation. Deportations have skyrocketed, especially after the IIRIRA passed in 1996 (National Research Council, 2011, p. 52; also see Figure 2-1 in Chapter 2). In 2013, the United States deported more than 438,000 people.

The majority of undocumented workers are confined to low-wage occupations either because of their lower human capital or because their status makes it difficult to find jobs commensurate with their skills and education or keeps them from accessing educational opportunities. This puts undocumented workers at unique risk for labor violations by employers (Bernhardt et al., 2013, p. 725). A 2008 survey of low-wage workers in Chicago, Los Angeles, and New York indicated that 31 percent of immigrant workers experienced a violation of minimum-wage laws compared with only 16 percent among native-born workers; among the undocumented the figure was 37 percent compared with 21 percent among those with work authorization (Bernhardt et al., 2009). Another survey of immigrant workers in New Orleans found that 41 percent had experienced wage theft by those who presumably had hired them (Fussell, 2011).

Undocumented immigrants are also subjected to hostility from the American public at large and to racial profiling by authorities, which makes their integration much more difficult. For instance, the rise of anti-immigrant sentiment and intensification of immigration enforcement appear to be taking a toll on the health of undocumented Mexican migrants, who are positively selected for good health when they leave for the United States but display worse health than otherwise similar nonmigrants when they return (Ullmann et al., 2011; Barcellos et al., 2012). In addition, there is a strong connection between anti-immigrant sentiment and the level of Hispanic segregation and neighborhood isolation across metropolitan areas (Rugh and Massey, 2014). And Hall and Stringfield (2014) showed that segregation of Hispanics from non-Hispanic white Americans rises as the estimated prevalence of undocumented migrants in the population increases.

Undocumented Status and "Crimmigration"

Undocumented immigrants are often called "illegal aliens" and many, if not most, Americans believe that it is a crime to reside in the United States as an undocumented immigrant. Yet the law is much more complex. Currently it is a civil matter to overstay a visa, a misdemeanor to illegally enter the country, and a felony to re-enter the country after having been previously caught here illegally and deported. While many people describe the process of expelling people from the United States as "deportations," the legal term is "removal." The Supreme Court ruled in 1893 in *Fong Yue Ting v. United States*, 149 U.S. 698 (1893) that "the order of deportation is not punishment for a crime." Therefore undocumented immigrants who are deported do not have "criminal" trials but rather "administrative hearings," and they are not allowed the protections of U.S. criminal law: the right to a lawyer, the right to a warrant before the police can search them, or other aspects of due process.

Thus, the 40+ percent of the undocumented who overstayed their visas did not thereby actually commit a crime. And among those who do cross the border illegally, most are not charged with a criminal offense; instead they are offered voluntary departure, which does not create a criminal record (National Research Council, 2011). These are usually people found within 100 miles of the Mexican border who "voluntarily" agree to be taken back over the border and are released with no further sanctions or charges. They do not see an immigration judge, and the decision to remove them comes from Department of Homeland Security (DHS) personnel. In other cases, undocumented immigrants are ordered removed by DHS personnel (accelerated removal) or can be detained and then see an immigration judge who issues a removal ruling (standard formal removal). This creates a record of removal, which has serious implications if immigrants are apprehended crossing the border again. "Unlawful re-entry" after removal is now categorized as a felony offense, expanding the criminalization of undocumented immigrants.

The passage of the IIRIRA and the Antiterrorism and Effective Death Penalty Act in 1996 greatly expanded the list of deportable crimes, as well as expanding the authority of state and local police to enforce federal immigration policies. More recently, the Secure Communities Program made it easier for local and state police to communicate about arrestees' immigration status with the federal government (discussed in Chapter 2). Consequently there has been a large increase in the detention of undocumented people, deportations and removals, and the general "criminalization" of undocumented status (Gladstein et al., 2005; Douglas and Sáenz, 2013).

On an average day, U.S. federal deportation authorities now hold in custody over 33,000 noncitizens and manage more than 1.71 million people in various stages of immigration removal proceedings (U.S. Department of Homeland Security, 2012). Nearly 400,000 individuals are deported annually, double the rate of a decade ago (Simanski, 2014). These numbers represent some of the largest numbers of deportations or removals in the history of the United States.

Immigration and Customs Enforcement does not exercise direct control over most of the noncitizens in its custody. Rather, it contracts with local jails and state and private prisons, which hold approximately 84 percent of its detainees (Amnesty International, 2007). This growth in detentions in prisons and in other facilities includes many people with no criminal records. A recent study using Immigration and Customs Enforcement data found that 58 percent of the 32,000 detainees in custody as of January 29, 2009, did not have any criminal record. Four hundred people who had no criminal record had been held for over a year's time (Kerwin and Lin, 2009). Those who had committed crimes had often been found guilty of relatively minor crimes such as traffic-related violations (13 percent) and immigration-related offenses (6 percent)" (Kerwin and Lin, 2009). The most common criminal conviction was driving under the influence of alcohol. Nevertheless, these detainees were primarily held in facilities designed for people who have committed serious crimes: 70 percent were in state and local prisons, while only 27 percent were in contract detention facilities or service processing centers.[15]

The significant increase in detentions and deportations of undocumented immigrants has profound effects on these immigrants' ability to integrate, and in many ways that is the intended effect. Yet the number of undocumented immigrants in the United States continued to soar after

---

[15]The remaining 5 percent were in federal prisons or in "soft" detention centers such as medical centers (Kerwin and Lin, 2009).

1996 and only fell (slightly) in response to the economic deprivations of the Great Recession.

Attitudes Toward Undocumented Immigrants

An important aspect of the context of reception for undocumented immigrants that affects their integration prospects is the attitude of the native-born toward them. While Americans have generally preferred to decrease the number of immigrants coming to the United States, they have also tended to resist mass deportation as the solution to the problem of undocumented immigration. For example, in the *CBS/New York Times Poll* in 2006 and 2007, the proportion favoring a pathway to legal status for undocumented immigrants was consistent at around 62 percent,[16] while the proportion favoring deportation was considerably lower, at around 33 percent.[17] In later years nearly one-half supported a pathway to citizenship, while less than a third of respondents preferred deportation (see Chapter 2).

Despite the often negative rhetoric surrounding undocumented immigration, there is some public support both for more lenient and more punitive actions toward the undocumented. Support for President Obama's Executive action on DACA ranged from 41 percent to 54 percent in 2015, depending on how the question was worded.[18] Yet support for tougher laws such as Arizona's Support our Law Enforcement and Safe Neighborhoods Act [19] was at 69 percent in 2010.

Majorities of both Latino and Asian Americans agree that granting legal status to undocumented immigrants would strengthen the U.S. economy and improve the lives of undocumented immigrants, and support for a pathway to citizenship among Asian Americans increased significantly between 2008 and 2012 (Ramakrishnan and Lee, 2013). Yet majorities of these groups are also concerned that granting legal status might lead

---

[16] Support for legalization was 62 percent in May 2006, 60 percent in March 2007, 61 percent in May 2007, and 65 percent in June 2007. See http://www.cbsnews.com/htdocs/pdf/poll_bush_050906.pdf, http://www.cbsnews.com/htdocs/pdf/052407_immigration.pdf, and http://www.cbsnews.com/htdocs/pdf/062807_immigration.pdf [August 2015].

[17] Support for deportation was 33 percent in May 2006, 36 percent in March 2007, 35 percent and 28 percent in May 2007. CBS News Poll, see http://www.cbsnews.com/htdocs/pdf/poll_bush_050906.pdf, http://www.cbsnews.com/htdocs/pdf/052407_immigration.pdf, and http://www.cbsnews.com/htdocs/pdf/062807_immigration.pdf [August 2015].

[18] See http://www.cnn.com/2014/11/26/politics/cnn-immigration-poll/, http://www.wsj.com/articles/wsj-nbc-poll-finds-americans-want-parties-to-work-together-1416439838, and http://www.washingtonpost.com/politics/polling/united-states-obama-undocumented/2015/01/04/154e034a-86c9-11e4-abcf-5a3d7b3b20b8_page.html [August 2015].

[19] This Arizona law is often called "SB 1070." See http://www.cbsnews.com/htdocs/pdf/CBSNYTPoll_health_care_060712.pdf [August 2015].

to more undocumented immigration and would reward illegal behavior (Lopez et al, 2013, p. 3).

Perhaps not surprisingly, the issue of unauthorized immigration is far more personal for Latinos than for Asian Americans. The Pew Research Center found that 46 percent of Hispanics report that they are much more likely to fear that a family member or a close friend would be deported compared to 16 percent of Asian Americans. The contrast is even more stark among the foreign-born from these two regions of origin: 59 percent of Latino immigrants expressed this fear, compared to only 18 percent of foreign-born Asian Americans (Lopez et al., 2013, p. 2). Still, there is diversity of opinion on immigration by nativity (Lopez and Gonzalez-Barrera, 2013).

In summary, undocumented legal status poses the highest barrier to immigrant integration among the current statuses; in fact, the lack of legal status is intended to explicitly discourage integration by denying undocumented immigrants access to various social and economic benefits and leaving them vulnerable to deportation. Yet millions of undocumented immigrants continue to reside in the United States, working, starting families, seeking pathways to other legal statuses, and integrating into American society despite the obstacles.

SUMMARY AND CONCLUSIONS

Given the significant potential to alter individuals' life chances, legal status has become a new axis of social stratification, similar to other social markers such as social class, gender, and race (Gee and Ford, 2011; Massey, 2007, 2012; Menjívar, 2011). The research to date indicates that a strong positive relationship exists between naturalization and integration and that LPR status and other statuses with clear pathways to becoming an LPR offer significant benefits for integration. However, the barriers that legal statuses short of naturalization create for integration and the codification of these barriers in law mean that legal status sometimes trumps the effects of other social markers (Menjívar et al., in press). Legal status intensifies the effects of disadvantages that come from other social positions, such as those based on social class, gender, or race and ethnicity, while diminishing the benefits that an advantageous social position can have. Undocumented status, in particular, presents a formidable barrier to integration and economic progress, a situation exacerbated by criminalization of undocumented status and the unprecedented level of enforcement and deportations since 1996.

Conclusion 3-1 Legal status affects immigrant integration. Legal permanent resident status has a positive effect on integration, but temporary, discretionary, and especially undocumented status negatively affect immigrants' ability to integrate across various social dimensions. More research is needed to better understand the relationship between temporary legal statuses, in particular, and integration outcomes.

In addition, legal status has intergenerational impacts. For instance, the educational attainments of children whose parents eventually legalized were just as high as those whose parents entered the country legally, suggesting that the burdens of parental undocumented status on children (including U.S.-born children), while sizeable and debilitating, mostly disappear when legalization occurs (Bean et al., 2015). Given the ripple effects that legal status has for other family members, it is important that future research examine its effects in family and community contexts.

Conclusion 3-2 Parents' legal status affects the integration prospects of a significant proportion of the U.S.-born children of immigrant parents. Parents' undocumented status in particular can have negative effects on children's socioeconomic outcomes, cognitive development, and mental health.

REFERENCES

Abrego, L.J. (2006). I can't go to college because I don't have papers: Incorporation patterns of Latino undocumented youth. *Latino Studies, 4*(3), 212-231.

Abrego, L.J. (2014). *Sacrificing Families: Navigating Laws, Labor, and Love Across Borders.* Stanford, CA: Stanford University Press.

Amnesty International. (2007). *Jailed Without Justice: Immigration Detention in the USA.* Available: http://www.amnestyusa.org/pdfs/JailedWithoutJustice.pdf [August 2015].

Armenta, A. (2012). From sheriff's deputies to immigration officers: Screening immigrant status in a Tennessee jail. *Law & Policy, 34*(2), 191-210.

Aptekar, S. (2015). *The Road to Citizenship: What Naturalization Means for Immigrants and the United States.* New Brunswick, NJ: Rutgers University Press.

Balcazar, A.J., Grineski, S.E., and Collins, T.W. (2015). The durability of immigration-related barriers to health care access for Hispanics across generations. *Hispanic Journal of Behavioral Sciences, 37*(1), 118-135.

Barcellos, S.H., Goldman, D.P., and Smith, J.P. (2012). Undiagnosed disease, especially diabetes, casts doubt on some of reported health "advantage" of recent Mexican immigrants. *Health Affairs, 31*(12), 2727-2737.

Batalova, J., Hooker, S., and Capps, R. (2013). *Deferred Action for Childhood Arrivals at the One-Year Mark: A Profile of Currently Eligible Youth and Applicants.* Washington, DC: Migration Policy Institute. Available: http://www.migrationpolicy.org/research/deferred-action-childhood-arrivals-one-year-mark-profile-currently-eligible-youth-and [August 2015].

Batalova, J., Hooker, S., Capps, R., and Bachmeier, J.D. (2014). *Deferred Action for Childhood Arrivals at the Two-Year Mark: A National and State Profile of Youth Eligible and Applying for Deferred Action.* Washington, DC: Migration Policy Institute.

Bean, F.D., Leach, M.A., Brown, S.K., Bachmeier, J.D., and Hipp, J.R. (2011). The educational legacy of undocumented migration: comparisons across U.S. immigrant groups in how parents' status affects their offspring. *International Migration Review, 45*, 348-385.

Bean, F.D., Brown, S.K., Leach, M.A., Bachmeier, J.D., and Van Hook, J. (2013). *Unauthorized Mexican Migration and the Socioeconomic Integration of Mexican Americans.* US2010 Report. New York: Russell Sage Foundation. Available: http://www.scribd.com/doc/145926497/Unauthorized-Mexican-Migration-and-the-Socioeconomic-Integration-of-Mexican-Americans [September 2015].

Bean, F.D., Brown, S.K., and Bachmeier, J.D. (2015). *Parents Without Papers: The Progress and Pitfalls of Mexican American Integration.* New York: Russell Sage Foundation.

Bernhardt, A., Milkman, R., Theodore, N., Heckathorn, D., Auer, M., DeFilippis, J., González, A.L., Narro, V., Perelshteyn, J., Polson, D., and Spiller, M. (2009). *Broken Laws, Unprotected Workers: Violations of Employment and Labor Laws in America's Cities.* New York: National Employment Law Project. Available: http://www.nelp.org/content/uploads/2015/03/BrokenLawsReport2009.pdf?nocdn=1 [September 2015].

Bernhardt, A., Spiller, M., and Polson, D. (2013). All work and no pay: Violations of employment and labor laws in Chicago, Los Angeles, and New York City. *Social Forces, 91*(3), 725-746.

Bhuyan, R., and Senturia, K. (2005). Understanding domestic violence resource utilization and survivor solutions among immigrant and refugee women: Introduction to the Special Issue. *Journal of Interpersonal Violence, 20*(8), 895-901. Available: http://jiv.sagepub.com/content/20/8/895.full.pdf [September 2015].

Bloemraad, I., and Trost, C. (2008). It's a family affair: Intergenerational mobilization in the spring 2006 protests. *American Behavioral Scientist, 52*(4), 507-532.

Bosniak, L. (2007). Being here: Ethical territoriality and the rights of immigrants. *Theoretical Inquiries in Law, 8*(2), 389-410.

Brabeck, K., and Xu, Q. (2010). The impact of detention and deportation on Latino immigrant children and families: A quantitative exploration. *Hispanic Journal of Behavioral Sciences, 32*(3), 341-361.

Bruno, A. (2015). *Refugee Admissions and Resettlement Policy.* Washington, DC: Congressional Research Service. Available: https://www.fas.org/sgp/crs/misc/RL31269.pdf [August 2015].

Calavita, K. (2005). *Immigrants at the Margins: Law, Race, and Exclusion in Southern Europe.* Cambridge, UK: Cambridge University Press.

Capps, R., Fortuny, K., and Fix, M. (2007). *Trends in the Low-Wage Immigrant Labor Force, 2000-2005.* Washington, DC: The Urban Institute.

Castañeda, H., and Melo, M.A. (2014). Health care access for Latino mixed-status families: Barriers, strategies, and implications for reform. *American Behavioral Scientist, 58*(14), 1891-1909.

Chavez, L.R. (2001). *Covering Immigration: Popular Images and the Politics of the Nation.* Berkeley: University of California Press.

Chavez, L.R. (2007). The condition of illegality. *International Migration, 45*(3), 192-196.

Cummings, K.J., and Kreiss, K. (2008). Contingent workers and contingent health: Risks of a modern economy. *Journal of the American Medical Association, 299*(4), 448-450.

Donato, K.M., and Massey, D.S. (1993). Effect of the Immigration Reform and Control Act on the wages of Mexican migrants. *Social Science Quarterly, 74*(3), 523-541.

Donato, K.M., and Sisk, B. (2012). Shifts in the employment outcomes among Mexican migrants to the United States, 1976-2009. *Research in Social Stratification and Mobility, 30*(1), 63-77.

Donato, K.M., Durand, J., and Massey, D.S. (1992). Changing conditions in the U.S. labor market. *Population Research and Policy Review, 11*(2), 93-115.

Donato, K.M., Wakabayashi, C., Hakimzadeh, S., and Armenta, A. (2008). Shifts in the employment conditions of Mexican migrant men and women. *Work and Occupations, 35*(4), 462-495.

Douglas, K.M., and Sáenz, R. (2013). The criminalization of immigrants and the immigration-industrial complex. *Daedalus, 142*(3), 199-227.

Dreby, J. (2012). The burden of deportation on children in Mexican immigrant families. *Journal of Marriage and Family, 74*(4), 829-845.

Dreby, J. (2015). U.S. immigration policy and family separation: The consequences for children's well-being. *Social Science & Medicine, 132*, 245-251.

Drever, A.I., and Blue, S.A. (2011). Surviving sin papeles in post-Katrina New Orleans: An exploration of the challenges facing undocumented Latino immigrants in new and re-emerging Latino destinations. *Population, Space and Place, 17*(1), 89-102.

Ellis, M., Wright, R., and Townley, M. (2014). The great recession and the allure of new immigrant destinations in the United States. *International Migration Review, 48*(1), 3-33.

Enchautegui, M.E. (2013). *More than 11 Million: Unauthorized Immigrants and Their Families.* Washington, DC: Urban Institute.

Enchautegui, M.E., and Menjívar, C. (2015). Paradoxes of family immigration policy: Separation, reorganization, and reunification of families under current immigration laws. *Law & Policy, 37*(1-2), 32-60.

Enriquez, L.E. (2015). Multigenerational punishment: Shared experiences of undocumented immigration status within mixed-status families. *Journal of Marriage and Family, 77*(4), 939-953.

Erez, E., and Globokar, J. (2009). Compounding vulnerabilities: The impact of immigration status and circumstances of battered immigrant women. *Sociology of Crime, Law, and Deviance, 13*, 129-145.

Espenshade, T.J., Baraka, J.L., and Huber, G.A. (1997). Implications of the 1996 Welfare and Immigration Reform Acts for U.S. immigration. *Population and Development Review, 23*(4), 769-801.

Fix, M., and Zimmerman, W. (2001). All under one roof: Mixed-status families in an era of reform. *International Migration Review, 35*(2), 397-419.

Flippen, C. (2014). Intersectionality at work: Determinants of labor supply among immigrant Latinas. *Gender & Society, 28*(3), 404-434.

Fox, C. (2012). *Three Worlds of Relief: Race, Immigration, and the American Welfare State from the Progressive Era to the New Deal: Race, Immigration, and the American Welfare State from the Progressive Era to the New Deal.* Princeton, NJ: Princeton University Press.

Fussell, E. (2011). The deportation threat dynamic and victimization of Latino migrants: Wage theft and robbery. *The Sociological Quarterly, 52*(4), 593-615.

Gee, G.C., and Ford, C.L. (2011). Structural racism and health inequities. *Du Bois Review: Social Science Research on Race, 8*(01), 115-132.

Gentsch, K., and Massey, D.S. (2011). Labor market outcomes for legal Mexican immigrants under the new regime of immigration enforcement. *Social Science Quarterly, 92*(3), 875-893.

Gladstein, H., Lai, A., Wagner, J., and Wishnie, M.J. (2005). *Blurring the Lines: A Profile of State and Local Police Enforcement of Immigration Law Using the National Crime Information Center Database, 2002–2004.* Washington, DC: Migration Policy Institute.

Gleeson, S., and Gonzales, R.G. (2012). When do papers matter? An institutional analysis of undocumented life in the United States. *International Migration, 50*(4), 1-19.

Gonzales, R.G. (2011). Learning to be illegal: Undocumented youth and shifting legal contexts in the transition to adulthood. *American Sociological Review, 76*(4), 602-619.

Gonzales, R.G., and Chavez, L.R. (2012). Awakening to a nightmare. *Current Anthropology,* *53*(3), 255-281.

Gonzales, R.G., and Bautista-Chavez, A.M. (2014) *Two Years and Counting: Assessing the Growing Power of DACA.* Washington, DC: American Immigration Council. Available: http://www.immigrationpolicy.org/sites/default/files/docs/two_years_and_counting_assessing_the_growing_power_of_daca_final.pdf [August 2015].

Gonzales, R.G., Terriquez, V., and Ruszczyk, S. (2014). Becoming DACAmented: Assessing the short-term benefits of DACA (Deferred Action for Childhood Arrivals). *American Behavioral Scientist, 58,* 1852-1872.

Gonzalez-Barrera, A., Lopez, M.H., Passel, J.S., and Taylor, P. (2014). *The Path Not Taken.* Washington, DC: Pew Research Center.

Hacker, K., Chu, J., Leung, C., Marra, R., and Pirie, J. (2011). The impact of immigration and customs enforcement on immigrant health: Perceptions of immigrants in Everett, Massachusetts, USA. *Social Science & Medicine, 73*(4), 586-594.

Hagan, J., Rodriguez, N., Capps, R., and Kabiri, N. (2003). The effects of recent welfare and immigration reforms on immigrants' access to health care. *International Migration Review,* 444-463.

Hagan, J.M., Rodriguez, N., and Castro, B. (2011). Social effects of mass deportations by the United States government, 2000–2010. *Ethnic and Racial Studies, 34*(8), 1374-1391.

Hall, M., and Stringfield, J. (2014). Undocumented migration and the residential segregation of Mexicans in new destinations. *Social Science Research, 47,* 61-78.

Heyman, J.M. (2013). "Illegality" and the U.S.-Mexico border. *Constructing Immigrant Illegality: Critiques, Experiences, and Responses,* 111.

Hill, N.E., and Torres, K. (2010). Negotiating the American dream: The paradox of aspirations and achievement among Latino students and engagement between their families and schools. *Journal of Social Issues, 66*(1), 95-112.

Jasso, G. (2011). Migration and stratification. *Social Science Research, 40,* 1292-1336.

Jones-Correa, M., and de Graauw, E. (2013). The illegality trap: The politics of immigration and the lens of illegality. *Daedalus, 142*(3), 185-198.

Kandula, N.R., Grogan, C.M., Rathouz, P.J., and Lauderdale, D.S. (2004). The unintended impact of welfare reform on the Medicaid enrollment of eligible immigrants. *Health Services Research, 39*(5), 1509-1526.

Kanstroom, D. (2007). *Deportation Nation: Outsiders in American History.* Cambridge, MA: Harvard University Press.

Kerwin, D., and Lin, S.Y.Y. (2009). *Immigrant Detention: Can ICE Meet Its Legal Imperatives and Case Management Responsibilities?* Washington, DC: Migration Policy Institute. Available: http://www.migrationpolicy.org/research/immigrant-detention-can-ice-meet-its-legal-imperatives-and-case-management-responsibilities [September 2015].

Kunz, E.F. (1973). The refugee in flight: Kinetic models and forms of displacement. *International Migration Review, 7,* Summer.

Landale, N., Thomas, K.J.A., and Van Hook, J. (2011). The living arrangements of children of immigrants. *The Future of Children, 21*(1), 43-70

Lee, J., and Foreman, K. (2014). *U.S. Naturalizations: 2013.* Office of Immigration Statistics Annual Flow Report. Available: http://www.dhs.gov/sites/default/files/publications/ois_natz_fr_2013.pdf [August 2015].

Longazel, J.G. (2013). Moral panic as racial degradation ceremony: Racial stratification and the local-level backlash against Latino/a immigrants. *Punishment & Society, 15*(1), 96-119.

López, J.L. (2015). Impossible families: Mixed-citizenship status couples and the law. *Law & Policy, 37*(1-2), 3-118.

Lopez, M.H., and Gonzalez-Barrera, A. (2013). *High Rate of Deportations Continue Under Obama Despite Latino Disapproval.* Washington, DC: Pew Research Center.

Lopez, M.H., Taylor, P., Funk, C., Gonzalez-Barrera, A., and Oats, R. (2013). *On Immigration Policy, Deportation Relief Seen as More Important Than Citizenship: A Survey of Hispanics and Asian Americans.* Washington, DC: Pew Research Center.

Marquardt, M., Steigenga, T., Williams, P., and Vasquez, M. (2011). *Living "Illegal": The Human Face of Unauthorized Immigration.* New York: The New Press.

Martin, D.C., and Yankay, J.E. (2014). *Refugees and Asylees: 2013.* Annual Flow Report. Office of Immigration Statistics, U.S. Department of Homeland Security. Available: http://www.dhs.gov/sites/default/files/publications/ois_rfa_fr_2013.pdf [August 2015].

Massey, D.S. (2007). *Categorically Unequal: The American Stratification System.* New York: Russell Sage Foundation.

Massey, D.S. (2012). *Immigration and the Great Recession.* The Russell Sage Foundation and the Stanford Center on Poverty and Inequality. Available: https://web.stanford.edu/group/recessiontrends/cgi-bin/web/sites/all/themes/barron/pdf/Immigration_fact_sheet.pdf [September 2015].

Massey, D.S., and Gelatt, J. (2010). What happened to the wages of Mexican immigrants and quest; Trends and interpretations. *Latino Studies, 8*(3), 328-354.

Massey, D.S., Durand, J., and Malone, N.J. (2002). *Beyond Smoke and Mirrors: Mexican Immigration in an Era of Economic Integration.* New York: Russell Sage Foundation.

McBrien, J.L. (2005). Educational needs and barriers for refugee students in the United States: A review of the literature. *Review of Educational Research, 75*(3), 329-364.

McConnell, E.D. (2013). Who has housing affordability problems?: Disparities in housing cost burden by race, nativity, and legal status. *Race and Social Problems, 5*(3), 173-190.

McConnell, E.D. (2015). Hurdles or walls? Nativity, citizenship, legal status and Latino homeownership in Los Angeles. *Social Science Research, 53,* 19-33.

McConnell, E.D., and Marcelli, E.A. (2007). Buying into the American Dream? Mexican immigrants, legal status, and homeownership in Los Angeles County. *Social Science Quarterly, 88*(1), 199-221.

Menjívar, C. (2000). *Fragmented Ties: Salvadoran Immigrant Networks in America.* Berkeley: University of California Press.

Menjívar, C. (2006). Liminal legality: Salvadoran and Guatemalan immigrants' lives in the United States. *American Journal of Sociology, 111*(4), 999-1037.

Menjívar, C. (2011). The power of the law: Central Americans' legality and everyday life in Phoenix, Arizona. *Latino Studies, 9*(4), 377-395.

Menjívar, C., and Abrego, D. (2009). Parents and children across borders. In N. Foner (Ed.), *Across Generations: Immigrant Families in America* (pp. 160-189). New York: New York University Press.

Menjívar, C., and Abrego, L. (2012). Legal violence: Immigration law and the lives of Central American immigrants. *American Journal of Sociology, 117*(5), 1380-1421.

Menjívar, C., Abrego, L., and Schmalzbauer, L. (forthcoming). *Immigrant Families.* Hoboken, NJ: Wiley.

Menjívar, C., and Lakhani, S.M. (n.d.). Transformative Effects of Immigration Law: Migrants' Personal and Social Metamorphoses Through Regularization. Submitted to the *American Journal of Psychology.*

Messick, M., and Bergeron, C. (2014). *Temporary Protected Status in the United States: A Grant of Humanitarian Relief that Is Less than Permanent.* Available: http://www.migrationpolicy.org/article/temporary-protected-status-united-states-grant-humanitarian-relief-less-permanent [September 2015].

Mexican Migration Monitor. (2012). *Hitting Home: The Impact of Immigration Enforcement.* Tomas Rivera Policy Institute and Colegio de la Frontera Norte. Available: http://www.migrationmonitor.com/3-article/ [July 2015].

Migration Policy Institute. (2014). *As Many as 3.7 Million Unauthorized Immigrants Could Get Relief from Deportation under Anticipated New Deferred Action Program.* Press release. Available: http://migrationpolicy.org/news/mpi-many-37-million-unauthorized-immigrants-could-get-relief-deportation-under-anticipated-new [September 2015].

Motomura, H. (2007). *Americans in Waiting: The Lost Story of Immigration and Citizenship in the United States.* New York: Oxford University Press.

National Immigrant Women's Advocacy Project. (2012). *Social Science Documents the Need for VAWA Self-Petitions and U-Visas.* Available: http://www.ncdsv.org/images/NIWAP_SocialScienceResearchDocumentsTheNeedForpercent20VAWASelf-Petitions AndU-Visas_12-6-2012.pdf [September 2015].

National Research Council. (2011). *Budgeting for Immigration Enforcement: A Path to Better Performance.* Committee on Estimating Costs of Immigration Enforcement in the Department of Justice. S. Redburn, P. Reuter, and M. Majmundar, Eds. Committee on Law and Justice, Division of Behavioral and Social Sciences and Education. Washington, DC: The National Academies Press.

O'Brien, M. (2013). High-skilled immigration debate grows over stark gender imbalance, favoring men for H-1B visas. *San Jose Mercury News.* Available: http://www.mercury news.com/politics-government/ci_22819054/high-skilled-immigration-debate-grows-over-stark-gender [September 2015].

Office of Immigration Statistics, U.S. Department of Homeland Security. (2014). *Yearbook of Immigration Statistics, 2013.* Available: Available: http://www.dhs.gov/yearbook-immigration-statistics-2013-refugees-and-asylees [October 2015].

O'Leary, A.O., and Sanchez, A. (2011). Anti-immigrant Arizona: Ripple effects and mixed immigration status households under "policies of attrition" considered. *Journal of Borderlands Studies, 26*(1), 115-133.

Orellana, M.F., Dorner, L., and Pulido, L. (2003). Accessing assets: Immigrant youth's work as family translators or "paraphrasers." *Social Problems, 50*(4), 505-524.

Orrenius, P., and Zavodny, M. (2014). *The Impact of Temporary Protected Status on Immigrants' Labor Market Outcomes.* Federal Reserve Bank of Dallas, Research Department, Working paper 1415. Available: http://www.dallasfed.org/assets/documents/research/papers/2014/wp1415.pdf [September 2015].

Ortega, A.N., Horwitz, S.M., Fang, H., Kuo, A.A., Wallace, S.P., and Inkelas, M. (2009). Documentation status and parental concerns about development in young U.S. children of Mexican origin. *Academic Pediatrics, 9*, 278-282.

Park, L. S-H. (2005). *Consuming Citizenship: Children of Asian Immigrant Entrepreneurs.* Stanford, CA: Stanford University Press.

Passel, J., and Cohn, D. (2014) *Unauthorized Immigrant Total Rises in 7 States, Falls in 14.* Available: http://www.pewhispanic.org/files/2014/11/2014-11-18_unauthorized-immigration.pdf [July 2015].

Passel, J., Cohn, D., Krogstad, J.M., and Gonzalez-Barrera, A. (2014) *As Growth Stalls, Unauthorized Immigrant Population Becomes More Settled.* Washington, DC: Pew Hispanic Institute.

Phillips, J.A., and Massey, D.S. (1999). The new labor market: Immigrants and wages after IRCA. *Demography, 36*(2), 233-246.

Portes, A., and Zhou, M. (1993). The new second generation: Segmented assimilation and its variants. *The ANNALS of the American Academy of Political and Social Science, 530*(1), 74-96.

Portes, A., and Zhou, M. (2014). The new second generation: Segmented assimilation and its variants. In M. Suárez-Orozco, C. Suárez-Orozco, and D. Qin-Hilliard (Eds.), *The New Immigrant in American Society: Interdisciplinary Perspectives on the New Immigration* (volume 1). New York: Routledge.

Potochnick, S.R., and Perreira, K.M. (2010). Depression and anxiety among first-generation immigrant Latino youth: Key correlates and implications for future research. *The Journal of Nervous and Mental Disease, 198*, 470-477.

Ramakrishnan, S.K., and Lee, T. (2013). *Opinions of Asian Americans and Pacific Islanders: Federal Immigration Policy.* Supplement to the Policy Priorities and Issue Preferences of Asian Americans and Pacific Islanders. The National Asian American Survey. Available: http://www.naasurvey.com/resources/Home/NAAS12-immigration-jan2013.pdf [September 2015].

Raymond-Flesch, M., Siemons, R., Pourat, N., Jacobs, K., and Brindis, C.D. (2014). There is no help out there and if there is, it's really hard to find: A qualitative study of the health concerns and health care access of Latino "DREAMers." *Journal of Adolescent Health, 55*(3), 323-328.

Regets, M.C. (2007). *Research Issues in the International Migration of Highly Skilled Workers: A Perspective with Data from the United States.* Working paper SRS 07-203. Arlington, VA: National Science Foundation.

Rodriguez, N., and Hagan, J.M. (2004). Fractured families and communities: effects of immigration reform in Texas, Mexico, and El Salvador. *Latino Studies, 2*(3), 328-351.

Rosenblum, M. (2015). *Understanding the Potential Impact of Executive Action on Immigration Enforcement.* Washington, DC: Migration Policy Institute. Available: http://www.migrationpolicy.org/research/understanding-potential-impact-executive-action-immigration-enforcement [July 2015].

Rosenblum, M.R., and McCabe, K. (2014). *Deportation and Discretion: Reviewing the Record and Options for Change.* Washington, DC: Migration Policy Institute.

Rugh, J.S., and Massey, D.S. (2014). Segregation in post-civil rights America. *Du Bois Review: Social Science Research on Race, 11*(02), 205-232.

Ruiz, N.G. (2013). *America's Foreign Students and Immigration Reform.* Washington, DC: Brookings Institution Press. Available: http://www.brookings.edu/blogs/up-front/posts/2013/04/09-foreign-students-ruiz [August 2015].

Salcido, O., and Adelman, M. (2004). He has me tied with the blessed and damned papers: Undocumented-immigrant battered women in Phoenix, Arizona. *Human Organization, 63*(2), 162-172.

Salcido, O., and Menjívar, C. (2012). Gendered paths to legal citizenship: The case of Latin American immigrants in Phoenix, Arizona. *Law & Society Review, 46*(2), 335-368.

Santos, C., Menjívar, C., and Godfrey, E. (2013). Effects of SB 1070 on children. In L. Magaña and E. Lee (Eds.), *Latino Politics and Arizona's Immigration Law SB 1070* (pp. 79-92). New York: Springer.

Schmalzbauer, L. (2011). "Doing gender," ensuring survival: Mexican migration and economic crisis in the rural mountain West. *Rural Sociology, 76*(4), 441-460.

Schueths, A.M. (2012). Where are my rights? Compromised citizenship in mixed-status marriage—A research note. *Journal of Sociology and Social Welfare, 39*(4), 97-110.

Simanski, J.F. (2014). *Immigration Enforcement Actions: 2013.* Office of Immigration Statistics Annual Report. Available: http://www.dhs.gov/sites/default/files/publications/ois_enforcement_ar_2013.pdf [August 2015].

Singer, A., and Wilson, J. (2007). *Refugee Resettlement in Metropolitan America.* Washington, DC: Migration Policy Institute. Available: http://www.migrationpolicy.org/article/refugee-resettlement-metropolitan-america [September 2015].

Singer, A., Svajlenka, N.P., and Wilson, J.H. (2015). *Local Insights from DACA for Implementing Future Programs for Unauthorized Immigrants.* Washington, DC: Brookings Institution Press. Available: http://www.brookings.edu/research/reports/2015/06/04-local-insights-daca-singer-svajlenka-wilson [August 2015].

Sladkova, J., Garcia Mangado, S.M., and Reyes Quinteros, J. (2011). Lowell immigrant communities in the climate of deportations. *Analyses of Social Issues and Public Policy, 12*(1), 78-95.

Solis, J., Fernandez, J.S., and Alcala, L. (2013). Mexican immigrant children and youth's contributions to a community centro: Exploring civic engagement and citizen constructions. *Sociological Studies of Children and Youth, 16,* 177-200.

Steil, J.P., and Ridgley, J. (2012). Small-town defenders: The production of citizenship and belonging in Hazleton, Pennsylvania. *Environment and Planning D: Society and Space, 30,* 1028-1045.

Stewart, J. (2012). Fiction over facts: How competing narrative forms explain policy in a new immigration destination. In K. Cerulo (Ed.), *Sociological Forum, 27*(3):591-616). Hoboken, NJ: Blackwell.

Stumpf, J.P. (2006). The crimmigration crisis: Immigrants, crime, and sovereign power. *American University Law Review, 56,* 367.

Suárez-Orozco, C., Yoshikawa, H., Teranishi, R., and Suárez-Orozco, M. (2011). Growing up in the shadows: The developmental implications of unauthorized status. *Harvard Educational Review, 81*(3), 438-473.

Takei, I., Saenz, R., and Li, J. (2009). Cost of being a Mexican immigrant and being a Mexican non-citizen in California and Texas. *Hispanic Journal of Behavioral Sciences, 31*(1), 73-95.

Teranishi, R., Suárez-Orozco, C., and Suárez-Orozco, M. (2015). *In the Shadows of the Ivory Tower: Undocumented Undergraduates in the Uncertain Era of Immigration Reform.* Los Angeles: Institute for Immigration, Globalization, and Education, University of California.

Thronson, D.B. (2008) Creating crisis: Immigration raids and the destabilization of immigrant families. *Wake Forest Law Review.* Available: http://wakeforestlawreview.com/2008/04/creating-crisis-immigration-raids-and-the-destabilization-of-immigrant-families/ [September 2015].

Ullmann, S.H., Goldman, N., and Massey, D.S. (2011). Healthier before they migrate, less healthy when they return? The health of returned migrants in Mexico. *Social Science and Medicine, 73*(3), 421-428.

U.S. Citizenship and Immigration Service. (2013). *Characteristics of H1B Specialty Occupation Workers: Fiscal Year 2012 Annual Report to Congress.* Available: http://www.uscis.gov/sites/default/files/USCIS/Resources/Reports percent20and percent20Studies/H-1B/h1b-fy-12-characteristics.pdf [September 2015].

U.S. Citizenship and Immigration Services. (2015). *Characteristics of H-1B Specialty Occupation Workers. Fiscal Year 2014 Annual Report to Congress, October 1, 2013–September 30, 2014.* Available: http://www.uscis.gov/sites/default/files/USCIS/Resources/Reports%20and%20Studies/H-1B/h-1B-characteristics-report-14.pdf [September 2015].

U.S. Department of Homeland Security. (2012). *A Day in the Life of ICE Enforcement and Removal Operations.* U.S. Immigration and Customs Enforcement Fact Sheet. Available: http://www.ice.gov/doclib/news/library/factsheets/pdf/day-in-life-ero.pdf [August 2015].

Valenzuela, A. (1999). Gender roles and settlement activities among children and their immigrant families. *American Behavioral Scientist, 42*(4), 720-742.

Van Hook, J., and Balistreri, K.S. (2006). Ineligible parents, eligible children: Food stamps receipt, allotments, and food insecurity among children of immigrants. *Social Science Research, 35*(1), 228-251.

Viladich, A. (2012). Beyond welfare reform: Reframing undocumented immigrants' entitlement to health care in the United States. *Social Science & Medicine, 74*(6), 822-829.

Wasem, R.E. (2014). *Noncitizen Eligibility for Federal Public Assistance: Policy Overview and Trends.* Washington, DC: Congressional Research Service.

Wong, J., and Tseng, V. (2008). Political socialization in immigrant families: Challenging top-down parental socialization models. *Journal of Ethnic and Migration Studies, 34*(1), 151-168.

Wong, T., and Valdivia, C. (2014). *In Their Own Words: A National Survey of Undocumented Millenials.* Washington, DC: United We Dream. Available: http://unitedwedream.org/words-nationwide-survey-undocumented-millennials/ [September 2015].

Yoshikawa, H. (2011). *Immigrants Raising Citizens: Undocumented Parents of Young Children.* New York: Russell Sage Foundation.

Yoshikawa, H., and Kalil, A. (2011). The effects of parental documentation status on the developmental contexts of young children in immigrant families. *Child Development Perspectives, 5*, 291-297.

Yoshikawa, H., Weiland, C., Brooks-Gunn, J., Burchinal, M.R., Espinosa, L.M., Gormley, W.T., and Zaslow, M.J. (2013). *Investing in Our Future: The Evidence Base on Preschool Education.* Society for Research in Child Development and Foundation for Child Development. Available: http://fcd-us.org/sites/default/files/Evidence%20Base%20on%20Preschool%20Education%20FINAL.pdf [September 2015].

Zayas, L.H. (2015). *Forgotten Citizens: Deportation, Children, and the Making of American Exiles and Orphans.* New York: Oxford University Press.

Zhou, M. (2001). Contemporary immigration and the dynamics of race and ethnicity. *America Becoming: Racial Trends and Their Consequences, 1*, 200-242.

4

Political and Civic Dimensions
of Immigrant Integration

The integration of immigrants and their descendants plays out in both the civic and political life of the country. Becoming a U.S. citizen, voting, participating in a parent-teacher association, or volunteering at a local food bank can all be seen as markers of integration. Such activities also serve as way-stations to further integration and engagement in U.S. society and politics. Although naturalization is necessary for voting in almost all parts of the United States, acquiring citizenship does not guarantee political participation. Conversely, noncitizens can be engaged in their communities, for example, by participating in a parent-teacher association. Civic and political integration can occur together, or in distinct steps. Naturalization might spur new Americans to join a local town hall meeting, while an immigrant's prior participation in a religious faith community may provide the encouragement and assistance necessary to acquire U.S. citizenship or register to vote.

In this chapter, the panel summarizes the state of social science knowledge on (1) naturalization and citizenship; (2) political engagement (from voting and electoral participation to contacting officials or participating in peaceful protest); and (3) civic integration beyond formal politics (such as volunteering and participation in community-based organizations), including engagement in a globalized world.

Civic and political integration must be understood at three levels. First, integration involves individual actions and beliefs, such as whether an immigrant naturalizes, joins a community group, or votes. The degree of integration, or variations in integration among individuals, is often linked to individuals' attributes, such as level of education, an immigrant's ability to speak English, or the length of time they have spent in the United States. One important conclusion from available research is that despite a democratic ideal of equal participation, data on naturalization and voting suggest a divide in civic and political integration, with low-income immigrants who have modest education facing significant barriers to citizenship and participation.

At the same time, individual factors are only part of the story. The depth and breadth of civil society constitute a second marker of integration and can spur or hinder engagement. Immigrants' integration is affected by the degree to which community groups, political parties, religious institutions, and a host of other groups reach out to immigrants, as well as immigrants' capacity to create their own groups to develop civic skills, learn about current events, mobilize for common goals, and find community together. The majority of immigrants' organizational engagements are oriented to activities in the United States, from soccer clubs and cultural troupes to professional associations and advocacy organizations, but they also include transnational groups, such as home town associations that send development money back to places of origin. At a third level of analysis, civic integration is affected by the extent to which the political and civic institutions of the United States influence who becomes engaged and who remains on the sidelines of the nation's civic and political life. This perspective suggests that barriers to and inequalities in civic and political integration can be mitigated by partnerships among the voluntary sector, civil society, community-based organizations, the business sector, and government.

NATURALIZATION AND CITIZENSHIP

Most people in the United States acquire U.S. citizenship at birth by being born in the country or born to American parents living in a foreign country. In 2013, about 273 million of the almost 314 million U.S. residents (87%) were native-born citizens, a figure that includes 2.6 million people born abroad to American parents and 1.8 million people born in Puerto Rico or a U.S. territory.[1] The 14th Amendment of the U.S. Constitution guarantees the birthright of citizenship to almost everyone born in one of the 50 states, regardless of parents' legal status.[2] Congressional legislation determines citizenship for those born in U.S. territories or born

---

[1] These figures are from the 2013 3-year estimates from the American Community Survey.

[2] The relevant section of the Fourteenth Amendment reads, "All persons born or naturalized in the United States, and subject to the jurisdiction thereof, are citizens of the United States and of the state wherein they reside." In 1884, the Supreme Court, in *Elk v. Wilson*, 112 U.S. 94, focused on "subject to the jurisdiction," and held that children born to members of Indian tribes governed by tribal legal systems were not U.S. citizens. In 1924, the Congress extended citizenship to all American Indians by passing the Indian Citizenship Act, 43 Stat.

to U.S.-citizen parents abroad.[3] Birthright citizenship is one of the most powerful mechanisms of formal political and civic inclusion in the United States; without it, the citizenship status of 37.1 million second generation Americans living in the country (about 12% of the country's population), and perhaps many millions more in the third and higher generations, would be up for debate.[4]

Immigrants can acquire U.S. citizenship through the legal process of naturalization. The U.S. Constitution assigns power over naturalization to the federal Congress.[5] For much of the 19th century, the requirements for naturalization were simple: adult immigrants generally needed five years of residence, proof of good moral character, and a willingness to swear an oath of allegiance to the United States.[6] At the same time, the 1790 Naturalization Act specified that only a "free white person" was eligible for naturalization. In 1846, the Treaty of Guadalupe-Hidalgo ending the war between the United States and Mexico clearly specified that all Mexicans residing in the conquered territories would be considered U.S. citizens. Consequently, immigrants from Latin America were considered "white" for purposes of immigration and citizenship. The Naturalization Act of 1870 extended naturalization to "aliens of African nativity and to persons of African descent." Immigrants of Asian origins remained barred from naturalization, both through legislation such as the 1882 Chinese Exclusion Act and through a series of court cases that determined Asians were not "white" under the law. The Supreme Court's 1898 *U.S. v. Wong Kim Ark*

253, Ch. 233. Currently, those born within the 50 states who are deemed outside U.S. jurisdiction are primarily the children born here to foreign diplomats.

[3] Congress made Hawaiians eligible for citizenship in 1900, Puerto Ricans in 1917, and inhabitants of the Virgin Islands in 1927. The 1965 Immigration and Nationality Act, with subsequent amendments, determines the citizenship of children born to U.S. citizens abroad.

[4] Automatic birthright citizenship is prevalent in the Western hemisphere from Canada through the Caribbean and Latin America, but it is highly contested and more limited in Europe. See the EUDO Citizenship legal database at http://eudo-citizenship.eu/databases/modes-of-acquisition [March 2015].

Calculation of the second generation draws from two different sources. Using American Community Survey data, it is estimated that in 2013, 17.4 million children under the age of 18 (25% of all children in the United States) had at least one foreign-born parent. Data from the Current Population Survey suggest that 19.7 million adults (8% of all people 18 years and older) have one or more immigrant parents. ACS estimates are from http://www.migrationpolicy.org/article/frequently-requested-statistics-immigrants-and-immigration-united-states#7 [August 2015]. CPS estimates are from http://www.pewsocialtrends.org/2013/02/07/second-generation-americans/ [August 2015].

[5] The U.S. Constitution of 1878 empowered the federal government to "establish a uniform Rule of Naturalization" (Article 1, Section 8).

[6] The 1790 Naturalization Act set a residency requirement of two years, which was raised to 14 years in 1798. An 1802 law mandated a minimum of 5 years of residence in the United States; this 5-year requirement remains to the present, with some exceptions.

(169 U.S. 649) decision did, however, uphold the birthright citizenship of children born in the United States to Asian immigrant parents ineligible for naturalization. Race-based restrictions on some Asian immigrants' ability to acquire U.S. citizenship through naturalization started to fall during World War II. The 1952 Immigration and Nationality Act definitely eliminated all race criteria for naturalization.

Latinos' social status as "nonwhite" also mattered in acquiring citizenship in the early 20th century. Legally, Mexicans were eligible for citizenship through naturalization. Unlike European immigrants, however, their eligibility was a product of foreign relations and treaties rather than any common acceptance of their "whiteness" (Fox, 2012). In fact, in 1930, only 9 percent of Mexican men living in the United States had naturalized, compared to 60 percent of southern and eastern Europeans and 80 percent of northern and western Europeans. A statistical analysis of 1930 census data found that a substantial proportion of the gap between Mexican and European naturalization levels was likely related to discrimination, net of differences in literacy, English ability, veteran status, or proximity to the homeland (Fox and Bloemraad, 2015).

Since the category of "undocumented" immigrant did not yet exist in this period, any male white immigrant was eligible for naturalization. Women's status was more complicated. The law did not limit eligibility by sex, but not all courts honored women's right to petition for citizenship. Women's citizenship was also often tied to their marital status and the citizenship of their husband.[7] Because the federal government only established administrative control over naturalization in 1906, there are no reliable data on the exact number of naturalizations during the 19th century, but the figure can be inferred to be in the millions. For example, in 1900 the U.S. Census reported that, just among the adult male population (21 years and older), more than 2.8 million of the 5 million foreign-born men held U.S. citizenship through naturalization (Gibson and Jung, 2006, p. 58).

From 1907 to 2000, 18.1 million people acquired U.S. citizenship through naturalization (U.S. Department of Homeland Security, 2002, p. 202). An important point is that when parents naturalize, their underage foreign-born children also acquire "derivative" citizenship through their parents. This fine point of law has generated hundreds of thousands of new U.S. citizens not counted in naturalization statistics.[8]

---

[7]At some historical moments, women automatically became citizens upon their marriage to a U.S. citizen or upon their husband's naturalization. This "derivative citizenship" was not possible if a woman's husband was racially ineligible for naturalization; and at some point in time, American women lost their U.S. citizenship upon marriage to a noncitizen (Smith, 1998).

[8]The regulations determining derivative citizenship have changed over time. See http://www. uscis.gov/policymanual/PDF/NationalityChart3.pdf [October 2015]. For children born on or after February 27, 2001, any child living in the United States in the legal and physical custody

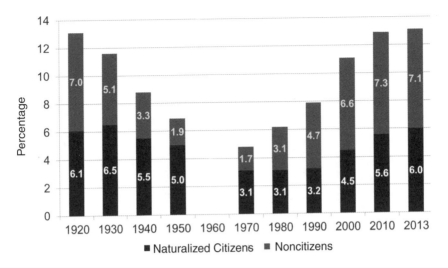

FIGURE 4-1 (Non)citizenship of the foreign-born in the United States (% of population).
SOURCE: Data from Gibson and Jung (2006); American Community Survey 2010, 2013.

Naturalization requirements have changed little since the 1952 Immigration Act, although the civics test underwent revisions in 2008 and the fee that would-be citizens must pay has increased substantially, from $95 in 1996 to $680 in 2015.[9] In 2013, 18.7 million immigrants, or 46 percent of the almost 40 million foreign-born residents living in the United States, had acquired U.S. citizenship through naturalization. This amounts to just under 6 percent of the U.S. population. Noncitizens, at over 22 million residents, constitute 7.1 percent of the U.S. population.[10]

The proportions of naturalized citizens and noncitizens in the population today almost exactly mirror the percentages in 1920, as shown in Figure 4-1, although the number of immigrants is much higher now. After

---

of a citizen parent currently derives citizenship from their parent if they are under the age of 18. An accurate count of these new child citizens is difficult to determine since the form filed for derivative citizenship, the N-600, is the same one filed by U.S.-citizen parents living abroad who seek proof of citizenship for their children. Some parents also never seek a Certificate of Citizenship but acquire passports for their children by showing their child's foreign birth certificate and the parent's naturalization certificate. Over the 10-year period from 2004 to 2013, USCIS received 602,943 N-600 applications. (Personal communication to the panel from Delancey Gustin, August 2014, U.S. Citizenship and Naturalization Service.)

[9] The current fee (2015) is $595 for filing the N-400 form plus $85 for capturing required biometric data.

[10] These figures are from the 2013 3-year estimates from the American Community Survey.

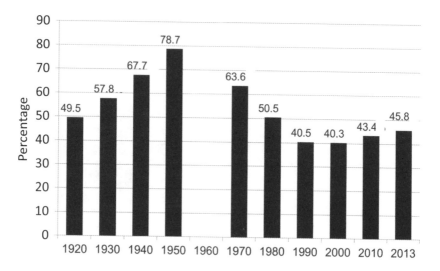

FIGURE 4-2 Naturalization levels among foreign-born residents of the United States, 1920-2013 (% naturalized).
SOURCE: Data from Gibson and Jung (2006); American Community Survey 2010, 2013.

immigration was curtailed in the 1920s and as the foreign-born population aged, the level of citizenship among the immigrant population increased, but the share of naturalized citizens and noncitizens in the general population declined. With the resumption of large-scale migration after 1965, citizenship levels among foreign-born residents dropped precipitously as newcomers flowed into the country, from 64 percent of all foreign-born in 1970 to 40 percent in 2000 (see Figures 4-1 and 4-2). Because citizenship levels are often calculated as the number of naturalized citizens among the total foreign-born population, some of the apparent decline in the fraction of foreign-born who are naturalized—though far from all of the decline—is due to an increase in the number of undocumented and temporary immigrants, groups that are barred from naturalization.

CITIZENSHIP IN A GLOBAL WORLD

Some observers note a decline in the importance of citizenship within a more global world (Jacobson, 1996; Schuck, 1998; Soysal, 1994; Spiro, 2010), which might reduce immigrants' interest in naturalization. Yet the advantages of U.S. citizenship remain significant and have arguably increased over the last 20 years, making it doubtful that this factor fully explains declines in naturalization over time. The benefits of U.S. citizenship include protection from deportation, broader rights in the judicial system, greater access to social benefits, the ability to sponsor immigrant parents or minor children to the United States outside the annual immigration quotas, greater access to educational loans and scholarships, the ability to travel with a U.S. passport, more favorable tax treatment for estate taxes, and the ability to vote and run for office. Another benefit is eligibility for certain jobs or occupations in government, the defense industry, and military that are barred to noncitizens. Research suggests that U.S. citizenship also improves employment outcomes, wage growth, and access to better jobs (Bratsberg et al., 2002; OECD, 2011; Mazzolari, 2009).[11] Across a range of studies, the wage premium of citizenship, holding other personal attributes constant, was estimated to be at least 5 percent (Sumpton and Flamm, 2012). Conversely, even if an immigrant is not a U.S. citizen, he or she is still obligated to pay taxes, obey all U.S. laws and, historically, noncitizens have been drafted into the U.S. military. Considering the advantages and the United States' long history as a nation of immigrants, the declining level of citizenship acquisition is surprising.

There is, however, evidence of a recent uptick in the level of citizenship. Estimates by the Office of Immigration Statistics of the immigrant population eligible for naturalization—adjusting for those who are not legal permanent residents or who have not met the 5-year residency requirement—suggest that in 2002, 50 percent of eligible immigrants held U.S. citizenship, while in 2012, the proportion had risen to 58 percent (see Figure 4-3). Some observers explain this increase as "defensive" or "protective" naturalization undertaken by immigrants worried about legislative changes that target noncitizens (Aptekar, 2015; Gilbertson and Singer, 2003; Massey and Pren, 2012; Nam and Kim, 2012). This effect might be especially dramatic among Latino immigrants, particularly as community-based and advocacy groups mobilize in the face of perceived anti-immigrant legislation (Cort 2012). From 2000 through 2009, over 6.8 million immigrants became U.S. citizens, and from 2010 through 2013, naturalizations averaged 713,000 per year.[12] Of course, these numbers do not include new citizens' foreign-born minor children, who automatically derive U.S. citizenship upon their parents' naturalization.

Despite the increase in naturalization since 2000, the level of citizenship in the United States—the proportion of naturalized citizens among

---

[11] Bratsberg and colleagues (2002) studied young male immigrants and found that following naturalization, these new U.S. citizens gain greater access to public-sector, white-collar, and union jobs, which helps accelerate wage growth.

[12] These data are from the 2013 *Yearbook of Immigration Statistics*, Table 20, Office of Immigration Statistics, U.S. Department of Homeland Security. See http://www.dhs.gov/publication/yearbook-immigration-statistics-2013-naturalizations [October 2015].

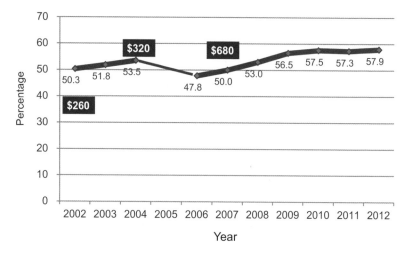

FIGURE 4-3 Percentage of immigrants who acquired U.S. citizenship among those eligible, and fees for I-40 application, 2002-2012.
SOURCE: Data from Office of Immigration Statistics "Estimates of the Legal Permanent Resident Population," for 2002 through 2012 (2005 missing).

the immigrant population—remains much lower than in some other major immigrant-receiving countries. The overall level of citizenship among working-age immigrants (15-64 years old) living in the United States for at least 10 years is, at 50 percent, below the average across 15 OECD countries, which stands at 61 percent (OECD, 2011, p. 28). After adjustments to account for the undocumented population, a group with very limited pathways to citizenship, naturalization among U.S. immigrants rises to slightly above the OECD average. Nevertheless, it still stands far below European countries such as the Netherlands (78%) and Sweden (82%), and much lower than traditional countries of immigration such as Australia (81%) and Canada (89%) (OECD, 2011, pp. 27-28). Cross-national differences in naturalization levels are in part due to compositional differences between countries based on variation in immigrants' origins, time in country, human capital, and migration status (Bloemraad, 2006a; Picot and Hou, 2011; OECD, 2011), as well as differences in citizenship laws, regulations, and bureaucratic cultures (Vink et al., 2013; Dronkers and Vink, 2012; Janoski, 2010). There is also some limited evidence that broader public policies related to multiculturalism and public-private partnerships around immigrant integration lead to higher levels of citizenship among immigrants, even after holding immigrants' characteristics and naturalization policy constant (Bloemraad, 2006b). The United States has relatively open citizenship policies, and even controlling for immigrants' characteristics, the level of naturalization in the United States appears to sit in the middle of the pack for highly developed, immigrant-receiving countries.

Who Naturalizes and Why?

When asked, the vast majority of immigrant respondents to surveys say that they want to naturalize. Two national surveys of Hispanic immigrants found that more than 9 in 10 noncitizen Latinos would want to naturalize if they could (Gonzalez-Barrera et al., 2013; Pantoja and Gershon, 2006). A survey of immigrant women born in Latin American, Asian, African, and Arab countries found that 84 percent of respondents wanted to be a U.S. citizen rather than remaining a citizen of their home country (New America Media, 2009, p. 31). Reasons for not naturalizing ranged from language, financial, and administrative barriers to not having had the time to apply or not understanding the application process. Of those who did apply for citizenship over a 10-year period from 2004 to 2013, 12 percent of applicants were denied, a percentage that is half of the 24 percent denied from 1990 to 2003 but still five or six times higher than denials in the 1970s and 1980s.[13] Gender also plays a role in naturalization. Women are more likely to naturalize than men (Ruiz et al., 2015), may have different motivations for naturalizing (Pantoja and Gershon, 2006), and experience the naturalization process differently (Salcido and Menjívar, 2012; Singer and Gilberston, 2003); all these factors contribute to gender differences in naturalization. Immigrants' previous statuses also influence their decisions: previous experience with undocumented status appears to be a motivating factor for immigrants' intention to stay in the United States, while immigrants who come to the United States on employment visas are the least likely to express an intention to stay (Jasso, 2011). Overall, moderate levels of naturalization in the United States appear to stem not from immigrants' lack of interest or even primarily from the bureaucratic process of applying for citizenship. Instead the obstacle to naturalization lies somewhere in the process by which individuals translate their motivation to naturalize into action, and research has so far failed to clearly identify this obstacle.

One of the strongest predictors of citizenship acquisition is time spent

---

[13]The data presented here are based on adjusted data on petition denials (data provided by personal communication to the panel by Michael Hoefner, August 2014, U.S. Citizenship and Immigration Service). This differs somewhat from published data (Table 20 of the 2013 *Yearbook*). Although historical calculations are tricky because what counts as a naturalization petition "denial" has changed over time, based on the available data it appears that petition denials climbed significantly in the 1990s and early 2000s and declined slightly in the past 5 years.

in the United States: the longer immigrants reside in the country, the more likely they are to become naturalized citizens (Bloemraad, 2006b). One reason is the requirement to prove 5 years of residence as an LPR before being allowed to naturalize.[14] On average, however, immigrants wait longer than 5 years before filing N-400 forms. In 2013, the median new citizen had held LPR status for 7 years, a bit longer than the 6-year median in 2008 and 2009 but shorter than the 9 years of LPR status for immigrants naturalizing in 1995 or 2000 (Lee and Foreman, 2014). Median years in LPR status does not, however, capture the length of stay among noncitizens, which can range from less than a year to decades. Other data hint that long-time noncitizens are naturalizing at increasing rates. In 2002, only 46.5 percent of immigrants eligible for citizenship who had lived in the United States for at least 12 years were naturalized citizens; in 2012, the level of citizenship among these long-term residents had increased to 58 percent.[15]

Length of residency also captures other integration processes. Over time, immigrants with limited English might improve their language skills sufficiently to feel confident about applying for citizenship. Some migrants who initially saw their move to the United States as temporary put down roots, have families, buy homes, and get settled, increasing their interest in naturalization. Immigrants provide myriad reasons for acquiring U.S. citizenship, including the desire to secure civil and legal rights, to travel on a U.S. passport, to access social benefits or economic opportunities, or to sponsor overseas family members to come to the United States (Aptekar, 2015; Bloemraad, 2006b; Gilbertson and Singer, 2003; Gonzalez-Barrera et al., 2013; New American Media, 2009). Although the evidence on political participation is mixed (e.g., New American Media, 2009, p. 32), some research suggests that stressing the importance of voting, civic engagement, and being politically informed could increase naturalization (Pantoja and Gershon, 2006).[16] Immigrants also naturalize to reflect a sense of American identity, a feeling of being at home or the belief that it is just "the right thing to do," even if they also retain, in many cases, a strong attachment to their homeland or national origin identity (Aptekar, 2015; Bloemraad, 2006a; Brettel, 2006).

---

[14]There are some exceptions to the 5-year minimum residency requirement for those in the military, and for the spouses of U.S. citizens. In the latter case, the minimum residency requirement is reduced to 3 years.

[15]Panel's calculations of percentages use data from Rytina (2004, 2012).

[16]Other studies have found a higher percentage of immigrants listing the right to vote as a major reason to acquire citizenship. Almost 7 in 10 naturalized U.S. citizens in a random-digit telephone survey in the Dallas-Fort Worth area mentioned voting as among the "major" reasons they naturalized (Brettell, 2006, p. 83), and in a nonprobability sample of immigrants exiting a USCIS office, 46 percent cited the right to vote (Aptekar, 2015, p. 69).

Diverging Integration Pathways? Barriers to Naturalization

Some observers wonder whether rising naturalization fees are hurting immigrants' integration as they are priced out of citizenship (Catholic Legal Immigration Network, Inc., 2007; Pastor et al., 2013; Emanuel and Gutierrez, 2013). In 1994, the cost of filing an N-400 form was $95. The fee rose to $225 in 1999, $320 in 2004, and $595 in 2007.[17] This fee does not include a mandatory biometric fee of $85. Fee increases reflect congressional intent that immigration services be cost-neutral to taxpayers; immigrants' filing fees are supposed to cover administrative costs. In 2010, the U.S. naturalization fee was the sixth most expensive of 34 countries across Europe, Australia, and Canada; the median fee in these countries was about $220 (Goodman, 2010, p. 24; Bogdan, 2012).[18] Surveys of Latino immigrants eligible for citizenship found that about one-fifth cite cost as a primary reason that they had not filed a naturalization application (Freeman et al., 2002; Gonzalez-Barrera et al., 2013).

A cursory glance at citizenship trends does not suggest a negative relationship between cost increases and naturalization. As noted above, the aggregate citizenship level in the United States has been rising over the last 15 years, albeit modestly (Haddal, 2007; Kandel and Haddal, 2010; Figure 4-3). However, there is clear evidence of "bumps" in N-400 filings shortly before announced fee increases, and some sensitivity to the relative cost of renewing LPR status (filing the I-90 form) versus the cost of naturalization.[19] Immigrants likely have some "price sensitivity" to naturalization fees.[20] In response to concerns about fees, the White House Task Force

---

[17]USCIS adjusted its fee schedule at least 14 times between 1969 and 2007. Most were minor adjustments to reflect inflation. The 1998, 2004, and 2007 adjustments were significant increases beyond the inflation rate. In 2007, USCIS increased fees by an average of 88 percent for each immigration benefit (Haddal, 2007).

[18]The median naturalization fee was about 163 Euros; this equaled US$ 222 based on the exchange rate in November 2010.

[19]Lawful permanent residents must renew their "green cards" every 10 years by filing an I-90 form. From 1994 to 2007, the N-400 fee rose from $95 to $595, an increase of 626 percent; the fee for the I-90 rose from $75 to $290, or an increase of 387 percent (Pastor et al., 2013, p. 6). The difference was mitigated somewhat in 2011, when the I-90 fee rose to $365 but the N-400 filing fee remained stable.

[20]Wait times in processing naturalization applications can also be a frustration, though there is no evidence that this poses a hard barrier to citizenship. In the mid-1990s, the Immigration and Naturalization Service was projecting 3-year wait periods to citizenship. In 2001, the U.S. General Accounting Office estimated backlogs of 21 months for would-be citizens (U.S. General Accounting Office, 2001, pp. 6, 23). Current processing times range from 5 months in places such as Charlotte, North Carolina, and Boston, Massachusetts, to 9 months in Santa Ana, California, and Atlanta, Georgia. Processing time information is from March 6, 2015, as posted on the USCIS website at https://egov.uscis.gov/cris/processTimesDisplayInit. do [October 2015].

on New Americans (2015) recently recommended that USCIS assess the potential for expanding its fee waiver program, as well as allowing naturalization applicants to pay fees with credit cards. However, the effects of these potential changes are not yet known.

Price sensitivity raises important questions over inequities in civic and political integration. The recent uptick in naturalization appears to hide a deepening divide in the path to citizenship, a path that is relatively smooth for more affluent, educated immigrants and a bumpy, obstacle-ridden road for those facing more significant personal and financial barriers.

Immigrants with less education, lower incomes, and poorer English skills are less likely to acquire U.S. citizenship (e.g., Aptekar, 2014; Bueker, 2006; Bloemraad, 2006b; Chiswick and Miller, 2008; Logan et al., 2012; Pantoja and Gershon, 2006). Currently, immigrants with an income below 150 percent of the poverty level or who have a qualified family member receiving means-tested benefits can ask for a fee waiver in filing the N-400 form.[21] The panel made a formal request to USCIS for data on how many ask for and receive fee waivers, but USCIS was unable to provide the data. A recent analysis did find that while 32 percent of the population eligible to naturalize fell below this poverty threshold, poor immigrants only made up 26 percent of those who naturalized in 2011 and 2012 (Pastor et al., 2015, p. 7). In contrast, those with incomes two and a half times the poverty line or higher made up 53 percent of those recently naturalized, but only 45 percent of the pool of eligible immigrants. Thus, low or modest income might be a barrier to naturalization despite the fee waiver.

Differences become starker when it comes to education. Democratic equality is predicated on the idea that all citizens are equal, regardless of income or education. But limited education makes it less likely that an immigrant acquires U.S. citizenship. Language requirements tend to be a bigger barrier for those with less than a high school degree; government forms are complex and written in technical language; and those with less education often worry about passing the civics test (Bloemraad, 2006a; Gonzalez-Barrera et al., 2013). Although success rates for the English and civics test appear high—91 percent of those who took these tests in November 2014 passed—many immigrants with limited education and low English proficiency probably never reach the test stage because they are afraid to do so or the administrative process appears too daunting.[22]

---

[21] For details, see http://www.uscis.gov/feewaiver [October 2015].

[22] USCIS publishes the national pass rate and average naturalization processing time on its webpage. See http://www.uscis.gov/us-citizenship/naturalization-test/applicant-performance-naturalization-test [March 2015]. Some observers have wondered whether the redesigned civics test, introduced in 2008, created higher barriers to citizenship acquisition. Analysis of pass rates among those who took the test in 2010 compared to two earlier groups shows greater success in 2010 (ICF International, 2011). While the analysis could not directly judge

Educational barriers might also be getting worse. One analysis, based on Decennial Census and American Community Survey data from 1970 to 2000, found that the educational penalty for those with less than a high school education, holding other naturalization determinants constant, increased between 1970 and 2000 (Aptekar, 2014, p. 350). In 1970, the probability that an immigrant with less than a high school degree held U.S. citizenship was 0.42; by 2000, this had plummeted to 0.18.[23] The drop moderates after attempts to adjust for undocumented migration, but the trend remains: a naturalization probability of 0.45 in 1970 for someone with less than a high school education falls to 0.31 in 2000 (Aptekar, 2014, p. 352). Strikingly, over this period, citizenship levels in Canada increased regardless of educational background: the probability of becoming a Canadian citizen for an immigrant with less than a high school education was 0.43 in 1971; in 2001, it was 0.76 (Aptekar, 2014, p. 352). A different analysis, using more recent 2011 American Community Survey data, suggests a similar story of growing educational inequality. Immigrants in the United States with limited education—less than a high school education—became less likely to naturalize from 1996 to 2010; over this same period, those with high levels of education—a bachelor degree or beyond—became more likely to acquire citizenship (Pastor et al., 2013, p. 13; Logan et al., 2012).

It is not the case, however, that the immigrants most likely to become U.S. citizens are the rich and very highly educated. Foreign-born residents with 4-year college degrees and especially those with professional or advanced academic degrees are less likely to naturalize than foreign-born high school graduates or those with only an associate degree, holding other factors constant (Logan et al., 2012; Pastor et al., 2013). Immigrants from rich countries with high levels of political freedom and economic development are also less likely, all else considered, to naturalize (Bueker, 2006; Chiswick and Miller, 2008; Logan et al., 2012; OECD, 2011). It is possible, given significant educational resources and affluent, safe countries to which they can return, that the most privileged immigrants see fewer advantages in U.S. citizenship. A survey of a cohort of immigrants who received lawful permanent resident status in 2003 found that while 78 percent of the entire cohort intended to stay in the United States indefinitely, the percentage who were uncertain or did not foresee staying was the largest, at 34 percent,

---

if test success varied by applicants' level of education, other demographics—by gender, age and region of origin—all showed higher pass rates in 2010. The analysis could not evaluate whether certain groups were less likely to file for citizenship given the redesigned test.

[23] These predicted probabilities hold constant other potential determinants of naturalization, such as age, length of residence in the country, marital status, gender, and income.

among those gaining LPR status through employment pathways, a path dominated by the high-skilled.[24]

Conversely, among those most likely to naturalize are immigrants who serve in or are veterans of the U.S. military. According to Barry (2014), the Immigration and Nationality Act of 1952 gives the President authority to expedite naturalization for noncitizen service members. Residency periods, usually 5 years, can be cut to 3 years or even a day of active-duty service; in some cases, citizenship is bestowed posthumously to a service member killed in the line of duty. Physical presence requirements can be a roadblock to naturalization for those serving overseas, but especially during times of conflict, application fees have been waived and special processing centers set up at military installations. This was the case during World War I and more recently during conflicts in Iraq and Afghanistan. Barry (2014) notes that during World War I, over 500,000 immigrants were drafted into military service and more than 192,000 immigrants acquired citizenship through military service, accounting for over half of all naturalizations during the period. Analysis of census data from 1930 confirms that veteran status was a significant predictor of men's naturalization, even controlling for personal resources and country of origin (Fox and Bloemraad, 2015). This predictive power for veteran status appears to be continuing. An analysis of 1980 Decennial Census data underscored the significant influence of veteran status on citizenship acquisition (Yang, 1994); more recent research estimated that veteran status is associated with a 13 percentage point increase in the probability of naturalization among men and an 8 percentage point increase for women (Chiswick and Miller, 2008, p. 116). In the 75 years from 1939 through 2013, 424,315 members of the U.S. armed forces became U.S. citizens (1.9% of all successful naturalizations).[25] Between September 2002 and May 2013, 89,095 noncitizens serving in U.S. armed forces naturalized, with 10,719 naturalizations occurring at USCIS citizenship ceremonies in 28 countries, including Afghanistan, Djibouti, El Salvador, Haiti, Iraq, Kenya, Mexico, the Philippines, and South Korea (Barry, 2014).[26]

---

[24] Calculated from data provided by Guillermina Jasso in personal communication to the panel, March 2015.

[25] Panel's calculation from data reported in the 2013 *Yearbook of Immigration Statistics*, Table 20, Office of Immigration Statistics, U.S. Department of Homeland Security. See http://www.dhs.gov/publication/yearbook-immigration-statistics-2013-naturalizations [October 2015].

[26] See http://www.uscis.gov/news/fact-sheets/naturalization-through-military-service-fact-sheet [August 2015].

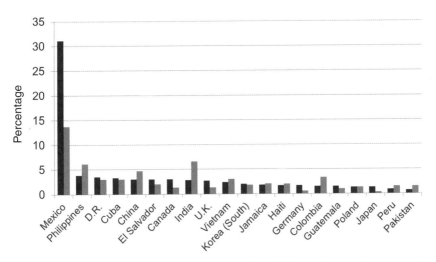

FIGURE 4-4 National origin proportions in the eligible and naturalized populations, 2011.
NOTE: Dark shading = eligible populations, light shading = naturalized populations.
SOURCES: Panel's calculations from Lee and Foreman (2014, Table 1); Rytina (2012, Table 4).

National Origins and Global Changes Around Multiple Citizenship

Of all immigrants who acquired citizenship in 2013, the largest group, almost 100,000 people out of 780,000 successful applicants, were born in Mexico (Lee and Foreman, 2014). Not surprisingly, other countries among the top five from which new citizens originate are also among the largest sources of migration to the United States: India, the Philippines, the Dominican Republic, and the People's Republic of China. However, their relative share of immigrants in the pool eligible to naturalize does not necessarily reflect that country's share of immigrants who acquire U.S. citizenship. For 2011, the Office of Immigration Statistics estimated that 31.1 percent of all LPRs eligible for naturalization were born in Mexico. But data on successful naturalization applications indicate that only 13.7 percent of immigrants receiving U.S. citizenship in 2011 were Mexican born.[27] Relative to their share of the eligible LPR population, immigrants from El Salvador and Guatemala were also less likely to naturalize, as were immigrants from Canada, Japan, and the United Kingdom. Conversely, as Figure 4-4 shows, the proportion of new American citizens from India,

---

[27]These statistics, and those that follow, are drawn from comparing Rytina (2012), Table 4, with Lee and Foreman (2014), Table 1.

Colombia, and Pakistan was more than twice each country's proportion in the pool of eligible LPRs in 2011. For example, those born in India were 2.8 percent of all eligible LPRs, but the Indian-born made up 6.6 percent of all newly naturalized Americans in 2011.

These differences by country of origin are explained in part by factors discussed earlier. Immigrants from certain countries are more likely to have modest levels of education, which depresses the rate of naturalization, while nationals of wealthy, stable democracies such as Japan and the United Kingdom might see fewer benefits to acquiring U.S. citizenship. Proximity to the United States and a concomitant belief that an immigrant will return to his or her home country probably also play a role: those born in Canada and Mexico have, over the past 35 years, consistently had low levels of naturalization and among the longest median wait times between acquiring LPR status and acquiring U.S. citizenship. In contrast, migrants who arrive as refugees are more likely to naturalize (Fix et al., 2003; Woodrow-Lafield et al., 2004). Research suggests that they are more likely to appreciate the security of U.S. citizenship, more likely to be escaping desperate conditions in their country of origin, and more likely to feel a strong sense of gratitude or attachment to the country that gave them refuge (Bloemraad, 2006a; Portes and Curtis, 1987). Legal status also plays a role because immigrants who are undocumented or present with various temporary statuses are barred from applying for LPR and therefore naturalizing—a barrier that affects a greater proportion of immigrants from Latin America than from other regions (see Chapter 3).

The citizenship laws of immigrants' homelands also affect naturalization in the United States. Countries around the world increasingly allow nationals who migrate and seek another citizenship to hold dual or multiple nationalities. Legal changes permitting dual citizenship appear to increase immigrants' propensity to naturalize (Chiswick and Miller, 2008; Jones-Correa, 2001a; Mazzolari, 2009; Naujoks, 2012). Mazzolari (2009) estimated a 10 percentage point increase in the 1990s in naturalization among migrants from Colombia, the Dominican Republic, Ecuador, Costa Rica, and Brazil when those countries changed their laws. Naujoks (2012) calculated a 2 to 13 percentage point increase in naturalization of immigrants from India following creation of the "Overseas Citizenship of India" status in 2005. Dual citizenship laws may also lead to racial differences in naturalization rates by increasing the probability of naturalization for Latino and Asian immigrants, but it might not do the same for non-Hispanic white or black immigrants, holding other factors constant (Logan et al., 2012). To the extent that naturalization promotes career gains and income benefits, home-country dual citizenship laws produce the largest increase in naturalization and employment success among more educated immigrants

(Mazzolari, 2009), perhaps because these immigrants can best leverage the benefits of transnational activities.

The U.S. recognizes but does not encourage multiple nationality. Immigrants who naturalize in the United States pledge, when swearing the Oath of Allegiance, to "absolutely and entirely renounce and abjure all allegiance and fidelity to any foreign prince, potentate, state, or sovereignty, of whom or which I have heretofore been a subject or citizen."[28] Through the early 1960s, the U.S. State Department could strip away the citizenship of an American who acquired another nationality. However, Supreme Court decisions have upheld the legality of multiple citizenships, and today the U.S. State Department explicitly advises that "U.S. law does not mention dual nationality or require a person to choose one nationality or another. . . . The U.S. Government recognizes that dual nationality exists but does not encourage it as a matter of policy because of the problems it may cause."[29] Since people can acquire multiple nationalities in a variety of ways, including marriage to a foreign national, having a parent or grandparent of another nationality, or the birth country's continued presumption of nationality even after acquisition of U.S. citizenship, many Americans, both immigrants and native-born, may legally hold multiple citizenships, even if they do not formally request multiple passports.

The Social and Civic Context of Naturalization

Academic research and policy attention have focused primarily on how the rules and regulations of naturalization, such as the filing fee or civics and language tests, affect immigrants' interest in and ability to acquire citizenship, or how personal factors, such as limited formal education, might make it more difficult for some immigrants to become citizens than others. Missing from these accounts is the important role played by family and friends; the immigrant community; nonprofit organizations; and other groups including for-profit businesses, employers, and unions in encouraging and helping immigrants become citizens and thereby fostering civic and political integration.

When asked to elaborate on their path to citizenship, immigrants—especially those who face the highest barriers to naturalization—often tell stories of how a child, family member, or local nonprofit organization helped them to study for the language or civics exam and how a community social service provider, a refugee resettlement agency or a for-profit

---

[28] The full text of the oath can be found at http://www.uscis.gov/us-citizenship/naturalization-test/naturalization-oath-allegiance-united-states-america [October 2015].

[29] Full text available at http://travel.state.gov/content/travel/english/legal-considerations/us-citizenship-laws-policies/citizenship-and-dual-nationality/dual-nationality.html [October 2015].

notario helped them to fill in paperwork (Bloemraad, 2006a; Plascencia, 2012). Consistent with such stories, statistical analyses of census data have found that a 1 percent increase in the share of co-ethnic immigrants who are naturalized in a metropolitan area increases an individual immigrant's odds of naturalization by 2.5 percent (Logan et al., 2012, p. 548; see also Liang, 1994). In one targeted effort, the Open Society Institute received $50 million from philanthropist George Soros to facilitate citizenship, distributing grants through the Emma Lazarus Fund to organizations, such as the Catholic Legal Immigration Network, Inc., Council of Jewish Federations, National Council of La Raza, and International Rescue Committee. The Open Society Institute estimated that within 2 years over half a million immigrants had been assisted in beginning the naturalization process (Catholic Legal Immigration Network, Inc., 2007, p. 106).

More recently, the New American Workforce initiative, through the National Immigration Forum, is working with businesses to assist their eligible immigrant employees with the citizenship process.[30] This assistance continues a tradition from a century earlier, when major employers such as Bethlehem Steel and Ford Motor Company provided English-language classes to their immigrant workforce, a practice continued in the 21st century by some manufacturers, grocery stores, and hospitals, in partnership with local nonprofits or community colleges (Catholic Legal Immigration Network, Inc., 2007, p. 169; Schneider, 2011).

Civil society initiatives can be carried out by nonprofits, businesses, religious institutions, ethnic media, schools, or other organizations in partnership with multiple levels of government, from the local and county levels to state and federal government. Civil society initiatives might be particularly effective when done in partnership with government, as happens with refugee resettlement (Bloemraad, 2006a). A national study estimated that refugees are one and a half times more likely to become citizens than are eligible legal immigrants with similar socioeconomic and demographic characteristics (Fix et al., 2003, p. 6). In one case, the Office of Refugee Resettlement worked with Catholic Legal Immigration Network, Inc., to help 5,385 refugees file naturalization applications (Catholic Legal Immigration Network, Inc., 2007, p. 111). Similar public-private partnerships—often but not always targeting refugees or elderly immigrants—have been spearheaded by state governments in Florida, Illinois, and Massachusetts.

Beyond the refugee community, federal leadership in U.S. citizenship promotion has only developed recently, and at a very modest level. Various observers, ranging from academics and nonprofit leaders to the U.S. Government Accountability Office, have underscored that the United States has no articulated or coordinated integration policy, including policy on citizen-

---

[30] See http://immigrationforum.org/programs/new-american-workforce/ [June 2015].

ship promotion, but rather that federal involvement is characterized by a patchwork of policies, agencies, and actors and a largely *laissez-faire* orientation (e.g., Bloemraad and de Graauw, 2012; Catholic Legal Immigration Network, Inc., 2007; U.S. Government Accountability Office, 2011). For instance, the White House Task Force on New Americans (2015) identified 58 immigrant integration programs administered by 10 different federal agencies in its recent report.

The Office of Citizenship, a branch of USCIS, was established by the Homeland Security Act of 2002 with the mission "to engage and support partners to welcome immigrants, promote English language learning and education on the rights and responsibilities of citizenship, and encourage U.S. citizenship." A 2007 analysis concluded that with a budget of $3 million, the Office of Citizenship had produced useful informational products (Catholic Legal Immigration Network, Inc., 2007, p. 128), but given a budget equivalent to what the state of Illinois spent that year on citizenship promotion, such educational activities were inadequate to a task that spans the entire nation. The recent report from the White House Task Force on New Americans (2015) recommends that USCIS explore additional opportunities to inform LPRs of their potential eligibility for naturalization, expand its citizenship outreach efforts, offer mobile services, and create online tools to assist naturalization preparation and application filing. It is unclear whether any additional funding will become available for these efforts.

In more recent years, federal support for naturalization through the Office of Citizenship remains anemic, and demand for these grants far outstrips the available funding. In fiscal 2009, for example, the program received 293 applications for $1.2 million in grants, with only 13 organizations funded. In 2011, 324 applications were received and 42 organizations were granted a total of $9 million (U.S. Government Accountability Office, 2011, p. 15). As Table 4-1 shows, the total of all grants awarded under this program for the six fiscal years from 2009 through 2014 was $43.2 million. This is less than the $50 million granted by the privately funded Lazarus Fund initiative and far less than neighboring Canada spends on integration efforts, even though the United States has many more immigrants than Canada.[31] Furthermore, since the Citizenship and Integration Grant Program has no authorizing statute, officials in the Office of Citizenship are unsure year to year whether the program can continue.

Public support for integration not only provides assistance in navigating the naturalization process but also sends the message that governments welcome and want to encourage civic integration. The lack of such federal support in the United States might partially explain the substantial gap in

---

[31] Leslie Seidle (2010, p. 4) estimates that in Canada's 2010-2011 fiscal year, the Canadian federal government allocated over CAD$1 billion to promoting the integration of newcomers.

TABLE 4-1 Grants Awarded by the Office of Citizenship through the USCIS Citizenship and Integration Grant Program

Fiscal Year	Number of Organizations Funded	Total Grants Awarded (in $)
2009	13	1,200,000
2010	78	8,100,000
2011	42	9,000,000
2012	31	5,000,000
2013	40	9,900,000
2014	40	10,000,000

SOURCE: Data from U.S. Department of Homeland Security, Office of Citizenship data. Available: http://www.uscis.gov/archive/archive-citizenship/citizenship-and-integration-grant-program-archives [August 2015].

citizenship levels compared with Canada, as well as the starker differences in naturalization between less-educated and more educated immigrants in the United States discussed above in this chapter (Bloemraad, 2006a; Aptekar, 2010).

Some research does suggest that immigrants living in more welcoming environments are more likely to become U.S. citizens. Following devolution of public assistance programs in 1996 (see Chapter 2), immigrant naturalization increased not just among poorer immigrants who might have wanted to secure benefits but also among all LPR residents. And there is evidence that acquisition of U.S. citizenship increased most for those with more education and better economic situations (Van Hook et al., 2006; Nam and Kim, 2012). Furthermore, naturalization among immigrants living in states with the strongest anti-immigrant attitudes among the general population, as measured by responses to General Social Survey (GSS) questions on immigration, rose less than among immigrants in states with more positive attitudes, a finding that holds whether researchers use data from the Survey of Program Dynamics (Van Hook et al., 2006) or use U.S. Census 2000 microfile data (Logan et al., 2012). States with lower political participation barriers have higher naturalization rates, perhaps because a more open institutional environment signals that civic and political engagement is encouraged and valued (Jones-Correa, 2001b). An analysis of longitudinal data in Los Angeles County indicated that anti-immigrant legislation might spur a modest increase in immigrants' likelihood to take out citizenship as a defensive measure, but that citizenship levels go up more dramatically after the perceived threat diminishes (Cort, 2012). All these studies support a conclusion that the acquisition of citizenship is not just a matter of immigrants' personal characteristics but also depends on the welcome they are given by the native-born populations and by organizations in the broader civil society.[32]

Beyond Legal Citizenship: Feeling American

Holding U.S. citizenship is a legal status, but it can also be considered a marker of national identity. Asked in the GSS whether having American citizenship is important for being "truly American," 94 percent of U.S.-born respondents in 1996 and 80 percent in 2004 answered affirmatively. Immigrants, however, might feel or identify as American without citizenship. In the same GSS surveys, a majority of foreign-born respondents (76% in 1996 and 59% in 2004) said that citizenship was not important for being "truly American." Interviews with immigrants engaged in the naturalization process find that many feel American not because they are becoming citizens but because they have built a life in their adopted country. They see citizenship as a natural and commonsense step in their overall settlement process (Aptekar, 2015). Thus immigrants who are not citizens—and indeed, not to have legal status—may nonetheless feel American (Bloemraad, 2013).[33]

Like naturalization, feeling American is a story both about the personal views and orientations of immigrants and about the attitudes of native-born citizens. An extensive survey undertaken in 2004 asked over 2,700 U.S. residents what should be important in making someone "truly American" (Schildkraut, 2011). Almost one in five respondents said being Christian should be very important. When asked whether having European ancestors or being white should be very or somewhat important, 17 and 10 percent, respectively, answered yes. These percentages are small but represent a view of "being American" that excludes large segments of the immigrant population. More positively, 80 percent of respondents said that "respecting other people's cultural differences" should be very important to being truly American, and 73 percent agreed that "seeing people of all backgrounds

---

[32] There is evidence that in the early 20th century the naturalization of European immigrants was also linked to how warmly, or punitively, a state treated noncitizens. More punitive contexts, which raised the cost of noncitizenship, did not encourage higher levels of naturalization; rather, immigrants were more likely to acquire citizenship where the local political and social context was more welcoming (Bloemraad, 2006c).

[33] In perhaps the most prominent example of redefining what it means to be American, Jose Antonio Vargas, an undocumented immigrant from the Philippines, started the "Define American" project in 2011, to craft a narrative of American identity based on social membership and contributions to American society. See http://www.defineamerican.com/page/about/about-defineamerican [October 2015].

as American" was very important. Comparing the answers given by different people who participated in the survey, Schildkraut (2011) concluded that there is significant overlap between the views of people from different ethnoracial backgrounds and immigrant generations; to the extent that different views exist about what ought to be at the heart of being American, differences tend to align with people's political partisanship, ideologies, and level of education, not their ethnic or immigrant background. Thus both immigrants and native-born Americans tend to agree with a vision of being American that is not based on culture, religion, or even citizenship status. Instead, there is broad agreement that being American is defined by a common commitment to the ideals of diversity and multiculturalism. This suggests a more open culture of acceptance of immigrants and their descendants beyond legal definitions of belonging, with differences in attitudes on these measures explained more by ideology than by race or ethnicity.

Naturalization as Part of Civic and Political Integration

In sum, a striking drop in the share of immigrants taking up U.S. citizenship from 1970 through to 2000 seems to be reversing course, albeit slowly. Although clear explanations for the low naturalization rate among eligible immigrants are still lacking, research does indicate that socioeconomic status matters: for example, those with more education—a frequently used indicator of socioeconomic status—have an easier time with the process, while those who already face other barriers to integration also have more difficulty with the naturalization process. Legal status also matters, as one in four immigrants in the United States is prevented by law from pursuing citizenship (see Chapter 2). This legal barrier is problematic because the vast majority of immigrants, when surveyed, report wanting to become a U.S. citizen. It also flies in the face of a democratic ideal of civic equality, regardless of background or personal resources. Given some evidence linking naturalization with better labor market outcomes, and current laws preventing noncitizens from voting or running for office, lack of citizenship also implicates weaker economic and political integration.

A bright spot in this mixed picture is civic integration through the Fourteenth Amendment, which guarantees the birthright of citizenship to virtually everyone born in the United States, regardless of origins or parents' legal status. This "birthplace citizenship" ensures a basic level of political incorporation of the second generation and, given the advantages citizenship provides, carries implications for social and economic integration. High levels of naturalization among refugees also hint at how public-private partnerships to encourage and assist with citizenship could pay civic dividends and mitigate inequalities in naturalization and political integration.

Voting and Other Forms of Political Engagement

Although naturalization might seem the logical antecedent to voting, the U.S. Constitution does not forbid noncitizens from voting in federal elections. As discussed in the introduction to Chapter 2, historically, some states and localities allowed noncitizens to vote, often as an incentive to encourage settlement (Bloemraad, 2006c; Hayduk, 2006; Raskin 1993). These laws "reflected both an openness to newcomers and the idea that the defining principle for political membership was not American citizenship but the exclusionary categories of race, gender, property, and wealth" (Raskin, 1993, p. 1395). By 1926, however, all states had repealed such policies, given nativist sentiment following World War I and labor unrest at home (Murray, 1955; Raskin, 1993).

Today, except for a handful of localities, the right to vote is restricted to adult citizens. Noncitizens, even those who are lawful permanent residents, are effectively shut out of participating in key parts of the political system: they cannot vote for a political candidate, run for office, or participate in direct democracy through referenda, recalls, or ballot initiatives. There are some important exceptions, as lawful permanent residents are allowed to make campaign contributions to federal, state, and local elections (Federal Election Commission, 2003) and noncitizens can contact elected officials about issues of concern, attend protests, and persuade others to vote.

Voting As a Measure of Political Integration

While naturalization is, at present, the first step to voting for the foreign-born, there are other steps that immigrants must navigate. Unlike in countries such as Australia, where voter registration is automatic and voting is mandatory, the United States leaves these decisions to individuals. Jurisdictions within the United States also vary in their requirements for maintaining a current and valid voter registration. Stricter voter identification requirements in some jurisdictions have generated reductions in voter turnout (U.S. Government Accountability Office, 2014), but their systematic effects on voting among naturalized citizens have not yet been examined (although a prior literature suggests that stricter registration rules may dampen voting among naturalized citizens, see Jones-Correa, 2001b).[34] The United States is also unlike most other advanced, industrialized democracies in that it has a comparatively weak party system with candidate-centered elections and a far greater number of offices for election, ranging from

---

[34] There is some debate over the disproportionate impact of these laws on turnout among Latinos and Asian Americans (Cobb et al., 2012), and there have been no studies of how voter identification ("voter ID") laws affect voting patterns with respect to the birthplace of voters (e.g., U.S-born compared with naturalized citizens by region of origin).

federal and state seats, to county supervisors and city councilors, to judges, school board members, insurance commissioners, and so on. Often, these many and varied elections are held at different times, further depressing voting turnout (Hajnal and Lewis, 2003).

Even when it comes to presidential and congressional midterm elections, voter turnout is relatively low in the United States relative to other countries. Low voter turnout is characteristic of both native-born and foreign-born citizens, although turnout tends to be somewhat lower among foreign-born citizens, with some exceptions. Since reports of voter turnout collected by state officials do not contain information on voters' birthplace, analysts have to rely on self-reports of registration and voting, such as responses to questions in the Current Population Survey Voting and Registration Supplement (CPS-VRS), which is conducted in November of every midterm and presidential election year. The panel's analyses of 1996-2012 CPS-VRS data indicate that voting among first generation immigrants has been consistently lower than voting among those in the second or later generations.[35] In 1996, there was a pattern of "second generation advantage" in voting, relative to third and later generation Americans, but this 'advantage' disappeared after 2000, due largely to the changing age and racial composition of the second generation. Analysis of midterm election years revealed voting gaps between foreign-born and native-born citizens even greater than the gaps found in presidential election years.[36] Naturalized citizens are also much less likely than second or third generation citizens to report voting regularly in local elections such as for a mayor or school board.

There are, however, some exceptions to generational voting patterns by race and ethnicity, according to the panel's analysis. Among Latino adult citizens, from 1996 to 2012, voting was higher among first generation immigrants (averaging 52% across the last five presidential elections) when compared to second generation Latinos (46%) and higher than those in the third or subsequent generations (45%). For Asian Americans and blacks, there was no statistically significant difference in presidential voting by immigrant generation, while for non-Hispanic whites, voting was lowest among first generation immigrants (averaging 57% in the last five presidential elections), with a "second generation advantage" pattern of higher

---

[35] See https://catalog.data.gov/dataset/current-population-survey-voting-and-registration-supplement [August 2015].

[36] This difference is more apparent in proportional terms than absolute terms. For example, voting among adult naturalized citizens was 36.8 percent, compared to 46.4 percent among those in the third generation and higher. This difference of 10 percentage points is roughly equal to the difference in voting rates found in the 2012 presidential election (53.3% versus 62.9%), but the proportional difference is significantly greater in the case of midterm elections (from the panel analysis of CPS-VRS data outlined above).

voting among second generation adult citizens (70%) than among those in the third generation and higher (64%).

Analyses reported in the literature have also found gender differences in voting and political participation among immigrants. Women are somewhat more likely to register to vote than men, although this varies across racial and ethnic groups (Bass and Casper, 2001a; Lien, 1998). There is also evidence that Latina immigrants are more politically involved than Latino men (Hardy-Fanta, 1993; Bass and Casper, 2001b).

What accounts for lower voting participation of naturalized citizens? Answering this question requires attention to participation gaps at each stage of the voting process: citizenship, voter registration, and voter turnout among registered voters. The foreign-born account for a 50 percent smaller share of the voting population than does the native-born population. The citizenship stage has by far been the most important barrier, accounting for 88 percent of the gap in voting participation between foreign-born and native-born in 2012. But voting requires two additional stages after acquiring citizenship: registration and actually turning out to vote. Differential levels of registration accounted for 12 percent of the voting gap in 2012. In comparison, voter turnout among foreign-born registered voters in 2012 was comparable to the turnout among native-born registered voters. Previous research (DeSipio, 1996, Ramakrishnan, 2005) also indicates that voting gaps between immigrants and the native-born are much larger at the registration stage than at the turnout stage.

Gaps in voting between foreign-born and native-born citizens are also significantly related to the following factors:

- *English proficiency*: Voting is lower among citizens who have limited English proficiency (Tam Cho, 1999; Ramakrishnan, 2005).
- *Age structure*: Controlling for age makes the first generation deficit in voting even worse, as naturalized citizens are older, on average, than the U.S.-born electorate (U.S. Census Bureau, 2012).[37]
- *Educational attainment:* The positive relationship between education and voting is weaker among first generation immigrants than it is for higher generations, but is nevertheless statistically significant (Jones-Correa, 1998; Tam Cho, 1999; Ramakrishnan, 2005). The weaker relationship between education and voting among first generation immigrants is most likely due to the fact that most of them have attained their college degrees outside the United States, and the content of civic education learned in another country might transfer imperfectly to the political system of the United States (Tam Cho, 1999; Wong et al., 2013).

---

[37] Analysis of 2012 Current Population Survey Voter Supplement.

- *Party identification*: Naturalized citizens have significantly lower levels of partisanship, which may lead in turn to lower rates of voting (Wong, 2000; Wong et al., 2011).[38]
- *Past experiences with democracy*: Ramakrishnan (2005) found that immigrants to the United States who come from countries with nondemocratic regimes are generally less likely to vote than immigrants from democratic countries, and a similar result was found in studies of immigrants to Canada and Australia (Bilodeau, 2008).

Other Forms of Political Engagement

Beyond voting, immigrants can get involved in the democratic process by contacting elected officials, making campaign contributions, attending public hearings, signing petitions, engaging in protest activities, and encouraging others to vote, among other activities. Immigrants do not need to be U.S. citizens to engage in these activities, although the limited data available suggest that participation among naturalized citizens is significantly higher than among noncitizens (Leal, 2002; Wong et al., 2011).[39] The latest data from the CPS Civic Engagement Supplement in November 2013 show that 6 percent of naturalized citizens had contacted or visited elected officials to express their opinions, while only 2 percent of noncitizens had done so.[40] Naturalized immigrants were also twice as likely as noncitizens to have boycotted a product or service because of the company's social or political values (7.2% versus 3.4%), and slightly more likely to express their political views online (22% for naturalized citizens versus 17% for noncitizens).

Data from other surveys are largely consistent with the above results from the November 2013 CPS Civic Engagement Supplement in finding that political participation is higher among naturalized citizens than among noncitizens (Leal, 2002; Martinez, 2005). Protest activity might, however, be one exception to this general pattern, especially for Latino immigrants in the last decade. A 2012 survey of Latino noncitizens living in mixed-status households with at least one citizen adult found that the noncitizens were more likely than the naturalized citizens to participate in protest activity, and they were about as likely to attend community meetings (Jones-Correa

---

[38] Importantly, among Latinos, lower party identification among first generation immigrants (Hajnal and Lee, 2011) is not reflected in their voting behavior (Pantoja, Segura, and Ramizez, 2001; Ramakrishnan 2005).

[39] A study by Barreto and Munoz (2003) found that among Mexican immigrants, there was no significant difference in electoral nonparticipation between citizens and noncitizens after controlling for age, gender, income, education, and other factors.

[40] See http://catalog.data.gov/dataset/current-population-survey-civic-engagement-supplement [August 2015].

and McCann, 2015).[41] Unions that actively cultivate immigrant membership have also become a starting point for immigrants' political and civic participation (Milkman and Voss, 2004; Terriquez, 2011). The bulk of academic research indicates, however, that even though many political activities are open to immigrants regardless of U.S. citizenship, a significant difference in participation exists based on immigrants' citizenship status (Hochschild et al., 2013; Leal, 2002; Martinez, 2005; Ramakrishnan, 2005).

Beyond citizenship status, immigrant generation also bears a significant relationship to political engagement. Survey data indicate that participation rates among naturalized first generation immigrants are lower than among the native-born. For example, the 2008 American National Election Study[42] found that naturalized Latinos were significantly less likely than native-born Latinos to sign petitions, either on paper or online, and were also less likely to make campaign contributions.[43] By contrast, there was no significant difference between naturalized Latino immigrants (first generation) and native-born Latinos in terms of attending public meetings or protests. Similarly, the 2008 National Asian American Survey found significant differences in political participation by immigrant generation, with first generation immigrants less likely than higher generations to make campaign contributions, discuss politics with family and friends, and discuss politics online.[44] This lower level of participation among first generation immigrants occurred whether the analysis examined only naturalized citizens or all foreign-born adults in the survey, and even after controlling for education and household income.

Political Representation of Immigrants

Beyond participation, political integration can also be evaluated through representation. There are different ways to think about the representation of immigrants in the American system of representative democracy, from immigrants being counted as part of the population for the purpose of drawing congressional districts (apportionment) to immigrants running for office and exerting influence on legislative decision making.

---

[41]This might be a recent phenomenon as a study of data from 1989-1990 found that 8.5 percent of Latino citizens said they had attended a rally, compared to only 2 percent of Latino noncitizens who said they had done so (Leal, 2002; see also Martinez, 2005).

[42]See http://www.electionstudies.org/studypages/2008prepost/2008prepost.htm [August 2015].

[43]Nativity differences in the rate of political contributions among Latinos are statistically significant at the .10 level but not the .05 level.

[44]Ramakrishana et al. (2011) found no statistically significant relationship between nativity and low-propensity activities such as contacting officials or participating in protests.

Representation via apportionment Even though noncitizens do not currently have the right to vote in most jurisdictions, the U.S. Constitution still provides for an implicit expectation of noncitizen representation via apportionment. In Article I, Section 2, the Constitution stipulates that apportionment be based on a count of persons, regardless of citizenship.[45] There have been some attempts to limit the representation of noncitizens via apportionment, and the Supreme Court is currently reviewing equality of representation in *Evenwel v Abbot*.[46] The United States still has the implicit expectation that all persons, citizen or otherwise, are to be represented in Congress.

Representation through election to office Another way for immigrants to gain representation is by running for elected office. Indeed, one of the remarkable, early stories of representation among Asian immigrants is that of Dalip Singh Saund, who campaigned for Indians to qualify for naturalization in the 1940s, won elected office just a year after being granted citizenship, and in 1957 was the first Asian American elected to Congress.[47] At the same time, there are limits in the U.S. Constitution to immigrant representation. While naturalized U.S. citizens may hold virtually all elected offices in the United States, the presidency and vice presidency are restricted to "natural born" citizens: one of the only areas in which a U.S. citizen's path to citizenship makes a legal difference in his or her rights and life opportunities.

The available evidence underscores that immigrants are relatively rare in the halls of congress. Throughout the 20th century, the prevalence of foreign-born Representatives and Senators in Congress has always been less than the proportion of foreign-born in the general population (Bloemraad, 2006a, p. 56-63). The highest proportion of foreign-born Representatives in any given Congress, 5.4 percent of all House members in 1910, was still only about a third of the percentage of immigrants in the general population that year (14.7%). In 1940, the proportion of foreign-born members in Congress, as compared to the proportion of foreign-born citizens in the

---

[45] Of course, initially not all persons were treated equally for purposes of apportionment: slaves were counted as three-fifths of a person until the abolition of slavery and the passage of the 14th Amendment, and "Indians not taxed" were not counted for purposes of apportionment until the Indian Citizenship Act of 1924 (Anderson and Seltzer, 2001).

[46] More recent attempts to chip away at noncitizens representation via apportionment have failed, such as a case petitioned to the U.S. Supreme Court in December 2012, *Lepak v. City of Irving*, which sought to allow cities and states to exclude noncitizens for the purposes of drawing legislative districts of equal size. In addition, two U.S. Senators attempted, without success, to mandate a question on citizenship in the 2010 census, to lay the groundwork for court challenges and perhaps constitutional amendments to exclude noncitizens (Roberts, 2009).

[47] See http://www.infoplease.com/spot/apahmfirsts.html [October 2015].

country, hit a high point with 3.9 percent of Representatives foreign-born (17 individuals) compared to 5.5 percent of foreign-born among all citizens.[48] With the resumption of large-scale immigration in the late 1960s, the ratio of foreign-born representation in the house to the total foreign-born population fell—perhaps surprisingly—with only a very modest increase in the 1990s. Relative to other major Western immigrant-receiving countries, immigrant representation in the United States in the national legislature is not among the lowest, but also not among the nations whose ratios are closest to parity (Alba and Foner, 2015; Bloemraad, 2011).

Today, although naturalized citizens account for about 7 percent of voters, only one U.S. Senator out of 100 is a naturalized citizen—Mazie Hirono (D-HI), born in Japan—and only 5 out of 435 members (1%) in the House of Representatives are naturalized citizens: Ileana Ros-Lehtinen (R-FL) and Albio Sires (D-NJ), both born in Cuba; Ted Lieu (D-CA) born in Taiwan; Raul Ruiz (D-CA) born in Mexico; and Norma Torres (D-CA) born in Guatemala.[49] Thus, the percentage of naturalized citizens in Congress (1 percent) is considerably lower than their percentage of the electorate (7%). This is far lower than the representation gaps for Latinos and Asian Americans more generally, however, suggesting that there is greater incorporation through the second and later generations.

Perhaps surprisingly, very few of the foreign-born members of the U.S. House of Representatives come from the largest source countries for naturalized citizens today: China, India, Mexico, the Philippines, and Vietnam. In the first half of the 20th century, about half of the foreign-born U.S. Representatives were born in the United Kingdom or Canada (Bloemraad, 2006a). By the beginning of the 21st century in the 107th Congress (2001-2003), no Senator was born outside the United States and of the six foreign-born representatives—born in Cuba, Hungary, Japan, the Netherlands, or Taiwan—none came from a top-five immigrant-sending country (Amer, 2001).[50]

---

[48] These statistics consider the Congress sitting at the time of each decennial census, comparing members of the House of Representatives to the general U.S. population. These data for the entire 20th century are not able to take into account foreign-born Representatives who were citizens at birth due to their U.S. citizen parents, as in the case of politicians born to military service members or diplomats stationed abroad (for more on the methodology, see Bloemraad, 2006a).

[49] For full list, see http://library.clerk.house.gov/documents/Foreign_Born.pdf and http://www.senate.gov/pagelayout/reference/three_column_table/Foreign_born.htm [October 2015]. In the House, an additional eight members were born to U.S. parents abroad. And as noted by the U.S. Senate reference bureau, Bennet (R-CO), Cruz (R-TX), and McCain (R-AZ) were all born to American parents abroad.

[50] Information on the foreign-born in the 107th Congress from Amer (2001). This report does not distinguish, in counting Congress people born abroad, between those who held birthplace U.S. citizenship and those who naturalized.

There is little systematic data on foreign-born state legislators, but one might expect somewhat greater representation at this level given the presence of term limits in several states (Peverill and Moncrief, 2009), as opposed to the U.S. Congress, which has no term limits. At the municipal level, one would expect greater immigrant representation, especially in large, immigrant-receiving cities. The barriers to election are likely lower compared to the networks, experience and campaign financing needed to win national office. The more concentrated residence of immigrants at the municipal level can also facilitate local mobilization of immigrant-origin voters.

Perhaps surprisingly, then, the available research indicates that foreign-born representation in large cities is still limited. De Graauw and collegues (2013) reported that in 2009, only 8 percent of city councilors in New York were foreign-born, compared to 37 percent foreign-born in the city's population. The corresponding percentages for Chicago were 4 and 22 percent, respectively; for San Francisco, 9 and 36 percent; for Los Angeles 7 and 40 percent; and for Houston, 7 and 28 percent (de Graauw et al., 2013, p. 1882). If the comparison is extended beyond the immigrant generation to include the second and third generations, and also enlarged to include consider African Americans as well, the representation of ethnic and racial minorities in these cities becomes much somewhat closer to parity (de Graauw et al., 2013). For example, ethnoracial minorities made up 49 percent of the New York City council in 2009, in a city where 63 percent of all residents are ethnoracial minorities (de Graauw et al., 2013, p. 1882). Across the five major U.S. cities that de Graauw studied, the biggest representation gap occurred in Houston, where the 71 percent of the city's population is classified as of ethnoracial minority background compared to 43 percent of city council; the only city that achieved representation slight above parity was San Francisco in 2009: the proportion of all these minorities in elected office, 55 percent, was slightly higher than their share of the city's population, 52 percent (de Graauw et al., 2013, p. 1882).

Representation through the legislative process While the proportion of foreign-born elected officials is a type of "descriptive" or demographic representation, evaluation of "substantive" or issue representation is also important. Despite comparatively low participation rates and very low rates of proportional representation, certain members of Congress might still be responsive to immigrant voters due to the profile of residents in their districts. Elected officials from districts with a high proportion of naturalized citizens may be likely more supportive of initiatives deemed important to immigrants, such as more expansive immigration policy. The proportion of *noncitizens* in a Congressional district might also matter for legislative votes on immigration policy. This may be the case if noncitizens share the same preferences on immigration policy as naturalized citizens, or attempt to influence citizen voters, thereby gaining representation "through proxy."

Nationwide surveys of Latinos and Asian Americans show that noncitizens and citizens who self-identify with these racioethnic identities share similar policy priorities and preferences, particularly on matters such as education and immigration (Fraga et al., 2012; Ramakrishnan et al., 2009). The panel does not have similar opinion data at the level of congressional districts, but did have data on whether members of congress with significant proportions of noncitizen constituents vote differently from those who have comparatively few noncitizen constituents. To distinguish between the direct political power of noncitizens versus "representation by proxy" through citizens holding similar preferences, the panel controlled for the proportion of naturalized citizens in the district.[51] The panel's examination of House votes on three enforcement-related bills in 2006 and the American DREAM Act legislation in 2010 indicates that the share of noncitizens in the district is significantly related to House votes at the bivariate level, and in a direction that suggests a member of congress with more noncitizens in his or her district is less likely to vote for restrictive legislation, and more likely to vote for the American DREAM Act.[52] Even after controlling for a member's party and the naturalized share of the electorate, the noncitizen share of the district is still important in explaining the final vote on enforcement-oriented HR 4437 in 2006 and the final vote on the American DREAM Act in 2010. There is, however, a partisan split in the importance of noncitizens in the electorate. Democratic House members with more noncitizens in their district were more likely to vote for the American DREAM Act, and less likely to vote for HR 4437, while among Republican members the opposite was true.[53]

---

[51] If noncitizens do indeed wield political influence, one would expect such influence to be greatest on issues related to immigration. So far, the literature on Congressional roll call votes is largely silent on the potential representation of noncitizen constituents on immigration, with far greater attention being paid to the role of partisanship (Jeong et al., 2011), the economic characteristics of member districts (Facchini and Steinhardt 2011), member ideology (McCarty et al., 2006), and national interest group activity (Tichenor, 2002).

[52] In 2006, the House voted on a series of restrictive measures that were heavy on enforcement, including HR 4437, which was introduced by James Sensenbrenner (R-WI) and sought to make felons of anyone who is an undocumented immigrant or who assists someone who is an undocumented immigrant. In 2010, the House got another chance to vote on immigration, this time on a permissive bill, the American Dream Act (H.R. 1751), which would have legalized those who became undocumented immigrants when they were children. This bill was introduced in the House in May 2010 and was passed by the House during the "lame duck session" of Congress in December 2010 before failing a cloture vote in the Senate.

[53] Other researchers have found a positive correlation between the proportion of voting-age noncitizens in a state's population and spending by that state on redistributive social policy, net of the naturalized population, unemployment in the state, the state's racial composition and other factors known to influence spending on social benefits (Fox et al., 2013). To the

Representation through bureaucratic incorporation Beyond legislative representation, immigrants may also have their interests represented through bureaucratic actors. Social scientists have begun to focus on a growing phenomenon of "bureaucratic political incorporation" whereby government officials respond directly to the needs of immigrant residents (de Graauw, 2014, 2015; Jones-Correa, 2008; Lewis and Ramakrishnan, 2007; Marrow, 2009). This response mode contrasts with the more traditional model of electoral representation, where immigrant residents attempt to persuade elected representatives (either in the executive or legislative branch), who then push bureaucracies to be more responsive, via legislative oversight, executive policy, or both.

These studies have shown that heads of government agencies—particularly school administrators, librarians, and police chiefs—are likely to implement programs in a manner that addresses the needs of immigrants (de Graauw 2014, 2015; Jones-Correa 2008; Lewis and Ramakrishnan 2007; Marrow 2009, 2011). In places where immigrant residents are a smaller share of the electorate, this kind of bureaucratic implementation may stem from a sense of professional mission, norms reinforced through initial training and ongoing professional development, or the need to achieve particular goals (such as a reduction in crime) that require cooperation from immigrant residents. However, there are limits to bureaucratic incorporation: it may be subject to overrule by elected officials as political dynamics change, and it may be more vulnerable to cuts in agency budgets because there is less of a voting constituency to apply pressure to maintain funding necessary for incorporation activities.

CIVIC VOLUNTEERISM AND COMMUNITY ORGANIZATIONS

While political acts constitute a significant aspect of civic engagement in American society, it is also important to examine the ways that immigrants are involved in their communities more generally, through acts of volunteerism and social participation. Studies of immigrant civic participation have drawn attention to a wide array of formal and informal institutions, such as indigenous dance groups, hometown associations, mutual assistance groups, and family or clan networks (de Graauw, 2015; Cordero-Guzman, 2005; Ramakrishnan and Bloemraad, 2008, Ramakrishnan and Viramontes, 2010; Terriquez, 2011; Wong, 2006).

Studies of volunteerism from about a decade ago indicated large gaps in participation by nativity, with volunteering substantially higher among

---

extent that immigrants experience, on average, higher poverty rates than the native-born, this might be another example of noncitizens influencing political decision making despite disenfranchisement.

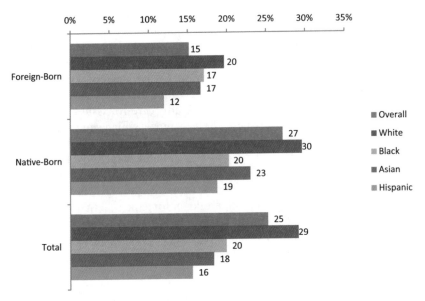

FIGURE 4-5 Volunteerism by nativity and race, 2014.
SOURCE: Current Population Survey Supplement, 2014. Available: https://catalog.
data.gov/dataset/current-population-survey-volunteers-supplement [October 2015].

native-born residents than among the foreign-born (Ramakrishnan, 2006, Foster-Bey, 2008), as well as for membership in civic organizations (Han, 2004). These gaps in participation were more marked than racial gaps in volunteerism, and also showed that naturalized citizens were much more likely to be civically involved through community organizations than those who were not U.S. citizens. The latest available data from the CPS Volunteer Supplement show these patterns to be persistent (see Figure 4-5), with rates of volunteerism nearly twice as high for all native-born (27%) than for all foreign-born (15%), and that native-born in all ethnoracial groups were more likely to volunteer than their foreign-born peers. Importantly, other data from the same CPS-VS round indicate that volunteerism is higher among naturalized citizens (18%) than among noncitizens (13%), and that length of stay in the United States matters: long-term immigrant residents—i.e., those living in the United States for 20 years or more—have significantly higher rates of volunteerism (18%) than those living in the United States for 10 years or fewer (11%). In addition to differences in volunteerism by nativity, there were significant racial gaps in participation, although as Figure 4-5 indicates, these gaps are much greater among the native-born than among the foreign-born. Finally, while these gaps in participation by race and nativity diminish when controlling for education and income, they still remain statistically significant.

Examining individuals' volunteer activities is but one side of understanding civic engagement; immigrant integration also depends on the breadth, depth, and openness of civil society. Civil society comprises the groups, organizations, and informal associations that offer a sense of community, provide services and information, advocate for issues or policies, and take action on a host of issues. These groups—which can range from a local food bank to a political action committee—are neither public institutions nor for-profit businesses; they instead inhabit what some have called a "third sector" of American society. Mirroring the tensions between enforcement and integration outlined in Chapter 2, U.S. civil society groups can either advance agendas and undertake enforcement activities meant to keep immigrants out of the United States, work actively to help immigrants integrate into the economic, social and political spheres of their new communities, or ignore or be blind to immigrant populations—neither working for exclusion nor for inclusion.

On the enforcement side, America's long history of immigration parallels a tradition of organizing to reduce or restrict immigration, from fears about Catholic, Jewish, and Asian immigrants and concerns about political radicals in the 19th and early 20th centuries (Higham, 1955) to worries about undocumented migration and foreign terrorists in the 21st century. Today, some Americans feel that there is insufficient staffing on the U.S.-Mexico border by the Border Patrol, and they therefore organize themselves as a civilian extension of the agency, conducting volunteer patrols (Elcioglu, 2014; Shapira, 2013). Far inland, long-time residents of some smaller communities experiencing rapid population growth have organized to pass ordinances seeking to deter immigrants' settlement, as in the case of Prince William County, Virginia. The community group Help Save Manassas worked with other civil society organizations at the national and local levels to convince the County Board of Supervisors to pass Resolution 07-609, directing police to inquire about the immigration status of anyone detained and to enter into a 287(g) agreement with the Department of Homeland Security (Singer et al., 2009).

At the same time, civil society groups have long been the backbone of integration efforts. This was as true in the 19th century, a time when governments had limited engagement with immigrant residents and nonprofit and civil society organizations did much of the day-to-day settlement work, animated by volunteer efforts, public contracts, and private donations. Broadly speaking, a similar pattern applies today. Historically, religious institutions spanning faiths helped newcomers find housing, jobs, and community; initiatives that were also carried out by settlement houses, associations organized around particular hometowns or kin networks, and myriad other organizations. When the U.S. government initiated a concerted effort to resettled displaced people following World War II, it entered into partnership with voluntary agencies ("VOLAGs") to carry out the resettlement. This partnership continues today with organizations such as Church World Service, the Hebrew Immigrant Aid Society, the International Rescue Committee, and the U.S. Conference of Catholic Bishops.[54] Today, civic integration and mobilization can occur through congregations and faith communities (Ecklund, 2008; Heredia, 2011; Mora, 2013), unions (Gleeson, 2009; Milkman, 2000; Terriquez, 2011), nonprofit service agencies (de Graauw, 2014, 2015; Cordero-Guzmán, 2005), or a host of other organizations, from sports and recreation groups to arts and cultural associations, business associations, or school-based parent groups (Ramakrishnan and Bloemraad, 2008).

Research on the civic and organizational foundations of immigrants' integration is underdeveloped, but the evidence thus far suggests that civil society groups—whether organized by immigrants or predominantly organized by native-born citizens who include immigrant members—can facilitate integration. A denser and more active civil society infrastructure helps low-income immigrants access health and human services, for themselves and vulnerable children (Cordero-Guzmán, 2005; de Graauw, 2008; Flores et al., 2005; Yoshikawa et al., 2014), provides information and resources to make legal claims against discriminatory employment practices (Gleeson, 2009), facilitates citizenship acquisition and political engagement (Bloemraad, 2006a; Cordero-Guzmán et al., 2008; Wong, 2006), and provides a way for immigrants—including noncitizens—to secure some measure of policy representation (de Graauw, 2008; 2015). Membership in voluntary organizations such as athletic and social clubs can also provide immigrants with resources that aid integration in other domains, such as information about employment opportunities (Massey et al., 1987).

Many American civil society groups—probably the majority—are oriented neither to enforcement nor to integration. This is understandable to the extent that many groups have a purpose or a mission not centered on immigrants or immigration; one can think of groups such as a choral society, baseball league, volunteer fire department, high school debate society, nonprofit health clinic, or environmental advocacy organization. However, given that increasing immigration is a reality in a growing number of communities across the United States, these groups' lack of involvement

---

[54]The nine officially recognized voluntary agencies with which the Office of Refugee Resettlement works today are the Church World Service, Ethiopian Community Development Council, Episcopal Migration Ministries, Hebrew Immigrant Aid Society, International Rescue Committee, U.S. Committee for Refugees and Immigrants, Lutheran Immigration and Refugee Services, U.S. Conference of Catholic Bishops, and World Relief Corporation.

with immigrant populations can be a lost opportunity to build bridges, share information and resources, and generate new feelings of community. Even in traditional regions of immigration, researchers have found that suburban areas have engaged in very limited public-private partnerships with immigrants and immigrant organizations, even when the proportion of the municipality's population is 40 percent foreign-born (de Graauw et al., 2013; see also Joassart-Marcelli, 2013). This raises the possibility of potentially troubling inequalities and civic stratification by nativity and residential location, as well as inequalities between immigrant-origin national origin groups based on the groups' resources (educational, linguistic, and financial) and inequalities by legal status (Gleeson and Bloemraad, 2013; Joassart-Marcelli, 2013; Ramakrishnan and Bloemraad, 2008). Especially as immigrants move to new destinations, a lack of civic capacity and limited support for building immigrant organizations might impede integration in the future. On the flip side, research in rural areas and new immigrant destinations found that immigrant civic engagement was higher in places with a prior history of refugee resettlement and in places that have large, supportive nonprofits and public universities (Andersen, 2010). The positive experience of private-public partnerships around refugee resettlement provides a template for successful engagement with civil society around immigrant integration.

"LEARNING" CIVIC AND POLITICAL ENGAGEMENT

All democratic countries need residents who are knowledgeable about their government institutions, current issues, and ways to be engaged to keep democratic legitimacy and accountability strong. Such democratic "learning" is as relevant to the native-born population as it is to immigrant populations. But for the foreign-born, especially those who come to the United States as adults, processes of civic and political learning can occur along different pathways, such as through non-English ethnic media, or they do not occur as fully, as the participation gaps between native-born and foreign-born outlined above suggest. In particular, for adult immigrants, an individual's level of education is not as strong a predictor of political participation as it is among the native-born population (Cho, 1999; Ramakrishnan, 2005), perhaps because the content of civic education learned in another country might transfer imperfectly to the political system of the United States. Substituting for the role that schools play for native-born children (discussed below), unions (Han, 2004; Milkman and Terriquez, 2012; Terriquez, 2011), ethnic media (Felix et al., 2008), religious institutions (Heredia, 2011; Mora, 2013; Stoll and Wong, 2007) and workplaces (Verba et al., 1993) can provide contexts in which adult immigrants can learn about and be mobilized into civic and political engagement.

Attention to immigrant origins and engagement also raises questions for second generation youth or immigrant children who arrive in the United States at a young age. For native-born citizens with native-born parents, political and civic learning often takes place in the family, as parents talk about politics (or not) with their children, model behaviors such as voting and volunteering, or bring children to rallies or protests. Foreign-born parents can also engage in such parent-to-child learning, but the inter-generational transmission of political attitudes, behaviors, and civic involvements might be weaker, given a limited knowledge of how things work in the United States. Especially if immigrant parents are noncitizens, or perhaps not even lawful permanent residents, immigrant-origin youth might be less likely to learn about, or take an interest in, American politics and civic life. Research on this topic is sparse, but available evidence suggests that the children of immigrants are no less likely—and no more likely—to engage in volunteer activities or to vote than similarly situated children of native-born parents, even in the case of undocumented parents (Callahn and Muller, 2013; Humphries et al., 2013; Terriquez and Kwon, 2014).

Schools appear to play an important role in equalizing civic and political engagement among young people, regardless of parents' immigrant background. In the 19th century, the American common school emerged as an institution to teach both basic skills for work and democratic participation. Today, these twin roles continue. Schools can provide places to develop political identities, learn about government and citizenship, and be encouraged to volunteer or perform community service. Research shows that extracurricular involvement and volunteering shape adolescents' social and civic experiences equally, regardless of parents' nativity (Niemi et al., 2000; Stepik and Stepik, 2002. However, while parents' socioeconomic status predicts nonimmigrant students' engagement, in at least one longitudinal dataset of youth transitioning to adulthood, that association was weaker among immigrant-origin youth; instead, exposure to social studies in high school appeared to have a significant, positive effect on these young people's likelihood of voting, registering to vote, and identifying with a political party (Callahan and Muller 2013; Humphries et al., 2013). Other findings underscore the importance of schools in immigrant-origin youths' civic and political integration, an influence which can have spill-over effects for parents, especially mothers, who have contact with school programs and school officials, from teachers to guidance counselors (Terriquez, 2012).

Outside of schools, youth who are members of community-based organizations with strong advocacy orientations and leadership training are more likely to be politically active, and they might even pass along their knowledge to parents (Terriquez and Kwon, 2014). Indeed, the children of immigrants, educated in American schools, might engage in "reverse" political socialization, teaching their immigrant parents about the electoral college and ballot measures (Wong and Tseng, 2007) or encouraging them to participate in peaceful immigrant rights rallies (Bloemraad and Trost, 2008).

Political and civic engagement—and the learning of skills and cultivation of interest in politics and community issues—can also occur across international boundaries. Some observers have worried that immigrants' activism in their home countries, whether around homeland elections or in raising funds for community development, might impede engagement in and learning about U.S. politics and civic affairs. But research has found no such trade-off between U.S.-based and homeland engagements. Some scholars have concluded that participation in transnational organizations (DeSipio, 2006; Portes et al., 2008) and attention to homeland concerns (Chung et al., 2013; Karpathakis, 1999; Wong et al., 2013) have a positive effect on participation and interest in U.S. political life. And overall, only a very small proportion of immigrants appear to be actively engaged in homeland political activities, even if they continue to send money or travel to their home country (Guarnizo et al., 2003; Waldinger, 2008). As with multiple citizenship, it appears that those with more education and more secure economic situations are more likely to engage in political and civic activities spanning borders (Lessinger, 1995; Ong, 1999; Guarnizo et al., 2003).

SUMMARY AND CONCLUSION

If the naturalization rate is the best marker of immigrants' political integration into the United States, then the research cited above indicates that there is reason for concern, despite slight increases in naturalization rates since 2000. There are notable disparities in who becomes a citizen by socioeconomic status, and evidence exists that the naturalization process itself makes it more difficult for immigrants who already face barriers to integration to achieve citizenship, despite their desire to do so. Meanwhile legal status bars many immigrants from citizenship, a burden that falls disproportionately on immigrants from Mexico and Central America. But despite these correlations, there are no clear explanations for low naturalization rates, particularly for those who have higher socioeconomic status.

Conclusion 4-1 Overall, moderate levels of naturalization in the United States appear to stem not from immigrants' lack of interest or even primarily from the bureaucratic process of applying for citizenship. Instead the obstacle to naturalization lies somewhere in the process by which individuals translate their motivation to naturalize into action. Further research is needed to clearly identify this barrier.

In addition, foreign-born representation at all levels of government is disproportionately low. This poses a challenge to the American democratic ideal of civic equality and has implications for dimensions beyond political integration, such as labor market participation.

The decentralized nature of the U.S.'s immigrant integration "system" may also hinder immigrants' political and civic integration (see Chapter 2). While civil society groups have historically been the backbone of grassroots integration efforts and continue to provide invaluable services in areas where there is established organizational presence, in new immigrant destinations a lack of engagement between civil society organizations and immigrants or immigrant organizations leaves a void in many communities. However, successful models of public-private partnerships could provide a template for successful engagement with civil society around immigrant integration, even in places where these efforts are currently absent. And other social institutions, perhaps most importantly schools, continue to provide invaluable tools for political and civic integration for immigrants and the second generation.

REFERENCES

Alba, R., and Foner, N. (2015) *Strangers No More: Immigration and the Challenges of Integration in North America and Western Europe.* Princeton, NJ: Princeton University Press.

Amer, M. (2001). *Membership of the 107th Congress: A Profile.* Washington, DC: Congressional Research Service.

Anderson, M., and Seltzer, W. (2001). The dark side of numbers: The role of population data systems in human rights abuses. *Social Research,* 481-513.

Aptekar, S. (2010). *Immigrant Naturalization and Nation-Building in North America.* Princeton, NJ: Princeton University Press.

Aptekar, S. (2014). Citizenship status and patterns of inequality in the United States and Canada. *Social Science Quarterly, 95*(2), 343-359.

Aptekar, S. (2015). *The Road to Citizenship: What Naturalization Means for Immigrants and the United States.* New Brunswick, NJ: Rutgers University Press.

Barreto, M.A., and Muñoz, J.A. (2003). Reexamining the "politics of in-between": Political participation among Mexican immigrants in the United States. *Hispanic Journal of Behavioral Sciences, 25*(4), 427-447.

Barry, C. (2014). *Immigrants, Their Children and the U.S. Military: Current Enlistment Trends and Post-Service Trajectories.* Paper commissioned by the Panel on Integration of Immigrants into American Society, October, National Academies of Sciences, Engineering, and Medicine, Washington, DC.

Bass, L.E., and Casper, L.M. (2001a). Impacting the political landscape: Who registers and votes among naturalized Americans? *Political Behavior, 23*(2), 103-130.

Bass, L.E., and Casper, L.M. (2001b). Differences in registering and voting between native-born and naturalized Americans. *Population Research and Policy Review, 20*(6), 483-511.

Bilodeau, A. (2008). Immigrants' voice through protest politics in Canada and Australia: Assessing the impact of pre-migration political repression. *Journal of Ethnic and Migration Studies, 34*(6), 975-1002.

Bloemraad, I. (2006a). *Becoming a Citizen: Incorporating Immigrants and Refugees in the United States and Canada*. Berkeley: University of California Press.

Bloemraad, I. (2006b). Becoming a citizen in the United States and Canada: Structured mobilization and immigrant political incorporation. *Social Forces 85*(2):667-695.

Bloemraad, I. (2006c). Citizenship lessons from the past: The contours of immigrant naturalization in the early twentieth century. *Social Science Quarterly, 87*(5), 927-953.

Bloemraad, I. (2011). "We the people" in an age of migration: Multiculturalism and immigrants' political integration in comparative perspective. In R. Smith (Ed.), *Citizenship, Borders, and Human Needs* (pp. 250-272). Philadelphia: University of Pennsylvania Press.

Bloemraad, I. (2013). Being American/becoming American: Birthright citizenship and immigrants' membership in the United States. *Studies in Law, Politics, and Society, 60*, 55-84.

Bloemraad, I., and de Graauw, E. (2011). *Immigrant Integration and Policy in the United States: A Loosely Stitched Patchwork*. Washington, DC: Institute for Research on Labor and Employment.

Bloemraad, I., and Trost, C. (2008). It's a family affair: Intergenerational mobilization in the spring 2006 protests. *American Behavioral Scientist, 52*(4), 507-532.

Bogdan, N.B. (2012). *Shaping Citizenship Policies to Strengthen Immigrant Integration*. Washington, DC: Migration Information Source. Available: http://www.migrationpolicy.org/article/shaping-citizenship-policies-strengthen-immigrant-integration [March 2015].

Bratsberg, B., Ragan, J.F., and Nasir, Z.M. (2002). The effect of naturalization on wage growth: A panel study of young male immigrants. *Journal of Labour Economics 20*(3), 568-579.

Brettell, C.B. (2006). Political belonging and cultural belonging: Immigration status, citizenship and identity among the four immigrant populations in a Southwestern city. *American Behavioral Scientist, 59*(1), 70-99.

Bueker, C.S. (2006). *From Immigrant to Naturalized Citizen*. New York: LFB Scholarly.

Callahan, R.M., and Muller, C. (2013). *Coming of Political Age: American Schools and the Civic Development of Immigrant Youth*. New York: Russell Sage Foundation.

Catholic Legal Immigration Network, Inc. (2007). *A More Perfect Union: A National Citizenship Plan*. Washington, DC: Author.

Chiswick, B.R., and Miller, P.W. (2008). Citizenship in the United States: The roles of immigrants characteristics and country of origin. *Research in Labor Economics 29*, 91-130.

Cho, W.K.T. (1999). Naturalization, Socialization, Participation: Immigrants and (Non)Voting. *The Journal of Politics, 61*(4), 1140-1155.

Chung, A.Y., Bloemraad, I., and Tejada-Peña, K.I. (2013). Reinventing an authentic "ethnic" politics: Ideology and organizational change in Koreatown and Field's Corner. *Ethnicities, 13*(6), 838-862.

Cobb, R.V., Greiner, D.J., and Quinn, K.M. (2012). Can voter ID laws be administered in a race-neutral manner? Evidence from the city of Boston in 2008. *Quarterly Journal of Political Science, 7*(1), 1-33.

Cordero-Guzmán, H.R. (2005). Community-based organizations and migration in New York City. *Journal of Ethnic and Migration Studies, 31*(5), 889-909.

Cordero-Guzmán, H.R, Martin, N., Quiroz-Becerra, V., and Theodore, N. (2008). Voting with their feet nonprofit organizations and immigrant mobilization. *American Behavioral Scientist, 52*(4), 598-617.

Cort, D.A. (2012). Spurred to action or retreat? The effects of reception contexts on naturalization decisions in Los Angeles. *International Migration Review, 46*, 483-516.

de Graauw, E. (2008). Nonprofit organizations: Agents of immigrant political incorporation in urban America. *Civic Hopes and Political Realities: Immigrants, Community Organizations, and Political Engagement*, 323-350.

de Graauw, E. (2014). Municipal ID cards for undocumented immigrants: Local bureaucratic membership in a federal system. *Politics & Society, 42*(3), 309-330.

de Graauw, E. (2015). *Making Immigrant Rights Real: Nonprofit Advocacy and Immigrant Integration in San Francisco.* Ithaca, NY: Cornell University Press.

de Graauw, E., Gleeson, S., and Bloemraad, I. (2013). Funding immigrant organizations: Suburban free-riding and local civic presence. *American Journal of Sociology, 119*(1), 75-130.

DeSipio, L. (1996). Making citizens or good citizens? Naturalization as a predictor of organizational and electoral behavior among Latino immigrants. *Hispanic Journal of Behavioral Sciences 18*(2).

DeSipio, L. (2006). Transnational politics and civic engagement: Do home-country political ties limit Latino immigrant pursuit of U.S. civic engagement and citizenship? In T. Lee, S.K. Ramakrishnan, and R. Ramirez (Eds.), *Transforming Politics, Transforming America* (pp. 106-128). Charlottesville: University of Virginia Press.

Dronkers, J., and Vink, M.P. (2012). Explaining access to citizenship in Europe: How citizenship policies affect naturalization rates. *European Union Politics, 13*(3), 390-412.

Ecklund, E.H. (2008). Religion and spirituality among scientists. *Contexts, 7*(1), 12-15.

Elcioglu, E.F. (2014). Popular sovereignty on the border: Nativist activism among two border watch groups in southern Arizona. *Ethnography, 0*(00), 1-25. Available: http://eth.sage pub.com/content/early/2014/10/09/1466138114552951.full.pdf+html [September 2015].

Emanuel, R., and Gutierrez, L.V. (2013). Priced out of citizenship. (Op-Ed.) *New York Times,* April 3. Available: http://www.nytimes.com/2013/04/04/opinion/priced-out-of-citizenship.html?_r=0 [June 2015].

Facchini, G., and Steinhardt, M.F. (2011). What drives U.S. immigration policy? Evidence from congressional roll call votes. *Journal of Public Economics, 95*(7), 734-743.

Federal Election Commission. (July 2003). *Foreign Nationals.* Available: http://www.fec.gov/pages/brochures/foreign.shtml [January 2015].

Felix, A., Gonzalez, C., and Ramírez, R. (2008). Political protest, ethnic media, and Latino naturalization. *American Behavioral Scientist, 52*(4), 618-634.

Fix, M., Passel, J.S., and Sucher, K. (2003). *Trends in Naturalization.* Washington, DC: Urban Institute. Available: http://webarchive.urban.org/publications/310847.html [July 2015].

Foster-Bey, J. (2008). *Do Race, Ethnicity, Citizenship and Socio-economic Status Determine Civic-Engagement?* CIRCLE Working paper# 62. Medford, MA: Center for Information and Research on Civic Learning and Engagement.

Fox, C. (2012). *Three Worlds of Relief: Race, Immigration, and the American Welfare State from the Progressive Era to the New Deal:.* Princeton, NJ: Princeton University Press.

Fox, C., and Bloemraad, I. (2015). White by law, not in practice: Explaining the gulf in citizenship acquisition between Mexican and European immigrants, 1930. *Social Forces.* Available: http://sf.oxfordjournals.org/content/early/2015/02/11/sf.sov009.full.pdf [September 2015].

Fox, C., Bloemraad, I., and Kesler, C. (2013). Immigration, political participation and redistributive social policy. In D. Card and S. Raphael (Eds.), *Immigration, Poverty, and Socioeconomic Inequality* (pp. 381-420). New York: Russell Sage Foundation.

Fraga, L.R., Garcia, J.A., Hero, R., Jones-Correa, M., Martinez-Ebers, V., and Segura, G.M. (2012). *Latino National Survey (LNS), 2006 ICPSR 20862.* Ann Arbor, MI: Inter-university Consortium for Political and Social Research. Available: http://www.research-gate.net/publication/228806926_Latino_National_Survey_(LNS)_2006_ICPSR_20862 [September 2015].

Freeman, G., Plascencia, L.F.B, and Baker, S.G. (2002). Explaining the surge in citizenship applications in the 1990s: Lawful permanent residents in Texas. *Social Science Quarterly, 83*(4), 1013-1025.

Gibson, C., and Jung, K. (2006). *Historical Census Statistics on the Foreign-Born Population of the United States: 1850 to 2000*. Working paper no. 18. Washington, DC: U.S. Census Bureau, Population Division.

Gilbertson, G., and Singer, A. (2003). The emergence of protective citizenship in the USA: Naturalization among Dominican immigrants in the post-1996 welfare reform era. *Ethnic and Racial Studies, 26*(1), 25-51.

Gleeson, S. (2009). From rights to claims: the role of civil society in making rights real for vulnerable workers. *Law & Society Review, 43*(3), 669-700.

Gleeson, S., and Bloemraad, I. (2013). Assessing the scope of immigrant organizations: Official undercounts and actual underrepresentation. *Nonprofit and Voluntary Sector Quarterly, 42*(2), 346-370.

Goodman, S.W. (2010). *Naturalization Policies in Europe: Exploring Patterns of Inclusion and Exclusion*. Florence, Italy: EUDO Citizenship Observatory. Available: http://eudo-citizenship.eu/docs/7-Naturalisation%20Policies%20in%20Europe.pdf [March 2015].

Gonzalez-Barrera, A., Hugo, M.L., Passel, J.S., and Taylor, P. (2013). *The Path Not Taken.* Washington, DC: Pew Hispanic Center. Available: http://www.pewhispanic.org/2013/02/04/the-path-not-taken/ [September 2015].

Grieco, E.M., Acosta, Y.D., de la Cruz, G.P., Gambino, C., Gryb, T., Larsen, L.J., Trevelyan, E.N., and Walters, N.P. (2012). *The Foreign-Born Population in the United States: 2010.* Washington, DC: U.S. Census Bureau. Available: https://www.census.gov/prod/2012pubs/acs-19.pdf [August 2015].

Guarnizo, L.E., Portes, A., and Haller, W. (2003). Assimilation and transnationalism: Determinants of transnational political action among contemporary migrants. *American Journal of Sociology, 108*(6), 1211-1248.

Haddal, C.C. (2007). *U.S. Citizenship and Immigration Services' Immigration Fees and Adjudication Costs: The FY2008 Adjustments and Historical Context.* Washington, DC: Congressional Research Service.

Hajnal, Z.L., and Lewis, P.G. (2003). Municipal institutions and voter turnout in local elections. *Urban Affairs Review, 38*(5), 645-668.

Hajnal, Z., and Lee, T. (2011). *Why Americans Don't Join the Party: Race, Immigration, and the Failure (of Political Parties) to Engage the Electorate.* Princeton, NJ: Princeton University Press.

Han, S. (2004). Ashore on the land of joiners: Intergenerational social incorporation of immigrants. *International Migration Review, 38,* 732-746.

Hardy-Fanta, C. (1993). *Latina Politics, Latino Politics: Gender, Culture and Political Participation in Boston*. Philadelphia: Temple University Press.

Hayduk, R. (2006). *Democracy for All: Restoring Immigrant Voting Rights in the United States*. New York: Routledge.

Heredia, L.L. (2011). From prayer to protest: The immigrant rights movement and the Catholic church. In I. Bloemraad and K. Voss (Eds.), *Rallying for Immigrant Rights* (pp. 101-122). Berkeley: University of California Press.

Higham, J. (1955). *Send These to Me: Jews and Other Immigrants in Urban America*. New York: Scribner.

Hochschild, J., Chatapadhyay, J., Gay, C., and Jones-Correa, M. (2013) *Outsiders No More? Models of Immigrant Political Incorporation*. New York: Oxford University Press.

Humphries, M., Muller, C., and Schiller, K.S. (2013). The political socialization of adolescent children of immigrants. *Social Science Quarterly, 94,* 1261-1282.

ICF International. (2011). *Records Study Comparison Report: U.S. Citizenship and Immigration Services' Records Study on Pass/Fail Rates for Naturalization Applicants.* Report prepared for U.S. Citizenship and Immigration Services. Fairfax, VA: Author. Available: http://www.uscis.gov/sites/default/files/USCIS/files/Records_Study_for_the_Naturalization_Test.pdf [April 2015].

Jacobson, D. (1996). *Rights Across Borders: Immigration and the Decline of Citizenship.* Leiden, Netherlands: Brill.

Janoski, T. (2010). *The Ironies of Citizenship: Naturalization and Integration in Industrialized Countries.* New York: Cambridge University Press.

Jasso, G. (2011). Migration and stratification. *Social Science Research*, 40(5), 1292-1336.

Jeong, G.H., Miller, G.J., Schofield, C., and Sened, I. (2011). Cracks in the opposition: Immigration as a wedge issue for the Reagan coalition. *American Journal of Political Science*, 55(3), 511-525.

Joassart-Marcelli, P. (2013). Ethnic concentration and nonprofit organizations: the political and urban geography of immigrant services in Boston, Massachusetts. *International Migration Review*, 47(3), 730-772.

Jones-Correa, M. (1998). *Between Two Nations: The Political Predicament of Latinos in New York City.* Ithaca, NY: Cornell University Press.

Jones-Correa, M. (2001a). Under two flags: Dual nationality in Latin America and its consequences for naturalization in the United States. *International Migration Review, 35,* 997-1029.

Jones-Correa, M. (2001b). Institutional and contextual factors in immigrant naturalization and voting. *Citizenship Studies, 5*(1), 41-56.

Jones-Correa, M. (2008). Race to the top? The politics of immigrant education in suburbia. In D. Massey (Ed.), *New Faces in New Places: The Changing Geography of American Immigration* (pp. 308-341). New York: Russell Sage Foundation.

Jones-Correa, M., and McCann, J.A. (2013). *The Effects of Naturalization and Documentation Status on the Participation of Latino Immigrants.* Presented at the American Political Science Association Meeting, Chicago, IL, August 28-September 1.

Kandel, W.A., and Haddal, C.C. (2010). *U.S. Citizenship and Immigration Services' Immigration Fees and Adjudication Costs: Proposed Adjustments and Historical Context.* Washington, DC: Congressional Research Service.

Karpathakis, A. (1999). Home society politics and immigrant political incorporation: The case of Greek immigrants in New York City. *International Migration Review, 33*(1), 55-78.

Leal, D.L. (2002). Political participation by Latino non-citizens in the United States. *British Journal of Political Science, 32,* 353-370.

Lee, J., and Foreman, K. (2014). *U.S. Naturalizations: 2013.* Annual Flow Report. Washington, DC: U.S. Department of Homeland Security, Office of Immigration Statistics.

Lewis, P.G., and Ramakrishnan, S.K. (2007). Police practices in immigrant-destination cities: Political control or bureaucratic professionalism? *Urban Affairs Review* 42(6), 874-900.

Liang, Z. (1994). Social contact, social capital, and the naturalization process: Evidence from six immigrant groups. *Social Science Research, 23,* 407-437.

Lien, P.T. (1998). Does the gender gap in political attitudes and behavior vary across racial groups? *Political Research Quarterly, 51*(4), 869-894.

Logan, J.R., Oh, S., and Darrah, J. (2012). The political and community context of immigrant naturalization in the United States. *Journal of Ethnic and Migration Studies, 38*(4), 535-554.

Marrow, H.B. (2009). Immigrant bureaucratic incorporation: The dual roles of professional missions and government policies. *American Sociological Review, 74*(5), 756-776.

Marrow, H.B. (2011). *New Destination Dreaming: Immigration, Race, and Legal Status in the Rural American South.* Stanford, CA: Stanford University Press.

Martinez, L.M. (2005). Yes we can: Latino participation in unconventional politics. *Social Forces, 84*(1), 135-155.

Massey, D.S., and Pren, K.A. (2012). Unintended consequences of US immigration policy: Explaining the post-1965 surge from Latin America. *Population and Development Review, 38*, 1-29.

Massey, D.S., Alcaron, R., Durand, J., and Gonzalez, H. (1987). *Return to Aztlan: The Social Process of International Migration from Western Mexico.* Berkeley: University of California Press.

Mazzolari, F. (2009). Dual citizenship rights: Do they make more and richer citizens? *Demography, 46*(1), 169-191.

McCarty, N., Poole, K.T., and Rosenthal, H. (2006). *Polarized America: The Dance of Ideology and Unequal Riches* (vol. 5). Cambridge, MA: MIT Press.

Milkman, R. (2000). *Organizing Immigrants: The Challenge for Unions in Contemporary California.* Ithaca, NY: Cornell University Press.

Milkman, R., and Terriquez, V. (2012). "We are the ones who are out in front": Women's leadership in the immigrant rights movement. *Feminist Studies, 38*, 645-647.

Milkman, R., and Voss, K. (2004). *Rebuilding Labor: Organizing and Organizers in the New Union Movement.* Ithaca, NY: Cornell University Press.

Mora, G.C. (2013). Religion and the organizational context of immigrant civic engagement: Mexican Catholicism in the USA. *Ethnic and Racial Studies, 36*(11), 1647-1665.

Murray, R.K. (1955). *Red Scare: A Study in National Hysteria, 1919-1920.* Minneapolis: University of Minnesota Press.

Nam, Y., and Kim, W. (2012). Welfare reform and elderly immigrants' naturalization: Access to public benefits as an incentive for naturalization in the United States. *International Migration Review, 46*(3), 656-679.

Naujoks, D. (2012). *Does Dual Citizenship Increase Naturalization?—Evidence from Indian Immigrants in the U.S.* Research paper 125. Hamburg, Germany: Hamburg Institute of International Economics.

New America Media. (2009). *Women Immigrants: Stewards of the 21st Century Family.* Available: http://www.in.gov/icw/files/immwomenexecsummary.pdf [July 2015].

Niemi, R.G., Hepburn, M.A., and Chapman, C. (2000). Community service by high school students: A cure for civic ills? *Political Behavior, 22*(1), 45-69.

OECD. (2011). *Naturalization: A Passport for the Better Integration of Immigrants?* Paris, France: Author. Available: http://www.oecd-ilibrary.org/social-issues-migration-health/naturalisation-a-passport-for-the-better-integration-of-immigrants_9789264099104-en [July 2015].

Pantoja, A.D., and Gershon, S.A. (2006). Political orientations and naturalization among Latino and Latina immigrants. *Social Science Quarterly, 87*(5), 1171-1187.

Pantoja, A.D., Ramirez, R., and Segura, G.M. (2001). Citizens by choice, voters by necessity: Patterns in political mobilization by naturalized Latinos. *Political Research Quarterly, 54*(4), 729-750.

Pastor, M., Sanchez, J., Ortiz, R., and Scoggins, J. (2013). *Nurturing Naturalization: Could Lowering the Fee Help?* Los Angeles, CA: Center for the Study of Immigrant Integration.

Pastor, M., Oakford, P., and Sanchez, J. (2015). *Profiling the Eligible to Naturalize.* Los Angeles, CA: Center for the Study of Immigrant Integration. Available: http://www.partnershipfornewamericans.org/storage/Report_Profiling-the-Eligible-to-Naturalize.pdf [July 2015].

Picot, G., and Hou, F. (2011). *Divergent Trends in Citizenship Rates among Immigrants in Canada and the United States.* Ottawa: Statistics Canada. Available: http://www.statcan.gc.ca/pub/11f0019m/11f0019m2011338-eng.pdf [September 2015].

Plascencia, L. (2012). *Disenchanting Citizenship: Mexican Migrants and the Boundaries of Belonging.* New Brunswick, NJ: Rutgers University Press.

Portes, A., and Curtis, J.W. (1987). Changing flags: Naturalization and its determinants among Mexican immigrants. *International Migration Review*, 352-371.

Portes, A., Escobar, C., and Arana, R. (2008). Bridging the gap: Transnational and ethnic organizations in the political incorporation of immigrants in the United States. *Ethnic and Racial Studies, 31*(6), 1056-1090.

Ramakrishnan, S.K. (2005). *Democracy in Immigrant America: Changing Demographics and Political Participation.* Stanford, CA: Stanford University Press.

Ramakrishnan, S.K. (2006). But do they bowl? Race, immigrant incorporation, and civic volunteerism in the United States. In T. Lee, S.K. Ramakrishnan, and R. Ramirez (Eds.), *Transforming Politics, Transforming America: The Political and Civic Incorporation of Immigrants in the United States* (pp. 243-259). Charlottesville: University of Virginia Press.

Ramakrishnan, S.K., and Bloemraad, I. (Eds.). (2008). *Civic Hopes and Political Realities: Immigrants, Community Organizations, and Political Engagement.* New York: Russell Sage Foundation.

Ramakrishnan, S.K., and Viramontes, C. (2010). Civic spaces: Mexican hometown associations and immigrant participation. *Journal of Social Issues, 66*(1), 155-173.

Ramakrishnan, S.K., Junn, J., Lee, T., and Wong, J. (2001). *National Asian American Survey.* Unpublished analysis of data. Ann Arbor, MI: Inter-university Consortium for Political and Social Research.

Ramakrishnan, S.K., Wong, J., Lee, T., and Junn, J. (2009). Race-based considerations and the Obama vote. *Du Bois Review: Social Science Research on Race, 6*(01), 219-238.

Raskin, J.B. (1993). Legal aliens, local citizens: The historical, constitutional, and theoretical meanings of alien suffrage. *University of Pennsylvania Law Review, 141*(4), 1391-1470.

Roberts, S. (2009). California would lose seats under census change. *The New York Times*, October 27. Available: http://www.nytimes.com/2009/10/28/us/politics/28census.html?_r=0 [August 2015].

Ruiz, A.G., Zong, J., and Batalova, J. (2015). Immigrant Women in the United States. Washington, DC: Migration Policy Institute. Available: http://www.migrationpolicy.org/article/immigrant-women-united-states [August 2015].

Rytina, N. (2004). *Estimates of the Legal Permanent Resident Population and Population Eligible to Naturalize in 2002.* Washington, DC: U.S. Department of Homeland Security, Office of Immigration Statistics.

Rytina, N. (2012). *Estimates of the Legal Permanent Resident Population in 2011.* Washington, DC: U.S. Department of Homeland Security, Office of Immigration Statistics.

Salcido, O., and Menjívar, C. (2012). Gendered paths to legal citizenship: The case of Latin American immigrants in Phoenix, Arizona. *Law & Society Review, 46*(2), 335-368.

Schildkraut, D.J. (2011). National identity in the United States. In *Handbook of Identity Theory and Research* (pp. 845-865). New York: Springer.

Schneider, D. (2011). *Crossing Borders: Migration and Citizenship in the Twentieth-Century United States.* Cambridge, MA: Harvard University Press.

Schuck, P.H. (1998). *Citizens, Strangers, and In-Betweens: Essays on Immigration and Citizenship.* Boulder, CO: Westview Press.

Seidle, F.L. (2010). *The Canada-Ontario Immigration Agreement: Assessment and Options of Renewal.* Toronto, ON: Mowat Centre for Policy Innovation, University of Toronto. Available: http://mowatcentre.ca/the-canada-ontario-immigration-agreement/ [March 2015].

Shapira, H. (2013). From the nativist's point of view. *The Sociological Quarterly, 54*(1), 35-50.

Singer, A., Wilson, J.H., and DeRenzis, B. (2009). *Immigrants, Politics, and Local Response in Suburban Washington.* Washington, DC: Brookings Institution Press.

Smith, M.L. (1998). Any woman who is now or may hereafter be married... Women and naturalization, ca. 1802-1940. *Prologue Magazine 30*(2). Available: http://www.archives.gov/publications/prologue/1998/summer/women-and-naturalization-1.html [March 2015].

Soysal, Y.N. (1994). *Limits of Citizenship: Migrants and Post-national Membership in Europe.* Chicago: University of Chicago Press.

Spiro, P.J. (2010). Dual citizenship as human right. *International Journal of Constitutional Law, 8*(1), 111-130.

Squire, P., and Moncrief, G. (2009). *State Legislatures Today: Politics Under the Domes.* London, UK: Longman.

Stepick, A., and Stepick, C.D. (2002). Becoming American, constructing ethnicity: Immigrant youth and civic engagement. *Applied Developmental Science, 6*(4), 246-257.

Stoll, M.A., and Wong, J.S. (2007). Immigration and civic participation in a multiracial and multiethnic context. *International Migration Review, 41*(4), 880-908.

Sumption, M., and Flamm, S. (2012). *The Economic Value of Citizenship for Immigrants in the United States.* Washington, DC: Migration Policy Institute.

Terriquez, V. (2011). Schools for democracy: Labor union participation and Latino immigrant parents' school-based civic engagement. *American Sociological Review, 76,* 581-601.

Terriquez, V. (2012). Civic inequalities?: Immigrant incorporation and Latina mothers' participation in their children's schools. *Sociological Perspectives, 55,* 663-682.

Terriquez, V., and Kwon, H. (2014). Intergenerational Family Relations, Civic Organisations, and the Political Socialisation of Second-Generation Immigrant Youth. *Journal of Ethnic and Migration Studies, 41*(3), 425-447.

Tichenor, D.J. (2002). *Dividing lines.* Princeton, NJ: Princeton University Press.

U.S. Department of Homeland Security. (2002). *Yearbook of Immigration Statistics, 2001.* Washington, DC: U.S. Government Printing Office.

U.S. General Accounting Office. (2001). *Immigration Benefits: Several Factors Impede Timeliness of Application Processing.* GAO-01-488. Available: http://www.gpo.gov/fdsys/pkg/GAOREPORTS-GAO-01-488/content-detail.html [August 2015].

U.S. Government Accountability Office. (2011). *Immigrant Integration: U.S. Citizenship and Immigration Services Could Better Assess Its Grant Program.* Washington, DC: Author. Available: http://www.gao.gov/products/GAO-12-274 [October 2015].

U.S. Government Accountability Office. (2014). *Elections: Issues Related to State Voter Identification Laws.* Available: http://www.gao.gov/assets/670/665966.pdf [October 2015].

Van Hook, J., Brown, S.K., and Bean, F. (2006). For love or money? Welfare reform and immigrant naturalization. *Social Forces, 85*(2), 643-666.

Verba, S., Schlozman, K.L., Brady, H., and Nie, N.H. (1993). Race, ethnicity and political resources: Participation in the United States. *British Journal of Political Science, 23*(04), 453-497.

Vink, M.P., Prokic-Breuer, T., and Dronkers, J. (2013). Immigrant naturalization in the context of institutional diversity: policy matters, but to whom? *International Migration, 51*(5), 1-20.

Waldinger, R. (2008). Between "here" and "there": Immigrant cross-border activities and loyalties. *International Migration Review, 42*(1), 3-29.

White House Task Force on New Americans. (2015). *Strengthening Communities by Welcoming All Residents: A Federal Strategic Action Plan on Immigrant and Refugee Integration.* Available: https://www.whitehouse.gov/sites/default/files/docs/final_tf_newamericans_report_4-14-15_clean.pdf [August 2015].

Wong, C. (2006). *Lobbying for Inclusion: Rights, Politics, and the Making of Immigration Policy.* Stanford, CA: Stanford University Press.

Wong, J., Ramakrishnan, S.K., Lee, T., and Junn, J. (2011). *Asian American Political Participation: Emerging Constituents and Their Political Identities*. New York: Russell Sage Foundation.

Wong, J., and Tseng, V. (2008). Political socialization in immigrant families: Challenging top-down parental socialization models. *Journal of Ethnic and Migration Studies, 34*(1), 151-168.

Wong, J.S. (2000). The effects of age and political exposure on the development of party identification among Asian American and Latino immigrants in the United States. *Political Behavior, 22*(4), 341-371.

Woodrow-Lafield, K., Xu, X., Kersen, T., and Poch, B. (2004). Naturalization of U.S. immigrants: Highlights from ten countries. *Population Research and Policy Review, 23*, 187-218.

Yang, P. (1994). Explaining immigrant naturalization. *International Migration Review, 28*(3), 449-477.

5

Spatial Dimensions of Immigrant Integration

National statistics sometimes hide or even obfuscate the nation's spatially uneven patterns of immigrant integration from one place to another. Indeed, where immigrants live shapes the integration experience in myriad ways. Every place—state, city, suburb, neighborhood or rural area—represents a unique context of reception that affects how immigrants, refugees, and their offspring are incorporated into neighborhoods, schools, local labor markets, and, ultimately, U.S. society. What is different today from the past is that unprecedented numbers of new immigrants and the foreign-born population have diffused spatially from traditional areas of first settlement (e.g., in the Southwest or in large gateway cities) to so-called "new destinations" in the Midwest and South, to suburbs previously populated largely by native-born Americans, to small but rapidly growing metropolitan areas, and even to rural communities (Lichter, 2012; Massey, 2008; Singer, 2013).

Perhaps paradoxically, this widespread geographic diffusion of immigrants also has occurred in tandem with population concentration in *specific* immigrant receiving areas (e.g., inner suburban neighborhoods, new Asian ethnoburbs, and Hispanic boom towns, as well as continued settlement in established destinations) with growing racial and ethnic minority populations that may not share the same culture, language, or education with the local native-born population. New immigration has left an outsized demographic and economic imprint on many communities, including on ethnoracial diversity, the provision of public assistance, school budgets, and local politics. Processes of assimilation and incorporation occur "in place," and these processes are expressed differently depending on the reception local communities give to groups of diverse national origins; that is, whether native-born populations and state and local policies are welcoming or antagonistic to new immigrants.

In this chapter, the panel emphasizes that the national picture of social integration of America's new immigrant groups outlined in Chapter 1 is the net result of offsetting positive and negative trajectories of immigrant integration that occur unevenly from one place to another. Scholars often focus on immigrant incorporation into U.S. society or the economic mainstream, but the experience of integration is, in reality, an inherently local one. As this chapter makes plain, the current research-based understanding of the local context of immigrant reception is regrettably incomplete and often superficial, especially for nontraditional receiving areas that are now attracting large immigrant populations of different national origins, different legal statuses (e.g., unauthorized and refugee populations), and different levels of social and political capital. The research literature nevertheless has identified some policy options—at the state and local level—that can shape immigrant trajectories of incorporation, now and into the future.

This chapter has three specific aims. First, it provides a general overview of current theory and research on spatial assimilation: the local incorporation of immigrant populations into the mainstream. The panel discusses both the canonical view, which was drawn from classical assimilation theory, and alternative (and less optimistic) views that some new immigrant groups are becoming "ghettoized" or have assimilated spatially with an urban underclass population in poor and segregated neighborhoods and communities (even rural communities).

Second, the chapter highlights recent patterns of spatial redistribution and internal migration among the immigrant and foreign-born populations. Spatial integration can be defined by the extent to which residence patterns among immigrants mirror those of the native-born population. This chapter highlights changes in patterns of population redistribution among immigrants, as well as their movement into nontraditional areas of first settlement. Spatial assimilation is now taking place at multiple but interlinked levels of geography (i.e., region, state, metropolitan, suburban, neighborhood, and rural). New immigrants have transformed the racial and ethnic composition of many cities and communities, while also providing a demographic lifeline to other slow-growing or economically declining areas, especially in rural areas.

Third, the chapter identifies how processes of social integration and assimilation are influenced by local economic and political contexts of reception. New destinations, in particular, represent natural laboratories for studying immigrant integration, ethnic conflict and majority-minority relations, and local politics and policy responses (Waters and Jiménez, 2005). In those places, where growth in the immigrant population is fast-paced and often unexpected by the resident population, policy reactions can be swift and strong. In response to the growing presence of immigrants in these new destinations and stalled efforts in Congress at comprehensive immigration reform, some states and municipalities have enacted inclusive policies and practices (e.g., sanctuary cities, like San Francisco), while others have created policies designed to restrict how and where some immigrants can work and live (e.g., in Arizona and Hazleton, Pennsylvania). How states and local communities assist or impede the incorporation of new immigrants into the larger community is important to understanding the process of immigrant integration at the local level.

SPATIAL INTEGRATION: BACKGROUND AND THEORY

The canonical view is that the spatial "assimilation" (as it has historically been called) of immigrants and minority groups is a product of increasing cultural and economic integration. That is, residential differences between immigrants and natives are expected to decline as immigrants—over time and across generations—experience upward social and economic mobility. Spatial assimilation theory holds that immigrants typically first settle in communities with others from similar backgrounds (e.g., enclaves where cultural and institutional support is ensured) but "move up and out" over time or across generations as they learn English, acquire new job skills, and become "Americanized" (Alba and Foner, 2015; Lichter et al., 2015; Massey, 2008). In this view, social and spatial mobility presumably go hand in hand. Spatial integration therefore both reflects and reinforces socioeconomic mobility among America's new immigrant populations, including Hispanics from Mexico and other parts of Latin America, culturally and economically diverse Asian foreign-born populations, and refugee populations from war-torn parts of sub-Saharan Africa, the Middle East, and Eastern Europe (the Balkans). That family income among immigrant populations is positively associated with neighborhood quality also gives empirical credence to this spatial assimilation model (Alba et al., 2014).

Indeed, a common inference today is that the new spatial diffusion of immigrant populations from traditional gateway states (e.g., Texas or California) and cities (e.g., El Paso, Texas, or Los Angeles, California) to new destinations reflects social and economic integration. To illustrate the point historically, Italian immigrants in New York City in the early 1900s gained an economic toehold living in the tenements in the lower East Side of Manhattan before their upwardly mobile descendants moved to better neighborhoods in New Jersey, Long Island, and elsewhere (Kasnitz et al., 2009). Today's recent immigrant movement to new destinations—many with little recent history of immigration—may similarly signal a pathway to immigrant integration in more affluent communities (Massey, 2008;

Massey et al., 2009). The movement of immigrants, especially Hispanics and Asians, to new or nontraditional destinations without an intermediate stop in traditional gateways suggests much greater similarity today than in the past in immigrants' residence patterns with the native population. Spatial integration implies greater access to society's rewards, including good schools, high-paying jobs, and safe neighborhoods.

An alternative view to the canonical model, a less optimistic one, is that new immigrants are remaining highly segregated and spatially isolated from the mainstream society. Indeed, low-income immigrant and refugee populations may be living in a "parallel society," metaphorically locked away in poor and segregated neighborhoods that are cut off from the rest of society and where opportunities to succeed are limited (Alba and Foner, 2015). The concern arising from this view is that these communities lack the most basic economic, cultural, and political ingredients needed to ensure immigrant success—for themselves and their children. Moving to new destinations is no economic panacea. Emerging empirical evidence indicates that some native whites and affluent populations are "fleeing" diversifying neighborhoods for predominantly white suburbs, gated communities in exurban developments, or returning to the city as part of the gentrification process (in Minneapolis, Washington, D.C., and elsewhere), leaving behind the poorest and most vulnerable populations to fend for themselves in economically declining communities (Crowder et al., 2011; Hall and Crowder, 2014). The fact that more immigrants are bypassing traditional gateways altogether (Lichter and Johnson, 2009, Singer et al., 2008) suggests that native-born populations and basic institutions like schools in some new destinations are being exposed, perhaps for the first time, to immigrant populations that lack basic education and English-language skills. This makes integration especially difficult and sometimes instills new anti-immigrant antipathies and discrimination that compound the problem (Massey and Sanchez, 2012). Many new destinations simply lack the institutional resources needed to effectively accommodate the needs of new arrivals. As described later in this chapter, state and local responses in the form of racial profiling, restrictive zoning, or other exclusionary policies have cropped up in communities across the United States, even as other states and localities have welcomed immigrants (Carr et al., 2012; Gelatt et al., 2015). The problem, of course, is that idiosyncratic patterns from state to state or from community to community are not easily summarized by highly aggregated national statistics on the "average" experiences of specific immigrants or immigration populations.

Finally, Alba and Foner (2015, p. 71) argue that our thinking about spatial assimilation or isolation is sometimes "turned on its head" by the idea of the immigrant enclave, where economically vulnerable immigrants find a safe haven in institutionally complete and highly functional ethnic communities (e.g., communities often known as Chinatown, Little Italy, Koreatown, or little Havana) that provide a permanent home or a launching point for someplace better. The immigrant enclave literature is large, well established, and typically based on local case studies, which can be idiosyncratic. Sweeping generalizations are best avoided, and caution in interpretation and lessons is required. For example, the establishment and growth of immigrant enclaves is sometimes viewed as a response to discrimination and the lack of good jobs. The important point is that all traces of "parallel society" in America are not regarded as especially problematic or as a source of fear among natives or local residences. In fact, ethnic neighborhoods are often regarded as a local attraction, providing native-born Americans with opportunities to experience a different culture (i.e., the people, language, music, and food of a foreign land) without leaving the United States.

Recent immigration settlement patterns have upended conventional theories of assimilation and integration (Waters and Jiménez, 2005). "Contexts of reception" clearly matter, and they matter now in ways heretofore unimagined because of the racial and ethnic diversity of America's new immigrant populations and the heterogeneity in the places they settle. Indeed, the context of reception operates at the national level through government immigration policy, but any positive effects trickle down unevenly across states, cities, suburbs, neighborhoods, and rural areas with widely different institutional resources and local labor market dynamics (Ellis and Almgren, 2009). Diverse economic, political, civic, and social characteristics, along with local culture, shape the experiences of immigration integration.

THE GEOGRAPHY OF IMMIGRATION

Immigration is driving rapid increases in racial and ethnic diversity across the United States. Texas joined California, the District of Columbia, Hawaii, and New Mexico between 2000 and 2010 as "majority-minority" states having more ethnoracial minorities than non-Hispanic whites (Humes et al., 2011). Of the nation's 3,143 counties, 348 are at least half minority. Most of America's 100 largest cities have majority-minority populations (Frey, 2015), and the numbers of diverse suburban and rural communities have also grown considerably over the past two decades (Lee et al., 2014; Lichter, 2012). Many newcomers, however, continue to concentrate or become residentially segregated in specific neighborhoods or communities across the metropolitan landscape (Iceland and Scopilliti, 2008). Immigration is thus driving two countervailing trends: new patterns of spatial dispersal are occurring at the same time that many immigrant populations are concentrating locally (Rugh and Massey, 2014; Holloway et al., 2012). Recent trends require that a thoughtful person recalibrate the

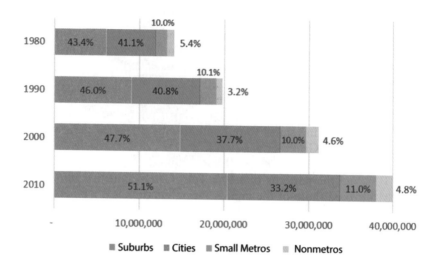

FIGURE 5-1 Change in geographic dispersal of immigrants by metro type, 1980-2010.
SOURCE: Adapted from Singer (2013a).

historical perspective that immigrants gradually disperse and integrate with U.S. society over time and generation after initially settling in inner cities.

Residential integration occurs at multiple levels of geography (Lee et al., 2014; Massey et al., 2009). Yet, the usual metro-centric approach focusing on big-city neighborhood segregation may be less appropriate than the past.[1] As illustrated below, immigrants are dispersing broadly across many different levels of geography—states, metropolitan cities, neighborhoods, and rural areas—and more than half of all immigrants are in the suburbs. This means that the usual generalizations based on the spatial assimilation model of big-city neighborhood segregation are incomplete and perhaps even misleading. Numerically speaking, the biggest shift in the distribution across places has been to the suburbs, where more than half of all immigrants currently live (see Figure 5-1) (Singer, 2013). A spatially inclusive approach to native-immigrant residence patterns is now required (Parisi et al., 2015). That is a key challenge for scholars today.

---

[1]Segregation is the degree to which one or more groups live separately from one another. For more details on how this is conceptualized and measured, see Denton and Massey (1992).

States

Recent census data reveal that in 2010 more than 25 percent of the foreign-born population lived in California, and almost two-thirds of all immigrants lived in just six states: California, Florida, Illinois, New Jersey, New York, and Texas (Grieco et al., 2012). The spatial concentration of immigrants is greater than among the native-born population. California accounted for 10.2 percent of the native-born population, and the top six immigrant-receiving states were home to only about 36 percent of all native-born people (Grieco et al., 2012).

In 2012, about 26 percent of all immigrants were undocumented (see Figure 3-1), and the patterns of settlement of undocumented immigrants generally mirrored those of the immigrant population as a whole. For example, the top six receiving states for all immigrants are the same for the undocumented; these states accounted for 62.3 percent of all unauthorized immigrants in 2012 (Center for Migration Studies, 2015). The estimated numbers of immigrants eligible for Deferred Action for Childhood Arrivals (DACA) and Deferred Action for Parental Accountability (DAPA) also follow these patterns very closely.

In 2012, Mexicans made up more than 28 percent of the immigrant stock (11.5 million out of a total foreign-born population of 40.7 million) and they are even more concentrated than the total foreign-born population. According to recent research by the Pew Research Center, more than 58 percent of all Mexican immigrants live in just two states: California (4.2 million) and Texas (2.5 million).[2] Immigrants from South and East Asia (principally immigrants from China, India, the Philippines, South Korea, and Vietnam) make up about a quarter of all immigrants: 10.4 million persons. These immigrants are more evenly distributed[3] across the states than are Mexicans, with the main concentrations occurring in California (3.3 million) and New York (1 million). About 3.9 million immigrants are from the Caribbean; these immigrants remain highly concentrated, with more than 40 percent in Florida and another 28 percent in New York. Notably, the 3.2 million Central American immigrants are more evenly distributed than Mexicans, in part because of the significant numbers of El Salvadorans who have settled in the greater Washington, D.C., metropolitan area. South American immigrants have an East Coast orientation with concentrations in Florida, New Jersey, and New York; California, nevertheless accounts for over 9 percent of South Americans in the United States.

As noted in Chapter 3, in 2013 about 70,000 new refugees were re-

---

[2] See http://www.pewhispanic.org/2014/04/29/statistical-portrait-of-the-foreign-born-population-in-the-united-states-2012/#foreign-born-by-state-and-region-of-birth-2012-a [August 2015].

[3] Measured using the Herfindahl index based on the percentage distribution across all states.

settled in the United States. This is roughly 5 percent of the total number of people who obtained lawful permanent residence status that year.[4] The country profile of refugees is very different from that of other immigrants. Bhutan, Burma, and Iraq accounted for more than 70 percent of all arriving refugees in both 2012 and 2013. The principal receiving states were California and Texas, followed by Florida, Michigan, New York, and Pennsylvania. The top six states accounted for about 37 percent of all the refugees who arrived in 2012 and 2013. Thus refugees are more evenly distributed than are immigrants, but they are still distributed in a slightly more concentrated pattern that the native-born population (Burt and Batalova, 2014). And unlike the native-born and nonrefugee immigrants, refugees are also directed to specific places of settlement by the federal government. Although these are overwhelmingly places with large foreign-born populations, the refugees are also settled in smaller metropolitan areas where they may be disproportionately represented among the immigrant population (Singer and Wilson, 2006).

The top immigrant-receiving states have been important gateways for new immigrants for some time, but other states have become new destinations over the past two decades. In 2010, the six states with the largest immigrant populations accounted for 65 percent of the foreign-born population. This figure is nevertheless down from 2000 (68%) and 1990 (73%). For example, Mexican-born immigrants during the 1990s started leaving California in large numbers or moving to other destinations in a marked shift from the past. Today, the states with the highest rates of growth in immigrant populations include some relatively small states such as Nevada and Utah in the West but also include seven southern states (see Figure 5-2). The fiscal and political implications of the new state geography of U.S. immigration are played out unevenly at the local level: in cities, suburban communities, and neighborhoods.

Whether the realignment of immigrants across states reflects a process of spatial assimilation is open to debate. On the one hand, the passage of the Immigration Reform and Control Act (IRCA) in 1986 provided a new freedom for many newly legalized immigrants to freely move beyond traditional gateway states and communities. Long-established immigrant populations (i.e., Latin American immigrants in California, Texas, and elsewhere) also had accumulated sufficient socioeconomic and cultural resources to leave gateway enclaves for better employment opportunities and housing elsewhere (Card and Lewis, 2007; Light, 2008). On the other hand, the exodus from traditional gateways was often spurred by state anti-migrant legislation. For example, in California, Proposition 187 ac-

---

[4] Another 29,000 individuals were granted asylum that year, with over a third of those coming from China. See Refugee and Asylee, Chapter 3.

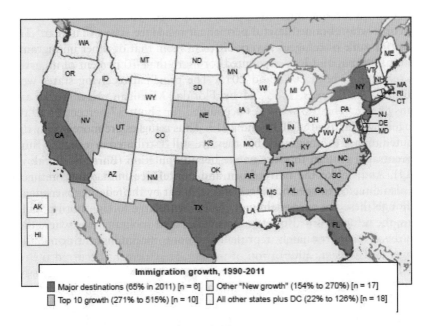

FIGURE 5-2 Immigration growth, 1990-2011.
SOURCE: Adapted from Jeff Passel, Pew Research Center, presentation to the panel, January 15, 2014.

celerated the departure of its foreign-born population, a circumstance that cannot be viewed as evidence of social and spatial integration. Moreover, the hardening of the border in the 1990s reduced illegal border entries in those heavily traveled areas and intentionally diverted flows to the Sonoran desert in Arizona, where authorities believed immigrants would be easier to catch (Nevins, 2010). The result was an unanticipated rise in death rates (Eschbach et al., 1999; Nevins, 2007) and a waning of California destinations as newer destinations held better opportunities. While an estimated 63 percent of all Mexican migrants arriving between 1985 and 1990 went to California, between 1995 and 2000 that figure shrank to just 28 percent (Massey and Capoferro, 2008). Clearly, state immigration policies contributed, perhaps unintentionally, to the spatial dispersal of new immigrants—both documented and undocumented—to nontraditional states in the Midwest and Southeast.

However, the continuing dispersal of immigrants from older gateway states to new, emerging destinations is by no means inevitable. Before the Great Recession, new gateway destinations drew significant numbers of foreign-born internal migrants as well as immigrants arriving directly from abroad. The recession and its aftermath tarnished the allure of new destinations (for both immigrants and the native born), as the economies in many emerging destinations were particularly hard hit (Ellis et al., 2014a).

Metropolitan Areas

Immigrants overwhelmingly live in America's largest metropolitan areas, which comprise cities and suburbs. In 2010, 85 percent of all immigrants lived in the 100 largest metropolitan areas, compared with 62 percent of the U.S.-born population (Singer, 2013, p. 81). The concentration of immigrants in metropolitan areas is not new. Immigrants historically have settled disproportionately in the nation's largest cities. In 1900, for example, two-thirds of all immigrants lived in the nation's largest 100 cities, compared to just 44 percent of the native-born population (Singer, 2013, p. 81). A significant proportion of immigrant settlement occurred then in just five metropolitan areas, and this has remained true for more than 100 years (see Figure 5-3).

In 2010, among the large metropolitan areas, 39 percent of Miami's population was foreign-born. San Jose (37%) ranked second, followed by Los Angeles (34%), San Francisco (30%), and New York (29%). Among metropolitan areas with populations over 1 million, the five with the small-

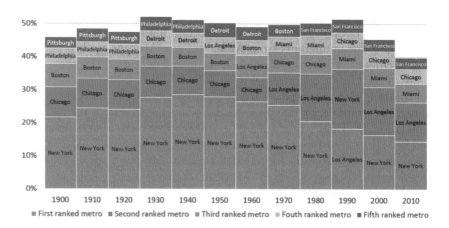

FIGURE 5-3 Five largest immigrant populations in metropolitan areas as a share of all metropolitan areas, 1900-2010.
SOURCE: Singer (2013, Fig. 1). Reprinted with permission.

est shares of immigrants in 2010 were Cincinnati, Cleveland, Pittsburgh, St. Louis, and Tulsa (Wilson and Singer, 2011).

Because the native-born population is predominantly white and the majority of immigrants are not, immigrants and their offspring are the main drivers of growing ethnic and racial diversity in the United States (Frey, 2015). Given the metropolitan orientation of U.S. immigration, this growing diversity is perhaps most often evident in cities and suburbs. All large metropolitan areas have become ethnically and racially more diverse since 1990 (Frey, 2015) and metropolitan areas with disproportionately large white populations are becoming a thing of the past: in 1990, 31 of the 53 largest metropolitan areas were 80 percent white, whereas in 2010, only 18 had populations more than 80 percent white. These changes are geographically uneven. In some metropolitan areas, especially those in the older industrial regions of the Northeast, whites remain numerically dominant, while other areas have rapidly diversified (Wright et al., 2013).

Immigrant-driven diversification itself is not uniform; different metropolitan areas have different immigrant and ethnic profiles. New York, for example, has a diverse set of immigrant populations, whereas immigrants from Asia, Central America, and Mexico are predominant in Los Angeles as well as major gateways such as Dallas-Fort Worth and Houston. Miami is also a major gateway, with more than 60 percent of Miami-Dade County residents claiming a Latino ethnicity, many of whom are foreign-born. Asian immigrants tend to concentrate in just three large immigrant gateways: San Francisco, Los Angeles, and New York. The metropolitan areas with the most immigrants from Africa (who make up about 4 percent of the total foreign-born population) are New York and Washington, D.C. Washington, D.C., is emerging as an important immigrant destination, but particularly for immigrants from Africa because Africans tend to perceive capital cities as centers for business, culture, and education—as they are in many of their home countries (Wilson and Habecker, 2008).

There is also geographic variation across metropolitan areas by legal status. For example, by mapping the undocumented share of the Mexican population, Hall and Stringfield (2014) showed that metropolitan areas that had had a longer history of Mexican settlement (in Southern California and Texas) had lower shares of undocumented immigrants than metropolitan areas in states with more recent Mexican immigration (e.g., Alabama, the Carolinas, Georgia, and Maryland).[5]

---

[5] The Center for Migration Studies' interactive website on the geography of the U.S. undocumented population adds further detail, see http://data.cmsny.org/ [August 2015].

Suburbs

What draws immigrants to different metropolitan areas has varied over time and is influenced by job opportunities (industrial restructuring and changing labor demand) in tandem with social networks. And where immigrants live *within* metropolitan areas also matters for their integration. Not only have immigrants found opportunities in many newer metropolitan destinations, they are no longer exclusively settling in inner-city neighborhoods of the largest metropolitan areas.

In 2010, 51 percent of all immigrants lived in the suburbs of the 95 largest metropolitan areas, while 33 percent lived within the city jurisdictions in those areas (Singer, 2013). As recently as 1980, similar shares lived in the cities and suburbs of the largest metros (41% and 43%, respectively). Overall trends in city and suburban settlements between 2000 and 2013 reveal that in the largest metropolitan areas, 76 percent of the growth in the immigrant populations occurred in the suburbs (Wilson and Svajlenka, 2014). In Chicago, Illinois; Cleveland, Ohio; Detroit and Grand Rapids, Michigan; Jackson, Mississippi; Los Angeles, California; Rochester, New York; and Ogden and Salt Lake City, Utah, virtually all of the metropolitan growth was in the suburbs (see Figure 5-4). These nine metropolitan

FIGURE 5-4 Foreign-born population growth in primary cities and suburbs, 2000-2013.
SOURCE: Wilson and Svajlenka (2014). Reprinted with permission.

areas reflect a mixture of former industrial powerhouses whose cities have been on the decline for decades and newer metropolitan areas, such as Salt Lake City, Ogden, and Jackson, where most of the population lives in suburbs. But Chicago and Los Angeles, which are well-established immigrant gateways, also saw all immigrant growth in the suburbs.

This suburban shift is partly related to the urban form of newer destinations that tend to be more suburban. In some suburban communities, it also reflects other metropolitan growth processes, such as out-migration and settlement shifts that include the native-born populations. In some cases, there is evidence of white flight from growing immigrant destination communities (Crowder et al., 2011). But another important factor is the restructuring of the U.S. economy: specifically, the decentralization of jobs and the rise of suburbs as the new locus of employment opportunity (Singer et al., 2008). Some metropolitan areas have developed strong knowledge-based industries, drawing high-skilled immigrants to the suburbs of Atlanta, Austin, Dallas, San Jose, Seattle, and Washington, D.C., where technology corporations are headquartered. During the economic expansion prior to the Great Recession, the growth of these industries also spawned housing and construction booms, drawing immigrant workers and making "the suburbs" more economically and racially diverse during the last immigration wave.

In some metropolitan areas, immigrant settlement is taking place almost entirely in the suburbs (Singer, 2013). Those areas with the highest shares of immigrants living in suburbs include places with small central cities, such as Atlanta (95% in suburbs) and Washington, D.C. (86% in suburbs), but also areas with central cities that have hemorrhaged population in recent years such as Detroit (87% in suburbs), Cleveland (86% in suburbs), and Dayton (83%). The newest immigrant destinations—mostly modest-sized metropolitan areas—have seen more than a doubling of the immigrant population in suburban areas. These places include Des Moines, Iowa; Indianapolis, Indiana; Jackson, Mississippi; Knoxville, Tennessee; Little Rock, Arkansas; and Louisville, Kentucky. Still, this is not a universal pattern. In 12 metro areas, including Asheville, North Carolina; Columbus, Ohio; Nashville, Tennessee; and Omaha, Nebraska, immigrant growth rates were faster in the city than in the suburbs. These are typically smaller metropolitan areas that have become new immigrant destinations over the past two decades.

The geography of job growth helps shape overall patterns of immigrant settlement. However, many of the fastest growing metropolitan immigrant destinations are places with small core cities and large suburbs, such as Atlanta and Washington, D.C. Others—including Austin, Texas; Charlotte, North Carolina; and Phoenix, Arizona—have large central cities developed through annexation and tend also to be sprawling, less dense communities organized around automobile transportation. While the role of the city center and ethnic residential neighborhoods within that center has declined for immigrants, it is not immediately clear how suburban settlement affects the integration prospects for immigrants or for the communities in which they choose to live. Suburban places often lack institutional support services (e.g., nonprofit organizations, churches, and other government services) that help immigrants adjust to their new surroundings (Roth et al., 2015). Moreover, many suburban communities lack public transportation services, day care, or after-school programs that can accommodate the routine daily activities and work schedules of immigrants. Under these circumstances, it is not surprising that rates of poverty have grown most rapidly over the past decade in suburban areas that have become home for America's new immigrant populations (Kneebone and Berube, 2013).

Neighborhoods

The impact of recent immigration into metropolitan areas is experienced first and foremost in the neighborhoods in which immigrants settle. Metropolitan areas with either large or fast-growing foreign-born populations have rapidly shifting patterns of immigrant concentrations and new forms of neighborhood racial and ethnic diversity (Holloway et al., 2012).[6] Immigration since the 1970s has produced a shift from historical black-white segregation patterns toward more complex geographies in what have become multiethnic metropolitan regions (Fong and Shibuya, 2005; Frey, 2015).

Although many new immigrants still concentrate in particular neighborhoods, other immigrants and their offspring are what Logan and Zhang (2010, p. 1069) call "pioneer integrators" of previously all-white spaces. The result is that many neighborhoods are more diverse than they have been for decades (e.g., Holloway et al., 2012; Logan and Zhang, 2010). Rugh and Massey (2014) assessed these competing trends for aggregate racialized groups living in U.S. metropolitan areas between 1970 and 2010. Black segregation and isolation declined overall, but in those areas with longer histories of high levels of segregation, black hyper-segregation per-

---

[6] See Mixed Metro U.S.: Mapping Diversity in the USA, a cooperative venture of the Departments of Geography at Dartmouth College, University of Georgia, and University of Washington at http://mixedmetro.us/ [August 2015].

sisted (Massey and Tannen, 2015).[7] Latino segregation increased slightly while Latino isolation rose substantially in this 40-year period. Asian segregation started at moderate levels and changed little. Although Asian isolation increased, it remained at comparatively low levels. Rugh and Massey (2014) also found that whites remained "quite isolated from all three minority groups in metropolitan America, despite rising diversity and some shifts toward integration from the minority viewpoint." The forces producing minority segregation and spatial isolation include density zoning ordinances that exclude low-income and minority populations (Rothwell and Massey, 2009, 2010), large or rising minority percentages, lagging minority socioeconomic status, and active expressions of anti-black and anti-Latino sentiment, especially in large metropolitan areas (Rugh and Massey, 2014). Places lacking these attributes are becoming more integrated, often relatively quickly (Rugh and Massey, 2014).

Immigrants generally tend to be more residentially segregated than their native-born counterparts, and segregation between immigrants and the native-born has increased since 1970 (Cutler et al., 2008). This suggests a lack of spatial assimilation, perhaps born of inequality in income, low levels of education, and cultural factors (e.g., poor English-language skills). One common empirical approach is to compare the patterns of neighborhood segregation of immigrants and immigrant groups with native-born whites. Iceland and Scopilliti (2008) measured residential segregation using the segregation index (on a scale from 0 for no segregation to 100 for complete segregation) across metropolitan areas.[8] In 2000, the segregation index between the foreign-born population and native-born white population was 44.3. This means that 44.3 percent of immigrants would be required to move to other neighborhoods for immigrants to achieve the same distribution across neighborhoods as the native-born white population (Iceland and Scopilliti, 2008).

In general, the foreign-born gradually become less segregated from

---

[7]Segregation is measured using two indices in the literature: dissimilarity and isolation. Segregation is measured using the Index of Dissimilarity (D). D_t is defined as

$$D_t = \tfrac{1}{2} \sum_{i=1}^{k} |m_{it} - w_{it}|$$

where m_{it} and w_{it} are the respective percentages of minorities and whites residing in census tract i at time t. This segregation index is based on pair-wise comparisons and varies from 0 (no segregation) to 100 (complete segregation). D indicates the percentage of minorities that would have to move to another neighborhood in order to achieve parity between minorities and whites in their percentage distributions across all neighborhoods. Isolation is a measure of the percentage of the population of a particular neighborhood or census tract who are of one racial or ethnic group. For example, an isolation index of 60 for Latinos means that Latinos, on average, live in neighborhoods that are 60 percent Latino.

[8]In this report, the panel uses "segregation index" in place of "dissimilarity index."

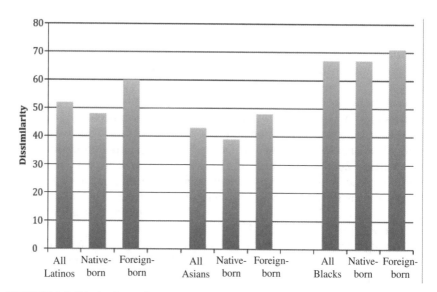

FIGURE 5-5 Dissimilarity from native-born whites by race/ethnicity and nativity in 2000.
SOURCE: Data from Iceland and Scopilliti (2008). Reprinted with permission.

native-born whites and more dispersed across residential neighborhoods as length of residence increases (Iceland and Scopilliti, 2008; Wright et al., 2005). For example, recently arrived immigrants tend to have higher levels of segregation from whites than immigrants who have lived in the country for 10 or 20 years (Iceland and Scopilliti, 2008). Thus, the segregation index for all recently arrived (past 10 years) immigrants compared to whites was 52, in contrast to an index of 31 for all immigrants (compared to whites) who had been in the country at least 20 years. This result provides clear evidence of spatial assimilation, at least at the metropolitan neighborhood level, and supports the idea that immigrant integration is following the historical pattern of initial settlement in ethnic enclaves, followed by subsequent dispersal to more diverse and "better" neighborhoods (Alba and Nee, 2003).

However, average segregation levels hide substantial heterogeneity by immigrant group. For example, Asian immigrants tend to be less segregated from native-born whites in metropolitan neighborhoods than are Hispanic or black immigrants (see Figure 5-5). According to Iceland and Scopilliti (2008), the segregation index for foreign-born Asians in 2000 was 47.7, compared with 59.9 among foreign-born Hispanics and 71.2 among foreign-born blacks. Segregation indices are lowest among foreign-born whites (D = 30.5). This racial hierarchy mirrors patterns of racial segregation nationally (Freeman, 2002; Logan et al., 2004), and highlights familiar patterns of black exceptionalism in integration processes. And, unlike the white, Hispanic, and Asian foreign-born populations, length of residence in the United States (as measured by year of arrival in the United States) was largely unrelated to foreign-born black-white declines in racial residential segregation (Iceland and Scopilliti, 2008; see also Wright et al., 2005). The implication for black immigrants is that improvements over time in socioeconomic status and other indicators of integration do not translate easily into spatial integration with native-born whites (or, by extension, into "better" neighborhoods).[9]

What accounts for these racialized patterns? The neighborhood has long been used as the starting point for understanding the integration process. Historical analysis and the research on recent immigration demonstrate that this process should not be measured in terms of years but rather decades or generations of immigrants (Brown, 2007). Even so, there is no simple one-to-one correspondence between immigrant social integration and segregation. Even considering just three aggregated racialized groups, patterns of immigrant concentration and the associated segregation from native-born whites varies by group (Figure 5-5). This reflects the long history of housing market discrimination against blacks in the United States that, along with poverty, has produced high levels of residential segregation (Massey and Denton, 1993). Immigrant blacks are not immune from these forces: foreign-born blacks are even more segregated from whites than are native-born blacks (Figure 5-5). The patterns for blacks are replicated for Latinos but with moderated levels of segregation from whites. Latinos also face housing market discrimination, historically and today (Turner et al., 2002). When these disadvantages are combined with low incomes, segregated residential patterns result. And heightened rates of residential segregation from whites are evident for foreign-born Latinos compared with native-born Latinos (Figure 5-5). In addition, Latinos of African origin (mostly from the Caribbean) are far more segregated than are white Latinos (Denton and Massey, 1989; Iceland and Nelson, 2008).

Yu and Myers (2007) also found differences by national origin when they tracked the residential assimilation of Chinese, Korean, and Mexican immigrants in Los Angeles. Each group exhibited a different trajectory and pace of assimilation. Chinese immigrants tended to rapidly enter into homeownership in predominantly suburban locations. Koreans were more likely than other immigrants to choose city residence and live in more

---

[9]Estimates of the segregation index by generation or for 2010 are currently unavailable, in part because nativity status was not included in the 2010 Decennial Census and spatially disaggregated estimates based on the American Community Survey are subject to substantial sampling variability.

mixed white-and-Latino neighborhoods. In contrast, Mexican homeowner-ship was more likely than the other groups to be associated with coethnic neighborhood residence (some implications of these patterns are discussed below).

In challenging the conventional narrative of dispersal and integration, another study found that the intermetropolitan *dispersal* of immigrants from traditional gateways was associated with heightened levels of immi-grant *segregation* in new metropolitan and nonmetropolitan destinations (Lichter et al., 2010; Hall, 2013). Earnings, occupation, or time of arrival in the United States can account for some but not all of the high levels of immigrant segregation from natives. Immigrant legal status does, however, play a role. For instance, Hall and Stringfield (2014) found that while the presence of undocumented immigrants is correlated with higher levels of segregation between Mexicans and whites, it has the opposite effect on Mexican-black segregation—contributing to residential sharing among these groups.

Immigrants continue to face challenges to residential integration in both new and established areas of settlement, both for the above reasons and because the migration behaviors of the native-born exacerbate resi-dential differences. Research examining how native-born white and black mobility relates to local immigrant concentrations, and how this relation-ship varies across metropolitan areas, indicates that as neighborhood im-migrant populations grow, the likelihood of neighborhood out-migration by the native-born increases (Crowder et al., 2011; Hall and Crowder, 2014). This finding is independent of the sociodemographic characteristics of householders or the types of neighborhoods and metropolitan areas stud-ied. Tellingly, this tendency to exit neighborhoods experiencing an influx of immigrants was most pronounced for the native-born who lived in metro-politan areas that were developing into notable immigrant gateway cities: that is, areas that were experiencing a rapid recent growth in foreign-born populations. The native-born in these areas who relocated tended to move to neighborhoods with smaller immigrant concentrations than the ones they left. This tendency was more pronounced in metropolitan areas that were developing into immigrant gateways than in other areas. Related research also reported growing immigrant neighborhood density produced native-born flight as well as slower housing price appreciation in immigrant-dense communities (Saiz and Wachter, 2011).

Despite changing attitudes toward racialized minorities and immi-grants, the dynamics of neighborhood change retain some very familiar processes associated with the native-born wanting to literally distance themselves from relatively poor nonwhite immigrants, some of whom will be undocumented. Consequently, traditional gateways as well as emerg-ing gateway metropolitan areas contain immigrant and second generation neighborhoods lacking amenities. These neighborhoods provide limited opportunities for immigrant integration. If immigrants continue to arrive with low levels of human capital or from impoverished backgrounds, spatial integration may be delayed, perhaps occurring most rapidly between the second and third generations (Bean et al., 2015; Brown, 2007). Places with large concentrations of poor immigrant populations may become part of a more permanent settlement system, one where "the potential for neighborhood improvement is modest" (Alba et al., 2014).

The recent subprime mortgage crisis further highlights the precarious position of poor, and especially poor Latino, immigrants in residential housing markets. Rugh (2015) found that Latinos were more likely than other groups to have been subject to especially risky low- and no-documentation lending. The probability that Latino borrowers experienced foreclosure during this crisis was about the same as that for blacks prior to the crisis or in the Rust Belt. But after the crisis, Latinos were significantly more likely than blacks to lose their homes because they were concentrated in states where the recession was particularly acute (i.e., Arizona, California, Florida, and Nevada).

Nonmetropolitan and Rural Areas

Until recently, rural and small-town America had been largely excluded from discussions associated with immigration and integration. But that has changed over the past decade or so because of the widespread spatial dispersion of immigrants into new rural areas and small towns (Kandel and Cromartie, 2004; Marrow, 2011; Zuniga and Hernandez-Leon, 2006). Population growth in nonmetropolitan America over the past decade was a direct result of new Latino immigration and the second-order effects of high fertility (Johnson and Lichter, 2010; Lichter, 2012). Between 2000 and 2010, Latinos accounted for 58 percent of all nonmetropolitan population growth, yet represented only about 7 percent of total population in these areas. In addition, many hired farmworkers are foreign-born. Kandel (2008, Table 1) estimated that in 2006 one-third of farmhands were noncitizens; of those, almost 95 percent were Latino. Farmwork is tied less than in the past to seasonal farm jobs performed by migrant workers. Agricultural workers have increasingly put down roots; for example, on dairy farms or working on year-round agricultural operations.

New immigrant populations have been a lifeline for many "dying" small towns experiencing chronic out-migration, especially in America's agricultural heartland (Carr et al., 2012). In a swath of counties from the Dakotas in the north to the Texas Panhandle in the south, the growth of the Latino immigrant population slowed overall population loss or overcame population loss of the native-born (Donato et al., 2008; Johnson and

Lichter, 2008). In the nonmetropolitan Midwest, for example, just 7 percent of counties accounted for 50 percent of Latinos (Lichter, 2012), many of whom are foreign-born. One consequence has been that the growth in some small rural communities has been extraordinary. As one example, Worthington, Minnesota experienced a Latino population increase from 392 in 1990 to 3,058 in the late 2000s.[10] In 1990, Latinos accounted for only about 4 percent of Worthington's population.[11] In 2012, Latinos made up nearly one-third of Worthington's population of nearly 13,000 people, and almost half were foreign-born.[12]

In nonmetropolitan areas, Latino growth and diversity have typically occurred in places where employment is linked to a few clearly defined industries (Parrado and Kandel, 2008). Some communities in the Midwest and Southeast with meat processing or meat packing plants now represent geographic "hot spots" for Latino growth (Gouveia et al., 2005; Griffith, 2005). Latino immigrants do the "dirty" and dangerous work that native workers apparently eschew. Latino growth is linked directly to rural industrial restructuring (especially in nondurable manufacturing, which include food processing) and, more generally, to the rapidly globalizing agro-food system. Recent studies found that, for Latino workers, relocating to small towns and rural areas has been a route to upward economic mobility, with few economic downsides for native-born workers (e.g., in the form of higher unemployment or lower wages), including low-wage, low-skilled black workers (Crowley et al., 2015; Turner, 2014).

New destinations are natural laboratories for studying highly located processes of social integration of immigrant communities. For instance, Massey and Capoferro (2008) showed that, between 1985 and 1990, only 10 percent of recently arrived immigrants from Mexico settled in new destinations (defined at the state level). However, a decade later during the 1995-2000 period, this percentage increased to 30 percent of Mexican immigrants.

The new growth of urban-origin Latino in-migrants into nonmetropolitan areas raises new integration challenges for many small towns unaccustomed to minority or foreign-born populations. Because of high Latino fertility (Lichter, 2012), and an aging-in-place native-born white population, generational strains have grown between older whites and the younger minority populations who often account for most new births and much of the school-age population. Schools may be less well equipped—in funding

---

[10]Panel-derived estimates based on data from the 2005-2009 American Community Survey.
[11]See http://www.census.gov/population/www/documentation/twps0029/twps0029.html [September 2015].
[12]Panel analysis of data is from http://www.city-data.com/races/races-Worthington-Minnesota.html [August 2015].

and personnel—to accommodate immigrant children who are disproportionately poor and who in many cases are being raised by parents who have
little or no education and who may be undocumented (see Chapters 1 and
8). Large shares of undocumented rural immigrants are at risk of joining a
permanent underclass that may prevent their children from moving ahead
in American society (Green, 2003). Undocumented workers are overrepresented in the rural labor force, which arguably makes economic, political,
and cultural incorporation more difficult (Kandel and Cromartie, 2004;
Southern Poverty Law Center, 2010).

Rural immigrants risk becoming socially and culturally isolated from
mainstream institutions, and often face strong anti-immigrant sentiment
from natives (Maldonado, 2014; Southern Poverty Law Center, 2010). In
Perry, Iowa, new Latino immigrants and migrants report becoming hyper-
visible; that is, "a sense of 'standing out' associated with their physical presence as Latino-looking and Latino-sounding bodies moving in and through
community spaces" (Maldonado, 2014, p. 1934). In this small town, Latino
integration "is frail at best" (Maldonado, 2014, p. 1942).

Segregation indexes in new rural destinations in the 2000s remain
high—rivaling rates found in metropolitan cities and suburbs (Parisi et al.,
2011). In addition, Latino immigrants seem to be integrating more rapidly
with blacks than whites, as measured by changes in small town segregation
in the 1990s and 2000s. Segregation also seems to be especially high if immigrants lack authorization and legal recourse or a welfare safety net (Hall
and Stringfield, 2014), and unauthorized immigrants are overrepresented
in rural areas, where they often work at low pay in meat packing or other
food processing plants, dairy farms, and agriculture. New immigrants from
Mexico and Latin America, in particular, may face other hardships, including job discrimination and exploitation in the workforce. Anti-immigrant
sentiment may be especially high in rural areas (e.g. Fennelly, 2008). Indeed, emerging evidence shows that native-born whites, especially those
with school-age children, are exiting communities with growing immigrant
populations (Crowder et al., 2011; Hall and Crowder, 2014). Research-
based understanding of processes of immigrant integration and native reactions in rural Latino "boom towns" is clearly incomplete (Waters and
Jiménez, 2005).

INTEGRATION "IN PLACE"

Immigrants work, go to school, worship, consume, recreate, and pro-
create in specific places—in big cities, suburban communities, and small
rural towns. These places vary not only in population size but also in
demographic makeup, labor force dynamics and job opportunities, and
racial and ethnic diversity and relations. For the children of immigrants, the

context of reception affects the type and quality of schooling, peer group interactions, and avenues for upward mobility. Immigrant newcomers initially join friends and family in ethnic enclaves, segregated neighborhoods, or minority communities. There, they become exposed to local employment opportunities, housing markets, and customs and language. Some stay while others eventually disperse into the majority society as part of the integration process (Alba and Nee, 2003).

Where immigrant populations live often changes over time and across the generations (Goodwin-White, 2015; Kritz and Gurak, 2015). Immigrants are drawn to specific receiving areas for a variety of reasons, but they also invariably affect communities and neighborhoods in ways that ultimately reshape processes of social integration and incorporation. The key substantive question seems clear. What is it about specific places—contexts of reception—that attracts new immigrants and affects the pace of social integration, as measured by schooling, employment patterns, poverty, and the provision of social services? Which kinds of places successfully accommodate immigrants? Answers to these questions are incomplete. The relevant research literature is inchoate and ultimately unsatisfying, but it nevertheless provides some important and basic lessons about spatial integration of immigrants and their offspring.

For example, much of the relevant recent literature has focused on the question of whether the recent widespread movement of immigrants to "new destinations" reflects the positive selectivity of upwardly mobile immigrants, where migration represents an investment in human capital that is ultimately rewarded with better schools for their children, better jobs, and more affluent communities. In other words, does spatial mobility reinforce a process of integration that is already well under way (Hall, 2013)? Here the panel considers research on spatial variation in two key indicators of social integration—academic achievement and various economic outcomes (including access to jobs). The research literature is most mature on these topics. Other indicators of integration at the local level, such as political participation or intermarriage, have received much less research attention.

The fact that immigrant families often settle in economically disadvantaged communities and neighborhoods—where they can afford to live—also means that they are typically served by inadequately funded school districts and few institutional support services. For example, in their review, Perreira and colleages (2006) claimed that minority and immigrant youth living in disadvantaged neighborhoods complete fewer years of schooling, drop out of high school at higher rates, and perform poorly on math and reading achievement tests. Moreover, in ethnic enclaves, the competing obligations of strong kinship and peer networks may dampen academic aspirations and achievement. Perreira and colleagues (2006) in fact showed that immigrants living in segregated and racially mixed neighborhoods were significantly more likely to drop out of school than their co-ethnics in less segregated neighborhoods. Much of the neighborhood effect was indirect, operating through other forms of cultural and social capital (e.g., neighborhood quality affects parenting styles, such as parental supervision, and the characteristics of schools).

More recently, attention has turned to new destinations and to questions such as whether out-migration from gateway states and cities to these new destinations is selective of more highly educated groups (a pattern consistent with the canonical model of spatial assimilation) or whether children in new destinations benefit or are harmed by relocating in nontraditional receiving areas (Fischer, 2010; Stamps and Bohon, 2006). On the question of immigrant educational selectivity among Hispanics, Lichter and Johnson (2009) found a clear educational gradient, with the least-educated Hispanics overrepresented in established gateways. In established areas, for example, the percentage of high school graduates among nonmovers was about 37 percent, compared with about 46 percent among out-migrants from these areas. The most educated group of Hispanics, regardless of migrant status, lived in "other" areas—neither in gateways nor new destinations but in areas that were composed of mostly non-Hispanics. These results provide some evidence of spatial assimilation. Still, there is little evidence on the question of whether the quality of life (variously measured) is "better" in new destinations than in the communities and neighborhoods from which out-migrants moved.

On the question of whether the children of immigrants actually benefit from moving to new destinations, there is likewise little scholarly consensus on empirical approach or findings. For example, Dondero and Muller (2012) showed that schools in new destinations generally provided more favorable educational opportunities for immigrant children, albeit with fewer linguistic support services than schools in established destinations. Yet they also reported larger within-school Latino versus non-Hispanic-white gaps in advanced math courses in new destinations than in established gateways. However, the differences between Latino students in new versus established destinations were small. Other research that is done at different levels of geography have drawn different conclusions. On one side, Potochnick (2014) found that 10th grade math and reading test scores among the children of immigrants were highest in the new high-immigration states. But Fischer (2010) reported that immigrant children in new destinations compared unfavorably with their counterparts in established destinations, where the children of immigrants were less likely to drop out of high school.

These studies are difficult to compare. They typically highlight generational differences in educational outcomes, but do not control for race and ethnicity and therefore short-circuit evidence of differences among immigrants from different national origin groups. A recent meta-analysis by Duong and colleagues (2015) of 53 studies makes this point, emphasizing the substantial racial and ethnic variation in the context of immigrant reception, including the availability of community and school resources. The authors claimed that "Latino and Black children face greater risk for academic failure, as they are more likely to reside in neighborhoods with high rates of delinquency and community violence, face discrimination and racism, struggle against negative stereotypes regarding their academic ability, and encounter peer pressure for antischool attitudes" (Duong et al., 2015, p. 5).

The evidence and conclusions for Hispanic immigrants contrast sharply with the high educational achievement of Asian immigrant populations (see Chapter 6), where empirical studies have typically focused on culture (e.g., family and social capital, educational values and practices, and Confucianism) rather than on structural opportunities or deficits (e.g., impoverished neighborhoods or poorly resourced schools) that promote or limit educational success (Zhou et al., 2008; Zhou, 2009). Indeed, big-city Asian ethnic enclaves—Chinatowns and Koreatowns—often have well-established community resources (e.g., afterschool language programs and Saturday day schools) that foster upward mobility among these immigrant groups. Asian immigrants have "put down roots," unlike many low-skilled transient Hispanic workers and their families, who must move to where the jobs are (i.e., in construction or food processing) or follow the harvest seasons. In their study of Chinese and Korean immigrants, Zhou and Kim (2006, p. 21) argued that "the cultural attributes of a group feed on the structural factors, particularly ethnic social structures that support community forces and social capital."

Not unlike the evidence on school outcomes, studies of spatial heterogeneity in economic integration are similarly difficult to summarize neatly across diverse immigrant populations. By definition, immigrants seeking employment and higher wages tend to relocate or settle in local labor markets experiencing rapid population and job growth. Perhaps not surprisingly then, immigrants, on average, tend to have higher rates of employment than their native-born ethnic counterparts (see Chapter 6). But, even here, it is often difficult to separate evidence of positive community or neighborhood effects from the positive selectivity of new immigrants. Moreover, employment opportunities are played out unevenly over geographic space and national origin groups. They are shaped by the ebb and flow of local labor market conditions and the demand for low-skill labor.

Industrial restructuring in the meat packing industry provides a clear case in point (Kandel and Parrado, 2005). The growth in beef, pork, and poultry processing plants in rural areas reflects America's changing meat consumption habits, energy technology, and marketing strategies (e.g., cut-up meat products on site rather than by local butchers), new anti-union management strategies designed to hire unorganized, poorly educated, and low-skilled workers (including new immigrants and undocumented workers in remote settings), and the realization of new savings on transportation costs from locating slaughter houses and processing plants closer to where the animals are raised. For the meat processing industry, Kandel and Parrado (2005) showed that the share of Hispanic workers increased from 8.5 to 28.5 percent between 1980 and 2000, while the shares of the foreign-born among Hispanic workers increased from 50 percent to 82 percent over the same period. About 70 percent of Hispanic workers had less than a high school education. This is a clear case of Hispanic immigrant labor following job growth in rural America. Hispanics are also following jobs in the dairy industry (e.g., in the agricultural Midwest and elsewhere) and in apple orchards, vineyards, and vegetable farms (Cross, 2006; Gozdziak and Bump, 2004).

The demographic and economic impacts of new immigration on rural America have been obvious. Many previously declining small towns have boomed since 1990, and Hispanic immigrants have generally benefited economically in comparison to their counterparts in Mexico and other parts of Latin America and in traditional urban gateways. For example, Donato and colleagues (2007) identified 59 nonmetropolitan counties that, between 1990 and 2000, experienced overall population growth but only because of the growth of the foreign-born population, thus offsetting population decline. Over the decade, the shares of foreign-born Mexicans in these "offset counties" who spoke English well declined, as did the shares with a high school diploma or more. Despite declines in human capital, poverty rates nevertheless declined over the decade, and median household income and wage rates increased.

But these relative economic gains may have been reversed as a result of the Great Recession in the late 2000s. In a recent study of Hispanic growth in the nonmetropolitan South over the 1990-2010 period, Crowley and colleagues (2015) showed significantly higher Hispanic employment rates in new destinations (71.1%) than in established gateways (61.6%). However, in 2010 poverty rates across different population groups (children, female heads of household, and others) tended to be significantly higher in new destinations than traditional gateways—a much different pattern from 2000, when differences were generally small and statistically insignificant. This finding speaks indirectly to the low and declining wages among Hispanic workers since 2000 in many new destination labor markets. Still, Hispanic homeownership increased, compared to the 2000s, as many immigrants "put down roots" and crowding (measured by persons per room) decreased. The test of integration will ultimately depend on whether places with fast-growing Hispanic populations can serve the children of immigrant families as launching points for upward mobility or whether those children will become "trapped in place," reproducing the economic circumstances and hardships of their parents. And what happens when boom goes bust in such areas?

Small rural labor markets, often dominated by a single industry, provide a suitable but incomplete venue for assessing the local economic incorporation of low-skill Hispanic immigrant populations. To be sure, the situation in many rural boom towns is decidedly different from the diverse economic experiences of immigrants in large metropolitan and suburban areas, where most Hispanic, Asian, and other refugee populations actually live and work. For example, suburbanization typically has connoted upward mobility and the attainment of the "American Dream." This is still true today (especially among Asian immigrant groups), but with some important caveats. The first is that the term "suburbs" covers a diverse set of places regarding economic status, housing prices, access to transit, job growth, and proximity to central cities. The rise of poverty in the suburbs has accelerated, and although residents of central cities are more likely to be poorer than their suburban counterparts, there are now more persons living in poverty in the suburbs than in cities (Kneebone and Berube, 2013). The second caveat is that as suburbs have been changing both economically and racially, some of that change is attributable to immigrant settlement. Suburban job growth has been a factor, as low-wage workers have been drawn to live closer to their jobs. In addition, post-recession job loss, particularly in the construction and manufacturing sectors, hit the suburbs especially hard (Singer and Wilson, 2010). However, Suro and colleagues (2011) found that although immigrants accounted for almost a third (30 percent) of overall population growth in the suburbs in the 2000s, they contributed less than a fifth (17%) of the increase in the poor population.

For immigrants in the inner suburban ring and in exurbia, housing may be readily available and more affordable, but the institutional support services that have historically helped promote social integration in established gateways may be lacking (Allard and Roth, 2010). Indeed, access to public transportation is often a problem—to get to work, to shop, and to perform routine daily activities (e.g., drop the children off at preschool programs or daycare, go to the doctor, attend religious services, or participate in civic events) (Ray, 2003). Suburbanization under these circumstances arguably is less an indicator of social integration than of spatial and social isolation of new immigrant populations.

The problem is that the current literature lacks a clear or compelling narrative of the changing economic circumstances and social integration of immigrants living in the suburbs. Moreover, it is hard to distinguish selection from causation, namely, whether suburbs are attracting different socioeconomic profiles of immigrants or instead contributing positively (or negatively) to economic integration. Are (some) immigrant populations becoming ghettoized in economically declining suburbs?

Other recent studies have focused on the lack of public transportation and its corollary: the "spatial mismatch" between where immigrants live and where good jobs are located. But recent studies typically have focused on specific metropolitan areas from which broad or compelling generalizations are difficult to draw (e.g., McKenzie, 2013; Painter et al., 2007). For example, Liu (2009) found that suburban residence in the Chicago, Los Angeles, and Washington, D.C., metropolitan areas was positively associated (compared with the central cities in their respective metropolitan areas) with employment rates among immigrant populations. She also observed positive enclave effects both in the city and suburbs. Large scale cross-city or comparative studies of the economic trajectories of suburban immigrants of different national origins are surprisingly rare. Other studies have found little or only mixed evidence in support of "enclave effects" on economic outcomes (see Xie and Gough, 2011).

Virtually all of the recent literature on new destinations has focused on disadvantaged Hispanic populations. An exception is a recent study by Flippen and Kim (2015), who focused on the relationship between Asian settlement patterns in new and traditional destinations and socioeconomic attainment (earnings and occupational status) in metropolitan areas. Their analysis revealed higher socioeconomic status among some Asian populations (Chinese, Filipinos, Indians, and Japanese) in new destinations vis-à-vis established gateways. For other Asian populations (i.e., Koreans and Vietnamese), the reverse was true (Flippen and Kim, 2015).

The panel's review of this research raises many more questions than it answers. Simple or straightforward generalizations are difficult to identify or neatly summarize, because just as "immigrants" do not represent a group with a uniform set of characteristics, "the suburbs," cities, and other geographies where they reside are not monolithic; the opportunity structures vary from one location to another. As America's immigrant populations disperse spatially and put down roots, it will become increasingly important to monitor local processes of integration for different national origin groups. Evidence of integrational mobility among immigrant populations is key; social integration will be played out at the local level and in emerging patterns of geographic mobility. This will also require up-to-date and longitudinal data at the community and neighborhood level (see Chapter 10). The current literature is developing rapidly but is still immature.

STATE AND LOCAL CONTEXTS AND POLICY RESPONSES

One of the most significant trends of the last decade has been the effort by some state and local governments to wrest control over immigration from federal authority and develop legislation on immigration and immigrants within their borders (see Chapter 2). Since 2000, new trends in immigrant settlement have stirred social conflict and anxiety over job competition and the costs of providing publicly funded services such as health care and schooling to undocumented immigrants and their children. These trends, combined with the frustration of state and local officials with the lack of efforts by Congress to take up comprehensive immigration reform, have produced a rash of local legislation. The result, discussed in detail in Chapter 2, has been a type of federalism around policies that affect immigrants, as states and localities pursue their own management and control over immigration. Thus, since the early 2000s, immigration policy activism across state and local jurisdictions has produced policies and programs that exclude and expel immigrants in some places but welcome immigrants and support their integration in other places.

For instance, many states, cities, and counties have responded to federal inaction to change immigration policy and have proposed or passed laws intended to exclude or deflect immigrants. These actions include laws that penalize employers who knowingly employ immigrants who are unauthorized to work; laws that forbid landlords from renting to undocumented immigrants; laws that do not allow immigrants to congregate in informal day labor sites; and laws that prevent undocumented residents from getting state-issued driver's licenses, business licenses, and in-state tuition and scholarships (Varsanyi, 2010; Walker, 2015). In addition to state and local measures, new federal policies require coordination with policing at the local level, and the variable response of local police forces to these policies have produced what scholars have labeled a "multilayered jurisdictional patchwork" of immigration enforcement—a landscape complicated by varying and overlapping responsibilities of local authorities (Varsanyi et al., 2012; Walker, 2015).

However, President Obama's Executive actions in November 2014 changed the enforcement system by re-prioritizing categories of undocumented immigrants that are to be removed (with the aim of targeting the more serious threats to public safety) and replacing the Secure Communities Program with a new more tailored Priority Enforcement Program (PEP) (Rosenblum, 2015). Because the Secure Communities Program engendered considerable resistance in many communities, including some that refused to participate, the Department of Homeland security will, under PEP, work with individual communities "to develop protocols that stipulate agreed-upon enforcement practices" (Rosenblum, 2015).

While it is difficult to assess the effectiveness of such policies, one can reasonably assume that they will not serve to further the integration of immigrants, especially if immigrants flee from areas perceived as pursuing enforcement more stringently. Arizona has been ground zero in efforts to expel immigrants, and some evidence exists that Arizona's laws worked. As noted in Chapter 2, SB 1070, passed in 2010, made it a crime to be present in the state without legal status and authorized local police to check the immigration status of anyone the police suspected of being in the country without authorization. Two years earlier, Arizona enacted the Legal Arizona Worker's Act (LAWA), making it the first state that required all public and private employers to authenticate the legal status of their workers using the federal employment verification system known as E-Verify. While laws like LAWA and local restrictions target undocumented immigrants, most of whom are from Latin America, other immigrants experience the laws' effects, such as those living in mixed status households.

Although the Supreme Court pulled much of the teeth from SB 1070 (*Chamber of Commerce of the United States v. Whiting*, 131 S. Ct. 1968, 2011; see Table 2-2 in Chapter 2) and similar legislation in other states, the message conveyed by SB 1070 and LAWA that Arizona had become intolerant of undocumented immigrants created fear and anxiety among immigrants and their families (see Chapter 3). As noted in Chapter 2, LAWA likely prompted some Latinos to move to other states (Bohn et al., 2014; Lofstrom et al., 2011). In addition, Ellis and colleagues (2014b) found that after LAWA, noncitizen foreign-born Latinos exited Arizona at higher rates relative to other states. They found weaker evidence of outmigration for other Latino groups who might experience fear, or resent LAWA's requirements: U.S.-born Latinos did leave Arizona at higher rates in 2008 but naturalized Latinos did not. Nevertheless, the results suggest that state-level immigration policy can alter the settlement geography and integration experience of the foreign-born.

These differing orientations to local immigrant integration have led to a jumble of policies and practices across local jurisdictions. While demographic, economic, and political contexts are important for understanding both settlement patterns and immigrant integration, measuring such contexts is difficult across places and time (see Gelatt et al., 2015, for a good discussion of efforts to measure and describe the range of state and local policy contexts).

There are several potential explanations for the differing approaches to "managing" immigration at the local level. While there are case studies of local anti-immigrant policy activism (see for example Varsanyi, 2008), it seems likely that a range of factors, including population change, local politics, and economic conditions, are needed to explain how particular places move toward more-restrictive or less-restrictive policies. For example, Hazleton, Pennsylvania, was the first municipality that instituted an ordinance that penalized landlords who knowingly rented property to undocumented immigrants (Flores, 2014). Places with rapidly growing foreign-born populations and with a relatively high percentage of owner-occupied housing have been more likely to introduce such exclusionary policies. In contrast, municipalities with better-educated populations have been more likely to adopt inclusionary policies (Walker and Leitner, 2011). Region matters also, as exclusionary policies are often associated with sudden and rapid immigrant growth. Municipalities in the South and outside central cities also tend to impose exclusionary policies (Walker and Leitner, 2011).[13]

Ramakrishnan and Wong (2007) found that the factors compelling local action include the size and growth of the Latino population; the attendant challenges to schools, housing, and neighborhoods; unease or prejudice among resident populations; and the presence of partisanship and politicization of immigration at the local level. A case study of Prince William County, Virginia in suburban Washington, D.C. (DeRenzis et al., 2009), concluded that the confluence of several factors, including swift population change and growth of the immigrant population, local activism and discourse around the problems of undocumented workers and residents, and unseasoned local government, coupled with the lack of an immigrant service and advocacy infrastructure. These factors combined with upcoming election pressures to heighten the issue's importance, resulting in an enforcement regime that was the most stringent in the country at the time of its passage (Singer et al., 2008).

On the other end of the spectrum of local responses, places that have developed pro-immigrant integration policies or have local (nongovernmental) programs appear to fall into two types. The first type comprises those localities that have long-established, large immigrant and refugee populations, well-developed supportive services, and strong identities as immigrant gateways, such as San Francisco and New York. In these places, deep infrastructure supports programs for immigrants, aimed at helping to alleviate poverty and providing adult education, language training, credentialing, civic engagement, and legal services. The second type comprises places with low levels of immigration and slow or declining population growth that aspire to receive and retain more immigrants as a way to stem population loss and increase economic activity. For example, a group of 20 Midwestern cities has created a network with the mission: "to strengthen the work, maximize the impact, and sustain the efforts of local economic and community development initiatives across the region that welcome, retain, and empower immigrant communities as valued contributors to the region's shared prosperity." These initiatives seek to retain international students, facilitate entrepreneurship, and support the credentialing

---

[13] Flores (2015) found that proposals of anti-immigrant legislation are correlated with increased gun sales across counties in Pennsylvania and South Carolina, perhaps reflecting political rhetoric linking immigrants to crime and social disorder.

of highly skilled immigrants who were trained outside the United States. These contexts are important for understanding how a locality develops pro- or anti-immigrant policies, yet there are no definitive studies providing evidence across places.[14]

Ramakrishnan and Gulasekaram (2014) argued that the tide has turned against local restrictive efforts. They cited as evidence the growing number of places passing laws that aid in integration and limit cooperation with federal authorities seeking to enforce deportation orders and the Supreme Court ruling (*Arizona v United States* 567 U.S., 2012), in which the majority of justices voted for the reassertion of federal authority over state actions to control immigration. They also cited the 2012 Presidential election, in which Republican candidate Mitt Romney, whose immigration platform centered on "attrition through enforcement" to promote self-deportation of undocumented immigrants, lost to President Barack Obama by record margins among Latino and Asian American voters. Moreover, as discussed in Chapter 4, research indicates that immigrants are more likely to naturalize in places where the context of reception is relatively welcoming. However, election cycles matter, and immigration policy appears to be an increasingly vocal and contentious issue for the November 2016 elections.

It is difficult to measure the direct impact that state and local policies have on the integration of immigrants, both as first- and second-order consequences. Additionally, policy stances can shift quickly over time, making it difficult to collect and measure the dynamic policy landscape (Gelatt et al., 2015). However, the panel concludes, from the evidence cited above, that place matters in ways that are directly tied to the policies, programs, and service infrastructure in particular localities.

SUMMARY AND CONCLUSION

The spatial integration of immigrants and racial and ethnic minority populations arguably is an increasingly important indicator of integration into American society. Where immigrants live reflects and reinforces social integration and shapes access to good schools, safe neighborhoods, and good jobs. Moreover, different national origin groups have differing distributions in geographic space and face different and often unequal access to society's rewards and different community responses from the native-born populations residing in the same locality. For much of the 20th century, the majority of immigrants concentrated overwhelmingly in a small number of gateway states and large metropolitan areas. Today, growing opportuni-

---

[14] An exception is the study by Flores (2015), mentioned in the preceding footnote, on the association among anti-immigrant attitudes, political rhetoric claiming a link between immigrants and crime, and increased gun sales counties of Pennsylvania and South Carolina.

ties outside traditional gateways have attracted immigrants to what have become known as "new immigrant destinations," which include many suburbs and rural areas as well as urban areas that have little or no recent history of immigration. Immigration—and social integration—has become a national issue as recent immigrants have spread throughout the nation.

The local context of reception shapes immigrant integration into American society. This issue is perhaps more important than ever as America's immigrant population has grown and dispersed spatially. Indeed, the migration of America's foreign-born population to "new destinations" has upended conventional interpretations of the link between spatial and social mobility. Yet new patterns of spatial dispersal are occurring at the same time that individual immigrant groups (by source country) are concentrating in particular locations. Are some immigrants increasingly "trapped" in economically declining areas, joining a minority underclass, or do immigrant gateways (still) represent landing and launching pads for something better in new destinations—for both the first generation immigrants and their children? It is much too early to tell, especially in the new destinations now dominated by recently arrived immigrants and their growing children.

As a result, the panel's review yielded incomplete and rather mixed messages about place-to-place patterns of social integration. Today's widespread spatial diffusion of immigrants implies greater spatial integration, but there is also evidence of important variations by race and national origin with respect to neighborhood segregation.

> **Conclusion 5-1** Neighborhoods are more diverse than they have ever been, and the number of all-white census tracts has fallen. Yet racial segregation is still quite prevalent throughout the country, with black immigrants experiencing the most residential segregation from non-Hispanic whites, followed by Hispanic immigrants and then Asian immigrants. Spatial integration is mediated by race, and improvements over time in socioeconomic status and other indicators of integration (e.g., education or earnings) do not translate easily into spatial integration with native-born whites (or, by extension, into "better" neighborhoods), particularly for black immigrants.

National portraits of immigration and immigrant integration—in its myriad forms—may also increasingly mask idiosyncratic patterns that are shaped mostly by local social, economic, and political conditions. New destinations in particular provide natural laboratories for better understanding how immigrant integration is shaped by the context of reception, the presence of other co-ethnics, good job opportunities, residential segregation, anti-immigrant sentiment, and inclusively or exclusionary public policies. There is much more work to be done to understand the day-to-day experiences of immigrants and their descendants in different places and facing diverse contexts of reception.

REFERENCES

Alba, R., and Foner, N. (2015) *Strangers No More: Immigration and the Challenges of Integration in North America and Western Europe.* Princeton, NJ: Princeton University Press.

Alba, R., and Nee, V. (2003). *Remaking the American Mainstream: Assimilation and Contemporary Immigration.* Cambridge, MA: Harvard University Press.

Alba, R., Deane, G., Denton, N., Disha, I., McKenzie, B., and Napierala, J. (2014). The role of immigrant enclaves for Latino residential inequalities. *Journal of Ethnic and Migration Studies, 40*(1), 1-20.

Allard, S.W., and Roth, B. (2010). *Strained Suburbs: The Social Service Challenges of Rising Suburban Poverty.* Washington, DC: Brookings Institution Press. Available: http://www.brookings.edu/~/media/research/files/reports/2010/10/07-suburban-poverty-allard-roth/1007_suburban_poverty_allard_roth.pdf [August 2015]

Bean, F.D., Brown, S.K., and Bachmeier, J.D. (2015). *Parents Without Papers: The Progress and Pitfalls of Mexican American Integration.* New York: Russell Sage Foundation.

Bohn, S., Lofstrom, M., and Raphael, S. (2014). Did the 2007 Legal Arizona Workers Act reduce the state's unauthorized immigrant population? *The Review of Economics and Statistics, 96*(2), 258-269.

Brown, S.K. (2007). Delayed spatial assimilation: Multigenerational incorporation of the Mexican-origin population in Los Angeles. *City & Community, 6,* 193-209.

Burt, L., and Batalova, J. (2014). *Refugees and Asylees in the United States.* Washington, DC: Migration Information Source. Available: http://www.migrationpolicy.org/article/refugees-and-asylees-united-states [March 2015].

Card, D., and Lewis, E.G. (2007). The diffusion of Mexican immigrants during the 1990s: Explanations and impacts. In G.J. Borjas (Ed.), *Mexican Immigration to the U.S.* (pp. 193-227). Chicago, IL: University of Chicago Press.

Carr, P.J., Lichter, D.T., and Kefalas, M.J. (2012). Can immigration save small-town America? Hispanic boomtowns and the uneasy path to renewal. *The ANNALS of the American Academy of Political and Social Science, 641*(1), 38-57.

Center for Migration Studies. (2015). *2013 U.S. Unauthorized Population.* New York: Author. Available: http://cmsny.org/researchprojects/democratizingdata/us/unauthorized tables/#table1a [March 2015].

Cross, J.A. (2006). Restructuring America's dairy farms. *Geographical Review, 96*(1), 1-23.

Crowder, K., Hall, M., and Tolnay, S.E. (2011). Neighborhood immigration and native out-migration. *American Sociological Review, 76*(1), 25-47.

Crowley, M., Lichter, D.T., and Turner, R.N. (2015). Diverging fortunes? Economic well-being of Latinos and African Americans in new rural destinations. *Social Science Research, 51,* 77-92.

Cutler, D.M., Glaeser, E.L., and Vigdor, J.L. (2008). Is the melting pot still hot? Explaining the resurgence of immigrant segregation. *The Review of Economics and Statistics, 90*(3), 478-497.

Denton, N.A., and Massey, D.S. (1989). Racial identity among Caribbean Hispanics: The effect of double minority status on residential segregation. *American Sociological Review, 54,* 790-808.

DeRenzis, B., Singer, A., and Wilson, J. (2009). *Prince William County Case Study: Immigrants, Politics, and Local Response in Suburban Washington.* Washington, DC: Brookings Institution Press. Available: http://www.brookings.edu/research/reports/2009/02/25-immigration-singer [September 2015].

Donato, K.M., Tolbert, C.M., Nucci, A., and Kawano, Y. (2007). Recent immigrant settlement in the nonmetropolitan United States: Evidence from internal census data. *Rural Sociology, 72*(4), 537-559.

Donato, K.M., Tolbert, C., Nucci, A., and Kawano, Y. (2008). Changing faces/changing places: The emergence of nonmetropolitan immigrant gateways. In D.S. Massey (Ed.), *New Faces in New Places: The Changing Geography of American Immigration* (pp. 75-98). New York: Russell Sage Foundation.

Dondero, M., and Muller, C. (2012).School stratification in new and established Latino destinations. *Social Forces, 91*(2), 477-502.

Duong, M.T., Badaly, D., Liu, F.F., Schwartz, D., and McCarty, C.A. (2015). Generational differences in academic achievement among immigrant youths: A meta-analytic review. *Review of Educational Research, XX*(X), 1-39. Available: http://rer.sagepub.com/content/early/2015/03/30/0034654315577680.full.pdf+html [September 2015].

Ellis, M., and Almgren, G. (2009). Local contexts of immigrant and second-generation integration in the United States. *Journal of Ethnic and Migration Studies, 35*(7), 1059-1076.

Ellis, M., Wright, R., and Townley, M. (2014a). The great recession and the allure of new immigrant destinations in the United States. *International Migration Review, 48*(1), 3-33.

Ellis, M., Wright, R., Townley, M., and Copeland, K. (2014b). The migration response to the Legal Arizona Workers Act. *Political Geography, 42*, 46-56.

Eschbach, K., Hagan, J., Rodriguez, N., Hernandez-Leon, R., and Bailey, S. (1999). Death at the border. *International Migration Review, 33*(2), 430-454.

Fennelly, K. (2008). Prejudice toward immigrants in the Midwest. In D. Massey (Ed.), *New Faces in New Places: The Changing Geography of American Immigration* (pp. 151-178). New York: Russell Sage Foundation.

Fischer, M.J. (2010). Immigrant educational outcomes in new destinations: An exploration of high school attrition. *Social Science Research, 39*(4), 627-641.

Flippen, C., and Kim, E. (2015). Immigrant context and opportunity: New destinations and socioeconomic attainment among Asians in the United States. *The ANNALS of the American Academy of Political and Social Science, 660*(1), 175-198.

Flores, R.D. (2014). Living in the eye of the storm: How did Hazleton's restrictive immigration ordinance affect local interethnic relations? *American Behavioral Scientist, 58*(13), 1743-1763.

Flores, R.D. (2015). Taking the law into their own hands: Do local anti-immigrant ordinances increase gun sales? *Social Problems, 62*(3). Available: http://socpro.oxfordjournals.org/content/62/3/363 [September 2015].

Fong, E., and Shibuya, K. (2005). Multiethnic cities in North America. *Annual Review of Sociology*, 285-304.

Freeman, L. (2002). Does spatial assimilation work for black immigrants in the U.S.? *Urban Studies, 39*(11), 1983-2003.

Frey, W. (2015). *Diversity Explosion: How New Racial Demographics are Remaking America.* Washington, DC: Brookings Institution Press.

Gelatt, J., Bernstein, H., and Koball, H. (2015). *Uniting the Patchwork: Measuring State and Local Immigrant Contexts.* Washington DC: Urban Institute.

Goodwin-White, J. (2015). *Is Social Mobility Spatial? Characteristics of Immigrant Metros and Second Generation Outcomes: 1940-1970 and 1970-2000.* California Center for Population Research On-Line Working Paper Series. Available: http://papers.ccpr.ucla.edu/papers/PWP-CCPR-2015-001/PWP-CCPR-2015-001.pdf [September 2015].

Gouveia, L., Carranza, M.A., and Cogua, J. (2005). The Great Plains migration: Mexicanos and Latinos in Nebraska. In V. Zúñiga and R. Hernández-León (Eds.), *New Destinations: Mexican Immigration in the United States* (pp. 23-49). New York: Russell Sage Foundation.

Gozdziak, E.M., and Bump, M.N. (2004). Poultry, apples, and new immigrants in the rural communities of the Shenandoah Valley: An ethnographic case study. *International Migration, 42*(1), 149-164.

Green, P.E. (2003). The undocumented: Educating the children of migrant workers in America. *Bilingual Research Journal, 27*(1), 51-71.

Grieco, E.M., Trevelyan, E., Larsen, L., Acosta, Y.D., Gambino, C., de la Cruz, P., Gryn, T., and Walters, N. (2012). *The Size, Place of Birth, and Geographic Distribution of the Foreign-Born Population in the United States: 1960 to 2010.* Working Paper No. 96. Washington, DC: U.S. Census Bureau, Population Division.

Griffith, D.C. (2005). Rural industry and Mexican immigration and settlement in North Carolina. In V. Zúñiga and R. Hernández-León (Eds.), *New Destinations: Mexican Immigration in the United States* (pp. 50-75). New York: Russell Sage Foundation.

Hall, M. (2013). Residential integration on the new frontier: Immigrant segregation in established and new destinations. *Demography, 50*(5), 1873-1896.

Hall, M., and Crowder, K. (2014). Native out-migration and neighborhood immigration in new destinations. *Demography, 51*(6), 2179-2202.

Hall, M., and Stringfield, J. (2014). Undocumented migration and the residential segregation of Mexicans in new destinations. *Social Science Research, 47*(1), 61-78.

Holloway, S., Wright, R., and Ellis, M. (2012). The racially fragmented city? Neighborhood racial segregation and diversity jointly considered. *The Professional Geographer, 63*(4), 1-20.

Humes, K.R., Jones, N.A., and Ramirez, R.R. (2011). *Overview of Race and Hispanic Origin: 2010.* 2010 Census Briefs. Washington, DC: U.S. Census Bureau. Available: http://www.census.gov/prod/cen2010/briefs/c2010br-02.pdf [August 2015].

Iceland, J., and Nelson, K. A. (2008). Hispanic segregation in metropolitan America: Exploring the multiple forms of spatial assimilation. *American Sociological Review, 73*(5), 741-765.

Iceland, J., and Scopilliti, M. (2008). Immigrant residential segregation in U.S. metropolitan areas, 1990–2000. *Demography, 45*(1), 79-94.

Jang, W., and Yao, X. (2014). Tracking ethnically divided commuting patterns over time: A case study of Atlanta. *The Professional Geographer, 66*(2), 274-283.

Johnson, K.M., and Lichter, D.T. (2008). Natural increase: A new source of population growth in emerging Hispanic destinations in the United States. *Population and Development Review, 34*(2), 327-346.

Johnson, K.M., and Lichter, D.T. (2010). Growing diversity among America's children and youth: Spatial and temporal dimensions. *Population and Development Review, 36*(1), 151-176.

Johnson, K.M., and Lichter, D.T. (2012). Rural natural increase in the new century: America's third demographic transition. In *International Handbook of Rural Demography* (pp. 17-34). Dordrecht, Netherlands: Springer.

Kandel, W. (2008). *Profile of Hired Farmworkers: A 2008 Update.* ERS Report EER-60. Washington, DC: U.S. Department of Agriculture, Economic Research Service. Available: http://www.ers.usda.gov/publications/err-economic-research-report/err60.aspx [August 2015].

Kandel, W., and Cromartie, J. (2004). *New Patterns of Hispanic Settlement in Rural America.* Washington, DC: U.S. Department Agriculture, Economic Research Service.

Kandel, W., and Parrado, E.A. (2005). Restructuring of the U.S. meat processing industry and new Hispanic migrant destinations. *Population and Development Review, 31*(3), 447-471.

Kasnitz, P., Mollenkopf, J.H., Waters, M.C., and Holdaway, J. (2009). *Inheriting the City: The Children of Immigrants Come of Age.* New York: Russell Sage Foundation.

Kneebone, E., and Berube, A. (2013). *Confronting Suburban Poverty in America.* Washington, DC: Brookings Institution Press.

Kritz, M.M., and Gurak, D.T. (2015). U.S. immigrants in dispersed and traditional settlements: National origin heterogeneity. *International Migration Review, 49*(1), 106-141.

Lee, B.A., Iceland, J., and Farrell, C.R. (2014). Is ethno-racial residential integration on the rise? Evidence for metropolitan and micropolitan America since 1980. In J. Logan (Ed.), *Diversity and Disparities: America Enters a New Century* (pp. 415-456). New York: Russell Sage Foundation. Available: https://www.russellsage.org/sites/all/files/logan/logan_diversity_chapter13.pdf [July 2015].

Lichter, D.T. (2012). Immigration and the new racial diversity in rural America. *Rural Sociology, 77*(1), 3-35.

Lichter, D.T., and Johnson, K. M. (2009). Immigrant Gateways and Hispanic Migration to New Destinations1. *International Migration Review, 43*(3), 496-518.

Lichter, D.T., Parisi, D., Taquino, M.C., and Grice, S.M. (2010). Residential segregation in new Hispanic destinations: Cities, suburbs, and rural communities compared. *Social Science Research, 39*(2), 215-230.

Lichter, D.T., Parisi, D., and Taquino, M.C. (2015). Spatial assimilation in U.S. cities and communities? Emerging patterns of Hispanic segregation from blacks and whites. *The ANNALS of the American Academy of Political and Social Science, 660*(1), 36-56.

Light, I. (2008). *Deflecting Immigration.* New York: Russell Sage Foundation.

Liu, C.Y. (2009). Ethnic enclave residence, employment, and commuting of Latino workers. *Journal of Policy Analysis and Management, 28*(4), 600-625.

Lofstrom, M., Bohn, S., and Raphael, S. (2011). *Lessons from the 2007 Legal Arizona Workers Act.* San Francisco: Public Policy Institute of California.

Logan, J.R., and Zhang, C. (2010). Global neighborhoods: New pathways to diversity and separation. *American Journal of Sociology, 115*(4), 1069-1109.

Logan, J.R., Stults, B.J., and Farley, R. (2004). Segregation of minorities in the metropolis: Two decades of change. *Demography, 41*(1), 1-22.

Maldonado, M.M. (2014). Latino incorporation and racialized border politics in the Heartland: Interior enforcement and policeability in an English-only state. *American Behavioral Scientist, 58*(14), 1927-1945.

Marrow, H.B. (2011). *New Destination Dreaming: Immigration, Race, and Legal Status in the Rural American South.* Stanford, CA: Stanford University Press.

Massey, D.S. (2008). *New Faces in New Places: The Changing Geography of American Immigration.* New York: Russell Sage Foundation.

Massey, D.S., and Capoferro, C. (2008). The geographic diversification of American immigration. In D.S. Massey (Ed.), *New Faces in New Places: The Changing Geography of American Immigration* (pp. 25-50). New York: Russell Sage Foundation.

Massey, D.S., and Tannen, J. (2015). A research note on trends in black hypersegregation. *Demography, 52*, 1025-1034.

Massey, D.S., Rothwell, J., and Domina, T. (2009). The changing bases of segregation in the United States. *The ANNALS of the American Academy of Political and Social Science, 626*, 74-90.

McKenzie, B.S. (2013). Neighborhood access to transit by race, ethnicity, and poverty in Portland, Oregon. *City & Community, 12*(2), 134-155.

Nevins, J. (2007). Dying for a cup of coffee? Migrant deaths in US Mexico border region in a neoliberal age. *Geopolitics, 12*(2), 228-247.

Nevins, J. (2010). *Operation Gatekeeper and Beyond: The War On "Illegals" and the Remaking of the U.S.* New York: Routledge.

Painter, G., Liu, C. Yang, and Zhuang, D. (2007). Immigrants and the spatial mismatch hypothesis: Employment outcomes among immigrant youth in Los Angeles. *Urban Studies, 44*(13), 2627-2649.

Parisi, D., Lichter, D.T., and Taquino, M.C. (2011). Multi-scale residential segregation: Black exceptionalism and America's changing color line. *Social Forces, 89*(3), 829-852.

Parrado, E.A., and Kandel, W. (2008). New Hispanic migrant destinations: A tale of two industries. In D.S. Massey (Ed.), *New Faces in New Places: The Changing Geography of American Immigration* (pp. 99-123). New York: Russell Sage Foundation.

Perreira, K.M., Mullan Harris, K., and Lee, D. (2006). Making it in America: High school completion by immigrant and native youth. *Demography, 43*(3), 511-536.

Potochnick, S. (2014). The academic adaptation of children of immigrants in new and established settlement states: The role of family, schools, and neighborhoods. *Population Research and Policy Review, 33*(3), 335-364.

Ramakrishnan, S.K., and Gulasekaram, P. (2014). *Understanding Immigration Federalism in the United States.* Washington, DC: Center for American Progress.

Ramakrishnan, S.K., and Wong, T. (2007). Immigration Policies Go Local: The Varying Responses of Local Governments to Undocumented Immigration. Unpublished paper, University of California, Riverside.

Ray, B. (2003). The role of cities in immigrant integration. *Migration Information Source* (feature article, October). Available: http://www.migrationpolicy.org/article/role-cities-immigrant-integration [September 2015].

Rosenblum, M. (2015). *Understanding the Potential Impact of Executive Action on Immigration Enforcement.* Washington DC: Migration Policy Institute.

Roth, B.J., Gonzales, R.G., and Lesniewski, J (2015). Building a stronger safety net: Local organizations and the challenges of serving immigrants in the suburbs. *Human Service Organizations: Management, Leadership & Governance, 39*(4), 348-361.

Rothwell, J., and Massey, D.S. (2009). The effect of density zoning on racial segregation in U.S. urban areas. *Urban Affairs Review, 44*, 799-806.

Rothwell, J., and Massey, D.S. (2010). Density zoning and class segregation in U.S. metropolitan areas. *Social Science Quarterly, 91*(5), 1123-1143.

Rugh, J.S. (2015). Double jeopardy: Why Latinos were hit hardest by the U.S. foreclosure crisis. *Social Forces, 93*(3), 1139-1184.

Rugh, J.S., and Massey, D.S. (2014). Segregation in post-civil rights America: Stalled integration or end of the segregated century? *DuBois Review: Social Science Research on Race, 11*(2), 205-232.

Saiz, A., and Wachter, S. (2011). Immigration and the neighborhood. *American Economic Journal: Economic Policy, 3*(2), 169-188.

Singer, A. (2013). Contemporary immigrant gateways in historical perspective. *Daedalus, 142*(3), 76-91.

Singer, A., and Wilson, J.H. (2006). *From "There" to "Here": Refugee Resettlement in Metropolitan America.* Washington, DC: Brookings Metropolitan Policy Program.

Singer, A., Hardwick, S., and Brettell, C. (2008). *Suburban Immigrant Gateways: Immigration and Incorporation in New U.S. Metropolitan Destinations.* Washington, DC: Brookings Institution Press.

Southern Poverty Law Center. (2010). *Injustice on Our Plates. SPLC Report.* Montgomery, AL: Author. Available: https://www.splcenter.org/20101108/injustice-our-plates [August 2015.]

Stamps, K., and Bohon, S.A. (2006). Educational attainment in new and established Latino metropolitan destinations. *Social Science Quarterly, 87*(5), 1225-1240.

Suro, R., Wilson, J.H., and Singer, A. (2011). *Immigration and Poverty in America's Suburbs.* Washington, DC: Brookings Metropolitan Policy Program.

Turner, M.A., Ross, S., Galster, G.C., and Yinger, J. (2002). *Discrimination in Metropolitan Housing Markets: National Results from Phase 1 of the Housing Discrimination Study (HDS).* Submitted to U.S. Department of Housing and Urban Development. Available: http://www.huduser.gov/portal/Publications/pdf/Phase1_Report.pdf [September 2015].

Turner, R.N. (2014). Occupational stratification of Hispanics, whites, and blacks in Southern rural destinations: A quantitative analysis. *Population Research and Policy Review, 33*(5), 717-746.

U.S. Census Bureau. (1993). *1990 Census of Population: Social and Economic Characteristics, Minnesota.* Washington, DC: U.S. Department of Commerce Economics and Statistics Administration.

Varsanyi, M.W. (2008). Immigration policing through the backdoor: City ordinances, the "right to the city," and the exclusion of undocumented day laborers. *Urban Geography, 29*(1), 29-52.

Varsanyi, M.W. (2010). *Taking Local Control: Immigration Policy Activism in U.S. Cities and States.* Stanford, CA: Stanford University Press.

Varsanyi, M.W., Lewis, P.G., Provine, D.M., and Decker, S. (2012). A multilayered jurisdictional patchwork: Immigration federalism in the United States. *Law & Policy, 34,* 138-158.

Walker, K.E. (2015). The spatiality of local immigration policies in the United States. *Tijdschrift voor Economische en Sociale Geografie, 106*(4), 486-498.

Walker, K.E., and Leitner, H. (2011). The variegated landscape of local immigration policies in the U.S. *Urban Geography, 32,* 156-178.

Waters, M.C., and Jiménez, T.R. (2005). Assessing immigrant assimilation: New empirical and theoretical challenges. *Annual Review of Sociology,* 105-125.

Waters, M.C., Kasnitz, P., and Asad, A. (2014). Immigrants and African Americans. *Annual Review of Sociology, 40,* 369-390.

Wilson, J.H., and Habecker, S. (2008). The lure of the capital city: An anthro-geographical analysis of recent African immigration to Washington, D.C. *Population, Space, and Place, 14,* 433-448.

Wilson, J.H., and Singer, A. (2011). *Immigrants in 2010 Metropolitan America: A Decade of Change.* Washington, DC: Brookings Institution Press.

Wilson, J.H., and Svaljenka, N.P. (2014). *Immigrants Continue to Disperse, with Fastest Growth in the Suburbs.* Washington, DC: Brookings Institution Press. Available: http://www.brookings.edu/research/papers/2014/10/29-immigrants-disperse-suburbs-wilson-svajlenka [July 2015].

Wright, R., Ellis, M., and Parks, V. (2005). Re-placing whiteness in spatial assimilation research. *City and Community, 4*(2), 111-135.

Wright, R., Ellis, M., Holloway, S., and Wong, S. (2013). Patterns of racial segregation and diversity in the United States: 1990-2010. *The Professional Geographer, 66*(2), 173-182.

Xie, Y., and Gough, M. (2011). Ethnic enclaves and the earnings of immigrants. *Demography, 48*(4), 1293-1315.

Yu, Z., and Myers, D. (2007). Convergence or divergence in Los Angeles: Three distinctive ethnic patterns of immigrant residential assimilation. *Social Science Research, 36*(1), 254-285.

Zhou, M. (2009). *Contemporary Chinese America: Immigration, Ethnicity, and Community Transformation.* Philadelphia, PA: Temple University Press.

Zhou, M., and Kim, K. (2006). Community forces, social capital, and educational achievement: The case of supplementary education in the Chinese and Korean immigrant communities. *Harvard Educational Review,* 76(1), 1-29.

Zhou, M., Lee, J., Vallejo, J. A., Tafoya-Estrada, R., and Sao Xiong, Y. (2008). Success attained, deterred, and denied: Divergent pathways to social mobility in Los Angeles's new second generation. *The ANNALS of the American Academy of Political and Social Science,* 620(1), 37-61.

Zuniga, V., and Hernández-León, R. (2006). *New Destinations: Mexican Immigration in the United States.* New York: Russell Sage Foundation.

6

Socioeconomic Dimensions of Immigrant Integration

Immigrants come to the United States for many reasons, but the predominant one is to make a better life for themselves and their children. European immigrants and their descendants experienced a great deal of social mobility throughout the 20th century. Immigrants from countries such as Germany, Greece, Ireland, Italy, and Poland often arrived with no possessions and very little or no education. Through hard work and the opportunities provided by an expanding labor market, they achieved some socioeconomic progress in their own lives and remarkable progress by the second and third generation. By the 1980s, groups that had started out in dire poverty and without skills and formal education saw their grandchildren achieve parity and then surpass other third generation native-born whites (Alba, 1985; Lieberson, 1980; Lieberson and Waters, 1988). The sociologist Andrew Greeley (1976) called this the "Ethnic Miracle."

Have recent immigrants who have come from Asia, Latin America, Africa, and the Caribbean experienced the same socioeconomic mobility? Will their children do better than their immigrant parents? Will they also achieve parity with other native-born Americans? Today's immigrants bring with them many of the same attributes as their European predecessors: ambition, a capacity for hard work and sacrifice, and a strong belief in America as a land of opportunity. Immigrants are actually more likely to believe in the American dream than the native-born (see Chapter 7). In 2014, almost 70 percent of immigrant parents said their children will prosper relative to themselves, compared with only 50 percent of native-born parents.[1] They also are less uniformly poor than earlier waves of immigrants, with a large proportion of highly educated immigrants who enter the labor market in high status occupations (Foner, 2000). Yet there are also reasons to worry about their advancement, especially for the one-third of immigrants who have less than a high school education and thus have a long way to go to reach the middle class. Immigrants today face different conditions than their predessors, including rising income inequality and declining wages for unskilled workers, greater racial and ethnic discrimination, failing and segregated public schools, and a legal regime that leaves large proportions of some groups in temporary or undocumented statuses.

This chapter examines the integration of immigrants and their children in education, occupation, earnings, and poverty. As the panel did in other domains, we examined change over time for the immigrants themselves and intergenerational change across the first, second, third, and later generations. As detailed below, we found a great deal of progress for immigrants and their descendants over time and generationally. Yet the panel's ability to draw reasoned conclusions was hampered by substantial gaps in the available data. Because the American Community Survey lacks a question on parental birthplace, the panel had to rely instead on aggregated data from the Current Population Survey (CPS) to derive estimates for the second generation of major national origin groups. In addition, the panel could not separate the third generation specifically from all later generations in federal data sources, and we found no information on legal status for the first generation (the foreign-born). These gaps make it hard to interpret some of the trends for later generation Mexican-Americans in particular, a topic discussed in depth below.

CHANGING CONDITIONS IN AMERICAN SOCIETY

As discussed in Chapter 1, European immigrants in 1910 came with very little education and had, on average, half the education of native-born Americans of that time, with high rates of illiteracy in many groups. The second generation of children of these immigrants entered the labor market at the height of the Great Depression. Yet the children and grandchildren of these immigrants were ultimately able to achieve upward social mobility during the remarkable post–World War II expansion of the American economy from the 1940s through the 1970s, an expansion that particularly benefited those at the bottom of the economic distribution. This period has been called the "Great Compression" because the wage structure nar-

---

[1] Data from NORC's General Social Survey (GSS) at http://www3.norc.org/Gss+website/ [September 2015].

rowed and became more equal than at any time since (Goldin and Margo, 1992), and for immigrants and their children it created opportunities to rise to the middle class and beyond. With rising real wages at the bottom of the distribution, the low-skilled and low-educated saw their wages rise over time. Immigrants and their children with higher levels of educational attainment reaped the rewards of their own effort as well as the structural uplift of rising real wages.

The situation for immigrants and their children who entered the labor market since the early 1970s is exactly the opposite. Those at the bottom of the distribution, particularly men, who maintain the same level of education and skill have seen their real wages decline over time. Real hourly earnings for men without a high school education dropped 22 percent between 1980 and 2012; for high school graduates, they dropped by 11 percent. Only those with a college degree or higher have seen increases (Autor, 2014). And while real wages for women with less than a college degree did not decline over this period, they experienced very modest growth.

Rising inequality in the labor market and the increasing returns to higher education in recent decades mean that immigrants and especially their children need rapid growth in educational attainment to experience rising incomes over time. While Italians, for instance, took three or four generations to reach educational parity with the general population of native-born whites, there was an abundance of jobs that paid a family wage for men with less than a college degree. Descendants of these immigrants had the luxury of time to catch up educationally with other Americans, and they did (Perlmann, 2005). Education is much more highly valued in today's labor market, and the children of immigrants with low education must not only surpass their parents' educational attainment but make large strides beyond them just to stay in place (Goldin and Katz, 2008; Card and Raphael, 2013). One consequence of this focus on educational attainament is that the public schools serving the children of low-skilled immigrants are incredibly important to their chances for social mobility—an issue the panel returns to later in the chapter.

EDUCATIONAL ATTAINMENT AMONG IMMIGRANTS

As described in Chapter 1, immigrants are still overrepresented at the bottom of the educational distribution, but a sizeable proportion now come with advanced educational credentials. These differences in educational attainment also map onto source countries, with Asia and Africa sending relatively more immigrants with high educational attainment, while Latin America and the Caribbean send relatively more immigrants with low attainment. Tables 6-1 and 6-2 show educational attainment among first and second generation men and women, respectively, ages 25-59, by country of

TABLE 6-1 Educational Attainment of First and Second Generation Men, Ages 25-59, by Source Country

Source Country	First Generation				Second Generation			
	Avg. Educ.	% with Education:		Sample Size	Avg. Educ.	% with Education:		Sample Size
		< 12	16+			< 12	16+	
Mexico	9.4	55.2	5.4	24,371	12.6	15.2	14.9	5,545
Cuba	12.9	13.6	24.7	1,614	14.2	3.5	40.4	599
Dominican Republic	11.8	26.7	15.8	1,303	13.4	7.3	23.3	254
Central America	9.8	48.0	9.5	6,414	13.4	8.1	25.7	665
South America	13.2	12.6	31.6	4,718	14.3	1.7	42.9	803
China	14.7	10.7	58.3	2,409	15.4	3.4	67.8	672
India	16.3	2.7	83.2	3,878	15.9	2.2	76.7	389
Japan	15.6	0.5	72.7	456	14.3	4.5	42.8	529
Korea	15.4	0.9	68.8	1,510	15.0	2.2	60.5	378
Philippines	14.4	2.5	49.1	2,977	14.3	2.2	42.7	1,168
Vietnam	13.0	15.2	30.1	2,062	14.4	4.9	48.9	256
Haiti	12.8	13.9	22.1	844	13.9	2.9	32.9	131
Jamaica	13.0	10.9	20.9	980	14.1	4.3	36.8	203
Africa	14.3	5.3	48.1	3,551	14.7	2.2	50.1	429
Canada	15.0	3.1	57.4	1,419	14.1	4.2	38.8	2,856
Europe	14.4	5.2	47.4	8,177	14.5	2.8	46.1	10,519
All Countries	12.1	28.2	28.4	78,471	13.9	7.1	35.6	29,631

NOTE: The first generation samples include foreign-born men ages 25-59, excluding those born abroad of an American parent. The second generation samples include U.S.-born men ages 25-59 who have at least one foreign-born parent. Sampling weights were used in the calculations. See Duncan and Trejo (2015) for further details on methodology.

SOURCE: Adapted from Duncan and Trejo (2015, p. 119). Data from 2003-2013 CPS outgoing rotation group data.

TABLE 6-2 Educational Attainment of First and Second Generation Women, Ages 25-59, by Source Country

Source Country	First Generation				Second Generation			
	Avg. Educ.	% with Education:		Sample Size	Avg. Educ.	% with Education:		Sample Size
		<12	16+			<12	16+	
Mexico	9.5	53.9	6.5	21,762	12.8	14.6	18.2	6,034
Cuba	13.2	9.5	26.3	1,612	14.5	3.7	46.4	594
Dominican Republic	11.9	27.1	16.8	2,071	14.0	6.6	36.2	297
Central America	10.2	43.0	10.9	6,124	14.0	5.4	36.7	751
South America	13.4	10.2	33.1	5,495	14.5	2.3	45.8	860
China	14.2	11.5	52.6	2,918	15.4	1.9	70.1	689
India	15.8	4.0	78.1	3,445	16.1	2.4	79.8	397
Japan	14.8	0.6	53.4	874	14.7	2.0	47.8	518
Korea	14.5	3.9	53.7	2,267	15.3	2.1	65.3	387
Philippines	14.7	2.9	57.2	4,753	14.6	2.1	49.8	1,244
Vietnam	12.5	19.3	25.9	2,340	14.8	2.5	59.5	250
Haiti	12.6	17.0	21.0	975	14.7	5.8	53.3	158
Jamaica	13.4	10.6	28.4	1,408	14.7	2.1	46.2	274
Africa	13.5	9.9	37.9	3,201	15.0	2.4	58.1	443
Canada	14.8	2.2	51.4	1,707	14.4	3.0	43.4	2,920
Europe	14.4	4.9	47.0	9,316	14.6	2.3	46.3	11,015
All Countries	12.3	24.8	29.8	83,028	14.0	6.4	38.9	31,608

NOTE: The first generation samples include foreign-born women ages 25-59, excluding those born abroad of an American parent. The second generation samples include U.S.-born women ages 25-59 who have at least one foreign-born parent. Sampling weights were used in the calculations. See Duncan and Trejo (2015) for further details on methodology.
SOURCE: Data from 2003-2013 Current Population Survey outgoing rotation group data.

origin for the largest source countries of immigrants to the United States.[2] The tables provide the average educational attainment (years of schooling), percentage with less than a high school degree (< 12), and percentage with a college degree or more (16+). Among men (Table 6-1), Mexicans have the lowest average educational attainment (9.4 years), and 55 percent of the first generation from Mexico have less than a high school degree, while only 5 percent have a college degree. The average educational attainment of Central American men is also very low in the first generation (9.8 years); 48 percent have less than high school, while only 10 percent have a college education. Men from the Dominican Republic are less disadvantaged but still have overall low levels, averaging 11.8 years of education; 27 percent with less than high school, and 16 percent with a college degree.

The highest educational attainments among first generation men are among immigrants from Asia, followed closely by Africa, Canada, and Europe (Table 6-1). Indians are the most educated with an average of 16.3 years of education, and 83 percent of Indian immigrant men having a college degree. They are followed by Japanese, Koreans, and Filipinos, who also display high average levels of education, low percentages of people with less than high school attainment (less than 1% of Koreans and Japanese), and high shares with college attainments and beyond. Chinese and Vietnamese immigrant men have high percentages at the top of the educational distribution (58% and 30% with college degrees, respectively) but also relatively high percentages at the bottom of the distribution (11% and 15%, respectively, with less than high school).

The patterns for women are quite similar to those of men in all groups, with average levels of education being somewhat lower for women among Asian and African groups and modestly higher for women among Latino groups (Table 6-2).

Overall, the educational profiles of these groups vary extensively by source country and could also be associated with percentage of immigrants with undocumented status, which cannot be ascertained in most datasets. Mexicans and Central Americans have both the lowest educational attain-

---

[2]The panel is very grateful to Brian Duncan, Department of Economics, University of Colorado Denver, for his help with much of the data analysis reported in this chapter. These calculations are similar to those presented for second generation men in Duncan and Trejo (2015, Table 1), but here Tables 6-1 and 6-2 incorporate additional years of data and report results for the first generation as well as the second and for women as well as for men. The tables use microdata from all months of the Current Population Survey (CPS) from January 2003 through December 2013. The CPS is a monthly survey of about 60,000 households that the U.S. government administers to estimate unemployment rates and other indicators of labor market activity. The sampling universe for this survey is the civilian noninstitutionalized population of the United States. Pooling together these 11 years of monthly CPS data substantially increases sample sizes and improves the precision of the estimates.

ments in the first generation, by all three measures shown in Tables 6-1 and 6-2, and the highest proportion of undocumented people (Passel and Cohn, 2009). Among Asian immigrants, the profile of high education among immigrants bodes well for the second generation, as the best predictor of a child's educational outcomes is the educational attainment of the child's parents (Sewell and Hauser, 1975; Mare, 1981; Haveman and Wolfe, 1994; Mulligan, 1997; Schiller et al., 2002).

Educational Outcomes in the Second Generation

The second generation shows remarkable educational progress compared with the first generation. Overall, the average educational attainment for men increases from 12.1 years in the first generation to 13.9 in the second, surpassing the average educational attainment of 13.8 years for the general population of third generation and higher white Americans. For women the second generation has an average educational attainment of 14.0 years, also surpassing the average of 13.9 years for all third generation and higher white Americans (Table 6-2).

For the groups with overall low levels of education in the first generation, both men and women gain substantially in education from the first to the second generation. Among Mexican American men for instance, average education rises from 9.4 years to 12.6 years in the second generation. Among women the average education rises from 9.5 to 12.8 years. The percentage with less than a high school education falls from 55 percent in the first generation to 15 percent in the second for men and from 54 percent to 15 percent for women. Equivalent strides are made by Central American men, who improve their average educational attainment from 9.8 to 13.4 years, and women, who improve from 10.2 to 14.0 years of education. The percentage with less than a high school education among Central American men falls from 48 percent to 8 percent and among women from 43 percent to 5 percent. These changes represent an impressive amount of upward educational mobility in one generation.

Among the Asian groups with exceptionally high educational attainment in the first generation, the Indians, Koreans, and Japanese show a decline between the first and second generations in the percentage with education above a college degree. This likely reflects the selectivity among the first generation, as well as differing patterns of immigration over time. The second generation descendants of Japanese immigrants, for instance, include many elderly people whose parents immigrated before World War II, as well as the children of more recent, highly selected immigrants. In other words, these cross-sectional generations do not represent true generational cohorts. Most of the other groups show modest increases in education by generation, which equal or exceed the educational attainment of the general population of third generation and higher native-born whites.

To better approximate true parental and child cohorts, Figures 6-1 and 6-2 plot the average education in years of first and second generation men and women, respectively, restricting the first generation to people ages 50-59 and the second generation to people ages 25-34. The solid regression lines in the figures highlight the central tendencies of the relationships between the average education levels of second-generation individuals from a particular source country and those of their immigrant ancestors. The dashed horizontal and vertical lines represent the average educational attainment for all non-Hispanic third generation and higher white Americans in the younger (25-34 years of age) cohort: 13.7 years of education for men and 14.2 years for women. The R-squared statistic for each regression line suggests that the parents' cohort educational attainment predicts the child's attainment quite well for men (.58) and somewhat less well for women (.39).

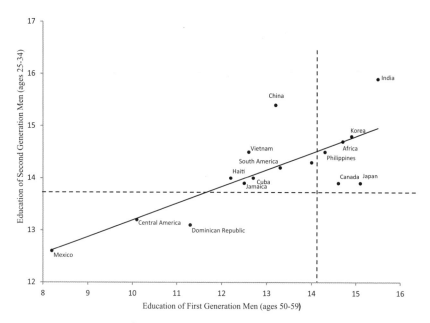

FIGURE 6-1 Average education (in years) of first and second generation men.
NOTE: The first generation samples include foreign-born men ages 50-59, excluding those born abroad of an American parent. The second generation samples include U.S.-born men ages 25-34 who have at least one foreign-born parent. Sampling weights were used in the calculations.
SOURCE: Adapted from Duncan and Trejo (2015). Data from 2003-2013 Current Population Survey outgoing rotation group data.

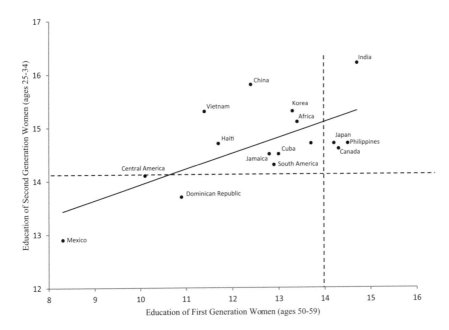

FIGURE 6-2 Average education (in years) of first and second generation women. NOTE: The first generation samples include foreign-born women ages 50-59, excluding those born abroad of an American parent. The second generation samples include U.S.-born women ages 25-34 who have at least one foreign-born parent. Sampling weights were used in the calculations.
SOURCE: Adapted from Duncan and Trejo (2015. Data from 2003-2013 Current Population Survey outgoing rotation group data.

The groups with the lowest educational attainment among the young-cohort second generation men (Figure 6-1) are Mexicans, Central Americans, and Dominicans. Among the young-cohort women (Figure 6-2), Mexicans and Dominicans are still below the third generation and higher white American reference group, but Central American women are almost equal to their reference group. The relatively low educational attainment of most of these groups reflects the lower educational attainment of their immigrant parents, but may also be attributed to a variety of factors, including discrimination (Telles and Ortiz, 2008; Brenner and Graham, 2011), residential instabililty (Green, 2003; Bohon et al., 2005; Palerm, 2006), limited English proficiency (Crosnoe and Lopez-Turley, 2011; Terriquez, 2012), and cultural differences (González et al., 2013; Valenzuela, 2000). Context of reception also matters: immigrants who come in with socioeconomic disadvantages often come to live in poor neighborhoods with underfunded schools (Portes and Rumbaut, 2001; Suárez-Orozco and Suárez-Orozco, 2002).

The "hyperselectivity" of Asian immigrants (i.e., the highly educated and highly selective background of these immigrants) also factors into cumulative advantages in immigrant integration compared to Latin American groups (Lee and Zhou, 2014). However, it is important to note that sharp contrasts between the educational outcomes of Mexican and Central American children of immigrants on the one hand and of Asian Americans on the other obscure the situation of Asian immigrants like the Hmong (Xiong, 2012), whose socioeconomic background and educational outcomes more closely resemble the Mexican immigrants than the Chinese and Korean immigrants in other studies.

Overall this analysis suggests that the second generation of all groups are converging with the native-born in terms of educational attainment and that the remaining deficits among the three Latino second generation groups are primarily due to the very low starting point of their immigrant parents. All of this is positive evidence of rapid educational integration.

Assessing Education Patterns in the Third+ Generation

Examining patterns of educational attainment in the third generation requires the use of a different categorization system for the population. While the Current Population Survey (CPS) data analyzed above provides data on the first generation (based on the birthplace question) and the second generation, (based on the birthplace of parents question) there is no birthplace of grandparents question that allows analysts to identify the true third generation: the grandchildren of immigrants. In order to examine patterns of integration beyond the second generation, the panel instead used the CPS self-identification questions on race and Hispanic origin. Using their responses to these questions, each individual is assigned to one of five mutually exclusive and exhaustive racial/ethnic groups: Hispanic (of any race), and non-Hispanic white, black, Asian (including Native Hawaiian and Pacific Islander), and a residual "other race" category. Hispanics are disaggregated further by national origin group (Mexican, Cuban, Central/South American, or Other Hispanic). Those whom the panel could not identify as first or second generation through the birthplace questions noted above were classified by default as third+ generation members of their racial/Hispanic origin category.

For Mexican Americans, this might include the "true" third generation—people whose grandparents immigrated from Mexico, but because Mexican migration has occurred over centuries, it would also include, fifth, sixth, and seventh generation Mexicans, including those people whose ancestors never "immigrated" but instead remained in the Southwest as it changed hands from Mexico to the United States via the Treaty of Guadalupe Hidalgo at the end of the Mexican American War in 1848. For blacks, this analysis would capture the true third generation grandchildren of immigrants from countries such as Jamaica and Trinidad, along with people who are descendants of slaves brought to the United States in the 16th through 18th centuries. Therefore these categories are very heterogeneous for whites, blacks, and Hispanics. Because Asian immigration is generally more recent, the third+ generation is less varied but still contains higher generations than the third within the category.

Table 6-3 provides data on average education by race/ethnicity, sex, and generation for Hispanic subgroups and for whites, blacks and Asians. Among all groups, the data show generational progress between the first and second generations, but the data suggest little progress and even some decline between the second and third+ generations. For instance, among non-Hispanic white men, average education declines from 14.4 to 13.8 between the second and third+ generations, among blacks it declines from 13.9 years to 12.9, and for Asians it declines from 15.0 to 14.3 years. Among Mexicans there is no change from the second to the third+ generation. A similar pattern of stagnation or decline appears for all of the groups examined among women.

However, Smith (2003) and Borjas (1993, 2006) pointed out that cross-sectional data do a poor job of matching immigrant parents and grandparents with their offspring to measure true generational progress. Smith (2003, 2006, 2012) examined educational progress by birth cohort—beginning with the first generation born in 1880-1884 and continuing through to immigrants born in 1940-1944—and by age to better match generations across time. He concluded that "measured across all three or just two generations and for men and women alike, the education advances made by Latinos are actually greater than those achieved by either European or Asian migrants" (Smith, 2012, p. 24). Table 6-4 presents a similar type of analysis using the CPS data available to the panel. Specifically, we compared age/generation groups that potentially match parents with their children (i.e., by moving northwest [diagonally up and to the right] between the connected cells with similar shading in Table 6-4). With this analysis, one begins to see educational gains for Mexicans after the second generation. Among men, for example, average schooling rises slightly from 12.4 years for the older, second generation to 12.6 years for the younger, third+ generation. The analogous educational increase between the second and third+ generations is larger for women, from 12.2 to 12.9 years. Moreover, calculating schooling progress between the first and second generations in this same way produces larger gains than those shown in Table 6-3: gains of 4.4 years for men and 4.6 years for women. Despite these intergenerational advances,

TABLE 6-3 Average Education, Ages 25-59, by Race/Ethnicity, Sex, and Immigrant Generation

Race/Ethnicity	Men, by Immigrant Generation			Women, by Immigrant Generation		
	First	Second	Third+	First	Second	Third+
Hispanic (aggregate)	10.2	12.9	12.7	10.5	13.1	12.8
	(0.02)	(0.02)	(0.02)	(0.02)	(0.02)	(0.02)
Mexican	9.4	12.6	12.6	9.5	12.8	12.7
	(0.02)	(0.03)	(0.02)	(0.03)	(0.03)	(0.02)
Cuban	12.9	14.2	13.8	13.2	14.5	13.8
	(0.07)	(0.11)	(0.21)	(0.07)	(0.11)	(0.18)
Central or South American	11.1	13.7	13.2	11.6	14.1	13.6
	(0.04)	(0.07)	(0.14)	(0.04)	(0.07)	(0.13)
Other Hispanic	11.8	13.5	13.1	12.2	13.5	13.1
	(0.15)	(0.12)	(0.05)	(0.13)	(0.12)	(0.04)
Non-Hispanic: White	14.3	14.4	13.8	14.1	14.5	13.9
	(0.02)	(0.02)	(0.004)	(0.02)	(0.02)	(0.004)
Black	13.4	13.9	12.9	13.1	14.4	13.2
	(0.04)	(0.08)	(0.01)	(0.04)	(0.07)	(0.01)
Asian	14.7	15.0	14.3	14.2	15.2	14.4
	(0.04)	(0.08)	(0.01)	(0.04)	(0.07)	(0.01)
Other race	14.1	14.2	13.0	14.4	14.6	13.3
	(0.16)	(0.08)	(0.02)	(0.14)	(0.08)	(0.02)
All Race/Ethnic Groups	12.1	13.9	13.6	12.3	14.0	13.8
	(0.01)	(0.01)	(0.004)	(0.01)	(0.01)	(0.003)

NOTE: Standard errors are reported in parentheses. The samples include people ages 25-59. The "first generation" consists of foreign-born individuals, excluding those born abroad of an American parent. The "second generation" consists of U.S.-born individuals who have at least one foreign-born parent. Remaining persons are members of the "third+ generation" (i.e., the third and all higher generations), which consists of U.S.-born individuals who have two U.S.-born parents. Sampling weights were used in the calculations. See Duncan and Trejo (2015) for further details on methodology.
SOURCE: Data from 2003-2013 Current Population Survey outgoing rotation group data.

TABLE 6-4 Average Education of Mexicans Ages 25-34 and 50-59, by Sex and Immigrant Generation

National Origin and Age Group	Men, by Immigrant Generation			Women, by Immigrant Generation		
	First	Second	Third+	First	Second	Third+
Mexican						
Ages 25-34	9.8	12.6	12.6	10.0	12.9	12.9
	(0.04)	(0.04)	(0.04)	(0.04)	(0.04)	(0.03)
Ages 50-59	8.2	12.4	12.4	8.3	12.2	12.3
	(0.07)	(0.11)	(0.06)	(0.08)	(0.11)	(0.05)

NOTE: Standard errors are reported in parentheses. The samples include people ages 25-34 and 50-59. The "first generation" consists of foreign-born individuals, excluding those born abroad of an American parent. The "second generation" consists of U.S.-born individuals who have at least one foreign-born parent. Remaining persons are members of the "third+ generation" (i.e., the third and all higher generations), which consists of U.S.-born individuals who have two U.S.-born parents. Sampling weights were used in the calculations. See Duncan and Trejo (2015) for further details on methodology.
SOURCE: Data from 2003-2013 Current Population Survey outgoing rotation group data.

young third- and higher-generation Mexican Americans continue to trail the average schooling of their non-Hispanic white peers by more than a year.

Explaining Mexican American Educational Outcomes in the Third Generation

Because Mexican Americans are the largest immigrant group to the United States and have one of the longest histories of migration, an important question is whether their educational gains continue after the second generation, as Smith (2012) suggested, or stall or stagnate as other scholars have argued, such as Telles and Ortiz (2008). This issue has been much debated in the immigration literature (Perlmann, 2005; Portes, 2006; Telles and Ortiz, 2008; Alba et. al., 2011a; Haller et al., 2011a, 2011b; Perlmann, 2011; Alba et al., 2014; Park et al., 2014; Bean et al., 2015; Duncan and Trejo, 2015).

There are two interpretations of the outcomes among third generation and higher Mexican Americans. One is that the outcomes found are due in large part to measurement error stemming from the problem of identifying this group in the available data. The second interpretation holds that there has not in fact been progress beyond the second generation in educational attainment and explains this outcome in terms of both the legacy of high levels of undocumented immigration across generations and the reality of racial and ethnic discrimination in the United States toward Latinos, including educational segregation and poor quality schooling for Mexican American children. Both interpretations and their supporting arguments are examined below.

Accurately Measuring the Third Generation

Intermarriage and selective identification among mixed ancestry individuals is a serious obstacle when using self-identification data such as the CPS data on third and higher generation Mexican Americans. Mexican Americans have had relatively high levels of intermarriage with other American ethnic groups, especially in later generations, and the children of such intermarriages are less likely to self-identify as Mexican than are the children of two Mexican-origin parents (Alba and Islam, 2009; Duncan and Trejo, 2009). This phenomenon, known as ethnic attrition, can bias estimates of characteristics such as education. Alba and Islam (2009) call this problem the "missing Mexicans." Duncan and Trejo (2007, 2009, 2011a, 2011b) have extensively examined this phenomenon and found that this ethnic attrition is "highly selective, because Mexican Americans who intermarry tend to have much higher education and earnings than Mexican Americans who do not intermarry.[3] Consequently, available data for third- and higher-generation Mexicans, who usually can be identified only by their subjective responses to questions about Hispanic ethnicity, understate the socioeconomic attainment of this population." (Duncan and Trejo, 2015, p. 125). They concluded that "those Mexicans who intermarry tend to have higher levels of education and earnings, and many of the resulting children are not identified as Mexican in census data. In this way, selective intermarriage interacts with the intergenerational transmission of human capital and ethnic identity to create a situation in which available data for later-generation Mexican Americans may omit an increasingly large share of the most successful descendants of Mexican immigrants" (Duncan and Trejo, 2015, p. 126).

The complexity of ethnic identity among third generation Mexicans is evident in the analysis of CPS data on Mexican-ancestry children living with both parents (Duncan and Trejo, 2015). Only 17 percent of these children have a majority of their grandparents born in Mexico, and about 30 per-

---

[3] The panel notes that although most of the research on ethnic attrition has studied Mexican Americans, and Mexican Americans are the focus of the analysis in this section of ther report, there is evidence that ethnic attrition occurs for other post-1965 immigrant groups, including other groups with Latin American origins (Duncan and Trejo, 2012; Emeka and Vallejo, 2011; Rumbaut, 2004) and Asian origin groups (Duncan and Trejo, 2012). Ethnic attrition may therefore be an important part of the explanation for third generation "stalling" or decline in socioeconomic progress of other immigrant groups, as well.

cent of third generation Mexican American children do not self-identify as Mexican. This is highly selective on education, and the high school dropout rate is 25 percent higher if the sample is limited to only those who self-identify as Mexican (Duncan and Trejo, 2015, p. 127). Research that has tried to correct for this ethnic attrition has found that educational attainment levels for third-only generation Mexican American groups are higher than those for second generation groups (Alba et al., 2011b; Bean et al., 2015). The hypothesis of ethnic attrition suggests that there is in fact educational progress in the third generation, but it is difficult to measure it well.

Explanations for Slow Educational Progress

The other interpretation of apparent Mexican American educational "stagnation" is to accept that there is less progress for the third generation and attempt to explain it through discrimination, racialization, and other factors such as family socialization. There is substantial historical evidence of third generation stagnation among Mexican Americans. Using data from a 1965 study of Mexican Americans in Los Angeles and San Antonio, Telles and Ortiz (2008) tracked down many of the original respondents and also found their children and grandchildren. The original respondents were mostly immigrants who settled in the United States before 1929 and their children. The children of these respondents grew up in the 1940s and 1950s, and their grandchildren came of age in the 1960s and 1970s.

The analysis by Telles and Ortiz of these data, comparing actual grandparents, parents and children, found that the third generation experienced little or no educational mobility, which they attributed to racial discrimination and exclusion. Alba and colleagues (2014) reanalyzed these data and noted that educational attainment among Mexican Americans was particularly low in Texas as compared to California. They attributed this in part to higher degrees of discrimination and exclusion in Texas as a result of the legacies of "conquest and colonization." Until the civil rights movement in the 1960s, Mexican American children in Texas attended segregated schools and had very low levels of educational attainment. Although it was less intense, Mexican Americans in California also experienced significant discrimination well into the civil rights era (Obregon Pagan, 2006; Fox, 2012). Whether similar patterns of discrimination and exclusion will limit educational attainment among the grandchildren of post-1970 Mexican and Central American immigrants is hotly debated and difficult to resolve, since the third generation of that wave of immigrants is very young and their educational attainment will not be measurable for several more decades.

Educational progress within and across generations for youth of recent immigrant ancestry depends on both school and family characteristics, so inequalities in American schools constitute a source of concern. A national study found that Mexican-origin students are overrepresented, for example, in schools that are larger, have lower levels of teacher experience on average, and have higher concentrations of low-income students, compared with schools that have higher levels of students from other low-income immigrant or native-born backgrounds (Crosnoe, 2005). Other research found that teachers of students who are of immigrant origin and who have limited English proficiency not only have less teaching experience but also are more likely to report not feeling prepared to teach their students, compared with teachers of the native-born (Samson and Lesaux, 2015). In another study, although first generation Latino parents held relatively high expectations for the quality of U.S. schooling, teacher expectations for Latino immigrant students were lower than expectations for other pan-ethnic groups, such as East Asian immigrant students (Tenenbaum and Ruck, 2007).

Recent research has found that legal status is another important factor in socioeconomic integration and that the legacy of parents' undocumented status can reverberate across generations (e.g., Bean et al., 2011, 2015). And undocumented status was found to hinder socioeconomic advancement not just for the undocumented immigrants themselves but also for their U.S.-born children (Bean et al., 2015). This handicap of legal status is relevant in considering the low educational attainment of second generation Mexicans and Central Americans, both of which are groups with high rates of undocumented status in the immigrant generation.

The legacies of earlier low levels of education can also influence children through family socialization practices that lead to slower intergenerational advancement in education. For example, higher levels of the kinds of parental stimulation that can aid cognitive development in early childhood—reading picture books with children, interactive play, singing songs—were observed among immigrant parents with higher levels of education (Cabrera et al., 2006). In other studies, immigrant mothers who increased their own education also appeared to engage more with their children's schools (Crosnoe and Kalil, 2010; Kalil and Crosnoe, 2009). And parents from immigrant groups with lower levels of education, on average, were found to have young children with lower levels of cognitive skills than those from groups with higher levels (Cabrera et al., 2006; Crosnoe, 2007). In another study, such parents were also less likely to enroll their children in preschool education, which can help reduce early school-readiness disparities in cognitive skills between low-income immigrant-origin children and their higher-income, native-born counterparts (Yoshikawa et al., 2013).

Parents' support of learning among older children can encompass a range of behaviors, including not just the traditional forms of academic socialization such as homework help but also behaviors that depend less on language proficiency, such as structuring household routines, emphasizing academic values, ensuring attention to schoolwork, enrolling children in extracurricular activities, and engagement with children's schools. Researchers have found that these behaviors differ by cultural group (e.g., Caplan et al., 1991; Chao, 1994), with some commonalities such as emphasis on obedience and proper behavior at school across the more often-studied Latino and Asian immigrant groups (Chao, 1994; González et al., 2013; Valenzuela, 2000). Others reported that socioeconomic class had a powerful influence across immigrant-origin and native-born groups in parents' investments in learning opportunities such as supplemental lessons and after-school programs (Kornrich and Furstenberg, 2013; Lareau, 2011) and in time spent with children (Guryan et al., 2008).

However, barriers have been found to academic socialization of immigrant-origin parents, especially if they had limited English proficiency (Hill and Torres, 2010; Terriquez, 2012). Communication barriers between teachers, very few of whom were Latino, in high-concentration Latino schools and the students' parents were an issue that researchers thought could be responsible for a disconnect between understanding of and intervention for students with low levels of achievement (Suárez-Orozco et al., 2015). Cultural differences in parent-teacher relationships in immigrants' origin countries were also reported to impede efforts at academic socialization (Smith et al., 2008; Sohn and Wang, 2006). However, another study found that, with increasing time in the United States, immigrant parents' involvement in their children's schools increased (Terriquez, 2012).

Relevant to this debate, recent research highlights three promising trends. The first is rising high school completion rates for U.S.-educated Hispanics from 1990 to 2010, with particularly large gains during the second half of this period (Murnane, 2013). In another study, the dropout rate in 2012 fell to a record low of 15 percent (Lopez and Fry, 2013). Second, steady and substantial improvement from 2003 to 2013 were found in how Hispanic fourth and eighth graders scored on standardized math tests (Pane, 2014). Finally, Lopez and Fry (2013) reported that among recent high school graduates, for the first time a greater share of Hispanic graduates (49%) than white graduates (47%) were enrolled in college. And although the same researchers found that college completion rates for Hispanics continued to lag behind their white counterparts (Fry and Lopez, 2012), these recent results, if confirmed as continuing trends, point to rising educational levels for young Hispanic Americans.

In sum, although there is historical evidence to worry about the educational progress of Hispanic American youth, and Mexican American generations over time, recent studies provide reasons to be more optimistic. Nonetheless, the significant number of second generation immigrants with undocumented parents tempers this optimism. In the end, the current data do not allow the panel to project with confidence what the long term patterns of educational advance will be for Mexican Americans and others of Hispanic ancestry.

EMPLOYMENT

Unlike many European countries, the United States has a very open labor market, and immigrants, even undocumented ones, have ready access to employment (Gautie and Schmitt, 2009). Table 6-5 provides employment rates, based on statistical sampling of CPS data, by generation and education for both men and women. Throughout this discussion, an employment rate represents the percentage of individuals of the stated group who were employed during the week they were surveyed by the CPS. For the period from 2003 through 2013, the employment rate for all males and all educational levels was slightly higher for the foreign-born (86%) than for U.S.-born generations (83% for the second generation and 82% for the third and higher generations). Among women, the pattern is reversed, with a substantially lower employment rate for immigrants (61%) than for the native born (roughly 72% for both the second generation and the third and higher generations).[4]

For the first generation, prior research found that employment integration occured relatively quickly, with immigrant employment rates rising sharply (e.g., by as much as 20 percentage points) during the first few years after arrival in the United States; thereafter, employment rates did not change much with further time in the country.[5] As a result, if one disregards recent arrivals and instead focuses on the employment rates of immigrants who have been here long enough to be past the initial period of adjustment to the U.S. labor market, employment rates for the foreign-born are a few percentage points higher than those shown in Table 6-5 (Duncan and Trejo, 2012).

These modest overall differences obscure the dramatic differences in employment at the bottom of the educational attainment distribution. For just men with low education, the differentials in employment by generation in Table 6-5 are very large. Among males with less than 12 years of schooling, the average employment rate of the first generation during 2003-2013 (84%) exceeded that of the second generation by 21 percentage points and

---

[4]Perhaps not surprisingly, U.S. employment rates were lower during this period for immigrant women originating in countries with more traditional gender roles and lower levels of female participation in labor-market work (Antecol, 2000; Blau and Kahn, 2011; Blau et al., 2011). A large share of U.S. immigration originates in such countries, which helps to explain the lower overall employment rate of foreign-born women relative to U.S.-born women.

[5]See, for example, Chiswick and colleagues, (1997), Funkhouser and Trejo (1998), Schoeni (1998a), Funkhouser (2000), and Antecol and colleagues (2006).

TABLE 6-5 Employment Rates (percentage), Ages 25-59, by Education Level, Sex, and Immigrant Generation

Education Level	Men, by Immigrant Generation			Women, by Immigrant Generation		
	First	Second	Third+	First	Second	Third+
Years of education:						
< 12	83.9	63.4	58.2	47.5	42.9	40.8
	(0.25)	(1.09)	(0.30)	(0.35)	(1.15)	(0.32)
12	84.9	80.0	78.3	59.7	65.6	66.6
	(0.24)	(0.44)	(0.11)	(0.32)	(0.54)	(0.13)
13-15	84.0	83.0	83.6	68.1	73.1	73.6
	(0.33)	(0.41)	(0.11)	(0.38)	(0.45)	(0.12)
16+	89.0	89.8	91.3	70.4	80.1	81.1
	(0.21)	(0.29)	(0.08)	(0.29)	(0.36)	(0.10)
All education levels	85.7	83.2	82.3	61.4	72.1	71.9
	(0.13)	(0.22)	(0.06)	(0.17)	(0.25)	(0.07)

NOTE: The reported figures give the percentage of individuals who were employed during the week they were surveyed by the CPS. Standard errors are reported in parentheses. The samples include people ages 25-59. The "first generation" consists of foreign-born individuals, excluding those born abroad of an American parent. The "second generation" consists of U.S.-born individuals who have at least one foreign-born parent. Remaining persons are members of the "third+ generation" (i.e., the third and all higher generations), which consists of U.S.-born individuals who have two U.S.-born parents. Sampling weights were used in the calculations. See Duncan and Trejo (2015) for further details on methodology.
SOURCE: Data from 2003-2013 Current Population Survey outgoing rotation group data.

exceeded that of the third and higher generations by 26 percentage points. The data for women did not show such dramatic differences, even among women with less than 12 years of schooling, where the immigrant employment rate exceeds that of natives by just 5-7 percentage points.

The high employment levels for the least educated immigrants indicates that employer demand for low-skilled labor remains high. There are still many jobs in the United States for low skilled workers (Lockard and Wolf, 2012). Among the important reasons cited for this high demand have been the substantial shrinkage since 1990 of the U.S.-born, younger, less-skilled working-age population (those who are native born, ages 25-44, and with educational attainment of a high school diploma or less), owing to the aging of Baby Boomers; higher educational attainment among the U.S.-born; and a fertility rate below the replacement rate for the U.S.-born (Alba, 2009; Bean et. al., 2011; Bean et al., 2015). In other words, immigrants appear to be taking low-skilled jobs that natives are either not available or unwilling to take.

Next, the panel uses CPS data sampled over the same period, 2003-2013, to explore how employment patterns vary across racial/ethnic groups. Figures 6-3 (for men) and 6-4 (for women) show how employment patterns varied across racial/ethnic groups by generation, comparing them to the reference group of third and higher generation, non-Hispanic whites. A negative differential implies that the reference group had a higher employment rate than the group in question, whereas a positive differential indicates the opposite. The top panel of each figure displays the employment differentials that remain after using regression analysis to control for the influence of age, geographic location, and survey month/year. The bottom panel of each figure shows what happens to the estimated employment differentials when the underlying regressions also control for education level.

Figure 6-3 indicates that, for men, in spite of the low educational levels of Hispanic immigrants in general and Mexican immigrants in particular, these two groups had employment rates very similar to those of third and higher generation non-Hispanic whites. Second generation and third and higher generation Hispanic and Mexican men did have modest employment deficits relative to the reference group, but the bottom panel of Figure 6-3 suggests that these deficits are explained in large part by the lower education levels of U.S.-born Hispanics and Mexicans relative to the reference group. Asian men of all generations exhibit employment propensities similar to those of third and higher generation non-Hispanic whites.[6] However, employment rates for black men are much lower; the corresponding employment deficits are modest (4 percentage points) for

---

[6]Though not shown in Figure 6-3, employment rates for non-Hispanic white men are almost identical across generations, with or without controls for education.

A. Not Controlling for Education

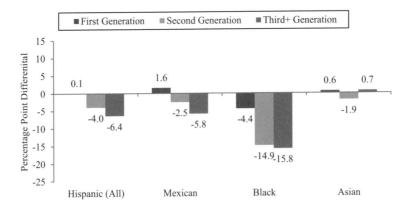

B. Controlling for Education

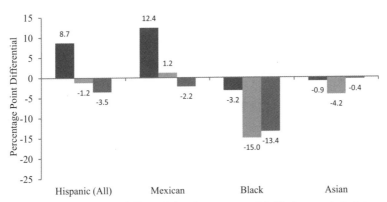

FIGURE 6-3 Employment differentials of men, ages 25-59, by race/ethnicity and immigrant generation (relative to third+ generation, non-Hispanic whites).

NOTE: The reported figures represent employment rate differentials between each race/ethnicity and immigrant generation group and the reference group of third+ generation, non-Hispanic whites. These differentials are estimated from least squares regressions in which the dependent variable is a dummy identifying individuals who were employed during the CPS survey week. The samples include men ages 25-59. All regressions include controls for age, geographic location, and survey month/year. The differentials shown in the bottom panel are from regressions that also control for education level.

SOURCE: Data from 2003-2013 Current Population Survey outgoing rotation group data.

A. Not Controlling for Education

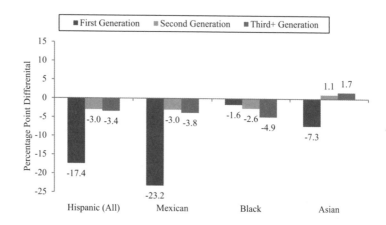

B. Controlling for Education

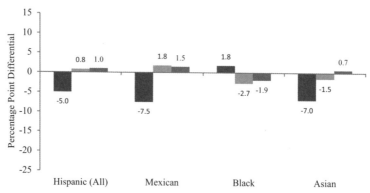

FIGURE 6-4 Employment differentials of women, ages 25-59, by race/ethnicity and immigrant generation (relative to third+ generation, non-Hispanic whites).

NOTE: The reported figures represent employment rate differentials between each race/ethnicity and immigrant generation group and the reference group of third+ generation, non-Hispanic whites. These differentials are estimated from least squares regressions in which the dependent variable is a dummy identifying individuals who were employed during the CPS survey week. The samples include women ages 25-59. All regressions include controls for age, geographic location, and survey month/year. The differentials shown in the bottom panel are from regressions that also control for education level.

SOURCE: Data from 2003-2013 Current Population Survey outgoing rotation group data.

black male immigrants but much larger (15 percentage points) for the second and later generations. Conditioning on education has only minor effects on these deficits.[7]

For women, Figure 6-4 shows that employment rates were relatively low for first-generation Hispanics, especially for immigrants from Mexico. For first-generation Hispanic women, the employment deficit relative to the reference group of third generation and higher non-Hispanic white women is 17 percentage points; for first-generation Mexican women the deficit climbs above 23 percentage points. These deficits shrink considerably, to 5 and 7.5 percentage points, respectively, after accounting for the low education levels of Hispanic immigrant women (see lower half of Figure 6-4). The corresponding employment deficits are much smaller for foreign-born black (2 percentage points) and Asian (7 percentage points) women. Boyd (1984) concluded that immigrant women are particularly disadvantaged in the labor market due to their gender. Schoeni (1998b) cited immigrant women's lower human capital as a limiting factor on their employment prospects, while Donato and colleagues (2014) cited marital status. Among U.S.-born women, however, the employment rates in Figure 6-4 do not vary much by race/ethnicity, particularly after conditioning on education.[8]

EARNINGS

When they first arrive, immigrants earn less than natives of comparable skill levels. This may be because they are not sufficiently proficient in English or because they lack knowledge that is valued by the U.S. labor market. Early research on the economic integration of immigrants focused on how long it would take for immigrant earnings to catch up with the native-born. Chiswick (1978) concluded that immigrants would catch up within 15 years as they acquired language and U.S.-specific labor market experience. Borjas (1985) pointed out that these conclusions were based on cross-sectional data but were making longitudinal cohort conclusions; he suggested that Chiswick had been overly optimistic and that recent immigrants would not catch up to the native-born over time. More recently, research by Lubotsky (2007) examined true longitudinal data on immigrants earnings using Social Security records. He found that immigrants do experience earnings growth as length of residency increases, but they do

---

[7] Research by Donato and colleagues (2015) indicates that black immigrants of both genders from the Caribbean actually have higher employment rates than do the black native-born, suggesting within-race variation based on country or region of origin.

[8] Among non-Hispanic white women, employment rates, determined as in Figures 6-3 and 6-4, were about 9 percentage points lower for immigrants than for U.S.-born women, with little variation between the second and later generations of the U.S.-born (not shown in Figure 6-4). Controlling for education did not alter this pattern.

not fully catch up to the native-born. He concluded that "over their first 20 years in the United States, immigrant earnings grow by 10-15 percent relative to the earnings of native-born workers" (Lubotsky, 2007, p. 864).

Consistent with other research (Borjas, 1995; Trejo, 2003; Blau and Kahn, 2007; Borjas and Katz, 2007), Lubotsky also found that earnings assimilation is considerably slower for Hispanic (predominantly Mexican) immigrants than for other immigrants. A majority of Mexican immigrants currently present in the United States are undocumented, and one possible reason for the slower wage growth among Mexican immigrant workers, beyond their low educational levels, is the effect of being undocumented on wages. Studies show that the 1986 Immigration Reform and Control Act (IRCA), which criminalized the hiring of undocumented workers, and the massive increase in the number of undocumented migrants in labor markets throughout the United States have put substantial downward pressure on the wages not just of undocumented migrants but of all immigrant workers (Donato and Massey, 1993; Donato et al., 2008; Massey and Gelatt, 2010; Massey and Gentsch, 2014; Warren and Warren, 2013). Whereas undocumented status did not negatively affect earnings prior to IRCA, afterward it carried a 21 percent wage penalty (Phillips and Massey, 1999). Caponi and Plesca (2014) found that, in addition to lowering wages among immigrant workers, undocumented status itself carries a substantial wage penalty. Hall and colleagues (2010) estimated a 17 percent wage disparity between documented and undocumented Mexican immigrant men and a 9 percent wage disparity among Mexican immigrant women, as well as large differences in returns to human capital by legal status. Gentsch and Massey (2011) likewise found that the shift to a new and more intense regime of harsh border and internal enforcement coincided with a drop in the economic returns to a variety of forms of human and social capital, constraining both occupational attainment and earnings. The high proportion of undocumented immigrants therefore may drag down Mexican immgrants' overall earnings.

Another potential barrier to earnings mobility among immigrants is skin color discrimination. Using data from the New Immigrant Survey, Hersch (2008) demonstrated that wages systematically decline as skin color darkens. After controlling for education, English-language ability, source country occupation, family background, ethnicity, race, and country of birth, she found that immigrants with the lightest skin color earned 17 percent more than those with the darkest skin color. In a later analysis of the spouses of main respondents to the New Immigrant Survey, Hersch (2011) found that compared to immigrants with the darkest skin tone, those with the lightest experienced 16 to 23 percent greater earnings, even after controlling for labor market conditions in addition to respondent characteristics. Moreover, the skin color penalty did not disappear with time spent in the United States, underscoring the persistence of color stratification in U.S. labor markets.

What about earnings mobility beyond the immigrant generation? To illustrate some basic patterns relevant for this question, Figures 6-5 (for men) and 6-6 (for women) present weekly earnings differentials similar to the employment differentials shown previously in Figures 6-3 and 6-4.[9] As before, the reported differentials are all relative to the reference group consisting of non-Hispanic whites in the third and higher generations.[10] Because the outcome is weekly earnings, these differentials measure the cumulative effect of differences in both hourly wages and hours worked per week.

For Hispanics overall and for Mexicans in particular, the earnings deficits in Figures 6-5 and 6-6 display a similar pattern across generations as the education data presented earlier (see Table 6-3): large gains for the second generation over the first, with little or no evidence of further gains for third and higher generations. Among men, for example, the Hispanic earnings deficit (relative to third and higher generation non-Hispanic whites) drops from about 50 percent for the first generation to 22 percent for the second generation, but there is no additional decline for third and higher generations. The corresponding pattern for Mexican men is quite similar. However, comparing the top and bottom panels of Figure 6-5, the earnings deficits for Hispanic and Mexican men of every generation shrink by more than half after controlling for education. Earnings gains for Hispanic and Mexican women between the first and second generations are even larger than for men, and earnings deficits all but disappear for U.S.-born Hispanic and Mexican women when controlling for education (see Figure 6-6). On the whole, these results suggest that the educational disadvantage of Hispanics accounts for much of their earnings deficit. In addition, Hispanic gains in educational attainment between the first and second generations appear to play an important role in the earnings progress between these generations.

Among the U.S.-born groups, third and higher generation black men stand out, with earnings deficits that remain large even after controlling for

---

[9]Here, the dependent variable for the underlying regressions is the natural logarithm of weekly earnings from wage and salary work (the CPS outgoing rotation group data do not report self-employment income), and the samples include individuals ages 25-59 who are employed in civilian wage and salary jobs. Otherwise, these regressions are the same as those described previously for employment.

[10]For ease of exposition, we will refer to the estimated log earnings differentials as if they represented percentage earnings differences. Strictly speaking, however, log differentials closely approximate percentage differences only when the log differentials are on the order of .25 or less in absolute value. For larger differentials, the implied percentage difference can be calculated as $e^c - 1$, where c is the log differential and e is Euler's number (i.e., the base of natural logarithms).

A. Not Controlling for Education

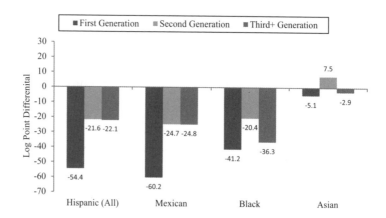

B. Controlling for Education

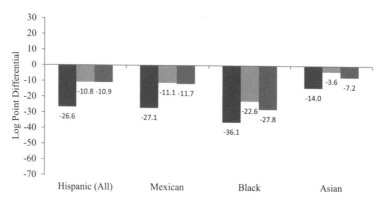

FIGURE 6-5 Weekly earnings differentials of men, ages 25-59, by race/ethnicity and immigrant generation (relative to third+ generation, non-Hispanic whites).

NOTE: The reported figures represent log weekly earnings differentials between each race/ethnicity and immigrant generation group and the reference group of third+ generation, non-Hispanic whites. These differentials are estimated from least squares regressions in which the dependent variable is the natural logarithm of weekly earnings. The samples include men ages 25-59 employed in civilian wage and salary jobs. All regressions include controls for age, geographic location, and survey month/year. The differentials shown in the bottom panel are from regressions that also control for education level.

SOURCE: Data from 2003-2013 Current Population Survey outgoing rotation group data.

A. Not Controlling for Education

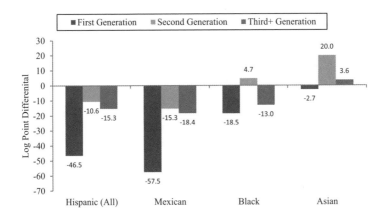

B. Controlling for Education

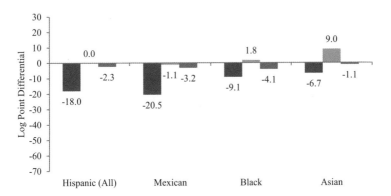

FIGURE 6-6 Weekly earnings differentials of women, ages 25-59, by race/ethnicity and immigrant generation (relative to third+ generation, non-Hispanic whites). NOTE: The reported figures represent log weekly earnings differentials between each race/ethnicity and immigrant generation group and the reference group of third+ generation, non-Hispanic whites. These differentials are estimated from least squares regressions in which the dependent variable is the natural logarithm of weekly earnings. The samples include women ages 25-59 employed in civilian wage and salary jobs. All regressions include controls for age, geographic location, and survey month/year. The differentials shown in the bottom panel are from regressions that also control for education level.
SOURCE: Data from 2003-2013 Current Population Survey outgoing rotation group data.

educational attainment. Third and higher generation black men earn about 28 percent less than their non-Hispanic white counterparts with similar education. The corresponding deficit is much smaller for Hispanics (11% overall, 12% for Mexicans). These findings corroborate other research suggesting that, among men, U.S. labor market opportunities for Hispanics are more similar to those of whites than are the opportunities for blacks (Trejo, 1997; Grogger and Trejo, 2002; Duncan et al., 2006). The bottom panel of Figure 6-6 shows that, after controlling for education, earnings of U.S.-born women do not vary much with race/ethnicity.

In contrast with blacks and Hispanics, earnings deficits (relative to third and higher generation non-Hispanic whites) are either small or nonexistent for first and second generation white immigrants (not shown in the figures) and for Asian immigrants of all generations. However, earnings comparisons for Asians become less favorable after controlling for education. As others have noted (Sakamoto et al., 2009), the schooling advantage of native-born Asian Americans can obscure the fact that, at least among men, they tend to earn somewhat less than non-Hispanic whites with the same level of education.

OCCUPATION

Immigrants make up 13 percent of the population overall, but 16 percent of the civilian workforce ages 16-64 (Singer, 2012). There is a longstanding tendency of immigrants to concentrate in certain occupations and industries. Most Americans would instantly recognize these concentrations: Filipino American nurses, Mexican American farmworkers, Korean American shopkeepers. These ethnic concentrations have been a springboard for the first generation and sometimes have persisted for several generations (Lieberson and Waters, 1988). Such concentrations occur throughout the occupational structure, but immigrants make a special contribution to highly skilled, creative, and scientific occupations. The panel highlights these concentrations by examining Census Bureau data from 1950-2010 on detailed occupations by nativity, focusing on the subset of occupational roles that correspond to positions of high achievement and creativity.[11]

In the panel's analysis, immigrants did not dominate any single occupation. Even in immigrant niches, such as private household workers

---

[11] The Census Bureau data analyzed here are actually random samples (usually 1%) of the total population, and the samples are restricted to persons ages 25 to 64 in the experienced labor force, who reported an occupation. The 2010 data are based on the American Community Survey, which has replaced the long form census. Some persons are missed (undercounted) in censuses, and the foreign-born are probably more likely to be undercounted than the nativeborn. These sampling errors are estimated by the Census Bureau to be small (1% to 3%), however, and are unlikely to affect any of the patterns reported here.

(42%) and farm laborers (30%), immigrants were still a minority, although it is possible that in some regions of the country and in more detailed occupational categories immigrants do make up a much larger share. In the highly skilled professions of science and technology, immigrants comprised about one-fifth to one-third of all workers. While immigrants comprised an important, and perhaps a critical, share in some highly skilled occupations, native-born Americans still comprised the majority of workers in these roles.

The summary occupational classification in Table 6-6 contains 7 major and 25 detailed occupational categories.[12] In collapsing categories, the panel has highlighted the occupations of immigrant concentration ("niches") and immigrant participation in scientific and cultural professions. At the least-skilled end of the occupational structure, we have combined two of the largest groups, *Operatives and Laborers* into one major category. At the top of the earnings distribution, we identified seven detailed occupations within the major group of *Managerial and Professional Specialty Occupations*. *Military Occupations* is only included for the sake of completeness among all workers in the Experienced Labor Force, since relatively few immigrants are in military occupations.

In 1950, immigrants comprised about 8 percent of the experienced labor force, and this figure shrank to 5.2 percent in the 1970s as the wave of early 20th century immigrants aged and left the workforce. From 1970 to 2010, the relative share of foreign-born workers increased by 2 to 3 percentage points each decade, reaching 15 percent of all workers in 2010, triple the 1950 level (see Table 6-6).To create a consistent measure of relative immigrant concentration in occupations that is independent of these historical fluctuations in the size of the foreign-born population and the size of each occupation, the panel created an index of immigrant concentration relative to the native-born for each occupation and for each census year in (Table 6-6).[13] For managerial or professional specialty occupations in 1950, for instance, the number 1.23 means that immigrants were 23 per-

---

[12]These are based on the IPUMS USA variable in *OCC 1990* (Ruggles et al., 2010). *OCC 1990* was constructed by the Minnestoa Population Center to be a consistent occupational classification across all U.S. censuses and surveys since 1950. For further details, see https://usa.ipums.org/usa/chapter4/chapter4.shtml [September 2015].

[13]Specifically, each cell in Table 6-10 shows the ratio of the percent of all immigrants in an occupation to the percent of all native-born workers in the same occupation:

Index of immigrant concentration = $[(FB_i/FBt)/(NB_i/NB_t)]$

Where FB_i = the number of foreign-born workers in occupation i

FB_t = the total number of foreign-born workers in the experienced labor force with a reported occupation

NB_i = the number of native-born workers in occupation i

NB_t = the total number of native-born workers in the experienced labor force with a reported occupation.

TABLE 6-6 Index of Relative Occupational Concentration of Foreign-Born Workers, Ages 25-64, of Experienced Labor Force, United States, 1950 to 2010

IPUMS Codes		Total Experienced Labor Force with Reported Occupation
003-200		MANAGERIAL AND PROFESSIONAL SPECIALTY OCCUPATIONS
003-037	1	Exec., Admin., and Managerial and Related
043-059	2	Engineers, Architects, and Surveyors
064-068	3	Mathematical and Computer Scientists
069-083	4	Natural Scientists
084-089	5	Physicians and Other Health Diagnosing
183-200	6	Writers, Artists, Entertainers, and Athletes
095-179, 200	7	Health, Teachers, Lawyers, Religious and Other Related Professionals
201-400		TECHNICAL, SALES, AND ADMINISTRATIVE SUPPORT OCCUPATIONS
203-235	8	Technicians and Related Support Occupations
243-283	9	Sales Occupations
303-389	10	Administrative Support Occupations, Clerical
401-470		SERVICE OCCUPATIONS
405-407	11	Private Household Occupations
415-427	12	Protective Service Occupations
434-444	13	Food Preparation and Service Occupations
445-447	14	Health Service Occupations
448-455	15	Cleaning and Building Service, Except Households
456-469	16	Personal Service Occupations
471-500		FARMING, FORESTRY, AND FISHING OCCUPATIONS
473-476	17	Farm Operators and Managers
479-498	18	Other Agricultural and Related Occupations

Index of Relative Occupational Concentration						
1950	1960	1970	1980	1990	2000	2010
1.23	1.04	1.02	0.96	0.87	0.82	0.86
1.54	1.16	0.94	0.89	0.84	0.80	0.84
0.86	1.12	1.52	1.53	1.43	1.32	1.42
0.98	0.87	0.85	1.14	1.23	1.06	1.17
0.73	1.23	1.84	1.50	1.52	2.22	2.38
1.36	2.21	2.93	2.74	2.00	1.88	1.83
1.12	1.24	1.40	1.18	0.99	0.86	0.88
0.66	0.72	0.86	0.79	0.68	0.64	0.69
0.63	0.76	0.86	0.82	0.82	0.79	0.79
0.83	0.92	1.10	1.06	1.02	1.09	1.13
0.83	0.91	0.88	0.80	0.86	0.85	0.82
0.52	0.66	0.83	0.79	0.76	0.70	0.68
1.38	1.23	1.15	1.20	1.33	1.31	1.36
2.12	1.93	1.41	1.97	2.66	3.10	4.09
0.95	0.58	0.40	0.47	0.50	0.47	0.45
1.50	1.30	1.36	1.36	1.54	1.49	1.42
0.60	0.73	0.87	1.02	1.03	1.12	1.28
1.97	1.71	1.36	1.19	1.46	1.56	1.58
1.23	1.15	0.96	1.17	1.19	1.12	1.24
0.54	0.82	0.88	1.18	1.60	1.98	1.85
0.40	0.43	0.33	0.30	0.39	0.36	0.27
0.72	1.23	1.32	1.83	2.36	2.74	2.41

continued

TABLE 6-6 Continued

IPUMS Codes		Total Experienced Labor Force with Reported Occupation
501-700		**PRECISION PRODUCTION, CRAFT, AND REPAIR OCCUPATIONS**
503-549	19	Mechanics and Repairers
558-599	20	Construction Trades
666-674	21	Precision Textile, Apparel, and Furnishings
686-688	22	Precision Food Production Occupations
657-659, 614 - 684, 693-699	23	All Other Precision and and Craft Occupations
701-900	24	**OPERATORS, FABRICATORS, AND LABORERS**
095	25	**MILITARY OCCUPATIONS**

NOTES:
Unemployed and other workers without a reported occupation are excluded:
Index of immigrant concentration = $[(FB_I/FB_t) / (NB_I/NB_t)]$

   Where FB_I = the number of foreign-born workers in occupation i

   FB_t = the total number of foreign-born workers in the experienced labor force with a reported occupation

   NB_I = the number of native-born workers in occupation i

   NB_t = the total number of native-born workers in the experienced labor force with a reported occupation

SOURCE: Ruggles et al. (2010).

cent more likely than native-born workers to be working in a managerial or professional occupation in 1950. In 2010 the number was 0.86, meaning immigrant workers were 14 percent less likely than the native-born to be working in these occupations, although there is great variability across sub-categories.

The trends across rows in Table 6-6 can be used to divide the displayed occupations into three categories: (1) *consistent immigrant occupations*, or occupations in which immigrants have been overrepresented for the entire period (all index values in that row in Table 6-6 are greater than 1); (2) *consistent non-immigrant occupations*, in which immigrants have always been underrepresented during this period, relative to natives (all index values in the row are less than 1) ; and (3) *occupations in transition*, or occupations that have shifted from underrepresentation (a value less than

Index of Relative Occupational Concentration						
1950	1960	1970	1980	1990	2000	2010
1.27	1.40	1.07	0.97	0.99	1.02	1.04
0.86	0.91	0.77	0.82	0.86	0.85	0.80
1.25	1.16	1.04	0.84	0.95	1.09	1.26
4.03	3.81	4.95	4.43	4.56	3.69	3.98
2.64	2.73	2.31	1.95	1.76	2.31	2.27
1.28	1.18	1.03	0.99	0.89	0.82	0.75
1.13	1.03	1.10	1.21	1.22	1.33	1.30
0.44	0.37	0.60	0.75	0.60	0.59	0.46

1) to overrepresentation (a value greater than 1), or the opposite, between 1950 and 2010.

As Table 6-6 indicates, in general immigrants are overrepresented in the lower ranks of blue collar jobs, including Operators (of machines) and Laborers, Farm Laborers (except in 1950), and Service Workers (Table 6-6, Rows 18 and 24). Consistent immigrant occupations include service workers in private households, food preparation, and in cleaning and building services. Immigrants are also overrepresented in some skilled trades including textiles and apparel (e.g., garment workers and tailors) and food production (e.g., meatpacking) (Table 6-6, Rows 21 and 22). Foreign-born workers are often recruited for work in these industries, and lack of English proficiency is less of a barrier to employment in these occupations (Rodriguez, 2004). The one high status occupation that has always had a consistent overrepresentation of immigrants is physicians (which include other highly trained health-diagnosing occupations) (Table 6-6, Row 5). In contrast, immigrants are typically underrepresented in most other higher and medium status occupations such as teachers, lawyers, clerical and administrative support workers, sales workers, protective service workers, farm operators and managers, and mechanics (Table 6-6, Rows 7, 17, 19).

As shown in Table 6-6, the concentration of immigrants in all managerial and professional occupations declined, albeit unevenly, from overrepresentation (index of 1.23) in 1950 to underrepresentation (0.86) in 2010. The overall decline is primarily due to the sharp drop in managers. The foreign-born are also underrepresented for teachers, health (not physicians), lawyers, religious and other related professionals, the second largest group in managerial and professional occupations (Table 6-6, Row 7). There are, however, interesting trends in some of the specialized professional occupations. The foreign-born were overrepresented in "'Writers, Artists, Entertainers, and Athletes" (panel category 6 in Table 6-6) in the early post–World War II era, but were underrepresented in recent decades.

Instead, the overrepresentation of immigrants in areas of exceptional contribution to American society has shifted over time from cultural and artistic fields (Writers, Artists, Entertainers, and Athletes) in the period 1950-1980 to engineering, computing, and scientific professions since 1980.[14] As shown in Table 6-6, immigrants are a growing presence in highly skilled scientific and technical professions, including Engineers and Architects (row 2), Mathematical and Computer Scientists (row 3), and Natural Scientists (row 4). Somewhat related, there has also been increasing representation of immigrants in Technicians and Related Support Occupations (row 8) and in Health Service Occupations (row 14). Immigrants were overrepresented in Construction Trades (row 20) during the early years of this period (1950s and 1960s) and recently in 2000 and 2010.

---

[14]Two additional qualifications to the findings in Table 6-6 should be noted. The concentration of immigrants in specific occupational niches (including highly skilled professions) is not related to the size or growth of specific occupations. Each of the highly skilled professions are very small (about 1 to 2% or less of the experienced labor force), some have grown rapidly, such as computer scientists, while others have only grown modestly, such as engineers, natural scientists, and physicians. Many rapidly growing occupations, including sales, highly skilled executives and managers, teachers, and protective service, have a below-average representation of immigrants. But a few rapidly growing occupations, including technicians and health service workers, have attracted immigrants. Immigrants have also become more concentrated in many declining occupations (in relative size), such as private household workers and operators and laborers. Other occupations, which have no clear trend of growth or decline, have also become immigrant niches, such as farm laborers and the construction trades. The forces that shape immigrant participation appear to be largely independent of those affecting occupational growth and decline.

Intergenerational Change in Occupations

The occupational distributions of the first and second generations reveal a picture of intergenerational change and stability similar to the ones presented above for education and earnings. The ethnoracial and regional origin groups in the immigrant generation that are concentrated in low-status occupations improve their occupational position substantially in the second generation but still fall short of parity with third and later generation Americans (see Table 6-7). The groups whose immigrants are unusually clustered in high-level occupations, mostly professional and technical, maintain their above-average position in the second generation. These groups increase their representation in jobs in "management, business, and financial" occupations that typically require more proficiency in the English language and in the mainstream culture than most immigrants can manage.

Some of the major Latin American groups, such as Mexicans and Central Americans, illustrate the first pattern. The immigrants from Mexico and Central America are more likely to take jobs in the lower tiers of the occupational hierarchy (Brick et al., 2011). They are most overrepresented in the service, construction, and agricultural categories. They are also more likely than other workers to have nonstandard, and more precarious, forms of employment, taking for example short-term jobs or working for contractors (Luthra and Waldinger 2010). Few are in management or other business and financial occupations or in "professional" positions (a category that includes numerous scientific, teaching, health and arts-related occupations as well). For instance, as shown in Table 6-7, approximately 7 percent of Mexican-born men and 9 percent of men born in Central America work at jobs in these categories; by comparison, 36 percent of all third and higher generation men work at such jobs.

As the table shows, the Mexican and Central American second generations make a large leap in occupational terms, relative to the first generation in this dataset. Twenty-two percent of second generation Mexican men and 31 percent of second generation Central American men were in professional or managerial positions; the latter figure is intermediate between that for third generation Hispanic men and third generation Anglo men. The panel's analysis of the CPS data indicates that second generation men are, like their immigrant fathers, overrepresented in service jobs (but have largely left agricultural ones). The leap for second generation women is even greater than for men of that generation, and the gap separating them from third and later generation women narrows greatly (even closing in the case of second generation Central American women). Moreover, the job situations of the second generation are improved, relative to the immigrant generation, in other ways: second generation Mexican men are less likely than their immigrant parents to take informal jobs (Waldinger et al., 2007),

TABLE 6-7 Representation of Groups in Professional and Managerial Occupations, by Generation

	1st Generation			2nd Generation			3rd Generation		
	Prof.	Manag.	Both	Prof.	Manag.	Both	Prof.	Manag.	Both
Men									
Hispanics	4.9	5.8	10.7	12.9	12.6	25.5	12.5	11.9	24.4
Mexicans	2.7	4.1	6.8	11.5	10.4	21.9			
Central Americans	4.2	5.1	9.3	15.6	15.6	31.2			
Cubans	11.3	13.4	24.7	21.5	23.0	44.5			
Asians	34.3	17.0	51.3	35.1	20.8	55.9	27.6	18.8	46.4
Chinese, incl HK and Tn	41.7	18.4	60.1	39.7	24.8	64.5			
Filipino	27.3	11.2	38.5	28.1	15.8	43.9			
Indians	52.6	21.9	74.5	47.3	24.3	71.6			
Black	17.5	10.1	27.6	26.5	12.0	38.5	13.0	9.6	22.6
White	24.4	20.4	44.8	23.9	23.2	47.1	19.0	19.8	38.8
Women									
Hispanics	10.4	6.3	16.7	23.7	13.5	37.2	21.2	12.5	33.7
Mexicans	6.8	4.5	11.3	21.9	12.4	34.3			
Central Americans	8.4	5.6	14.0	28.7	16.0	44.7			
Cubans	18.9	13.0	31.9	36.1	19.7	55.8			
Asians	30.9	15.2	46.1	38.0	20.3	58.3	32.5	19.1	51.6
Chinese, incl HK and Tn	33.4	19.5	52.9	45.5	19.7	65.2			
Filipino	36.4	12.8	49.2	30.6	19.6	50.2			
Indians	49.3	17.8	67.1	50.5	24.7	75.2			
Black	25.9	9.0	34.9	34.1	13.3	47.4	22.1	11.8	33.9
White	29.2	16.1	45.3	33.2	19.7	52.9	30.0	16.7	46.7

NOTE: The table is limited to individuals between the ages of 25 and 59 who are in the labor force. Generational definitions are the same as in prior tables. In the first and second generations, national-origin groups are identified by the birthplaces of respondents and their parents; in the third+ generation, ethnoracial categories are self-identifications (see discussion in "Assessing Education Patterns in the Third+ Generation"). For further details on methodology, see Farley and Alba (2002).

SOURCE: Data from 2003-2013 Current Population Survey outgoing rotation group data.

and they are much more likely to receive health and retirement benefits through their employment, although not as likely as other third and later generation men (Luthra and Waldinger, 2010). However, one issue that has been inadequately addressed is the extent to which the second generation moves ahead through bilingualism, which gives the U.S.-raised children of immigrants advantages in dealing with Spanish-speaking customers and workers (Hernández-León and Lakhani, 2013).

Some Asian groups enter the U.S. labor market at very high occupational levels (Table 6-7), so the question pertinent to their second generations is whether this favorable occupational placement can be maintained. For example, Table 6-7 shows that half of Indian immigrant men and women in the dataset held professional jobs. Chinese immigrant men and women were also overrepresented in the professional category in comparison to other groups, despite the substantial proportion of Chinese immigrants who hold low-wage jobs in such workplaces as restaurants and garment factories (Zhou, 2009). The second generations of these groups generally maintain a high level of concentration in professional positions and often attain above-average representation in managerial and other business-related jobs (Table 6-7). Among Asian women overall, almost one-third of the immigrants hold professional occupations, but the figure rises to almost 40 percent in the second generation, and twenty percent of the second generation has managerial jobs.

The robust representation of the first and second generations throughout the occupational spectrum implies that the U.S. workforce increasingly relies on immigrants and their children to staff higher-level jobs. This dependence on immigration is likely to grow as the baby boom cohorts complete their retirement over the next two decades (Alba 2009). At the beginning of the second decade of the century, the first and second generations made up a quarter of workers ages 25-54, and 28 percent of those under 45 years of age.

The presence of the foreign-born and their children among younger workers in professional and managerial occupations is impressive. The role of immigration with respect to professional positions, particularly in science, technology, engineering, and mathematics (STEM) jobs, is by now a well-known story (Ruiz et al., 2012; Stine and Matthews, 2009), but its contribution to management and business occupations, where familiarity with U.S. culture and native English proficiency are presumed to be assets, is equally important. In 2010-2013, the first and second generations constituted 23 percent of workers under the age of 45 in managerial positions, compared to 17 percent of older workers in such positions. The diversity of origins of the younger first and second generation managerial workers is also impressive. According to the panel's analysis, the two largest aggregate groups among them, at about 7.5 percent, come from Canada and Europe, on the one hand, and from Latin America, on the other. Asian origins account for 6.5 percent.

POVERTY

Public concerns about immigration often center on questions of poverty and economic dependency, namely, whether immigrants are disproportionately poor and dependent on public assistance. The Office of Management and Budget (OMB) uses a set of dollar values that define poverty income thresholds that vary by family size and composition (DeNavas-Walt and Proctor, 2014). For example, a four-person family (with two adults and two children) required an annual income of at least $23,624 in 2013 to meet the income poverty threshold. The income threshold for a single mother and two children was $18,769. In 2013, 45.3 million people, or 14.5 percent of the U.S. population, lived in families with incomes below poverty.[15]

Immigrant-Native Differentials in Poverty

The data shown in Table 6-8 are baseline poverty estimates for the native-born and foreign-born populations in 2013 (based on family income reported in 2014).[16] They indicate that the poverty rate among foreign-born persons was 18.4 percent in 2013, or roughly 30 percent higher than the native-born poverty rate of 13.8 percent. The differences in poverty rate for foreign-born groups compared with their native-born counterparts vary widely across racial and ethnic groups. Poverty was overrepresented among Hispanic Americans (23.5%), but the difference between immigrant and native-born Hispanic Americans was negligible. Among blacks, the poverty rate for immigrants was lower than for the native-born (22 vs. 27.7%). For these two historically disadvantaged ethnic and racial groups, these 2013 data show that immigrants suffer disproportionately from poverty compared with the general population, albeit at somewhat lower rates than their native-born counterparts.

Among non-Hispanic white and Asian immigrant populations, the poverty rates among the foreign-born were higher than for their native-born counterparts (see Table 6-8). For example, among foreign-born non-Hispanic whites, the poverty rate was 14.8 percent in 2013, or more than

---

[15]These estimates and the data presented in Tables 6-8 through 6-10 are drawn for the 2014 *Current Population Survey*'s Annual Social and Economic Supplement (ASEC), a nationally representative survey of nearly 68,000 households that define the resident, noninstitutionalized population of the United States. See https://www.census.gov/hhes/www/poverty/publications/pubs-cps.html [September 2015].

[16]The panel thanks Youngmin Yi, a doctoral student in Sociology at Cornell University, for conducting the analyses on poverty reported in this section.

TABLE 6-8 Percentage in Poverty (using federal poverty level), 2013, by Immigrant Generation, Race, and Hispanic Origin

	Poverty Status	Total	Native-Born	Foreign-Born
Total	Poverty	14.5	13.8	18.4
	Deep poverty	6.3	6.2	7.2
Hispanic	Poverty	23.5	23.5	23.5
	Deep poverty	9.4	9.9	8.6
Non-Hispanic	Poverty	14.5	12.6	23.5
	Deep poverty	12.6	12.4	14.1
White	Poverty	9.6	9.4	14.8
	Deep poverty	4.3	4.2	6.6
Black	poverty	27.2	27.7	22.0
	Deep poverty	12.3	12.9	7.4
Asian	Poverty	10.4	9.5	10.9
	Deep poverty	5.2	4.9	5.3
Other, Two or More	Poverty	19.2	19.6	10.4
	Deep poverty	9.2	9.5	4.1

SOURCE: Data from 2014 March Current Population Survey. Table was created courtesy of Youngmin Yi, Department of Sociology, Cornell University.

55 percent greater than the 9.4 percent poverty rate among native-born non-Hispanic whites. Still, poverty among non-Hispanic white immigrants was roughly the same as the overall U.S. poverty rate of 14.5 percent. Among the foreign-born, Asians had the lowest poverty rates of the racial and ethnic groups considered in Table 6-8. Their poverty rate was 10.9 percent, well below the U.S. poverty rate but slightly higher than the 9.5 prcent rate observed among their native-born Asian counterparts. Based on these data, racial and ethnic background is a much larger source of variation in poverty than nativity (foreign-born versus native-born).

Of course, the usual emphasis on poverty rates as a summary measure of economic deprivation hides extremes at the bottom of the income distribution. In an additional analysis for the panel, a common measure of "deep poverty" was calculated, defined as the share of the population below one-half of the poverty income threshold. These deep poverty rates are included in Table 6-8. In 2013, 6.3 percent of the U.S. population was living in households that were in deep poverty by this defintion. This percentage represents over 40 percent of the U.S population living under the poverty threshold. Interestingly enough, there is little if any evidence that native-born and foreign-born poor populations vary widely in the shares of the poor who are deeply impoverished. For example, about 44 percent of the native-born poor can be counted among those in deep poverty. The corresponding figure for the foreign-born population is 39.4 percent. Table 6-8 shows similar patterns of deep poverty across the racial and ethnic groups in the table.[17]

Generational Differences in Poverty

The above differences in poverty rates for the foreign-born compared with native-born counterparts suggest there may be potentially large generation-to-generation differences as well. Tables 6-9 and 6-10 provide 2013 poverty rates by generation (i.e., foreign-born or first generation, second generation, and third generation and higher for adults and children, respectively. The analysis separated adults from children because families often have members from multiple generations. Indeed, second generation children are economically dependent on their foreign-born parents, with whom they share the same income status. This means that poverty rates for second generation children are determined by the economic circumstances of their immigrant parents. To avoid these interpretative problems, the analysis separates children from adults.

Poverty Among Adults

Overall, poverty rates among adults in the United States in 2013 were highest among immigrants (18.8%) but dropped to 13.6 percent in the second generation and to 11.5 percent in the third and higher generations (see Table 6-9). These declines in poverty for different cross-sectional generations[18] are clearly consistent with canonical models of immigrant economic incorporation. Similar generational patterns were observed among Hispanic adults. That is, poverty rates were highest for first generation Hispanic

---

[17]At the other end of the income distribution, native-born versus foreign-born disparities are much larger than at the bottom of the income distribution. In some additional analyses (not shown in the tables), 36.1 percent of all persons in the United States in 2013 lived in families with incomes at 400 percent or more of the income poverty threshold. Only 28.1 percent of all foreign-born persons were also this far above the poverty threshold, and only 14.3 percent were among the Hispanic foreign-born population. In contrast, among the foreign-born non-Hispanic whites and Asians, 43.1 and 40.7 percent, respectively, were living in families at this range in the income distribution. Indeed, these percentages exceed that for the U.S. population overall, as well as for the native-born population (37.3%).

[18]The generation-to-generation changes in poverty rate in Table 6-9 should not be interpreted as indicating the experience of particular families over time. These are cross-sectional generations as of the time of the 2013 survey, not longitudinally linked generations.

TABLE 6-9 Percentage of Adults in Poverty, 2013, by Immigrant Generation, Race, and Hispanic Origin

	Poverty Status	Total	Foreign-Born	Native 2nd Generation	3rd+ Generation	Total Native
Total	Poverty	12.8	18.8	13.6	11.5	11.7
	Deep poverty	5.6	7.6	5.8	5.1	5.2
Hispanic	Poverty	21.6	25.0	18.1	17.4	17.6
	Deep poverty	8.3	9.1	7.3	7.6	7.5
Non-Hispanic	Poverty	11.3	13.1	9.0	11.2	11.1
	Deep poverty	5.1	6.3	4.4	5.0	5.0
White	Poverty	9.0	12.9	8.8	8.9	8.8
	Deep poverty	4.0	6.2	3.1	4.0	4.0
Black	Poverty	22.8	18.8	--*a*	23.6	23.3
	Deep poverty	10.1	8.8	--*a*	10.4	10.3
Asian	Poverty	11.0	11.5	9.1	9.1	9.1
	Deep poverty	5.7	5.6	6.0	5.8	6.0

NOTE: *a* denotes cell with 30 or fewer cases.

SOURCE: Data from 2014 March Current Population Survey. Table was created courtesy of Youngmin Yi, Department of Sociology, Cornell University.

TABLE 6-10 Percentage of Children in Poverty, 2013, by Immigrant Generation, Race, and Hispanic Origin

			Native		
Poverty Status	Total	Foreign Born	2nd Generation	3rd+ Generation	Total Native
Total					
Poverty	19.8	30.2	29.1	17.6	19.8
Deep poverty	8.8	13.1	10.5	8.2	8.8
Hispanic					
Poverty	30.2	37.0	38.3	23.8	30.2
Deep poverty	12.7	14.1	14.2	11.6	12.7
Non-Hispanic					
Poverty	16.5	25.0	14.6	16.4	16.5
Deep poverty	7.5	12.3	4.6	7.6	7.5
White					
Poverty	10.6	28.6	13.4	10.2	10.6
Deep poverty	4.5	17.9	5.3	4.3	4.5
Black					
Poverty	38.9	39.7	30.3	39.8	38.9
Deep poverty	19.0	13.8	9.5	20.3	19.0
Asian					
Poverty	10.2	16.8	7.9	10.5	10.2
Deep poverty	4.1	8.3	2.0	6.1	4.1

SOURCE: Data from 2014 March Current Population Survey. Table was created courtesy of Youngmin Yi, Department of Sociology, Cornell University.

Americans and lowest for third and higher generation Hispanic Americans. The decline in the poverty rate was largest between the first and second generation, while the further decline for the third and higher generation was comparatively small, less than 1 percentage point.

For non-Hispanic white and Asian adults, generational differences in poverty rates in 2013 were small compared with the differences between Hispanic adult generations (see Table 6-8). Declines in poverty rate were observed only between the first and second generations. For example, both the second generation and third and higher generation Asians had poverty rates of 9.1 percent. This is about 20 percent less than the poverty rate for Asian adult immigrants. Among blacks, most adults in the survey were either foreign born or third and higher generation native born. For black adults, the immigrant generation had a lower poverty rate than did the third and higher generation blacks (18.8 versus 23.3%). With respect to models of integration, these two generations are not relevant. Most third and higher generation native-born black Americans have ancestral roots in American slavery dating back more than two centuries and in racial and economic oppression over much of the pre-Civil Rights era after the emancipation. An obvious but unanswered question is whether the offspring of today's first generation black immigrants will experience patterns of poverty similar to today's third and higher generation black Americans.

Poverty Among Children

Because the majority of infants born in the United States today are children of racial or ethnic "minorities," the poverty rates among these children are especially germane (Lichter et al., 2005; Thomas, 2011; Van Hook et al., 2004). Their economic circumstances, as measured by poverty rates, provide a window to the future (Lichter et al., 2015), especially during a period of growing income inequality, crystallizing class boundaries, and declining intergenerational mobility. The data in Table 6-9 reveal substantially higher rates of poverty among America's children (ages 0-17) than for the general population (compare Table 6-7). In 2013, 19.8 percent of America's children lived in households whose income met the official definition of living in poverty. Foreign-born children as a group experienced an exceptionally high poverty rate—30.2 percent, a figure nearly 60 percent higher than the poverty rate for all foreign-born (18.4%) in Table 6-7. In a recent study, Lichter et al. (2015) noted that the poverty rate for families with newborn infants was particularly high among Mexican-origin populations in new destinations, especially in rural areas.

As shown in Table 6-10, in 2013, poverty rate gaps between foreign- and native-born children varied considerably by race. Among Asians, household poverty rates were ony slightly higher for foreign-born children

(11.5%) than for native-born children (10.2%). Among Hispanics, the gap was larger: 37.0 percent of foreign-born Hispanic children were poor, compared to 30.2 percent of their native born counterparts. The poverty rate gap between foreign-born and native-born children was especially large among whites: 28.6 percent of white foreign-born children lived in households below the poverty line, compared with only 10.6 percent of native-born white children.

It is also instructive to compare the circumstances of first, second, and third and higher generation children in the CPS data for 2013. Nationally, a large decline in child poverty appears to occur between the second and third generations. This overall pattern of large declines in poverty was particularly observed among households with second generation to third generation Hispanic children. As with adults living in households in poverty, the exception to this general rule of poverty declines is found among black children. For the native-born children of black native-born parents, the poverty rate was nearly 40 percent (39.8%). For second generation black children, the poverty rate was nearly 25 percent lower at 30.3 percent. These poverty rates are very high, but are nevertheless lower than rates among second generation Hispanic children (38.3%). However, as noted above, there are limitations to generational comparisons among blacks. Finally, second generation Asian children fare better than their native-born counterparts with native-born Asian parents. This reflects the relatively low rates of poverty among today's Asian immigrant families (and the parents of these children). Yet despite these ethnoracial differences, large numbers of immigrant children start life's race well behind the starting line, which raises important questions about prospects for upward socioeconomic mobility and social integration as these children make their way to adulthood and productive roles.

Supplemental Poverty Measure, 2012

The debate about how best to measure poverty—how to establish appropriate poverty income thresholds—has been ongoing and often contentious over the past several decades (National Research Council, 1995). The official poverty measure has been appropriately criticized for its limitations. Among these criticisms are that the official measure does not take into account income-in-kind (e.g., food stamps or housing vouchers), it fails to accurately reflect economies of scale from one family to the next, it does not adjust for geographic differentials in the cost-of-living or in consumption patterns, and it is based on the family as the unit of income generation and consumption (National Research Council, 1995). In 2009, an Interagency Technical Working Group on Developing a Supplemental Poverty Measure (SPM) was charged with developing an experimental poverty measure that

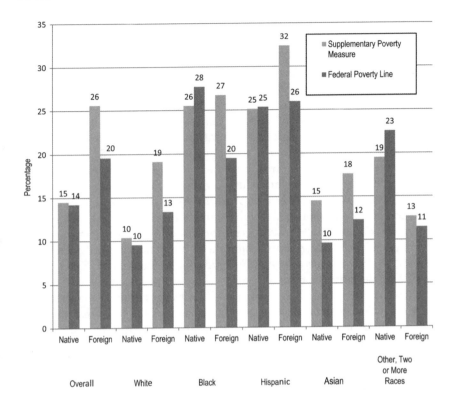

FIGURE 6-7 Percentage in poverty, comparison of FPL and SPM, 2012, by nativity status, race, and Hispanic origin.
SOURCE: Data from Supplementary Poverty Measure and Current Population Survey.

defines income thresholds and resources based on recommendations made by a 1995 National Research Council Panel on Poverty and Family Assistance that addressed the shortcomings listed above (National Research Council, 1995).

Figure 6-7 shows differences in the percentages of foreign-born and native-born households with incomes at or below the poverty level based on the SPM for 2012 data from the 2013 CPS (hereafter, "SPM in 2012") and the percentaged when the 2013 official poverty measures are used.[19] The SPM in 2012 yielded lower overall (i.e, not broken down by ethnoracial group) poverty rates than the official rate (14.9% versus 16.0%, not shown

---

[19] At this writing, the 2013 SPM is not available. The panel compare alternative poverty estimates for 2012, based on the 2013 CPS.

in Figure 6-7). But for the foreign-born overall, the SPM-based figure was 26 percent compared with 20 percent using the official rates. Although the differences between the SPM and the official poverty rate for foreign-born versus native-born are a matter of degree rather than kind, they are hardly negligible. Indeed, they tended to indicate much larger poverty gaps among immigrants when using the SPM (which presumably reflects differences in access to resources). For example, the official poverty rate revealed a native-immigrant disparity of 6 percentage points in 2012 (20 vs. 14%). The SPM, however, indicated a gap of 11 percentage points (26 vs. 15%).

Whereas the gap between native- and foreign-born Hispanics was only 0.7 percentage points (favoring natives) using the official poverty level, the gap using the SPM levels was much larger at 7.3 percentage points. For non-Hispanic whites, the gap between immigrants and native-born was only 3.8 percentage points using the official poverty measure, but the gap was 8.7 percentage points using the SPM measures. For foreign-born blacks, the SPM levels show 26.8 percent in poverty in 2013, compared with 19.5 percent using the official poverty measure.

The key point of these comparisons is that the official poverty level arguably underestimates the extent of poverty and economic hardship for certain groups, even as it tends to overstate the poverty rate for the nation as a whole. The implication is that the official poverty rates may misrepresent the degree of family hardship among immigrant populations, especially if immigrant groups do not have access to government resources (e.g., SNAP or TANF) or if the economies of family size implied by current poverty income thresholds do not accurately gauge the economic implications of characteristic features of immigrant families (e.g., large size and household extension in multi-generation households). In a recent study by Lichter and colleagues (2015), for example, only 11.9 percent of poor Hispanic children lived in family households receiving cash assistance from the government (TANF). For immigrant populations, questions of eligibility for government assistance may distort comparisons of welfare based on the official poverty measure.

SUMMARY AND CONCLUSIONS

The evidence summarized in this chapter indicates that substantial socioeconomic integration is occurring for immigrants to the United States and especially for their U.S.-born descendants. Compared to the general population of third and higher generation native-born, the foreign-born are much more varied in their skill levels, including not only a large segment with little formal schooling and without the ability to speak English but also a disproportionate share of highly educated workers concentrated in science, technology, engineering, and health fields. The robust representation of the first and second generations across the occupational spectrum in these analyses implies that the U.S. workforce has been welcoming immigrants and their children into higher-level jobs in recent decades. This pattern of workforce integration appears likely to continue as the baby boom cohorts complete their retirement over the next two decades.

Notwithstanding this heterogeneity within the first generation, socioeconomic integration is remarkably high in general for the second generation (i.e., the U.S.-born children of immigrants).

Conclusion 6-1 Despite large differences in starting points among the first generation, there has been strong intergenerational progress in educational attainment. Second generation members of most contemporary ethnoracial immigrant groups meet or exceed the schooling level of the general population of third and higher generation native-born Americans. This is true for both men and women. However, there are important variations between and within these ethnoracial groups that reflect the different levels of human capital their immigrant parents bring to the United States. The children of Mexican and Central American immigrants, in particular, progress a great deal relative to their parents, but they do not reach parity with the general population of native-born.

Conclusion 6-2 Immigrant men have an employment advantage compared to men in the second generation and the third+ generations. This employment advantage is especially dramatic among the least-educated immigrants, who are much more likely to be employed than comparable native-born men, indicating that they are filling an important niche in our economy. For second and later generation men, employment varies by ethnicity and race: Hispanic men still have high employment rates when their lower education is taken into account, and Asian men are integrating into the non-Hispanic white population by this measure, but the employment rates for second generation blacks appear to be moving toward those for the general black native-born population, for whom higher education does not translate into higher employment rates. Among women the above pattern is reversed, with a substantially lower employment rate for immigrants than for the native-born in general. But employment rates for second and higher generation women, regardless of ethnoracial group, approach parity with the general native-born population of women.

Conclusion 6-3 Foreign-born workers' earnings improve relative to the native-born the longer they reside in the United States. These overall patterns, however, are still shaped by racial and ethnic stratification. Immigrants experience a substantial earnings penalty as skin color darkens. Earnings assimilation is also considerably slower for Hispanic (predominantly Mexican) immigrants than for other immigrants. And although Asian immigrants and their descendants appear to do just as well as native-born whites, these comparisons become less favorable after controlling for education.

Conclusion 6-4 The occupational distributions of the first and second generations reveal a picture of intergenerational improvement similar to that for education and earnings. The groups concentrated in low-status occupations in the first generation improve their occupational position substantially in the second generation, although they do not reach parity with third and later generation Americans. Second generation men are overrepresented in service jobs, but they have largely left agricultural ones. The occupational gains for second generation women relative to the first generation are even greater than for second generation men, and the gap separating them from the general population of third and higher generation women narrows greatly. Second generation men are also less likely than their immigrant parents to take jobs in the informal sector, and they are more likely to receive health and retirement benefits through their employment. The robust representation of the first and second generations across the occupational spectrum implies that the U.S. workforce has increasingly welcomed immigrants and their children into higher-level jobs in recent decades. This pattern of workforce integration is likely to continue to increase as the baby boom cohorts complete their retirement over the next two decades.

Conclusions about the socioeconomic integration of the third generation and beyond are harder to draw. Available nationally representative datasets are problematic for assessing progress after the second generation because such data almost always rely on subjective ethnic identification and also typically cannot distinguish the "true" third generation from later generations. Some evidence suggests that samples of later-generation Hispanics identified from subjective ethnic responses will understate the attainment of the descendants of Hispanic immigrants (Alba and Islam, 2009; Duncan and Trejo, 2011a, 2012). Pooling together individuals from the third and later generations might hide progress for Mexican Americans because many of those in generations beyond the third have ancestors who grew up in places and times (e.g., Texas in the 19th and early 20th centuries) in which discrimination against Mexican ethnics was widespread and often institutionalized (Foley, 1997; Montejano, 1987)—a factor likely to impede socioeconomic mobility in such families. Ambitious data collection efforts and detailed analyses of Mexican American families in particular locations have attempted to overcome these and other problems in tracking intergenerational progress, with mixed findings (e.g., Telles and Ortiz, 2008; Bean et al., 2015).[20] Although we have learned a great deal from recent research, the amount of socioeconomic mobility experienced by the descendants of Mexican immigrants beyond the second generation remains an important open question.[21]

Black immigrants and their descendants also face additional barriers to socioeconomic integration. Black immigrants from the Caribbean and Africa arrive with relatively high levels of schooling, and second generation members of these groups meet or exceed, on average, the educational attainment of third and higher generation Americans in general, but other things being equal, black immigrants experience a substantial earnings penalty in excess of 16 percent as skin color darkens. Second generation black men have substantial employment and earnings deficits similar to those of third and higher generation African American men, and these deficits are much larger for U.S.-born blacks than they are for U.S.-born Hispanics, especially after controlling for education. Although the U.S.-born descendants of black immigrants do achieve labor market integration, it is into the racialized space occupied by African Americans in U.S. society rather than into the non-Hispanic white mainstream (Waters, 1999). In the same way, the evidence discussed earlier suggesting the possibility of socioeconomic stagnation for Mexicans after the second generation could be interpreted as assimilation into the disadvantaged minority position of U.S. Hispanics. Given the composition of contemporary immigrant flows, the collection of data that would allow generational change to be identified within racial and ethnic categories would go a long way toward answering these questions (see Chapter 10).

The variation in the rate of socioeconomic integration among different groups is not unprecedented. As the panel noted at the beginning of this chapter, Italians, for instance, took several generations to achieve parity with other immigrant-origin and native-born groups. But although there are parallels between the economic conditions the second generation faced in the past and what today's second generation faces, ongoing economic stagnation, rising income inequality, failing public schools, ongoing racial and ethnic discrimination; and a much more complicated and restrictive legal structure create higher barriers to integration for today's immigrants, particularly for those who arrive with fewer skills and resources (see Chap-

---

[20] An important issue with subnational studies of socioeconomic mobility is the potential selectivity of who chooses to locate initially in a particular region and who chooses to remain there. Such selectivity can color interpretation of the results of these studies (Alba et al., 2014).

[21] Two other influential studies of particular locations focus instead on the second generations from a wide range of national origin groups. Portes and Rumbaut (2001) collect and analyze data on the children of immigrants living in Miami and San Diego, and Kasinitz et al. (2008) do the same for New York City.

ters 2, 3, and 5). Researchers and policymakers need to take this context of reception into account when analyzing immigrant integration, and they need to understand the complicated nature of comparisons to immigrant groups from the past.

REFERENCES

Alba, R.D. (1985). *Italian Americans: Into the Twilight of Ethnicity*. Columbus, OH: Prentice-Hall.

Alba, R.D. (2009). *Blurring the Color Line: The New Chance for a More Integrated America*. Cambridge, MA: Harvard University Press.

Alba, R.D., and Islam, T. (2009). The case of the disappearing Mexican Americans: An ethnic-identity mystery. *Population Research and Policy Review, 28*(2), 109-121.

Alba, R.D., Abdel-Hady, D., Islam, T., and Marotz, K. (2011a). Downward assimilation and Mexican Americans: An examination of intergenerational advance and stagnation in educational attainment. In R.D. Alba and M.C. Waters (Eds.), *The Next Generation: Immigrant Youth in a Comparative Perspective* (Part II, Chapter 5). New York: New York University Press.

Alba, R.D., Kasinitz, P., and Waters, M.C. (2011b). The kids are (mostly) alright: Second generation assimilation. Comments on Haller, Portes, and Lynch. *Social Forces, 89*(3), 733-762.

Alba, R.D., Jimenez, T.R., and Marrow, H.B. (2014). Mexican Americans as a paradigm for contemporary intra-group heterogeneity. *Ethnic and Racial Studies, 37*(3), 446-466.

Antecol, H. (2000). An examination of cross-country differences in the gender gap in labor force participation rates. *Labour Economics, 7*(4), 409-426.

Antecol, H., Kuhn, P., and Trejo, S.J. (2006). Assimilation via price or quantities? Sources of immigrant earnings growth in Australia, Canada, and the United States. *Journal of Human Resources, 8*(4), 821-840.

Autor, D. (2014). *Polanyi's Paradox and the Shape of Employment Growth*. Cambridge, MA: National Bureau of Economic Research.

Bean, F.D., Leach, M., Brown, S.K., Bachmeier, J., and Hipp, J. (2011). The educational legacy of unauthorized migration: Comparisons across U.S.-immigrant groups in how parents' status affects their offspring. *International Migration Review, 45*(2), 348-385.

Bean, F.D., Brown, S.K., and Bachmeier, J.D. (2015). *Parents Without Papers: The Progress and Pitfalls of Mexican-American Integration*. New York: Russell Sage Foundation.

Blau, F.D., and Kahn, L.M. (2007). Gender and assimilation among Mexican Americans. In G.J. Borjas (Ed.), *Mexican Immigration to the United States* (pp. 57-106). Chicago: University of Chicago Press.

Blau, F.D., and Kahn, L.M. (2011). *Substitution Between Individual and Cultural Capital: Pre-Migration Labor Supply, Culture and U.S. Labor Market Outcomes Among Immigrant Woman*. NBER Working Paper 17275. Cambridge, MA: National Bureau of Economic Research.

Blau, F.D., Kahn, L.M., and Papps, K.L. (2011). Gender, source country characteristics, and labor market assimilation among immigrants. *Review of Economics and Statistics, 93*(1), 43-58.

Bohon, S.A., Macpherson, H., and Atiles, J.H. (2005). Educational barriers for new Latinos in Georgia. *Journal of Latinos and Education, 4*(1), 43-58.

Borjas, G.J. (1985). Assimilation, changes in cohort quality, and the earnings of immigrants. *Journal of Labor Economics, 3*(4), 463-489.

Borjas, G.J. (1993). The intergenerational mobility of immigrants. *Journal of Labor Economics, 11*(1), 113-135.

Borjas, G.J. (1995). Assimilation and changes in cohort quality revisited: What happened to immigrant earnings in the 1980s? *Journal of Labor Economics, 13*(2), 201-245.

Borjas, G.J. (2006). Making it in America: Social mobility in the immigrant population. *The Future of Children, 16*(2), 55-71.

Borjas, G.J., and Katz, L.F. (2007). The evolution of the Mexican-born workforce in the United States. In G.J. Borjas (Ed.), *Mexican Immigration to the United States* (pp. 13-55). Chicago: University of Chicago Press.

Boyd, M. (1984). At a disadvantage: The occupational attainments of foreign-born women in Canada. *International Migration Review, 18*(4), 1091-1119.

Brenner, A.D., and Graham, S. (2011). Latino adolescents' experiences of discrimination across the first 2 years of high school: Correlates and influences on educational outcomes. *Child Development, 82*(2), 508-519.

Brick, K., Challinor, A.E., and Rosenblum, M.E. (2011). *Mexican and Central American Immigrants in the United States*. Washington, DC: Migration Policy Institute and European University Institute.

Cabrera, N.J., Shannon, J.D., West, J., and Brooks-Gunn, J. (2006). Parental interactions with Latino infants: Variation by country of origin and English proficiency. *Child Development, 77*(5), 1190-1207.

Caplan, N.S., Choy, M.H., and Whitmore, J.K. (1991). *Children of the Boat People: A Study of Educational Success*. Ann Arbor: University of Michigan Press.

Caponi, V., and Plesca, M. (2014). Empirical characteristics of legal and illegal immigrants in the USA. *Journal of Population Economics, 27*(4), 923-960.

Card, D., and S. Raphael. (2013). *Immigration, Poverty, and Socioeconomic Inequality*. New York: Russell Sage Foundation.

Chao, R.K. (1994). Beyond parental control and authoritarian parenting style: Understanding Chinese parenting through the cultural notion of training. *Child Development, 65*(4), 1111-1119.

Chiswick, B.R. (1978). The effect of Americanization on the earnings of foreign-born men. *Journal of Political Economy, 86*(5), 897-921.

Chiswick, B.R., Cohen, Y., and Tzippi, Z. (1997). The labor market status of immigrants: Effects of the unemployment rate at arrival and duration of residence. *Industrial and Labor Relations Review, 50*(2), 289-303.

Crosnoe, R. (2005). Double disadvantage or signs of resilience? The elementary school contexts of children from Mexican immigrant families. *American Educational Research Journal, 42*(2), 269-303.

Crosnoe, R. (2007). Early child care and the school readiness of children from Mexican immigrant families. *International Migration Review, 41*(1), 152-181.

Crosnoe, R., and Kalil, A. (2010). Educational progress and parenting among Mexican immigrant mothers of young children. *Journal of Marriage and Family, 72*(4), 976-990.

Crosnoe, R., and Turley, R.N.L. (2011). K-12 educational outcomes of immigrant youth. *The Future of Children, 21*(1), 129-152.

DeNavas-Walt, C., and Proctor, B.D. (2014). *Income and Poverty in the United States: 2013*. Current Population Reports P-60 249. Washington, DC: U.S. Census Bureau.

Donato, K. M., and Massey, D.S. (1993). Effect of the Immigration Reform and Control Act on the wages of Mexican migrants. *Social Science Quarterly, 74*(3), 523-541.

Donato, K.M., Wakabayashi, C., Hakimzadeh, S., and Armenta, A. (2008). Shifts in the employment conditions of Mexican migrant men and women: The effect of U.S. immigration policy. *Work and Occupations, 35*(4), 462-495.

Donato, K.M., Piya, B., and Jacobs, A. (2014). The double disadvantage reconsidered: Gender, immigration, marital status, and global labor force participation in the 21st century. *International Migration Review, S1*(Fall), S335-S376.

Donato, K.M., Jacobs, A., and Hearne, B. (2015). *The Immigrant Double Disadvantage among Blacks in the United States.* Paper prepared for the Population Association of America 2015 Annual Meeting, San Diego, CA, April 30-May 2. Available: http://paa2015.princeton.edu/uploads/153392 [July 2015].

Duncan, B., and Trejo, S.J. (2007). Ethnic identification, intermarriage, and unmeasured progress by Mexican Americans. In G.J. Boras (Ed.), *Mexican Immigration to the United States* (Chapter 7). National Bureau of Economic Research Conference Report. Chicago: University of Chicago Press.

Duncan, B., and Trejo, S.J. (2009). Ancestry versus ethnicity: The complexity and selectivity of Mexican identification in the United States. *Research in Labor Economics, 29*, 31-66.

Duncan, B., and Trejo, S.J. (2011a). Intermarriage and the intergenerational transmission of ethnic identity and human capital for Mexican Americans. *Journal of Labor Economics, 29*(2), 195-227.

Duncan, B., and Trejo, S.J. (2011b). Tracking intergenerational progress for immigrant groups: The problem of ethnic attrition. *American Economic Review: Papers and Proceedings, 101*(3), 603-608.

Duncan, B., and Trejo, S.J. (2011c). *Selectivity and Immigrant Employment.* Available: http://paa2013.princeton.edu/papers/130581 [September 2015].

Duncan, B., and Trejo, S.J. (2012). *The Complexity of Immigrant Generations: Implications for Assessing the Socioeconomic Integration of Hispanics and Asians.* Available: http://www.rand.org/content/dam/rand/www/external/labor/seminars/adp/pdfs/2013/trejo.pdf [September 2015].

Duncan, B., and Trejo, S.J. (2015). Assessing the socioeconomic mobility and integration of U.S. immigrants and their descendants. *The ANNALS of the American Academy of Political and Social Science, 657*(1), 108-135.

Duncan, B., Hotz, V.J, and Trejo, S.J. (2006). Hispanics in the U.S. labor market. In National Research Council, *Hispanics and the Future of America* (pp. 228-290). M. Tienda and F. Mitchell, Eds., Panel on Hispanics in the United States. Committee on Population, Division of Behavioral and Social Sciences and Education. Washington, DC: The National Academies Press.

Foley, N. (1997). *The White Scourge: Mexicans, Blacks, and Poor Whites in Texas Cotton Culture.* Berkeley: University of California Press.

Foner, N. (2000). From Ellis Island to JFK. *New York's Two Great Waves of Immigration.* New Haven, CT: Yale University Press.

Fox, C. (2012). *Three Worlds of Relief: Race, Immigration, and the American Welfare State from the Progressive Era to the New Deal.* Princeton, NJ: Princeton University Press.

Fry, R., and Lopez, M.H. (2012). IV. College graduation and Hispanics. *Pew Research Center Hispanic Trends.* Available: http://www.pewhispanic.org/2012/08/20/iv-college-graduation-and-hispanics/ [July 2015].

Funkhouser, E. (2000). Convergence in employment rates of immigrants. In G.J. Borjas (Ed.), *Issues in the Economics of Immigration* (Chapter 4). Chicago: University of Chicago Press.

Funkhouser, E., and Trejo, S.J. (1998). Labor market outcomes of female immigrants in the United States. In National Research Council, *The Immigration Debate: Studies on the Economic, Demographic, and Fiscal Effects of Immigration* (pp. 239-288). J.P. Smith and B. Edmonston (Eds.), Panel on the Demographic and Economic Impacts of Immigration. Committee on Population and Committee on National Statistics, Commission on Behavioral and Social Sciences and Education. Washington, DC: National Academy Press.

Gautié, J., and Schmitt, J. (2009). *Low-Wage Work in Wealthy Countries*. New York: Russell Sage Foundation.

Gentsch, K., and Massey, D.S. (2011). Labor market outcomes for legal Mexican immigrants under the new regime of immigration enforcement. *Social Science Quarterly, 92*(3), 875-893.

Goldin, C., and Katz, L.F. (2008). Transitions: Career and family life cycles of the educational elite. *The American Economic Review*, 363-369.

Goldin, C., and Margo, R.A. (1992). Wages, prices, and labor markets before the Civil War. In C. Goldin and H. Rockoff (Eds.), *Strategic Factors in Nineteenth Century American Economic History: A Volume to Honor Robert W. Fogel* (pp. 67-104). Chicago: University of Chicago Press.

González, N., Moll, L.C., and Amanti, C. (Eds.). (2013). *Funds of Knowledge: Theorizing Practices in Households, Communities, and Classrooms*. New York: Routledge.

Greeley, A. (1976).The ethnic miracle. *Public Interest*, Fall, 20-36.

Green, P.E. (2003). The undocumented: Educating the children of migrant workers in America. *Bilingual Research Journal: The Journal of the National Association for Bilingual Education, 27*(1), 51-71.

Grogger, J., and Trejo, S.J. (2002). *Falling Behind or Moving Up? The Intergenerational Progress of Mexican Americans*. San Francisco: Public Policy Institute of California.

Guryan, J., Hurst, E., and Kearney, M.S. (2008). *Parental Education and Parental Time with Children*. Working Paper No. w13993. Cambridge, MA: National Bureau of Economic Research.

Hall, M., Greenman, E., and Farkas, G. (2010). Legal status and wage disparities for Mexican immigrants. *Social Forces, 89*(2), 491-513.

Haller, W., Portes, A., and Lynch, S.M. (2011a). Dreams fulfilled, dreams shattered: Determinants of segmented assimilation in the second generation. *Social Forces, 89*(3), 733-762.

Haller, W., Portes, A., and Lynch, S.M. (2011b). On the dangers of rosy lenses; Reply to Alba, Kasinitz, and Waters. *Social Forces, 89*(3), 775-782.

Haveman, R., and Wolfe, B. (1994). *Succeeding Generations: On the Effects of Investments in Children*. New York: Russell Sage Foundation.

Hernández-León, R., and Morando Lakhani, S. (2013). Gender, bilingualism, and early occupational careers of second-generation Mexicans in the South. *Social Forces, 92*, 59-80.

Hersch, J. (2008). Profiling the new immigrant worker: The effects of skin color and height. *Journal of Labor Economics, 26*, 345-386.

Hersch, J. (2011). The persistence of skin color discrimination for immigrants. *Social Science Research, 40*, 1337-1349.

Hill, N.E., and Torres, K. (2010). Negotiating the American dream: The paradox of aspirations and achievement among Latino students and engagement between their families and schools. *Journal of Social Issues, 66*(1), 95-112.

Kalil, A., and Crosnoe, R. (2009). Two generations of educational progress in Latin American immigrant families in the U.S. In E. Grigorenko and R. Takanishi (Eds.), *Immigration, Diversity, and Education* (pp.188-204). New York: Routledge.

Kasinitz, P., Mollenkopf, J.H., Waters, M.C., and Holdaway, J. (2008). *Inheriting the City: The Children of Immigrants Come of Age*. New York: Russell Sage Foundation.

Kornrich, S., and Furstenberg, F. (2013). Investing in children: Changes in parental spending on children, 1972-2007. *Demography, 50*(1), 1-23.

Lareau, A. (2011). *Unequal Childhoods: Class, Race, and Family Life*. Oakland: University of California Press.

Lee, J., and Zhou, M. (2014). The success frame and achievement paradox: The costs and consequences for Asian Americans. *Race and Social Problems, 6*(1), 38-55.

Lichter, D.T., Qian, Z., and Crowley, M.L. (2005). Child poverty among racial minorities and immigrants: Explaining trends and differentials. *Social Science Quarterly, 86*(S1,) 1037-1059.

Lichter, D.T., Sanders, S.R., and Johnson, K.M. (2015). Hispanics at the starting line: Poverty among newborn infants in established gateways and new destinations. *Social Forces, 94*(1), 209-235.

Lieberson, S. (1980). *A Piece of the Pie: Blacks and White Immigrants Since 1880.* Berkeley: University of California Press.

Lieberson, S., and Waters, M.C. (1988). *From Many Strands: Ethnic and Racial Groups in Contemporary America.* New York: Russell Sage Foundation.

Lockard, C.B., and Wolf, M. (2012). *Occupational Employment Projections to 2020.* U.S. Bureau of Labor Statistics. Available: http://www.bls.gov/opub/mlr/2012/01/art5full.pdf [September 2015].

Lopez, M.H., and Fry, R. (2013). *Among Recent High School Grads, Hispanic College Enrollment Rate Surpasses that of Whites.* Washington, DC: Pew Research Center. Available: http://www.pewresearch.org/fact-tank/2013/09/04/hispanic-college-enrollment-rate-surpasses-whites-for-the-first-time/ [August 2015].

Lubotsky, D. (2007). Chutes or ladders? A longitudinal analysis of immigrant earnings. *Journal of Political Economy, 115*(5), 820-867.

Luthra, R. Reichl, and Waldinger, R. (2010). Into the mainstream? Labor market outcomes of Mexican-origin workers. *International Migration Review, 44*, 830-868.

Mare, R. (1981). Change and stability in educational stratification. *American Sociological Review, 46*(1), 72-87.

Massey, D.S., and Gelatt, J. (2010). What happened to the wages of Mexican immigrants? Trends and interpretations. *Latino Studies, 8*(3), 328-354.

Massey, D.S., and Gentsch, K. (2014). Undocumented migration to the United States and the wages of Mexican immigrants. *International Migration Review, 48*(2), 482-499.

Montejano, D. (1987). *Anglos and Mexicans in the Making of Texas: 1836-1986.* Austin: University of Texas Press.

Mulligan, C.B. (1997). *Parental Priorities and Economic Inequality.* Chicago: University of Chicago Press.

Murnane, R.J. (2013). U.S. high school graduation rates: Patterns and explanations. *Journal of Economic Literature, 51*(2), 370-422.

National Research Council. (1995). *Measuring Poverty: A New Approach.* C.F. Citro and R.T. Michael, Eds., Panel on Poverty and Family Assistance: Concepts, Information Needs, and Measurement Methods. Committee on National Statistics, Commission on Behavioral and Social Sciences and Education. Washington, DC: National Academy Press.

Obregon Pagan, E. (2006). *Murder at the Sleepy Lagoon: Zoot Suits, Race, and Riot in Wartime L.A.* Chapel Hill: University of North Carolina Press.

Palerm, J. (2006). *Immigrant and Migrant Farm Workers in the Santa Maria Valley, California.* Working paper. Santa Barbara: University of California, Center for Chicano Studies.

Pane, N.E. (2014). *Math Scores Add Up for Hispanic Students: States and School Districts Notable for Recent Gains by Hispanic Students in Mathematics.* Publication #2014-59. Bethesda, MD: Child Trends Hispanic Institute.

Park, J., Myers, D., and Jimenez, T.R. (2014). Intergenerational mobility of the Mexican-origin population in California and Texas relative to a changing regional mainstream. *International Migration Review, 48*(2), 442-481.

Passel, J.S., and Cohn, D. (2009). A portrait of unauthorized immigrants in the United States. *Pew Research Center Hispanic Trends.* Available: http://www.pewhispanic.org/2009/04/14/a-portrait-of-unauthorized-immigrants-in-the-united-states/ [September 2015].

Perlmann, J. (2005). *Italians Then, Mexicans Now: Immigrant Origins and Second-Generation Progress, 1890-2000*. New York: Russell Sage Foundation.

Perlmann, J. (2011). The Mexican American second generation in Census 2000: Education and earnings. In R. Alba and M.C. Waters (Eds.), *The Next Generation: Immigrant Youth in a Comparative Perspective* (Chapter 4). New York: New York University Press.

Phillips, J.A., and Massey, D.S. (1999). The new labor market: Immigrants and wages after IRCA. *Demography, 36*(2), 233-246.

Portes, A. (2006). Review essay: Paths of assimilation in the second generation. *Sociological Forum, 21*(3), 499-504.

Portes, A., and Rumbaut, R.G. (2001). *Legacies: The Story of the Immigrant Second Generation*. Berkeley: University of California Press.

Rodriguez, N. (2004). Workers wanted: Employer recruitment of immigrant labor. *Work and Occupations, 31*(4), 453-473.

Ruggles, S.J., Trent, A., Genadek, K., Goeken, R., Schroeder, M.B., and Sobek, M. (2010). *Integrated Public Use Microdata Series: Version 5.0* [machine-readable database]. Minneapolis: University of Minnesota.

Ruiz, N.G., Wilson, J.H., and Choudhury, S. (2012). *The Search for Skills: Demands for H-1B Immigrant Workers in the U.S. Metropolitan Areas*. Washington, DC: Brookings Institution Press. Available: http://www.brookings.edu/~/media/research/files/reports/2012/7/18-h1b-visas-labor-immigration/18-h1b-visas-labor-immigration.pdf [September 2015]

Sakamoto, A., Goyette, K.A., and Chang Hwan K. (2009). Socioeconomic attainments of Asian Americans. *Annual Review of Sociology, 35,* 255-276.

Samson, J., and Lesaux, N. (2015). Disadvantaged language-minority students and their teachers: A national picture. *Teachers College Record, 117*(2), 1-26.

Schoeni, R.F. (1998a). Labor market assimilation of immigrant women. *Industrial and Labor Relations Review, 51*(3), 483-504.

Schoeni, R.F. (1998b). Labor market outcomes of immigrant women in the United States: 1970 to 1990. *International Migration Review, 32*(1), 57-77.

Schiller, K.S., Khmelkov, V.T., and Wang, X.Q. (2002). Economic development and the effects of family characteristics on mathematics achievement. *Journal of Marriage and the Family, 64*(3), 730-742.

Sewell, W., and Hauser, R. (1975). *Education, Occupation, and Earnings: Achievement in the Early Career*. New York: Academic Press.

Singer, A. (2012). *Immigrant Workers in the U.S. Labor Force*. Washington, DC: Brookings Institution Press.

Smith, J.P. (2003). Assimilation across the Latino generations. *American Economic Review, 93*(2), 315-319.

Smith, J.P. (2006). Immigrants and the labor market. *Journal of Labor Economics, 24*(2), 203-233.

Smith, J.P. (2012). The human capital (schooling) of immigrants in America. In B.R. Chiswick and P.W. Miller (Eds.), *Handbook in Economics: Economics of International Migration* (pp. 183-210). Oxford, UK: Elseivier.

Smith, J., Stern, K., and Shatrova, Z. (2008). Factors inhibiting Hispanic parents' school involvement. *The Rural Educator, 29*(2), 8-13.

Sohn, S., and Wang, X.C. (2006). Immigrant parents' involvement in American schools: Perspectives from Korean mothers. *Early Childhood Education Journal, 34*(2), 125-133.

Stine, D.D., and Matthews, C.M. (2009). *The U.S. Science and Technology Workforce*. Congressional Research Service, paper 57. Available: http://digitalcommons.unl.edu/cgi/viewcontent.cgi?article=1056&context=crsdocs [September 2015].

Suárez-Orozco, C., and Suárez-Orozco, M.M. (2002). *Children of Immigration.* Cambridge, MA: Harvard University Press.

Suárez-Orozco, C., Yoshikawa, H., and Tseng, V. (2015). *Intersecting Inequalities: Research to Reduce Inequality for Immigrant-Origin Children and Youth.* New York: William T. Grant Foundation.

Telles, E.E., and Ortiz, V. (2008). *Generations of Exclusion: Mexican Americans, Assimilation, and Race.* New York: Russell Sage Foundation.

Tenenbaum, H.R., and Ruck, M.D. (2007). Are teachers' expectations different for racial minority than for European American students? A meta-analysis. *Journal of Educational Psychology, 99,* 253-273.

Terriquez, V. (2012). Civic inequalities? Immigrant incorporation and Latina mothers' participation in their children's schools. *Sociological Perspectives, 55*(4), 663-682.

Thomas, K.J.A. (2011). Familial influences on poverty among young children in black immigrant, U.S.-born black, and nonblack immigrant families. *Demography, 48*(2), 437-460.

Trejo, S.J. (1997). Why do Mexican Americans earn low wages? *Journal of Political Economy, 105*(6), 1235-1268.

Trejo, S.J. (2003). Intergenerational progress of Mexican-origin workers in the U.S. labor market. *Journal of Human Resources, 38*(3), 467-489.

Valenzuela, A. (2000). The significance of the TAAS test for Mexican immigrant and Mexican American adolescents: A case study. *Hispanic Journal of Behavioral Sciences, 22*(4), 524-539.

Van Hook, J., Brown, S.I., and Ndigume Kwenda, M. (2004). A decomposition of trends in poverty among children of immigrants. *Demography, 41*(4), 649-670.

Waldinger, R., Lim, N., and Cort, D. (2007). Bad jobs, good jobs, no jobs? The employment experience of the Mexican American second generation. *Journal of Ethnic and Migration Studies, 33*(1), 1-35.

Warren, R., and Warren, J.R. (2013). Unauthorized immigration to the United States: Annual estimates and components of change, by state, 1990 to 2010. *International Migration Review, 47*(2), 296-329.

Waters, M.C. (1999). *Black Identities: West Indian Immigrant Dreams and American Realities.* New York: Russell Sage Foundation.

Xiong, Y.S. (2012). Hmong Americans' educational attainment: Recent changes and remaining challenges. *Hmong Studies Journal, 13*(2), 1.

Yoshikawa, H., Weiland, C., Brooks-Gunn, J., Burchinal, M., Espinosa, L., Gormley, W., Ludwig, J.O., Magnuson, K.A., Phillips, D.A., and Zaslow, M.J. (2013). *Investing in Our Future: The Evidence Base on Preschool Education.* New York: Foundation for Child Development and Ann Arbor, MI: Society for Research in Child Development.

Zhou, M. (2009). *Contemporary Chinese America: Immigration, Ethnicity, and Community Transformation.* Philadelphia, PA: Temple University Press.

7

Sociocultural Dimensions of
Immigrant Integration

In this chapter, the panel reviews research bearing on some key questions about the social and cultural dimensions of immigration. In doing so, we consider issues that often arouse popular fears and concerns, just as they did in earlier historical eras when massive numbers of new arrivals, the vast majority from Europe, were settling in this country. Today, as in the past, some worry that immigrants and their children do not share the same social values as the native-born, that they will not learn English and the dominance of English in the United States is under threat, and that immigrants are increasing crime rates. Some Americans experience discomfort about the introduction of new and unfamiliar religions. These fears generally are concentrated among a minority of Americans, but they often drive public discourse about immigration (see Chapter 1).

Since 2004, the Pew Research Center has conducted surveys that asked whether respondents believe that a "Growing number of newcomers from other countries strengthens American society, or threatens traditional American customs and values." Although the results for responses to this question vary over time, the belief that immigrants threaten traditional American values and customs has generally been a minority opinion, averaging about 43 percent in 2013, while the proportion who believed that immigrants strengthen American society was 52 percent.[1] There are significant differences in opinion by age, education, and partisanship (with older respondents, those without high school degrees, and Republicans more likely

---

[1] See http://www.people-press.org/files/legacy-pdf/3-28-13%20Immigration%20Release.pdf [November 2015].

than others to say that immigrants threaten traditional American values and customs). Those Americans who do worry about immigration's effect on American society are most concerned about Latinos and the Spanish language in particular (Brader et al, 2008; Hartman et al., 2014; Valentino et al., 2013; Hopkins et al., 2014).

In the sections below, the panel addresses these concerns by examining integration across several different sociocultural dimensions: public attitudes, language, religion, and crime. As the data and literature reviewed below suggest, today's immigrants and their descendants do not appear to be very different from earlier waves of immigrants in their overall pace of integration. However, there are differences—both between historical and current immigrant groups and in the context in which they are integrating—that present new challenges for integration.

PUBLIC ATTITUDES

One measure of the extent to which immigrants and their descendants are becoming culturally integrated into the United States is the extent to which their attitudes about political and social issues converge with higher-generation native-born (Branton, 2007; de la Garza et al., 1996; Fraga, 2012; Fuchs, 1990; Hajnal and Lee, 2011). Data on attitudes on policy issues among immigrants and the native born are available from various sources. Most notably, the General Social Surveys from 1977 to 2014 asked questions about political ideology and opinions on key issues, including the role of the federal government, same-sex marriage, and access to the American Dream. [2] The 2005-2006 Latino National Survey and the 2008 National Asian American Survey also contain sizable samples of immigrants to provide comparisons of attitudes by nativity for various national-origin groups. Overall, these data show that immigrants tend to support more government services, have weaker party identification, and are less likely to support same-sex marriage than the native-born. At the same time, there is significant convergence in attitudes between the native-born and foreign-born as individual immigrants spend longer time in the United States (Fraga et al., 2012; Lien et al., 2001; Wong, 2000; Wong et al., 2011).

Political Ideology and Party Identification

Two topics that have received close scrutiny because of their impact on the U.S. political system are the political ideologies and political partisanship of immigrants and their descendants (e.g., Alvarez and Bedolla, 2003;

---

[2] See NORC's General Social Survey website for variables and wording of questions at http://www3.norc.org/GSS+Website/Browse+GSS+Variables/Subject+Index/ [November 2015].

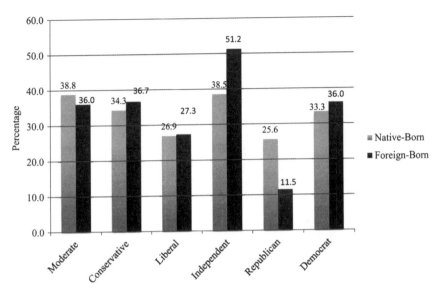

FIGURE 7-1 Political ideologies and party identification by nativity, 2012.
SOURCE: Data from General Social Survey.

Wong et al., 2011). The evidence suggests that immigrants are converging with the native-born in terms of political ideology, although immigrants tend to be less committed to one political party than the native-born (see Figure 7-1). In 2014, the largest percentage of both the foreign-born (44%) and native-born (39%) consider their political views to be *moderate*, while 38 percent of the native-born and 31 percent the foreign-born judge their views to be *conservative*. Approximately one-quarter of both groups state they hold *liberal* views. The political ideology of foreign-born respondents show more variation over time in comparison to the native-born, but the basic distribution across the three categories of political views (liberal, moderate, and conservative) is largely the same.

Yet when it comes to political parties, immigrants are much more likely to describe themselves as "independent" than the native-born, a finding that is borne out in surveys of both Latinos and Asian Americans (Figure 7-1). Unlike native-born citizens, immigrants did not grow up in households where they learned about U.S. politics from their parents, leaving them with weaker attachments to political parties. At the same time, immigrants tend to develop stronger party identification as they spend more years in the United States (Wong et al., 2011), although this depends to some extent on outreach by political parties and the extent to which they differentiate themselves on issues that immigrants care about (Wong, 2000; 2006; Hajnal and Lee, 2011).

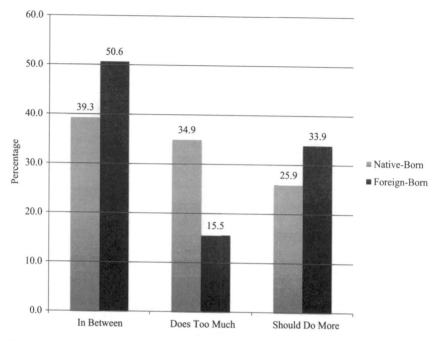

FIGURE 7-2 Beliefs about the proper role of the federal government by nativity, 2012.
SOURCE: Data from General Social Survey.

The Role of Government

The proper role of the federal government, meanwhile, is a central issue in most national policy debates and has become an increasingly salient issue in political campaigns (see Figure 7-2).[3] On average about one-third of the native-born agree that "the government in Washington is trying to do too many things that should be left to individuals and private businesses" and one quarter disagree, stating that the government should do more to help with the country's problems. Immigrants tend to diverge from the native-born on this issue, as they are significantly more likely to believe that the government should do more (36%) than to believe that it does too much (15%)—a near reversal of the opinion from the native-born. The largest percentage of both immigrants and the native-born held opinions that fell somewhere in between these two more extreme positions, and in fact immigrants were much more likely to be in the middle.

---

[3] See http://www.ropercenter.uconn.edu/pdf/Health%20care%20issue.pdf [November 2015].

Same-sex Marriage

Dramatic shifts have occurred in American public attitudes toward the acceptance of same-sex marriage in the last two decades, an issue that remains contested in U.S. society, despite the recent Supreme Court ruling (*Obergefell v. Hodges* 576 U.S.__, 2015) striking down laws limiting marriage to opposite-sex couples. In the 2000 and 2004 elections, same-sex marriage was used as a "wedge issue" in several states, perhaps helping Republican candidates in closely contested local races and in the race for the White House (Taylor, 2006). However, in the years since those elections, the American public's views on gay rights have changed at a rapid pace, with support for "marriage equality" increasing from little more than 10 percent in 1988, when the GSS first began asking about whether homosexuals should have the right marry, to 56 percent in 2014.[4] The extent to which foreign- and native-born opinions about gay marriage are generally moving in the same direction is therefore an interesting indicator of immigrant integration.

Response patterns over time are similar for both the native born and the foreign born. The percentage of respondents in both groups who thought that same-sex couples should be allowed to marry trended up between 2002 and 2012, from 12 percent to 59 percent for the native-born and from 17 percent to 36 percent for the foreign-born (see Figure 7-3). Also, the percentage of both groups who oppose same-sex marriage has generally trended downward, in particular for respondents who say they highly disagree with the statement that same-sex couples should be allowed to marry. Further research indicates that the same trend holds true for Latinos and Asians more generally, suggesting that the views of second and higher generation immigrants are evolving in the same direction as those of higher-generation native-born Americans in general on this issue (Abrajano, 2010; Lewis and Gossett, 2008; Lopez and Cuddington, 2013).

The American Dream

One way in which immigrants may be more American than the native-born is in their steadfast belief in the American dream. The foreign-born are increasingly likely to believe that their children's standard of living will surpass theirs. In 2014, almost 70 percent voiced this optimism (up from 60% in 1994). The percentage of native-born who feel their children will prosper relative to their parents remains much lower, even though it rose slightly from 47 percent in 1994 to 50 percent in 2014. Majorities of both

---

[4] See http://www.apnorc.org/PDFs/SameSexStudy/LGBT%20issues_D5_FINAL.pdf [November 2015].

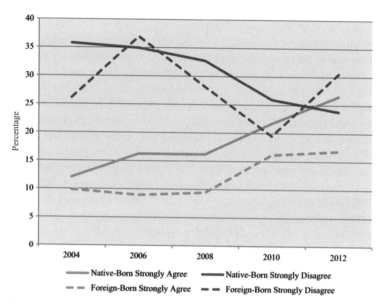

FIGURE 7-3 Beliefs about whether same-sex couples should marry by nativity, 2002-2012.
SOURCE: Data from General Social Survey.

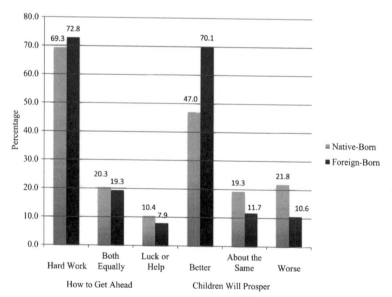

FIGURE 7-4 Beliefs about the American dream by nativity, 2012.
SOURCE: Data from General Social Survey.

the native-born and foreign born agree that *hard work* is the key to getting ahead economically (see Figure 7-4).

Overall, both survey data and the research on public attitudes indicate that immigrants, their descendants, and the general population of native-born Americans are not far from one another when it comes to attitudes and beliefs about social issues, and as immigrants and their descendants spend more time in the United States, even these differences diminish. If anything, immigrants are more optimistic about their prospects for success and less tied to partisan politics—attitudes that may further assist their sociocultural integration. Unfortunately, there are few data on how the attitudes immigrants bring with them affect the values and beliefs of the native-born, and this is an area that deserves further research (for information on native-born attitudes toward immigration, see Chapter 1).

LANGUAGE

The vast majority of Americans (over 90%), regardless of nativity status, agree that it is very or fairly important to be able to speak English. In a Pew Research Center/*USA Today* survey from June 2013, 76 percent of Americans said that they would require learning English as a precondition for immigrant legalization (Pew Research Center, 2013).[5] English-language acquisition is both a key indicator of integration (Bean and Tienda, 1987) and an underlying factor that impacts one's ability to integrate in other domains.

Language is also a sensitive topic that continues to be an important component in debates over immigration and immigrant integration. While one side of the debate views English as central to social cohesion and sees other languages and their speakers as a threat to American cultural dominance and native-born power, the other side argues that linguistic diversity and bilingualism contribute to American dynamism and aid innovation (Huntington, 2004; Alba, 2005). In fact, language diversity has grown with the immigrant population: since 1980, there has been a 158 percent increase in the number of residents who do not speak English at home (Ryan, 2013; Gambino et al., 2014). However, this diversity and concerns about its effects are not new. Similar debates and rhetoric emerged during earlier immigration waves (Crawford, 1992; Foner, 2000). As Rumbaut and Massey (2013) pointed out, the revival of immigration after the 1960s has simply restored language diversity to something approaching the country's historical status quo. The major difference, discussed below, is the prevalence and perhaps endurance of Spanish.

---

[5] See http://www.people-press.org/files/legacy-pdf/6-23-13%20Immigration%20Release%20Final.pdf November 2015].

Language has a strong and well-demonstrated effect on the ability of immigrants and their descendants to integrate across various social dimensions. Recent research has documented how English proficiency affects employment opportunities and earnings (Batalova and Fix, 2010; Bleakley and Chin, 2004; Borjas, 2013; Chiswick and Miller, 2009; Hamilton, 2014; Shin and Alba, 2009; Wilson, 2014) and educational outcomes (Bleakley and Chin, 2008; Kieffer, 2008; Suárez-Orozco et al., 2008, 2010). Lack of English ability limits residential choices (Iceland and Scopilliti, 2008; Toussaint-Comeau and Rhine, 2004) and even foreign accents can lead to housing discrimination (Purnell et al., 1999; Massey and Denton, 1987). Difficulty in communicating effectively with health care providers and social isolation have been found to negatively affect immigrants' health and socioemotional well-being (Kang et al., 2014; Yoo et al., 2009; Yu et al., 2003; Zhang et al., 2012). Language ability also mediates the exposure of immigrants and their descendants to mainstream American culture, influencing, for instance, marriage patterns (Duncan and Trejo, 2007; Oropesa and Landale, 2004; Stevens and Swicegood, 1987) and fertility decisions (Lichter et al., 2012; Swicegood et al., 1988). And it affects their ability to engage in native civic organizations, understand political discourse, and naturalize (Bloemraad, 2006; Chenoweth and Burdick, 2006; Stoll and Wong, 2007).

A major source of concern is what the Census Bureau and other researchers term "linguistic isolation." Households are linguistically isolated when none of their adult members (over age 14) speak English very well (Siegel et al., 2001). In 2013, 4.5 percent of households in the United States were linguistically isolated. The largest proportion of such households was Asian and Pacific Islander, followed by households speaking Spanish (see Figure 7-5). In addition, 22 percent of children living in immigrant families in 2013 lived in linguistically isolated households.[6] Linguistic isolation has important implications for immigrant and second generation integration, because it limits immigrants' social capital and their access to various resources; it also contributes to anxiety (Nawyn et al., 2012). Children from linguistically isolated households are more likely to be in English-Language Learner (ELL) classes and to face higher barriers to educational attainment due to their parents' limited ability to communicate with school staff and monitor their children's educational progress (Batalova and Fix, 2010; Fix and Capps, 2005; Gifford and Valdes, 2006). Linguistically isolated house-

---

[6] "Children in immigrant families" are children who are themselves foreign-born or are living with at least one foreign-born parent. For more information and data sources, see http://datacenter.kidscount.org/data/tables/129-children-living-in-linguistically-isolated-households-by-family-nativity?loc=1&loct=2#detailed/2/2-52/true/36,868,867,133,38/78,79/472,473 [November 2015].

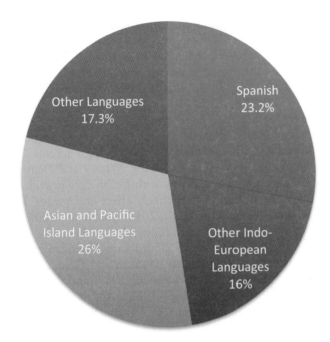

FIGURE 7-5 Linguistically isolated households by language spoken, 2013.
SOURCE: Data from 2013 American Community Survey.

holds are also more likely to be impoverished, which has negative consequences for children's cognitive abilities (Glick et al., 2013). High levels
of linguistic isolation in new immigrant destinations have also been linked
with higher homicide rates for Latinos (Shihadeh and Barranco, 2010).

Notably, the importance of English proficiency does not negate the potential positive effects of bilingualism. Retention of parents' mother tongue
in the second generation is linked to better educational outcomes (Bankston
and Zhou, 1995; Olsen and Brown, 1992; Portes and Rumbaut, 2001) and
expanded opportunities for employment (Hernandez-Leon and Lakhani,
2013; Morando, 2013). Although there may currently be limited economic
returns to bilingualism (Saiz and Zoido, 2005; Shin and Alba, 2009), this
may change in the face of increasing globalization. Various studies have
found that bilingualism is associated with positive cognitive outcomes,
including increased attentional control, working memory, metalinguistic
awareness, and abstract and symbolic representation skills (Adesope et al.,
2010). And bilingualism may benefit children's social and emotional health
(Halle et al., 2014).

Language Integration in the Immigrant Generation

The languages spoken by immigrants at home reveal contemporary linguistic diversity. In 1980, the first time the decennial census included the household language question, 70 percent of the foreign-born spoke a language other than English at home.[7] Twenty-eight percent of these respondents spoke Spanish, which was already the largest foreign-language group in the United States. By 2012, 85 percent of the foreign-born population spoke a language other than English at home (Gambino et al., 2014, p. 2). Sixty-two percent spoke Spanish at home, while Chinese languages came in a distant second at 4.8 percent (Ryan, 2013). Just over three-fourths of both Latinos and Asians spoke a language other than English at home, compared to 6 percent of non-Hispanic whites (Johnson et al., 2010). However, there was significant variation by country of origin: more than 90 percent of Dominicans, Guatemalans, and Salvadorans spoke Spanish at home, while Colombians and Mexicans matched the average for Latinos. Among Asians, 89 percent of Vietnamese spoke a non-English language at home, compared to only 46 percent of Japanese (Johnson et al., 2010). There are also regional and state variations, with significantly higher proportions of the foreign-born in Texas, California, Illinois, Nebraska, New Mexico, and Nevada speaking a language other than English at home (Gambino et al., 2014, p. 4).

The current data on English proficiency indicate that 66 percent of the foreign-born who use a foreign language at home speak English "very well" or "well," 23 percent speak it "not well, and 11 percent speak English "not at all" (see Figure 7-6) (Gambino et al., 2014, p. 3). The foreign-born from Latin America and the Caribbean generally have lower English-language proficiency compared to immigrants from other regions and are most likely to speak English "not at all" (Gambino et al., 2014, p. 7).

English-language proficiency among immigrants is strongly correlated with age of arrival (Bleakley and Chin, 2010); and duration of stay in the United States (Batalova and Fix, 2010). Not surprisingly, immigrants who arrive as young children and those who have resided in the United States for longer periods tend to speak English well (Stevens, 2014). Citizenship status (Johnson et al., 2010) and education are also positively associated with English proficiency (Gambino et al., 2014). In addition, English-language ability is strongly associated with occupational status in the United States (Akresh et al., 2014). Other research indicates that place of settlement (Singer, 2004); household context (Thomas, 2010); and gender (Batalova

---

[7] See https://www.census.gov/population/www/documentation/twps0029/tab05.html [November 2015].

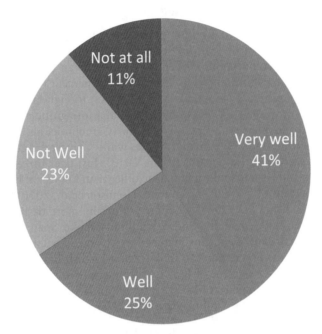

FIGURE 7-6 English-speaking ability of the foreign-born who speak a language other than English at home, 2013.
SOURCE: Data from 2013 American Community Survey; Gambino et al. (2014).

and Fix, 2010; Thomas, 2010; Hernandez-Leon and Lakhani, 2013) also influence immigrants' English-language abilities.

Despite popular concerns that immigrants are not learning English as quickly as earlier immigrants, the data on English proficiency indicate that today's immigrants are actually learning English faster than their predecessors (Fischer and Hout, 2008). One factor is the increase in English-language acquisition before migration. Many of today's immigrants arrive from countries where English is the official or common language, including migrants from the English-speaking West Indies, India, Pakistan, the Philippines, and former British colonies in West Africa such as Nigeria and Ghana. Immigrants from these countries are often well educated and relatively highly skilled (Anderson, 2015). In addition, English has become the lingua franca of international trade and politics (Crystal, 1997; Pennycook, 2014), and is embedded in many non-English speaking cultures, especially among those in the higher tiers of the economy and polity (Park, 2009; Song, 2010). English is now taught in primary and secondary schools across the world (e.g., Warschauer, 2000). Akresh and colleagues (2014) found that experience with English is common among immigrants from non-English speaking countries, with 38 percent of new legal immigrants saying they had taken a class in English and nearly everyone having consumed at least one form of English-language media prior to departure. These experiences yielded a 48 percent rate of English proficiency upon arrival.

Language Integration Across Generations

If the rate of language integration among the foreign-born over the course of their lifetime is important, the rate of linguistic integration across generations is just as significant. The current evidence suggests that the second and third generations are integrating linguistically at roughly the same rates as their historical predecessors, with complete switch to English and loss of the ability to speak the immigrant language generally occurring within three generations (Alba et al., 2002; Alba, 2005; Portes and Hao, 1998). However, there are differences based on immigrants' first language; specifically, Spanish-speakers and their descendants appear to be integrating more slowly in terms of both gaining English language and losing the ability to speak the immigrant language than other immigrant groups (Alba, 2005; Borjas, 2013).

A major reason is the larger size and frequent replenishment of the Spanish-speaking population in the United States (Linton and Jimenez, 2009). As noted above, Spanish is by far the most common non-English household language in the United States due to the enormous increase in immigration from Spanish-speaking countries since 1970. Spanish speakers appear to become English proficient at a slower pace than other immigrants (Alba, 2005; Borjas, 2013). Bilingualism is more common among second generation Latinos, and English monolingualism is less common, than it is for Asians and Europeans in the third generation (Alba, 2005; Portes and Schauffler, 1994; Telles and Ortiz, 2008). Thomas (2011) found that among descendants of Caribbean immigrants, the transition to English monolingualism was faster for French speakers than for Spanish speakers.

Even so, Rumbaut and colleagues (2006), using data IMMLA and CILS data from Southern California, show that the vast majority of children of Spanish-speaking immigrants are fluent in English and that by the third generation most are monolingual English speakers. Even in the large Spanish-speaking concentration in Southern California, Mexican Americans' transition to English dominance was all but complete by the third generation: only 4 percent still spoke Spanish at home, although 17 percent reported they still spoke it very well (Rumbaut et al., 2006). And although most Mexican Americans favor bilingualism, Spanish fluency is "close to extinct" by the fifth generation (Telles and Ortiz, 2008, p. 269). Although the prevalence of Spanish among immigrants is historically exceptional, the extent to which this impedes English proficiency or encourages its retention in succeeding generations remains an open question.

Ethnic and Foreign-Language Media

Ethnic and foreign-language media has a long and storied history in the United States: Benjamin Franklin printed the first German-language Bible in the United States, in addition to widely available German hymnals and textbooks (Pavlenko, 2002). By the turn of the 20th century, "every major ethnic community had a number of dailies and weeklies," many of which also published literary works and serialized novels (Pavlenko, 2002, p. 169). Today's immigrants also have access to a range of foreign-language television channels, many originating in their native countries, as well as other channels, such as Telemundo and Univision, produced in the United States and with content specifically designed for residents of this country. Lopez and Gonzalez-Barrera (2013) found that a majority of Latino adults say they get at least some of their news in Spanish, although that number was declining. And while the panel found no comparable data on general news consumption among Asian Americans, Wong and colleagues (2011) reported that the consumption of news about politics shows a significantly higher proportion of Asian Americans than Latino Americans who get their political news exclusively in English.

Foreign-language media can play a role in immigrant integration, although it may simultaneously impede or slow down assimilation. For instance, Zhou and Cai (2002) find that while Chinese language media may contribute to ethnic isolation, it also helps orient recent immigrants to their new society and promotes social mobility goals like entrepreneurship and educational achievement. Felix and colleagues (2008) suggested that Spanish-language media may play a role in encouraging immigrants to mobilize politically and eventually naturalize. And Shah and Thornton (2003) noted that while mainstream media coverage of interethnic conflict and immigration tended to reinforce the dominant racial ideology and fears about immigration, ethnic newspapers provided their readers with an alternative perspective to this ideology and its associated fears about immigrants. The extent to which ethnic and foreign-language media may promote social and economic integration, even as it helps immigrants maintain their native language and ties to their country of origin, is an issue that needs to be studied further.

Two-Way Exchange

Absent from most discussions about language and immigrant integration is the two-way exchange between American English and the languages immigrants bring with them. Evidence of this two-way exchange occurs in education trends and in additions to American English itself. Dual language and two-way immersion programs in languages such as Spanish and Chinese that include both native-born English speakers and first or second-generation Limited English Proficient (LEP) students are becoming increasingly popular (Fortune and Tedick, 2008; Howard et al., 2003). And enrollment in modern foreign-language courses in colleges and universities has grown since 2002 (Furman et al., 2010). Spanish course enrollments are by far the largest, but there has been significant growth in enrollment for Arabic, Chinese, and Korean, even as enrollment in classical languages has fallen (Furman et al., 2010). It is unclear whether native-born Americans are becoming proficient in these languages, but a majority of Americans feel that learning a second language is an important, if not necessarily essential, skill (Jones, 2013).

Other evidence of two-way exchange includes the incorporation of words or expressions into American English. Linguistic "borrowing", in which words or parts of words are imported or substituted, is a common phenomenon when languages come into contact (Appel and Muysken, 2005). Just as expressions such a "kosher" and "spaghetti" became common after large waves of Jewish and Italian immigrants arrived at the turn of the 20th century (Thomason and Kaufman, 1988), today native-born Americans may serve "guacamole" at Super Bowl parties or take their children to taekwondo. In addition, there are "hybridized" linguistic expressions and dialects that combine English and other languages, most notably Spanglish but also "Hinglish"(Hindi and English) and "Taglish" and "Englog" (Tagalog and English) that immigrants from countries formerly colonized by English-speaking nations bring with them to the United States (Bonus, 2000; Lee and Nadeau, 2011; Perez, 2004; Stavans, 2003). It is also worth noting here that, according to a recent analysis by the Pew Research Center, 2.8 million non-Hispanics speak Spanish at home, the majority born in the United States and with ancestry in non-Spanish speaking countries (Gonzalez-Barrera and Lopez, 2013). Although it is unclear why so many non-Hispanics speak Spanish at home (many may be married to Hispanics), this number reconfirms that Spanish holds a special place in the American linguistic landscape.

Conclusion

The current research on language integration suggests that today's immigrants and their descendants are strikingly similar to previous waves of immigrants, despite the differences in their countries of origin and the dominance of Spanish among current immigrants. The panel agrees with Rumbaut and Massey (2013, p. 152) who concluded that the mother tongues of immigrants today will probably "persist somewhat into the second generation, but then fade to a vestige in the third generation and expire by the fourth, just as happened to the mother tongues of the southern and eastern European immigrants who arrived between 1880 and 1930." Although the Spanish-speaking second and third generations may retain their dual language abilities longer than others, Rumbaut and Massey (2013, pp. 152-153) pointed out that even in Southern California, Spanish effectively dies out by the fourth generation, and Asian languages disappear even faster. Meanwhile, as discussed above, an increasing number of native-born Americans are learning the languages immigrants bring with them, while immigrant cultural forms and expressions continue to alter the American cultural landscape.

Although the outlook for linguistic integration is generally positive, the lack of English proficiency among many in the recently arrived first generation, particularly in low-skilled, poorly educated, and residentially segregated immigrant populations, coupled with barriers to English acquisition, can impede integration. Funding for English-language classes has declined even as the population of limited English proficient residents has grown (Wilson, 2014). Tellez and Waxman (2006) found significant state variation in English as a second language (ESL) certification of primary and secondary school teachers and how schools manage ESL education. Batalova and Fix (2010) reported that the supply of adult ESL and basic skills learning opportunities has not kept up with demand; nearly two-thirds of immigrants with very limited English proficiency had never taken an ESL class. As discussed in Chapter 2, ESL instruction is most readily available for refugees, and the Workforce Innovation and Opportunity Act was explicitly designed to address the needs of adult English language learners. But there are barriers to receiving English-language education, particularly for low-income immigrants (see Chapter 2). Delays in English-language acquisition significantly diminish immigrants' ability to integrate across various dimensions and may have long-term deleterious effects not only on their opportunities but also on their children's life chances.

RELIGION

Religion and religious institutions have long helped immigrants adjust to American society and have facilitated the integration process for immigrants and their descendants. This was true a hundred years ago, when the vast majority of immigrants were from Europe, and is still true today, when immigrants mostly come from Latin America, Asia, and the Caribbean. The integration of the descendants of turn-of-the-20th-century eastern, southern, and central European immigrants and eventual acceptance of their predominant religions—Catholicism and Judaism—into the

American mainstream helped to create a more welcoming environment for non-Western religions that a minority of immigrants bring with them today.

Because the U.S. Census Bureau is not allowed to ask questions on religious affiliation, researchers have to rely on various other surveys for data on immigrants' religious affiliations. In 2014, according to one survey, the vast majority of immigrants—68 percent—were Christian, while 4 percent were Muslim, 4 percent Buddhist, 3 percent Hindu, 1 percent Jewish, and 2 percent a mix of other faiths (Pew Research Center, 2015) (see Figure 7-7). Immigrants are more Catholic than the U.S.-born (39% foreign-born adults are Catholic versus 18% of U.S.-born adults) and less Protestant (foreign-born adults are about half as likely, 25%, to be Protestant as are U.S.-born adults, 50%) (Pew Research Center, 2015). This is not surprising given the high proportion of immigrants from predominantly Catholic Latin America and the significant numbers of Catholics from other countries such as the Philippines. Interestingly, foreign-born Protestants have a much

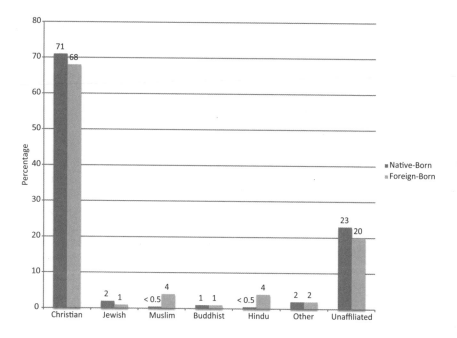

FIGURE 7-7 Religious affiliation of native-born and foreign-born adults in the United States, 2014.
SOURCE: Data from Pew Research Forum (2015). Available: http://www.pew forum.org/2015/05/12/chapter-4-the-shifting-religious-identity-of-demographic-groups/pr_15-05-12_rls_chapter4-01/ [November 2015].

lower tendency to belong to evangelical groups (16%) than do U.S.-born Protestants (28%), although a survey of very recent arrivals found a much higher fraction (41%) identifying as Evangelical or Pentecostal. A large proportion came from Central America, where evangelical Protestants have made substantial inroads in recent years (Pew Research Center, 2014). In a 2013 Pew survey, 16 percent of foreign-born Latinos identified as evangelical Protestant, about half of them becoming "born again" after coming to the United States (Pew Forum on Religion and Public Life, 2008; Massey and Higgins, 2011; Pew Research Center, 2014).

The post-1965 immigration has led to the growing prominence of new religions on the American landscape. According to the Pew Forum on Religion and Public Life (2011), 63 percent of the nation's estimated 2.75 million Muslim Americans are first generation immigrants and 15 percent are second generation (about one in eight Muslim Americans in 2011 were African Americans). Around 40 percent of Muslim Americans are from the Middle East and North Africa, and about a quarter are from the South Asian region (Pew Forum on Religion and Public Life, 2011). A total of 86 percent of the nation's Hindus, and a quarter of the Buddhists, are foreign-born. Most Hindu immigrants are from India, while immigrant Buddhists are mostly from Vietnam, with a significant proportion from China (Pew Forum on Religion and Public Life, 2008).

How religious are immigrants? In 2014, 80 percent of immigrants were affiliated with a religious group or faith, compared to 77 percent of the U.S.-born (Pew Research Center, 2015). Unfortunately, we know little about the strength of religious beliefs among those who are affiliated. Data on religious service attendance is available from the New Immigrant Survey (NIS) of immigrants receiving permanent residence documents in 2003. Overall, a little more than a quarter (27%) of all Christian immigrants in the survey (30% of Catholics and 22% of Protestants) attended religious services once or twice a month, with about the same percentages never attending; the percentages never attending were much higher for Muslims (68%) and Buddhists (68%) (Massey and Higgins, 2011). By comparison, about six in ten (62%) of all Christians in the United States say they attend religious services at least once or twice a month (Pew Research Center, 2013). However, other research found that some immigrant groups did show high rates of church attendance. Massey and Higgins (2011) reported that 70 percent of Korean Protestant immigrants and around 40-50 percent of Filipino and Vietnamese Catholics and Salvadoran Protestants attend religious services at least four times a month.

According to the NIS data, for every major religious group (except Jews), immigration was associated with a drop in the frequency of religious service attendance in the United States. In all the groups, the percentage never attending religious services rose in the United States, with especially high levels of nonattendance among non-Christians, more than two-thirds for Muslims and Buddhists. The NIS study also found low rates of congregational membership among the recently arrived non-Christian immigrants (10%) as well as Catholics (19%) as compared to nearly half (49%) of Protestants.

The declines in religious attendance may reflect reduced access to appropriate religious facilities in the United States as well as the disruptive experience and time-consuming process of initial settlement and long hours spent at work. Some immigrants do not intend to stay permanently, so they may be less motivated to get involved in religious groups (Massey and Higgins, 2011). An open question is whether, and to what extent, immigrants become more involved in religious groups the longer they reside in and become more used to life in the United States. The data on Muslim immigrants cited below do point in this direction.

Among the second generation, a substantial minority appear to be engaged with religious congregations, although here, too, the data are limited. One source is the Children of Immigrants Longitudinal Study, which is conducted in San Diego and south Florida and is heavily weighted toward Catholics, given the high proportion of Latin Americans and Filipinos in these areas (Portes and Rumbaut 2001). More than 50 percent of the children of immigrants interviewed in the third wave of the study (when the average age of the cohort was 24) were Catholic, fewer than 10 percent were Protestant. While nearly 20 percent in the survey never took part in religious services, about a third were regular church-goers, attending at least once a month (more than a fifth attended at least once a week). The most regular attenders were Afro-Caribbeans, especially Haitians; Chinese and other Asians (Cambodians, Laotians, and Vietnamese, although not the mostly Catholic Filipinos) had very high rates of nonattendance (Portes and Rumbaut 2014). Other research points to high rates of church involvement among young adults with Korean immigrant parents; in a New York survey, more than 80 percent of 1.5 generation and second generation Korean Protestants attended church once a week or more (Min, 2010, p. 139).

Role of Religious Institutions in Integration

Historical studies of U.S. immigrants argued that religious participation helped turn European Jewish and Catholic immigrants into Americans in the past, with Will Herberg (1960, pp. 27-28) famously writing that it was "largely in and through . . . religion that . . . the immigrant], or rather his children and grandchildren, found an identifiable place in American life." Herberg's themes continue to have relevance today, as a substantial share of contemporary immigrants "become American" through participating in religious and community activities of churches and temples. Religion provides a way for many immigrants to become accepted in the United States—or, perhaps more accurately, religious institutions are places where they can formulate claims for inclusion in American society (Portes and Rumbaut, 2014; Alba et al., 2009).

Membership in religious groups offers immigrants the "3Rs": a refuge (a sense of belonging and participation in the face of the strains and stresses of adjusting to life in a new country); an alternative source of respectability for those who feel denied social recognition in the United States; and an array of resources such as information about jobs, housing, and classes in English (Hirschman, 2004; see also Ebaugh and Chafetz, 2000; Menjívar, 2003; Min, 2001). For many immigrants, religious groups represent one of the most welcoming institutions in the new society (Alba and Foner, 2015). Religious groups can be a place where immigrants build a sense of community and receive material help and emotional solace (Hirschman 2004). Central American religious communities in the United States represent continuity, since immigrants may join a church of the same, or a similar, denomination or faith community as they belonged to back home (Menjívar, 2003). But they also enable change, as these immigrants become involved with new institutions and new co-worshippers in this country. In fact, some Latin American immigrants have left Catholicism for smaller evangelical churches that provide more opportunity to develop personal and supportive relationships than do larger Catholic or mainline Protestant congregations (Menjívar, 1999, 2003).

Immigrant churches, mosques, and temples can, in addition, build civic skills, encourage active civic engagement, and provide a training ground for leadership; some provide citizenship classes and programs to register people to vote and encourage volunteer services in the wider community (Foley and Hoge, 2007). As discussed in Chapter 2, many of the organizations that partner with the federal government to assist refugees are religiously affiliated. In some cases, religious groups increase the second generation's upward mobility prospects by providing a variety of classes, including in English and SAT preparation. Even classes in home-country languages can encourage habits of study (Lopez, 2009). Involvement in church may also shield young people from gangs and negative aspects of American culture (Zhou and Bankston, 1998) and some churches have developed programs that explicitly target youth at risk of engaging in drugs or gangs (Menjívar, 2002). While Catholic parochial schools have provided a pathway to upward mobility for some of the second generation in the Northeast and Midwest today, as they did for many Irish and Italian Americans in the past (Kasinitz et al., 2008), the Catholic school system, only weakly developed in the Southwest, did not operate this way for the Mexican second generation there in earlier years, and it has not been doing so today (Lopez, 2009).

Furthermore, asserting a religious identity may be an acceptable way to be different and American at the same time, a dynamic captured by the title of Prema Kurien's article, "Becoming American by Becoming Hindu" (1998) (see also Kibria, 2011). Menjívar (2002) asserted that religious involvement may enable second generation Central American youth to better appreciate their parents' origins while also helping them to navigate their place in the United States. At the same time, there is a trend toward Americanization—and the development of congregational forms—in immigrant religious institutions as leaders often consciously attempt to become more "American" in response to the exigencies of everyday life, including immigrants' work schedules (Warner and Wittner, 1998; Ebaugh and Chafetz, 2000; Kibria, 2011). Muslim women are much more likely to attend Friday prayers at a mosque than in their home countries, and English is often used at least some of the time in many congregations (Connor, 2014). In addition, some immigrants, as surveys of Asian Americans indicate for the Korean and Chinese communities, have converted to Christianity, many after they arrived in the United States (Kasinitz et. al., 2008; Pew Forum on Religion and Public Life, 2012b).

Another issue related to integration concerns the extent to which immigrants, especially Christians, worship and thus have opportunities to mix with long-established native born Americans in religious congregations. Ethnographic studies suggest a predominant pattern of Asian and Latino immigrants worshipping with their own group, although these studies are selective (Kasinitz et.al. 2008; Chai Kim, 2006). There is also evidence from in-depth studies that religious groups can foster pan-ethnic ties and identities. For example, a study of Salvadoran immigrants frequenting large Catholic churches found that as they prayed with other Latinos, pan-ethnic (Latino) sentiments developed and strengthened among church members (Menjívar, 1999). Language, culture, and social networks are among the factors drawing Asian and Latino immigrants to Protestant and Catholic ethnic (and among Latinos, pan-Latino) congregations; their U.S.-born children may continue to feel more comfortable in ethnic or pan-ethnic congregations in adulthood, as is the case among many second generation Korean Protestants in the New York and Boston areas who attend Korean churches with services and programs available in English (Chai, 1998; Min, 2010). Just how common this pattern is among the second generation in other heavily Protestant (or Catholic) immigrant-origin groups is uncertain.

Muslim Immigrant Integration

Of particular interest when it comes to non-Western religions is the relation between Islam and integration into U.S. society. Research on Muslim Americans reveals signs of considerable integration although, at the same time, prejudice remains a barrier. The Pew Forum on Religion and Public

Life report on Muslim Americans (2011) found high rates of naturalization among the first generation; 70 percent of foreign-born Muslims were naturalized citizens (95% of those who came in the 1980s and 80% of those arriving in the 1990s). The Muslim foreign-born also had high educational attainment: nearly a third (32%) had graduated from college and a quarter were currently enrolled in college or university classes. Thirty-five percent of foreign-born Muslims had annual household incomes of at least $50,000, with 18 percent over $100,000—about the same as the general public. According to the Pew survey, religion is very important in the lives of Muslim immigrants and their children: 65 percent of the first generation and 60 percent of the second generation (i.e., native-born non–African Americans) perform the Salah, or ritual prayer, every day; 43 percent of the first generation and 47 percent of the second attended services at a mosque at least once a week. Nearly a third (30%) of foreign-born Muslim women in the United States reported always wearing a head cover or hijab when out in public.

At the same time, the Pew Research Center report revealed signs of growing Muslim American involvement in American society. As Kibria (2011, p. 57) noted, many Islamic American leaders have encouraged Muslim Americans to "assert their rights as Americans and claim their American identity." In the Pew survey, 57 percent of foreign-born Muslims said they wanted to adopt U.S. customs and ways of life, although about half of the foreign-born (48%) and second generation (51%) thought of themselves first as Muslim rather than American (to put this in context, 46% of Christians in the United States think of themselves first as Christian). Among foreign-born Muslims, 53 percent said that all or most of their close friends were Muslim. The survey revealed strong support among Muslim Americans of both generations for women working outside the home (90%); most (64%) saw little support among Muslim Americans for violence and extremism.

Less happily, many (37% of foreign-born Muslims and 61% of non–African American native-born Muslims) reported being victims of one or more acts of hostility in the past year because they were Muslim. A smaller proportion of native-born non–African American Muslims (37%) than immigrants (58%) said that Americans were friendly to Muslim Americans.

Evidence from surveys of native-born Americans reveals unease among a minority about the non-Christian religions increasingly in their midst. In a 2002-2003 national survey reported by Wuthnow (2005), about a third of respondents said they would not welcome a stronger presence of Muslims, Hindus, and Buddhists in the United States. About 4 in 10 said they would not be happy about a mosque being built in their neighborhood (about a third also would be bothered by the idea of a Hindu temple being nearby), and almost a quarter favored making it illegal for Muslim groups to meet (a fifth in the case of Hindus or Buddhists). In a 2009 Gallup poll, more than 40 percent Americans said they felt at least a little prejudice toward Muslims, more than twice the number who said the same about Jews (Gallup Center for Muslim Studies, 2010).

Since the September 11, 2011, terrorist attacks (9/11), cases of discrimination, hate crimes, and bias incidents against Muslims have increased. Indeed, anti-Muslim discourse is acceptable in American public life in a way that no longer is true for anti-black rhetoric (Alba and Foner, 2015). Yet religion has not become a deep divide between contemporary immigrants and the native-born in the United States as it has in much of western Europe, and religion is not a frequent subject of public debate about immigrant integration (Alba and Foner, 2015). By and large, religion is an accepted avenue for immigrants and their children's inclusion in American society. Immigrant debates in the United States, according to Cesari (2013), have not been Islamicized, or systematically connected with anti-Islamic rhetoric, as they have been in western Europe. Alba and Foner (2015) found that, in the United States, Muslims are often framed as an external threat, as an enemy from outside the country committing acts of terrorism and threatening national security, not as an enemy from within undermining core national values, which is a view they said looms larger in western Europe.

Alba and Foner (2015, 2008) suggested three reasons for this difference:

1. Only a tiny proportion of the foreign-born are Muslim in the United States as compared to Europe. Also, unlike in Europe, the migration flow of Muslims to the United States has been more selective, and Muslim immigrants have done fairly well, with many of them well-educated and in the middle class.
2. The United States, characterized by unusually high levels of religious belief and behavior relative to much more secular western Europe, has less trouble recognizing claims based on religion.
3. Historically rooted relations and arrangements between the state and religious groups in the United States, especially foundational Constitutional principles of religious freedom and separation of church and state, make it less difficult to incorporate and accept new religions than has been true in Europe, with its long history of entanglement of Christian religious institutions and the state.

Two-Way Exchange

As the data above suggest, immigrants are adding new diversity to the nation's religious mosaic. Immigrants and their children are also adding new members to the Catholic church and to Protestant denominations, no doubt keeping some congregations alive, especially in numerous inner-city and inner-suburban neighborhoods that, absent immigration, would have witnessed dramatic population decline (Foner, 2013; Singer, 2004). As the panel noted above, both the foreign-born and the U.S.-born are very likely to be religiously affiliated (80% and 77% respectively), and the proportion of religiously unaffiliated is growing at a faster pace among the native-born than among immigrants (Pew Research Center, 2015). Nationwide, almost a quarter of the Catholics in the United States are foreign-born, as are nearly two-fifths of the Greek and Russian Orthodox; only 5-7 percent of Protestants, mainline and evangelical, are foreign-born (Pew Forum on Religion and Public Life, 2008). Although secularism appears to be increasing for both groups, the stronger religiosity of the foreign-born means that immigrants may play an even larger role in sustaining religious organizations in the United States in the future.

As for the incorporation of non-Christian religions into the American mainstream, it is unclear whether history will repeat itself. When Catholic and Jewish immigrants arrived from Europe in the past, Protestant denominations were more or less "established" and they dominated the public square. Those earlier immigrants experienced virulent anti-Catholic nativism and anti-Semitism (Higham, 1955). By the mid-20th century, however, Jews and Catholics had been incorporated into the system of American pluralism and Americans had come to think in terms of a tripartite perspective—Protestant, Catholic, and Jew. The very transformation of the United States into a "Judeo-Christian" nation and the decrease in religious affiliation among the native-born has meant that post-1965 immigrants enter a more religiously open society than their predecessors did 150 years ago (Pew Research Center, 2015; Alba and Foner, 2015).

An important question is whether the new religions, and Islam in particular, will eventually attain the charter status now occupied by Protestantism, Catholicism, and Judaism. It is too early to tell. The ongoing controversies over zoning for mosques near Ground Zero in New York City and in localities across the country indicates that 9/11 continues to strongly influence Americans' perception of Islam as an existential threat and Americans' reception of Muslims in their communities (Cesari, 2013; Goodstein, 2010). Despite pockets of opposition, however, more than 40 percent of the mosques in the United States have been built just since 2000 (Pew Research Center, 2012). Although it took more than a century, the United States was able to overcome its fear of the "Catholic menace" in the past. This history offers hope that the nation may be able to do so with regard to Islam as well. Perhaps as the historian Gary Gerstle (2015) notes, we will be talking about America as an Abrahamic civilization, a phrase joining Muslims with Jews and Christians. We are at present a long way from that formulation of American national identity, but no further than America once was from the Judeo-Christian one."

CRIME

Americans have long believed that immigrants are more likely than natives to commit crimes and that rising immigration leads to rising crime (Kubrin, 2014; Gallagher, 2014; Martinez and Lee, 2000). This belief is remarkably resilient to the contrary evidence that immigrants are in fact much *less likely* than natives to commit crimes. These contemporary beliefs have strong historical roots. Common stereotypes of immigrants in the late 19th and early 20th centuries were that immigrants were much more likely to be criminals than the native-born.

The criminal stereotype applied to a number of different ethnic groups. The term "paddy wagon," slang for a police van to transport prisoners, began as an ethnic slur against the "criminal" Irish in the mid-19th century. Stereotypes about Italian Americans have focused on organized criminal activity and the mafia; but all southern and eastern European immigrants were commonly thought to bring crime to America's cities. European immigrants were generally poor, and their neighborhoods were thought to be highly disorganized and anomic, leading to higher crime rates. Historical studies have shown that this belief was wrong (Moehling and Piehl, 2009). Then, as now, immigrants were less crime prone than native-born Americans.

Today, the belief that immigrants are more likely to commit crimes is perpetuated by "issue entrepreneurs" who promote the immigrant-crime connection in order to drive restrictionist immigration policy (Ramakrishnana and Gulasekaram, 2012; Gulasekaram and Ramakrishnan, 2015), and media portrayals of non-whites and immigrants as prone to violence and crime (Gilliam and Iyengar, 2000; Rumbaut and Ewing, 2007; Sohoni and Sohoni, 2014; Subveri et al., 2005). The criminalization of certain types of migration also contributes to this perception (see Chapter 3 for discussion of "crimmigration"). Although native-born Americans' attitudes about immigration and immigrants are often conflicting (see Chapter 1), the negative perception of immigrants' criminality continues to endure, potentially posing a barrier to integration, particularly for the first generation. The historical evidence suggests that immigrants' descendants were able to overcome these negative stereotypes, but if Latinos, in particular, continue to be racialized and discriminated against, this stereotyping may present a more formidable barrier to their successful integration in the future.

An empirical assessment of the relationship between immigration and crime involves two key questions. First, are immigrants more likely than the native-born to commit crime? And second, do immigrants adversely affect the aggregate crime rate? Distinguishing between these two questions is critical (Mears, 2002, p. 285). For example, it is plausible that at the individual level immigrants are far less criminal than nonimmigrants but that an influx of immigrants could cause increased crime among the native-born by disrupting the structure of local labor markets (Reid et al., 2005, p. 761) or by displacing other native-born minorities, which could lead to an increase in the criminality of the displaced groups (Wilson, 1996), in either case leading to an increase in the crime rate. In other words, immigrants may have an adverse effect on crime by crowding natives out of the legal employment sector and increasing criminal behavior among natives (Butcher and Piehl, 1998b; Reid et al., 2005).

The hypothesis that immigrants would be more likely to commit crime than natives at the individual level appears at least plausible to social scientists because immigrants have a number of characteristics associated with higher crime: they are disproportionately male and young. They also tend to have lower education levels and wages than the rest of the population (Butcher and Piehl, 1998a); both these factors are correlated with commission of crimes (Harris and Shaw, 2000).

While both ideas that immigrants themselves might be more likely to commit crime and that the presence of immigrants might be more likely to raise the crime rate in a given area, are plausible as hypotheses to examine, recent empirical evidence, discussed below, shows that both hypotheses are false. Immigrants are in fact much *less likely* to commit crime than natives, and the presence of large numbers of immigrants seems to *lower* crime rates.

The vast majority of research in this area has focused on the individual-level question of whether immigrants have higher crime, arrest, and incarceration rates than native-born individuals. In 1931, the National Commission on Law Enforcement, also known as the Wickersham Commission, devoted an entire report to the topic of "Crime and the Foreign-born," reaching the conclusion that, when controlling for age and gender, the foreign-born committed proportionally fewer crimes than the native-born (National Commission on Law Observance and Enforcement, 1931). Contemporary empirical studies continue to find that crime and arrest rates are lower among immigrants (Bersani, 2014; Butcher and Piehl, 1998a, p. 654; Hagan and Palloni, 1999, p. 629; MacDonald and Saunders, 2012; Martinez and Lee, 2000; Martinez, 2002; Olson et al., 2009; Sampson et al., 2005; Tonry, 1997). In an extensive review of the literature, Martinez and Lee (2000, p. 496) concluded that: ". . . the major finding of a century of research on immigration and crime is that immigrants . . . nearly always exhibit lower crime rates than native groups."

Similarly, research reveals that the rate of judicial institutionalization in the United States is lower among immigrants than among the native-born. Butcher and Piehl (1998a, 2007), for example, report that among U.S. men 18-40 years old, immigrants were less likely than the native-born to be institutionalized (i.e., in correctional facilities, mental hospitals, or other institutions) and much less likely to be institutionalized than native-born men with similar demographic characteristics. They further noted that when controls are included for characteristics that correlate with labor market opportunities and criminal justice enforcement, "institutionalization rates are *much* lower for immigrants than for natives" (Butcher and Piehl, [1998a], p. 677, emphasis in original). A recent analysis of California in-carceration rates by nativity status shows the dramatic differences between the foreign-born and U.S.-born (see Figure 7-8).

This finding on individual propensity to commit crime seems to apply to all racial and ethnic groups of immigrants, as well as applying over different decades and across varying historical contexts. Rumbaut and colleagues (2006) compared incarceration rates for the foreign-born and U.S.-born men, ages 18-39, and found that the incarceration of the foreign-born was one-fourth that of the native born. Rumbaut and Ewing (2007) compared the U.S.-born and foreign born incarceration rates in the 2000 census by racial ethnic groups. They found dramatic differences. Foreign-born Hispanic men had an incarceration rate that was one-seventh of U.S.-born Hispanic men. These large differences in rates held within specific Hispanic groups as well. Using 2010 ACS Census data, Ewing and colleagues (2015, pp. 6-7) found that 1.6 percent of immigrant males, ages 18-39, are incarcerated, compared to 3.3 percent of the native-born. And these figures include immigrants who were incarcerated for immigration violations. In other words, young native-born men are much more likely

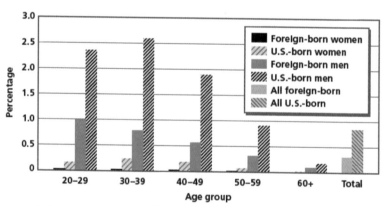

Source: Authors' calculations from California Department of Corrections and Rehabilitation Data, 2005.
Note: Does not include federal inmates.

FIGURE 7-8 Percentage incarcerated in California, by age and place of birth.
SOURCE: Butcher and Piehl (2008). Reprinted with permission.

to commit crimes than comparable foreign-born men. This disparity also holds for young men most likely to be undocumented immigrants: Mexican, Salvadoran, and Guatemalan men. Ewing and colleagues (2015, p. 7) found that "[I]n 2010, less educated native born men age 18-39 had an incarceration rate of 10.7 percent—more than triple the 2.8 percent rate among foreign born Mexican men, and five times greater than the 1.7 percent rate among foreign born Salvadoran and Guatemalan men." Sampson and colleagues (2005) studied crime by generation in Chicago neighborhoods for the period 1995-2002. They found that adjusting for family and neighborhood background, first generation immigrants were 50 percent less likely to commit crime than the third generation comparison group. And the second generation was 25 percent less likely to commit violent crime than the comparison group. This kind of finding has been called the immigrant paradox, or the "counterintuitive finding that immigrants have better adaptation outcomes than their national peers despite their poorer socioeconomic conditions" (Sam et al., 2006, p. 125) and "despite community conditions that sociologists traditionally associated with 'social disorganization'" (Lee and Martinez, 2006, p. 90).

However, a related observation from this research is that the individual-level association between immigrants and crime appears to wane across generations. That is, the children of immigrants who are born in the United States have higher rates of judicial "offending" than the immigrant generation does (Lopez and Miller, 2011; Morenoff and Astor, 2006; Rumbaut et al., 2006 p. 72; Sampson et al., 2005; Taft, 1933). Although the second generation has higher crime rates than the first generation, their rates are generally lower than or very similar to the crime rate of the native-born in general (Berardi and Bucerius, 2014; Hagan et al., 2008; Bersani, 2014). Similarly, research has found that assimilated immigrants (defined as those who have been in the United States longer, those who are more fluent in English; and those who are likely to be naturalized citizens, and those who are more highly acculturated to the United States) have higher rates of criminal involvement compared to unassimilated immigrants (Alvarez-Rivera et al., 2014; Bersani, 2014). The risk of incarceration is higher not only for the children of immigrants but also for immigrants themselves, the longer they reside in the United States (Rumbaut and Ewing, 2007, p. 11). Butcher and Piehl (1998b) found that in both 1980 and 1990, those immigrants who arrived earlier were more likely to be institutionalized than were more recent entrants.

Findings such as these have led scholars to describe an "assimilation paradox" (Rumbaut and Ewing, 2007, p. 2), where the crime problem reflects "not the foreign born but their children" (Tonry, 1997, p. 20). Some researchers have suggested that the children of immigrants may have higher crime rates than their parents in large part because they are more assimilated into American culture, including into "deviant subcultural values of youth gangs which young people joined as a source of self-identification and self-esteem" (Tonry, 1997, pp. 21-22). However, few studies have data available on first and second generation criminal behaviors, so the mechanisms that would account for the changes in crime rate are still unexplained (Berardi and Bucerius, 2013).

Immigration and the Crime Rate

Polling data show that Americans believe immigration increases crime at the aggregate level. Multiyear polling data by Gallup asking the following question: "Please say whether immigrants to the U.S. are making the crime situation better, worse, or not having much effect?" In 2001, before 9/11, 50 percent of polled respondents believed that immigrants will worsen the crime situation. By 2007 that response had reached 58 percent, with 63 percent of whites believing immigrants will worsen the crime situation in the United States. Nonetheless, a large body of evidence demonstrates that this belief is wrong. The research shows that immigration is associated with decreased crime rates at both the city and neighborhood levels.

The number of studies that examine the immigration-crime relationship across various levels of aggregation has grown in recent years. There have been numerous contemporary studies estimating the relationship between immigration and urban violent crime in the United States (Butcher and Piehl, 1998; 2007; Martinez, 2000; Reid et al., 2005; Piehl, 2007; Ousey and Kubrin, 2009; Stowell, 2010; Wadsworth, 2010; Bersani, 2010; Leerkes and Bernasco, 2010). All of these studies found that immigration *inversely* relates to crime rates: that is, the more immigrants in an area, the lower the crime rate tends to be. Using a wide range of methods, data, and levels of aggregation, these studies also found that the crime drop observed between 1990 and 2000 can partially be explained by increases in immigration. Although these studies include investigations of entire metropolitan areas and cities (Butcher and Piehl, 1998a; Martinez, 2000; Ousey and Kubrin, 2009; Reid et al., 2005; Stowell and Martinez, 2009; Wadsworth, 2010), more common are neighborhood-level studies that examine whether, and to what extent, immigration and crime are associated at a more local level. This literature has produced a fairly robust finding in criminology: areas, and especially neighborhoods, with greater concentrations of immigrants have lower rates of crime and violence, all else being equal (Akins et al., 2009; Chavez and Griffiths, 2009; Desmond and Kubrin, 2009; Feldmeyer and Steffensmeier, 2009; Graif and Sampson, 2009; Kubrin and Ishizawa, 2012; Lee and Martinez, 2002; Lee et al., 2001; MacDonald et al., 2013; Martinez et al., 2004, 2008, 2010; Nielsen and Martinez, 2009; Nielsen et al., 2005; Stowell and Martinez, 2007; 2009; Velez, 2009; Kubrin and Desmond, 2014) .

The finding that immigrant communities have lower rates of crime and violence holds true for various measures of immigrant concentration (e.g., percent foreign-born, percent recent foreign-born, percent linguistic isolation) as well as for different outcomes (e.g., violent crime, property crime, delinquency). The correlations of a variety of measures of immigration on homicide, robbery, burglary, and theft are consistent. "Even controlling for demographic and economic characteristics associated with higher crime rates, immigration either does not affect crime, or exerts a negative effect" (Reid et al., 2005, p. 775). Finally, the finding that areas with high concentrations of immigrants have lower rates of crime and violence holds true not just in cross-sectional but also in longitudinal analyses of the immigration-crime nexus (Ousey and Kubrin, 2009; 2014; Stowell and Martinez., 2009; Martinez et al., 2010; Wadsworth, 2010).

While the research is conclusive on the statistical relation between immigration and crime, there is still a lot to be learned because of limitations in the available data. The extent to which this relationship is truly generalizable or robust *for all immigrant groups* needs further study. Nearly all macro-level research focuses on "immigrant concentration," generally defined as a single measure of immigrant concentration: the percentage of foreign-born in an area. Other studies combine several measures, such as percentage of foreign born, percentage who are Latino, percentage of persons who speak English not well or not at all, to create an "immigrant concentration index" (Desmond and Kubrin, 2009; Kubrin and Ishizawa, 2012; Lee and Martinez, 2002; Lee et al., 2001; Martinez, 2000; Martinez et. al., 2004, 2008; Morenoff and Sampson, 1997; Nielsen et al., 2005; Sampson et al., 1997; Reid et al., 2005; Sampson et al., 2005; Stowell and Martinez, 2007; but see Stowell and Martinez, 2009 for an attempt to identify ethnic-specific effects on crime).

Because research has not yet uncovered the mechanisms by which immigrant concentration leads to less crime in neighborhoods, what remains unproven is *why* this is the case. One hypothesis put forward by Sampson (2008) is that the decline in crime in recent decades in American cities is partly due to the influx of immigrants. Using time-series techniques and annual data for metropolitan areas over the 1994-2004 period, Stowell and Martinez (2009) found that violence tended to decrease as metropolitan areas experienced gains in their concentration of immigrants. Likewise, Wadsworth (2010) employed pooled cross-sectional time-series models to determine how changes in immigration influenced changes in homicide and robbery rates between 1990 and 2000. He found that cities with the largest increases in immigration between 1990 and 2000 experienced the largest decreases in homicide and robbery during that time period. Ultimately, both of these studies concluded that growth in immigration *may have been* responsible, in part, for the crime drop. Still, much more research is needed to reach a definitive conclusion on the mechanisms involved in the well-documented results on the association of immigration with decreased crime rates.

SUMMARY AND CONCLUSIONS

As this chapter reveals, the evidence for integration of immigrants and their descendants across various sociocultural dimensions is more positive than some fear. The beliefs of both immigrants and the second generation are converging with native-born attitudes on many important social issues. Indeed, immigrants are actually more optimistic than native-born Americans about achieving the American Dream.

Meanwhile, current research indicates that immigrants and their descendants are learning English, despite some people's fears to the contrary.

Conclusion 7-1 Although language diversity among immigrants has increased even as Spanish has become the dominant immigrant language, the available evidence indicates that today's immigrants are learning English at the same rate or faster than earlier immigrant waves.

Meanwhile, the potential cognitive and economic benefits of bilingualism, both among immigrants and the native-born, are just beginning to be understood and appreciated, potentially altering the debate about language acquisition in the future.

A serious cause for concern, however, is the underfunding of ESL and ELL programs:

Conclusion 7-2 Since 1990, the school-age population learning English as a second language has grown at a much faster rate than the school-age population overall. Today, nearly 5 million students in K-12 education—9 percent of all students—are English-language learners. The U.S. primary-secondary education system is not currently equipped to handle the large numbers of English-language learners, potentially stymying the integration prospects of many immigrants and their children.

Just as in the past, recent immigration has made the country's religious landscape more diverse. However, the overwhelming majority of immigrants identify as Christian.

Conclusion 7-3 Although immigrants involved in non-Western religions, especially Islam, may confront unease and prejudice, research also shows that participation in religious organizations helps immigrants integrate into American society in a wide variety of ways, and immigration may in fact shore up support for religious organizations as native-born Americans' religious affiliation and participation declines.

Crime rates are another source of concern for Americans, and the criminal propensity of immigrants is currently being widely discussed (see Chapter 1). However, popular perceptions about immigrants' criminality are not supported by the data.

Conclusion 7-4 Far from immigration increasing crime rates, studies demonstrate that immigrants and immigration are associated *inversely* with crime. Immigrants are less likely than the native-born to commit crimes, and neighborhoods with greater concentrations of immigrants have much lower rates of crime and violence than comparable nonimmigrant neighborhoods. However, crime rates rise among the second and later generations, perhaps a negative consequence of adaptation to American society.

The research presented in this chapter also explores ways in which integration is a process of two-way exchange, in which immigrants and their descendants alter the social and cultural environment even as they become more like the native-born. For instance, the increases in dual immersion education programs, in which both native-born English-language speakers and immigrant LEP students learn together in two languages, and in enrollment in Spanish at the college level suggest that more native-born Americans are learning to communicate in non-English languages and may increasingly value bilingual ability. Meanwhile, immigrants are sustaining Christian religious congregations in many communities where native-born attendance has declined precipitously, even as less familiar religions such as Islam, Buddhism, and Hinduism become more visible and part of mainstream discussions about religious diversity and accommodation.

Although immigrants actually commit fewer crimes that the native-born; public perceptions about immigrants' higher potential for criminality continue to endure, spurred on by media and highly visible political actors. These inaccurate perceptions remain salient to the public because of the large number of immigrants currently residing in the United States and the rapid increase in undocumented immigration between 1990 and 2006.

Historical precedents show that religious minorities and very large groups of immigrants and their descendants were still able to successfully integrate despite their differences and the prejudices against them, in part by reshaping the American mainstream. It remains to be seen whether today's immigrants and their children can repeat those success stories or if racial and religious differences will present more formidable barriers to integration.

REFERENCES

Abrajano, M. (2010). Are blacks and Latinos responsible for the passage of Proposition 8? Analyzing voter attitudes on California's proposal to ban same-sex marriage in 2008. *Political Research Quarterly, 63*(4), 922-932.

Adesope, O.O., Lavin, T., Thompson, T., and Ungerleider, C. (2010). A systematic review and meta-analysis of the cognitive correlates of bilingualism. *Review of Educational Research, 80*(2), 207-245.

Akresh, I.R., Massey, D.S., and Frank, R. (2014). Beyond English proficiency: Rethinking immigrant integration. *Social Science Research, 45*, 200-210.

Akins, S., Rumbaut, R.G., and Stansfield, R. (2009). Immigration, economic disadvantage, and homicide: A community-level analysis of Austin, Texas. *Homicide Studies, 13*(3), 307-314.

Alba, R. (2005). *Bilingualism Persists, But English Still Dominates.* Washington, DC: Migration Policy Institute.

Alba, R., and Foner, N. (2015). *Strangers No More: Immigration and the Challenges of Integration in North America and Europe.* Princeton, NJ: Princeton University Press.

Alba, R., Logan, J., Lutz, A., and Stults, B. (2002). Only English by the third generation? Loss and preservation of the mother tongue among the grandchildren of contemporary immigrants. *Demography, 39*(3), 467-484.

Alba, R., Raboteau, A., and DeWind, J. (2009). Introduction: Comparisons of migrants and their religions, past and present. In R. Alba, A. Raboteau, and J. DeWind (Eds.), *Immigration and Religion in America: Comparative and Historical Perspectives* (pp. 1-24). New York: New York University Press.

Alvarez, R.M., and Bedolla, L.G. (2003). The foundations of Latino voter partisanship: Evidence from the 2000 election. *Journal of Politics, 65*(1), 31-49.

Alvarez-Rivera, L.L., Nobles, M.R., and Lersch, K.M. (2014). Latino immigrant acculturation and crime. *American Journal of Criminal Justice, 39*(2), 315-330.

Anderson, M. (2015). *A Rising Share of the U.S. Black Population Is Foreign Born.* Washington, DC: Pew Research Center. Available: http://www.pewsocialtrends.org/2015/04/09/a-rising-share-of-the-u-s-black-population-is-foreign-born/ [July 2015].

Appel, R., and Muysken, P. (2005). Introduction: Bilingualism and language contact. In R. Appel and P. Muysken (Eds.), *Language Contact and Bilingualism* (pp. 1-9). Amsterdam, Netherlands: Amsterdam University Press.

Bankston, C.L., III, and Zhou, M. (1995). Effects of minority-language literacy on the academic achievement of Vietnamese youths in New Orleans. *Sociology of Education, 68*(1), 1-17.

Batalova, J., and Fix, M. (2010). A profile of limited English proficient adult immigrants. *Peabody Journal of Education, 85*(4), 511-534.

Bean, F.D., and Tienda, M. (1987). *The Hispanic Population of the United States.* New York: Russell Sage Foundation.

Berardi, L., and Bucerius, S. (2013). Immigrants and their children: Evidence on generational differences in crime. In S. Bucerius and M. Tonry (Eds.), *The Oxford Handbook of Ethnicity, Crime, and Immigration* (pp. 551-583). New York: Oxford University Press.

Bersani, B.E. (2010). *Are Immigrants Crime Prone? A Multifaceted Investigation of the Relationship between Immigration and Crime in Two Eras.* Available: http://drum.lib.umd.edu/bitstream/handle/1903/10783/Bersani_umd_0117E_11419.pdf?sequence=1&isAllowed=y [August 2015].

Bersani, B.E. (2014). An examination of first and second generation immigrant offending trajectories. *Justice Quarterly, 31*(2), 315-343.

Bersani, B.E., Loughran, T.A., and Piquero, A.R. (2014). Comparing patterns and predictors of immigrant offending among a sample of adjudicated youth. *Journal of Youth and Adolescence, 43*(11), 1914-1933.

Bleakley, H., and Chin, A. (2004). Language skills and earnings: Evidence from childhood immigrants. *Review of Economics and Statistics, 86*(2), 481-496.

Bleakley, H., and Chin, A. (2008). What holds back the second generation? The intergenerational transmission of language human capital among immigrants. *Journal of Human Resources, 43*(2), 267-298.

Bleakley, H., and Chin, A. (2010). Age at arrival, English proficiency, and social assimilation among U.S. immigrants. *American Economic Journal: Applied Economics, 2*(1), 165-192.

Bloemraad, I. (2006). *Becoming a Citizen: Incorporating Immigrants and Refugees in the United States and Canada.* Berkeley: University of California Press.

Bonus, R. (2000). *Locating Filipino Americans: Ethnicity and the Cultural Politics of Space.* Philadelphia, PA: Temple University Press.

Borjas, G.J. (2013). *The Slowdown in the Economic Assimilation of Immigrants Aging and Cohort Effects Revisited Again.* NBER Working Paper 19116. Cambridge, MA: National Bureau of Economic Research.

Brader, T., Valentino, N.A., and Suhay, E. (2008). What triggers public opposition to immigration? Anxiety, group cues, and immigration threat. *American Journal of Political Science, 52*(4), 959-978.

Branton, R. (2007). Latino attitudes toward various areas of public policy: The importance of acculturation. *Political Research Quarterly, 60*(2), 293-303.

Butcher, K.F., and Piehl, A.M. (1998a). Recent immigrants: Unexpected implications for crime and incarceration. *Industrial and Labor Relations Review, 51*(4), 654-679.

Butcher, K.F., and Piehl, A.M. (1998b). Cross-city evidence on the relationship between immigration and crime. *Journal of Policy Analysis and Management, 17*(3), 457-493.

Butcher, K.F., and Piehl, A. M. (2007). *Why Are Immigrants' Incarceration Rates so Low? Evidence on Selective Immigration, Deterrence, and Deportation.* NBER No. 13229. Cambridge, MA: National Bureau of Economic Research.

Butcher, K.F., and Piehl, A.M. (2008). *Crime, Corrections, and California: What Does Immigration Have to Do with It?* San Francisco: Public Policy Institute of California. Available: http://www.ppic.org/main/publication.asp?i=776 [October 2015].

Cesari, J. (2013). *Why the West Fears Islam.* New York: Palgrave Macmillan.

Chai, K. (1998). Competing for the second generation: English-language ministry at a Korean Protestant church. In R.S. Warner and J. Wittner (Eds.), *Gatherings in Diaspora: Religious Communities and the New Immigration* (Part IV, Ch. 9). Philadelphia, PA: Temple University Press.

Chai, K. (2006). Chinatown or uptown? Second-generation Chinese American Protestants in New York City. In P. Kasinitz, J.H. Mollenkopf, and M.C. Waters (Eds.), *Becoming New Yorkers: Ethnographies of the New Second Generation* (pp. 257-280). New York: Russell Sage Foundation.

Chavez, J.M., and Griffiths, E. (2009). Neighborhood dynamics of urban violence: Understanding the immigration connection. *Homicide Studies, 13*(3), 261-273.

Chenoweth, J., and Burdick, L. (2006). *Citizenship for Us: A Handbook on Naturalization and Citizenship* (4th ed.) Washington, DC: Catholic Legal Immigration Network.

Chiswick, B.R., and Miller, P.W. (2009). The international transferability of immigrants' human capital. *Economics of Education Review, 28*(2), 162-169.

Connor, P. (2014). *Immigrant Faith: Patterns of Immigrant Religion in the United States, Canada, and Western Europe.* New York: New York University Press.

Crawford, J. (1992). *Hold Your Tongue: Bilingualism and the Politics of English Only.* Boston, MA: Addison Wesley.

Crystal, D. (1997). *English as a Global Language.* New York: Cambridge University Press.

de la Garza, R.O., Falcon, A., and Garcia, F.C. (1996). Will the real Americans please stand up: Anglo and Mexican-American support of core American political values. *American Journal of Political Science, 40*(2), 335-351.

Desmond, S.A., and Kubrin, C.E. (2009). The power of place: Immigrant communities and adolescent violence. *The Sociological Quarterly, 50*(4), 581-607.

Duncan, B., and Trejo, S.J. (2007). Ethnic identification, intermarriage, and unmeasured progress by Mexican Americans. In G.J. Borjas (Ed.), *Mexican Immigration to the United States* (pp. 229-268). Chicago: University of Chicago Press.

Ebaugh, H.R., and Chafetz, J.S. (2000). *Religion and the New Immigrants: Continuities and Adaptation in Immigrant Congregations.* Walnut Creek, CA: Altamira.

Ewing, W.A., Martinez, D. E., and Rumbaut, R.G. (2015). *The Criminalization of Immigration in the United States.* Washington, DC: American Immigration Council.

Feldmeyer, B., and Steffensmeier, D. (2009). Immigration effects on homicide offending for total and race/ethnicity-disaggregated populations (white, black, and Latino). *Homicide Studies, 13*(3), 211-226.

Félix, A., González, C., and Ramírez, R. (2008). Political protest, ethnic media, and Latino naturalization. *American Behavioral Scientist, 52*(4), 618-634.

Fischer, C., and Hout, M. (2008). *Century of Difference: How America Changed in the Last One Hundred Years.* New York: Russell Sage Foundation.

Fix, M., and Capps, R. (2005). *Immigrant Children, Urban Schools, and the No Child Left Behind Act.* Washington, DC: Migration Policy Institute.

Foley, M. and Hoge, D. (2007). *Religion and the New Immigrants: How Faith Communities Form Our Newest Citizens.* New York: Oxford University Press.

Foner, N. (2000). *From Ellis Island to JFK: New York's Two Great Waves of Immigration.* New Haven, CT: Yale University Press.

Foner, N. (2003). (Ed.). *One Out of Three: Immigrant New York in the Twenty-First Century.* New York: Columbia University Press.

Foner, N., and Alba, R. (2008). Immigrant religion in the U.S. and Western Europe: Bridge or barrier to inclusion? *International Migration Review, 42*(2), 360-392.

Fortune, T.W., and Tedick, D.J. (Eds.). (2008). *Pathways to Multilingualism: Evolving Perspectives on Immersion Education.* Volume 66. Tonawanda, NY: Multilingual Matters.

Fraga, L.R., Garcia, J.A., Hero, R.E., Jones-Correa, M., Martinez-Ebers, V., and Segura, G.M. (2012). *Latinos in the New Millennium: An Almanac of Opinion, Behavior, and Policy Preferences.* New York: Cambridge University Press.

Fuchs, L.H. (1990). *The American Kaleidoscope: Race, Ethnicity, and the Civic Culture.* Hanover, NH: University Press of New England.

Furman, N., Goldberg, D., and Lusin, N. (2010). *Enrollments in Languages Other Than English in United States Institutions of Higher Education.* New York: Modern Language Association of America.

Gallagher, C.A. (2014). Blacks, Jews, gays, and immigrants are taking over: How the use of polling data can distort reality and perpetuate inequality among immigrants. *Ethnic and Racial Studies, 37*(5), 731-737.

Gallup Center for Muslim Studies. (2010). *In U.S., Religious Prejudice Stronger Against Muslims.* Analysis by the Gallup Center for Muslim Studies. January 21. Available: http://www.gallup.com/poll/125312/religious-prejudice-stronger-against-muslims.aspx [September 2015].

Gambino, C.P., Acosta, Y.D., and Grieco, E.M. (2014). *English-Speaking Ability of the Foreign-Born Population in the United States: 2012.* No. ASC-26. Washington, DC: U.S. Census Bureau.

Gerstle, G. (2015). The contradictory character of American nationality: A historical perspective. In N. Foner and P. Simon (Eds.), *Fear, Anxiety, and National Identity: Immigration and Belonging in North America and Western Europe* (Intro.). New York: Russell Sage Foundation.

Gifford, B.R., and Valdes, G. (2006). The linguistic isolation of Hispanic students in California's public schools: The challenge of reintegration. *Yearbook of the National Society for the Study of Education, 105*(2), 125-154.

Gilliam, F.D., Jr., and Iyengar, S. (2000). Prime suspects: The influence of local television news on the viewing public. *American Journal of Political Science,* 560-573.

Glick, J.E., Walker, L., and Luz, L. (2013). Linguistic isolation in the home and community: Protection or risk for young children? *Social Science Research, 42*(1), 140-154.

Gonzalez-Barrera, A., and Lopez, M.H. (2013). *Spanish Is the Most Spoken Non-English Language in U.S. Homes, Even among Non-Hispanics.* Washington, DC: Pew Research Center. Available: http://www.pewresearch.org/fact-tank/2013/08/13/spanish-is-the-most-spoken-non-english-language-in-u-s-homes-even-among-non-hispanics/ [August 2015].

Goodstein, L. (2010). Across nation, mosque projects meet opposition. *The New York Times,* August 7. Available: http://www.nytimes.com/2010/08/08/us/08mosque.html [July 2015].

Graif, C., and Sampson, R.J. (2009). Spatial heterogeneity in the effects of immigration and diversity on neighborhood homicide rates. *Homicide Studies, 13*(3), 242-260.

Gulasekaram, P., and Ramakrishnan, S.K. (2015). *The New Immigration Federalism.* Cambridge, UK: Cambridge University Press.

Hagan, J., and Palloni, A. (1999). Sociological criminology and the mythology of Hispanic immigration and crime. *Social Problems 46*(4), 617-632.

Hagan, J., Levi, R., and Dinovitzer, R. (2008). The symbolic violence of the crime-immigration nexus: Migrant mythologies in the Americas. *Criminology and Public Policy, 7*(1), 95-112.

Hajnal, Z.L., and Lee, H. (2011). *Why Americans Don't Join the Party: Race, Immigration, and the Failure (of political parties) to Engage the Electorate.* Princeton, NJ: Princeton University Press.

Halle, T.G., Whittaker, J.V., Zepeda, M., Rothenberg, L., Anderson, R., Daneri, P., Wessel, J., and Buysse, V. (2014). The social–emotional development of dual language learners: Looking back at existing research and moving forward with purpose. *Early Childhood Research Quarterly 29*(4), 734-749.

Hamilton, T.G. (2014). Selection, language heritage, and the earnings trajectories of black immigrants in the United States. *Demography 51*(3), 975-1002.

Harris, A.R., and Shaw, J.A.W. (2000). Looking for patterns: Race, class, and crime. In J.F. Sheley (Ed.), *Criminology: A Contemporary Handbook* (3rd ed., pp. 129-163). Belmont, CA: Wadsworth.

Hartman, T.K., Newman, B.J., and Bell, C.S. (2014) *Anti-Hispanic Prejudice Drives Opposition to Immigration in the U.S.* The London School of Economics and Political Science Daily Blog on American Politics and Policy. Available: http://blogs.lse.ac.uk/usappblog/ [August 2015].

Herberg, W. (1960). *Protestant Catholic Jew.* (2nd ed.) Chicago: University of Chicago Press.

Hernández-León, R., and Lakhani, S.M. (2013). Gender, bilingualism, and the early occupational careers of second-generation Mexicans in the South. *Social Forces, 92*(1), 59-80.

Higham, J. (1955). *Strangers in the Land: Patterns of American Nativism, 1860-1925.* New Brunswick, NJ: Rutgers University Press.

Hirschman, C. (2004). The role of religion in the origins and adaptation of immigrant groups in the United States. *International Migration Review, 38*(3), 1206-1233.

Hopkins, D.J., Tran, V.C., and Williamson, A. F. (2014). See no Spanish: Language, local context, and attitudes toward immigration. *Politics, Groups, and Identities, 2*(1), 35-51.

Howard, E.R., Sugarman, J., and Christian, D. (2003). *Trends in Two-Way Immersion Education: A Review of the Research.* Baltimore, MD: Center for Research on the Education of Students Placed At Risk.

Huntington, S.P. (2004). The Hispanic challenge. *Foreign Policy, 141*(2), 30-45.

Iceland, J., and Scopilliti, M. (2008). Immigrant residential segregation in U.S. metropolitan areas, 1990-2000. *Demography, 45*(1), 79-94.

Johnson, T.D., Rios, M., Drewery, M.P., Ennis, S.R., and Kim, M.O. (2010). *People Who Spoke a Language Other Than English at Home by Hispanic Origin and Race: 2009.* Washington, DC: U.S. Census Bureau.

Jones, J. (2013). *Most in U.S. Say It's Essential That Immigrants Learn English.* Washington, DC: Gallup. Available: http://www.gallup.com/poll/163895/say-essential-immigrants-learn-english.aspx [August 2015].

Kang, H.S., Haddad, E., Chen, C., and Greenberger, E. (2014). Limited English proficiency and socio-emotional well-being among Asian and Hispanic children from immigrant families. *Early Education and Development, 25*(6), 915-931.

Kasinitz, P., Mollenkopf, J., Waters, M., and Holdaway, J. (2008). *Inheriting the City: The Children of Immigrants Come of Age.* New York and Cambridge, MA: Russell Sage Foundation and Harvard University Press.

Kibria, N. (2011). *Muslims in Motion: Islam and National Identity in the Bangladeshi Diaspora.* New Brunswick, NJ: Rutgers University Press.

Kieffer, M.J. (2008). Catching up or falling behind? Initial English proficiency, concentrated poverty, and the reading growth of language minority learners in the United States. *Journal of Educational Psychology 100*(4), 851-868.

Kubrin, C. (2014). *Crime and Immigration: Reviewing the Evidence and Charting Some Promising New Directions in Research.* Paper commissioned for the Panel on Integration of Immigrants into American Society, October, National Academies of Sciences, Engineering, and Medicine, Washington, DC.

Kubrin, C.E., and Desmond, S.A. (2014). The power of place revisited: Why immigrant communities have lower levels of adolescent violence. *Youth Violence and Juvenile Justice, 13*(4), 345-366.

Kubrin, C.E., and Ishizawa, H. (2012). Why some immigrant neighborhoods are safer than others: Divergent findings from Los Angeles and Chicago. *The ANNALS of the American Academy of Political and Social Science, 641*(1), 148-173.

Kurien, P. (1998). Becoming American by becoming Hindu: Indian Americans take their place at the multicultural table. In R.S. Warner and J. Wittner (Eds.), *Gatherings in Diaspora: Religious Communities and the New Immigration* (pp. 37-70). Philadelphia, PA: Temple University Press.

Lee, J.H.X., and Nadeau, K.M. (2011). (Eds.). *Encyclopedia of Asian American Folklore and Folklife.* Santa Barbara, CA: ABC-CLIO.

Lee, M.T., and Martinez, R. (2002). Social disorganization revisited: Mapping the recent immigration and black homicide relationship in northern Miami. *Sociological Focus, 35*(4), 363-380.

Lee, M.T., and Martinez, R. (2006). Immigration and Asian homicide patterns in urban and suburban San Diego. In R. Martinez and A. Valenzuela (Eds.), *Immigration and Crime: Race, Ethnicity, and Violence* (pp. 90-116). New York: New York University Press.

Lee, M.T., Martinez, R., Jr., and Rosenfeld, R. (2001). Does immigration increase homicide? Negative evidence from three border cities. *Sociological Quarterly, 42*(4), 559-580.

Leerkes, A., and Bernasco, W. (2010). The spatial concentration of illegal residence and neighborhood safety. *Journal of Urban Affairs, 32*(3), 367-392.

Lewis, G.B., and Gossett, C.W. (2008). Changing public opinion on same sex marriage: The case of California. *Politics & Policy, 36*(1), 4-30.

Lichter, D.T., Johnson, K.M., Turner, R.N., and Allison, C. (2012). Hispanic assimilation and fertility in new U.S. destinations. *International Migration Review, 46*(4), 767-791.

Lien, P., Collet, C., Wong, J., and Ramakrishnan, S.K. (2001). Asian Pacific-American public opinion and political participation. *Political Science & Politics, 34*(3), 625-630.

Linton, A., and Jimenez, T.R. (2009). Contexts for bilingualism among U.S.-born Latinos. *Ethnic and Racial Studies, 32*(6), 967-995.

Lopez, D. (2009). Whither the flock? The Catholic Church and the success of Mexicans in America. In R. Alba, A. Raboteau, and J. DeWind (Eds.), *Immigration and Religion in America: Comparative and Historical Perspectives* (Part I, Ch. 3). New York: New York University Press.

Lopez, M.H., and Cuddington, D. (2013). *Latino's Changing Views of Same-Sex Marriage.* Washington, DC: Pew Research Center. Available: http://www.pewresearch.org/fact-tank/2013/06/19/latinos-changing-views-of-same-sex-marriage/ [July 2015].

Lopez, M.H., and Gonzalez-Barrera, A. (2013). *A Growing Share of Latinos Get Their News in English.* Washington, DC: Pew Hispanic Center-Pew Research Center. Available: http://www.pewhispanic.org/files/2013/07/latinos_and_news_media_consumption_07-2013.pdf [August 2015].

Lopez, K.M., and Miller, H.V. (2011). Ethnicity, acculturation, and offending: Findings from a sample of Hispanic adolescents. *The Open Family Studies Journal 4,* 27-37.

MacDonald, J.M., Hipp, J.R., and Gill, C. (2013). The effects of immigrant concentration on changes in neighborhood crime rates. *Journal of Quantitative Criminology, 29*(2), 191-215.

MacDonald, J.M., and Saunders, J. (2012). Are immigrant youth less violent? Specifying the reasons and mechanisms. *The ANNALS of the American Academy of Political and Social Science, 641*(1), 125-147.

Martinez, R. (2000). Immigration and urban violence: The link between immigrant Latinos and types of homicide. *Social Science Quarterly, 81*(1), 363-374.

Martinez, R. (2002). *Latino Homicide: Immigration, Violence and Community.* New York: Routledge.

Martínez, R., Jr., and Lee, M.T. (2000). On immigration and crime. In National Institute of Justice, *Criminal Justice 2000: The Nature of Crime* (NCJ 182408, vol. 1, pp. 485-524). Washington, DC: U.S. Department of Justice, Office of Justice Programs. Available: https://www.ncjrs.gov/criminal_justice2000/vol_1/02j.pdf [July 2015].

Martinez, R., Lee, M.T., and Nielsen, A.L. (2004). Segmented assimilation, local context and determinants of drug violence in Miami and San Diego: Does ethnicity and immigration matter? *International Migration Review, 38*(1), 131-157.

Martinez, R., Stowell, J.I., and Cancino, J.M. (2008). A tale of two border cities: Community context, ethnicity, and homicide. *Social Science Quarterly, 89*(1), 1-16.

Martinez, R., Stowell, J., and Lee, M. (2010). Immigration and crime in an era of transformation: A longitudinal analysis of homicides in San Diego neighborhoods, 1980-2000. *Criminology, 48*(3), 797-829.

Massey, D., and Higgins, M.E. (2011). The effect of immigration on religious beliefs and practice: A theologizing or alienating experience? *Social Science Research, 40*(5), 1371-1389.

Massey, D.S., and Denton, N.A. (1987). Trends in the residential segregation of blacks, Hispanics, and Asians: 1970-1980. *American Sociological Review, 52*(6), 802-825.

Mears, D.P. (2002). Immigration and crime: What's the connection? *Federal Sentencing Reporter, 14*(5), 284-288.

Menjívar, C. (1999). Religious institutions and transnationalism: A case of Catholic and evangelical Salvadoran immigrants. *International Journal of Politics, Culture, and Society, 12*(4), 589-612.

Menjívar, C. (2002). Living in two worlds? Guatemalan-origin children in the United States and emerging transnationalism. *Journal of Ethnic and Migration Studies, 28*(3), 531-552.

Menjívar, C. (2003). Religion and immigration in comparative perspective: Catholic and evangelical Salvadorans in San Francisco, Washington, DC, and Phoenix. *Sociology of Religion, 64*(1), 21-45.

Min, P.G. (2001). Koreans: An institutionally complete community in New York. In N. Foner (Ed.), *New Immigrants in New York* (pp. 173-200, 2nd ed.) New York: Columbia University Press.

Min, P.G. (2010). *Preserving Ethnicity Through Religion in America: Korean Protestants and Indian Hindus across Generations.* New York: New York University Press.

Moehling, C., and Piehl, A.M. (2009). Immigration, crime, and incarceration in early twentieth-century America. *Demography, 46*(4), 739-763.

Morando, S.J. (2013). Paths to mobility: The Mexican second generation at work in a new destination. *Sociological Quarterly, 54*(3), 367-398.

Morenoff, J.D., and Astor, A. (2006). Immigrant assimilation and crime: Generational differences in youth violence in Chicago. In R. Martinez and A. Valenzuela (Eds.), *Immigration and Crime: Race, Ethnicity, and Violence* (pp. 36-63). New York: New York University Press.

Morenoff, J.D., and Sampson, R.J. (1997). Violent crime and the spatial dynamics of neighborhood transition: Chicago, 1970-1990. *Social Forces, 76*(1), 31-64.

National Commission on Law Observance and Enforcement. (1931). *Report on Crime and the Foreign Born.* Washington, DC: U.S. Government Printing Office.

Nawyn, S.J., Gjokaj, L., Agbényiga, D.L., and Grace, B. (2012). Linguistic isolation, social capital, and immigrant belonging. *Journal of Contemporary Ethnography, 41*(3), 255-282.

Nielsen, A.L., Lee, M.T., and Martinez, R. (2005). Integrating race, place and motive in social disorganization theory: Lessons from a comparison of black and Latino homicide types in two immigrant destination cities. *Criminology, 43*(3), 837-872.

Nielsen, A.L., and Martinez, R. (2009). The role of immigration for violent deaths. *Homicide Studies, 13*(3), 274-287.

Olsen, S.A., and Brown, L.K. (1992). The relation between high school study of foreign languages and ACT English and mathematics performance. *ADFL Bulletin, 23*(3), 47-50.

Olson, C.P., Laurikkala, M.K., Huff-Corzine, L., and Corzine, J. (2009). Immigration and violent crime: Citizenship status and social disorganization. *Homicide Studies, 13*(3), 227-241.

Oropesa, R.S., and Landale, N.S. (2004). The future of marriage and Hispanics. *Journal of Marriage and Family, 66*(4), 901-920.

Ousey, G.C., and Kubrin, C.E. (2009). Exploring the connection between immigration and violent crime rates in U.S. cities, 1980-2000. *Social Problems, 56*(3), 447-473.

Ousey, G.C., and Kubrin, C.E. (2014). Immigration and the changing nature of homicide in U.S. cities, 1980-2010. *Journal of Quantitative Criminology, 30*(3), 453-483.

Park, J.S.-Y. (2009). *The Local Construction of a Global Language: Ideologies of English in South Korea.* Volume 24. Berlin, Germany: Walter de Gruyter.

Pavlenko, A. (2002). We have room for but one language here: Language and national identity in the U.S. at the turn of the 20th century. *Multilingual, 21*(2-3), 163-196.

Pennycook, A. (2014). (orig. pub. 1994). *The Cultural Politics of English as an International Language.* New York: Routledge.

Perez, B. (2004). *Becoming Biliterate: A Study of Two-Way Bilingual Immersion Education.* Mahwah, NJ: Lawrence Erlbaum Associates.

Pew Forum on Religion and Public Life. (2008). *U.S. Religious Landscape Survey.* Washington, DC: Pew Research Center. Available: http://www.pewforum.org/files/2013/05/report-religious-landscape-study-full.pdf [July 2015].

Pew Forum on Religion and Public Life. (2011). *Muslim Americans: No Signs of Growth in Alienation or Support for Extremism.* Washington, DC: Pew Research Center. Available: http://www.people-press.org/files/2011/08/muslim-american-report.pdf [July 2015].

Pew Forum on Religion and Public Life. (2012a). *Faith on the Move: The Religious Affiliation of International Migrants.* Washington, DC: Pew Research Center. Available: http://www.pewforum.org/faith-on-the-move.aspx [July 2015].

Pew Forum on Religion and Public Life. (2012b). *Asian Americans: A Mosaic of Faiths.* Washington, DC: Pew Research Center. Available: http://www.pewforum.org/files/2012/07/Asian-Americans-religion-full-report.pdf [July 2015].

Pew Research Center. (2012). *Controversies Over Mosques and Islamic Centers Across the U.S.* Washington, DC: Author. Available: http://www.pewforum.org/files/2012/09/2012Mosque-Map.pdf [July 2015].

Pew Research Center. (2013). *A Portrait of Jewish Americans.* Washington, DC: Author. Available: http://www.pewforum.org/files/2013/10/jewish-american-survey-full-report.pdf [July 2015].

Pew Research Center. (2014). *The Shifting Religious Identity of Latinos in the United States.* Washington, DC: Author. Available: http://www.pewforum.org/files/2014/05/Latinos-Religion-07-22-full-report.pdf [July 2015].

Pew Research Center. (2015). *American's Changing Religious Landscape.* Washington, DC: Author. Available: http://www.pewforum.org/files/2015/05/RLS-05-08-full-report.pdf [July 2015].

Portes, A., and Hao, L. (1998). E pluribus unum: Bilingualism and loss of language in the second generation. *Sociology of Education,* 269-294.

Portes, A., and Rumbaut, R.G. (2001). *Legacies: The Story of the Immigrant Second Generation.* Berkeley: University of California Press.

Portes, A., and Rumbaut, R.G. (2014). *Immigrant America* (4th ed.). Berkeley: University of California Press.

Portes, A., and Schauffler, R. (1994). Language and the second generation: Bilingualism yesterday and today. *International Migration Review,* 640-661.

Purnell, T., Idsardi, W., and Baugh, J. (1999). Perceptual and phonetic experiments on American English dialect identification. *Journal of Language and Social Psychology, 18*(1), 10-30.

Ramakrishanan, S.K., and Gulasekaram, P. (2012). The importance of the political in immigration federalism. *Arizona State Law Journal 44*(1431). Legal Studies Research Paper No. 4-13. Available: http://ssrn.com/abstract=2209311 [September 2015].

Reid, L.W., Weiss, H.E., Adelman, R.M., and Jaret, C. (2005). The immigration-crime relationship: Evidence across U.S. metropolitan areas. *Social Science Research, 34*(4), 757-780.

Rumbaut, R.G., and Ewing, W.A. (2007). *The Myth of Immigrant Criminality and the Paradox of Assimilation: Incarceration Rates among Native and Foreign-Born Men.* Washington, DC: American Immigration Law Foundation, Immigration Policy Center.

Rumbaut, R.G., Gonzales, R.G., Komaie, G., Morgan, C.V., and Tafoya-Estrada, R. (2006). Immigration and incarceration: Patterns and predictors of imprisonment among first- and second-generation young adults. In R. Martinez and A. Valenzuela (Eds.), *Immigration and Crime: Race, Ethnicity, and Violence* (pp. 64-89). New York: New York University Press.

Rumbaut, R.G., and Massey, D.S. (2013). Immigration and language diversity in the United States. *Daedalus, 142*(3), 141-154.

Rumbaut, R.G., Massey, D.S., and Bean, F.D. (2006). Linguistic life expectancies: Immigrant language retention in Southern California. *Population and Development Review, 32*(3), 447-460.

Ryan, C. (2013). *Language Use in the United States: 2011.* Washington, DC: U.S. Census Bureau.

Saiz, A., and Zoido, E. (2005). Listening to what the world says: Bilingualism and earnings in the United States. *Review of Economics and Statistics, 87*(3), 523-538.

Sam, D.L, Vedder, P., Ward, C., and Horenczyk, G. (2006). Psychological and socio-cultural adaptation of immigrant youth. In J.W. Berry, J.S. Phinney, D.L. Sam, and P. Vedder (Eds.), *Immigrant Youth in Cultural Transition: Acculturation, Identity, and Adaptation across National Contexts* (pp. 117-142). New York: Lawrence Erlbaum Associates.

Sampson, R.J. (2008). Rethinking crime and immigration. *Contexts, 7*(1), 28-33.

Sampson, R.J., Raudenbush, S.W., and Earls, F. (1997). Neighborhoods and violent crime: A multilevel study of collective efficacy. *Science, 277*(5328), 918-924.

Sampson, R.J., Morenoff, J.D., and Raudenbush, S. (2005). Social anatomy of racial and ethnic disparities in violence. *American Journal of Public Health, 95*(2), 224-232.

Shah, H., and Thornton, M.C. (2003). *Newspaper Coverage of Interethnic Conflict: Competing Visions of America.* Thousand Oaks, CA: Sage.

Shihadeh, E.S., and Barranco, R.E. (2010). Latino immigration, economic deprivation, and violence: Regional differences in the effect of linguistic isolation. *Homicide Studies, 14*(3), 336-355.

Shin, H.J., and Alba, R. (2009). The economic value of bilingualism for Asians and Hispanics. *Sociological Forum, 24*(2), 254-275.

Siegel, P., Martin, E., and Bruno, R. (2001). *Language Use and Linguistic Isolation: Historical Data and Methodological Issues.* Washington, DC: U.S. Census Bureau.

Singer, A. (2004). *The Rise of New Immigrant Gateways.* Washington, DC: Brookings Institution Press.

Sohoni, D., and Sohoni, T.W.P. (2014). Perceptions of immigrant criminality: Crime and social boundaries. *Sociological Quarterly, 55*(1), 49-71.

Song, J. (2010). Language ideology and identity in transnational space: Globalization, migration, and bilingualism among Korean families in the USA. *International Journal of Bilingual Education and Bilingualism, 13*(1), 23-42.

Stavans, I. (2003). *Spanglish: The Making of a New American Language.* New York: Harper Collins.

Stevens, G. (2014). Trajectories of English acquisition among foreign-born Spanish-language children in the United States. *International Migration Review.* Available: http://online library.wiley.com/doi/10.1111/imre.12119/full [August 2015].

Stevens, G., and Swicegood, G. (1987). The linguistic context of ethnic endogamy. *American Sociological Review, 52*(1), 73-82.

Stoll, M.A., and Wong, J.S. (2007). Immigration and civic participation in a multiracial and multiethnic context. *International Migration Review, 41*(4), 880-908.

Stowell, J.I. (2010). Immigration and the recent violent crime drop in the United States: A pooled, cross-sectional time-series analysis of metropolitan areas. *Criminology, 47,* 889-928.

Stowell, J.I., and Martinez, R. (2007). Displaced, dispossessed, or lawless? Examining the link between ethnicity, immigration, and violence. *Journal of Aggression and Violent Behavior, 5*(12), 564-581.

Stowell, J.I., and Martinez, R. (2009). Incorporating ethnic-specific measures of immigration in the study of lethal violence. *Homicide Studies, 13*(3), 315-324.

Suárez-Orozco, C., Gaytán, F.X., Bang, H.J., Pakes, J., and Rhodes, J. (2010). Academic trajectories of newcomer immigrant youth. *Developmental Psychology, 46*(3), 602-618.

Suárez-Orozco, C., Suárez-Orozco, M., and Todorova, T. (2008). *Learning a New Land: Immigrant Children in American Society.* Cambridge, MA: Harvard University Press.

Subervi, F., Torres, J., and Montalvo, D. (2005). *Network Brownout Report: The Portrayal of Latinos and Latino Issues on Network Television News, 2004 with a Retrospect to 1995.* Report prepared for the National Association of Hispanic Journalists. Washington, DC: National Association of Hispanic Journalists. Available: http://www.nahj.org/nahjnews/articles/2005/june/nahjbrownout0616.pdf [July 2015].

Swicegood, G., Bean, F.D., Stephen, E.H., and Opitz, W. (1988). Language usage and fertility in the Mexican-origin population of the United States. *Demography, 25*(1), 17-33.

Taft, D.R. (1933). Does immigration increase crime? *Social Forces, 12*(1), 69-77.

Taylor, P. (2006). *Wedge Issues on the Ballot: Can State Initiatives on Gay Marriage, Minimum Wage Affect Candidate Races?* Washington, DC: Pew Research Center. Available: http://www.pewresearch.org/2006/07/26/wedge-issues-on-the-ballot/ [July 2015].

Telles, E., and Ortiz, V. (2008). *Generations of Exclusion: Mexican Americans, Assimilation, and Race.* New York: Russell Sage Foundation.

Téllez, K., and Waxman, H. C. (Eds.). (2006). *Preparing Quality Educators for English-Language Learners: Research, Policy, and Practice.* London, UK: Routledge.

Thomas, K.J.A. (2010). Household context, generational status, and English proficiency among the children of African immigrants in the United States. *International Migration Review, 44*(1), 142-172.

Thomas, K.J.A. (2011). Socio-demographic determinants of language transition among the children of French- and Spanish-Caribbean immigrants in the U.S. *Journal of Ethnic and Migration Studies, 37*(4), 543-559.

Thomason, S.G., and Kaufman, T. (1988). *Language Contact, Creolization, and Genetic Linguistics.* Berkeley: University of California Press.

Tonry, M. (1997). Ethnicity, crime, and immigration. *Crime & Justice,* 21, 1-29.

Toussaint-Comeau, M., and Rhine, S. L. (2004). The relationship between Hispanic residential location and homeownership. *Economic Perspectives-Federal Reserve Bank of Chicago, 28*(3), 2.

Valentino, N.A., Brader, T., and Jardina, A.E. (2013). Immigration opposition among US Whites: General ethnocentrism or media priming of attitudes about Latinos? *Political Psychology, 34*(2), 149-166.

Velez, M.B. (2009). Contextualizing the immigration and crime effect: An analysis of homicide in Chicago neighborhoods. *Homicide Studies, 13*(3), 325-335.

Wadsworth, T. (2010). Is immigration responsible for the crime drop? An assessment of the influence of immigration on changes in violent crime between 1990 and 2000. *Social Science Quarterly, 91*(2), 531-553.

Warner, R.S., and Wittner, J. (1998). (Eds.). *Gatherings in Diaspora: Religious Communities and the New Immigration.* Philadelphia, PA: Temple University Press.

Warschauer, M. (2000). The changing global economy and the future of English teaching. *Tesol Quarterly,* 511-535.

Wilson, J.H. (2014). *Investing in English Skills: The Limited English Proficient Workforce in U.S. Metropolitan Areas.* Washington, DC: Brookings Institution Press.

Wilson, W.J. (1996). *When Work Disappears: The World of the New Urban Poor.* New York: Alfred A. Knopf.

Wong, J.S. (2000). The effects of age and political exposure on the development of party identification among Asian American and Latino immigrants in the United States. *Political Behavior, 22*(4), 341-371.

Wong, J.S. (2006). *Democracy's Promise.* Ann Arbor: University of Michigan Press.

Wong, J., Ramakrishnan, S.K., Lee, T., and Junn, J. (2011). *Asian American Political Participation: Emerging Constituents and their Political Identities.* New York: Russell Sage Foundation.

Wuthnow, R. (2005). *America and the Challenges of Religious Diversity.* Princeton, NJ: Princeton University Press.

Yoo, H.C., Gee, G.C., and Takeuchi, D. (2009). Discrimination and health among Asian American immigrants: Disentangling racial from language discrimination. *Social Science and Medicine, 68*(4), 726-732.

Yu, S.M., Huang, Z.J., Schwalberg, R.H., Overpeck, M., and Kogan, M.D. (2003). Acculturation and the health and well-being of U.S. immigrant adolescents. *Journal of Adolescent Health, 33*(6), 479-488.

Zhang, W., Hong, S., Takeuchi, D.T., and Mossakowski, K.N. (2012). Limited English proficiency and psychological distress among Latinos and Asian Americans. *Social Science and Medicine, 75*(6), 1006-1014.

Zhou, M., and Bankston, C., III. (1998). *Growing Up American: How Vietnamese Children Adapt to Life in the United States.* New York: Russell Sage Foundation.

Zhou, M., and Cai, G. (2002). Chinese language media in the United States: Immigration and assimilation in American life. *Qualitative Sociology, 25*(3), 419-441.

8

Family Dimensions of Immigrant Integration

The family is a fundamental institution of human societies, but family structure—size, composition, and a family's set of interconnected social relationships—can shift rapidly over time, as it has in the United States (Cherlin, 2010; Sassler, 2010), and can vary enormously from one society to another (Lesthaeghe, 2010). However, all families serve the basic functions of regulating sexual expression and procreation, providing child care and socialization, and imposing agreed-upon social roles and rules of lineage on family members. For this report, "providing socialization" refers to the fact that all families transmit culture—including social mores and customs, language, and belief systems, from parental to filial generations. Immigrant families are therefore cornerstones of the process of social integration (Clark et al., 2009; Glick, 2010). Families and kin networks provide a cultural safe haven for immigrants to this country, but they are also a launching point for integrating their descendants into American society. Immigrant families are where the second generation first learns to become Americans, separating themselves from the cultural repertoires of their foreign-born parents, who are located at a different, typically earlier, point along the integration continuum.

In this chapter, the panel examines patterns of marriage and family formation among immigrants and their descendants. We begin by examining recent patterns of immigrant marriage, including documenting the extent to which foreign-born populations marry natives of the same cultural or racial backgrounds. Next, we examine recent patterns and differentials in immigrant fertility, which are sometimes viewed as cultural expressions of

345

familialism[1] (especially among some Hispanic immigrant groups). Finally, we look at differences and similarities in household structure between native-born and immigrant groups, and we discuss how these factor into immigrant integration.

INTERMARRIAGE AND IMMIGRANT INTEGRATION

Intermarriage refers to marriages between partners from different ethnic or racial groups, socioeconomic backgrounds, religious affiliations, or national origins (Kalmijn, 1998; Schwartz, 2013). Intermarriage of immigrants with native-born Americans who differ in any one or more of these characteristics arguably represents a form of social integration, as immigrants and native-born of differing backgrounds merge within families and blur cultural distinctions and national-origin differences in their new American identity. Historically, intermarriage between racial- and ethnic-minority immigrants and native-born whites has been considered the ultimate proof of integration for the former and as a sign of "assimilation"[2] (Gordon, 1964; Alba and Nee, 2003). When the rate of interethnoracial or interfaith marriage is high (e.g., between Irish Americans and non-Irish European Americans or between Protestants and Catholics), as happened by the late 20th century for the descendants of the last great immigration wave, the significance of group differences generally wanes (Alba and Nee, 2003). Intermarriage stirs the ethnic melting pot and blurs the color lines. Because a large share of the post-1965 wave of immigrants is perceived as "nonwhite," intermarriage of these immigrants and their descendants with native-born non-Hispanic whites has the potential to transform racial and ethnic boundaries even further.

The marriage and intimate partner choices of immigrants and the second generation shed light on the strength or permeability of social boundaries separating them from the mainstream or the host society. The boundary concept alludes to the everyday social distinctions that orient our ideas about, attitudes toward, and behavior in relation to others. It distinguishes "us" from "them," insiders from outsiders, and it defines at a societal level who can relate to whom, in what way, and under what circumstances.

---

[1] Familialism is the cultural value that emphasizes close family relationships (e.g., Campos et al., 2008).

[2] Assimilation in this context refers to Milton Gordon's (1964, pp. 80-81) classic conceptualization of structural assimilation, meaning the entry of members of an ethnic minority into "the social cliques, clubs, and institutions of the core society at the primary group level." In this formulation, intermarriage between ethnic minorities and majority non-Hispanic whites was both a sign and an outcome of assimilation, which in turn diminished the importance of minority ethnic identity and relaxed social boundaries. For further discussion of this concept and Gordon's influence on this field, see Alba and Nee (1997).

Yet intermarriage is not only affected by such social boundaries; it can in turn diminish or even redefine existing social and cultural boundaries. Marriage is not just an intimate, co-residential relationship between two individuals; it brings together distinct family and friendship networks that, in light of the marriage, now overlap in significant ways. In this chapter, we discuss three types of intermarriage and their implications for immigrant integration: internativity, meaning marriage between a foreign-born person and a native-born person; ethnoracial, meaning marriage between two persons of two different ethnoracial backgrounds, one of whom may be foreign-born or both of whom may be native-born; and intergenerational, meaning intermarriage between two people of the same ethnoracial group who are from different immigrant generations. These categories often overlap: for instance, many internativity intermarriages are also ethnoracial intermarriages.

Intermarried couples—particularly in ethnoracial intermarriages—represent associational bridges between the two populations, connecting family and friends with different or unfamiliar backgrounds. Through childbearing, ethnoracial intermarriage can also give rise to a new generation of Americans whose experiences and identities are novel compounds of two or more ethnoracial backgrounds (Alba and Foner, 2015). Intermarriage may contribute to a "blurring" of social boundaries and lead to more hybrid forms of cultural and social identity. Mixed-race individuals in an ethnoracial intermarriage may operate on both sides of the boundary or may not be fully accepted by either side.

Incidence of Intermarriage

Trends in intermarriage of immigrants with the general population of native-born therefore provide an indirect measure of social integration. The frequency of ethnoracial intermarriages between immigrants and native-born is profoundly affected by the boundaries of race and of Hispanic ethnicity, which remain distinct in today's multiracial, multicultural society. The fact that the majority of immigrants to the United States are ethnoracial minorities (see Chapter 1) might therefore lead one to conclude that internativity marriages occur relatively infrequently. Yet more than half of the marriages involving immigrants between 2008 and 2012 included a native-born partner (Lichter et al., 2015a). While the odds of endogamous marriages (among natives and among immigrants) are about 30 times greater than the odds of exogamous marriages (between natives and immigrants) (Lichter et al., 2015a), the overall picture suggests that marriages between immigrants and the native-born have increased significantly over time. Social and cultural boundaries between native- and foreign-born populations are therefore perhaps less clearly defined than in the past. Ethnoracial intermarriage is also on the rise: today about one of every seven marriages (15.1% in 2010) is an interracial or interethnic marriage, more than twice the rate in 1980 (6.7%) (Wang, 2012; Frey, 2014) and many of these are internativity intermarriages or involve the descendants of post-1965 immigrants. Immigrants have therefore contributed enormously to America's shifting patterns of racial mixing in intimate and marital relationships.

Intermarriage Rates by Race and Ethnicity

Although both internativity and ethnoracial intermarriage is increasing, ethnoracial background still clearly shapes trajectories of intermarriage between immigrants and the native-born. For instance, Lichter and colleagues (2015a) found that non-Hispanic white immigrants were far more likely to marry the native-born than were immigrants from other racial groups (see Table 8-1).[3] Non-Hispanic white immigrants were also much more likely to marry native-born non-Hispanic whites than were other ethnoracial immigrant groups. Native-born non-Hispanic whites were the most endogamous of any group studied: around 90 percent of them married another native-born non-Hispanic white person.

Native-born Hispanics follow a different pattern: the number of native-born Latino/as who marry foreign-born Hispanics (17.8% of native-born women and 13.3% of native-born women) is much larger than the percentage of native-born non-Hispanic whites who married foreign-born non-Hispanic whites (Table 8-1). Hispanic native-born individuals, through marriage with their foreign-born counterparts, may provide a "helping hand" in the integration process of U.S. Hispanics. Native-born Hispanics are also much more likely than their non-Hispanic white counterparts to marry outside of their ethnoracial group: for instance, 33.6 percent of native-born Hispanic men and 32.4 percent of native-born Hispanic women married non-Hispanic whites (Table 8-1). This suggests that the social boundaries between Hispanics and non-Hispanic whites may be waning.

Native-born blacks are also less likely than native-born non-Hispanic whites to be endogamous when it comes to internativity marriages, although they are more likely to marry other native-born blacks than Hispanics or Asians (Table 8-1). However, the data on ethnoracial marriages between blacks and other groups reinforce the idea that the so-called black-white color line operates similarly for immigrants as it does for natives, at least with respect to out-marriage patterns. Black immigrant women, in particular, are far less likely than other immigrant women to cross racial/ethnic lines and integrate through marriage with non-Hispanic whites,

---

[3] Table 8-1 includes only those marriages formed in the United States, which best reflects contemporary U.S. marriage market conditions and processes of marital integration.

despite high levels of education among black immigrants from Africa and the Caribbean (Thomas, 2009). And Asian and Hispanic immigrants are much less likely to enter into intermarriages with blacks than they are with non-Hispanic whites. The results suggest that the continuing significance of race in America affects new immigrant minorities whose ancestors did not experience slavery or its aftermath directly, but who nevertheless now experience the long-standing consequences of this history in the form of inequality and racial hierarchy.

These data also demonstrate the overall asymmetrical gender patterns of internativity and ethnoracial intermarriage among Asians. Among all foreign-born, immigrant Asian men were most likely to be endogamous by nativity and race (75.8%). In contrast, only 54.4 percent of immigrant Asian women married other Asian immigrants; nearly one-third married non-Hispanic white men (29.5%) (Table 8-1). Native-born Asian men were also less likely than Hispanic and black native-born men to marry non-Hispanic whites, while the opposite was true for native-born Asian women. These patterns may be explained in part by cultural definitions of physical attractiveness, by patrilineal lines of descent among Asian populations, and by America's previous military actions (e.g., during the Vietnam conflict) and the continuing (mostly male) military presence in parts of East and Southeast Asia. More recently, the rise of internet dating services has "rationalized" the marital search process while reinforcing marital preferences that sometimes favor Asian women (Feliciano et al., 2009).

The racial and ethnic difference in intermarriage rates between and among immigrants and the native born suggest that race continues to be a very salient factor in marriage decisions in the United States. Gender also plays a role: black immigrant women and Asian immigrant men in particular, have lower rates of intermarriage, both with the native-born and with other ethnoracial groups, which may affect their prospects for integration. Asian women, on the other hand, appear to be integrating faster than any other group by this measure of integration. The evidence from both internativity and ethnoracial intermarriage indicates that the changing racial mix of new immigrants is changing patterns of native-immigrant intermarriage and shifting its historical role in the assimilation process.

Generational Shifts in Ethnoracial Intermarriage

Generational distinctions in ethnoracial intermarriage, especially between immigrants and their descendants, also provide a window to America's future (Alba and Foner, 2015). Many immigrants are already married when they arrive, and others sometimes lack the prerequisites needed for easy interaction with the native born population (e.g., English-language skills). The situation of the second generation, born and raised in the

TABLE 8-1 Percentage Distributions of Immigrants and Natives Who Married in the Previous Year, 2008-2012 (multiracial individuals excluded)

| | Marriages Formed in the Previous Year | | | | | | | |
| | Same Race | | | | | | | |
	Native-Born	Foreign-Born	White	Black	American Indian	Asian	Hispanic	N
Native-born								
Men								
White	89.9	1.6	—	0.6	0.5	2.0	4.2	60,440
Black	73.7	2.3	14.7	—	0.5	1.3	5.6	6,233
American Indian	43.3	0.3	47.9	1.1	—	2.0	4.7	669
Asian	35.6	26.4	28.7	0.6	0.1	—	6.1	967
Hispanic	46.6	13.3	33.6	2.0	0.6	2.4	—	6,039
Women								
White	90.2	1.5	—	1.6	0.5	0.8	4.2	60,229
Black	85.8	4.3	6.0	—	0.1	0.3	2.6	5,355
American Indian	40.8	0.0	46.6	4.6	—	0.6	6.7	711
Asian	31.5	17.7	37.5	3.6	0.6	—	6.9	1,093
Hispanic	42.5	17.8	32.4	4.8	0.3	1.0	—	6,622

Foreign-born

Men							
White	47.3	37.2	—	1.3	0.3	5.4	6.7	1,948
Black	23.6	55.2	12.7	—	0.1	1.6	5.3	973
American Indian	—	—	—	—	—	—	—	5
Asian	8.9	75.8	11.1	0.7	0.1	—	2.1	2,174
Hispanic	22.5	62.4	12.5	0.9	0.2	1.2	—	5,229
Women							
White	50.2	37.6	—	2.4	0.2	1.8	6.6	1,926
Black	18.7	68.8	7.2	—	0.1	0.7	3.3	780
American Indian	—	—	—	—	—	—	—	8
Asian	8.4	54.4	29.5	1.9	0.2	—	4.4	3,025
Hispanic	16.8	68.3	11.6	1.7	0.2	0.7	—	4,774

NOTE: "White" in this table actually means non-Hispanic white.
SOURCE: Adapted from Lichter et al. (2015a).

United States, is much different (Lichter et al., 2011; Telles and Ortiz, 2008). Unfortunately, the decennial censuses and the American Community Survey do not provide information on the generational status of the U.S. population (see Chapter 10), but intergenerational patterns of ethnoracial intermarriage can be crudely gleaned from the March Current Population Survey (Brown et al., 2008; Lichter et al., 2011), by aggregating multiple annual files in order to identify sufficient numbers of (currently) intermarried couples (Brown et al., 2008).

Using this data, Lichter and colleagues (2008, 2011) showed that ethnoracial intermarriage, as a measure of integration with native-born non-Hispanic whites, increased from generation to generation among immigration populations. Generation-to-generation improvements in education (reported in Chapter 6) may also raise the likelihood of intermarriage with native-born non-Hispanic whites because education at the postsecondary level is often "liberating" with respect to influences of social origins, and is associated with exposure to others from a wider range of backgrounds (Alba and Nee, 2003; Qian and Lichter, 2007). Ethnoracial intermarriage is also strongly associated with other well-known proxies of social integration: length of time in the country, and naturalization status (Lichter et al., 2015a).

More specifically, second and third generation Hispanic American women are less likely to marry other Hispanics than are first generation Hispanic women (see Table 8-2). Whereas 94.4 percent of first generation Latinas ages 18-34 married other Hispanics between 1995 and 2008, these percentages declined to 81.3 percent in the second generation and to 67.7 percent in third and higher generations. By the third and higher generations, most ethnoracial intermarriage among Hispanic American women was to non-Hispanic white men (27.3%). Only a small percentage (10.5%) of third and higher generation Hispanic American women married Hispanic immigrants. In contrast, only 4.6 percent of Hispanic immigrant women married non-Hispanic white men. Most (84.6%) married other Hispanic immigrants. Similar but less pronounced generational differences are also found among Asians, especially between the second and third generations (Lichter et al., 2008).[4] The relatively high rates of intermarriage between native-born Hispanic Americans, Asian Americans and non-Hispanic white Americans (discussed in more detail below) point to relaxing of social boundaries between these groups and to the influence that post-1965 immigrants and their descendants, the majority of whom are Hispanic or Asian, have on transforming social and cultural boundaries.

---

[4]Nearly 85 percent of first generation Asian women married Asian men. Endogenous marriages declined to 48 percent and 49 percent, respectively, for second and third generation Asian women (Lichter et al., 2008).

TABLE 8-2 Marriage Patterns of Hispanic Women by Generation, Ages 18-34, 1995-2008

| | Generation | | | |
Married to:	1st	2nd	3rd and Higher	Total
Hispanics	94.4	81.3	67.8	86.3
1st	84.6	39.7	10.5	60.5
2nd	7.8	28.3	12.1	12.6
3rd and higher	2.1	13.4	45.1	13.2
Non-Hispanics	5.6	18.7	32.2	13.7
White	4.6	14.8	27.3	11.3
Non-White	0.9	4.0	4.9	2.4
Total percent	100.0	100.0	100.0	100.0
N	4,927	1,528	1,811	8,266

SOURCE: Data from Lichter et al. (2011), based on concatenated files of the March Current Population Survey (1995-2008).

One caveat is that patterns and trends in ethnoracial intermarriage may be influenced by America's recent uptick in cohabiting unions. Today, roughly 70 percent of the first unions of young adults are cohabiting unions rather than marriages (Manning et al., 2014), and cohabiting unions are more likely to be composed of ethnoracially mixed couples (Blackwell and Lichter, 2000). We discuss rates of cohabitation across racial/ethnic groups and their potential impacts in the section on family living arrangements below.

Factors Affecting Intermarriage

The growth of intermarriage—and integration—is being affected by (and in turn affecting) changing values and attitudes, including increasing tolerance for family members of other racial backgrounds. In a 2009 Pew Research poll, nearly two-thirds of respondents said they would be "fine" if a family member married someone of another race, regardless of the partner's racial background (Wang, 2012). During the 1970s, by contrast, when the General Social Survey asked about a "close relative" marrying someone of another race, three-quarters said they would be at least "somewhat uneasy."[5] However, not all backgrounds were equally "fine" in the

---

[5] See http://www3.norc.org/GSS+Website/ [November 2015].

2009 results. White (meaning non-Hispanic white) partners were the most welcome (acceptable to 81% of nonwhites), and blacks were the least (acceptable to just 66% of nonblacks). Whites also were much more likely to accept interracial partners for others than for themselves (Herman and Campbell, 2012). Unfortunately, studies of changing marital preferences or attitudes about the desirability of dating or marrying immigrants across ethnoracial lines are limited, and further research on these topics needs to be done.

The frequency of ethnoracial intermarriage is affected by a variety of factors that operate through three main mechanisms: societal constraints on partner choice (e.g., antimiscegenation laws), exposure to potential partners, and preferences for partner characteristics. First and foremost, the increase in ethnoracial intermarriages must be seen against the long shadow cast by the pre-Civil Rights era, when antimiscegenation laws barred marriages between whites and members of other races, including Mexicans, in many states. These laws were invalidated in 1967 by a Supreme Court decision (*Loving v. Virginia*, 388 U.S. 1). Not surprisingly, ethnoracial intermarriage did not increase appreciably until the 1970s, even though interracial sexual intimacy dates back to slavery (Gullickson, 2006).

Internativity intermarriages historically were also constrained by the lack of opportunities to interact with potential spouses as co-equals. The recent rise in this kind of intermarriage implies greater opportunities than in the past. Many immigrants living in the United States today came to the United States to study or work temporarily, and U.S. natives often spend time abroad for similar reasons (Lichter et al., 2015a; Stevens et al., 2012). These international flows create new opportunities for interaction and a platform for intimacy, dating, cohabitation, and marriage between native and immigrant populations. America's military presence in a large number of countries and wars fought in Korea, Vietnam, and the Middle East have also given native-born Americans the opportunity to meet and befriend potential spouses from around the globe. For immigrants, marriage to an American citizen is a route to a permanent U.S. visa and citizenship, which means that current immigration laws play a potentially large role in creating conditions that can either favor or discourage immigrant integration through marriage to an American citizen (Bohra-Mishra and Massey, 2015). Moreover, new social media and Internet dating sites increasingly serve as a new form of the traditional marriage broker, aiding matches between foreigners and U.S. citizens. The globalism of electronic communication systems has created a global marriage market, where a promise of marriage made through the Internet can be the "cause" of immigration (Lichter et al., 2015a).

Massive immigration and growing racial and ethnic diversity over the past three decades also means that opportunities to marry within one's own ethnoracial or nationality group have increased, even as the opportunities to out-marry among native-born non-Hispanic whites has grown. Group size is an important factor accounting for immigrant-native variation in ethnoracial intermarriage. Generally, members of small groups are more likely to intermarry, partly because their members have more difficulty finding another group member who can satisfy the range of their preferences (e.g., education level, earning potential, age, physical appearance). A corollary is consequential for recent trends: as groups grow (or decline) in size, their rates of intermarriage decline (or grow). Intermarriage rates for Asians and Hispanics—populations with large immigrant shares—have recently declined or stalled (Qian and Lichter, 2007, 2011), even as they have increased among the non-Hispanic white, native-born population.

A narrow focus on broad pan-ethnic groups of immigrants hides substantial diversity in the processes of marital assimilation and social integration. And education may serve a different integrating function for some populations than others (e.g., Asian groups, where the majority achieves a high level of education). Although marriage has historically been regarded as the final step in the assimilation process (Gordon, 1964), intermarriage does not appear to be a large component of marriages in some immigrant groups (i.e., Indians) that are doing very well by other measures of integration. In such cases, it is perhaps inappropriate to regard intermarriage with non-Hispanic whites as a "final step." Rather, marriage may simply be another indicator of social integration that is only loosely associated with other characteristics, such as education, which paves the most direct pathway to full membership in the American society.

Finally, individual preferences, including religious preferences, also represent a constraint on partnership choice. Religion's influence is often disguised in the data about ethnoracial intermarriage, because the Census Bureau is prevented by law from collecting data on religion. Preferences for partners of the same religion, when they exist, may depress the likelihood of ethnoracial intermarriage, although evidence over time suggests that religion is less constraining than in the past. It is most relevant to Asian intermarriage, since some Asian groups have the most members of such non-Judeo-Christian religions as Buddhism, Hinduism, and Islam. Other large immigrants groups, such as Mexicans, are largely Christian, which may promote intermarriage with America's Christian majority (Qian et al., 2012). Nevertheless, the United States is not witnessing much second-generation transnational marriage, a phenomenon associated with Muslim groups in Europe, whose second generation members frequently choose partners who come directly from their parents' home regions (Alba and Foner, 2015; Bean and Stevens, 2003). Marriage migration occurs at lower rates in the United States than other developed countries, which tend to include those with lowest-low fertility rates (e.g., South Korea).

Consequences of Intermarriage

An important impact of internativity and interracial intermarriage is on family networks, which become more racially mixed. The magnitude of this impact is larger than the rate of intermarriage because of a multiplier effect: any single individual has a "risk" of exposure to a racially different relative through multiple marriages of close kin (Goldstein, 1999). A recent survey indicates that more than a third (35%) of Americans say that one of their "close" kin is of a different race (Wang, 2012).

Another powerful impact of intermarriage is mixed-race children. The share of multiracial infants in the United States rose from 1 percent in 1970 to 10 percent in 2013 (Pew Research Center, 2015). The growth of multiracial children was especially large among the newborn children of black-white and Asian-white couples, whose numbers almost doubled over a decade (Frey, 2014). However, the number of mixed-race children is undoubtedly underestimated, because many multiracial couples identify their children as single race, a legacy of the "one drop rule" (Frey, 2014; Lee and Bean, 2010).

The social and economic implications of racial identity—especially mixed-race identity—are often unclear. There is some evidence that mixed-race children, for example, tend to have higher rates of poverty than white children, but children of white intermarried parents often enjoy higher socioeconomic status (SES) than children of minority parents (Bratter and Damaske, 2013). Minority-white couples have more income on average than do endogamously married couples of the same minority origin. This difference is especially large for Hispanics, and Asian-white couples have the highest income of all (Wang, 2012).

One indicator of mixed-race children's circumstances is where they live. An analysis of residential segregation patterns of mixed-race individuals in the United States shows that mixed-race individuals are "in-between" the single race groups (Bennett, 2011). Those who are a mixture of Asian and white are less segregated from whites than single-race Asians and less segregated from Asians than single-race whites. The same is true for individuals with both black and white heritage (Bennett, 2011).

Additional insight comes from the personal experiences of mixed-race children—the degree to which they feel accepted in mainstream settings and the choices they make in terms of marriage partners. In-depth interviews indicate that mixed-race young adults with non-Hispanic white and Asian or Hispanic ancestry may not perceive any impediments to mixing in the mainstream society and feel they have the option to identify along ethnic lines or as non-Hispanic whites, without having their decisions questioned by outsiders or institutions (Lee and Bean, 2010). Children of black-white unions, however, find that they are often seen as mainly black, underscoring the continued stigma attached to African ancestry in the United States (Lee and Bean, 2010; Childs, 2005).

Data on the partnership patterns of children of mixed unions are scant, but Telles and Ortiz (2008) found that individuals with one Mexican and one non-Mexican parent have intermarriage rates with non-Hispanic white partners five times higher than individuals whose parents were both Mexican. This suggests that mixed Mexican/non-Hispanic white individuals are raised in much more mainstream contexts, and generally find acceptance there. Analysis of out-marriage frequencies by Asians when individuals of mixed Asian/non-Hispanic white ancestry are included suggests a similar conclusion for them (Qian and Lichter, 2011).

The Paradoxes of Intermarriage

The rise of ethnoracial intermarriage in recent decades is "normalizing" marriage across major racial and ethnic boundaries. In many parts of the country, intermarriage has become sufficiently common that many native-born Americans know intermarried couples, in family or friendship networks, or at school or work, or encounter them in public places. This normalization is reflected in the profound shift toward more accepting attitudes since the 1970s.

The rise in ethnoracial intermarriage is likely to continue, if only for demographic reasons. The demographic shifts in the young adult population will enhance the relative roles of the U.S.-born Asian and Hispanic populations, which have relatively high ethnoracial intermarriage rates, and depress the relative size of the U.S.-born non-Hispanic white population, thereby generating demographic pressures for increased ethnoracial intermarriage by its members. In addition, the size of the mixed-race group among young adults will grow, and its members' marriages, almost by definition, contribute to additional mixing in family networks.

Yet the ethnoracial intermarriage rates of the largest immigrant-origin groups, Asians and Hispanics, may be simultaneously leveling off as a result of continuing immigration. There is no numerical contradiction between an overall rise in intermarriage and stability, even some decline, in these key rates. There are several structural forces operating on them: expanding sizes of groups, which tend to depress ethnoracial intermarriage, and advancing generational distributions and rising education levels among Hispanics and some Asians, which tend to lift them.

Currently, the ethnoracial intermarriage rates of the Asian and Hispanic groups are far short of the intermarriage rates of earlier European-origin groups. Intermarriage among European-origin immigrant groups were sufficiently high in the 20th century—around 80 percent for U.S.-born Italians (Alba and Nee, 2003)—to undermine group distinctions among the great majority of whites. Today, the intermarriage rates of U.S.-born Asians and Latinos are generally in the 30-50 percent range, depending on the specific group and the generation. We cannot expect the same level of group dissolution that occurred for the descendants of the earlier waves of immigrants any time in the near future.

Moreover, marriage across ethnoracial lines may not always be an integrating force, as the evidence about black-white marriages suggests. It is important to avoid the assumption that intermarriages hold a uniform significance for intergroup relations. In an intermarriage with a non-Hispanic white partner, the minority partner may not be fully accepted by white family members (Childs, 2005; Song, 2010; Parker and Song, 2009). The mixed-race children of an intermarriage may not gain acceptance in the mainstream society; they may be marginalized and forced to find their home in the minority community. Yet the increase in intermarriage and the growth of the mixed-race population indicates that while intermarriage may not yet be dissolving ethnoracial group boundaries to the extent that it did for the last wave of European immigrants, it is nevertheless having a pronounced effect on the society as a whole.

CHILDBEARING AND FAMILY FORMATION AMONG IMMIGRANTS

The childbearing patterns of immigrants—average family size, parity distribution, and timing of fertility (e.g., teen fertility)—are often distinctive, but they are transformed as immigrant populations become more fully incorporated into American society (Parrado, 2011; Parrado and Morgan, 2008). The high rates of fertility among some new immigrant populations (especially Hispanics) represent a large second-order demographic effect of massive new immigration in America. Immigrant fertility has helped offset below-replacement levels of fertility among America's non-Hispanic white majority, the effects of which include rapid population aging and widespread natural decrease in many parts of the United States (Johnson and Lichter, 2008). Immigrant fertility has augmented the size of America's newest generation, but, just as importantly, it has contributed to rapid changes in America's ethnic and racial composition through generational replacement. Indeed, growing racial and ethnic diversity starts from the "bottom-up"—with newborn infants and children (Lichter 2013). The majority of newborn babies today have minority parents (Frey, 2014). It is these families—and the children they bear and rear—who will ultimately determine America's place in the global economy. It is immigrant families who will perform the essential tasks of providing economic support and good parenting to insure their children's ultimate success and integration as fully engaged citizens in American society (Alba and Holdaway 2013; Glick 2010).

U.S. immigration policies are guided by principles of family reunification that provide an orderly pathway to legal residence for immigrant families. But the experiences and adaptation of immigrants also sometimes reflect the traumatic influences of conditions they escaped from their native countries (e.g., war, religious or ethnic oppression, and economic displacement). The experience of immigration itself also generates a unique set of influences on family formation processes, often through their effects on spousal separation and economic dislocations (Parrado and Flippen, 2012). For unauthorized immigrants, fertility also results in growing numbers of families with mixed-legal status (Passel and Taylor, 2010). America's immigration and refugee policies, which determine who gets to come and who gets to stay, often on the basis of marriage and other kin relationships, therefore affect family structure and family formation (Landale et al., 2011). For migrants who come to America and stay, exposure to new cultural and behavioral norms about family formation in immigrant receiving areas also means that fertility patterns play out unevenly in established immigrant gateways and new destinations.

Immigrant Childbearing

Immigration draws mostly on men and women in early adulthood, which means that immigration has an out-sized effect on the age distribution—and fertility—at the destination. Immigration increases the concentration of women in the reproductive ages (Lichter et al., 2012), even as the size of America's majority of non-Hispanic white females of reproductive age has declined absolutely (Johnson and Lichter, 2008, 2010). Although immigration is a disruptive process that initially leads to short-time declines in fertility, immigrants still have higher fertility levels than US-born women (Choi, 2014; Frank and Heuveline, 2005; Lichter et al., 2012). Immigrant women today are among the few population groups whose fertility is at or above the U.S. replacement level of 2.1 (Dye, 2008; Jonsson and Rendall, 2004; Parrado, 2011).

The Total Fertility Rate (TFR) perhaps best captures the differences between immigrant and native-born fertility.[6] Table 8-3 provides TFRs based on analyses from the 2012 American Community Survey (ACS) data on births in the previous year. These data confirm the higher fertility among

---

[6]The TFR indicates how many children women today would bear if they lived out their reproductive lives following 2012 age-specific fertility rates.

TABLE 8-3 Total Fertility Rates for Immigrants and U.S.-Born Natives

	Immigrants	U.S.-Born
Hispanic	2.54	2.01
Black	2.48	1.83
White	2.05	1.84
Asian	2.10	1.69
All	2.31	1.86

SOURCE: Data from the 2012 American Community Survey.

immigrants than natives.[7] The TFR was 2.31 for immigrant women and 1.86 for natives. This large native-immigrant differential is also observed for each major racial and ethnic group (see Table 8-3). Such high rates of immigrant fertility are not unprecedented historically. For example, the percentage of U.S.-born children with immigrant mothers is quite similar to the corresponding proportion observed during the era of rapid immigration from Europe (Livingstone and Chon, 2012). Period estimates of fertility such as the TFR are however limited by their inability to capture changes in the timing of childbearing that are usually associated with migration processes (Choi, 2014; Parrado 2011).

Another perspective focuses on changing childbearing patterns across immigrant generations. Discussions about intergenerational trends typically center on Hispanics, an immigrant population for which previous studies often find inconsistent evidence of the usual generational declines in fertility (e.g., Frank and Heuveline, 2005), perhaps because traditional cross-sectional measures of immigrant generations do not effectively capture intergenerational changes in fertility or other demographic events (Parrado and Morgan 2008; Smith 2003). Aligning immigrant and biological generations to approximate childbearing differences between the foreign-born and their offspring indicates that there is in fact a consistent pattern of intergenerational fertility declines among Hispanics (Choi 2014; Parrado and Morgan 2008). Among Mexican-origin Hispanics, for example, Choi (2014) reported that fertility levels decreased within and across generations "as immigrants deviate from their pre-migration fertility patterns and increasingly adopt those of whites" (Choi, 2014, p. 703). Similar trajectories

---

[7] The main advantage associated with using ACS data is that they allow us to use data on births and the female population in the reproductive ages from the same source. Research indicates that fertility rates can be biased if they are estimated using data on births from vital registration sources and female population size from other sources (Parrado 2011).

of intergenerational fertility declines are evident historically when using estimates of Completed Fertility Rates (CFR) among married women. These estimates provide additional evidence of cultural assimilation, as Hispanic fertility levels have dropped from generation to generation. Of course, these historical estimates cannot be extrapolated neatly to the situation today, where continuing immigration of Hispanics may be reinforcing high fertility in some immigrant receiving areas through a cultural replenishment (Jiménez, 2010; Lichter et al., 2012).

It appears that among Asians, too there is a decline in completed fertility between the first and third generations (although the absence of data identifying Asians in the 1986 and 1988 June CPS makes it impossible to fully construct generational trends in Asian fertility). In general, very little attention is given to the fertility outcomes of Asian immigrants in the existing literature. An exception is a recent working paper by Alvira-Hammond and Guzzo (2014) based on data from the June fertility supplement of the Current Population Survey (2000-2010), which documented exceptionally low completed fertility (at ages 40-44) among Asian immigrants. For each generation—first, second, and third and higher—Asian fertility rates were below replacement levels, but especially in the second generation.

Other available evidence supports a few additional observations. South East Asian refugee groups usually have high fertility levels after their arrival but with increasing U.S. residence have fertility outcomes that converge with those of natives (Kahn, 1994). Furthermore, Asian immigrants from low-fertility contexts such as mainland China have lower overall fertility levels than Asian immigrants from Hong Kong, Vietnam, and Taiwan (Hwang and Saenz 1997). When only post-immigration outcomes are considered, a clear pattern of comparatively higher fertility is observed among Chinese immigrants compared to immigrants from these countries (Hwang and Saenz, 1997).

Differentials in Fertility among Immigrants

Fertility rates vary considerably among America's new immigrant populations, a fact that implies uneven patterns of cultural integration and economic incorporation (i.e., because of the strong links between SES and fertility). As we noted above, Hispanic immigrant fertility is well above both overall U.S. rates and the fertility rates for other immigrant groups (Lichter et al., 2012). Foreign-born Hispanics had a General Fertility Rate[8] (GFR) of 84 births per 1000 women in 2005-2009, while native-born Hispanics had a GFR of 71, and the overall U.S. GFR was 58. But fertility also varies considerably by national origin. A recent study by Lichter et al.

---

[8]The GFR is defined as the number of births per 1000 women of reproductive age (15-50).

(2012) showed that the Mexican-origin population had higher rates of fertility (GFR = 85) than Hispanic fertility overall (GFR = 77). High Hispanic fertility rates are being driven largely by fertility among the Mexican-origin population. One possible explanation is that Mexican–origin immigrants, in anticipation of moving to the United States, have lowered their fertility but subsequently resumed their higher fertility to compensate for a fertility shortfall caused by immigration (Choi 2014).

The age and marital status profiles of immigrant fertility also matter. Early childbearing is positively associated with cumulative fertility and completed family size; teen childbearing may also disrupt schooling and upend prospects for upward socioeconomic mobility and economic incorporation, particularly as early fertility is higher for women of lower SES. Moreover, most childbearing today among teenagers is overwhelmingly composed of out-of-wedlock births, although this is less true among Hispanics than other population groups. Significantly, not unlike the U.S. teen population overall, Hispanic teen fertility rates have recently plummeted, dropping from 65 per 1000 women ages 15-19 in 1990 to 38 in 2012 (Martin et al., 2015). Teen fertility rates among Hispanics were also lower among the foreign-born than the native-born in 1994 and 2005 (DeLeone, Lichter, and Strawderman 2009). Teen and unmarried pregnancies are associated with preterm deliveries and low birthweight, which represents a public health concern for minority populations, including new immigrant mothers and children. Despite the decline in teen pregnancy, in 2013 53.2 percent of all Hispanic births occurred to unmarried women (Martin et al., 2015), compared with 40.6 percent for the overall U.S. population. However, a large share of Hispanic out-of-wedlock births, perhaps two-thirds, occur within stable marriage-like co-residential unions (Lichter et al., 2014).

The geographic spread of Hispanics into "new destinations" also suggests that the spatial patterning of fertility (and incorporation) among new immigrants may be uneven (Parrado and Morgan 2008; Waters and Jimenez 2005). Among Hispanics, fertility rates are considerably higher on average in new immigrant destinations than in established gateways.[9] In 2005-2009, the GFR among foreign-born Hispanics living in new destinations was 94, compared with 78 in established gateways (Lichter et al., 2012). In new destinations, fertility rates were especially high among Hispanics who arrived in the United States 1-5 years ago (GFR = 1.34), but much lower among those who arrived within the past year (GFR = 46),

---

[9] Lichter et al. (2012) defined new destinations on the basis of unusually rapid Hispanic population growth and a new presence in consolidated Public Use Microdata Areas (PUMAs) (i.e., multicounty areas) over the 1990-2000 time period. Established destinations also typically have rapid population growth rates, but, unlike new destinations, they had large Hispanic populations in 1990 (i.e., exceeding the national percentage of Hispanics).

suggesting a short-term "disruption effect" on fertility that is subsequently made up (Choi 2014; Lichter et al., 2012). The GFR for native-born Hispanics in new and established destinations were 76 and 70, respectively, indicating a similar geographic effect.

These high rates of fertility in new destinations cannot be explained by differences in age composition or by observed deficits in language ability or education. A subsequent follow-up study (Lichter et al., 2015b) showed that roughly 40 percent of Hispanic infants in new Hispanic destinations were "born poor," that is, they were born to mothers who were defined by U.S. Census Bureau definitions as living in families with incomes below the official poverty income threshold. Limited availability of publicly funded family planning clinics, lack of foreign-language capacity among health care providers, and restrictions on access to health care by legal status may also contribute to higher fertility rates among lower-income and immigrant Hispanic women, particularly in new destinations (DeRose et al., 2007; Kearney and Levine, 2009). Hispanic children born impoverished in new destinations begin life's race behind the "starting line," while undermining America's promise of intergenerational mobility among second generation Hispanics.

FAMILY LIVING ARRANGEMENTS AMONG IMMIGRANTS

Families are transformed during immigration processes in ways that leave them significantly different from their counterparts in origin countries. For example, non-kin families are more prevalent among Mexican immigrants than in Mexico (Brown et al., 2008) while more integrated Asian immigrants are more likely to live in cohabiting unions than are the nonmigrants in many Asian countries (Brown et al., 2008). Immigrant family forms are therefore less a reflection of cultural preferences tied to immigrants' ethnic origins than they are products of the social milieu at their destinations and the exigencies of immigrant life.

Immigrant Children

Among the specific influences that affect family dynamics are the unique challenges of immigration processes and the degree of integration. These challenges are particularly important for immigrant children and the elderly who are in the dependent stages of the life course (Kriz et al., 2000). During immigration families are relocated from the traditional sources of social support provided by members of their extended family and their friends in their origin countries (Suárez-Orozco et al., 2015). Furthermore, the rules of social engagement in their new societies are typically unclear, constraining the adjustment of immigrant families to their new communities (Suárez-Orozco et al., 2015).

These barriers have significant implications for the socialization of children in new immigrant families. One implication is that the barriers limit the ability of parents to provide guidance to their children in educational and institutional contexts at a time when such guidance is needed to navigate new social spaces (Suárez-Orozco et al., 2008, 2015). New immigrants face additional challenges in their efforts to establish new networks while navigating short-term economic constraints after their arrival. They are more likely to live in extended-family households than their long-term immigrant peers (Leach, 2014). Extended-family households subsequently experience increased rates of turnover after meeting these temporary needs. Moreover, successful integration increases the rates at which immigrants leave their families to marry and form their own independent households (Leach, 2014; Van Hook and Glick, 2007).

Immigrant family configurations are perhaps most consequential in childhood, when the need for parental support is greatest. However, as shown in Table 8-4, there are a number of structural differences between the familial environments of the children of immigrants (both first and second generation) and those of their third and higher-generation peers. In the first generation, for example, there is a significant concentration of children in two-parent families in the major racial groups. These families are associated with lower risks of poverty, more effective parenting practices, and lower levels of stress (Landale et al., 2011; Amato, 2005). First generation children therefore largely live in families that provide them with a number of important contextual advantages. The prevalence of two-parent families continues to be high for second generation children; nevertheless, as shown in these estimates, the percentage of children in these families declines substantially between the second and third and higher generations. Among third and higher generation children, for example, approximately 40 percent of Hispanic children and 60 percent of black children live in single-parent households.

Another feature of the living arrangements of first generation children of immigrants is their overrepresentation in family households without a co-residential parent, especially among Hispanics and blacks. The overall Hispanic percentages reflect the relatively high percentage of children from Central America who live separately from their parents (9%), while among blacks, residence in households without a co-residential parent is more highly prevalent among children from the Caribbean (12.7%).

TABLE 8-4 Living Arrangements of Children by Race and Generation Status (children between ages 0 and 17)

	Two parent	Single parent	No resident Parent
Hispanic			
First generation	70.0	23.0	7.0
Second generation	67.5	28.9	3.6
Third+ generation	54.1	40.1	5.8
Asian			
First generation	82.1	13.7	4.2
Second generation	84.9	13.5	1.7
Third+ generation	75.3	21.4	3.3
Black			
First generation	60.2	32.5	7.3
Second generation	58.7	37.8	3.6
Third+ generation	30.9	60.5	8.6
Non-Hispanic White			
First generation	83.1	13.7	3.2
Second generation	82.2	16.6	1.3
Third+ generation	75.1	22.3	2.6

SOURCE: Data from 2005-2014 March Community Population Survey.

Immigrant Adults

Family formation among adult immigrants may either precede or follow migration to the United States. Regardless of when it occurs, however, family formation processes have a significant bearing on adult living arrangements. Integration presents a number of union status options to immigrants. Among them is the retreat from marriage along with an increased emphasis on nonmarital cohabiting relationships. As immigrants adopt new social norms, they may also increasingly view divorce and separation as normatively acceptable alternatives to a bad marriage (Qian 2013; Glick 2010). Declines in marriage and increases in union dissolution increase the likelihood that immigrants would live alone or in other nonfamily households.

Indeed, in the prime union formation ages (i.e., 20 to 34) shifts in living arrangements—from family to nonfamily households—are consistently observed across generations, especially between the first and second generation, and across ethnoracial groups. For example, data from the Current

Population Survey, reported in Table 8-5, indicate that married spouses living together are the statistical if not cultural norm among first generation immigrants. Except among blacks, approximately half of all foreign-born individuals live with married spouses. Nevertheless, these living arrangements decline between the first and second generations, and although they rebound slightly in the third and higher generation, they still remain less prevalent than they were in the first generation.

Another feature of these living arrangements is the tendency for some immigrants to live in households with absentee spouses. Such households are mainly found among blacks and Hispanics. This phenomenon underscores the potential for spousal separation across borders during the immigration process. The resulting families are often deemed transnational, and have toeholds in both the United States and their native land.

In contrast to marriage, however, cohabiting relationships have become more prevalent in the generations after immigration.[10] Table 8-5 shows that among Asians, for example, the prevalence of cohabitation is twice as high in the third generation than in the first. Some scholars suggest that because Asian cohabitation rates are higher among females, this differential reflects the possible role of cohabitation as an arrangement preceding the distinctively high levels of intermarriage between Asian women and non-Hispanic white men (Brown et al., 2008).

Across ethnoracial groups, the prevalence of cohabitation is highest among Hispanics, except among individuals in the second generation. High levels of cohabitation among Hispanics are a reflection of several influences. One of them is their disadvantaged socioeconomic profile. Hispanics have low levels of education and income, both of which are associated with a higher likelihood of cohabitation (Qian, 2013). Furthermore, Hispanics are distinguished by their tendency to view cohabitation as a step toward subsequent marriage rather than as an alternative to marriage (Oropesa, 1996). More generally, Qian (2013) found that about a third of all immigrants in cohabiting unions were previously divorced or separated. Thus, cohabitation may also play an important role in facilitating immigrant transitions between marriages. An important question is whether these cohabiting unions represent a new pattern of Americanization, one characterized by less stable families and by weaker associational linkages between (racially

---

[10]When comparing the marriage and cohabitation rates of immigrants and natives, it is important to note that, in many cases, important cultural differences exist in the definition of marriage between both groups. For example, research indicates that common-law marriages are very common among Caribbean immigrants, although these marriages may not be legally recognized in the United States as legal marriage (Grace and Sweeney 2014; Lincoln et al., 2008). In general, differences in the definition of marriage could result in the underestimation of marriage rates among immigrants and may understate the decline in marriage between the first and second generations.

TABLE 8-5 Percentage Living with or without Married Spouses, Alone, in Other Arrangements, or Cohabiting (individuals ages 20 to 34)

	Married, Spouse Present	Married, Spouse Absent	Cohabiting	Lives Alone	Lives with Other Family Members	Lives with Others in Nonfamily Households
Hispanic						
First generation	49.6	3.8	7.9	3.3	23.7	11.8
Second generation	30.7	1.6	8.4	4.8	46.4	8.1
Third+ generation	32.1	1.3	12.3	6.3	37.9	10.1
Asian						
First generation	49.7	3.4	3.7	8.6	23.5	11.1
Second generation	20.5	1.0	6.5	9.6	48.5	13.9
Third+ generation	21.8	0.8	7.8	7.7	44.7	17.2
Black						
First generation	32.9	4.8	5.5	12.4	34.8	9.7
Second generation	13.0	0.7	6.8	12.6	58.3	8.6
Third+ generation	18.7	1.2	9.4	12.1	51.1	7.5
White						
First generation	54.0	2.0	6.8	7.8	19.2	10.3
Second generation	38.8	0.9	9.5	8.8	32.0	10.0
Third+ generation	44.4	0.8	11.5	7.2	25.1	11.0

SOURCE: Data from 2005-2014 March Community Population Survey.

diverse) family and kinship networks than is the case among married couples.

Immigrants without marital and cohabiting partners may choose to live with other related or unrelated individuals (e.g., Van Hook and Glick, 2007). Indeed, across ethnoracial groups, the percentage of immigrants living in such contexts increased from the first to second generation (Table 8-5). However, immigrants are more likely to live with other family members (e.g., siblings) than with nonrelatives in nonfamily households (Table 8-5).

The changing living arrangements of immigrant populations are consistent with generational shifts in marriage, and, more generally, from America's continuing retreat from marriage overall. In fact, these estimates suggest that as marriage rates have declined, the percentage of immigrants who have chosen to live with other family members even exceeds the percentage living in cohabiting relationships. Finally, although there are fewer immigrants living with other nonfamily members than with members of their families, living with nonrelated persons is generally a more preferred option compared to living alone, except among blacks (Table 8-5).

For elderly immigrants, families are particularly important for providing access to economic resources as well as being contexts in which they can provide and receive care (Treas and Mazumdar, 2002). Yet, the evidence on their living arrangements shown in Table 8-6 suggests that the significance of these functions varies widely across immigrant generations. First generation elderly immigrants, for example, mostly involve co-residence with both their spouses and their children. This is perhaps unsurprising; many foreign-born elderly do not participate in U.S. social benefit programs (Kritz et al., 2000; Hu, 1998). Co-residence with immediate family members may provide them with needed economic support in old age. In the second and third generations, however, the elderly are less likely to live with both spouses and children. Instead, they are increasingly more concentrated in households in which they live only with their spouses or by themselves.

The prevalence of these arrangements varies across race; for example, elderly blacks are most likely to live alone in the second and third generations, while their Asian, Hispanic, and non-Hispanic white peers most often live only with their spouses. More generally, elderly immigrants are considerably more likely to co-reside with members of their immediate families. However, there is little ethnoracial variation in the prevalence of these other arrangements across immigrant generations.

Family Functioning and Practices

Immigration is also associated with transformations in familial norms and the adoption of U.S. family ideals. For example, divorce increases dur-

TABLE 8-6 Living Arrangements of Elderly Immigrants Age 65 and Above by Race and Generation Status

	Alone	With Spouse Alone	With Spouse and Children	Other Arrangements
Hispanic				
First generation	18.1	28.4	34.6	19.0
Second generation	25.1	36.8	22.1	16.0
Third generation	24.2	37.4	22.2	16.2
Asian				
First generation	13.9	32.3	38.8	15.0
Second generation	24.0	38.4	20.7	17.0
Third generation	19.3	38.5	28.9	13.3
Black				
First generation	26.3	20.3	31.1	22.3
Second generation	43.2	20.5	15.2	21.2
Third generation	36.4	25.5	16.7	21.5
Non-Hispanic White				
First generation	26.3	44.8	18.1	10.7
Second generation	35.5	44.6	10.0	9.9
Third generation	28.1	50.2	11.4	10.3

SOURCE: Data from 2005-2014 March Community Population Survey.

ing immigrant integration even among immigrants from countries with low rates of divorce (Glick, 2010). With increasing female labor force participation, improvements in the economic fortunes of immigrant women result in the adoption of more egalitarian gender roles within immigrant families (Foner, 1997; Menjívar, 2003). Increasing integration is also accompanied by notable shifts in immigrant parenting practices: immigrant families typically shift from using traditional practices such as corporeal punishment of children to a combination of less controversial parenting practices, consistent with widely accepted American norms (Waters and Sykes, 2009; Foner and Dreby, 2011).

Another consequence of immigration processes is the emergence of transnational families that reflect the dispersion of family members across international borders. These families are created by a number of specific circumstances including the decision of one or more family members to migrate leaving other family members, typically children, behind (Dreby, 2007, 2010; Nobles, 2011). In other cases immigrant parents send children back to the parents' origin countries to ensure that their adolescent socialization occurs outside the United States (Orellana et al., 2001). Today, an increasing number of transnational families are a consequence of the deportation of undocumented immigrants who leave their U.S.-born children behind (Dreby, 2012).

Although transnational families are separated by international borders, many of them continue to invest in the cultivation of familial relationships and use them for instrumental purposes (Orellana et al., 2001). Their members are able to leverage resources, share caregiving responsibilities, and perform other social and economic functions, despite their residence in different countries (Abrego, 2009; Menjívar and Abrego, 2009; Suárez-Orozco et al., 2015). There is no conclusive evidence regarding how these arrangements affect immigrant integration. On the one hand, transnational families that send remittances to kin back home have fewer resources to use to support the welfare of their children here (Suárez-Orozco et al., 2015). On the other hand, transnational ties do decline as generational status increases (Levitt and Waters, 2002). As a result, even if these ties are maintained by immigrant parents, they could receive less emphasis among second generation children who are more fully incorporated into society (Levitt and Jaworsky, 2007; Portes, Guarnizo, and Landolt, 1999).

Like native families, immigrant families are dynamic; they encounter ever-changing concerns within the context of rapid U.S. demographic and social changes, which in turn require family adaptation and cultural change. In addition, legal structures and policies may work to strengthen families or separate them (see Chapters 2 and 3). For instance, until recently, immigration laws did not recognize the gay and lesbian partners of immigrants under its definition of spouses (Romero, 2005). However, since the U.S. Supreme Court ruled in 2013 that Section 3 of the Defense of Marriage Act was unconstitutional, eligible individuals have been able to petition for the immigration of their same-sex spouses (Avanzado, 2013). What social scientists know about the ensuing consequences of these unions for integration remains limited, but based on the available evidence on immigrant families it seems clear that they generally go through critical transformations as they adjust to their new environments. These transformations are important and further research is needed to better understand how they adapt to their changing social circumstances.

SUMMARY AND CONCLUSIONS

The historical record makes clear that with each successive generation, immigrant populations have adapted to their new environments by assuming patterns of family structure—size and composition—that resemble those of their native-born counterparts and the majority white population. This occurred during the last century as the diverse families of European ethnic groups merged through intermarriage and patterns of fertility and family living arrangements converged with the native-born population. Similar trends among today's immigrants exist today, although racial barriers clearly have slowed the growth of ethnoracial intermarriage between some immigrants and natives. But while the rise in ethnoracial intermarriage among Hispanics and Asian populations has slowed over the past decade or two (Qian and Lichter, 2007, 2011), the share of the U.S. non-Hispanic white population that has married with other ethnoracial groups and immigrants has grown considerably, as opportunities to meet and befriend new immigrant minorities has increased.

Conclusion 8-1 Marriages between the native-born and immigrants, most of whom are ethnoracial minorities, appear to have increased significantly over time. Today, about one of every seven new marriages is an interracial or interethnic marriage, more than twice the rate a generation ago. Perhaps as a result, the social and cultural boundaries between native-born and foreign-born populations in the United States are much less clearly defined than in the past. Moreover, second and third generation individuals from immigrant minority populations are far more likely to marry higher-generation non-Hispanic whites than are their first generation counterparts. These intermarriages also contribute to the increase in mixed-race Americans.

Immigrant integration also means that the families of new arrivals may increasingly reflect the unprecedented shifts in marriage and family life in the United States and other rich countries over the past several decades, which include the "retreat from marriage," more childbearing outside marriage, higher rates of nonmarital cohabitation, and increasing divorce and remarriage (Landale, Oropesa, and Bradatan, 2006; Sassler, 2010). Household or family extension among some immigrant populations also has slowly given way to the nuclear family system and the rise in nonfamily households (including cohabitation and living alone).

Conclusion 8-2 Immigrants' divorce rates and out-of-wedlock birth rates start out much lower than native-born Americans, but over time and generations these rates increase, while the likelihood of their living in extended families with multiple generations under one roof declines. Thus immigrant and second generation children are much more likely to live in families with two parents than are third and later generation children, where the proportion of single-parent families converges toward the percentage for native-born children in U.S. families generally. Since single-parent families are more likely to be impoverished, this is a disadvantage going forward.

Generational differences in family forms and demographic processes therefore may become larger in the future. Indeed, if benchmarked against the typical or average American family, immigrant integration clearly is a two-edged sword. The typical or average "family" today is a rapidly moving target. As America moves inexorably toward becoming a majority-minority society, the strong family and kinship networks often acknowledged among America's largest immigrant groups, especially Mexicans and Asians, may increasingly influence national indicators of marriage, cohabitation, and fertility, slowing the decline in two-parent families in the United States. The continuing rise in ethnoracial intermarriages also suggests a possible melding of family life and demographic processes across America's culturally diverse populations.

The potential influences on family life are hardly asymmetrical, that is, only extending from natives to immigrants (Alba and Nee, 2002). Instead, the future is likely to bring new growth of family forms and patterns of kin relations that reflect bidirectional influences among population groups with culturally different patterns of family life. The speed and form in which this occurs, however, is unclear. This will depend heavily on the nature of social, economic, and political integration of today's new immigrants and their children. It will also depend on patterns of intergroup exposure—in the neighborhoods and communities in which immigrants settle.

REFERENCES

Abrego, L. (2009). Economic well-being in Salvadoran transnational families: How gender affects remittance practices. *Journal of Marriage and Family*, 71(4), 1070-1085.

Alba, R., and Foner, N. (2015). Mixed unions and immigrant-group integration in North America and Western Europe. *The ANNALS of the American Academy of Political and Social Science*.

Alba, R., and Holdaway, J. (2013). The integration imperative., In R. Alba and J. Holdaway (Eds.), *The Children of Immigrants at School: A Comparative Look at Integration in the United States and Western Europe* (pp. 1-38). New York: New York University Press.

Alba, R., and Nee, V. (1997). Rethinking assimilation theory for a new era of immigration. *International Migration Review*, 31(4), 826-874.

Alba, R., and Nee, V. (2003). *Remaking the American Mainstream. Assimilation and Contemporary Immigration*. Cambridge, MA: Harvard University Press.

Alvira-Hammond, M., and Guzzo, K.B. (2014). *Fertility Differentials Across Race-Ethnicity and Generational Status: Incorporating Non-Hispanic Immigrants*. Working Paper. Bowling Green, OH: Bowling Green University Center for Family and Demographic Research.

Amato, P.R. (2005). The impact of family formation change on the cognitive, social, and emotional well-being of the next generation. *The Future of Children*, 15(2), 75-96.

Avanzado, D.M. (2013). *U.S. Citizens Can File Form I-130 for Their Same-Sex Partners*. U.S. Citizenship and Immigration Services. Available: http://www.uscitizenship.info/blog/us-citizens-can-file-form-i-130-for-their-same-sex-partners [September 2015].

Bean, F., and Stevens, G. (2003). *America's Newcomers and the Dynamics of Diversity.* New York: Russell Sage Foundation.

Bennett, P. (2011). The social position of multiracial groups in the United States: Evidence from residential segregation. *Ethnic and Racial Studies, 34*(4), 707-729.

Blackwell, D.L., and Lichter, D.T. (2000). Mate selection among married and cohabiting couples. *Journal of Family Issues, 21*(3), 275-302.

Bohra-Mishra, P., and Massey, D.S. (2015). Intermarriage among new immigrants in the USA. *Racial and Ethnic Studies, 38*, 734-758.

Brown, S.L., Van Hook, J., and Glick, J.E. (2008). Generational differences in cohabitation and marriage in the U.S. *Population Research and Policy Review, 27*(5), 531-550.

Campos, B., Schetter, C.D., Abdou, C.M., Hobel, C.J., Glynn, L.M., and Sandman, C.A. (2008). Familialism, social support, and stress: Positive implications for pregnant Latinas. *Cultural Diversity and Ethnic Minority Psychology, 14*(2), 155.

Cherlin, A.J. (2010). Demographic trends in the United States: A review of research in the 2000s. *Journal of Marriage and Family, 72*, 403-419.

Childs, E. (2005). *Navigating Interracial Borders: Black-White Couples and Their Social Worlds.* New Brunswick: Rutgers University Press.

Choi, K. (2014). Fertility in the context of Mexican migration to the United States. *Demographic Research, 30*(24), 703-738.

Clark, R.L., Glick, J.E., and Bures, R.M. (2009). Immigrant families over the life course research directions and needs. *Journal of Family Issues, 30*, 852-872.

DeLeone, F.Y., Lichter, D.T., and Strawderman, R.L. (2009). Decomposing trends in nonmarital fertility among Latinas. *Perspectives on Sexual and Reproductive Health, 41*(3), 166-172.

Derose, K.P., Escarce, J.J., and Lurie, N. (2007). Immigrants and health care: Sources of vulnerability. *Health Affairs, 26*(5), 1258-1268.

Dreby, J. (2007). Children and power in Mexican transnational families. *Journal of Marriage and Family, 69*(4), 1050-1064.

Dreby, J. (2012). The burden of deportation on children in Mexican immigrant families. *Journal of Marriage and Family, 74*(4), 829-845.

Dye, J.L. (2008). Fertility of American women: 2006. *Current Population Reports* #P20-563. Available: https://www.census.gov/prod/2010pubs/p20-563.pdf [September 2015].

Feliciano, C., Robnett, B., and Komaie, G. (2009). Gendered racial exclusion among white internet daters. *Social Science Research, 38*, 39-54.

Foner, N. (1997). The immigrant family: Cultural legacies and cultural changes. *International Migration Review, 31*(4), 961-974.

Foner, N., and Dreby, J. (2011). Relations between the generations in immigrant families. *Annual Review of Sociology, 37*, 545-564.

Frank, R., and Heuveline, P. (2005). A crossover in Mexican and Mexican-American fertility rates: Evidence and explanations for an emerging paradox. *Demographic Research, 12*(4), 77.

Frey, W.H. (2014). *Diversity Explosion: How New Racial Demographics Are Remaking America.* Washington, DC: Brookings Institution Press.

Glick, J.E. (2010). Connecting complex processes: A decade of research on immigrant families. *Journal of Marriage and Family, 72*(3), 498-515.

Glick, J.E., and Van Hook, J. (2011). Does a house divided stand? Kinship and the continuity of shared living arrangements. *Journal of Marriage and Family, 73*(5), 1149-1164.

Goldstein, J.R. (1999). Kinship networks that cross racial lines: The exception or the rule? *Demography, 36*(3), 399-407.

Gordon, M.M. (1964). *Assimilation in American Life: The Role of Race, Religion, and National Origins.* New York: Oxford University Press.

Grace, K., and Sweeney, S. (2014). Pathways to marriage and cohabitation in Central America. *Demographic Research, 30,* 187-226.

Gullickson, A. (2006). Education and black-white intermarriage. *Demography, 43*(4), 673-689.

Herman, M., and Campbell, M.E. (2012). I wouldn't but you can: Attitudes toward interracial relationships. *Social Science Research, 41*(2), 343-358.

Hu, W.Y. (1998). Elderly immigrants on welfare. *Journal of Human Resources, 90*(2), 711-741.

Hwang, S.S., and Saenz, R. (1997). Fertility of Chinese immigrants in the U.S.: Testing a fertility emancipation hypothesis. *Journal of Marriage and the Family, 59*(1), 50-61.

Jiménez, T.R. (2010). *Replenished Ethnicity: Mexican Americans, Immigration, and Identity.* Oakland: University of California Press.

Johnson, K.M., and Lichter, D.T. (2008). Natural increase: A new source of population growth in emerging Hispanic destinations in the United States. *Population and Development Review, 34*(2), 327-346.

Johnson, K.M., and Lichter, D.T. (2010). Growing diversity among America's children and youth: Spatial and temporal dimensions. *Population and Development Review, 36*(March), 151-175.

Jonsson, S.H., and Rendall, M.S. (2004). The fertility contribution of Mexican immigration to the United States. *Demography, 41*(1), 129-150.

Kahn, J.R. (1994). Immigrant and native fertility during the 1980s: Adaptation and expectations for the future. *The International Migration Review, 28*(3), 501-519.

Kalmijn, M. (1998). Intermarriage and homogamy: Causes, patterns, trends. *Annual Review of Sociology, 24,* 395-421.

Kearney, M.S., and Levine, P.B. (2009). Subsidized contraception, fertility, and sexual behavior. *Review of Economics and Statistics, 91*(1), 137-151.

Kritz, M.M., Gurak, D.T., and Chen, L. (2000). Elderly immigrants: Their composition and living arrangements. *Journal of Sociology and Social Welfare, 27,* 85-114.

Landale, N.S., Oropesa, R.S., and Bradatan, C. (2006). Hispanic families in the United States: Family structure and process in an era of family change. In National Research Council, *Hispanics and the Future of America* (pp. 138-178). M. Tienda and F. Mitchell, Eds., Panel on Hispanics in the United States. Committee on Population, Division of Behavioral and Social Sciences and Education. Washington, DC: The National Academies Press.

Landale, N.S., Thomas, K.J., and Van Hook, J. (2011). The living arrangements of children of immigrants. *The Future of Children/Center for the Future of Children, 21*(1), 43-70.

Leach, M.A. (2014). A burden of support? Household structure and economic resources among Mexican immigrant families. *Journal of Family Issues, 35*(1), 28-53.

Lee, J., and Bean, F. (2010). *The Diversity Paradox: Immigration and the Color Line in Twenty First Century America.* New York: Russell Sage Foundation.

Lesthaeghe, R. (2010). The unfolding story of the second demographic transition. *Population and Development Review, 36,* 211–251.

Levitt, P., and Jaworsky, B.N. (2007). Transnational migration studies: Past developments and future trends. *Annual Review of Sociology, 33,* 129-156.

Levitt, P., and Waters, M.C. (2002). *The Changing Face of Home: The Transnational Lives of the Second Generation* New York: Russell Sage Foundation.

Lichter, D.T. (2013). Integration or fragmentation? Racial diversity and the American future. *Demography, 50*(2), 359-391.

Lichter, D.T., Carmalt, J.H., and Qian, Z. (2008). *Who Marries Immigrants? Generational Differences in Marital Endogamy.* Paper presented at the Annual Meeting of the Population Association of America, New Orleans, LA.

Lichter, D.T., Carmalt, J.H., and Qian, Z. (2011). Immigration and intermarriage among Hispanics: Crossing racial and generational boundaries. *Sociological Forum, 26,* 241-264.

Lichter, D.T., Johnson, K.M., Turner, R.N., and Churilla, A. (2012). Hispanic assimilation and fertility in new U.S. destinations. *International Migration Review, 46*(4), 767-791.

Lichter, D.T., Sassler, S., and Turner, R.N. (2014). Cohabitation, post-conception unions, and the rise in nonmarital fertility. *Social Science Research 47,* 134-147.

Lichter, D.T., Qian, Z., and Tumin, D. (2015a). Who do immigrants marry? Emerging patterns of intermarriage and integration in the United States. *The ANNALS of the American Academy of Political and Social Sciences.*

Lichter, D.T., Sanders, S.R., and Johnson, K.M. (2015b). Hispanics at the starting line: Poverty among newborn infants in established gateways and new destinations. *Social Forces, 94*(1), 209-235.

Lincoln, K.D., Taylor, R.J., and Jackson, J.S. (2008). Romantic relationships among unmarried African Americans and Caribbean Blacks: Findings from the National Survey of American Life. *Family Relations, 57*(2), 254-266.

Livingston, G., and Cohn, D. (2012). U.S. birth rate falls to a record low; decline is greatest among immigrants. *Pew Research Center Social & Demographic Trends.* Available: http://www.pewsocialtrends.org/2012/11/29/u-s-birth-rate-falls-to-a-record-low-decline-is-greatest-among-immigrants/ [September 2015].

Manning, W.D., Brown, S.L., and Payne, K.K. (2014). Two decades of stability and change in age at first union formation. *Journal of Marriage and Family, 76*(2), 247-260.

Martin, J.A., Hamilton, B.E., Osterman, M.J., Curtin, S.C., and Mathews, T.J. (2015). Births: Final data for 2013. *National Vital Statistics, 64*(1). Available: http://www.cdc.gov/nchs/data/nvsr/nvsr64/nvsr64_01.pdf [September 2015].

Menjívar, C. (2003). (Ed.). *Through the Eyes of Women: Gender, Social Networks, Family and Structural Change in Latin America and the Caribbean.* Ontario, Canada: De Sitter.

Menjívar, C., and Abrego, D. (2009). Parents and children across borders: Legal instability and intergenerational relations in Guatemalan and Salvadoran families. In. N. Foder (Ed.), *Across Generations: Immigrant Families in America* (pp. 160-189). New York: New York University Press.

Nobles, J. (2011). Parenting from abroad: Migration, nonresident father involvement, and children's education in Mexico. *Journal of Marriage and Family, 73*(4), 729-746.

Oropesa, R.S. (1996). Normative beliefs about marriage and cohabitation: A comparison of non-Latino whites, Mexican Americans, and Puerto Ricans. *Journal of Marriage and the Family, 58,* 49-62.

Orellana, M.F., Thorne, B., Chee, A., and Lam, W.S.E. (2001). Transnational childhoods: The participation of children in processes of family migration. *Social Problems, 48*(4), 572-591.

Parker, D., and Song, M. (2009). New ethnicities and the internet: Belonging and the negotiation of difference in multicultural Britain. *Cultural Studies, 23*(4), 583-604.

Parrado, E.A. (2011). How high is Hispanic/Mexican fertility in the United States? Immigration and tempo considerations. *Demography, 48*(3), 1059-1080.

Parrado, E.A., and Flippen, C.A. (2012). Hispanic fertility, immigration, and race in the twenty-first century. *Race and Social Problems, 4*(1), 18-30.

Parrado, E.A., and Morgan, S.P. (2008). Intergenerational fertility among Hispanic women: New evidence of immigrant assimilation. *Demography, 45*(3), 651-671.

Passel, J.S., and Taylor, P. (2013). *Unauthorized Immigrants and Their U.S.-Born Children.* Washington, DC: Pew Research Center.

Pew Research Center. (2015). *Multiracial in America: Proud, Diverse and Growing in Numbers.* Available: http://www.pewsocialtrends.org/2015/06/11/multiracial-in-america/#fnref-20523-3 [July 2015].

Portes, A., Guarnizo, L.E., and Landolt, P. (1999). The study of transnationalism: pitfalls and promise of an emergent research field. *Ethnic and Racial Studies, 22*(2), 217-237.

Qian, Z. (2013). *Divergent Paths of American Families.* Available: http://www.s4.brown.edu/ us2010/Data/Report/report09112013.pdf [September 2015].

Qian, Z., and Lichter, D.T. (2001). Measuring marital assimilation: Intermarriage among natives and immigrants. *Social Science Research, 30*(2), 289-312.

Qian, Z., and Lichter, D.T. (2007). Social boundaries and marital assimilation: Interpreting trends in racial and ethnic intermarriage. *American Sociological Review, 72*(1), 68-94.

Qian, Z., and Lichter, D.T. (2011). Changing patterns of interracial marriage in a multiracial society. *Journal of Marriage and Family, 73*(5), 1065-1084.

Qian, Z., Glick, J.E., and Batson, C.D. (2012). Crossing boundaries: Nativity, ethnicity, and mate selection. *Demography, 49*(2), 651-675.

Romero, V.C. (2005). Asians, gay marriage, and immigration: Family unification at a crossroads. *Immigration & Nationality Law Review, 26,* 337-347.

Sassler, S. (2010). Partnering across the life course: Sex, relationships, and mate selection. *Journal of Marriage and Family, 72*(3), 557-575.

Schwartz, C.R. (2013). Trends and variation in assortative mating: Causes and consequences. *Annual Review of Sociology, 39,* 451-470.

Smith, J.P. (2003). Assimilation across the Latino generations. *American Economic Review, 93,* 315-319.

Song, M. (2010). Does race matter? A study of mixed race siblings' identifications. *The Sociological Review, 58*(2), 265-285.

Stevens, G., Ishizawa, H., and Escandell, X. (2012). Marrying into the American population: Pathways into cross-nativity marriages. *International Migration Review, 46*(3), 740-759.

Suárez-Orozco, C., Suárez-Orozco, M.M., and Todorova, I. (2008). *Learning a New Land: Immigrant Students in American Society.* Cambridge, MA: Harvard University Press.

Suárez-Orozco, C., Yoshikawa, H., and Tseng, V. (2015). *Intersecting Inequalities: Research to Reduce Inequality for Immigrant-Origin Children and Youth.* New York: William T. Grant Foundation.

Telles, E., and Ortiz, V. (2008). *Generations of Exclusion: Mexican Americans, Assimilation and Race.* New York: Russell Sage Foundation.

Thomas, K. (2009). Parental characteristics and the schooling progress of black immigrant and native-born children. *Demography, 46*(3), 513- 534

Treas, J., and Mazumdar, S. (2002). Older people in America's immigrant families: Dilemmas of dependence, integration, and isolation. *Journal of Aging Studies, 16*(3), 243-258.

Van Hook, J., and Glick, J.E. (2007). Immigration and living arrangements: Moving beyond economic need versus acculturation. *Demography, 44*(2), 225-249.

Wang, W. (2012). *The Rise of Intermarriage.* Washington, DC: Pew Research Center.

Waters, M.C., and Jimenez, T. (2005). Assessing immigrant assimilation: New empirical and theoretical challenges. *Annual Review of Sociology, 31,* 105-125.

Waters, M.C., and Sykes, J.E. (2009). Spare the rod, ruin the child: First-and second-generation West Indian childrearing practices. In N. Foner (Ed.), *Across Generations: Immigrant Families in America* (pp. 72-98). New York: New York University Press.

9

Health Status and Access to Care

The health of immigrants and its implications for American society have long been discussed, commented on, and at times, hotly contested. In the early part of the 20th century, immigrants were portrayed as sickly, likely to transmit infectious diseases, and a burden to local governments (Markel and Stern, 1999). Research eventually showed that infectious diseases had less to do with immigration and more to do with the neighborhood conditions, where immigrants frequently resided in cramped, crowded tenements with unsafe drinking water and unsanitary sewage removal systems (Garb, 2003). More recently, another picture has emerged that depicts immigrants from some countries as healthier and hardier than U.S.-born residents and less likely to access health care (Derose et al., 2007; Jasso et al., 2004; Paloni and Arias, 2004).

This chapter provides a summary review of some of the key evidence about the health status of immigrants and their capacity to access health care. The chapter (a) compares the rates of mortality and morbidity outcomes between immigrants and the native-born; (b) describes the association between some dimensions of immigrant integration and health; (c) focuses on the disparities in health care access between immigrants and the native-born, with an emphasis on health insurance coverage; (d) discusses the Patient Protection andAffordable Care Act (ACA) and its consequences for immigrants; and (e) identifies some future issues that may affect the health and well-being of immigrants.

HEALTH AND ILLNESS AMONG IMMIGRANTS

Comprehensive analyses on immigrant health status using eight federal national datasets[1] show that immigrants have better infant, child, and adult health outcomes than the native-born in general and the native-born members of the same ethnoracial groups (Singh et al., 2013). Immigrants, compared to the native-born, are less likely to die from cardiovascular disease and all cancers combined and have a lower incidence of all cancers combined, fewer chronic health conditions, lower infant mortality rates, lower rates of obesity, lower percentages who are overweight, fewer functional limitations, and fewer learning disabilities. Other studies show that immigrants have lower prevalence of depression, the most common mental disorder in the world, and alcohol abuse than the native-born (Alegria et al., 2007a; Brown et al., 2005; Szaflarski et al., 2011; Takeuchi et al., 2007; Williams et al., 2007).

Another example of the difference between immigrants and the native-born in health is life expectancy. Life expectancy is a widely used summary indicator that gauges the health of a population or group using a measure of the number of years a person is expected to live based on mortality statistics for a given time period. In one example of relevant research (Singh et al., 2013), national birth and death records were linked to provide life expectancy data. The data were reported for people living in 1999-2001 and included death records up to 2010, adjusted for age and gender. This study found that immigrants had a life expectancy of 80.0 years, which was 3.4 years higher than the native-born population (see Figure 9-1). Across the major ethnic categories (non-Hispanic whites, blacks, Asian/Pacific Islanders, and Hispanics), immigrants showed a life expectancy advantage over their native-born counterparts. This life expectancy advantage for immigrants over the native-born ranges from 0.7 years for whites and Asian/Pacific Islanders to a high of 7.4 years for blacks. The immigrant life expectancy advantage is comparable to that reported for an earlier time period (1989-1991) (Singh et al., 2013).

This pattern does not suggest that immigrants are free from infectious diseases, chronic illnesses, disabilities, mental disorders, or other health problems, but rather they show a general health advantage when compared to the native-born. Some exceptions are evident to this overall pattern. Immigrant males and females, for example, were more likely to die from stomach and liver cancer than native-born males and females (Singh et

---

[1] The datasets used in the research discussed here include the American Community Survey, National Health Interview Survey, National Health and Nutrition Examination Survey, National Linked Birth and Infant Death Files, National Longitudinal Mortality Study, National Notifiable Disease Surveillance System, National Survey of Children's Health, and National Vital Statistics Systems.

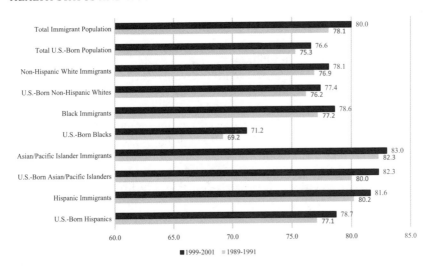

FIGURE 9-1 Life expectancy at birth (average lifetime in years) by race/ethnicity and immigrant status, United States, 1989-2001.
SOURCE: Data from the U.S. National Vital Statistics System, 1989-2001; Singh et al. (2013).

al., 2013). Chinese, Mexican, and Cuban immigrants were more likely to report their children's health as poor/fair compared to their native-born counterparts. Asian Indian, Central American, Chinese, Cuban, Mexican, and South American immigrants reported higher levels of poor/fair health in contrast to native born co-ethnics (Singh et al., 2013). It is also possible that some health problems among recent immigrants, such as diabetes, are not properly diagnosed (Barcellos et al., 2012).

There is only limited research on elderly immigrants and the interaction among immigrant status, age, and health. Elderly immigrants compose a heterogeneous group, and more research about how they age and their subsequent health care needs is essential to inform future policies and programs. One example of the research available is a study of the elderly who worked in low skilled jobs. Hayward and colleagues (2014) found that both foreign-born and native-born Hispanics have lower mortality rates but higher disability rates than non-Hispanic whites; their disability rates are similar to the rates of non-Hispanic blacks. The researchers concluded Hispanics, including the foreign-born, will have an extended period of disability in their elder years. Similarly, Gurak and Kritz (2013) found that older Mexican immigrants in rural areas had twice as many health limitations as other immigrants. It is likely that manual labor leads to functional limitations and disability in later life, and elderly immigrants may have high demand for health care in their elderly years (Population Reference Bureau, 2013).

The legal status of immigrants is also associated with health status (Landale et al, 2015b). Naturalized immigrants do better than noncitizen inmmigrants on some mobility measures such as acquiring higher levels of education, better paying jobs, and living in safer and better resourced neighborhoods (Aguirre and Saenz, 2002; Bloemraad, 2000; Gonzalez-Barrera et al., 2013). Gubernskaya and colleagues (2013) also found that naturalization has a differential association with health depending on the age of immigration. Among immigrants who came as children and young adults, naturalized citizens had better functional health at older ages than noncitizens. Conversely, among immigrants who came to the United States at middle or older ages, naturalized citizens fared worse on functional health measures than noncitizens. While the precise reasons for this differential effect cannot be determined from the datasets used in the analyses, the authors suggested that naturalization at later stages of life may not confer social and political integration advantages that are positive factors for better health outcomes.

Refugees, unlike immigrants in general, are leaving their home country because they face persecution, and are often escaping wars or political turmoil. People can apply for and receive refugee status if they meet two essential criteria: (1) they are unable or unwilling to return to their home country because of past persecution or fear of persecution and (2) the reason for persecution is associated with race, religion, nationality, membership in a particular social group, or political opinion. After 1 year, refugees must apply for a green card. The circumstances under which refugees exit their home country are associated with trauma, extreme stress, hunger, and living in cramped unsanitary conditions, especially in refugee camps and prior to settling in the United States. It is not surprising that studies find that refugees tend to have relatively high levels of different health problems related to major depression, general anxiety, panic attacks, and post-traumatic stress disorder (Birman et al., 2008; Carswell et al., 2011; Hollifield et al., 2002; Keyes, 2000; Lustig et al., 2004; Murray et al., 2010; Taylor et al., 2014). A recent Centers for Disease Control and Prevention (2013) report, for example, found that the estimated age-adjusted suicide rate among Butanese refugees resettled in the United States was 24.4 per 100,000, which is higher than the annual global suicide rate for all persons (16.0 per 100,000) and the annual suicide rates of U.S. residents (12.4 per 100,000).

The health of undocumented immigrants is more difficult to assess than immigrants as a whole because their legal status is generally not available on health administrative records or in community surveys. Some studies have found that undocumented immigrants have better health outcomes and positive health behaviors than the native-born (Dang et al., 2011; Kelaher and Jessop, 2002; Korinek and Smith, 2011; Reed et al., 2005). Other studies have found that undocumented immigrants had higher rates on some negative health outcomes (Landale et al., 2015a; Wallace et al., 2012). Despite these mixed results, there seems to be agreement that even if undocumented immigrants have better physical health status than the native-born, they may experience a faster decline of their mental health. Their undocumented status creates a social stigma, fear of discovery and deportation, and related stressors that have negative consequences for adults and their children (Gonzales et al., 2013; Suárez-Orozco et al., 2011; Sullivan and Rehm, 2005; Yoshikawa, 2011; also see Chapter 3).

International Comparisons

It is difficult to compare health indicators across countries because of different data collection methods and systems, differences in the measurement of health and immigrant status, and the frequency of data collection efforts. Despite these challenges, it is possible to make a broad assessment of this issue. The available evidence suggests that the immigrant pattern in the United States is not consistently found across different countries. Canada is similar to the United States, with Canadian immigrant men and women having a lower incidence of chronic conditions than Canadian-born men and women (McDonald and Kennedy, 2004). Canadian immigrants have lower rates of depression and alcohol dependence than the Canadian-born (Ali, 2002), although this pattern does not hold true for all immigrant populations (Islam, 2013). In Europe, the association between immigrant status and health is not as consistent (Domnich et al., 2012). One study examined the health of adults 50 years and older and found that immigrants were comparatively worse off on various dimensions of health than the native-born population across 11 European countries (Sole-Auro and Crimmins, 2008). Moullan and Jusot (2014) found that immigrants in France, Belgium, and Spain reported poorer health status than the native-born in their respective countries. Italian immigrants, on the other hand, reported better health than Italian native-born. Noymer and Lee (2013), in a study of immigrant status and self-rated health across 32 countries, found only two countries have poorer immigrant health than native-born (Macedonia and Switzerland), whereas three countries (Moldova, Nigeria, and Ukraine) have better immigrant health compared to the native-born in each country. The authors concluded that the age structure of immigrants compared to the native-born population may explain some of the variation found in health status between groups.

Possible Explanations for the Health Advantage among Immigrants

The terms "immigrant paradox" or "epidemiological paradox" are frequently used to refer to the pattern that immigrants tend to have better health outcomes than the native born. This paradox is especially pertinent for immigrants who come to the United States with low levels of education and income. Yet the sources of this paradox are not well understood, and are a subject of debate in the literature (Jasso et al., 2004; Markides and Rote, 2015). Below, the panel discusses some potentially relevant data sources that help account for this pattern of immigrant health.

Immigrants may endure difficulties and hardships as they grow accustomed to the social norms and lifestyles in the United States. They may encounter difficulties securing permanent residences in safe neighborhoods, earning decent wages for their work, finding resources for their social and health care needs, creating opportunities to expand their social networks, and sending their children to good schools. The transition may be made even more difficult if communities are not receptive to them. These difficulties may create conditions and stressors that are often associated with disease. Since low levels of education and income are strongly associated with poor health, immigrants with limited economic and social means are expected to be at even greater risk for health problems. But despite these elevated risks, even socioeconomically disadvantaged immigrants generally have better health outcomes than the general population of native-born.

Some immigrants arrive from countries that enjoy better health outcomes than the United States. Although the United States spends considerably more on medical technologies and clinical care than many other countries, these expenditures have not resulted in a healthier population. In 2011, for example, health care expenditures as a percentage of gross domestic product (GDP) were about 2.5 times higher than the average of all OECD countries and 50 percent higher than Switzerland and Norway, the next two highest health care spenders (OECD, 2013). Yet the United States has higher rates of cancer, HIV/AIDS, and obesity-related illnesses like diabetes and heart disease compared with other OECD member countries (OECD, 2013). And it has higher rates of disease and injury from birth to age 75 years for men and women and across ethnoracial groups than many other developed countries, including Canada and the United Kingdom (Woolf and Aron, 2013). These poorer health outcomes are evident even for people with high incomes, college educations, health insurance, and healthy lifestyles compared to their peers in other wealthy countries (Woolf and Aron, 2013). Thus, part of the explanation for the "paradox" may be that although immigrants may come to the United States for the perceived social and economic advantages relative to their home countries, better health is not necessarily one of them.

Two related explanations for any immigrant health advantage compared to native-born peers are the selection effect and the "salmon bias," or return migration. The selection effect occurs when people who are healthier than residents of the sending country migrate to the United States more frequently than their fellow residents who are less healthy. For instance, Jasso and colleagues (2004) compared average life expectancy of immigrants and residents in sending countries. They found a substantial potential selection effect, with male immigrants to the United States having longer life expectancies than the general population of males born in the sending countries. Male Asian immigrant life expectancy in the United States, for example, may be as much as 10 years greater than the average for the male population in Asian sending countries. Among Hispanics, although immigrant males show a life expectancy advantage over native-born Hispanics, the difference is only about 5 years. Abraido-Lanza and colleagues (1999) take a different approach, comparing foreign-born Latino males and females with their foreign-born white counterparts. They find that Latino foreign-born have lower mortality rates than the white foreign-born, challenging the selection effect explanation for the immigrant health advantage. If a selection effect exists, it holds for Latinos and Asians, but not white immigrants.

It is difficult to test for a selection effect since most datasets on immigrants do not collect data on health of people before migration, but, some creative analyses of existing datasets provide insights about a possible selection effect. For example, Akresh and Frank (2008) analyzed data from the first round of the New Immigrant Survey 2003 Cohort to assess how health selectivity differs across regions of origin. Their analyses showed evidence of a health selection effect, based on comparisons of self-rated health, for all sending countries. Immigrants from all regions were more likely to experience positive health selection than negative selection, with western European and African immigrants having the highest proportion of positive selection and Mexican immigrants the lowest. But when socioeconomic controls were added to the analyses, the differences in positive health selection among different sending regions were substantially reduced. Selectivity is a complex process that may have differential effects on different health conditions and other social factors such as gender (Martinez and Aguayo-Tellez, 2014).

Return migration works in the opposite direction from the selection effect: sicker or less fit immigrants return to their home countries, leaving a healthier immigrant population in the United States. Immigrants, especially older adults, may return to access health care they are more familiar with, seek the support and care of family members and friends, or to die in their place of birth. For instance, Palloni and Arias (2004) found that older Mexican-born immigrants did return to Mexico when ill, and this return migration may affect the life expectancy rates of immigrants who remained in the United States. Other researchers found a modest return bias (Turra and Elo, 2008; Riosmena et al., 2013). However, Abraido-Lanza and colleagues (1999) did not find evidence for a return bias in explaining the Latino mortality advantage.

Social and cultural factors constitute another set of explanations for the immigrant health advantage, particularly in explaining why their health status may worsen over time. Immigrants may come to the United States with behaviors and values that lead to healthy diets and lifestyles, but over time, they and their children learn U.S. norms and practices that may be less healthy in the long term, such as a diet of frequent fast foods, heavy alcohol and substance consumption, and less involvement in family life (Abraido-Lanza et al., 2005; Dubowitz et al., 2010). Immigrants coming at earlier ages, especially during childhood, have the longest risk period. With more years in the United States, diet and physical inactivity of immigrant youth approach those of the native-born (Gordon-Larsen et al., 2003). Immigrant children may also have a larger set of social groups and networks available to them than older immigrants and, as a result could experience a greater amount of negative stressors and influences that lead to detrimental health outcomes as they mature and become adults.

Smoking is a lifestyle factor that has a large effect on mortality rates. Immigrants in the UnitedStates have lower rates of smoking rates than the native-born of the same ethnicity or the general native-born population (Larisey et al., 2013; Shankar et al., 2000; Unger et al., 2000). New migrants to the United States also tend to have lower rates of smoking than do people in their countries of origin (Bosdriesz et al., 2013), but over time the risk of smoking increases as they stay in the United States (Singh et al., 2013). Some recent research attributes as much as 50 percent of the difference in life expectancy at 50 years between foreign- and native-born men and 70 percent of the difference between foreign- and native born women to lower smoking-related mortality (Blue and Fenelon, 2011; Cantu et al., 2013).

Worksite environments and the safety in workplaces may partially explain the worsening health status among immigrants over time. Immigrants who are poor or have low levels of skills may take jobs in neighborhoods with high levels of pollutants, near toxic dump sites, or with frayed water and sanitation infrastructure that are at risk for collapse when natural or manmade disasters occur (Pellow and Park, 2002). They may also work in hazardous jobs or in settings where harmful chemicals are present, such as in some agricultural occupations or in nail salons (Park and Pellow, 2011). While immigrants may not necessarily work in the most hazardous jobs compared to the native-born, they may not receive the best training and counseling to manage their safety and well-being in these workplace or neighborhoods (Hall and Greenman, 2014). The constant exposure to physical harm and chemicals can take its toll on the body and on mental health, potentially leading to declining health.

Despite these promising and noteworthy findings, there is no single definitive explanation why immigrants generally have better health outcomes than the native-born when they first arrive, or why their health eventually declines over time and over generations. Past research on these topics tends to use different datasets, conceptual models, analytic samples, measures, and time periods. Most existing datasets that include large samples of immigrants do not include extensive information about health status and other social conditions prior to the migration experience. Moreover, existing datasets are unable to track immigrants to fully capture how health changes over time and what factors may contribute to these changes. There is evidence, however, that selection, return migration, and social and cultural factors contribute to some extent to the immigrant health advantage and the changes in health over time.

IMMIGRANT INTEGRATION AND HEALTH

Immigrants may have an initial health advantage when they first arrive in the United States, but this advantage tends to decrease when some dimensions of integration are considered. The research on these dimensions establishes an association with health but not necessarily the causal effects. Accordingly, it is possible that while a statistically significant association can be demonstrated between some dimensions of integration and health, other factors may actually be responsible for the effect. One common dimension of integration in health research is the time spent in the United States. Research has documented higher rates of different health problems including hypertension, chronic illness, smoking, diabetes, and heavy alcohol use as length of residency increases (Alegria et al., 2007a; Jackson et al., 2007; Moran et al., 2007; O'Brien et al., 2014; Ro, 2014; Singh et al., 2013; Takeuchi et al., 2007). Since length of residence is often correlated with integration across other dimensions, this research suggests that increased integration may have a negative effect on health. Yet despite this general finding, it is not possible to conclude that the length of residence in the United States shows a linear association with health problems because the studies vary in how length of residence is categorized (e.g., in 5-year, 10-year, or 20-year intervals), in the health outcome measured, and in the immigrant group under consideration (Ro, 2014; Zsembik and Fennell, 2005). More clearly defined research that allows results to be linked across studies on this topic is warranted. In addition, negative health outcomes may result from the challenges to integration, for example, the accumulated stress resulting from discrimination, poor working conditions, undocumented legal status, and limited English proficiency (Finch and Vega, 2003;

Yoo et al., 2009). Lack of access to health insurance and adequate health care may also play a role, as discussed below.

Another important integration measure is generational status, since the expectation is that second and subsequent generations will be more integrated into American society than their parents. While data on the health of the children of immigrants are somewhat scarce, the empirical literature suggests a pattern of declining health status after the immigrant generation, although the pattern may differ depending on the health outcome and the ethnic group (Marks et al., 2014). For example, second generation Hispanic and Asian adolescents have shown much higher rates of obesity than the first generation (Popkin and Udry, 1998; Singh et al., 2013). Children of recent immigrants have encountered weight problems across socioeconomic (SES) status, and this was especially so for sons of non-English speaking parents (Van Hook and Baker, 2010).

Three national studies of black, Asian, and Latino immigrant adults found some generational association with mental disorders. Second and third generation Caribbean blacks had higher rates of psychiatric disorders than the first generation; the third generation had substantively higher rates of psychiatric disorders (Williams et al., 2007). Third generation Latinos also had significant higher rates of psychiatric disorders than the first and second generations (Alegria et al., 2007a), and the generational pattern for Asian Americans was similar (Takeuchi et al., 2007). A decline in health status for the third generation was also found in surveys in which respondents self-reported on their health status (self-rated health). Data from the Current Population Survey showed that the third generation had higher odds of reporting poor/fair self-rated health than the first generation. This effect was particular strong for blacks and Hispanics, but not for Asians (Acevedo-Garcia et al., 2010).

Higher levels of educational attainment have often been associated with increased cognitive functioning, better quality and higher paying jobs, more integration into civic life, and access to broader social networks, all of which can lead to better health (Mirowsky and Ross, 2003). In many respects, researchers consider education to be the causal mechanism (or a major causal factor) that leads to economic and social rewards and a better quality of life, and increases in educational attainment have also corresponded with incremental improvements in health status (Adler et al., 1994; Edgerter et al., 2011). Education has also been positively correlated with immigrant integration (see Chapter 6).

Despite this robust association, not all groups have shown the same positive associations between rewarding outcomes and education (see Conley, 1999; Farmer and Ferraro, 2005; Massey, 2008; National Research Council, 2001; Oliver and Shapiro, 1997). For example, the education and health association has been markedly weaker among Latino and Asian immigrants than it has been for non-Hispanic whites (Acevedo-Garcia et al., 2007; Goldman et al., 2006; Kimbro et al., 2008; Leu et al., 2008; Walton et al., 2009). The reason for this weaker association is not clearly established yet, but one possible reason is that where one receives the major part of her/his education experiences matters for social mobility and health. Immigrants may find that their educational achievements are undervalued in the United States, and they may not receive the same compensation and prestige for their educational accomplishments (Zeng and Xie, 2004). Education in another country, when compared to schooling in the United States, constrains economic opportunities, reduces positive social interactions, and limits English proficiency; these factors in turn are associated with less-positive health status (Walton et al., 2009). In addition, the educational gradient (i.e., positive correlations between educational attainment and other positive risk factors or outcomes) in the United States may be weaker or reversed in some sending countries. For example, people at higher SES levels in Latin America were shown to be more likely to eat higher calorie foods, smoke tobacco, and consume alcohol. These behaviors, while not conducive to better health, may have been associated with higher social status. Accordingly, immigrants may engage in these behaviors as they climb the educational and economic ladder (Buttenheim et al., 2010).

The ability to speak English in the United States is another often used measure of immigrant integration. Proficiency in English allows immigrants to communicate with people who do not speak their ethnic language and to manage their daily routines, whereas inability to speak English can limit opportunities for jobs and schooling, reduce abilities to expand networks and communicate with others, and constrain access to social and health services. Given its importance for social interactions in the United States, it is not surprising that English proficiency has been found to be strongly associated with health among Asian, black, and Latino immigrants (Gee et al. 2010; Kimbro et al., 2012; Okafor et al., 2013). Equally important, the ability to communicate in both English and one's ethnic language has been strongly associated with positive health (Gee et al., 2010; Kimbro et al., 2012). Chen and colleagues (2008) found that bilingual proficiency provided access to resources in both immigrant and non-immigrant communities, creating more opportunities for social mobility.

Residency, generational status, education, and English-language proficiency are individual characteristics that have been associated with health. Measures of discrimination and ethnic density of residential neighborhoods capture facets of the societal receptivity and responses that influence the health of immigrants. Perceived discrimination is frequently considered a type of stressor that can cause wear and tear on the body and psyche and eventually lead to premature illness and death (Williams and Mohammed, 2009). Perceived discrimination has been associated with a wide range of health behaviors and outcomes, such as smoking, alcohol use, obesity, hypertension, breast cancer, depression, anxiety, psychological distress, substance use, and self-rated health across ethnoracial groups (Gee et al., 2009; Pascoe and Smart, 2009; Williams and Mohammed, 2009). While fewer studies have focused specifically on immigrants, their findings support the general pattern that perceived discrimination is significantly associated with health outcomes (Gee et al., 2006; Ryan et al., 2006; Yoo et al., 2009). For example, Yoo and colleagues (2009) found that perceived language discrimination (the perception that a person is unfairly treated because of accent or English-speaking ability) had a strong association with health, particularly for Asian immigrants living in the United States for 10 years or more. The overall body of this research suggests that the perception that others are not receptive to one's presence is strongly associated with health outcomes for different ethnic groups and immigrants.

Violence against women, including intimate partner violence, rape and sexual assault, and other forms of sexual violence, is a public health problem that has been associated with poor health of women including depression, suicidality, sexually transmitted diseases, and death. In the United States, immigrant women do not appear to experience higher rates of domestic violence than the native-born, but their social positions may exacerbate the consequences of these assaults (Menjívar and Salcido, 2002). Some women come to the United States already in a violent relationship (Salcido and Adelman, 2004), while others may encounter violence after immigration. Research has found that limited English proficiency, isolation from family and community members, uncertain legal status, lack of access to good and dignified jobs, and past experiences with authorities in the sending country and the United States are all factors that can prevent abused immigrant women from reporting the crime or from leaving the family situation (Erez, 2000; Menjívar and Salcido, 2002). Violence against women is a difficult topic to study because women and family members may not want to talk about it for these same reasons that constrain them from reporting it to authorities. However, because domestic violence has detrimental consequences for the health of immigrant women and their children, innovative methods and strategies to overcome research obstacles to assessing its occurrence and contributing factors will go a long way toward addressing this major public health challenge.

The past two decades have seen a renewed focus on how geographic locations or places influence health (Burton et al., 2011). "Place" refers to any geographically located aggregate of people, practices, and built/natural objects that is invested with meaning and value (Gieryn, 2000). In this sense, place is a social and ecological force with detectable and independent effects on social life and individual well-being (Habraken, 1998; Werlen, 1993). Places reflect and reinforce social advantages and disadvantages by extending or denying opportunities, life-chances, and social networks to groups located in salutary or detrimental locales (Gieryn, 2000). Massey (2003), for example, showed that racial segregation produces a high allostatic load[2] for African Americans that have dire consequences on well-being. An immigrant's place has been shown to have negative attributes, such as high levels of poverty, limited jobs and services, extensive violence and crime, concentration of environmental hazards such as air pollution, and low levels of commitment and trust (Williams and Collins, 2001). Yet place can also be positive and protect residents from discrimination while offering high levels of social support, access to social and health services, ample parks and recreational activities, and accessible markets with fresh produce (Moreland et al., 2006; Sallis and Glanz, 2006; Walton, 2014).

Immigrants may live in places with a high proportion of people from the same ethnic backgrounds, especially when they first arrive, and this ethnic density is expected to be positive and supportive (Mair et al., 2010). Most studies have not found an effect between ethnic density and health, but when they have, positive effects were more common than negative ones (Bécares et al., 2012). A majority of these studies focus on the physical health of African Americans and Mexican Americans, and very few include immigrants in the samples. But a recent study provides additional insights: Lee and Liechty (2014) found that ethnic density was associated with lower depressive symptoms for Latino immigrant youth, but not for non-immigrant Latino adolescents. This study raises the possibility that the effects of ethnic density may depend on nativity, developmental stage, health outcomes, and the history of the group in the community (Osypuk, 2012). Longitudinal studies are needed for additional research on the places where immigrants reside and the relationships among place, health status and access to care, and integration.

ACCESS TO HEALTH CARE AMONG IMMIGRANTS

Unlike the overall health advantage, immigrants are at a distinct disadvantage compared to the native-born when it comes to receiving adequate and appropriate care to meet their preventive and medical health needs (Derose et al., 2007). This is a consistent and robust finding of research that covers physical and mental health problems among Asian, Black, and Latino immigrants (Abe-Kim et al., 2007; Alegria et al., 2007b; Jackson

---

[2] Allostatic load is the cost, or "wear and tear," to the human body of stress response to everyday life. Allostatic load reflects "not only the impact of life experiences but also of genetic load; individual habits reflecting items such as diet, exercise, and substance abuse; and developmental experiences that set lifelong patterns of behavior and physiological reactivity" (McEwen and Seeman, 1999, p. 30).

et al., 2007; Singh et al., 2013; Wafula and Snipes, 2014). This finding also extends to the research on undocumented immigrants, who were found to be less likely than native-born or other immigrants to have a usual source of care, visit a medical professional in an outpatient setting, use mental health services, or receive dental care (Derose et al., 2009; Pourat et al., 2014; Rodriguez et al., 2009). Per capita health care spending has been found to be lower for all immigrants, including the undocumented, than it was for the native-born (Derose et al., 2009; DuBard and Massing, 2007; Stimpson et al., 2010).

The lack of health insurance or inadequate insurance coverage are often cited as a primary source of constraint preventing immigrants from using health care services in a timely manner. Singh and colleagues (2013) found that immigrants have consistently lower rates of health insurance coverage than native-born populations at different age groupings and countries of origin. Immigrants 18 years and younger have four times the proportion of uninsured than do the native-born (29% to 7%); among 18-64-year-old immigrants, the prevalence of uninsured was 38 percent, compared to 18 percent among the native-born (Singh et al., 2013). In the age 65 and older category, they found that the prevalence of uninsured was lower for both groups and the difference was not as striking (5% to 3%). Immigrants born in Latin American countries were the most likely to be uninsured among both the group under 18 years of age (41%) and among 18-64-year-olds (52%). Immigrants from African and Latin American countries had the highest uninsured rates in the 65 years and older age group, with approximately 9 percent of that group being without insurance coverage (Singh et al., 2013). Wallace and colleagues (2012) found that the estimated percentage of undocumented immigrants (all regions of origin) without insurance was substantial, at about 61 percent.

Despite its importance, insurance coverage is the not the sole barrier to access to health care for immigrants (Clough et al., 2013; Derose et al., 2007; Ku, 2014; Perreira, et al., 2012). Hospitals, clinics, and community health centers may not have the appropriate staffing and capabilities to adequately communicate and serve some immigrant groups. Costs for health care—including medication—are high, and immigrants, especially those without health insurance coverage, may not have the capacity to pay these costs. Some immigrants may have to work at multiple jobs just to pay for their daily living expenses and are unable to find the time to seek care for their health problems (Chaufan et al., 2012). Many immigrants may not speak English or may not speak it well enough to negotiate access to needed health services (Flores, 2006; Timmins, 2002). Language can also limit knowledge about community services, create misunderstandings between patient and medical staff, and reduce effective communication between patient and physician (Cristancho et al., 2008). Public tensions around immigration may create a stigma about immigrants and lead to biases against immigrants among health care providers and staff, causing immigrants to avoid health care in public settings (Cristancho et al., 2008; Derose et al., 2009; Lauderdale et al., 2006). In addition, the safety net for health care continues to shrink and public programs for immigrants may not be available especially in new destinations (Crowley and Lichter, 2009; Ku and Matani, 2001). Undocumented immigrants may avoid contact with medical personnel and settings because they fear they will be reported to authorities and eventually deported (Heyman et al., 2009). In addition, the complexities of health care and insurance in the United States may make it difficult even for those who have health insurance to access care (Ngo-Metzger et al., 2003).

These challenges to improving access to health care for immigrants have led to many innovative government and public programs at the national, local, and community levels. The most ambitious program is the ACA, which was passed in 2010 and is intended to help a large number of immigrants to access health insurance (see below). However, ACA is not expected to change the number of uninsured among undocumented immigrants (Zuckerman et al., 2011). While it is not possible in this report to document all the programs that address access to care among immigrants, Yoshikawa and colleagues (2014) provide insights about what successful community-based organizations (CBO) can do to increase access to quality care and to provide better care. Among their suggestions are the following: (1) take advantage of strong family and community networks within immigrant neighborhoods for outreach; (2) establish collaboration and regular communication between CBOs and government agencies; (3) coordinate multiple service providers in the same location; (4) train trusted community members to disseminate health information (e.g., through the *promotores* programs found in some Latino immigrant communities); (5) address barriers for unauthorized parents to enrolling their U.S.-citizen children; and (6) address immediate needs as an entry point to accessing broader services.

Immigrants and the Affordable Care Act[3]

The ACA seeks to expand health insurance coverage through Medicaid expansions, the creation of health insurance exchanges (marketplaces) coupled with federal tax subsidies, and a requirement that people have health insurance or pay a tax penalty.[4] Embedded in both its policy development and implementation were a variety of exceptions concerning policies for

---

[3] The following discussion of the Affordable Care Act is edited and condensed from a longer paper prepared for the panel (Ku, 2014).

[4] For more details on the Affordable Care Act, including the full text of the law, see http://www.hhs.gov/healthcare/rights/index.html [September 2015].

immigrants, particularly those who are undocumented. A fundamental goal of the ACA was to incrementally expand health insurance coverage, largely beginning in 2014.[5] Since immigrants, particularly Latinos, are disproportionately uninsured, they were important targets of insurance expansion efforts, but other factors, discussed below, may be making it hard to reach immigrant communities effectively.

Three major components of the law were

- Medicaid Expansion for Adults. Prior to the ACA, most states did not provide Medicaid to adults without dependent children, no matter how poor. In addition, most states have established Medicaid or State Children's Health Insurance Program (SCHIP) income eligibility for children at or above 200% of the poverty line. The ACA was designed to expand Medicaid for nonelderly adults up to 138 percent of the poverty line, including parents and childless adults. However, in the summer of 2012, the Supreme Court ruled that states had the option whether to expand Medicaid or not (*National Federation of Independent Business v. Sebelius*, 567 U.S.__, 132 S. Ct 2566).

- Health Insurance Exchanges and Federal Tax Credits. The ACA also established the development of health insurance exchanges (also called marketplaces), which are Internet-based marketplaces where individuals and small business can shop for health insurance. The marketplaces are divided into those for individuals and families and those for enrolling through small businesses (the Small Business Health Options Program or SHOP). Individuals who are not otherwise eligible for insurance (e.g., through an employer) and who purchase insurance through an exchange are eligible for federal tax credits if they have incomes between 100 percent and 400 percent of the poverty line. In states that expand Medicaid, the subsidy range is generally 138 percent to 400 percent of the poverty line. There are exchanges in all states, but only about one-third were established by state agencies. The others were established in whole or in part by the federal government because the state in question chose not to create an exchange.

- Individual Responsibility. The ACA also established a requirement that people must either have insurance or face a tax penalty, unless insurance is otherwise unaffordable. The Supreme Court upheld the constitutionality of this requirement.

In all three areas, there are differences in policies for immigrants based

---

[5] See http://www.hhs.gov/healthcare/facts/timeline/timeline-text.html [September 2015].

on legal status. The ACA clearly states that the undocumented are not eligible for the health insurance exchanges nor for the federal tax credits that accompany them, and they remain ineligible for Medicaid. This applies even for those who receive a temporary reprieve from deportation and work authorization through the Deferred Action for Childhood Arrivals (DACA) provisions. Nonetheless, the ACA creates major opportunities to increase health insurance coverage for *legal-status* noncitizen immigrants. The ACA makes millions of "lawfully present" immigrants eligible for the health exchanges and the federal tax credits on the same terms as citizens, which could greatly expand access to private insurance coverage (Ku, 2013). The "lawfully present" standard is broader than the prior legal standards established for Medicaid eligibility. All lawful permanent residents, including those who have been in the United States for less than 5 years, are "lawfully present" under the ACA and are eligible for exchanges and tax credits. In addition, many lawful noncitizens who lack LPR status are also lawfully present and eligible for the exchanges and tax credits, although there is a length-of-residency requirement (see Table 3-2 in Chapter 3). Lawfully present immigrants with incomes under 100 percent or 138 percent of poverty who are otherwise ineligible for Medicaid are also eligible for health exchanges and federal tax credits. Data from the Department of Homeland Security indicate that in 2011 there were about 4 million LPRs who were residents for under 5 years and 1.9 million "nonimmigrant" residents, such as those with work visas (Rytina, 2013). Thus, a conservative estimate is that as many as 6 million noncitizen immigrants may have gained eligibility for private health insurance coverage through health insurance exchanges under the ACA.

Preliminary Effects of the ACA on Immigrants' Insurance Coverage

Since the ACA insurance expansions only began in January 2014, it is likely that the full impact of this law will not be known for many years, as implementation continues and as evidence accumulates. Analysts, including the Congressional Budget Office,[6] generally expect enrollment in the health insurance exchanges and Medicaid to continue to gradually increase, as familiarity with the programs grows and administrative and political kinks are ironed out (Holohan, 2012). Nonetheless, some evidence has begun to accumulate about preliminary insurance enrollment and the effects on health insurance coverage. The key evidence falls into two categories: administrative reports and early household surveys. Both forms of evidence indicate that millions of people enrolled in health insurance exchanges and

---

[6]For Congressional Budget Office Baseline Projections, see https://www.cbo.gov/publication/43900 [September 2015].

that Medicaid enrollment has increased, particularly in states that expanded Medicaid eligibility (Blumenthal and Collins, 2014; Sommers et al., 2013, 2014a). Early household surveys have revealed that the percentage of the population that is uninsured has declined significantly between 2013 and 2014 (Blumenthal and Collins, 2014).

None of the early published reports document the extent to which immigrants have enrolled or gained insurance coverage (aside from press releases about documentation of citizenship status, discussed below). Some inferences may be drawn based on data about enrollment or insurance coverage of Latinos or Asian Americans, since the majority of U.S. immigrants are Latino or Asian. But inferences about immigration status are inherently imperfect because of the lack of actual data on immigrant or citizenship status. Substantial shares of the Latino and Asian immigrants (first generation) in the United States are either naturalized citizens or have lawful status. In general, these studies have found that, while health reform has led to substantial improvements in overall health insurance coverage, including gains for Latinos (Doty et al., 2014) and Asians (Ramakrishnan and Ahmad, 2014), there is some evidence that improvements for Latinos have lagged behind those of other groups (Doty et al., 2014; Ortega et al., 2015).

Administrative data indicate that between October 2013 and March 2014 over 8 million people enrolled (selected a health plan) in health insurance exchanges. A federal report provided racial/ethnic statistics for the 5.4 million who were enrolled in health insurance programs through the federally facilitated exchanges: 7.4 percent were Latino and 5.5 percent were Asian, but 31 percent of people did not report race/ethnicity (Office of the Assistant Secretary for Planning and Evaluation, 2013). By comparison, Ku (2014) found that Latinos constituted 17 percent of the U.S. population and 32 percent of the uninsured, while Asians were 5 percent of the population and 5 percent of the uninsured population. Thus, Latinos appear to be underrepresented in the federally facilitated exchanges, whereas Asian enrollment through these exchanges appears to be roughly in proportion to the overall population. Ku (2014) also reported that in California, a state-based exchange with the largest program in the nation, of the 1.0 million who enrolled by March 2014, 28 percent of exchange enrollees were Latino and 21 percent were Asian (4% did not report race/ethnicity). For California, Ku found that 38 percent of the population and 57 percent of the uninsured are Latino, while 14 percent of the population and 12 percent of the uninsured are Asian. Latinos in California therefore appear underrepresented in that state's enrollment through its exchange, while Asians appear somewhat overrepresented.

Medicaid administrative data show that Medicaid enrollment grew by 7.7 million (or 12.4%) from July-September 2013 to June 2014. The growth was much larger—6.3 million new enrollees or 18.5 percent—in the 26 states (and the District of Columbia) expanding Medicaid under the provisions of the ACA than in the 24 states that chose not expand Medicaid (approximately 1 million new enrollees total, or 4.0% growth rate) (Centers for Medicare & Medicaid Services, 2014). Data about changes in enrollment by race/ethnicity or immigration status are not yet available from the Centers for Medicare & Medicaid. Since a large proportion of uninsured people are in low-income households, it is plausible to expect higher minority participation as a result of Medicaid expansions (and publicity about health reform in general), but the relevant Medicaid administrative data to investigate this expectation are not yet available.

Household surveys, based on self-reported insurance status, are another way to gain insights about changes in insurance coverage. Typically, these data are reported on an annual basis after a survey-year has ended. For example, Census Bureau data for 2014 insurance status will probably be available in August or September 2015. But the nationwide interest in health reform has prompted the release of early findings based on the first few months of 2014.[7]

The largest of these early reports national daily poll on health issues, the Gallup-Healthways Well-being Index survey of households found that, among adults 18-64, the percentage uninsured fell from 21 percent in September 2013 to 16.3 percent in April of 2014, a decline of to 5.2 percent (Sommers et al, 2014b). Among Latinos, the percent uninsured fell by from 41.8 percent 2012 to 34.1 percent in 2014, an 18 percent reduction in the Hispanic insurance rate, see Figure 9-2). Among white non-Hispanics there was a 28 percent reduction in the uninsured rate, and a 30 percent reduction in the black non-Hispanic uninsured rate (Figure 9-2). Although the overall percentage point reduction was larger for Hispanics than for non-Hispanic white or black populations, the relative reduction in the uninsured was therefore smaller for Latinos The report on the early-month data from the survey also found that the reduction in the percent uninsured was much greater in states that expanded Medicaid in accordance with the ACA than in those states that chose not to expand.

The Urban Institute's Health Reform Monitoring Surveys provide a slightly different perspective from the Gallup-Healthways Well-being Index survey. Shartzer et al. (2014) compared characteristics of adults 18-64 who were uninsured in September 2013 with those who remained uninsured in June 2014. When the authors compared the uninsured by Hispanic ethnicity, the found that among all adults who were uninsured, the proportion who were Hispanic grew from 33 percent in 2013 to 37 percent in 2014. Similarly, the share of the uninsured who were primarily Spanish-speaking

---

[7]See http://kff.org/health-reform/poll-finding/data-note-measuring-aca-early-impact-through-national-polls/ [November 2015].

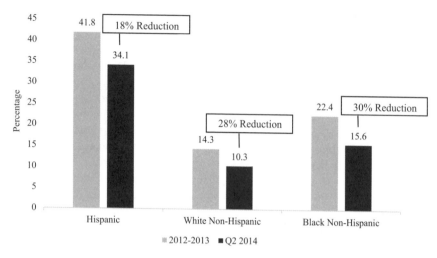

FIGURE 9-2 Changes in percentage of uninsured among adults, ages 18-64, following ACA Insurance Expansions, Gallup-Healthways Survey.
SOURCE: Data from Sommers et al. (2014). Original content from Ku (2014).

rose from 17 percent to 20 percent. Overall, self-identified Hispanic and Spanish-speaking adults had fewer improvements in insurance status than other ethnoracial groups. Since Spanish-speaking adults are particularly likely to be immigrants, this also indicates that insurance gains for Latinos lagged behind those of other groups.

Two other early reports have different results, however. The Commonwealth Fund's Affordable Care Act Tracking Survey[8] found larger reductions in the share of Latino adults who were uninsured than for white or black adults: the percentage of uninsured Latinos fell from 36 percent to 23 percent between July-September 2013 and April-June 2014, while the percentage of uninsured among white adults decreased from 16 percent to 12 percent and the percentage uninsured among blacks only decreased from 21 percent to 20 percent (Collins et al., 2014). Overall changes in the proportion of adults who were uninsured and the differences between Medicaid-expanding and non-expanding states in this survey were relatively

---

[8] The Affordable Care Act Tracking Survey examined the effect if ACA's open enrollment by interviewing nationally representative samples of 19-to-64-year-old adults at various points in time before and after open enrollment began. The April-June 2014 survey was conducted after the end of the second enrollment period and included a sample of adults who either had ACA marketplace or Medicaid coverage or might be eligible for that coverage. For further information on the methodology, see http://www.commonwealthfund.org/publications/issue-briefs/2015/jun/experiences-marketplace-and-medicaid [November 2015].

similar to the results reported above from other surveys, so it is not clear why there is a discrepancy in the race/ethnicity results.

Early results from the Centers for Disease Control and Prevention's National Health Interview Survey (NHIS) also show a somewhat larger expansion in insurance coverage for Latinos than whites or Asians, though less than for black adults (Figure 9-3) (Cohen and Martinez, 2014). As illustrated in Figure 9-3, the relative share of uninsured Latinos fell by 12 percent between 2013 and the first quarter of 2014, compared to a 7 percent reduction for white non-Hispanics, 19 percent for black non-Hispanics, and 4 percent for Asians. The NHIS data also suggest that the gains in insurance coverage for Latinos were related to increases in both public and private insurance coverage. Like the other surveys, the NHIS data indicate there were changes in the overall insurance coverage of adults and larger gains in Medicaid expansion states than states not currently expanding. The discrepancy in results across the surveys with respect to health insurance coverage of Latinos is puzzling and indicates that we will need to wait for more detailed analyses and longer survey periods to get clear insights into differences in insurance status changes by race or ethnicity or changes by immigrant status.

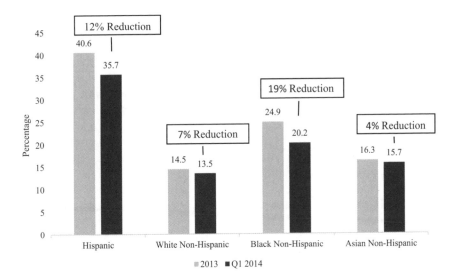

FIGURE 9-3 Changes in percentage of uninsured among adults, ages 18-64, following ACA Insurance Expansions, National Health Interview Survey.
SOURCE: Data from Cohen and Martinez (2014). Original content from Ku (2014).

Implementation Challenges

Initiating new programs can be challenging, and there is no question that the implementation of the ACA has been rocky. There were specific challenges that may have deterred participation by immigrants, most notably Latino immigrants, particularly at the beginning. First, eligibility and application policies and procedures about the new health insurance exchanges were complicated, and the rules about immigrant eligibility were especially complex. These rules were poorly understood not only by the public but even by public-sector and nonprofit-sector workers providing guidance on eligibility (Raymond-Flesch, 2015). Second, immigrants, especially those with limited English proficiency, had limited experience with the use of public benefits, including the concept of insurance; often live in immigrant enclaves, and may be socially isolated from other sources of information about public benefits (Perreira et al., 2012), even though the Navigator Program did attempt to address these challenges.[9] Third, as noted by Weissberg (2014), the websites designed to facilitate enrollment in the health insurance marketplaces and Medicaid were generally English-only, particularly at the beginning. Although the federal government eventually released a Spanish version of its healthcare.gov website, it was criticized for faulty translations and difficulty of use.

Another potential challenge has been the citizenship verification process (Perreira et al., 2012). Because the undocumented are prohibited by law from participating in the ACA exchanges, everyone who has who applied for insurance coverage via the exchanges has had to verify their citizenship/immigration status. A similar requirement already existed for Medicaid enrollment. If the data match process in the online system could not confirm that a person was a citizen or lawfully present immigrant, additional documentation was requested from the exchange user, even though that user may have entered the exchange on a provisional basis. However, the federal databases of citizens and lawfully present noncitizens are neither fully accurate nor up to date, and as of this report's publication, many states continued to experience challenges with citizenship verification (Weiss and Sheedy, 2015).

Finally, there are variations in access by state: California, Massachusetts, and New York, for example, allow people with DACA status to receive Medicaid services under that state's expansion of Medicaid. Most states do not have this policy. Given these challenges and the gradual mitigation of some of them over time, it will be important to continuing monitoring the response to ACA and its long-term effects in reducing the number

---

[9] See http://icirr.org/content/immigrant-communities-face-major-barriers-navigating-affordable-care-act [November 2015].

of uninsured and increasing access to health care for immigrant adults and children (both citizens and lawfully present noncitizens), including patterns of state variation in the insurance coverage and the relationships between those patterns and states' policies.

Although the ACA includes provisions that can help improve insurance coverage for millions of eligible immigrants, it is not clear how effective these policies have been in reaching this target population. This is partly due to the fact that the inevitable confusion that plagues initiation of any major policy made it harder to reach target populations in the first year of ACA implementation. In addition, a number of special barriers are likely to continue for immigrants, barriers that make it harder for them to be aware of or to apply for health insurance, even if they are uninsured and eligible under the law in its final form. These include language barriers, cultural misunderstanding, and fears about how a request for public benefits for which they may be eligible could jeopardize their immigration status. A combination of administrative remedies, such as better training of staff, bilingual or multilingual websites, enrollment information in multiple languages, and the availability of sufficiently knowledgeable and welcoming outreach and enrollment staff to help explain the new systems could reduce these barriers over time. Many of these remedies could be accomplished through the Navigator Program.

Immigrants' integration into American society tends to produce mixed results when health issues are considered. In general, immigrants tend to have a better health profile than the native-born, but there is evidence of a decline over time on a variety of health indicators. The flip side of this condition is that immigrants are more likely to access health insurance and health care, the more integrated they are into American society. Early data indicate that the ACA will help provide health insurance to immigrants who had not been previously covered, with the exception of undocumented immigrants. This may improve health outcomes for immigrants and their descendants, although any improvement will be conditioned on legal status. Finally, while health insurance is important, an insurance card by itself does not, in the United States at least, guarantee access to good quality health care.

TWO-WAY EXCHANGE

Integration involves a reciprocal relationship between immigrants and society. Immigrants make an indelible impact on public health in the United States, and three areas are especially noteworthy in this regard. First, immigrants contribute to the health of the U.S. population. For instance, Preston and Elo (2014) found that, from 1990 to 2010, life expectancy in New York City rose by 6.25 years for females and 10.49 years for males.

The gains for the rest of the United States were much smaller by comparison: 2.39 years for females and 4.49 years for males. The authors concluded that the influx of immigrants into New York City contributed substantially to this increase in longevity.

Given that immigrants have a health advantage when they first arrive, their higher life expectancy also offer clues about cultural practices that lead to healthy lifestyles. Satia (2009) noted that traditional diets that include organic fresh fruits and vegetables, fewer fatty foods, and lower reliance on fast foods and sugary drinks are associated with lower rates of obesity, cancers, hypertension, and heart disease. Immigrants have also brought with them different forms of stress relief and healing that have become relatively common in American life and in some health care practices, including acupuncture, yoga, tai-chi, meditation, and mindfulness.

At a global level, immigrants contribute to the health care workforce, but the extent of the contribution, measured in numbers of immigrants in the care provider population, varies by country. The United States falls in the middle of the global range for proportion of immigrants among nurses and, among OECD countries, at the higher end of the range for immigrants among physicians (OECD, 2007). These immigrants fill a pressing need because of the shortage of health care personnel in the United States (Schumacher, 2010). Foreign-born physicians, for example, fill a critical need for primary care physicians in rural and underserved areas (Hart et al, 2007). In 2010, about 11.1 million people in the United States were employed in health care occupations and 1.8 million or 16 percent were foreign-born. Immigrants were disproportionately represented among both lower skilled nursing aids and doctors (Singer, 2012). The foreign-born were 16 percent of registered nurses and 27 percent of the physicians and surgeons. Among the immigrant health care workforce, 75 percent were women and 40 percent came from Asian countries (McCabe, 2012). About a third of all registered nurses come from the Philippines (Schumacher, 2011). In 2010, approximately 66 percent of all immigrants in the U.S. health care workforce were naturalized citizens, including 70 percent of physicians and 72 percent of registered nurses. It is expected that immigrants will continue to make contributions to the health care workforce in the future, especially in long-term care (Lowell, 2013; McCabe, 2012). Long-term care, which allows people to live independently as possible when they can no longer perform everyday activities on their own, will increase in importance as the proportion of older adults in the United States increases (Institute of Medicine, 2008).

A frequently overlooked health contribution of immigrants is their support of Medicare. Medicare is the federal health insurance program for people 65 years and older, for certain younger people with long-term disabilities, and for people who have permanent kidney failure requiring dialysis or a transplant. More than 50 million Americans rely on Medicare as their primary health coverage. Zallman (2014) found that immigrants contribute more to Medicare than they receive in benefits. From 1996 to 2011, the contribution immigrants made to the Medical Hospital Insurance Trust Fund exceeded the benefits they received by $182.4 billion. By comparison, the native-born population produced an overall deficit in this part of Medicare of $68.7 billion over the same period. Without the contributions of immigrants to Medicare, the trust fund would be expected to become insolvent by the end of 2027 or 3 years earlier than currently estimated by the Medicare Trustees (Zallman, 2014).

Immigrants' positive impact on health care expenditures and the health care system may extend beyond Medicare. For instance, per capita health care expenditures for immigrants are 55% lower than expenditures for the native-born (Mohanty et al., 2005), and insured immigrants have much lower medical expenses than insured native-born, implying that immigrants' premiums may help subsidize insurance rates for the native-born (Ku, 2009). The taxes immigrants pay also contribute to funding for Medicaid, Title X for family planning, local health departments, and community clinics that serve both immigrants and the native-born.

SUMMARY AND CONCLUSIONS

Across various measures, immigrants in the United States are healthier than the native-born. The foreign-born show better infant, child, and adult health outcomes than the U.S.-born population in general and better outcomes than U.S.-born members of their ethnic group. In comparison with native-born Americans, the foreign born are less likely to die from cardiovascular disease and all cancers combined; they experience fewer chronic health conditions, lower infant mortality rates, lower rates of obesity, fewer functional limitations, and fewer learning disabilities. Immigrants also have a lower prevalence of depression, the most common mental disorder in the world, and of alcohol abuse. Foreign-born immigrants also live longer: they have a life expectancy of 80.0 years, 3.4 years higher than the native-born population. Across the major ethnic categories (non-Hispanic whites, blacks, Asian/Pacific Islanders, and Hispanics), immigrants have a life expectancy advantage over their native-born counterparts. However, these advantages diminish over time.

Conclusion 9-1 As length of residence and generational status increase, health advantages decline as their health status converges with the native-born. Further research should be done to identify the causal links between integration and health outcomes.

Conclusion 9-2 Immigrants are disadvantaged when it comes to receiving health care to meet their preventive and medical health needs. The ACA should improve this situation for lawfully present immigrants and naturalized citizens, but the undocumented are specifically excluded from all coverage under the ACA. In addition, the undocumented are not entitled to any nonemergency care in U.S. hospitals. Legal status therefore restricts access to health care, which may have detrimental effects for all immigrants' health.

Although past empirical studies have built a solid foundation for understanding the health status and access to health care among immigrants, most of this work has used cross-sectional studies that make it difficult to draw firm conclusions about the causal mechanisms for the demonstrated associations, how immigrants become integrated into U.S. society and its health care systems, and the factors that affect the pace at which this integration occurs. Equally important, it is difficult to determine what specific changes in norms, values, and lifestyles are associated with changes in health status and the use of health care, and what the impact of the policy climate is on health outcomes. Longitudinal studies, such as the New Immigrant Survey (http://nis.princeton.edu/project.html [November 2015]), that can track immigrants over time provide critical scientific and policy insights about immigrant integration and health outcomes (see Chapter 10).

REFERENCES

Abe-Kim, J., Takeuchi, D.T., Hong, S., Zane, N., Sue, S., Spencer, M.S., Appel, H., Nicdao, E., and Alegria, M. (2007). Use of mental health–related services among immigrant and native-born Asian Americans: Results from the National Latino and Asian American Study. *American Journal of Public Health, 97*(1), 91-98.

Abraido-Lanza, A.F., Dohrenwend, B.P., Ng-Mak, D.S., and Turner, J.B. (1999). The Latino mortality paradox: A test of the "salmon bias" and healthy migrant hypothesis. *American Journal of Public Health, 89*(10), 1543-1548.

Abraido-Lanza, A.F., Chao, M.T., and Flores, K.R. (2005). Do healthy behaviors decline with greater acculturation? Implications for the Latino mortality paradox. *Social Science and Medicine, 71*, 1243-1255.

Acevedo-Garcia, D., Mah-J. Soobader, M-J., and Berkman, L.F. (2007). Low birthweight among U.S. Hispanic/Latino subgroups: The effect of maternal foreign-born status and education. *Social Science and Medicine, 65*, 2503-2517.

Acevedo-Garcia, D., Bates, L.M., and Osypuk, T.L. (2010). The effect of immigrant generation and duration on self-rated health among U.S. adults 2003-2007. *Social Science and Medicine, 71*(6), 1161-1172.

Adler, N.E., Boyce, T., Cheshey, M.A., Cohen, S., Folkman, S., Kahn, R.L., and Syme, L.S. (1994). Socioeconomic status and health: The challenge of the gradient. *American Psychologist, 49*, 15-24.

Aguirre, B.E., and Saenz, R. (2002). Testing the effects of collectively expected durations of migration: The naturalization of Mexicans and Cubans. *International Migration Review*, 36, 103-124.

Akresh, I.R., and Frank, R. (2008). Health selection among new immigrants. *American Journal of Public Health*, 98(1), 2058-2064.

Alegria, M., Mulvaney-Day N., Torres, M., Polo, A., Cao, Z., and Canino, G. (2007a). Prevalence of psychiatric disorders across Latino subgroups in the United States. *American Journal of Public Health*, 97(1), 68-75.

Alegria, M., Mulvaney-Day, N., Woo, M., Torres, M., Gao, S., and Oddo, V. (2007b). Correlates of past-year mental health service use among Latinos: Results from the National Latino and Asian American Study. *American Journal of Public Health*, 97(1), 76-83.

Ali, J. (2002). *Mental Health of Canada's Immigrants*. Supplement to Health Reports, Volume 13. Ottawa: Health Statistics Division, Statistics Canada. Available: http://www.statcan. gc.ca/pub/82-003-s/2002001/pdf/82-003-s2002006-eng.pdf [October 2015].

Barcellos, S.H., Goldman, D.P., and Smith, J.P. (2012). Undiagnosed disease, especially diabetes, cast doubt on some of the reported health "advantage" of recent Mexican immigrants. *Health Affairs*, 31(12), 2727-2737.

Bécares, L., Shaw, R., Nazroo, J., Stafford, M., Albor, C., Atkin, K., Kierman, K., Wilkinson, R., and Pickett, K. (2012). Ethnic density effects on physical morbidity, mortality, and health behaviors: A systematic review of the literature. *American Journal of Public Health*, 102(12), e33-e66.

Birman, D., Beehler, S., Harris, E.M., Everson, M.L., Batia, K., Liautaud, J., Frazier, S., Atkins, M., Blanton, S., Buwalda, J., Fogg, L., and Cappella, E. (2008). International Family, Adult, and Child Enhancement Services (FACES): A community-based comprehensive services model for refugee children in resettlement. *American Journal of Orthopsychiatry*, 78(1), 121-132.

Bloemraad, R. (2000). Citizenship and immigration: a current review. *Journal of International Migration and Integration*, 1, 9-37.

Blue, L., and Fenelon, A. (2011). Explaining low mortality among U.S. immigrants relative to native-born Americans: The role of smoking. *International Journal of Epidemiology*, 40(3), 786-793.

Blumenthal, D., and Collins, S.R. (2014). Health care coverage under the Affordable Care Act—A progress report. *New England Journal of Medicine*, 371(3), 275-281.

Bosdriesz, J.R., Lichthart, N., Witvliet, W.B., Busschers, K.S. Stronks, K. and Kunst, A.E. (2013) Smoking prevalence among migrants in the U.S. compared to the native born and the population in countries of origin. *PLoS ONE*, 8(3), e58654.

Brown, J.M., Council, C.L., Penne, M.A., and Gfroerer, J.C. (2005). *Immigrants and Substance Use: Findings from the 1999-2001 National Surveys on Drug Use and Health*. DHHS Publication No. SMA 04-3909, Analytic Series A-23. Rockville, MD: Substance Abuse and Mental Health Services Administration.

Burton, L.M., Kemp, S., Leung, M., Matthews, S.A. and Takeuchi, D. (2011). (Eds.). (2011). *Communities, Neighborhoods, and Health: Expanding the Boundaries of Place*. New York: Springer-Verlag.

Buttenheim, A., Goldman, N., Pebley, A.R., Wong, R. and Chung, C. (2010). Do Mexican immigrants "import" social gradients in health to the U.S.? *Social Science & Medicine*, 7, 1268-1276.

Cantu, P.A., Hayward, M.D., Hummer, R.A., and Chiu, C-T. (2013). New estimates of racial/ethnic differences in life expectancy with chronic morbidity and functional loss: Evidence from the National Health Interview Survey. *Journal of Cross Cultural Gerontology*, 28, 283-297.

Carswell, K., Blackburn, P., and Barker, C. (2011). The relationship between trauma, post-migration problems and the psychological well-being of refugee and asylum seekers. *International Journal of Social Psychiatry, 57*, 1007.

Centers for Disease Control and Prevention. (2011). *Obesity: Halting the Epidemic by Making Health Easier.* Atlanta, GA: Author.

Centers for Medicare & Medicaid Services. (2014). *Medicaid and CHIP: June 2014 Monthly Applications Eligibility Determinations and Enrollment Report.* Washington, DC: Author.

Chaufan, C., Constantino, S., and Davis, M. (2012). "It's a full time job being poor": Understanding barriers to diabetes prevention in immigrant communities in the USA. *Critical Public Health, 22*(2), 147-158.

Chen, S.X., Benet-Martinez, V., and Bond, M.H. (2008). Bicultural identity, bilingualism, and psychological adjustment in multicultural societies: Immigration-based and globalization-based acculturation. *Journal of Personality, 76*(4), 803-838.

Clough, J., Lee, S., and Chae, D.H. (2013). Barriers to health care among Asian immigrants in the United States: A traditional view. *Journal of Health Care for the Poor and Underserved, 24*(1), 384-403.

Cohen, R., and Martinez, M. (2014). *Health Insurance Coverage: Early Reports of Estimates from the National Health Interview Survey, January-March 2014.* Atlanta, GA: Centers for Disease Control and Prevention.

Collins, S., Rasmussen, P., and Doty, M. (2014). *Gaining Ground: Americans' Health Insurance Coverage and Access to Care after the Affordable Care Act's First Open Enrollment Period.* New York: Commonwealth Fund.

Conley, D. (1999). *Being Black, Being in the Red: Race, Wealth and Social Policy in America.* Oakland: University of California Press.

Cristancho, S., Garces, D.M., Peters, K.E., and Mueller, B.C. (2008). Listening to rural Hispanic immigrants in the Midwest: A community-based participatory assessment of major barriers to health care access and use. *Qualitative Health Research, 18*(5), 633-646.

Crowley, M., and Lichter, D.T. (2009). Social disorganization in new Latino destinations. *Rural Sociology, 74*(4), 573-604.

Dang, B.N., Van Dessel, L., Hanke, J., and Hilliard, M.A. (2011). Birth outcomes among low-income women—documented and undocumented. *The Permanente Journal, 15*(2), 39-43.

Derose, K.P., Escarce, J.J., and Lurie, N. (2007). Immigrants and health care: Sources of vulnerability. *Health Affairs, 26*(5), 1258-1268.

Derose, K.P., Bahne, B.W., Lurie, N. and Escarce, J.J. (2009). Review: Immigrants and health care access, quality and costs. *Medical Care Research and Review, 66*(4), 355-408.

Domnich, A., Panatto, D., Gasparini, R. and Amicizia, D. (2012). The "healthy immigrant" effect: Does it exist in Europe today? *Italian Journal of Public Health, 9*(3), 1-7.

Doty, M.M., Blumenthal, D., and Collins, S.R. (2014). The Affordable Care Act and health insurance for Latinos. *Journal of the American Medical Association, 312*(17), 1735-1736.

DuBard, C.A., and Massing, M.W. (2007). Trends in emergency Medicaid expenditures for recent and undocumented immigrants. *Journal of the American Medical Association, 297*(10), 1085-1092.

Dubowitz, T., Bates, L.M., and Acevedo-Garcia, D. (2010). The Latino health paradox: Looking at the intersection of sociology and health. In C.E. Bird, P. Conrad, A.M. Fremont, and S. Timmermans (Eds.), *Handbook of Medical Sociology* (pp. 106-123). Nashville, TN: Vanderbilt University Press.

Edgerter, S., Braverman, P., Sadegh-Nobari, T., Grossman-Kahn, R., and Dekker, M. (2011). *Education and Health: Exploring the Social Determinants of Health.* Issue Brief #5. Princeton, NJ: Robert Wood Johnson Foundation.

Erez, E. (2000). Immigration, culture conflict and domestic violence/woman battering. *Crime Prevention and Community Safety: An International Journal*, 2(1), 27-36.

Farmer, M.M., and Ferraro, K. F. (2005). Are racial disparities in health conditional on socio-economic status? *Social Science & Medicine*, 60, 191-204.

Finch, B.K., and Vega, W.A. (2003). Acculturation stress, social support, and self-rated health among Latinos in California. *Journal of Immigrant Health*, 5(3),109-117.

Flores, G. (2006). Language barriers to health care in the United States. *New England Journal of Medicine*, 355(3), 229-231.

Garb, M. (2003). Health, morality, and housing: The "tenement problem" in Chicago. *American Journal of Public Health*, 93(9), 1420-1430.

Gee, G.C., Ryan, A., Laflamme, D.J., and Holt, J. (2006). Self-reported discrimination and mental health status among African descendants, Mexican Americans, and other Latinos in the New Hampshire REACH 2010 initiative: The added dimension of immigration. *American Journal of Public Health*, 96(10), 1821-1828.

Gee, G.C., Ro, A., Shariff-Marco, S., and Chae, D. (2009). Racial discrimination and health among Asian Americans: Evidence, assessment, and directions for future research. *Epidemiologic Reviews*, 31, 130-151.

Gee, G.C., Walsemann, K.M., and Takeuchi, D.T. (2010). English proficiency and language preference: Testing the equivalence of two measures. *American Journal of Public Health*, 100(3), 563-569.

Gieryn, T. (2000). A space for place in sociology. *Annual Review of Sociology*, 26, 463-496.

Goldman, N., Kimbro, R.T., Turra, C.M., and Pebley, A.R. (2006). Socioeconomic gradients in health for white and Mexican-origin populations. *American Journal of Public Health*, 96, 2186-2193.

Gonzales-Barrera, A., Lopez, M.H., Passel, J., and Taylor, P. (2013). *The Path Not Taken: Two-Thirds of Legal Mexican Immigrants Are Not U.S. Citizens*. Washington, DC: Pew Hispanic Center.

Gonzales, R.G., Suarez-Orozco, C., and Dedios-Sanguineti, M.C. (2013). No place to belong: Contextualizing concepts of mental health among undocumented immigrant youth in the United States. *American Behavioral Scientist*, 57(8), 1174-1199.

Gordon-Larsen, P., Harris, K.M., Ward, D.S., and Popkin, B.M. (2003). Acculturation and overweight-related behaviors among Hispanic immigrants to the U.S.: The National Longitudinal Study of Adolescent Health. *Social Science & Medicine*, 57(11), 2023-2034.

Gubernskaya, Z., Bean, F.D., and Van Hook, J. (2013). (Un)healthy immigrant citizens: naturalization and activity limitations in older age. *Journal of Health and Social Behavior*, 54(4), 427-443.

Gurak, D., and Kritz, M. (2013). Elderly immigrants in rural America: Trends and characteristics. In N. Glasgow and F.H. Berry (Eds.), *Rural Aging in the 21st Century* (pp. 331-352). New York: Springer-Verlag.

Habraken, J. (1998). *The Structure of the Ordinary: Form and Control in the Built Environment*. Cambridge, MA: MIT Press.

Hall, M., and Greenman, E. (2014). The occupational cost of being illegal in the United States: Legal status, job hazards, and compensating differentials. *International Migration Review, Fall*, 1-37.

Hart, L.G., Skillman, S.M., Fordyce, M., Thompson, M., Hagopian, A., and Konrad, T.R. (2007). International medical graduate physicians in the United States: Changes since 1981. *Health Affairs*, 26(4), 1159-1169.

Hayward, M., Hummer, R.A., Chiu, C-T., Gonzalez-Gonzalez, C., and Wong, R. (2014). Does the Hispanic paradox in the U.S. adult mortality extend to disability? *Population Research Policy Review*, 33, 81-96.

Heyman, J.M., Núñez, G.G., and Talavera, V. (2009). Healthcare access and barriers for unauthorized immigrants in El Paso County, Texas. *Family and Community Health*, 32(1), 4-21.

Hollifield, M., Warner, T.D., Lian, N., Krakow, B., Kesler, J., Stevenson, J., and Westermeyer, J. (2002). Measuring trauma and health status in refugees: A critical review. *Journal of the American Medical Association*, 288, 611-621.

Holahan, J. (2012). *The Cost and Coverage Implications of the ACA Medicaid Expansion: National and State-by-State Analysis*. Washington, DC: Urban Institute.

Institute of Medicine. (2008). *Retooling for an Aging America: Building the Health Care Workforce*. Committee on the Future Health Care Workforce for Older Americans, Board on Health Care Services. Washington, DC: The National Academies Press.

Islam, F. (2013). Examining the healthy immigrant effect for mental health in Canada. *University of Toronto Medical Journal*, 90(4), 169-175.

Jackson, J.S., Neighbors, H.W., Torres, M., Martin, L.A., Williams, D.R. and Baser, R. (2007). Use of mental health services and subjective satisfaction with treatment among black Caribbean immigrants: Results from the National Survey of American Life. *American Journal of Public Health*, 97(1), 680-687.

Jasso, G., Massey, D.S., Rosenzweig, M.R., and Smith, J.P. (2004). Immigrant health: Selectivity and acculturation. In National Research Council, *Critical Perspectives on Racial and Ethnic Differences in Health in Late Life* (pp. 227-266). N.B. Anderson, R.A. Bulatao, and B. Cohen (Eds.), Panel on Race, Ethnicity, and Health in Later Life. Committee on Population, Division of Behavioral and Social Sciences and Education. Washington, DC: The National Academies Press.

Keyes, E. (2000). Mental health status in refugees: An integrative review of current research. *Issues in Mental Health Nursing*, 21, 397-410.

Kelaher, M., and Jessop, D.J. (2002). Differences in low-birthweight among documented and undocumented foreign-born and native-born Latinas. *Social Science & Medicine*, 55(12), 2171-2175.

Kimbro, R.T., Bzostek, S., Goldman, N., and Rodriguez, G. (2008). Race, ethnicity, and the educational gradient in health. *Health Affairs*, 27, 361-372.

Kimbro, R.T., Gorman, B.K. and Schachter, A. (2012). Acculturation and self-rated health among Latino and Asian immigrants to the United States. *Social Problems*, 59(3), 341-363.

Korinek, K., and Smith, K.R. (2011). Prenatal care among immigrant and racial-ethnic minority women in a new immigrant destination: Exploring the impact of immigrant legal status. *Social Science & Medicine*, 72(10), 1695-1703.

Ku, L. (2009). Medical and dental utilization and expenditures under Medicaid and private health insurance. *Medical Care Research and Review*, 66(4), 456-471.

Ku, L. (2013). *Strengthening Immigrants' Health Access: Current Opportunities*. Issue Brief Washington, DC: George Washington University. Available: http://publichealth.gwu.edu/pdf/hp/current_opportunities_for_immigrants.pdf [October 2015].

Ku, L. (2014). *Immigrants' Access to Health Insurance and Care: The Role of Health Reform*. Washington, DC: George Washington University.

Ku, L., and Matani, S. (2001). Left out: Immigrants' access to health care and insurance. *Health Affairs*, 20(1), 247-256.

Landale, N.S., Hardie, J.H., Oropesa, R.S. and Hillemeier, M.M. (2015a). Behavioral functioning among Mexican-origin children: Does parental legal status matter? *Journal of Health and Social Behavior*, 56(1), 2-18.

Landale, N.S., Hardie, J.H., Oropesa, R.S. and Hillemeir, M.M. (2015b). Policy Brief. *Journal of Health and Social Behavior*, 56(1), 1.

Larisey, J.T., Hummer, R.A., Rath, J.M., Vallanti, A.C., Hayward, M.D. and Vallone, D.M. (2013). Race/ethnicity, nativity, and tobacco use among U.S. young adults: Results from a nationally representative sample. *Nicotine and Tobacco Research*, 15, 1417-1426.

Lauderdale, D.S., Wen, M., Jacobs, E.A., and Kandula, N.R. (2006). Immigrant perceptions of discrimination in health care: The California Health Interview Survey 2003. *Medical Care*, 44(10), 914-920.

Lee, M.J., and Liechty, J.M. (2014). Longitudinal associations between immigrant density, neighborhood processes, and Latino immigrant youth depression. *Journal of Immigrant and Minority Health*, 17(4), 983-991.

Leu, J., Yen, I.H., Ganskey, S.A., Walton, E., Adler, N., and Takeuchi, D.T. (2008). The association between subjective social status and mental health among Asian immigrants: Investigating the influence of age at immigration. *Social Science & Medicine*, 66, 1152-1164.

Lowell, L. (2013). The foreign born in the American healthcare workforce: Trends in this century's first decade. *Migration Letters*, 10(2), 180-190.

Lustig, S., Kia-Keating, M., Knight, W., Geltman, P., Ellis, H., Kinzie, D., Keane, T., and Saxe, G. (2004). Review of child and adolescent refugee mental health. *Journal of the Academy of Child and Adolescent Psychiatry*, 43(1), 24-36.

Mair, C., Diez Roux, A.V., Osypuk, T.L., Rapp, S.R., Seeman, T., and Watson, K.E. (2010). Is neighborhood racial/ethnic composition associated with depressive symptoms? The multiethnic study of atherosclerosis. *Social Science & Medicine*, 71, 541-550.

Markel, H., and Stern, A.M. (1999). Which face? Whose nation? Immigration, public health, and the construction of disease at America's ports and borders, 1891-1928. *American Behavioral Scientist*, 42(9), 1314-1331.

Markides, K.S., and Rote, S. (2015). Immigrant health paradox. In R.A. Scott, S.M. Kosslyn, and N. Pinkerton (Eds.), *Emerging Trends in the Social and Behavioral Sciences: An Interdisciplinary, Searchable, and Linkable Resource*. Wiley Online Library. Available: http://onlinelibrary.wiley.com/book/10.1002/9781118900772 [October 2015].

Marks, A.K., Ejesi, K., and García Coll, C. (2014). Understanding the U.S. immigrant paradox in childhood and adolescence. *Child Development Perspectives*, 8(2), 59-64.

Martinez, J.N., Aguayo-Tellez, E., and Rangel-Gonzales, E. (2014). *Explaining the Mexican-American Health Paradox Using Selectivity Effects*. Wiley Online Library. Available: http://onlinelibrary.wiley.com/doi/10.1111/imre.12112/abstract [October 2015].

Massey, D.S. (2003). Segregation and stratification: A biosocial perspective. *DuBois Review*, 1, 7-25.

Massey, D.S. (2008). *Categorically Unequal: The American Stratification System*. New York: Russell Sage Foundation.

McCabe, K. (2012). *Foreign-Born Health Care Workers in the United States*. Washington, DC: Migration Policy Institute. Available: http://www.migrationpolicy.org/article/foreign-born-health-care-workers-united-states [October 2015].

McDonald, J.T., and Kennedy, S. (2004). Insights into the "health immigrant effect": Health status and health service use of immigrants to Canada. *Social Science & Medicine*, 59(8), 1613-1627.

McEwen, B.S., and Seeman, T. (1999). Protective and damaging effects of mediators of stress: Elaborating and testing the concepts of allostasis and allostatic load. *Annals of the New York Academy of Sciences*, 896(1), 30-47.

Menjívar, C., and Salcido, O. (2002). Immigrant women and domestic violence: Common experiences in different countries. *Gender and Society*, 16(6), 898-920.

Mirowsky, J., and Ross, C.E. (2003). *Education, Social Status, and Health*. Hawthorne, NY: Aldine de Gruyter.

Mohanty, S.A., Woolhandler, S., Himmelstein, D.U., Pati, S., Carrasquillo, O., and Bor, D.H. (2005). Health care expenditures of immigrants in the United States: A nationally representative analysis. *American Journal of Public Health, 95*(8), 1431.

Moran, A., Diez Roux, A.V., Jackson, S.A., Kramer, H., Maniolo, T.A., Shrager, S. and Shea, S. (2007). Acculturation is associated with hypertension in a multiethnic sample. *American Journal of Hypertension, 20*, 354-363.

Morland, K., Diez Roux A. V. and Wing, S. (2006). Supermarkets, other food stores, and obesity: The Atherosclerosis Risk in Communities Study. *American Journal of Preventive Medicine, 30(4)*:333-339.

Moullan, Y., and Jusot, F. (2014). Why is the "healthy immigrant effect" different between European countries? *European Journal of Public Health, Supplement 1*, 80-86.

Murray, K., Davidson, G., and Schweitzer, R. (2010). Review of refugee mental health interventions following resettlement: best practices and recommendations. *American Journal of Orthopsychiatry, 80*(4), 576-585.

National Research Council. (2001). *America Becoming: Racial Trends and Their Consequences. Volume I.* N. Smelser, W.J. Wilson and F. Mitchell (Eds.). Commission on Behavioral and Social Sciences and Education. Washington, DC: National Academy Press.

National Research Council and Institute of Medicine. (2013). *U.S. Health in International Perspective: Shorter Lives, Poorer Health.* Panel on Understanding Cross-National Health Differences Among High-Income Countries, S.H. Woolf and L. Aron (Eds.). Committee on Population, Division of Behavioral and Social Sciences and Education. Board on Population Health and Public Health Practice, Institute of Medicine. Washington, DC: The National Academies Press.

Ngo-Metzger, Q., Massagli, M.P., Clarridge, B.R., Manocchia, M., David, R.B., Iezzoni, L.I., and Phillips, R.S. (2003).Linguistic and cultural barriers to care: Perspectives of Chinese and Vietnamese immigrants. *Journal of General Internal Medicine, 18*(1), 44-52.

Noymer, A., and Lee, R. (2013). Immigrant health around the world: Evidence from the World Values Survey. *Journal of Immigrant and Minority Health, 15*(3), 614-623.

O'Brien, M.J., Alos, V.A., Davey, A., Bueno, A., and Whitaker, R.C. (2014). Acculturation and the prevalence of diabetes in U.S. Latino adults, National Health and Nutrition Examination Survey 2007-2010. *Prevention of Chronic Disease, 11*. Doi: 10:5888/pcd11.140142. Available: http://www.cdc.gov/pcd/issues/2014/14_0142.htm [October 2015].

Office of the Assistant Secretary for Planning and Evaluation. (2013). *Health Insurance Marketplace: Summary Enrollment Report for the Initial Annual Open Enrollment Period for the Period October 1, 2013–March 31, 2014, May 1, 2014.* Washington, DC: Author.

OECD. (2013). *Health at a Glance 2013: OECD Indicators.* Paris, France: Author.

OECD. (2007). *Immigrant Health Workers in the Broader Context of Highly Skilled Migration 2007.* Paris, France: Author.

Okafor, M.T.C., Carter-Pokras, O.D., Picot, S.J., and Zhan, M. (2013). The relationship of language acculturation (English proficiency) to current self-rated health among African immigrant adults. *Journal of Immigrant and Minority Health, 15*(3), 499-509.

Oliver, M., and Shapiro, T. (1997). *Black Wealth, White Wealth.* New York: Routledge.

Ortega, A.N., Rodriguez, H.P., and Vargas Bustamante, A. (2015). Policy dilemmas in Latino health care and implementation of the Affordable Care Act. *Annual Review of Public Health, 18*(36), 525-544.

Osypuk, T.L. (2012). Invited commentary: Integrating a life-course perspective and social theory to advance research on racial segregation and health. *American Journal of Epidemiology, 168*(11), 1255-1258.

Palloni, A., and Arias, E. (2004). Paradox lost: Explaining the Hispanic adult mortality advantage. *Demography, 41*(3), 385-415.

Park, L.S-H, and Pellow, D.N. (2011). *The Slums of Aspen: Immigrants vs. the Environment in America's Eden.* New York: New York University Press.

Pascoe, E.A., and Smart, R.L. (2009). Perceived discrimination and health: a meta-analytic review. *Psychological Bulletin, 135*(4), 531-554.

Pellow, D.N., and Park, L.S-H. (2002). *The Silicon Valley of Dreams: Environmental Injustice, Immigrant Workers, and the High-Tech Global Economy.* New York: New York University Press.

Perreira, K.M., Crosnoe, R., Fortuny, K., Pedroza, J., Ulvestad, K., Weiland, C., Yoshikawa, H., and Chaudry, A. (2012). *Barriers to Immigrants' Access to Health and Human Services Program: ASPE Issues Brief.* Washington, DC: Office of the Assistant Secretary for Planning and Evaluation.

Popkin, B.M., and Udry, J.R. (1998). Adolescent obesity increases significantly in second and third generation U.S. immigrants: The National Longitudinal Study of Adolescent Health. *The Journal of Nutrition, 128*(4), 701-706.

Population Reference Bureau. (2013). Elder immigrants in the United States. *Today's Research on Aging, 29*(October), 1-9.

Pourat, N., Wallace, S.P., Hadler, M.W., and Ponce, N. (2014). Assessing health care services used by California's undocumented immigrant population in 2010. *Health Affairs, 33*(5), 840-847.

Preston, S.H., and Elo, I.T. (2014). Anatomy of a municipal triumph: New York City's upsurge in life expectancy. *Population and Development Review, 40*(1), 1-29.

Ramakrishnan, S.K, and Ahmad, F.Z. (2014). *State of Asian American and Pacific Islanders Series: A Multifaceted Portrait for a Growing Population.* Washington, DC: Center for American Progress. Available: https://cdn.americanprogress.org/wp-content/uploads/2014/04/AAPIReport-comp.pdf [September 2015].

Raymond-Flesch, M., Lucia, L., Jacobs, K., and Brindis, C. (2015). *Lessons from the ACA's Medicaid Expansion Front-Lines: Perspectives of Enrollment Workers.* Presented at the 143rd American Public Health Association Annual Meeting and Exposition, October 31-November 4, Chicago, IL.

Reed, M.M., Westfall, J.M., Bublitz, C., Battaglia, C., and Fickenscher, A. (2005). Birth outcomes in Colorado's undocumented immigrant population. *BMC Public Health, 5*(October), 100.

Riosmena, F., Wong, R., and Palloni, A. (2013). Migration selection, protection, and acculturation in health: A binational perspective on older adults. *Demography, 50*(3), 1039-1064.

Ro, A. (2014). The longer you stay, the worse your health? a critical review of the negative acculturation theory among Asian immigrants. *International Journal of Environmental Research and Public Health, 11*, 8038-8057.

Rodriguez, M.A., Bustamante, A.V., and Ang, A. (2009). Quality of care, receipt of preventive care, and usual source of health care among undocumented and other Latinos. *Journal of General Internal Medicine, 24*(Supplement 3), 508-513.

Ryan, A.M., Gee, G.C., and Laflamme, D.F. (2006). The association between self-reported discrimination, physical health and blood pressure: Findings from African Americans, black immigrants, and Latino immigrants in New Hampshire. *Journal of Health Care for the Poor and Underserved, 17*(2), 116-132.

Rytina N. (2013). *Population Estimate: Estimates of the Legal Permanent Resident Population in 2012.* Washington, DC: Office of Immigration Statistics, Department of Homeland Security.

Salcido, O., and Adelman, M. (2004). "He has me tied with the blessed and damned papers": Uncommented-immigrant battered women in Phoenix, Arizona. *Human Organization, 63*(2), 162-173.

Sallis, J.F., and Glanz, K. (2006). The role of built environments in physical activity, eating, and obesity in childhood. *Future Child, 16*(1), 89-108.

Satia, J.A. (2009). Diet-related disparities: Understanding the problem and accelerating solutions. *Journal of the American Dietary Association, 109*(4), 610-615.

Schumacher, E.J. (2011). Foreign-born nurses in the U.S. labor market. *Health Economics, 20*(3), 362-378.

Shankar, S., Gutierrez-Mohamed, M.L., and Alberg, A.J. (2000). Cigarette smoking among immigrant Salvadorans in Washington, DC: Behaviors, attitudes, and beliefs. *Addictive Behavior, 25*(2), 275-281.

Shartzer, A., Kenney, G.M., Long, S.K., Hempstead, K., and Wissoker, D. (2014). *Who Are the Remaining Uninsured as of June 2014?* Washington, DC: Urban Institute. Available: http://hrms.urban.org/briefs/who-are-the-remaining-uninsured-as-of-june-2014.html [October 2015].

Singer, A. (2012). *Immigrant Workers in the U.S. Labor Force.* Brookings Research Papers. Washington, DC: Brookings Institution Press.

Singh, G.K., Rodriguez-Lainz, A., and Kogan, M.D. (2013). Immigrant health inequalities in the United States: Use of eight major national data systems. *The Scientific World Journal, 2013*(Article ID 512313). Available: http://www.hindawi.com/journals/tswj/2013/512313/ [October 2015].

Sole-Auro, A., and Crimmins, E. (2008). Health of immigrants in European countries. *International Migration Review, 42*, 861-876.

Sommers, B.D., Buchmueller, T., Decker, S.L., Carey, C., and Kronick, R. (2013). The Affordable Care Act has led to significant gains in health insurance and access to care for young adults. *Health Affairs, 32*(1), 165-174.

Sommers, B.D., Musco, T., Finegold, K., Gunja, M.Z., Burke, A., and McDowell, A.M. (2014a). Health reform and changes in health insurance coverage in 2014. *New England Journal of Medicine, 371*(9), 867-874.

Sommers, B.D., Kenney, G.M., and Epstein, A.M. (2014b). New evidence on the Affordable Care Act: Coverage impacts of early Medicaid expansions. *Health Affairs, 33*(1), 78-87.

Stimpson, J.P., Wilson, F.A., and Eschblach, K. (2010). Trends in health care spending for immigrants in the United States. *Health Affairs, 29*(3), 544-550.

Suárez-Orozco, C., Yoshikawa, H., Yoshikawa, S.H., Teranishi, R.T., and Suárez-Orozco, M.M. (2011). Growing up in the shadows: The developmental implications of unauthorized status. *Harvard Educational Review, 81*(3), 438-472.

Sullivan, M.M., and Rehm, R. (2005). Mental health of undocumented Mexican immigrants: A review of the literature. *Advances in Nursing Science, 28*(3), 240-251.

Szaflarski, M., Cubbins, L.A., and Ying, J. (2011). Epidemiology of alcohol abuse among U.S. immigrant populations. *Journal of Immigrant and Minority Health, 13*(4), 647-658.

Taylor, E., Yanni, E.A., Pezzi, C., Guterbock, M., Rothney, E., Harton, E., Montour, J., Elias, C., and Burke, H. (2014). Physical and mental health status of Iraqi refugees resettled in the United States. *Journal of Immigrant and Minority Health, 16*, 1130-1137.

Timmins, C.L. (2002). The impact of language barriers on the health care of Latinos in the United States: A review of the literature and guidelines for practice. *Journal of Midwifery and Women's Health, 47*(2), 80-96.

Turra, C.M., and Elo, I.T. (2008). The impact of the salmon bias on the Hispanic mortality advantage: New evidence from Social Security data. *Population Research and Policy Review, 27*(5), 515-530.

Unger, J.B., Cruz, T.B., Rohrbach, L.A., Ribisl, K.M., Baezconde-Garbanati, L., Chen, X., and Johnson, C.A. (2000). English language use as a risk factor for smoking initiation among Hispanic and Asian American adolescents: Evidence for mediation by tobacco-related beliefs and social norms. *Health Psychology, 19*(5), 403-410.

Van Hook, J., and Baker, E. (2010). Big boys, little girls: Gender, acculturation, and weight among young children of immigrants. *Journal of Health and Social Behavior*, *51*, 200-214.

Wafula, E.G., and Snipes, S.A. (2014). Barriers to health care access faced by black immigrants in the U.S.: Theoretical considerations and recommendations. *Journal of Immigrant and Minority Health*, 16(4), 689-698

Wallace, S., Torres, J., Nobari, T.Z., Pourat, N., and Brown, E. (2012). *Undocumented and Uninsured: Barriers to Affordable Care for Immigrant Populations*. Los Angeles: University of California Center for Health Policy Research.

Walton, E. (2014). Vital places: Facilitators of behavioral and social health mechanisms in low-income housing neighborhoods. *Social Science and Medicine*, *122*, 1-12.

Walton, E., Takeuchi, D., Herting, J., and Alegria, M. (2009). Does place of education matter? Contextualizing the education and health association among Asian Americans. *Biodemography*, 55(1), 30-51.

Weiss, A.M., and Sheedy, K. (2015), *State Enrollment Experience: Implementing Health Coverage Eligibility and Enrollment Systems under the ACA*. National Academy for State Health Policy. Available: https://www.statereforum.org/system/files/nashp-brief-state-enrollment-aca1.pdf [September 2015].

Weissberg, J. (2014). The Spanish-language version of Healthcare.gov is a mess. *The Nation*, January 14. Available: http://www.thenation.com/article/spanish-language-version-healthcaregov-mess/ [October 2015].

Werlen, B. (1993). *Society, Action and Space: An Alternative to Human Geography*. London, UK: Routledge.

Williams, D.R., and Collins, C. (2001). Racial residential segregation: A fundamental cause of racial disparities in health. *Public Health Reports*, *116*, 404-416.

Williams, D.R., and Mohammed, S.A. (2009). Discrimination and racial disparities in health: Evidence and needed research. *Journal of Behavioral Medicine*, *32*, 20-47.

Williams, D.R., Haile, R., Gonzalez, H.M., Neighbors, H., Baser, R., and Jackson, J.S. (2007). The mental health of black Caribbean immigrants: Results from the National Survey of American Life. *American Journal of Public Health*, 97(1), 52-59.

Yoo, H.C., Gee, G.C., and Takeuchi, D. (2009). Discrimination and health among Asian American immigrants: Disentangling racial from language discrimination. *Social Science & Medicine*, 68(4), 726-732.

Yoshikawa, H. (2011). *Immigrants Raising Citizens: Undocumented Parents and Their Young Children*. New York: Russell Sage Foundation.

Yoshikawa, H., Weiland, C., Ulvestad, K., Perreira, K.M., and Crosnoe, R. (2014). *Improving Access of Low-Income Immigrant Families to Health and Human Services*. Washington, DC: Urban Institute.

Zallman, L. (2014). *Staying Covered: How Immigrants Have Prolonged the Solvency of One of Medicare's Key Trust Funds and Subsidized Care for U.S. Seniors*. Washington, DC: Partnership for a New American Economy.

Zeng, Z., and Xie, Y. (2004). Asian-Americans' earnings disadvantage reexamined: The role of place of education. *The American Journal of Sociology*, *109*, 1075-1108.

Zsembik, B.A., and Fennell, D. (2005). Ethnic variation in health and the determinants of health among Latinos. *Social Science & Medicine*, 61(1), 53-63.

Zuckerman, S., Waidmann, T.A., and Lawton, E. (2011). Undocumented immigrants, left out of health reform, likely to continue to grow as share of the uninsured. *Health Affairs*, 30(10), 1997-2004.

10

Data on Immigrants and Immigrant Integration

The study of immigrant integration requires reliable data on the foreign-born and their descendants, with the former providing information on the progress of immigrants with time spent in the United States, and the latter indicating progress toward integration between the first and second generations and beyond. By its very nature, integration is a process that unfolds over time. The pace of integration may be sped up or slowed down by individual characteristics, contexts of reception, or one's structural position in society, but it always also depends on the duration of exposure to the host country's culture and society (Alba and Nee, 2003; Portes and Rumbaut, 2014).

Among the most important information to gather to assess integration are data on birthplace/nativity, age and date of arrival, time spent in the United States, and legal status at present and upon entry. The many dimensions of integration (social, economic, political, civic, cultural) require different contextual, family/household, and individual-level data. This chapter focuses on data sources on the foreign-born and second generation, the measurement of the legal status of immigrants, including the undocumented, and challenges to the study of immigrant integration. It closes with recommendations to improve data collection, data access, and ultimately, the understanding of how well immigrants and their offspring are integrating into various arenas.

DATA ON IMMIGRANTS

The primary sources of data on immigrants are administrative data, government surveys, other nongovernmental national and local surveys, and qualitative studies.

Administrative Data

Administrative sources generally come from applications that immigrants file with the Department of Homeland Security (DHS) and/or the U.S. State Department in order to be admitted on either temporary or permanent visas into the United States. These data are produced annually and represent the "flow" of immigrants officially admitted into the United States. The Office of Immigration Statistics (OIS) in the Department of Homeland Security is the administrative home for annual data on all immigrants, both permanent and temporary, to the United States.[1] These aggregate data are useful for national-level questions about the number of documented immigrants arriving each year and the visa types on which they arrive.

Unfortunately the data OIS collects are neither very detailed nor very accessible. DHS collects very limited data on permanent residents as they arrive in the United States, and even less information is compiled upon the entry of temporary migrants. DHS lacks any consistent means of tracking immigrants as they move through different legal statuses. These data offer information about flows and numbers of immigrants in some legal statuses by various demographic characteristics, but are of limited use in assessing integration.

Surveys

For the study of immigrant *integration* in particular, researchers and policy makers need information beyond administrative data on the inflows of immigrants. That is, to study immigrants' economic integration, a survey or administrative data also need to capture detailed information on income, social benefits receipt, assets and debt, and so forth, while analysis of civic integration might ask about volunteerism, membership in organizations, and participation in community events. One of the easiest ways to expand the body of knowledge about immigrant integration is to make the collection of key migration variables—place of birth, year of arrival in the United

---

[1] The Department of Homeland Security is obviously unable to collect data on immigrants who "enter without inspection" (EWI) by a U.S. Customs officer. However, if and when these undocumented immigrants do apply for a legal status, their information is collected, and their administrative record should include their previous status as EWI.

States and parents' birthplace—part of most or all of the hundreds of surveys currently conducted to understand U.S. society. In addition, because a standard survey of U.S. residents with a bit over 1,000 sample respondents will, at best, include 100-200 immigrants, data collection should also consider oversampling the foreign-born population.

Government Surveys

The U.S. government also collects data on the characteristics of immigrants through the Census Bureau's surveys. These data represent the "stock" of the foreign-born and are identified in census and survey data from a question on respondent's place of birth. This type of question was included on U.S. censuses from 1850 through 2000 and since 2010 has been asked as part of the American Community Survey (ACS), which replaced the census long form. The birthplace question is also included on the Current Population Survey (CPS) and the Survey of Income and Program Participation (SIPP).

Most nationally representative statistics on immigrant integration currently come from the ACS, as its sample size alone among surveys is sufficient to enable statistically significant comparisons of integration outcomes across national origin groups and to consider patterns of integration at the regional, state, and local levels. Each year the ACS conducts around 2.5 million interviews and asks 24 questions about housing and 48 questions on the demographic, social, and economic characteristics of household members. Answers to these questions provide investigators with the major portion of the basic data used to assess immigrant integration.

ACS questions on country of birth, year of arrival, and naturalization enable researchers to examine indicators of immigrant integration by national origin, time since arrival, and citizenship and thus chart how social, economic, and housing characteristics change with time spent in the United States. Housing items of potential interest in assessing integration include kind of housing, age of housing, number of rooms, appliances and services, computer and Internet access, vehicle ownership, heating, utility costs, home value, home ownership, rent payments, tax payments, insurance costs, and mortgage payments. Socioeconomic characteristics of potential interest include educational attainment, foreign language usage, English ability, health insurance coverage, disabilities, marital status, marital history, childbearing, child care arrangements, veteran status, employment, occupation, hours worked, journey to work, and income from various sources.

The March CPS includes a demographic supplement that asks many of the same questions, often in greater detail, along with selected other items; but its sample size of 60,000 yields, on average, information on just 7,800 immigrants, which is sufficient for deriving national-level statistics for large national-origin groups but not for regional, state, and local estimates of smaller national-origin populations. The ACS is used to derive small-area estimates of the number and characteristics of immigrants for purposes of state and local planning, municipal decision making, and public service provision.

Nongovernment Surveys

Two private surveys particularly useful for studying immigrant integration are the New Immigrant Survey (NIS) and the Los Angeles Family and Neighborhood Study (LAFANS), although neither is nationally representative. With the addition of a supplemental sample of 511 immigrant families to the Panel Study of Income Dynamics in 1997/1999, that longitudinal survey is also now used to study integration, although the sample size is still too small for detailed studies and estimates below the national level. A list of all the surveys that collect data on immigration can be found at the UC Berkeley Population Center website (see http://www.popcenter.berkeley.edu/resources/migration_data_sets/data_by_region.php [November 2015]).

Qualitative Data Sources

There are many hundreds of qualitative studies of immigrant integration based on in-depth interviews or participant observation in immigrant communities, families, and institutions such as schools, churches, and workplaces. Most qualitative studies of immigrants in the United States only examine immigrants' lives in this country, but some span national borders to investigate the transnational lives of immigrants and their families and to compare life in the United States with life in the country of origin (Dreby, 2010; Levitt, 2001).

A growing number of qualitative studies focus on the second generation, and while many of these are based in the traditional gateway cities, qualitative researchers are increasingly examining the dynamics of immigrant integration in newer destinations (Marrow, 2011). The specific topics covered range widely from changing patterns of family life, the development of new identities, and the role of immigrant religious organizations to the difficulties facing undocumented immigrants and their children and the ethnic and racial barriers confronting legal immigrants and their children as well. A welcome development is that some studies have combined qualitative methods with local representative surveys (Kasinitz et al., 2008). Qualitative studies are an important resource, providing valuable insights into the attitudes, values, and beliefs as well as patterns of behavior among immigrants and their children that can provide the basis for further investigation through nationally representative surveys. One way that they could be improved in the future is if more researchers could deposit their qualitative data in publicly accessible archives, where the data could be used by other researchers to replicate studies or to explore new questions. It is often more difficult to do this with qualitative than with quantitative research because of privacy considerations, but when possible it should be encouraged.

Measuring Legal Status

As discussed throughout this report, legal status affects immigrants and the second generation in myriad ways, both as an outcome of integration and as a determinant of integration. For this reason, it is critical for researchers to have accurate and precise information about the number of people who acquire different legal statuses, especially citizenship and lawful permanent resident (LPR) status, the reasons they do so, the factors that influence acquisition of status, and the length of time it takes. Yet there are few sources of data about the legal status of immigrants that also capture viable information to understand integration. The lack of data stems at least in part from concerns that questions about legal status are sensitive in nature and will therefore yield invalid results or suppress participation (U.S. Government Accountability Office, 2006; Carter-Pokras and Zambrana, 2006). In their analysis of surveys posing questions on legal status, however, Bachmeier, Van Hook, and Bean (2014) found that item nonresponse rates were relatively small, ranging from 0 to 14 percent, and significantly below those typically observed on questions about income. Indeed, they found that after using standard imputation procedures to correct for nonresponse, survey questions on legal status produced estimates of undocumented population composition comparable to those obtained using the widely accepted residual methods employed by the Department of Homeland Security and the Pew Research Center. They recommended that future data collection efforts include questions about legal status to improve models of immigrant integration.

Although most surveys do not collect information about legal status, there are several sources of data on this variable that can aid the study of immigrant integration. These sources are outlined below. In addition, there has been strong interest in identifying immigrants who are living in the United States without legal status because of the disadvantages of this group and their descendants regarding chances for integration. Efforts to collect or estimate data on this population are also discussed below.

Administrative Data Sources on Legal Status

OIS does make available selective demographic information about some legal statuses via a variety of products. The most consistent is the annual Yearbook of Immigration Statistics, "a compendium of tables that provides data on foreign nationals who, during a fiscal year, were granted lawful permanent residence (i.e., admitted as immigrants or became legal permanent residents), were admitted into the United States on a temporary basis (e.g., tourists, students, or workers), applied for asylum or refugee status, or were naturalized."[2] The Yearbook offers basic statistical data on naturalized citizens, LPRs, refugees/asylees, nonimmigrants, and enforcement actions, but in general the breadth of these data is rather limited and their collection is limited to a single point in time (upon entry), making them of little use for studying immigrant integration.

Administrative data are most plentiful for LPRs and include annual information on country of origin, state and metropolitan area of U.S. residence, class of admission, age, sex, marital status, and occupation. No data are gathered on education or prior experience in the United States, which are critical factors to consider in any study of integration. For refugees and asylees, published tabulations include only country of origin, age, sex, and marital status. For nonimmigrants (those entering on temporary visas) these tabulations include country of origin, port of entry, category of admission, month of arrival, age, and sex. Data on undocumented migrants who are apprehended and deported include little more than country of origin.

U.S. Citizenship and Immigration Services (USCIS) also produces special reports on the H1B and H2B temporary visas. The H1B report is published annually and includes basic characteristics of workers in that status, but characteristics of H2B visa holders are only published for 2010. The U.S. State Department's annual Report of the Visa Office provides statistical data on immigrant and nonimmigrant visa issued by consular offices abroad. The U.S. Department of Labor also publishes annual data on labor certifications for various employment-based visas and Permanent Labor Certifications; however, labor certifications do not always translate into applications for visas, so these numbers are limited in their usefulness.

The U.S. Department of Justice publishes detailed statistics on cases the Executive Office for Immigration Review (EOIR) adjudicates each year in its Statistics Yearbooks, which provides some detailed information on grants of asylum. Other government agencies, including the Congressional Research Service, Congressional Budget Office, and Government Accountability Office also produce periodic reports on various legal statuses, but it

---

[2] See http://www.dhs.gov/yearbook-immigration-statistics [November 2015].

is unclear whether they use publicly available data from the sources listed above or nonpublic data only available within the federal government.

During the course of its work, the panel made a formal request to USCIS (one of the study's sponsors) for additional data on trends in naturalization rates and characteristics of naturalized citizens, estimates of eligible-to-naturalize populations and their characteristics, and information about assistance and fee waivers for applications for naturalization from USCIS. Some of these data were previously published in the Yearbook but no longer appear in the public data sources. Although USCIS did provide the panel with data on derivative naturalizations, none of the other data requests were met.

Survey Data on Legal Status

The only nationally representative survey that asks directly about legal status is the SIPP (Hall et al., 2010). The SIPP consists of a series of monthly panel surveys that began in 1984, with each panel lasting from 2.5 to 4 years. The most recent panel was fielded in 2014 and like prior surveys was a multistage stratified sample of the civilian, noninstitutionalized population. The SIPP is designed to compile detailed data on labor force status, program participation, and income to measure the economic situation of U.S. residents (U.S. Census Bureau, 2015). The study is designed as a continuous series of national panels, with sample size ranging from approximately 14,000 to 52,000 interviewed households.

For each person born abroad, the SIPP questionnaire asks "when [NAME] moved to the United States to live, what was his or her immigration status?" The response categories include immediate relative or family-sponsored permanent resident; employment-based permanent resident; other permanent resident; granted refugee status or granted asylum; nonimmigrant, such as a diplomatic, student, business, or tourist visa; and other. Respondents are then asked whether their status has changed to legal permanent residence. Undocumented status is estimated as a residual category inferred by process of elimination. Posing these questions produces very modest levels of nonresponse and has no significant effect on responses to subsequent questions or to survey follow-up rates. The questions appear to yield estimates of population characteristics comparable to the indirect methods described above (Bachmeier et al., 2014). The SIPP provides detailed data on labor force participation, income, assets, education, entitlement usage, and health insurance coverage and, given its large nationally representative sample, represents a potentially rich though underutilized source of information on the consequences of unauthorized status for immigrants and their families.

Although the SIPP is the only nationally representative survey of the entire U.S. population to contain questions on legal status, these questions have been asked on a variety of other surveys of specific populations or regions. Below, the panel reviews some of the most useful publicly available surveys, but the surveys we describe are not a comprehensive list.

LAFANS, a representative sample of Los Angeles County fielded between 2000 and 2002, also contained a module on legal status that has been used to infer a lack of documentation after eliminating a series of legal categories (see Prentice et al., 2005; Bachmeier et al., 2014). A series of five questions asks first whether the respondent is a U.S. citizen and if the answer is "no" goes on to ask in serial order whether the respondent has permanent residence; asylum, refugee status, or temporary protected status; a tourist visa, work visa, or other document permitting one to stay in the United States; and if the later document is still valid. Although LAFANS is representative for the area covered by its frame, it is not nationally representative; the relative size and composition of the undocumented population derived for Los Angeles County lines up closely with indirect estimates for that county using the residual approach (described below), at least with respect to age, sex, and national origin (Bachmeier et al., 2014). Given the wealth of data contained in LAFANS on households, adult and child members, neighborhoods, and schools, it offers a promising source for studying the consequences of unauthorized status in the nation's largest single undocumented population.

Another source of data on legal status is the NIS, which began with a representative pilot survey of 1,134 legal immigrants who acquired legal residence documents during July and August of 1996 and were followed for the next year. The pilot survey compiled detailed information about migratory experiences in the United States prior to admission as LPRs, enabling identification of those with prior undocumented status. Using these data, Massey and Malone (2002) estimated that 32 percent of all "new" LPRs had previously been undocumented migrants, roughly the same figure estimated by Jasso et al. (2008), although among groups such as Mexicans and Central Americans the figure was much higher.

The pilot survey was followed in 2003 with a probability sample of the entire cohort of LPRs who acquired their residence documents between May and November of 2003, including interviews with 8,573 adults, 810 parents of sampled child immigrants, and 4,915 spouses. Follow-up interviews were conducted with this cohort between June 2007 and December 2009, yielding data on 3,902 adults, 392 children, and 1,771 spouses. Although the full NIS did not include the detailed module on pre-arrival experiences administered in the pilot, it did identify previously unauthorized immigrants who were legalized under the Immigration Reform and Control Act's (IRCA's) registry provisions, suspension of deportation, cancellation of removal, and special legalization programs, again comprising around 32 percent of all immigrants. Both sources of data allow researchers to study the effects of legal status on integration (e.g., Weeraratne and Massey, 2014).

Another source of data on formerly unauthorized migrants is the Legalized Population Survey, a sample of 6,193 undocumented immigrants who sought LPR status through IRCA and were interviewed in 1989 with a follow-up survey of 4,012 respondents in 1992. The survey collected information on the labor market characteristics of those who gained legal status at three times: just prior to legalization while still undocumented, at legalization, and 5 years following legalization.

Although primarily designed to assess the progress of second generation immigrants, the Immigration and Intergenerational Mobility in Metropolitan Los Angeles Study (IIMMLA) included questions on legal status. The presence of undocumented parents and children in the Los Angeles study enabled work on the effects of legal status on the integration of undocumented migrants and their citizen children (see Bean et al., 2015).

Three specialized population surveys that also contain questions on legal status are the Latino National Survey, the National Agricultural Workers Survey, and the National Asian American Survey. The Latino National Survey is a representative national survey of some 8,634 Latino residents of the United States implemented in 2005-2006. Unfortunately, only a minority of respondents to the Latino National Survey are foreign-born, drastically reducing the sample size of immigrants and rendering it too small for all but national estimates on large groups such as Mexicans.[3]

The National Agricultural Workers Survey was an employment-based, random survey of U.S. crop workers. It collected demographic, employment, and health data in face-to-face interviews with over 56,000 workers in 1988-1989 and ascertained which respondents were undocumented and which had applied for legalization under IRCA's Special Agricultural Worker Program.

The National Asian American Survey was a telephone survey of 5,159 self-identified Asian or Asian American residents of the United States fielded in 2008. It included a direct question about current legal status but 93 percent of respondents reported either being U.S. citizens or legal visa holders, with just 5.2 percent saying they didn't know or refusing to answer, thus potentially identifying them as undocumented.

Finally, both the Mexican Migration Project (Durand and Massey, 2004) and the Latin American Migration Project (Donato et al., 2010) ask direct questions on legal status from representative samples of immigrants

---

[3]The sample size for the LNS is still the largest publicly available sample of the Latino foreign-born population, and some of the state subsamples should allow for national-origin level analysis of the foreign-born—e.g., California, Florida, and Texas.

from specific sending communities who are interviewed mostly in their countries of origin. Although neither dataset is necessarily representative of migrants from Mexico or other Latin American nations, systematic comparisons with objective sources suggest they cover their respective immigrant populations well (Massey and Zenteno, 2000; Massey and Capoferro, 2004), and both surveys have been used extensively to study the effect of legal status on labor market integration.

The above surveys all follow the best practice of making data publicly available in publicly accessible archives. All surveys of immigrants and the second generation should do this.

Qualitative Data on Legal Status

A variety of qualitative studies have examined the effects of legal status on immigrant integration, and many of these are cited in Chapter 3. Although qualitative datasets are generally too small to make broad generalizations about the effects of legal status on immigrant integration, they provide important guidance for how legal status might be measured and what types of social variables intersect with legal status to help or hinder immigrants' integration prospects. Qualitative studies can also help researchers assess the effects of legal status in particular local contexts and for smaller groups of immigrants.

Sources of Data on Undocumented Immigrants

Standard residual methods for measuring the undocumented have been perfected in recent decades to derive indirect estimates of the number, location, and basic demographic characteristics of undocumented migrants using the Decennial Census and the CPS and ACS surveys. Indirect estimates of the size and characteristics of the undocumented population are regularly published by OIS,[4] the Pew Research Center,[5] and the Center for Migration Studies.[6] The Migration Policy Institute has also published estimates for the undocumented at the national and select state and county level, including estimates of the population eligible for Deferred Action for Childhood Arrivals (DACA) and Deferred Action for Parental Accountability (DAPA, also called Deferred Action for Parents of Americans and Lawful Permanent Residents).

In order to derive an independent benchmark estimate of the undocu-

---

[4] See http://www.dhs.gov/immigration-statistics-publications [November 2015].

[5] See http://www.pewhispanic.org/category/publications/ [November 2015].

[6] See http://cmsny.org/researchprojects/democratizingdata/us/unauthorizedtables/ [November 2015].

mented population, the U.S. Government Accountability Office (2009) has recommended the application of a "two-card method" in conjunction with the CPS (see U.S. Government Accountability Office, 2009, for details). This method seeks to overcome concerns about asking about legal status because those without documents only admit to being in a category that contains undocumented migrants among several other legal statuses, making it impossible to identify any single person as being undocumented. Although this design feature guarantees privacy, it also makes it impossible to identify the characteristics of the undocumented population. As a result, the two-card method has been little used in research on immigrant integration to date.

In summary, the inability to identify legal status among the foreign-born enumerated in the Decennial Census or in the ACS and CPS leaves a major determinant of immigrant integration unmeasured, thus potentially biasing models estimated to predict how integration varies with time spent in the United States (Massey and Bartley, 2005). Among Mexican immigrants, in particular, one cannot know whether a relatively slow pace of socioeconomic integration is a general feature of the population or is simply the average of a fast pace of integration among legal immigrants and citizens and a slow pace among undocumented immigrants. Moreover, to the extent that the prevalence of undocumented migrants varies across national origins, differences in integration will be confounded with differences in the rate of legal documentation.

DATA ON THE SECOND GENERATION

As discussed throughout the report, family and household circumstances, as well as the general climate toward immigrants and the policy environment that immigrants enter, are critical in determining patterns and processes of social and economic integration for the second generation and beyond. In addition to the parents' own legal status, age and date of arrival, and time spent in the United States, other key variables affecting the integration of the second generation include whether both parents were foreign-born; what language is spoken at home; household socioeconomic and demographic composition; and general indicators of parental health, education, occupation, and income. In addition, more distal variables such as the general policy environment toward immigrants (welcoming or restrictive), neighborhood characteristics, the types of schools attended; and the availability and quality of English-as-a-Second-Language (ESL) programs and other social and health services affect immigrant integration and should be measured with respect to immigrant-descendent generation.

In general, resources accessible to children within the household while growing up can be expected to play an outsized role in determining the nature and extent of their later integration into American society. For older children of immigrants who no longer live at home, of course, a specific question on the birthplace of parents is required to identify members of the second generation but rarely is much additional information gathered about the parents or the family in which they came of age. Despite this information gap, circumstances in the family of origin are nonetheless critical to understanding current trajectories of integration among adult members of the second generation, underscoring the need for longitudinal data in studies of immigrant integration, especially in the second generation.

The second generation may be identified in one of two ways. Minor children of immigrants are easily identified as long as they remain in the household of their immigrant parents, who are themselves identified from the birthplace question. The adult children of immigrants, however, must be identified using a separate question on the birthplace of parents: a question that was asked on every Decennial Census from 1870 to 1970 but was eliminated on the 1980, 1990, and 2000 census forms and was not included on the ACS in 2010. Since 1996 a parental birthplace item has been asked in the March supplement to the CPS, but the small sample size makes it difficult to create reliable estimates for most second generation immigrant populations (for one potential method, see Ramakrishnan, 2005), especially at the state and local level. There are other limitations to the CPS that limit its usefulness for substate-level analysis: more than a third of county level identifiers are not available in the public release of the CPS due to concerns about privacy; other data might be available only through a handful of restricted data centers

At present there is no reliable source of information on adult second generation immigrants based on a large, nationally representative sample. As noted in Chapter 6, because the U.S. Census Bureau data relies on self-identification of race and Hispanic origin and because identity is related to socioeconomic status, the identification of the second and especially the third and higher generations may be increasingly inaccurate and may introduce systematic errors in measurements of intergenerational mobility.

To fill the gap, private organizations led by the Russell Sage Foundation have funded a series of specialized surveys of second generation immigrants in San Diego and Miami (Portes and Rumbaut, 2014), New York (Kasinitz et al., 2008), and Los Angeles (Brown et al., 2011). Telles and Ortiz (2008) used a survey of Mexican Americans in California and Texas, originally conducted in 1965, and then relocated the original respondents and their descendants. They demonstrated that having information on biological generations—tracing great-grandfathers, grandfathers, fathers, and sons—yielded a different trajectory of integration than measuring generation as time since immigration and examining cross-sectional differences among individuals of different immigrant generations but similar age cohorts. In addition, Grusky and colleagues (2015) recently recommended the creation of an "American Opportunity Study" to develop the capacity to link records across the Decennial Census, the ACS, and administrative records (see Box 10-1). These linkages would significantly enhance researchers' ability to monitor social mobility across generations, a key component in the measurement of immigrant integration. Overall, the lack of a parental birthplace on the ACS and its absence from the 1980-2000 census long forms constitutes a huge gap in the nation's statistical system and is the largest single barrier to studying the intergenerational integration of immigrants (Massey, 2010). As the third generation grows in size, the lack of a question on grandparents' place of birth also means that researchers are unable to trace intergenerational integration as it advances beyond the

---

BOX 10-1
American Opportunity Study

In June 2013, the National Research Council conducted a workshop to explore means of improving the measurement of social mobility in the United States (National Research Council, 2013). One of the key topics considered in the workshop was improving the means of measuring the intergenerational changes in the immigrant population, an important component in the measurement of immigrant integration.

An important outcome of this workshop and of the planning activities that followed it was the development of a proposal for a new American Opportunity Study (AOS; Grusky et al., 2015). The proposal stemmed from an understanding that social, behavioral, and economic research (surveys, experiments, evaluations) is making efficient and cost-saving linkages to Census Bureau and administrative data, yielding savings on survey costs, improving data accuracy, drastically increasing the ability to understand the long-term consequences of economic and social change, and ultimately improving the evidence base for policy.

In essence, the proposed data development would link the Decennial Census short and long forms from 1950 through 2010 and beyond, with the American Community Survey (ACS) substituting for the long form since 2010. Identification of immigrants would be facilitated by establishing a "Protected Identity Key" for the 1960-1990 data from the Decennial Censuses. In this manner, a protected longitudinal panel of the population, with identifiers for immigrants and later generations, could be constructed. From this linked file, linkages between federal administrative datasets and ongoing surveys could be established. The work would be carried out in restricted data environments, such as the Census Bureau's Research Data Centers. A significant amount of project development would be needed before this data linkage project could bear fruit, but the AOS would result in an important new information source to assist in understanding the processes and products of immigrant integration.

children of immigrants. During the greatest period of mass immigration since the early 20th century, when the population of immigrants rose from 14 to 40 million and the second generation proliferated, the nation has lacked a reliable means of assessing the progress and characteristics of the children of immigrants.

CHALLENGES TO THE STUDY OF IMMIGRANT INTEGRATION

Analyzing the progress of immigrants as individuals presents many challenges despite the existence of large, nationally representative sources of data on the foreign-born. In addition to the lack of data on legal status and the absence of a large nationwide sample of the second generation, additional challenges include the ambiguity in defining duration of U.S. experience among immigrants who undertake multiple trips in and out of the country, the difficulty of identifying the intention to settle in the United States and when settlement occurs, the relatively small share of immigrants in most general-population samples, and lack of data on contexts of reception.

Ambiguity in Duration and Intent to Settle

Beyond legal status, a key variable in all models of immigrant integration is an indicator of time spent in the United States. The 2000 Decennial Census long form and the 2010 ACS assessed time in the United States with the question "when did this person come to live in the United States?" The 1970 through 1990 Census long forms asked foreign-born person when they came to the United States "to stay." Most researchers simply subtract the date of entry (to live or to stay) from the date of the survey to estimate total time spent in the United States. However, recent research based on retrospective longitudinal data indicates that the vast majority of persons entering the United States as new LPRs are not arriving for the first time. For example, among the 2003 cohort of new legal resident aliens surveyed upon entry by the NIS, 66 percent had prior experience in the United States through a variety of pathways, and total time accumulated in the United States varied widely by legal status (Massey and Malone, 2002). The question itself tacitly assumes that foreign-born persons have indeed made a decision to settle in the United States, but in fact some LPRs and naturalized citizens use their residence documents as a convenience to come and go (Massey et al., 1987; Massey and Akresh, 2006). Even among those who intend to live out their lives in the United States, answering the question requires a judgment about when exactly it was that they came with the intention of settling (Massey and Malone, 2002).

Thus measures of time spent in the United States derived from government censuses and surveys may contain significant measurement error and considerable but unknown potential for bias across national-origin groups. Although total time accumulated in the United States and the total number of trips during this time are probably most relevant in determining integration outcomes, these quantities are generally not available from standard data sources. In sum, models of immigrant adaptation and integration estimated from the Decennial Census, ACS, or CPS are likely to be strongly affected by omitted variable bias (owing to the lack of information on legal status and parental birthplace) and measurement error (because of unreliability in accurately capturing time spent in the United States).

Small Sample Size

Moving beyond these standard sources of national data, the possibilities for studying immigrant integration are even more restricted given the relatively small size of the foreign-born population. The foreign-born presently constitute around 13 percent of the U.S. population, so that a representative national sample of 2,000 people would yield just 260 immigrants distributed across a wide variety of divergent groups. Unless non-Mexican Latinos and Asians or immigrants themselves are oversampled, standard surveys are unlikely to produce sufficient numbers of immigrants for meaningful analysis. There are some exceptions, including the National Health Interview Survey, the Panel Study of Income Dynamics, and the National Health and Nutrition Examination Survey. Other surveys target those of Latino and Asian origin and thus include a large number of immigrants by design (e.g., the Latino National Survey and Asian American National Survey). But even when surveys contain larger subsamples of immigrants, very few ask a question on parental birthplace, precluding studies of intergenerational integration.

Lack of Longitudinal Data

Another limitation is the lack of information about immigrants and their descendants in longitudinal data sources. One of the best ways to capture change over time, as is implicit in an idea such as "integration," is through longitudinal studies that reinterview the same respondents at multiple time points. This helps researchers identify whether economic, health, or civic integration happens gradually and steadily over time or if there are key inflection points in the process. One problem for cross-sectional surveys is that researchers face a much harder time identifying the temporal order of events that might point to potential mechanisms of change. For example, while the prior census enumerations captured whether a foreign-born resident was a U.S. citizen at the time of enumeration, as well as whether he or she was married, had a job, owned a home and so forth, one does not know whether marriage, employment, and homeownership occurred before or after acquiring citizenship. Recent changes to the ACS that ask respondents the year in which they naturalized will help to specify the determinants of citizenship, but longitudinal studies are a gold standard for understanding mechanisms of integration.

A model for how the United States could provide longitudinal data based on administrative records linking visa status and mode of entry to subsequent income is the Canadian government's Longitudinal Immigrant Database.[7] This database links taxation records with immigration records over time, allowing researchers to examine labor force participation, earnings, internal migration, and income over time by class of admission and other attributes such as language ability (Hiebert, 2009). The availability of these data allows researchers to provide evidence on the long-term integration of people admitted under different visa types. This type of database would not only allow U.S. researchers to more accurately describe integration over time, it would provide lawmakers with direct information about the effects of U.S. immigration law such as the relative costs and benefits over time of admitting different types of skilled workers.

Contexts of Reception

Even though there are difficulties in measuring changes to American society, the panel defined integration as a two-way process. To understand that process in both directions, data are needed not only on immigrants—their background, legal status, attitudes, economic condition, health status, and so forth—but also on the communities in which they live. In studies that include a detailed geographic identifier, researchers can embed the information about an individual in aggregate data on the individual's neighborhood, town, or metropolitan area, usually using Decennial Census data. However, such place-based data are often incomplete for some of the integration outcomes highlighted in this report. The research community needs better data, for example, on the civic or institutional infrastructure within immigrant communities—for instance, the number of religious institutions offering non-English services, the number of community-based social service agencies, the number of refugee resettlement organization, or the number of legal aid clinics, especially those able to process immigration paperwork. A few studies have begun to evaluate civic infrastructure using, for example, data on 501(c)(3) nonprofit organizations distributed by the National Center for Charitable Statistics, but these databases do not have

---

[7] See http://www23.statcan.gc.ca/imdb/p2SV.pl?Function=getSurvey&SDDS=5057 [November 2015].

consistent information on whether the organizations are focused on serving immigrant communities(see also de Leon and Roach, 2013).

Localities also vary in the degree to which they welcome or develop initiatives to facilitate immigrant integration (see White House Task Force on New Americans, 2015). Academics regularly compare the policy frameworks for immigrant integration across countries. One of the most developed is the MIPEX project,[8] which has 144 policy indicators across 38 countries over 8 years to track changes in policy and variation between countries. Other indicators, such as the Multiculturalism Policy Index[9] and the Citizenship Observatory[10] have generated cross-national policy comparisons for more focused topics such as diversity and citizenship policy. Using these indices, researchers can evaluate whether policy differences across countries tend to correlate with better or more problematic integration outcomes, such as naturalization or economic outcomes.

It would be valuable to extend this contextual approach to localities within the United States. A few studies have tried to see whether states or municipalities with harsher anti-immigrant ordinances impede immigrants' integration or, conversely, whether outreach policies have real effects on integration (see Mollenkopf and Pastor, 2013; Flores, 2014).

RECOMMENDATIONS

The most serious current gap in the U.S. statistical system on immigration is the lack of a question on parental birthplace for a large representative sample of the U.S. population. A question on the birthplace of parents would enable clear identification of second generation immigrants of all ages and enable researchers to assess their social, economic, and cultural integration not only within the United States as a whole but across various national origins in different regions, states, and metropolitan areas. Although it remains important to assess the relative progress of foreign-born immigrants as they adapt to life in the United States, the more critical issue for the nation is the progress of their U.S.-born children, since they are native citizens who in a very real way represent America's demographic future as they inevitably produce more citizens.

Recommendation 10-1 The U.S. Census Bureau should add a question on the birthplace of parents to the American Community Survey.

With millions of long-term U.S. residents lacking legal documentation and millions more children growing up in a household with one or more

---

[8] See http://www.mipex.eu/what-is-mipex [November 2015].

[9] See http://www.queensu.ca/mcp/immigrant.html [November 2015].

[10] See http://eudo-citizenship.eu/ [November 2015].

unauthorized parents, undocumented status clearly emerges as a major constraint on socioeconomic mobility among immigrants and thus a key determinant of the prospects for their children as well. A question by which respondents select among various well-defined legal statuses at entry or at present, leaving those in undocumented status to be identified by process of elimination, now appears on the SIPP and the LAFANS. The question provides important information on the status of immigrants. If the indirect estimation question functions well in the CPS, it could also be added to the ACS.

Recommendation 10-2 The U.S. Census Bureau should test, and if feasible, add a question on the monthly Current Population Survey by which respondents select among various well-defined legal statuses at entry or at present, leaving those in undocumented status to be identified by process of elimination.

As indicated by the New Immigrant Survey, the Mexican Migration Project, and other surveys, legal status is a dynamic variable that changes over time as immigrants move from temporary to permanent legal statuses or between unauthorized and authorized circumstances. The attainment of legal status and eventual citizenship are likely to be crucial steps in the process of economic and social integration, yet researchers presently lack the means to model them.

Recommendation 10-3 Following the example of the New Immigrant Survey, the Survey of Income and Program Participation, and the Los Angeles Family and Neighborhood Study, direct questions on legal status should be added to ongoing and proposed longitudinal surveys that contain significant numbers of foreign-born respondents, such as the Panel Study of Income Dynamics, the National Health Interview Survey, the National Educational Longitudinal Survey, and the National Health and Nutrition Examination Survey.

Just as the 1986 Immigration Reform and Control Act mandated a survey of the immigrants who legalized, any future legislation to address the legalization of millions of undocumented immigrants should do the same. A legalization program creates a targeted opportunity to learn more about the population of immigrants living in the United States without legal status. Data collection and analysis of the legalized population—how they entered the United States, where they fit into the labor market, demographic characteristics, family composition, use of social services, migration behavior and origins—in the 1986 program illuminated the behavior of a population for which there previously was little systematic information. Learning more about today's unauthorized population will help provide insights into an otherwise elusive population and assist in creating new policies to address undocumented immigration and immigrants.

> **Recommendation 10-4** Congress should prioritize the collection of data on the undocumented population by including a provision in the next immigration bill to survey the population. Data should be collected in two ways: USCIS should collect data on applicants who were previously out-of-status or entered without inspection, and government statistical agencies should conduct surveys similar to those conducted after IRCA.

A cost-effective way to improve data accuracy and aid research on intergenerational changes in immigrant integration is to link administrative data with Decennial Census and survey data. Records from the Survey of Income and Program Participation (SIPP) could link to respondents and their children and parents, to enable investigation into intergenerational and intragenerational issues, including but not limited to mobility, long-run outcomes of early life circumstances, and intergenerational effects for immigrants and their descendants. Matched individual-level records from Decennial Censuses (and the ACS) with income data from Internal Revenue Service and the Social Security Administration would allow for longitudinal studies of the socioeconomic progress of immigrants in American society and allow for the measurement of both intracohort change and intercohort (for cohorts based on time of arrival in the United States) change for successive waves of immigrants. Matched Census and USCIS records would allow for in-depth studies of pathways to legalization and also the impact of legal status on socioeconomic outcomes of individuals and their children.

> **Recommendation 10-5** The U.S. Census Bureau and U.S. Citizenship and Immigration Services should create a system that links administrative data to Census Bureau–administered surveys, including the Decennial Census, the American Community Survey, and the Survey of Income and Program Participation, following protocols that have recently been used to link Internal Revenue Service data to Census Bureau data and/or following protocols developed for the American Opportunity Study (National Research Council, 2013).

USCIS and other federal government agencies produce a range of administrative data about immigrants, including flows of new arrivals by visa status and data on newly naturalized U.S. citizens. However, the published data are aggregated with only some very basic cross-tabulations. It is impossible to use these data for more fine-grained analysis, for example, to compare whether women from specific countries over the age of 50 living in areas of the United States with more legal aid support in their native language are more likely to naturalize than similar female migrants living elsewhere. To support such finer grained analyses, researchers need micro-level data on individuals and the ability to link such data with additional information, such as aggregate data on localities.

> **Recommendation 10-6** U.S. Immigration and Citizenship Services and the Office of Immigration Statistics should make more administrative data available to researchers and the public. Sensitive data should be made available via Secure Data Centers.

Many common data sources for social science research lack large enough samples of Hispanics, Asians, or immigrants to effectively use in the study of immigrant integration. In recent years, however, a number of nationally representative studies have added oversamples of Hispanics and Asians or immigrants, including the National Health Interview Survey, the Panel Study of Income Dynamics, and the National Health and Nutrition Examination Survey. These surveys could provide a model for oversampling key populations.

> **Recommendation 10-7** The General Social Survey, the various National Longitudinal Surveys, the Adolescent Health Survey, and the National Survey of Family Growth should oversample the foreign-born, especially the smaller Asian and non-Mexican Hispanic groups that, when combined, make up a significant share of the immigrant population. In addition, the surveys cited above should add questions on parental birthplace.

Contexts of reception are critical for immigrant's integration prospects, not just on the national or state scale but also on the local and neighborhood scale. Researchers therefore need access to small-area data. In addition, researchers need these data in a timely manner if they are going to capture processes that are unfolding continuously.

> **Recommendation 10-8** The U.S. Census Bureau should enable researchers to access and analyze small-area data on first and second generation immigrants through the system of Regional Data Centers, taking steps to lower the cost of accessing the data; speed up the approval process; and permit researchers to access the data to address a larger range of research questions, not just research efforts than benefit the Census Bureau.

Population surveys continue to be an important source of health status and use of health services among immigrants and the U.S.-born. Unlike administrative and clinical data, population surveys are able to reach people who do not seek preventive or treatment services. Since there is a sizable portion of people who either do not access health care or do so irregularly, surveys provide data on people who are less likely to receive medical attention. Moreover, surveys are able to include more dimensions of social life that are important for understanding health status and health care (e.g., socioeconomic status, English language proficiency, country of origin, length of time in the United States, age of immigration).

Recommendation 10-9 The National Institutes of Health should offer continuing support for population health surveys. It should ensure that these surveys contain questions on date and age of arrival, time spent in the United States, and whenever possible and practical, legal status.

REFERENCES

Alba, R., and Nee, V. (2003). *Remaking the American Mainstream: Assimilation and Contemporary Immigration.* Cambridge, MA: Harvard University Press.

Bachmeier, J.D., Van Hook, J., and Bean, F.D. (2014). Can we measure immigrants' citizenship and legal status in surveys? Lessons from LAFANS and SIPP. *International Migration Review, 48*(2), 538-566.

Bean, F.D., Brown, S.K., and Bachmeir, J.D. (2015) *Parents Without Papers: The Progress and Pitfalls of Mexican-American Integration.* New York: Russell Sage Foundation.

Brown, S.K., Bean, F.D., Leach, M.A., and Rumbaut, R.G. (2011). Legalization and naturalization trajectories among Mexican immigrants and their implications for the second generation. In R. Alba and M.C. Waters (Eds.), *The Next Generation: Immigrant Youth in Comparative Perspective* (pp. 31-45). New York: New York University Press.

Carter-Pokras, O., and Zambrana, R.E. (2006). Collection of legal status information. *American Journal of Public Health, 96*(3), 399.

de Leon, E., and Roach, R. (2013). *Immigrant Legal-Aid Organizations in the United States.* Available: http://www.urban.org/research/publication/immigrant-legal-aid-organizations-united-states [October 2015].

Donato, K.M., Durand, J., Hiskey, J., and Massey, D.S. (2010). Migration in the Americas: Mexico and Latin America in comparative context. *The ANNALS of the American Academy of Political and Social Science, 630*, 6-17.

Dreby, J. (2010). *Divided by Borders: Mexican Migrants and Their Children.* Berkeley: University of California Press.

Durand, J., and Massey, D.S. (2004). *Crossing the Border: Research from the Mexican Migration Project.* New York: Russell Sage Foundation.

Flores, R.D. (2014). Living in the eye of the storm: How did Hazleton's restrictive immigration ordinance affect local interethnic relations? *American Behavioral Scientist, 58*(13), 1743-1763.

Grusky, D.B., Smeeding, T.M., and Snipp, C.M. (2015). A new infrastructure for monitoring social mobility in the United States. *The ANNALS of the American Academy of Political and Social Science, 657*(1), 63-82.

Hall, M., Greenman, E., and Farkas, G. (2010). Legal status and wage disparities for Mexican immigrants. *Social Forces,* 89, 491-514.

Hiebert, D. (2009). *The Economic Integration of Immigrants in Metro Vancouver.* Working Paper Series No. 09-08. Vancouver: Metropolis British Columbia Centre for Excellence for Research on Immigration and Diversity.

Jasso, G., Massey, D.S., Rosenzweig, M., and Smith, J.P. (2008). From illegal to legal: Estimating previous illegal experience among new legal immigrants to the United States. *International Migration Review,* 42, 803-843.

Kasinitz, P., Waters, M.C., Mollenkopf, J.H., and Holdaway, J. (2008). *Inheriting the City: The Children of Immigrants Come of Age.* New York: Russell Sage Foundation.

Levitt, P. (2001). *The Transnational Villagers.* Berkeley: University of California Press.

Marrow, H. (2011). *New Destination Dreaming: Immigration, Race, and Legal Status in the Rural American South.* Stanford: Stanford University Press.

Massey, D.S. (2010). Immigration statistics for the 21st century. *The ANNALS of the American Academy of Political and Social Science,* 631, 124-140.

Massey, D.S., and Akresh, I.R. (2006). Immigrant intentions and mobility in a global economy: The attitudes and behavior of recently arrived U.S. immigrants. *Social Science Quarterly,* 88, 30-47.

Massey, D.S., and Bartley, K. (2005). The changing legal status distribution of immigrants: A caution. *International Migration Review,* 34, 469-484.

Massey, D.S., and Capoferro, C. (2004). Measuring undocumented migration. *International Migration Review,* 38, 1075-1102.

Massey, D.S., and Malone, N. J. (2002). Pathways to legalization. *Population Research and Policy Review,* 21, 473-504.

Massey, D.S., and Zenteno, R. (2000). A validation of the Ethnosurvey: The case of Mexico-U.S. migration. *International Migration Review,* 34, 765-792.

Massey, D.S., Alarcón, R., Durand, J., and González, H. (1987). *Return to Aztlan: The Social Process of International Migration from Western Mexico.* Oakland: University of California Press.

Mollenkopf, J., and Pastor, M. (2013). *Struggling over Strangers or Receiving with Resilience? The Metropolitics of Immigrant Integration.* Working Paper. Available: http://brr.berkeley.edu/wp-content/uploads/2013/05/Mollenkopf-Pastor-struggling-strangers.pdf [October 2015].

National Research Council. (1985). *Immigration Statistics: A Story of Neglect. Panel on Immigration Statistics.* D.P. Levine, K. Hill, and R. Warren (Eds.). Committee on National Statistics, Commission on Behavioral and Social Sciences and Education. Washington, DC: National Academy Press.

National Research Council. (2013). *Developing New National Data on Social Mobility: A Workshop Summary.* A. Smith, Rapporteur. Committee on Population and Committee on National Statistics, Division of Behavioral and Social Sciences and Education. Washington, DC: The National Academies Press.

Portes, A., and Rumbaut, R.G. (2014). *Immigrant America: A Portrait, Updated and Expanded.* Oakland: University of California Press.

Prentice, J.C., Pebley, A.R., and Sastry, N. (2005). Immigration status and health insurance coverage: Who gains? Who loses? *American Journal of Public Health,* 95(1), 109-116,

Ramakrishnan, S.K. (2005). *Democracy in Immigrant America: Changing Demographics and Political Participation.* Stanford, CA: Stanford University Press

U.S. Census Bureau. (2015). *Survey of Income and Program Participation.* Available: http://www.census.gov/sipp/ [October 2015].

U.S. Government Accountability Office. (2006). *Estimating the Undocumented Population: A "Grouped Answers" Approach to Surveying Foreign-Born Respondents.* GAO-06-775. Report to the Subcommittee on Terrorism, Technology and Homeland Security, Committee on the Judiciary, U.S. Senate, Washington, DC.

U.S. Government Accountability Office. (2009). *Estimating Irregular Migration in a Survey: The "Two-Card Follow-Up" Method.* Working Paper No. ESA/P/WP.208. New York: United Nations, Department of Economic and Social Affairs, Population Division.

Weeraratne, B., and Massey, D.S. (2014). *Does Past Unauthorized Immigrant Status Result in a Wage Penalty for Legalized Immigrants?* Presented at the American Economic Association Annual Meeting, January 4, Philadelphia, PA.

White House Task Force on New Americans. (2015). *Strengthening Communities by Welcoming All Residents: A Federal Strategic Action Plan on Immigrant & Refugee Integration.* Available: https://www.whitehouse.gov/sites/default/files/docs/final_tf_newamericans_report_4-14-15_clean.pdf [October 2015].

Appendix

Biographical Sketches of Committee Members and Staff

MARY C. WATERS (*Chair*) is the M.E. Zukerman professor of sociology at Harvard University. She specializes in the study of immigration, intergroup relations, formation of racial and ethnic identity among the children of immigrants, challenges of measuring race and ethnicity, and the longitudinal impact of natural disasters. Currently, she is co-directing the RISK (Resilience in Survivors of Katrina) Study. This study includes pre-hurricane data on physical and mental health and follows survivors and their children wherever they have relocated. She is a member of the National Academy of Sciences and a fellow of the American Academy of Arts and Sciences. She has published extensively on race, ethnicity, and immigration and won the 2010 American Sociological Association Distinguished Contribution to Scholarship Award for her co-authored study of the children of immigrants, *Inheriting the City: The Second Generation Comes of Age*. She holds a B.A. in philosophy from Johns Hopkins University and an M.A. in demography, an M.A. in sociology, and a Ph.D. in sociology, all from the University of California, Berkeley.

RICHARD ALBA is a distinguished professor of sociology at the Graduate Center of the City University of New York. His teaching and research have a comparative focus, encompassing the immigration societies of North America and western Europe. He has published extensively on race, ethnicity, and immigration, and has carried out research with the support of Fulbright grants and fellowships from the Guggenheim Foundation, the German Marshall Fund, and the Russell Sage Foundation. He is a former elected president of the Eastern Sociological Society and vice president of the American Sociological Association. He is also the recipient of the Award for a Distinguished Career of Scholarship from the International Migration Section of the American Sociological Association. He holds a B.A. from Columbia College and a Ph.D. from Columbia University, both in sociology.

FRANK D. BEAN is distinguished professor of sociology and director of the Center for Research on Immigration, Population and Public Policy at the University of California, Irvine. His research focuses on demographic change and international migration, the social consequences of ethnoracial diversity, Mexican American integration, and the demography of the U.S. Hispanic population. He has been a Guggenheim fellow and a visiting scholar at the Russell Sage Foundation, the Transatlantic Academy in Washington, D.C., the American Academy in Berlin, the Research School of Social Sciences at the Australian National University, and the Center for U.S./Mexico Studies at the University of California, San Diego. He is a member of the Council on Foreign Relations. He is a recipient of the Distinguished Lifetime Scholarly Career Award in International Migration from the International Migration Section of the American Sociological Association. He attended Oberlin College and holds a B.A. from the University of Kentucky and an M.A. and a Ph.D. from Duke University.

IRENE BLOEMRAAD is professor of sociology at the University of California, Berkeley, and a scholar with the Canadian Institute for Advanced Research. Her main research interests are citizenship (including naturalization and dual nationality), immigrants' civic and political incorporation, multiculturalism and comparative political sociology. Her current research focuses on immigrants' civic and political engagement in the United States, immigrant political socialization, comparative minority representation, and the cross-national effects of immigrant-driven diversity on trust and engagement. She holds a B.A. in political science and an M.A. in sociology, both from McGill University, and a Ph.D. in sociology from Harvard University.

MICHAEL FIX is president of the Migration Policy Institute. His work focuses on immigrant integration, citizenship policy, immigrant children and families, the education of immigrant students, the effect of welfare reform on immigrants, and the impact of immigrants on the U.S. labor force. Previously, he was at the Urban Institute where he directed the Immigration Studies Program. His research there focused on immigrants and integration, regulatory reform, federalism, race, and the measurement of discrimination. He has also been a research fellow with IZA in Bonn, Germany and a New Millennium Distinguished visiting scholar at Columbia University's School of Social Work. He holds a B.A. from Princeton University and a J.D. from the University of Virginia.

NANCY FONER is distinguished professor of sociology at Hunter College and at the Graduate Center of the City University of New York. Her current work focuses on the comparative study of immigration: comparing immigration today with earlier periods in the United States, the immigrant experience in various American gateway cities, and immigrant minorities in the United States and Europe. She is a former president of the Eastern Sociological Society, a recipient of the Distinguished Career Award from the International Migration Section of the American Sociological Association, and an elected member of the American Academy of Arts and Sciences. She holds a B.A. in social anthropology from Brandeis University and an M.A. and Ph.D. in anthropology, both from the University of Chicago.

CHARLES HIRSCHMAN is Boeing International professor in the Department of Sociology at the Daniel J. Evans School of Governance and Public Policy at the University of Washington. Previously, he taught at Duke University and at Cornell University. As a social demographer, his interests are race and ethnicity, immigration to the United States, and social change in Southeast Asia. He has served as president of the Population Association of America and as chair of Social, Economic, and Political Sciences Section of the American Association for the Advancement of Science. He is an elected fellow of the American Academy of Arts and Sciences and of the American Association for the Advancement of Science. He holds a B.A. in sociology from Miami University and an M.S. and Ph.D. in sociology, both from the University of Wisconsin–Madison.

DANIEL T. LICHTER is the Ferris family professor in the Department of Policy Analysis and Management, a professor of sociology, and director of the Cornell Population Center, all at Cornell University. He is a past president of the Population Association of America and of the Rural Sociological Society. He has published widely on topics in population and public policy, including studies of concentrated poverty and inequality, intermarriage, cohabitation and marriage among disadvantaged women, and immigrant incorporation. His recent work has focused on changing ethnoracial boundaries, as measured by changing patterns of interracial marriage and residential segregation in the United States. His other work centers on new destinations of recent immigrants, especially Hispanics moving to less densely settled rural areas. He holds a B.A. from South Dakota State University, an M.A. from Iowa State University, and a Ph.D. from the University of Wisconsin–Madison, all in sociology.

DOUGLAS S. MASSEY is the Henry G. Bryant professor of sociology and public affairs, with a joint appointment in the Woodrow Wilson School, at Princeton University. He currently serves as director of the university's

Office of Population Research. His research focuses on international migration, race and housing, discrimination, education, urban poverty, stratification, and Latin America, especially Mexico. He is a member of the National Academy of Sciences, the American Academy of Arts and Sciences, and the American Philosophical Society. He is the current president of the American Academy of Political and Social Science and is a member of the Council of the National Academy of Sciences. He holds a B.A. in sociology, anthropology, psychology, and Spanish from Western Washington University and an M.A. and Ph.D. in sociology, both from Princeton University.

CECILIA MENJÍVAR is foundation distinguished professor of sociology at the University of Kansas. Her research has centered on immigration from Central America to the United States and violence in Latin America. She has studied the effects of immigration laws, at the federal, state, and local levels, on different aspects of immigrants' lives, such as family dynamics, the workplace and schools, family separations, educational aspirations, religious participation, and citizenship and belonging. She holds a B.A. in psychology and sociology and an M.S. in policy planning and international development, both from the University of Southern California, and an M.A. and a Ph.D. in sociology, both from the University of California at Davis.

MARISA GERSTEIN PINEAU is a program officer in the Division of Behavioral and Social Sciences and Education. She has worked with Academies' committees on a wide variety of topics, and co-edited several National Academies of Sciences, Engineering, and Medicine reports. She has also published on gender and family topics, and her dissertation was a sociological examination of breast milk banking in the United States. She won a dissertation research award from the Science of Generosity Initiative at Notre Dame, funded by the Templeton Foundation. She holds a B.A. in sociology from New College of Florida, and an M.A. and Ph.D. in sociology, both from the University of California, Los Angeles.

THOMAS PLEWES was director of the National Academies of Sciences, Engineering and Medicine's Committee on Population. Prior to this position, Plewes was study director at the Committee on National Statistics, where he directed a number of National Academies of Sciences, Engineering, and Medicine reports on topics such as research and development measurement and survey methodology. Previously, he was associate commissioner for employment and unemployment statistics of the Bureau of Labor Statistics. A member of the U.S. Army Reserve, he completed his service in 2002 as chief of the Army Reserve in the rank of Lieutenant General. He was a member of the Federal Committee on Statistical Methodology and is a fellow of the American Statistical Association, a senior fellow of the

Institute of Land Warfare, and a member of the Population Association of America. He has a B.A. in economics from Hope College and an M.A. in economics from George Washington University.

S. KARTHICK RAMAKRISHNAN is professor of public policy and political science at the University of California at Riverside, where he also serves as associate dean of the School of Public Policy. His research focuses on civic participation, immigration policy, and the politics of race, ethnicity, and immigration in the United States. He directs the National Asian American Survey and AAPI Data, which seeks to improve access to data on Asian Americans and Pacific Islanders. He has held fellowships at the Russell Sage Foundation, the Woodrow Wilson International Center for Scholars, and the Public Policy Institute of California, and he has provided consultation to public officials at the federal and local levels. He holds a B.A. in international relations and political science from Brown University and a Ph.D. in politics from Princeton University.

AUDREY SINGER is a senior fellow at the Brookings Metropolitan Policy Program. Her work focuses on international migration, U.S. immigration policy, demography, and urban and metropolitan change. She has written extensively on U.S. immigration trends, including the new geography of immigration, immigrant integration, undocumented migration, naturalization and citizenship, and the changing racial and ethnic composition of the United States. She recently completed a study of the implementation of the Deferred Action for Childhood Arrivals (DACA) Program in eight U.S. metropolitan areas. She has also studied he fastest growing immigrant populations among second-tier metropolitan areas including Washington, D.C., Atlanta, Dallas, Minneapolis-St. Paul, Sacramento, and Charlotte. She has served as chair of the International Migration Section of the American Sociological Association. She holds a B.A. in sociology from Temple University and an M.A. and a Ph.D. in sociology from the University of Texas at Austin.

DAVID T. TAKEUCHI is professor and the inaugural Dorothy Book scholar and associate dean for research at the Boston College School of Social Work. His research focuses on the social, structural, and cultural contexts that are associated with different health outcomes, especially among racial and ethnic minorities. He also examines the use of health services in different communities. He is a recipient of the legacy award from the Family Research Consortium for his research and mentoring and the Innovations Award from the National Center on Health and Health Disparities for his research. He is an elected member of the Washington State Academy of Sciences, the Sociological Research Association, and the American Academy of Social Work and Social Welfare. He currently serves as secretary-elect of the American Sociological Association and is a member of the National Advisory Committee for the Robert Wood Johnson Health and Society Program. He holds a B.A., an M.A., and a Ph.D. in sociology, all from the University of Hawaii.

KEVIN J.A. THOMAS is an associate professor of sociology, demography, and African studies at the Pennsylvania State University and a research associate at the university's Population Research Institute. Previously, he worked as a David Bell fellow at the Harvard Center for Population and Development Studies and as a research fellow at the Harvard Initiative for Global Health. He also worked with the Migration Policy Research Program of the International Organization for Migration and as a consultant for several organizations, including the Migration Policy Institute in Washington, D.C. His current research interests include migration and immigration processes, especially among African-origin populations, race and ethnic inequality, children and families, and international development. He holds a B.A. from Fourah Bay College at the University of Sierra Leone, an M.A. in development administration from Western Michigan University, and an M.A. and Ph.D. in demography from the University of Pennsylvania.

STEPHEN TREJO is a professor of economics at the University of Texas at Austin. His research focuses on public policy issues, including overtime pay regulation, the labor market experiences of immigrants, and obstacles to the economic progress of minority groups. He is the author of numerous articles concerning the status and mobility of Mexican Americans in the U.S. labor market. He holds a B.A. in economics from University of California at Santa Barbara and an M.A. and a Ph.D. in economics from the University of Chicago.

RICHARD WRIGHT is the Orvil E. Dryfoos professor of geography and public affairs at Dartmouth College. His major interest is in how immigrants fit into U.S. society. One focus of this work has been the study of labor market interactions of immigrants and migrants in and between the major metropolitan areas and regions of the United States, including the segmented nature of these labor markets and the impacts of state-level immigration statutes on the internal migration of the foreign born. Another focus has been housing markets and neighborhood segregation and diversity from the perspective of race and racism. He has been a Guggenheim fellow. He holds a B.Ed. from the University of Nottingham and an M.A. and a Ph.D. from Indiana University, all in geography.

HIROKAZU YOSHIKAWA is the Courtney Sale Ross university professor of globalization and education at the Steinhardt School at New York University and co-director of the university's Global TIES for Children Center. As a community and developmental psychologist, he studies the effects of public policies and programs related to immigration, early childhood, and poverty reduction on children's development, both in the United States and in low- and middle-income countries. He is serving as a presidentially appointed member of the National Board for Education Sciences. He also serves on the boards of the Russell Sage Foundation, the Foundation for Child Development, and the advisory boards for the UNESCO Global Monitoring Report and the Open Society Foundations Early Childhood Program. He holds a B.A. in English literature from Yale University and an M.A. and a Ph.D. in psychology, both from New York University.